Karen M. Jennison
Sociology

An Urban World

An Urban World

CHARLES TILLY

University of Michigan

with photographs by Steve Tilly

LITTLE, BROWN AND COMPANY   BOSTON · TORONTO

To
Otto Charles Tilly
and Naneth Rowena Tilly
my parents

Preface

At this moment, I doubt that anyone could write a textbook about cities which would be both coherent and faithful to the current state of knowledge. If I am wrong, so much the better: I'll cheer in surprise and admiration. Looking down my bookshelf, I get a strong feeling of rightness. The possibility of a coherent textbook, it seems to me, depends on one or both of two difficult conditions: (a) the availability of a single analytic scheme which provides an account of most of the phenomena which concern students of the subject, and/or (b) substantial consensus among investigators within each major subdivision of the topic, even if the concepts, methods, theories, and findings accepted in one subdivision do not fit well with those accepted in another. There have been times, like the 1930's, when students of cities and urbanization developed enough temporary agreement to make solid textbooks feasible. This is not one of those times.

Yet the urbanist can begin to see some areas of agreement forming which might eventually become the bases of a new synthesis. As the reader who goes through this book will soon discover for himself, I find the analyses of social networks which anthropologists and sociologists began developing in the 1960's especially promising. But there are other promising lines of argument and research in economics, geography, political science, demography, planning, and the other disciplines which deal with cities. A kind of impatience has therefore driven me to construct a textbook-reader when the time is not yet ripe. I find myself impatient with the confusion which issues from mishmash eclecticism, with premature intellectual imperialism, with the paltry contribution the social sciences have made so far toward making cities livable, with the time and effort it will probably take to form our existing fragments of knowledge into workable instruments of thought and action. At best, this book will speed things up a little. My hope is that it will help the student of communities, cities, and urbanization to do three things:

1. to deal with some particular but important aspects of the subject (such as patterns of land use, rural-urban migration, and world-wide variations in the character of urbanization) in a fairly systematic way;

2. to sort out the principal alternative ways of analyzing urban phenomena;

3. to identify and use some of the valuable new ideas investigators in the field have been developing.

For these purposes, the student needs to examine original contributions, and yet to have considerable guidance in examining them. A book of readings with a substantial amount of context and commentary seems a reasonable solution. That is what I have attempted here.

In selecting the readings, I have tried to find items which stand by themselves, are comprehensible to a student with little technical training in the social sciences, represent the chief theoretical alternatives now on the scene, and contain first-rate ideas. I admit to having been more generous to sociology than to other disciplines, to having emphasized Europe and, especially, North America more than the claim to discuss an urban *world* justifies, and to having reprinted papers of my own which I would probably have discarded if they had been someone else's.

My excuse for the over-emphasis on sociology is that I have done most of my teaching about cities and urbanization as a form of sociology and tend to approach urban phenomena as a sociologist rather than, say, as an economist or a planner. My defense for the concentration on Europe and North America is that I have seen and lived in a number of the cities of those two continents, and have only secondhand knowledge of cities in other parts of the world. My case for including so much of my own work is that the student thereby gets the chance to find out what happens when someone goes from the sorts of abstract ideas presented in the general sections of the book to their application in concrete cases.

My students at Toronto and Michigan helped make this book by arguing its general themes with me, carrying out investigations which taught me plenty about communities, cities, and urbanization, responding to many of the readings reprinted here, and working with some fragments of the text when they were circulated as classroom handouts and memoranda pretending to clarify difficult points in our discussions. Many of them will recognize portions of an essay which they have known for years, in various versions, under the title "Community: City: Urbanization," and which first came into being because my students in urban sociology at Toronto couldn't understand what I was driving at.

Edward Shorter gave acerbic and useful criticism to the initial drafts of this book's first three chapters. Anne V. O'Shea helped energetically with a series of editorial tasks. Steve Tilly made some fine photographs. Alex Inkeles offered encouragement without which I might well have abandoned the effort.

Contents

xi

Chapter
3
Communities

Chapter
4
Cities

Chapter
5
Changing the City

An Urban World

Chapter

1

Introduction

CITIES

In Paul Claudel's play *The City*, the poet Coeuvre and his former mistress Lala discuss the rebuilding of their city, which the disciples of the anarchist Avare have gutted:

> *Lala.* The city is the human form.
> What order and marvelous peace the human city will have
> When, meaning having returned to life, every man will have direct contact with every other one.
> And judging his needs from his position in life, having understood those needs he will not exceed them.
> And freely return the equivalent of what he has taken.
> Since there is no freedom except in necessity.
> Knowledge has put the world in man's hands and now you must see that to each man has been given all other men and that humanity as a whole forms a single body
> In the architecture of its members and the function of its organs,
> In the fullness of justice, in the power of life, in unshakable solidarity.
> *Coeuvre.* Well said.
> *Lala.* Then come with us, Coeuvre, and join with Avare and me
> So that having demolished this city
> We can use the beams and bricks for a new construction.

But Coeuvre cannot summon up the arrogance to impose his plans on other men; as a poet and observer, he must let life take its course:

> And what sort of impudence and foolhardiness does it take for those who do not bear the chief responsibility, to touch anything
> Which has the sacred fact of existence, and what madness

1

> To think you can build a better house, wielding the souls of men like
>   bricks
> Like beams whose size and strength you have calculated?[1]

Claudel wants us to see in the city—and in the possibility of its reconstruction—an image of life in general.

The passage from Claudel states the dilemmas of this book about cities. Any vision of a better life implies a reordering of human communities. That is why such Utopias as those of Thomas More or Lewis Mumford describe ideal communities. But it takes confidence—perhaps even arrogance and brutality—to smash what exists and then rebuild to shape the lives of other people.

To do nothing, however, means to leave our friends to their miseries. Should we join Avare in burning what we conceive to be evil, join Lala in building what we wish to be good, or join Coeuvre in observing and explaining whatever actually occurs? The urbanites of the world have never been able to escape those choices or their consequences.

The choices come every day, and the consequences last. That is obvious for public decisions: Should we tear down houses and stores to run an expressway downtown, dig an expensive subway which may not be used enough, or let cars and carbon monoxide fill the streets? Should we disband the school system, reorganize it radically at the possible expense of the children, or let it stagger along as it is? Should we refurbish the old, overgrown capital or erect a shining Brasilia in the midst of open land? Should we let people move into Warsaw as they want to (and thus overtax the city's supply of housing, transporation, welfare, and public health facilities) or admit only those who are obviously employable (and thus take on the job of policing clandestine migration and the peddling of rights to move)?

The cumulative effects of small decisions made by individuals and households are less obvious but just as powerful. The men who elect to drive to work on rainy days undermine the bus lines. The white families moving from New York to Boston who, for convenience of location, buy houses in all-white suburbs reinforce residential segregation. The youngsters who sneak back to Peking from their assignments in small towns reduce the overall productivity of the Chinese economy.

These are current examples, but they represent problems which grew large as soon as people began to build cities. The concentration of people and their activities in big, busy, complicated centers made most people vulnerable to the decisions of many other people, some of them far away. As collective creations, cities impose collective risks and collective responsibilities.

I have built this book on a simple premise: to recognize those risks and meet those responsibilities, we have to know how cities work. The questions the book deals with are also quite simple. The answers, however, are sometimes complicated, almost always tentative, now and then entirely speculative. A quick question-and-answer session will preview the book's main problems:

Q. What are cities, and why should we pay any particular attention to them?
A. Cities are special kinds of communities in which the coordination and

control of widely dispersed activities take place. Exactly which communities we single out as cities depends on which theoretical approach to community structure we adopt; right now we have four or five distinct ways of theorizing about cities, and no single one of them is clearly superior to all the rest. By any definition, however, cities came into being rather late in the long run of human existence, and only began to dominate the lives of most people in the world during the twentieth century. As cities become increasingly dominant, the need to understand them grows.

Q. Why and how do people concentrate in cities?

A. The how is easier than the why. Cities grow relative to other communities through migration, a favorable balance of births and deaths, and the transformation of other kinds of communities into cities. At one time or another, the concentration of political power, the expansion of trade, and the growth of industrial production have all promoted migration, favorable birth-death balances, and urbanization of community structures. The industrialization of the last century has accelerated the three city-building processes enormously and produced cities quite different in scale and character from their predecessors. The explanations of migration, birth-death balances, and transformations of community structure which make sense again depend on which theoretical approach we adopt. In general, people concentrate at the control points for large-scale dispersed activities because all sorts of resources and opportunities concentrate at those locations. But how much they concentrate also depends on the costs—social, political, and economic— of getting to cities and staying in them.

Q. What difference does the kind of community people live in make to their everyday experience?

A. A question for which we have conflicting answers. The closer people come to living out their entire lives in a single community, the more the response of the other members of the community to them determines the quality of their lives. Communities vary greatly in how closely they control the lives of their members. Yet every community has durable, definite patterns of activity in time and space which shape the opportunities of their members to produce, consume, form close relationships, find out what is going on, exert influence, and enjoy life.

Q. In particular, what difference do cities make?

A. Still a hard question whose answers vary from one theoretical approach to another. There is a lot of mythology on the impersonality and disorganization of urban life which has little basis in fact. City-dwellers tend to organize their lives in overlapping subcommunities: neighborhoods, ethnic groups, professional networks, clusters of friends, and so on. The subcommunities are only weakly linked to each other, but they interact through large structures such as markets, political systems, and mass communications.

Q. What are the strategic points of intervention for planned change in cities?

A. That depends on what you want to change. Given the nature of cities, however, changing the big connecting structures I just mentioned will ordinarily have a larger, more durable impact for a given amount of effort than will intervening in individual lives one by one. We have very little reliable information about the actual impact of large interventions such as the construction of superhighways or the building of great apartment complexes on the everyday lives of the people involved. Social scientists could play an important part in the tracing of those consequences.

Q. What are the pressing open questions about communities, cities, and urbanization we ought to be investigating?

A. The ones we have just asked. In addition to the standard ways of going at them, there are some promising new approaches to their study: Ideas drawn from biological ecology are beginning to yield insights into the operation of cities. The treatment of communities as networks of personal relationships instead of self-regulating systems has a number of advantages. And there are others.

The six questions and answers summarize the whole book. Of course the book contains plenty of elaborations, illustrations, qualifications, and corroborations of the six points. But they are the main themes. This introduction asks what cities are, and why we should study them. The other questions come later.

AN URBAN WORLD APPEARS

The building of an urban world is one of man's great adventures. It began seven or eight thousand years ago. It continues today. The adventure started with Middle Eastern settlements which a proud urbanite of our own time would dismiss as hopelessly rustic, unbearably primitive. Yet in those settlements for the first time there were a few positions completely freed from hunting, gathering, fishing, or farming. The people in these positions specialized in the control of activities and resources spread over an area larger than the settlement itself. They were priests, kings, tax-collectors, merchants, craftsmen, warriors—often more than one at a time.

Since those first days of city-building, cities have changed in form and scale. The constant, defining element of cities throughout their history has been their control and coordination of the surrounding areas. Control and coordination mean specialized organization, extensive lines of communication, accumulations of wealth, diverse populations, change, complexity—in short, civilization. They also mean adventure and joy.

To Americans accustomed to equating cities with filth, despair, and insoluble problems, the joy may seem hard to find. An old Western tradition which contrasts the genuineness of the countryside with the artificiality of the city makes pollution (of whatever variety) seem to be the inevitable condition of urban areas. John Donne laid out the contrast a long time ago:

Cities are Sepulchers; they who dwell there
Are carcases, as if no such there were.

And Courts are Theaters, where some men play
Princes, some slaves, all to one end, and of one clay.
The Country is a desert, where no good,
Gain'd (as habits, not borne,) is understood.
There men become beasts, and prone to more evils;
In cities blockes, and in a lewd court, devills.

("To Sir Henry Wotton," written 1597)

Donne is unable to choose between the oppressiveness of the city and the barbarity of the country. Those whose joy comes from change and complexity choose cities *despite* the serious costs.

What joy? I think of boarding a crowded bus on Spadina Avenue in Toronto, smelling the salami, Greek olives, fresh bread, and haddock in shopping bags around the bus, and then hearing animated conversations in Portuguese, Italian, Greek, Hungarian, Caribbean English, and German all going on at once. I think of strolling with a friend through the Tuileries in Paris, dropping in for an hour with the pictures in the impressionist museum at the corner of the park, stopping for a drink at a sidewalk cafe, hearing an open-air concert (cello, harp, and orchestra), then walking back across the Seine to the Left Bank, the night air cooler, the automobiles less ferocious, the city lights more harmonious, the people in the streets less numerous and less hurried than at the start of the evening. I remember brown Havana seen from a ship at anchor, blue San Francisco from the Golden Gate Bridge, gray New York from a helicopter. What costs? Heraclitus taught that no man can step into the same river twice, because the second time the man is a different man and the river a different river. The city is a bigger and faster flowing river than are other types of human community. The city-dweller must tolerate a good deal of change and diversity which he neither anticipates nor desires.

Large scale, too, has costs. In the city, petty failings—the habit of tossing away stale chewing gum, the careless honking of an automobile horn, the willingness of an official to give a friend a break—multiply into blights: garbage, noise, corruption. And the concentration in cities of complex activities of coordination and control guarantees that the major conflicts and divisions of the world at large will persist within the city and agitate the lives of its residents.

When summing up the character of cities, we have our choice of several common metaphors; each of them catches a certain part of the reality. We can call the city a nerve center, a melting pot, or a hub. I prefer to think of it as a node in a network (or, strictly speaking, the location of nodes in a great many networks). That metaphor, borrowed from communications theory, calls our attention to social relations inside and outside the city while avoiding the assumption that each city is the center of a well-defined system.

Centrality is nevertheless one of the main reasons for singling out cities for special study, as well as one of the main obstacles to their study. Their centrality makes them crucial locations for the study of all sorts of complex social processes, from the spread of rumors to the development of class conflict. That same centrality, however, guarantees that few social situations in any city will be self-contained; most will have effects reaching far outside the city. Anyone studying geographic mobility in industrial countries, for example, will find that cities act as the magnetic poles of short-term and long-term geographic movements; but anyone who deals with the migrants and commuters in a city soon discovers that a large part of what concerns him is actually going on elsewhere.

We have other good reasons for studying cities. An increasingly huge share of humanity lives in them. The social life of city-dwellers is readily observable without invasions of privacy (since much of it takes place in public spaces and leaves its traces in the physical structure, population distribution, public records, or daily routine of the city as a whole). Decisions about cities some few men are making now will shape the lives of millions of other people. We need desperately to know how and to what extent intervention affects the fates of city-dwellers. Finally, the joy of cities makes them worth examining for their own sake.

ANTHROPOLOGY ON THE TOWN

In recent years, anthropologists have come closer than other social scientists to bringing all these concerns together.[2] Sociologists, political scientists, and economists have been studying cities, but on the whole their reports convey less of the actual experience of urban life than those of anthropologists. Formerly anthropologists were thought of as spending all their time out in the bush smoking hemp with primitive people. Some of them may still be smoking hemp, but the old ethnocentric division between "primitive" and "civilized" peoples has almost disappeared. No one is sure which is which now. And many anthropologists have come to town. Some have gone on to cities, while others have simply realized that their methods apply to city-dwellers as well as to inhabitants of tiny villages.

Everyone knows what life is like in his own niche. The trouble is that we do not know enough about each other's worlds—how they overlap, how they differ, how they work together. Sociologists have been fairly successful at putting together pieces of individual lives to make up the big picture of land use, the location of nationalities within a city, or the distribution of crime.[3] Their sample survey is a convenient way of detecting the main trends and subdivisions in big-city populations. They have helped to design the biggest survey of them all—the census—and have invented some ingenious ways of using numbers from the census to find out where the city is going. The urban sociologist excels at averaging, at finding the main line.

It is important to know the averages in learning whether the population is getting more mobile, or if one national group is sending more of its children to college, or who is getting what during a general rise in prosperity. Once we know the averages, the deviations begin to matter. The urban anthropologist can tell us the way it feels to be at the average, or far away from it.

We can see the difference between the sociologist's approach and the anthropologist's in the study of North American urban poverty. The sociologists and economists have found out how many poor people there are, how the proportions have been changing, and roughly who the poor are. But they have often failed to analyze how people got into their various categories and what it is like to be there.

Three men—an anthropologist, a sociologist-planner, and a free-lance writer—have helped to remind students of cities of the need to examine the ways poor people face life in the city. Oscar Lewis, the anthropologist, began his work by studying everyday life in a Mexican village. Later he followed his villagers to the slums of Mexico City. There he lived with them and let them tell their own stories while his tape recorder turned. The result was a new kind of book, built almost entirely on the oral autobiographies of the people under study, and a new understanding of the distinct way of life Lewis called "the culture of poverty." Since then, the ideas and techniques Oscar Lewis put into such books as *Five Families* and *The Children of Sanchez* have turned up more and more in the study of North American cities.

The sociologist-planner was Herbert Gans, who lived in the West End of Boston. The West End was a low-income section, with many Italian families, slated for razing and replacement by a complex of expensive tall apartments. Gans' book, *The Urban Villagers*, reporting what he learned, did not appear in time to save the West End from destruction. But it raised prickly questions about outsiders' assumptions that the West End was "disorganized" and a "slum," that it was therefore good only for clearance, and that its residents had everything to gain through relocation. Since then, planners in Boston and elsewhere have taken much more seriously their responsibility for learning what kinds of communities they are proposing to renew.

Michael Harrington, the writer, tells how he went from a useful but distant statistical analysis of poverty to a firsthand exploration of its labyrinths:

> After I wrote my first article on poverty in America, I had all the statistics down on paper. I had proved to my satisfaction that there were around 50,000,000 poor in this country. Yet, I realized that I did not believe my own figures. The poor existed in the Government reports; they were percentages and numbers in long, close columns, but they were not part of my experience. I could prove that the other America existed but I had never been there.[4]

He went to the streets of New York and other cities to live with the poor. Harrington laid out the results of his inquiry in a powerful book, *The Other America*. And the American government had to listen as it established its antipoverty program.

Lewis, Gans, and Harrington all wrote influential books. But writing books is not all that comes of the anthropological approach to the city. When the group building the big new city of Guayana, in Venezuela, asked Lisa Redfield Peattie to join them as staff anthropologist, they probably thought she would feed back information about sore spots in people's adaptation to the city and explain what was going on to the natives. With her wide experience in rural Latin America, she certainly could have done this. In fact, she did become a good source of information about the poor people's neighborhoods in Guayana, but she did it by settling with her family in the local shacktown and helping its residents organize a successful protest against living conditions there. Then she taught city planners at Massachusetts Institute of Technology, and once again helped poor people—this time in Boston—articulate their demands for planning which would take their needs into account.

The implications for urban action in these investigations of poverty are obvious. It may be less obvious that they also contribute to our general understanding of how cities work. The title of Gans' book, for example—*The Urban Villagers*—states an important idea: the similarity between the social organization of many of the city's ethnic enclaves (urban villages) and of the small communities from which their members or their members' parents came. People have been noticing the diversity of cultures in North American cities for a century, but usually under the impression that they were transient residues of old-country customs. Gans establishes the durability of some of these village cultures and helps explain that durability. Thus, work with direct practical applications contributes to the theory of the city as well.

What do these urban anthropologists do besides settle in slums? That is an important beginning. It is a way of sharing an important experience and gaining acceptance. The trained participant-observer has a chance to see people when they take off their business faces and to accompany them through the full daily, weekly, or monthly round. He establishes some contact with all parts of the population he is dealing with, not just the talkative elite. He records what he sees systematically—in classified field notes, in a journal, or perhaps on cards representing different individuals or groups. He may very well take a "sociometric" approach, concentrating on the frequencies and kinds of contact among pairs of members of the group. Those observations he can sum up in diagrams of group structure such as Figure 1, a representation of visiting patterns among a group of housewives in adjoining houses.

Here, Mrs. Able and Mrs. Baker regularly exchange visits; Mrs. Able, Mrs. Baker, and Mrs. Cantor regularly visit Mrs. Dunn; and Mrs. Elkin stays by herself. We can do the same diagramming for other members of the families, or for different kinds of contact such as giving help, borrowing tools, or going shopping together.

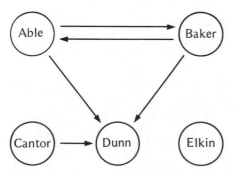

Figure 1. A Simple Friendship Network

The people involved don't need a diagram to tell them that A and B are close, that D is a center of attraction, or that E is an isolate. However, where the observer is a newcomer, where twenty or thirty households are involved, or where the question is whether the same kinds of clusters keep reappearing, only systematic recording and analysis will bring out the true state of affairs.

This technique has many versions. Under the heading of "network analysis" we will encounter several complicated forms of it in this book. It can neatly summarize which groups intermarry in a large city, what kinds of people form cliques in a high school, which individuals talk to each other most in an office. It is a natural starting point for a study of the flow of communications within a neighborhood. When done at a scale larger than the pairing of individuals, it helps us to distinguish three vitally different social arrangements, as in Figure 2.

The first might be the structure of a rooming-house district, the second the structure of a Chinese neighborhood, the third a high-rise apartment area.

Sociometric observation can be very complicated. There are simpler and faster ways to explore the social life in one section of a city or another. Very often an intelligent observer needs only to stroll through a neighborhood to spot the hangouts of the local population—doorsteps, bars, stores, clubs, churches. If they are public enough, he can station himself there and take a small part in local life. Or he can deliberately create his own social situations. Kevin Lynch, the city planner, tried to find out what kinds of roads and buildings made strong impressions on people. (His ideas appear in his article, "The Patterns of the Metropolis," reprinted in Chapter 4.) One of his devices was to stop people on the street and ask them directions to other sections of the city, noting what they used as their points of reference.

Lynch also adopted a slightly more formal way of finding out how people visualized their cities. He asked them to draw maps. His instructions went like this:

We would like to make a quick map of central Boston, inward or downtown from Massachusetts Avenue. Make it just as if you were making a rapid

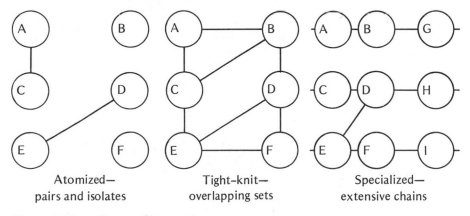

| Atomized— | Tight-knit— | Specialized— |
| pairs and isolates | overlapping sets | extensive chains |

Figure 2. Three Types of Networks

description of the city to a stranger, covering all the main features. We don't expect an accurate drawing—just a rough sketch.[5]

The interviewer was supposed to note the sequence in which the map was drawn. Everyone marked down Beacon Hill, the Common, the Charles River, and the Back Bay, but large areas of the central city simply disappeared from these maps for lack of what Lynch calls "imageability."

Allowing for skill in drawing and for visual imagination, we can learn about people's experience with the city from the maps they sketch. As an experiment, I asked my three eldest children to draw maps of central Toronto. They are not elegant, but they are revealing. The seven-year-old's world (Figure 3) is the path from home to school and its fringes, with her own block and the play areas she knows best blown up out of all proportion to their actual size. The nine-year-old (Figure 4) has grasped the grid pattern of the streets and has had enough experience

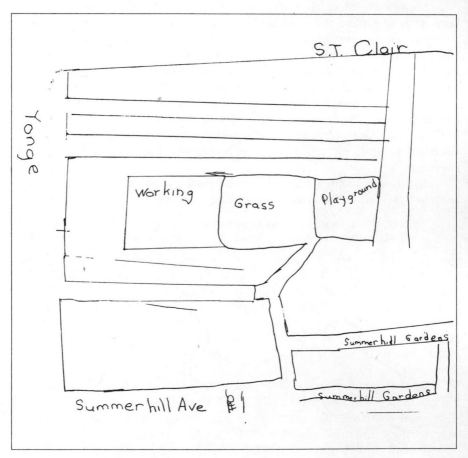

Figure 3. A Seven-Year-Old's Map of Toronto

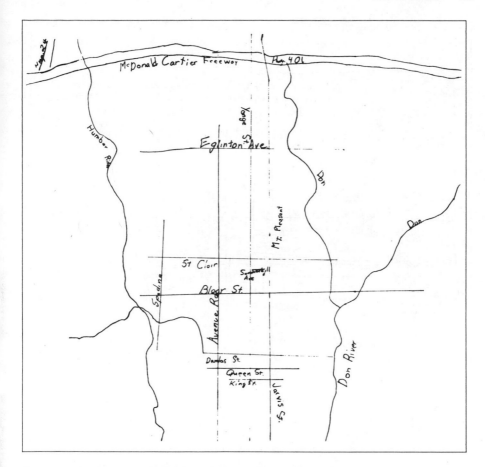

Figure 4. A Nine-Year-Old's Map of Toronto

with the downtown portions of the subway to put some important thoroughfares into the central business district; she probably learned the locations of the rivers and of Highway 401, however, in school. She still gives her own section of the city (From Bloor to Eglinton along Yonge) much more space than its due. The eleven-year-old (Figure 5) is aware of too many details for a map of this scale, so many that he gets some wrong and has trouble fitting others together. His map includes the lakefront, and shows places like the Royal Ontario Museum, the Exhibition Grounds, and the Airport as well as streets and waterways. Each child's view of the city is selective, but the older children can roam mentally through more of its territory, and they use different principles of selection.

Instead of starting with real cities, sociologist William Michelson asked people to map out ideal environments. He wondered what connection there was between

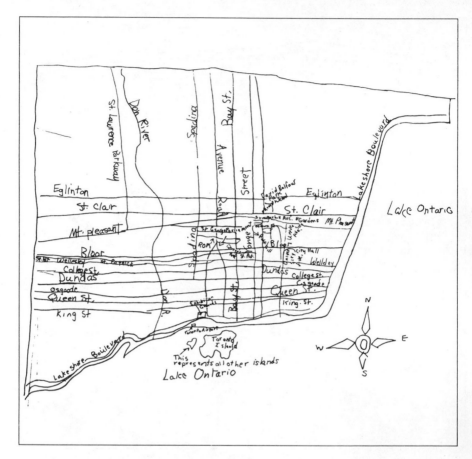

Figure 5. An Eleven-Year-Old's Map of Toronto

the things people wanted out of life in general and what sorts of neighborhoods they preferred, but his technique could be used for many other purposes.

The map drawer began with his own dwelling, placed a number of facilities such as schools, movies, shopping centers, and work places on the map, then drew a line around the area he would consider his neighborhood. Figure 6 contains a house with a yard about 200 feet square, a neighborhood including schools and a church within a fifteen-minute walk, and an area outside the neighborhood containing shopping facilities, a restaurant, and a job. Figure 7 shows only houses in the neighborhood, puts a post-office and a store just across its boundary, places a well-defined street between the house and all other facilities, and then traces detailed separate paths to a wide variety of centers of activity. These are rather different pictures of what the residential parts of cities should be like.

To complement this picture of the ideal world, people can tell us a great deal about what they do with the actual space of the city by recounting where they go,

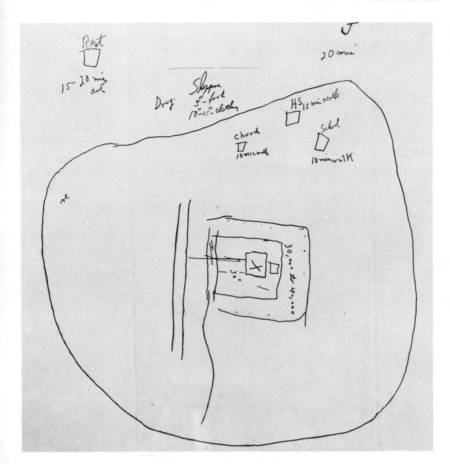

Figure 6. Ideal Environment #1

what they do and with whom, during an average day. One version of this is the "yesterday interview," in which the interviewer asks the person to give a history of yesterday from 6 A.M. to midnight, including each activity lasting ten minutes or more. Another version is the diary kept under the same rules. (Reiss' article, "Rural-Urban and Status Differences in Interpersonal Contacts," reprinted in Chapter 4, uses yet another variety of the same techniques.) Either one produces a valuable picture of how much time different kinds of people spend doing what, where, and with whom. The student of cities can learn from time-budgets when and where in a city the most people are likely to be in sociable contact with others, how much time is spent traveling, which activities most people do alone, which sections of the city are frequented by old people, rich people, or newcomers. How do the daily time-budgets of these individuals fit with the maps of the city they would draw?

Again we have moved from a simple notion to a complicated application.

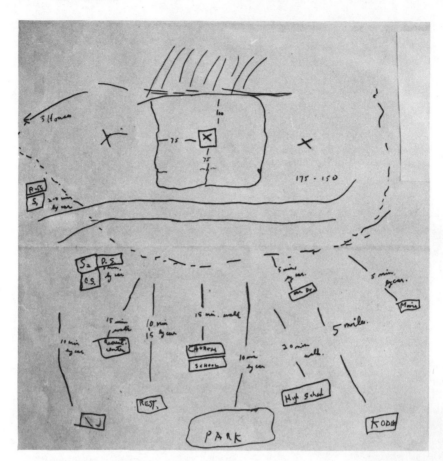

Figure 7. Ideal Environment #2

Some of these questions can be saved for a separate study. Who is on the street and when is fairly easy to observe. My students at the University of Toronto found they could make an informative first contact with a section of the city by going to a local intersection and recording who went by during scattered five-minute intervals. They set down not only how many people passed the corner, but also a rough judgment of age, sex, and whether they were alone or with others. They could do it by tallying within a grid, as shown in Table 1. These distributions vary sharply from place to place and from time to time.

If only the process of walking by could be slowed down, the observer could include the objects people are carrying, the way they are dressed, the languages they are speaking, how much they dawdle. A camera can catch some of these things very effectively. The photographs in Figure 8 show two locations about two miles apart on Bloor Street in Toronto. On the top is a fashionable downtown shopping apartment complex. On the bottom is a business street or an area heavily populated

TABLE 1
Tallying the Age and Sex of Passersby

	Male	Female
Alone		
Over 60		
20–60	1111	1
Under 20	1	1
In groups		
Over 60	111	1
20–60	1111	1
Under 20	11	11

by European immigrants, especially from Italy. The pictures show the two spots around noon in December on Friday, Saturday, and Sunday. The observer at the shopping-apartment area sees well-dressed women on Friday, couples and families on Saturday, an occasional solitary stroller on Sunday. Up the street, in the Italian neighborhood, he also sees women—but not so expensively dressed—on Friday, many mothers with their adolescent sons or daughters on Saturday, numerous groups of men roughly graded by age on Sunday. A series of photographs taken at intervals through the day would show the contrast even better. Even with only one time of day, the contrasts in activities and populations are obvious.

Of course, it takes a little bit of nerve to tally passers by or take pictures on the street. For observers with less nerve, observing the objects people leave around them is a good way to discover something important about their lives.

Here are some ideas culled from different research projects: count the proportion of door buttons pushed down in automobiles on the street in different areas in order to see how willing people are to leave their cars unlocked; notice how many backyards in a neighborhood contain grass, how many flower gardens, how many trash piles, and how many vegetable patches in order to get an idea of the local style of life; check the percentage of drawn blinds in order to judge how much people are shutting themselves off from others on the street; notice how many liquor bottles and what kind are thrown out on trash day in order to guess the home drinking patterns; record how many houses have outside Christmas decorations, and how elaborate they are, in order to gauge how much it is an occasion for public display.

Considering how much a part of everyday life these various sorts of observation are, it might seem that "urban anthropology" is nothing but a dressed-up version of common sense. Is it? It does deal with things everyone knows something about. It should build on good, common sense. But it also has more discipline and a greater focus than casual observation. The urban anthropologist's discipline shows up in his insistence on observing exactly how somebody says something or just how many people gather in a certain place, as well as his faithfulness in recording the

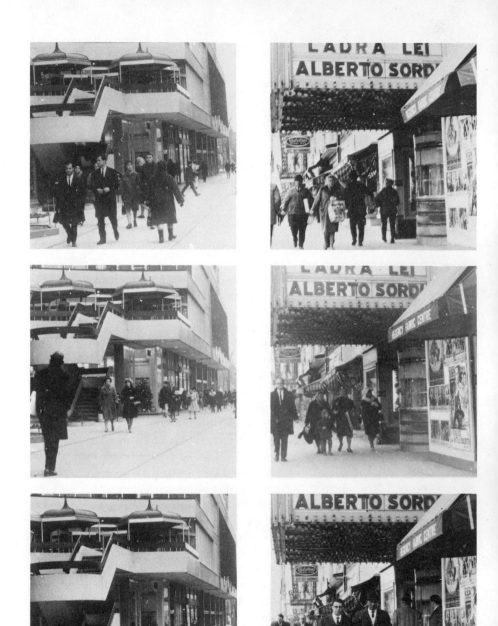

Figure 8. Two Toronto Street Scenes on Successive Days. *Top left:* Colonnade, Friday; *middle left:* Colonnade, Saturday; *bottom left:* Colonnade, Sunday; *top right:* Bloor St. West, Friday; *middle right:* Bloor St. West, Saturday; *bottom right:* Bloor St. West, Sunday.

observation for further reference. His focus is on social relations, especially on those revealing how groups are organized in the city.

Many pressing questions about cities need this systematic firsthand treatment. What difference does it make to people's social lives whether they live in separate houses, chains of garden apartments, or tall buildings? Does the dislocation caused by urban renewal wound people irreparably? Under what conditions do people have strong attachments to their neighborhoods? When are the dispossessed of the city likely to get together and protest their fate? What does it mean to become poor and to stay poor? How and when does assimilation work? Who and where are all the lonely people? Urban anthropology can produce at least some of the answers.

The anthropological approach to the city brings together theory, policy, action, and personal experience. Some city planners, uneasy at seeing almost all their colleagues working for governments and real estate developers, have started to organize groups of "advocate planners" to criticize official plans and offer alternative proposals on behalf of the people being planned for. We also need skilled and independent social researchers devoted to scrutinizing the facts and presumptions on which urban policies are based. Like Oscar Lewis, Herbert Gans, and Michael Harrington, they will have the chance to deal with vital theoretical issues along the way.

For the same reasons, urban anthropology has an important role in education. More than books about the history or the government of the city, it challenges the student to link his own fate and private experience to the life of the city as a whole. An inveterate city-walker myself, I often send my students out to walk a randomly assigned section of a city and report back on what they have seen. Even the life-time residents often find themselves in areas they have never really observed. Most of them learn something important about their city and about themselves.

The methods of urban anthropology leave room for the gifted amateur. I mean amateur in the exact sense of the word: someone who does something for the love of it. Survey research and much of the large-scale quantitative analysis so important to the study of cities depend on teams of specialists and expensive equipment. A few of the techniques I have described here are also easier to use with computers and other machines at hand. But most of the procedures are feasible for a person with a camera, a tape-recorder, a sketch pad, or just a quick eye and a ready notebook. Many of them consist of making observations most people make anyway, only more systematically.

THE PLACE OF THEORIES, CONCEPTS, AND TECHNIQUES

In order to know what to look for in cities and how to put together what we see, we also need good concepts, theories, and methods. That is where sharp observation and social scientific thinking intersect. Sooner or later, anyone who wants to produce comprehensive, systematic knowledge about cities will have to equip himself with some abstract theories, vocabularies, and technical skills which are not found in a city-dweller's everyday experience.

The sifting of census material, for example, recaptures very little of the day-to-day flavor of urban life, yet is essential for understanding changes in the city. Again, without careful conceptualization and measurement, it would be nearly impossible to determine whether racial segregation in a city over two or three years was increasing, decreasing, or holding steady. Finally, it takes a well-developed theory to anticipate the effect of rebuilding the downtown shopping area on the movement of people, goods, and traffic within the city. The social scientist has to weave informed observations of city life into systematic knowledge of urbanization, community structure, and cities; his loom is made of abstract theories, concepts, and analytic techniques.

The appropriate theories, concepts, and techniques are still developing. As a consequence, most generalizations about cities are debatable, apparent contradictions in research findings are commonplace, and reliable knowledge is fragmentary. We know much about traffic patterns in cities, about the effects of urban growth on agriculture in the surrounding areas, or about the way retailing varies from small towns to big cities. We know little about the impacts of different sorts of housing on the social lives of city-dwellers, the ways new family patterns spread from city to country, the conditions under which informal neighborhood ties draw people into crime or keep them out of it. Students of cities do not lack ideas, prejudices, even convictions on these questions; they lack systematic knowledge. The analyst of any one of these urban phenomena usually has several theories at his disposal—theories which are obviously different, yet which are too incomplete or poorly specified to permit a definitive test.

CONCEPTS

Students of urbanization have developed five main ways of identifying groups of men as communities. Let us call them:

1. ecological
2. normative
3. locational
4. interactional
5. holistic

The five definitions of community lead to five rather different ways of dealing with cities and with urbanization. They do not entirely exclude each other. Yet each has its own characteristic theories, rules of thumb, methods, styles of analysis, and difficulties.

All five build on the observation of a population acting—and interacting—within a defined territory. All five therefore pay attention to the relations of the same great clusters of variables: (1) population, (2) activity, and (3) territory. Every discussion of community structure, cities, and urbanization comes down to a way of talking about the interaction of these three. We can sketch them as a triangle whose sides represent interactions (see Figure 9).

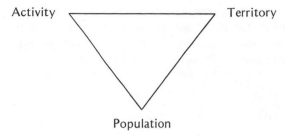

Figure 9. The Ecological Triangle

Except for the holistic approach, each of these lines of argument deals mainly with one side of the triangle. The *ecological* approach stresses the relationship of the population to the territory. The *normative* approach accents the orientation of the population to its activities. The *locational* approach concentrates on the distribution of activities with respect to territory. The *interactional* approach singles out the activities which link the members of the population. The *holistic* approach lumps them all together.

So we can place the five approaches on the triangle as shown in Figure 10. According to the diagram, the interactional and normative approaches overlap more than the others. The first emphasizes the identifiable links and interactions among persons or households, while the second underlines the beliefs and sentiments associated with the interactions. The distinction matters, since people who are linked to each other often differ in beliefs and sentiments, and people who have similar beliefs and sentiments often are unlinked to each other.

In all these approaches the community is the basic unit, the city is a special kind of community, and urbanization consists of the growing importance of the city. The definitions of community (and therefore of city and urbanization), however, differ sharply from one approach to another. Many people have tried to eliminate this variability by insisting that only one definition is right. Others have tried to find the common ground in all of them. We will do better to search for

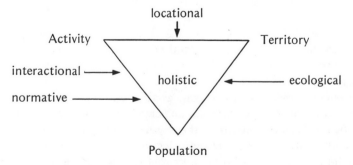

Figure 10. Approaches to the Ecological Triangle

consistency within each of the approaches; then we can redefine the problem by examining the effects of different forms of linkage on sentiments, of population distributions on distributions of activity, and so on. To that end, let us review in turn each of the major approaches to community, city, and urbanization.

ECOLOGICAL IDEAS OF CITY, COMMUNITY, URBANIZATION[6]

An *ecological* definition of community bears down on the common properties of human populations and other aggregates of animals or plants. According to a standard text in biological ecology, a community "includes all of the populations occupying a given area."[7] Human ecologist Amos Hawley offers a somewhat different definition: "Community ordinarily denotes a territorially localized population that carries on a collective life through a given set of institutions."[8]

Both biological and human ecologists begin with localized populations. The human ecologist adds common institutions. So long as the definition of "institutions" is not too stringent, neither separating one community from another nor deciding whether a certain collection of people really form a community poses much of a problem. Almost any localized population forms a community. Thus the demographer O.D. Duncan's essay, "Population Distribution and Community Structure" (found in Chapter 3 of this book), wades into the analysis of population patterns without much worry about the old question "What *is* a community?" The discussion of "Metropolis as Ecosystem" by the biologist Laurence Tilly in Chapter 5 concentrates on forms of interdependence within the metropolis rather than on the nature of its boundaries.

In order to insure some comparability from one case to the next, however, ecologists often block out the population to be studied through its sharing of a common niche (a mountain valley, an island, a lake shore) or through the pattern of density (the population ends where its density reaches a low point). This approach works quite well with small, self-contained populations. The trouble begins where the population is more or less continuously distributed over large territories or where the common institutions go far beyond any particular locality.

Human ecologists often consider any large, dense community to be a city. In his "Urbanism as a Way of Life," one of the most influential articles ever written on the subject, Louis Wirth added the adjective "heterogeneous" to a city's qualifications and then tried to show that size, density, and heterogeneity explained the predominant features of urban social life.

At first, this approach seems to offer a delightfully easy way to distinguish cities from other communities: just take the biggest and densest. Then it turns out that in order to decide how big or dense a population is the investigator first has to set some bounds to it. He usually does that either by judging for himself which groups of people depend on each other or by accepting someone else's delineation of municipalities, counties, and so on. In North America, one's ideas of the size and density of big cities change radically in switching from incorporated municipalities to metropolitan areas as the main units of analysis. France is considered more rural than it is in many international comparisons, because its census-takers use communes as their basic units and only start calling them "urban" when there are at least 2,000 people in the central settlement, regardless of how many more there are in the surrounding territory. Nevertheless, when the rules stay constant from one place to the next, size and density give us convenient, generally available criteria for singling out communities which unquestionably have some important features in common.

Urbanization, in this view, is the increasing concentration of a large territory's population in big, dense communities. The rate of urbanization can be thought of quite simply as the increase in proportion of the total population in communities above a certain size over a given period of time: say, percent increase per year of the proportion of a nation's entire population in places of 50,000 inhabitants or more. Kingsley Davis' general essay on the urbanization of the human population in Chapter 2 takes exactly that tack: he distinguishes sharply between *absolute* increase in urban population (which can easily occur with no change in the rural and urban proportions so long as the overall birth rate is high enough), and *relative* increase, which is true urbanization.

Davis' approach has the virtues of simplicity and precision. It does not work, however, unless the units called "urban" are reasonably comparable. Furthermore, it requires us to delineate precisely the territory and the population of the nation, region, or other large unit undergoing urbanization; the delineation does not pose any particular problems when the unit is a large, well-defined country like Brazil or the Soviet Union; when we start analyzing the urbanization of Hong Kong, Oceania, the American South, or some other such area with peculiar or indefinite boundaries, the going gets rougher. Where these problems can be met, Davis' procedure is the most practical and common way of indexing urbanization.

Within this framework, urbanization can occur through: (1) a higher rate of natural increase (excess of births over deaths) among the population already in cities than among the rest of the population, and/or (2) greater net migration (excess of in-migrants over out-migrants) to cities than to the rest of the territory. What commonly happens, in fact, is a small (or even negative) contribution from urban natural increase accompanied by a larger net migration from the rest of the territory to the city. So the student of urbanization working in this tradition ordinarily pays a great deal of attention to migration and the opportunities which encourage it.

This way of breaking down the subject matter helps explain the affinities of demography and human ecology. They both have more or less the same concerns and major variables. They share many definitions, assumptions, and sources of data. They have a common penchant for quantitative analysis and quantifiable problems. The demographic-ecological approach to communities, cities, and urbanization is, in short, already coherent and well established.

NORMATIVE IDEAS[9]

The *normative* approach has neither the unity nor the precision of the ecological approach, but it does have a distinct character. Normative definitions of community depend on the nature of the attachment of individuals to the groups of which they are members. I call them "normative" because they emphasize the extent and content of the norms binding men to their communities; the labels "cultural" or "sentimental" apply almost as well, since the sharing of a common culture or of sentiments of solidarity so regularly comes along with the sharing of norms.

MacIver's well-worn definition of a community singled out "any circle of people who live together, who belong together, so that they share, not this or that particular interest, but a whole set of interests wide enough and complete enough to include their lives."[10] This sort of notion makes sense of the common idea that recent urbanization, industrialization, and bureaucratization have destroyed the old-fashioned, integrated human community.[11] The territory doesn't matter very much here, even if some commentators feel that attachment to a small, well-defined territory somehow reinforces a population's shared interests. Unlike the ecologist, the follower of MacIver may well see a close analogy between highly organized occupational groups, like lawyers, or a distinct religious group, like Mormons, and territorial communities; he may well speak of occupational communities and religious communities. What matters is the shared interest, the sense of belonging, the commitment to the collectivity. Those who take this approach commonly assume that a shared culture and style of life accompany this shared commitment.

The normative definition of community is closer to common sense than the ecological one. It also has some of the weaknesses of common sense. The student of communities using a normative approach can only determine after a great effort whether the collection of people he has been observing "really" form a community. He is much more likely than the ecologist to get involved in asking people how they feel about things, in observing similarities in personal style or beliefs, in looking for psychological evidence, in collecting linguistic clues. (We can see a number of inquiries of this very kind yielding practical conclusions in the article by Michelson, "Social Insights to Guide the Design of Housing for Low Income Families," in Chapter 5.) He is much more likely to see a community as a mosaic of subcultures. He stands close to the way people themselves see their life in communities and therefore suffers from most of the uncertainties and contradictions of those perceptions.

In the normative line of thought, the city has two important aspects: as a place in which a certain kind of norm—or lack of norms—prevails, and as a place from which a certain way of life spreads. To be sure, the normative theorist often thinks large size produces impersonality, isolation, and flagging commitment, but to him not size but a certain quality of life is the essence of urbanity. Some small places have it, some big places lack it.

That "it" regularly spills out in a string of adjectives—secular, mobile, special-ized, impersonal, rational, instrumental, and so forth. As he conducted a famous series of Mexican community studies during the 1930's, Robert Redfield formu-lated just such a list in lining up his real communities between two poles: a small, personal, sacred "folk community" and its opposite, the city. Such complicated criteria sometimes work well in the hands of a skilled observer with a small number of cases, as in Redfield's Mexican studies. No one has applied them to the comparison of a large number of communities with any notable success. Nor has it been easy to get any two observers to agree how to apply them to complicated communities full of internal variations.

The extension to urbanization is obvious. Instead of a demographic process of agglomeration, urbanization becomes the production and diffusion of a way of life. The more people become involved in that way of life (whether they live in cities or not), the more we speak of their country as urbanized. Here there is nothing like the voluminous quantitative data or the standardized measures the ecologists have to work with. Yet as international sample surveys multiply, alternative indexes are coming into use. Changes in the degree of literacy, the proportion of people speaking the national language rather than a dialect, the extent of exposure to the mass media or the spread of information about international affairs might all be legitimate indexes of urbanization. (The analysis of the urbanization of Guaraní by Garvin and Mathiot in Chapter 2 suggests why linguistic cues would be helpful, while the discussion of the "civic bond" by Meier in Chapter 4 contains ideas for measurement.) We could even imagine a nation in which the proportion of the population in big settlements was declining, yet which by these standards could be said to be urbanizing.

That imaginary case points out the risks in a normative conception of urbanization. If the changes it emphasizes actually have little to do with the size of communities, perhaps they have little to do with the rest of community organiza-tion. If they are only incidentally related to the growth of cities, most likely some other word than "urbanization" would do better. In short, the normative approach to communities, cities, and urbanization gets at some fundamental processes the ecological approach by-passes, but it is hard to use systematically and often includes too much.

LOCATIONAL IDEAS[12]

Locational views of communities, cities, and urbanization shift the emphasis from persons to activities, thus exposing the junction between community structure and economic processes. Sociologists have rarely taken the locational view, but geographers have often done so. Its distinguishing feature is the singling out of spatial distributions of interdependent activities for analysis. The overwhelming bulk of the research and theorizing in the tradition has dealt with the activities of production and distribution.

Very likely the most serious and comprehensive attempt so far to apply a locational argument to a big urban complex was the New York Metropolitan Study.[13] In that study, Hoover, Vernon, and their collaborators made a great effort to order the whole range of activities of the metropolitan area in terms of the changing cost and accessibility of different locations and tried to treat the distribution of population at any point in time as a function of the distribution of activities. They showed, for example, the exceptional attachment to downtown locations of firms (like advertising agencies and small garment-makers) dependent on hour-to-hour contact with other organizations in the same field. Except for racial and ethnic segregation—which is, in New York, a glaring exception—the scheme worked impressively well.

Planners have launched some more modest but ingenious inquiries in the same direction. Some of them have examined how the geographic pattern of a household's activities varies with the kind of activity and the kind of household: whether old persons and poor families stay close to home, whether the journey to work is the only regular trip that takes some kinds of people out of the neighborhood, and so on. In Kevin Lynch's work (represented by "The Pattern of the Metropolis" in Chapter 4), we find the way individuals perceive different kinds of buildings, streets, or neighborhoods linked to the spatial pattern of the whole city. Another kind of planning analysis (William Alonso's "Historical and Structural Theories of Urban Form" in Chapter 5) attempts to pin down the dynamics of changes in activity patterns within the city in order to anticipate the effects of different sorts of deliberate change of land use. The current work of planners therefore points to a livelier and more useful version of a very old device: the map of land use or of population distribution.

The population distributed across the face of the map is, of course, fictitious—first, because almost all such maps take declared place of residence as the locus of each individual, when metropolitan residents spend a good half of their time somewhere else; second, because even those people who do spend much of their time in their declared residences are never all there at the same time. Years ago, Gerald Breese offered a mild and intelligent corrective by charting the *daytime* population of Chicago's central business district, but hardly anyone else followed his lead.[14] The convenience of census-defined populations was too great.

Likewise, the land-use map employs a fearsome abstraction, with its bold blues and yellows, strident cross-hatches and its rare chaste "mixed uses" assigning to one use at a time areas whose very essence is to have many things going on at once. I have sometimes daydreamed of a device for teaching and research which would offset some of this rigidity. It would be a series of filmed frames of an urban map representing persons carrying on various major activities (eating, sleeping, traveling, manufacturing, making love, trading, and so on) in their actual locations for successive hours of the day, days of the week, weeks of the year. Taken singly, the frames would look like combined land-use and population-distribution maps; put into motion, they would reveal the metabolism of the city (run the film slow for the daily rhythms, fast for the yearly ones).

Why not have a comparable map for sociability? When and where are people alone, in the company of strangers, engaged in business deals, surrounded by friends? At what time of the week, and where, are the maximum number of people alone or in the midst of strangers, as urbanites are supposed to be so often? Does that have anything to do with the pattern of suicide? Arthur Stinchcombe's essay in Chapter 3 tells us that differences in the patterns of public versus private space and their use in city and country produce substantially different varieties of police practice and consequently important rural-urban contrasts in reported crime. Does that effect show up on the sociability map? Since we know how foolish it is to relate spot maps of juvenile delinquency to other spot maps of residential characteristics when teenagers stray so far from home, perhaps we could examine the correspondence between activity distributions and spatial or temporal fluctuations in juvenile offenses.

These speculations are not absurd. If someone could reduce the difficulties of handling huge files of uncertain data, the great American metropolitan transportation surveys of the last few decades (which often have run into tens of thousands of interviews including detailed enumerations of trips by members of the households) could yield crude approximations of the fantastic film. Successive aerial photographs, of which many already exist, would at least catch the patterns of activity out in the open.

As the modest but informative study by A.J. Reiss in Chapter 4 shows, the old-fashioned time-budget has great possibilities. If researchers collecting time-budgets from individual urbanites were to code them carefully for location and social setting, then in the aggregate such bits of information about time, place, activity, and social setting would turn into something like the urban movie of my daydreams. My own work with time-budgets persuades me that the job would be irritating and expensive but by no means impossible. It would give new meaning to a locational view of community, city, and urbanization.

Location theorists eschew the word "community," partly because of their frequent insistence that the same principles operate at the local, regional, and national levels. Yet they have a local unit, variously called a *local system*, a *region*, a *spatial economy* or something else. It consists of a central place plus a tributary area, both depending on each other in the production and distribution of some set of goods and services. Presumably we would call the smallest or lowest-level unit of this kind a community. That is, in fact, approximately what the students of rural trade-center communities in the American Midwest used to single out for investigation.

Because of the requirement that there be both a node and a tributary area for that node, the locational conception is somewhat more exacting than the ecological one. The typical approach to delineating communities turns out, reasonably enough, to be the mapping of nodes (themselves identified by higher density, specialized activities, or maybe junctions of communication lines), followed by the division of the entire territory under examination into tributary areas. That assignment of tributary areas to nodes may be quite arbitrary. It may also depend on the estimation or measurement of dependence on the node, as in the classic rural sociological procedure of asking farmers where they go for banking, marketing, churching, and the like. The troubles in using a locational conception of community begin when nodes come too close to each other, when different interdependent activities have substantially different geographic distributions, and when the territories occupied by interdependent activities are not contiguous.

This notion of community expands easily to the idea of a hierarchy of local systems—each one identified by a node plus a tributary area, but higher-level ones including several nodes of lower-level systems within their tributary areas. A city then becomes the node of a higher-level system. Given such a beginning, the dividing line between city and town or city and country is no more than a convention. Likewise, one can think of the systems themselves as being more or less urban. Then the national system, if one exists, is the most urban of all, and its node the most citified.

There the difficulties begin. First, the requisite mapping of interdependent activities and sorting out of the hierarchy of central places is not only arduous but delicate. In practice geographers have been satisfied to show that the nodes of various sizes fall into a regular geographic pattern, and even that for no more than a region at a time. Second, both the logic and the practical procedures which follow from it put enormous difficulties in the way of identifying cities in a comparable manner within different societies. Third, the very logic of the analysis makes it very easy to identify the node and very hard to set any boundaries to it. We might be able to escape the difficulty by defining the city as *all* of the lowest-level system for which a node of a high-level system is also the node, but that way of doing it has its own peculiarities; in any case, so far as I know it has not been tried.

The locational approach does lead to a rather interesting notion of urbanization—that of the elaboration of the hierarchy of central places and their dependent systems. Thus the processes that fill in chinks in the system, regularize it, and add new levels to it are the processes of urbanization. We might imagine indexing urbanization through changes in the number of levels of markets, rather than the sheer number of markets. Or we might examine changes in the rank-size distribution of places, rather than the sheer sizes of communities. For the present, however, the theories, practices, and findings in this field of inquiry have too little shape to provide much guidance for the systematic comparison of large populations.

INTERACTIONAL IDEAS[15]

The *interactional* approach also shows unrealized promise. It brings the extent and form of the links among the members of a population into prominence, and gives less prominence to the territory as such. In his article in this book, Marc Fried speaks of a working-class community as "an overlapping series of close-knit networks situated in a single geographical or residential area." Two traditions of research—one which began with the study of friendship patterns in children's groups and moved on to investigations of solidarity, friendship, and influence in rural areas, the other starting with big-city studies of working-class life—have converged to produce the notion of a community as a localized social network.

The fundamental idea is fairly simple. We looked at its essentials earlier: any contract or relationship between two persons define a link. All such links within a population form a network with a definite pattern. We might, for example, imagine the two markedly different networks of friendship within a population of nine people shown in Figure 11. Group A has a great many cross-cutting links and two partly distinct cliques (1,2,4,5 and 5,6,8,9); Group B has relatively sparse connections arranged in long chains, so that breaking almost any link would cut several people off from the rest. If patterns A and B compounded to communities of 1,000 or 100,000 people, they would obviously have very different qualities of life.

Unfortunately, the actual tracing of networks of kinship, friendship, influence, and the like demands a great deal of effort and ingenuity. So far no one has done it on a sufficient scale to help much in the delineation of communities. It has been useful mainly in the identification of significant divisions *within* communities. In his analysis of the renewed-out-of-sight West End of Boston (see Chapter 5), for example, Marc Fried compares those residents of the neighborhood who were caught up in local close-knit networks (and thus hit exceptionally hard by the neighborhood's destruction) with others more loosely attached to the people of the area. More work of this kind is needed.

Looser forms of the interactional approach, however, have been part of the lore of community studies for half a century: the identification of all the people who use a common center of activity, the analysis of traffic patterns and flow of communication, the identification of friends, neighbors, relatives, or influentials by survey respondents. Anthropologists like Pitt-Rivers often have traced the clusters of friends, relatives, trading partners, or sharers of gossip within small communities

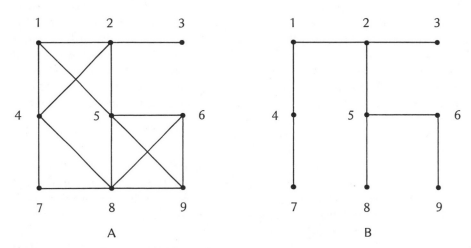

Figure 11. Two Contrasting Networks

(see Chapter 3). Students of traffic flows and of daily routines also have collected enough information to make possible the identification of groups of people sharing the same pacing of activity within a city, although this has not yet actually been done.

The strength of the interactional approach lies in its getting directly at social relations which are in principle observable and important. Its weaknesses come from the very complexity of social interactions. They are not only varied but also difficult to weigh (how do we compare an area where people know each other intimately through eavesdropping but rarely speak in public with an area where people live in relative isolation but are extensively connected by kinship?) and tricky to bound (if many mobile New Yorkers have close contacts in Philadelphia, are New York and Philadelphia the same community?). Network notions of communities are easier to use in theory than in practice.

Interactional concepts of the city rely especially on the scale and structure of personal networks. Rather than a big, dense place or one in which urbane norms prevail, we might consider a city to be the kind of community whose members often interact with others outside the community, and in which different activities (work versus recreation versus worship, for example) each generate different specialized networks of interaction. The comparison Reiss makes of rural and urban time budgets (Chapter 4), the distinctions between different ways of being attached to communities in America and Africa offered by the Mac Donalds (Chapter 3) and by Gutkind (Chapter 4), and the ingenious notions of the "civic bond" developed by Meier (Chapter 4) all suggest methods for indexing the urbanity of a community. The indexes now available, however, are mainly measures of communication and differentiation: mail flow per capita, population mobility, labor force distribution, extent of market activity, and so on.

The drawbacks of an interactional approach are subtle but serious. Even if he has developed a workable means of identifying and bounding individual communities, the student of cities in this tradition faces the weighting problem again. What *kinds* of social relations must be specialized and large in scale in order to qualify a community as urban? Is one sexual relationship worth twenty business contacts? And how do we get at the intensity or personal significance of various kinds of social relations? (Surely there is more influence per minute in contacts between parents and children than in contacts between fellow subway riders, but how do we compare them?) It is possible to weigh various social relations in terms of their influence and emotional content. Still, that job is much harder than learning the number of people living in the community.

The advantage, of course, is that an interactional approach to the city brings us much closer to what we already claim to know about other forms of social organization, such as kinship, industrial enterprise, or voluntary association. It makes the closing of the gap between the study of those phenomena and the analysis of the city that much easier.

What would an interactional description of urbanization look like? Scott Greer's treatment of urbanization as a growth in the scale of social relations offers a good example.[16] With Greer, we might think of urbanization largely in terms of the growth of specialized networks of social relations (one built around the job market, another around the commodity market, a third around formal politics, and so on) extending across whole continents and intersecting in complicated ways within any particular community. In this book, Warner's comparison of Philadelphia at three different points in time as well as my own analysis of American migration patterns (both reprinted in Chapter 4) rely on that general perspective. In this sense, urbanization can go on without any major physical movements of population—although that is unusual—and a small community can easily urbanize while remaining small. Changes in communication, mobility, and differentiation would all provide reasonable indexes of urbanization, especially if they summed up the experiences of communities instead of presenting some sort of average for all individuals. It is more to the point, for instance, to determine how many communities have highly differentiated labor forces, since in theory a highly differentiated nation could be made up of a number of one-industry towns.

When it comes to convenience and precision, the interactional approach to urbanization stands between the normative and ecological approaches. Its elements are easier to grasp and index than sentiments or ways of life are, but much harder to handle than community size, density, or net migration. Like the normative, the interactional approach runs a risk of veering off into the treatment of huge changes only loosely connected with the growth of cities. The issues it raises matter so much that they often drag in all the other big issues, and thus clog up the analysis. The more carefully the variables have been specified, however, the less likely this is to happen.

HOLISTIC IDEAS[17]

All the kinds of analysis we have discussed so far touch on the question of how the very large structures we loosely call "societies" operate. Some students of communities, cities, and urbanization compound all of them by thinking of what happens to any particular community primarily as a sample of what is happening to the entire society. Anthropologists have for generations settled down in small communities in order to sample large ways of life. As Lloyd Warner described his reasons for taking on the study of Yankee City:

> The immediate interest was in the community itself; the larger and more important purposes were to use the community as a convenient microcosm for field study, thus to gain new knowledge about the larger American social life, and with similar studies of other societies, to use the results comparatively.[18]

In itself, the holistic view does not provide much guidance for the delineation of individual communities. It has to begin with one of the other strategies. But at least it suggests that for any territorial group to be a community, it must contain a complete round of life; thus, a suburb or a military base becomes a dubious case.

When applied to cities, the holistic approach tends to lean on general ideas of the drift of change in the society as a whole; the cities are then the communities in which the big social changes have gone farthest. In his *Decline of the West*, Oswald Spengler portrayed the city as the last and most decadent expression of a dying society. In his deliberately contrary *Rise of the West*, William McNeill portrays the city as the leading edge of cultural accomplishment. The flaw in this way of identifying cities is that we must know the main direction of change in the society before deciding which communities embody it. We are usually in a better position to do that for the past than for the present. Yet despite its difficulties, this approach to cities does bring out two principles which ecological, normative, locational, and interactional approaches can easily miss: first, that every city sums up the civilization which produced it; second, that much of its special character lies in its relationship to the rest of the world.

Urbanization and large-scale social change, then, turn out to be about the same thing. We catch the whole sweep of social evolution by classifying societies (and the communities within them) as folk/feudal/urban. Caro Baroja's article in Chapter 5, "Reflections on Ancient Commonplaces," concerning enduring differences between rural and urban ways of life is nothing less than reflections on the nature of civilization itself.

In attempting to employ the holistic approach concretely, we may use multivariate indexes of modernization. Yet then we abandon the search for changes which are especially associated with the increasing preeminence of cities rather than the expansion of factory production or the growth of bureaucracy. Of course, this theoretical bundling together of different types of change has great advantages and some justification, since in the contemporary world all these transformations occur together with such complexity and confusion. But it is too soon to quit searching for the specific properties of communities, cities, and urbanization.

THE ALTERNATIVES

Up to this point we have seen that there are five main ways of conceiving of communities and that each one leads to a substantially different treatment of cities and urbanization. The ecological, normative, locational, interactional, and holistic approaches all have interesting advantages depending on what we are trying to find out. We could also adopt other ways of portraying communities: as systems of communication, organisms, art forms, markets, or as machines. Robert Redfield once wrote a brilliant little book laying out half a dozen distinct ways of understanding communities.[19]

The five approaches form the main threads of the remainder of this book—especially the first four, since the holistic approach is so much harder to use systematically. They are contrasting threads, and I will emphasize the contrasts below. The point is not to decide which is true or false. At their best, ecological, normative, locational, and interactional notions of the city are selective conceptual schemes, labeling some features of urban life conveniently and leaving others out completely. Each one selects differently, however; as a result, each one is useful for some purposes and worthless for others. Part of the book's task is therefore to match up purposes and approaches.

In the present state of knowledge, the approaches differ markedly in the ease with which we can observe and measure their most important variables. On the whole, ecological and locational schemes currently lend themselves to more precise measurement than normative and interactional schemes do. Furthermore, current theories about communities, cities, and urbanization framed in locational or eco- logical terms tend to be more elegant and more precise than others. The state of measurement and the state of theory combine to make it much easier to test hypotheses, new or old, within the ecological and locational frameworks.

At first glance, this looks like a powerful argument for junking normative and interactional approaches. The difficulty, of course, is that the others leave out features of urban life about which we have vital questions: how much and how inevitably urbanization produces cool, specialized, impersonal social relations; whether beyond some critical scale communities become oppressive, conflict-ridden, and ungovernable; under what conditions city life promotes social mobility; and so on. Perhaps we will finally discover that the answers to all these questions depend on basic effects of the distribution of populations and activities in space. In that case our fundamental theories of urbanism will take an ecological or locational form, and we will look back with respect to the many writers who are now emphasizing the analogies between such phenomena as the pathological behavior of laboratory animals forced to live at high densities and the frantic idiocies of city-dwellers.

Personally, I doubt that any of the more popular versions of such arguments will turn out to have much value, if only because of such evident difficulties as the fact that Americans (both in cities and outside them) live at exceptionally low densities by world standards, and that in the cities those densities are going down; yet those same Americans contribute more than their share to the world's urban ills. But even if current theories about the effects of density, mobility, size, and segregation turn out to be substantially correct, linking them to the texture and structure of social life will require us to take into consideration a wide range of variables which interactional and normative theorists now emphasize, but which locational and ecological theorists tend to ignore. So the confrontation of inter- actional, locational, ecological, and normative conceptions of urban phenomena is also a way of identifying the crucial sets of variables which adequate future theories of urban life will have to take into account.

To bring about that confrontation, we first deal with urbanization in a variety of perspectives. Then we move on to the analysis of community structure in general, following that by closing in on the city as a special type of community. Afterwards we ask questions about deliberate intervention in the lives of cities and city people. Finally comes a review of questions which are still open and crying for attention.

NOTES

1. Translated by permission from Paul Claudel, *La Ville,* 2nd version, © Mercure de France 1911.
2. With only minor alterations, the material which follows comes from Charles Tilly, "Anthropology on the Town," *Habitat,* 10 (Jan.–Feb. 1967), pp. 20–25. The articles in this book which most clearly illustrate an anthropological approach to cities and other communities are Garvin and Mathiot, "The Urbanization of the Guaraní Language" (Chapter 2), Pitt-Rivers, "Social Class in a French Village" (Chapter 3), Gutkind, "African Urbanism, Mobility, and the Social Network" (Chapter 4). See also Lisa Redfield Peattie, *The View from the Barrio* (Ann Arbor: University of Michigan Press, 1968).
3. The articles in this book which best illustrate the sociologists' usual way of looking at cities are Stinchcombe, "Institutions of Privacy in the Determination of Police Administrative Practice" (Chapter 3), Tilly, "Metropolitan Boston's Social Structure" (Chapter 3), Reiss, "Rural-Urban and Status Differences in Interpersonal Contacts" (Chapter 4), Tilly, "Migration to American Cities" (Chapter 4), Michelson, "Social Insights to Guide the Design of Housing for Low Income Families" (Chapter 5), and Fried, "Functions of the Working-Class Community in Modern Urban Society" (Chapter 5).
4. Michael Harrington, *The Other America* (New York: Macmillan, 1963), pp. 2–3.
5. Kevin Lynch, *The Image of the City* (Cambridge, Mass.: MIT Press, 1960), p. 141.
6. The clearest examples of this approach among the selections in this book are Davis, "The Urbanization of the Human Population" (Chapter 2), Abu-Lughod, "Urban-Rural Differences as a Function of the Demographic Transition" (Chapter 2), Duncan, "Population Distribution and Community Structure" (Chapter 3), and Tilly, "Metropolis as Ecosystem" (Chapter 5).
7. Eugene P. Odum, *Fundamentals of Ecology* (Philadelphia: Saunders 1971, 3rd edition), p. 5.
8. Amos H. Hawley, *Urban Society: An Ecological Approach* (New York: Ronald, 1971), p. 10.
9. Although there are normative elements in many of the articles, the papers in this book most clearly adopting the approach are Garvin and Mathiot, "The Urbanization of the Guaraní Language" (Chapter 2) and Caro Baroja "The City and the Country" (Chapter 5).
10. R. M. MacIver, *Society: Its Structure and Changes* (New York: Long and Smith, 1932), pp. 9–10.
11. For a lengthy and interesting presentation of this argument, including convenient summaries of a number of studies of American communities, see Maurice Stein, *The Eclipse of Community* (Princeton, N.J.: Princeton University Press, 1960).
12. The reader will find the most definite expressions of this perspective in Murphey, "Traditionalism and Colonialism" (Chapter 2), Lynch, "The Pattern of the Metropolis" (Chapter 4), and Alonso, "The Historical and the Structural Theories of Urban Form" (Chapter 5).
13. See, among other volumes, Edgar M. Hoover and Raymond Vernon, *Anatomy of a Metropolis* (Cambridge: Harvard University Press, 1959).
14. For a later report of this work, see Gerald M. Breese, "The Daytime Population of the Central Business District," in Ernest W. Burgess and Donald J. Bogue, eds., *Contributions to Urban Sociology* (Chicago: University of Chicago Press, 1964), pp. 112–128.
15. Interactional analyses appear most emphatically in MacDonald and MacDonald, "Chain Migration, Ethnic Neighborhood Formation, and Social Networks" (Chapter 3), Gutkind, "African Urbanism, Mobility and the Social Network" (Chapter 4), Meier, "The Civic Bond" (Chapter 5), Fried, "Functions of the Working-Class Community in Modern Urban Society" (Chapter 5).
16. Scott Greer, *The Emerging City* (New York: Free Press, 1962).
17. The only pure example of a holistic statement in this book is the sweeping historical survey by Mumford (Chapter 2), but that is a superb specimen. Precisely because of the nature of the holistic approach, it is hard to find short selections which convey its special features.
18. W. Lloyd Warner et al., *Yankee City* (New Haven, Conn.: Yale University Press, 1963; abridged one-volume edition), p. xiii.
19. Robert Redfield, *The Little Community* (Chicago: University of Chicago Press, 1955).

Selected Readings

These chapter-end bibliographies will emphasize: (1) books, (2) works in English, (3) writings more recent than the reviews of the field and detailed bibliographies listed here and at the end of Chapter 2, (4) writings which—both in themselves and through the sources they use—lead the reader to a wide range of time, place, perspective, and subject matter, (5) important writings rarely cited in American summaries of urban studies, (6) items which have some particular bearing on the themes of this book. This means that some excellent recent works are not on the list, while some mediocre works are, simply because they mention a considerable range of sources or because they are the best available in English. It also means that the user of these bibliographies—by exploring the most promising general publications shown, by looking at the specific items dealing most directly with his subject, and by scanning the footnotes of the relevant articles in this book—should be able to assemble efficiently an adequate list of sources for almost any special problem in the study of communities, cities, and urbanization.

GENERAL WORKS AND COLLECTIONS OF PAPERS

Abrams, Charles. *Man's Struggle for Shelter in an Urbanizing World.* Cambridge, Mass.: M.I.T. Press, 1964. World survey of housing problems.

Beshers, James. *Urban Social Structure.* New York: Free Press, 1962. Reviews previous work and states a simple theory of residential arrangements.

Bollens, John C., and Henry J. Schmandt. *The Metropolis: Its People, Politics, and Economic Life.* New York: Harper & Row, 1965. A vast compendium emphasizing politics and policy.

Breese, Gerald, ed. *The City in Newly Developing Countries: Readings on Urbanism and Urbanization.* Englewood Cliffs, N.J.: Prentice-Hall, 1969. A selection of the best recent writings strongly emphasizing sociological work.

Burgess, Ernest W., and Donald J. Bogue. *Contributions to Urban Sociology.* Chicago: University of Chicago Press, 1964. Excerpts from the best work of living members of the "Chicago School".

Chinitz, Benjamin, ed. *City and Suburb: The Economics of Urban Growth.* Englewood Cliffs, N.J.: Prentice-Hall, 1964.

Duhl, Leonard J., ed. *The Urban Condition.* New York: Basic Books, 1963. Diverse and lively essays converging on questions of mental health.

Friedmann, John, and William Alonso, eds. *Regional Development and Planning.* Cambridge, Mass.: M.I.T. Press, 1964. A reader.

Greer, Scott. *The Emerging City.* New York: Free Press, 1962. Imaginative treatise-text in the tradition of Social Area Analysis.

Hatt, Paul, and Albert J. Reiss, Jr., eds. *Cities and Society.* Glencoe, Ill.: Free Press, 1957. A reader with extensive systematic bibliography.

Higonnet, Patrice L. R. *Pont-de-Montvert: Social Structure and Politics in a French Village, 1700–1914.* Cambridge, Mass.: Harvard University Press, 1971. The time-span and sure handling of this developing community's history help bring out the connection between local experience and national transformation.

Johnson, James H. *Urban Geography: An Introductory Analysis.* New York: Pergamon Press, 1967. A solid, well-illustrated standard textbook.

Mayer, Harold M., and Clyde F. Kohn, eds. *Readings in Urban Geography.* Chicago: University of Chicago Press, 1959.

Meadows, Paul, and Ephraim H. Mizruchi, eds. *Urbanism, Urbanization, and Change: Comparative Perspective.* Reading, Mass.: Addison-Wesley, 1969. Abundant readings, mostly recent.

Mumford, Lewis. *The City in History.* New York: Harcourt, Brace, and World, 1961. Voluminous annotated bibliography.

Park, Robert E., et al. *The City.* Chicago: University of Chicago Press, 1966. Reprint of 1925 study, with an introduction by Morris Janowitz.

Reissman, Leonard. *The Urban Process*. New York: Free Press, 1964. One of the less objection-
able textbooks.
Schnore, Leo F., and Henry Fagin, eds. *Urban Research and Policy Planning*. Beverly Hills,
Calif.: Sage Publications, 1967. "Urban Affairs Annual Reviews", Vol. 1. Excellent and
up-to-date reviews of—you guessed—(a) urban research, (b) urban policy.
Smailes, Arthur E. *The Geography of Towns*. London: Hutchinson University Library, 1957.
Compact summary of urban geography.
Société Jean Bodin. *La Ville*. Brussels: Librairie encyclopedique, 1954–57. 3 vols. Learned and
specialized essays.
Sorokin, Pitirim A., and Carle C. Zimmerman. *Principles of Rural-Urban Sociology*. New York:
Holt, 1929. One of the classics.
Theodorson, George A., ed. *Studies in Human Ecology*. Evanston, Ill.: Row, Peterson, 1961. A
reader.
Warren, Roland L. *The Community in America*. Chicago: Rand McNally, 1972. Theoretically
sophisticated text.

BIBLIOGRAPHIES AND REVIEWS OF THE FIELD

Berry, Brian J. L., and Alan Pred. *Central Place Studies: A Bibliography of Theory and
Applications*. Philadelphia: Regional Science Research Institute, 1961.
Cahnman, Werner J. "The Historical Sociology of Cities: A Critical Review." *Social Forces*, 45,
No. 2 (December, 1966), pp. 155–160.
Castells, Manuel. "Structures sociales et processus d'urbanisation: analyse comparative inter-
sociétale," *Annales; Economies, Sociétés, Civilisations*, 25 (1970), 1155–1199. A long,
helpful, polemical review of the current literature on urbanization; one of many articles
in an issue devoted entirely to "urbanization and history."
Chiva, I. *Rural Communities*. Paris: UNESCO, 1959. Extensively commented systematic bibli-
ography.
Gutman, Robert, compiler. *Urban Sociology: A Bibliography*. New Brunswick, N.J.: Urban
Studies Center, Rutgers University, 1963.
Handlin, Oscar, and John Burchard, eds. *The Historian and the City*. Cambridge, Mass.: M.I.T.
Press and Harvard University Press, 1963. Includes an excellent systematic bibliography.
Hauser, Philip M., and Leo F. Schnore, eds. *The Study of Urbanization*. New York: Wiley,
1965. "State of the art" essays for history, geography, political science, sociology, and
economics, plus excellent surveys of major substantive problems.
Heyser, Erich, ed. *Bibliographie zur Städtegeschichte Deutschlands*. Cologne: Bohlau Verlag,
1969.
International Bibliography of Urban History. Denmark, Finland, Norway, Sweden. Stockholm:
Swedish Institute for Urban History, 1960.
Lampard, Eric. "American Historians and the Study of Urbanization," *American Historical
Review*, 1961, 1967:49–61.
Lessard, Marc-Andre and Jean-Paul Montminy. *L'Urbanisation de la société canadienne-
française*. Quebec: Presses de l'Université Laval, 1970. The state of the question for
research on urban Quebec.
Lorenz, Robert, Paul Medows, and Warner Bloomberg, Jr. *A World of Cities: A Cross-Cultural
Urban Bibliography*. Syracuse, N.Y.: Center for Overseas Operations and Research,
Maxwell Graduate School, Syracuse University, 1964. Very extensive, but without
annotation.
Pahl, R. E. "The Rural-Urban Continuum," *Sociologia ruralis*, 6 (1966), 299–329. A con-
venient review of the literature.
Schmandt, Henry J., and Warner Bloomberg, Jr., eds. *The Quality of Urban Life*. Beverly Hills,
Calif.: Sage, 1969. Urban Affairs Annual Reviews, No. 3.
Simms, Ruth P. *Urbanization in West Africa*. Evanston, Ill.: Northwestern University Press,
1965. A thorough review of the literature; extensive bibliographies.
Sjoberg, Gideon. "Comparative Urban Sociology", in Robert Merton and Leonard Cottrell,
eds., *Sociology Today*. New York: Basic Books, 1959.

STATISTICAL DATA AND TECHNICAL GUIDES

Bogue, Donald J. *The Population of the United States.* Glencoe, III.: Free Press, 1959. A compendium.

Chombart de Lauwe, P. H., et al. *Paris et l'agglomération parisienne.* Paris: Presses Universitaires de France, 1952. Largely methodological

Collier, John, Jr. *Visual Anthropology: Photography as a Research Method.* New York: Holt, Rinehart, and Winston, 1967.

Conant, Ralph, and Molly Apple Levin, eds. *Problems in Research on Community Violence.* New York: Praeger, 1969. Position papers on the major research problems, with considerable bibliography.

Dominion Bureau of Statistics. *Canada Year Book.* Ottawa: Queen's Printer, annual. A statistical summary, drawing especially on census material.

Duncan, Otis Dudley, Ray P. Cuzzort, and Beverly Duncan. *Statistical Geography.* Glencoe, III.: Free Press, 1961.

Gibbs, Jack P., ed. *Urban Research Methods.* Princeton, N.J.: Van Nostrand, 1961. A good set of readings.

Grytzell, Karl G. *The Demarcation of Comparable City Areas by Means of Population Density.* Lund, Sweden: Gleerup, 1963. Highly technical, but rewarding.

Hadden, Jeffry K., and Edward Borgatta. *American Cities: Their Social Characteristics.* Chicago: Rand McNally, 1965.

Hauser, Philip M., ed. *Handbook for Social Research in Urban Areas.* Paris: UNESCO, 1965. How-to-do-it for underdeveloped researchers.

International Statistics of Large Towns. The Hague: International Statistical Institute, 1954.

International Urban Research. *The World's Metropolitan Areas.* Berkeley: University of California Press, 1959. Data, data, data.

Isard, Walter. *Methods of Regional Analysis.* New York: Wiley, 1960. Technique, technique, technique.

Mols, Roger. *Introduction à la démographie historique des villes d'Europe du XIVe au XVIIIe siècles.* Louvain: Université de Louvain, 1955. 2 vols. Data, technique, history.

The Municipal Year Book. Chicago: International City Managers' Association, annual.

Olbricht, Konrad. "Die Vergrösstädterung des Abendlandes zu Beginn des Dreissigjährigen Krieges," *Petermanns Geographische Mitteilungen*, 85 (1939), 349–353. Scattered estimates on urban population before 1600.

Reinhard, Marcel, André Armengaud, and Jacques Dupâquier. *Histoire générale de la population mondiale.* Paris: Montchrestien, 1968. Well-documented demographic history, stronger on Europe than elsewhere. Lots of data.

Russell, J. C. *Late Ancient and Medieval Population.* Philadelphia: American Philosophical Society; Transactions of the American Philosophical Society, n.s., vol. 48, part 3. Mainly data, from a great variety of sources of highly varying reliability.

Spengler, Joseph J., and Otis Dudley Duncan, eds. *Demographic Analysis.* Glencoe, III.: Free Press, 1956. A reader.

Steinberg, S. H., ed. *The Statesman's Yearbook.* London: Macmillan, annual. An international statistical compilation, especially British Commonwealth.

United Nations statistical series: *Statistical Yearbook, Demographic Yearbook,* others indexed by country and/or subject in *United Nations Documents Index,* a periodical.

Urquhart, M. C., and K. A. H. Buckley, eds. *Historical Statistics of Canada.* Toronto: Macmillan, 1965. The first substantial and authoritative compilation.

U.S. Department of Commerce. *Statistical Abstract of the United States, 1970.* Washington: Government Printing Office, 1970. A guide to census and other statistical materials, with extensive tables.

Vital Statistics—Special Reports. Continuing series by National Office of Vital Statistics.

Chapter
2
Urbanization

INTRODUCTION[1]

"The foundation of every division of labor that is well developed, and brought about by the exchange of commodities," Karl Marx declared, "is the separation between town and country. It may be said, that the whole economic history of society is summed up in the movement of this antithesis."[2] Marx wrote off a good part of human experience with that remark. For the first 99 percent of his time on earth, after all, man lived without cities. Yet when it comes to the history we call "civilized," Marx did not err. In the last ten thousand years, man has made up for his long lack of cities. Since the new type of community grew out of the settled agriculture in the lands from the Bosporus to the Persian Gulf between 8,000 and 3,000 B.C., almost every increase in man's capacity to organize collective efforts and to exploit his physical environment has brought a new spurt of urban growth.

There have been lulls and even reversals of the trend toward cities. The period of European history which Westerners rather parochially call the Dark Ages is only one prominent example of deurbanization. On the whole, nevertheless, cities have expanded much more often than they have contracted. Their share of the world's population has grown enormously: practically nil in 3,000 B.C., under 1 percent in 100 A.D., less than 5 percent in 1800, perhaps a third in 1970. (Kingsley Davis' article in this chapter neatly summarizes the long-run trends.) Their range of influence over the population not actually living in cities has increased most of all. How many people are now really outside the range of a big city? By any reasonable test, less than one person in twenty.

The most sweeping of all the surges of urbanization the world has seen so far is still going on today. Kingsley Davis describes the process in his article:

> Before 1850 no society could be described as predominantly urbanized, and by 1900 only one—Great Britain—could be so regarded. Today, only 65 years

later, all industrial nations are highly urbanized, and in the world as a whole the process of urbanization is accelerating rapidly.

Indeed, the process has done nothing but accelerate in the years since Davis wrote those words.

The current wave of urbanization began around 1700. It was a joint product of the coming of large-scale industry and the emergence of national states. It spread through the world along with industrial organization, production for world markets, and political centralization. It seems unlikely to end before most of the world's people are living in cities. This chapter deals with three general questions raised by the current urbanization of the world. First, how and why does urbanization occur at all? Second, how uniform is urbanization? Third, if urbanization occurs, how great are its consequences for social life, and how predictable are they?

HOW AND WHY?

In trying to learn how and why something happens, we often do well to begin by observing when and where it happens; then we can see which explanations are consistent with the "when" and "where." In general, urbanization is closely tied to the growth of large-scale activities involving many people dispersed in space. It is not enough that many people in different places are doing the same thing; if it were, sex, sleep, fishing, hunting, and farming would all be great city-builders. The activities must be dispersed and numerous, but also interdependent and coordinated. Over the entire ten thousand years of human urbanization, trade, manufacturing, the creation of large political structures, and the growth of great religious cults have all played an important part. In our own time, manufacturing has gained enormous weight as a city-builder, but the commercial, political, and religious influences on urbanization have not disappeared. There are even relatively pure types of commercial, political, and religious city-building: trading cities like Dakar (Senegal), administrative cities like Islamabad (Pakistan), shrine cities like Mecca (Saudi Arabia). Whenever any of these activities has accelerated, so ordinarily has urbanization.

Let us be clear about a distinction stressed by Kingsley Davis in his article. If the population in a nation's cities increases at 2 percent per year, in over twenty-five years the nation will experience an urban growth of almost two-thirds (2 percent compounded twenty-five times comes to about 64 percent). But whether the nation *urbanizes* fast, slow, or not at all depends on how rapidly the rest of the population is growing. If the urban population increases more rapidly than the nonurban population, the proportion of the population in cities increases and the nation is urbanizing. If the urban and nonurban populations both grow at 2 percent per year, the proportion in cities remains constant and no urbanization occurs. If the urban population decreases, stays the same, or increases more slowly than the rest while the population as a whole is growing, then deurbanization is happening.

The statistics in Table 1 help make this distinction. They represent estimates

TABLE 1
European Population in Cities of 100,000 and More, 1500–1950

Date	Total Population of Europe (Millions)	Number of Cities of 100,000 +	Population in Cities of 100,000 + (Millions)	Percentage of Total Population in Cities of 100,000 +
1500	50–60	4	.75–.85	1.2–1.7
1550	65–75	7–10	1.10–1.65	1.5–2.5
1600	80–90	13–14	1.85–2.85	2.1–3.6
1650	95–105	11–12	2.35–2.50	2.2–2.6
1700	115–125	14	2.65–3.10	2.1–2.7
1750	135–145	13–15	3.35–3.75	2.3–2.8
1800	187	23	5.40	2.9
1850	226	43	12.66	4.8
1900	401	143	49.14	12.3
1950	548	374	119.19	21.8

Source: Charles Tilly, Karen Fonde, and Ann V. O'Shea, "Statistics on the Urbanization of Europe, 1500–1950," unpublished compilation circulated by the Center for Western European Studies, University of Michigan, 1972. Compiled from a wide variety of published sources.

of the total population of Europe and of the population in cities with 100,000 inhabitants or more at fifty-year intervals from 1500 to 1950. The ranges of the estimates before 1800 show how uncertain is our knowledge of even so elementary a matter as the total number of people before Europeans began taking a regular census in the nineteenth century. I have restricted the estimates to very large cities because for the earlier periods it is impossible to find figures for any substantial proportion of smaller places. It is reasonable to assume, however, that the population in cities of, say, 20,000 or more changed at roughly the same tempo.

With that assumption in mind, we can see how greatly industrial expansion accelerated urban growth in Europe after 1500. The four cities which had more than 100,000 inhabitants then were Constantinople, Naples, Paris, and Venice. All were crucial centers of trade; they also carried on manufacturing and political administration to varying degrees. Three centuries later, in 1800, there were 23 European cities in the large-size class, with seven or eight above 200,000: Constantinople, London, Moscow, Naples, Paris, St. Petersburg, Vienna, and possibly Amsterdam. Between 1500 and 1800 the population in cities of 100,000 or more had multiplied about 50 times, from perhaps 800 thousand to 5.4 million. In the century and a half from 1800 to 1950, it multiplied more than 20 times, to almost 120 million people. Urban growth from 1500 to 1800 was substantial, but from 1800 to 1950 it was tremendous.

Before going on to the urbanization which resulted from this urban growth, let us ask where the growth itself came from. Urban growth has three sources:

(1) *natural increase* in cities; (2) *net migration* to cities; (3) *structural transformation* of nonurban communities into cities. Natural increase is simply the difference between the number of births and the number of deaths in a given interval. It is convenient to express the relationship in rates. The Crude Birth Rate is the number of births per thousand population per year, the Crude Death Rate the number of deaths per thousand per year. (For reference: in 1970 most of the world's countries had CBRs between 20 and 45, CDRs between 10 and 30, with poorer countries generally being higher on both.) The rate of natural increase is the difference between them; if the CBR is 30 and the CDR 20, the rate of natural increase is 30 − 20 = 10 persons per thousand per year. For an urban population of 500 thousand, that rate would produce an increase of $(10/1,000) \times 500,000 = 5,000$ persons per year.

Net migration is the difference between the number of persons who move into an area (in-migration) during a given interval and the number who move out of the area (out-migration) during the same interval. In-migration, out-migration, and net migration also can be expressed in rates per thousand population. (Here there are no standard figures as in the case of birth and death rates, but it is not unusual for a city to receive the equivalent of a quarter of its population as in-migrants over a five-year interval, or to lose a quarter to out-migration.) If the rate of in-migration is 100 (persons per thousand population per year) and the rate of out-migration is 80, the rate of net migration will be 100 − 80 = 20; for an urban population of 500 thousand, a rate of 20 accounts for an increase of 10,000 persons per year. When a rapid acceleration of urban growth occurs, it is usually due to a rise in net migration rather than natural increase or structural transformation.

Structural transformation is the net effect of movements of whole communities into and out of the category "urban." If we are using a strictly numerical standard (such as a minimum population of 10,000 or 100,000) and the boundaries of the communities involved are both clear and constant, then the entire effect is due to the fact that during a given interval some communities pass the statistical threshold in one direction or the other. The annexation of areas adjacent to existing cities produces a related case; in that case, too, people who were there all along and whose behavior did not change much suddenly start being counted as "urban." If our test for "urban" communities includes nonnumerical items such as a particular composition of the labor force or the presence of a certain way of life, of course tracing the contribution of structural transformation to urban growth becomes more complicated at the same time as it becomes more crucial. That is one of the practical advantages the ecological approach to cities has over the normative, interactional, and locational approaches: it is easier to know how many residents a community has than to know how they organize their lives.

In all four approaches, the general account of urban growth follows the pattern shown in Figure 1. The differences among ecological, normative, interactional, and locational analyses of these processes lie in the definition of cities employed, the kinds of structural transformation singled out, and the causal connections proposed. When Garvin and Mathiot, in the article reprinted in this

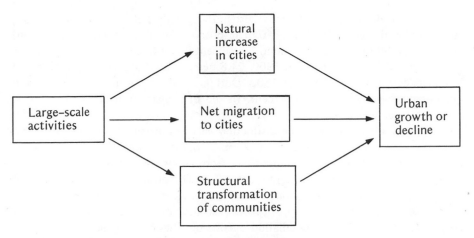

Figure 1. An Elementary Model of Urban Growth

chapter, equate the existence of a standard language (as opposed to folk speech) with "urban culture," they are using a normative criterion, not an ecological one. In fact, they propose to use language standardization as an index of urbanity. When Abu-Lughod (in this chapter) compares fertility, mortality, and other demographic variables for rural and urban areas in Egypt, she sticks to number of inhabitants as the test of rural versus urban. To exaggerate a bit: for Garvin and Mathiot, urban growth consists of changes in culture; for Abu-Lughod, urban growth consists of changes in size.

The exaggeration is useful even though it goes beyond what Garvin and Mathiot say in their article. It suggests a strictly normative account of urban growth. In the simplest version, we divide up all communities in the entire population into those where standard language is spoken, and those where folk language is spoken. (The "communities" do not even have to be territorial groups.) Obviously, both sets of communities can increase or decrease through natural increase and net migration. If we treat the substitution of standard speech for folk speech as "structural transformation," the account is complete. Urban growth occurs when natural increase, net migration, and structural transformation combine to produce a positive rate of growth for standard-language communities. We substitute a cultural characteristic—language spoken—for the size, density, and other population characteristics which prevail in ecological accounts.

In either case, *urbanization* relates urban growth to change in the total population under consideration. The simplest version is again ecological: urbanization is an increase in the proportion of the total population of an area which is living in cities; it occurs when the rate of growth in cities is higher than in the rest of the population. Obviously, urban growth can occur without urbanization; the rest of the population simply has to increase at the same rate or faster. Less obviously, urbanization can occur without urban growth; the rural population simply has to decline faster than the urban.

Look again at Table 1. Europe urbanized greatly between 1500 and 1950, especially in the century after 1850. The proportion of the total population in cities of 100,000 or more was around 1.5 percent in 1500, 2.9 percent in 1800, 4.8 percent in 1850, 12.3 percent in 1900, 21.8 percent in 1950. The proportion had less than doubled from 1500 to 1800. During the next century, the proportion quadrupled from 2.9 to 12.3 percent. In the fifty years from 1900 to 1950 it almost doubled again.

That is where we need the distinction between urban growth and urbanization. Between 1500 and 1950 the European population in cities of 100,000 or more multiplied more than a hundredfold, from about 800 thousand to about 120 million. That is *urban growth,* and plenty of it. The proportion living in cities of 100,000 or more multiplied about fifteen times, from around 1.5 to 22 percent. That is *urbanization.* The discrepancy between the two rates of growth is due, of course, to the fact that the population outside of cities of 100,000 also grew fast, especially after 1700.

It is even possible that Europe as a whole deurbanized during the century from 1600 to 1700, despite some urban growth. The best guess is that around 2.5 million Europeans lived in cities of 100,000 or more at the beginning of the century, and a little under 3 million at the end. Yet the continent's total population went from around 85 million to around 120 million in the same period. If these figures are correct, the proportion in large cities declined from 3 percent in 1600 to 2.4 percent in 1700. If they are correct, they fit with other things historians already know about Europe in the seventeenth century: that large parts of the continent underwent an economic crisis during the earlier years of the century; that between the waning of that crisis and the industrial revolution of the nineteenth century much of the expansion of European manufacturing occurred through the growth of cottage industries coordinated from cities but spread through the countryside; that some time before 1700 the surplus of births over deaths in the European countryside began to increase significantly, foreshadowing the population explosion of the eighteenth and nineteenth centuries. The balance between the rates of growth in the urban and nonurban segments of the population determines whether there will be urbanization, deurbanization, or no change in the proportion urban.

Why do large-scale, coordinated, dispersed activities promote urbanization? In the simplest terms, because they encourage the appearance of sets of interdependent specialists who can serve their own advantage by clustering together in space. The encouragement takes several forms. First, only a good-sized population with fairly efficient agriculture can release substantial numbers of people from food production to devote full time to trade, war, prayer, manufacturing, administration, conspicuous leisure, or any of the other characteristic urban occupations. Large-scale, coordinated, dispersed activities generally bring that potential base population into the same system, make possible the specialization of different localities within the system in crops and techniques calculated to raise the productivity of agriculture, and make it easier for a nonagricultural segment of the population to seize a portion of the increased product through trade, tribute, taxation, or rent.

Second, the coordination of large-scale, dispersed activities itself tends to be a full-time occupation which puts extensive resources in the hands of its holder. The resources may include goods, military might, land, labor, gold, control of prestigious symbols, information, tools, and communications lines. In any case, they give a few people the capacity to create personal retinues. The personal retinues likewise consist of individuals who are full-time specialists in nonagricultural activities, and who cluster near their powerful masters. They may be slaves or they may be disciples—but their concentration in space depends on someone else's accumulation of resources.

Third, specialized activities feed on each other: the presence of a crossroads market enhances the advantage of the nearby potter, who can sell pots to people arriving for the purchase of food. The presence of a number of soldiers, scribes, or artisans makes it possible for more people to survive by providing services to the soldiers, scribes, or artisans in exchange for some of the food which those specialists extract from the agricultural population. Trades themselves are interdependent: if there are full-time weavers, there must also be spinners, fullers, dyers, and cloth-merchants, although they need not all be full time.

In short, large-scale, coordinated activities which are dispersed in space (1) facilitate the creation and seizure of an agricultural surplus which will support a nonagricultural population, (2) concentrate enough resources under the control of a few people to permit them to create geographically clustered dependent populations devoted to the service of the few, (3) by permitting and promoting specialization within the major activity, promote the emergence of complementary specialties outside the major activity, and therefore (4) stimulate urbanization. The greater the mobilization of the agricultural surplus, the concentration of resources, and the specialization of activity, the greater the stimulus to urbanization.

Large-scale activity does not guarantee natural increase at the points of control. But it regularly causes the other two components of urban growth: net migration to those control points and structural transformation of the communities at those points into cities. The relationships are, of course, reciprocal. For example, the growth of cities creates a demand which makes agricultural specialization feasible, even though no cities are possible without an agricultural technology capable of producing more than farmers need to survive.

Through most of man's urban history, several different features of agriculture have held down the surplus available to feed cities: low labor productivity of agriculture; high costs of storing, processing, and shipping food to points of consumption; heavy commitment of whatever was being produced to particular families, communities, temples, landlords, and other groups outside the city. The low labor productivity meant that few hands could leave agriculture without a decline in per-capita food supply. The costs of delivering food restricted the size of the hinterland a particular city could draw on and therefore limited the absolute food supply available. The commitment of the crop meant that city-dwellers would starve, even in times of abundance, without strong economic and political leverage on the countryside. These problems are quite foreign to North Americans accustomed to mechanized farming, quick freezing, bumper crops, and subsidies to farmers who take land out of cultivation. But they are still pressing in Asia, Africa, and the Pacific, where large areas produce fewer than 2,000 calories of foodstuffs per person each day. That has been the normal situation of mankind until recently; it kept the vast majority of the population in the countryside and held all but a tiny number of tribute-exacting capital cities to a maximum size of 50 or 100 thousand people.

Consider the direct implications of this situation for urban growth. The shortage of food makes a high death rate in cities likely and may hold down the birth rate as well; the net effect is low, or even negative, natural increase. The need for labor in agriculture puts a strong brake on rural-to-urban migration, while the hunger and high prices of city living encourage a large counterflow from city to country; the effect is low net migration. The difficulty of supporting a specialized nonagricultural population and the risk, complexity, and effort of organizing the food supply of a large settlement make it costly for any community to make the structural transformation into a city. In these ways, the costs of urban living translate directly into a low rate of urban growth. Some of the costs concentrate more heavily in one of the components of urban growth; bad sanitation, for instance, throws up few obstacles to structural transformation, probably does not affect migration very greatly, and ordinarily has only minor effects on the birth rate; but it significantly affects the urban death rate from cholera, plague, dysentery, and other communicable diseases. Where such costs strike cities more heavily than other communities, they depress the rate of urbanization as well as the rate of urban growth: the costs may even produce deurbanization.

Every theory of urbanization contains, by implication, ideas about the relative costs and benefits some basic set of factors produces within each of the major components of urban growth—natural increase, net migration, and structural transformation—and then compares those costs and benefits within the urban and nonurban segments of the population. That gives us a way of decomposing and criticizing every theory that comes our way: for example, the idea that industrialization causes urbanization. How and why? If we are not able to specify the benefits and the costs within each of the three major components and their differential impact on the urban and nonurban worlds, the theory is incomplete.

In the case of Western industrialization, all three of the standard links between large-scale activity and urbanization clearly exist. The growth of manufacturing in eighteenth- and nineteenth-century Europe both stimulated and depended on a great expansion of the labor productivity of European agriculture; it likewise extended the search for food supplies into Asia, Africa, and, especially, the Americas. The growth of an industrial elite and the swelling of their staffs and servitors added to Western urban growth. The creation of a factory-based industrial labor force created further opportunities for employment in services, subsidiary industries, and administration.

These effects are very large. Despite the continued importance of trade or political centralization as a stimulus to urban growth in different parts of the world, the effects of industrialization are so great that the map of the urban world is coming increasingly to be the map of big industry.

The closeness of the connection in the contemporary world raises an important question: Is there a single, uniform process of urbanization? Assuming the growth of manufacturing in parts of the world which are now predominantly agricultural, can we anticipate the future course of urbanization? Before offering hasty answers, we should consider how much the nonindustrial forms of urbanization correspond to those which predominate today.

HOW UNIFORM IS URBANIZATION?

Even in the absence of dramatic changes in manufacturing, the quickening of trade, the forceful building of empires, the rise of new religious organizations, and even the conduct of agriculture on a large and bureaucratic scale have in their own ways regularly encouraged urban concentration. In his wide-ranging essay on early cities reprinted in this chapter, Lewis Mumford attributes the early development of cities to the appearance of the hunter-king, and the apparatus of control which came with him. Although scholars are still debating the precise character of that control, there is little doubt that the development of greater spans and degrees of control over the population outside any particular community by members of that community favored its formation of true urban characteristics: extensive division of labor, disposal of material surpluses, complex communication systems, high density. Manufacturing as such played no more than a secondary role in these transformations.

China, to consider a part of the world Mumford does not discuss, has only recently begun aggressive industrialization. Yet China has through most of human history been one of the most urban—and urbane—lands of the world; it is the very recent spurt of European and American urbanization which makes the balance seem to run in the other direction. Murphey's review of the changing roles of Asian cities in this chapter provides a corrective to Western prejudices concerning "rural" Asia:

> These capitals were intended as cosmic creations, substantive and symbolic pinnacles of and resplendent thrones for the Great Tradition, enshriners as well as administrators of a relatively homogeneous and particularistic culture, to which the market towns and the peasant villages of the Little Tradition also belonged. Their planned, monumental urban forms reaffirmed their role as the head pieces of unitary civilizations centered on their own cultural worlds. They were predominantly political and cultural rather than economic phenomena, functioning as microcosms of the national polity, symbols of authority, legitimacy, and power, creators and molders of literate culture, and seats of the dominant ideology. Commercial functions, both in the capitals and in the other traditional Asian cities, were for the most part secondary, and were in any case under varying degrees of control or manipulation by the state, whose chief monument was the city itself.

Japan's urban history is not quite so long as China's, but it antedates Japan's industrial growth by centuries. After a lapse of almost two hundred years, Tokyo is again about the largest city in the world. Industrial expansion has played an enormous part in its return to preeminence. In the few centuries after the emergence of the city in the 1500's, however, its first sensational expansion depended mainly on its role as capital and central market. The imperial palace was the nucleus from which the great city grew. Even today Tokyo's life seems to swirl around the palace more than any other focal point.

Such dominant structures often record the activities which have prevailed in the building of the city—the fortress and the temple in the traditional Japanese city, the cathedral in the older European town, the office building in the American metropolis. The shapes of cities and their social organizations vary significantly with the activities that build them. Compare (1) the medieval European trading city with its legal freedom, its governing corporation of merchants, its center preempted by a church and a city hall, both strategically near a vast marketplace and fairground, fed by tortuous streets blending shops and houses, with (2) the coal-burning nineteenth-century manufacturing city with its dominant factory area and central business district, its sharp separation of home from work, its geometric lines of transportation, and its incredible ebbs and flows of internal traffic; then compare both with (3) the traditional Islamic city: fortress, market, and central mosque placed at the intersection of two of the very few streets cutting through the entire city, quarters originating as the settlements of different tribes and nationalities living unto themselves (often walled off from each other) and reproducing in miniature the institutions of the city as a whole, hectic mixtures of land use, an unending tendency for private uses to take over nominally public space, an absence of formal arrangements for municipal government, a religious-intellectual elite, the *ulama*, mediating among the quickly shifting factions of the city and speaking to the sultan on behalf of its population. No single activity built any of these cities. Yet commerce marks the medieval town; mass production, the nineteenth-century city; and imperialism plus religion, the Islamic metropolis.

The same differences appear in the relations of these cities to their hinterlands and in the interaction between hinterland and city which we call urbanization. The medieval European city stood among landlord-run villages from which it drew surplus people as migrants and surplus food as subsistence, only slowly and incompletely drawing the villages into dependence, hardly affecting their techniques of daily living. The nineteenth-century industrial center grew in pace with energetic changes in agricultural production, rural landholding, and country life; drew rural people in swarms from short and long distances alike; relied for its vitality both on efficient transportation and on a constant extension of markets into the hinterland. In the old Islamic city, the military rulers commonly exacted tribute, food, and a measure of allegiance from the surrounding countryside; nomadic tribes maintained permanent bases in town; people forced off the land by famine, flood, disease, or war straggled to the cities; and the cities themselves grew by adding new, self-contained homogeneous settlements very much like the rural communities from which their inhabitants came. Even today (as the article by Abu-Lughod in this chapter makes clear) Middle Eastern cities like Cairo continue some of the same patterns—including the re-creation of villages within the metropolitan complex.

Variations of this last form, of course, appear far outside the Islamic world. One of the fundamental dimensions among the world's cities today includes those which are organized around a complex, specialized but partly unified and distinctly urban occupational structure as well as those which are largely agglomerations of transplanted villages and villagers. All real cities have something of both; there are still Algerian neighborhoods in Paris and Italian neighborhoods in New York, while Nigeria's Yoruba cities have many residents in specialized occupations who claim no tribal ties. Yet the difference in balance between the two forms of social organization produces a large contrast between the social life of Paris and the social life of Ibadan.

The two forms often confront each other with a special sharpness in colonial cities which used to be colonial outposts. They are divided much more than most settlements into dual dwelling areas, markets, communication systems, and living styles. One pole is the old, indigenous town; the other, the compound established by some European power during the eighteenth or nineteenth century for the purposes of trade and military control. Representing this type is Cairo, the labyrinthine native city in its eastern section, the strangely Parisian colonial city in its western half. There is prewar Shanghai, with the international quarter of tall buildings and spacious streets standing out from the low roofs and huddled houses of the Chinese city. Delhi, Old and New, splits into high density and low density, Eastern and Western, traditional and modern. Since such major colonial centers often become national capitals with the departure of the European governors, many postcolonial nations now either struggle to knit together the unwieldy halves of their ruling cities or attempt to move their governments to new planned, unified, and less clearly colonial settlements elsewhere.

Part of this powerful dualism of colonial outposts derives from the extractive role they have played in the larger territories under their control. All cities are extractive to some degree, first, because they always seize their substance, security, and population from some hinterland; and secondly, because they almost always act to accumulate, convert, and redistribute what surpluses of energy, goods, food power, and capital may exist in their dependent territories. Colonial outposts simply emphasize this sort of extraction more than most. They usually do it by concentrating on the exportation of raw materials and plantation-produced foodstuffs. Such a concentration (as compared, say, with the manufacture of textiles) draws a very distinct line between those involved in the trade or its protection and all others in the economy. The line passes through the colonial outpost itself, separating the traders and administrators from the rest of the population. In East Africa, the position of Dar es Salaam as an exporter of sisal, or of Zanzibar town as an exit first for slaves and then for cloves and coconuts, makes the point very well.

When successful, the exporting city concentrates a great deal of a country's resources, population, and power in a single location. Some scholars have called the most extreme cases "primate cities" to stress their overwhelming priority over other settlements in their areas. Bangkok, Jakarta, and Rangoon—all many times larger than their nearest competitors—are favorite examples. On the whole, city sizes in the larger Western countries fall into an intriguingly regular order with the largest city something like twice the size of the second largest, three times the size of the third, and so on. For that reason, North American geographers immediately take notice of the large share of all the urban population that Accra has in Ghana, that Colombo has in Ceylon, or even that Buenos Aires has in Argentina. Colonial history accounts for many of these primate cities; today countries exporting large volumes of raw materials are significantly more likely than others to have their populations, activities, and power concentrated in a single metropolis.

Whether such a concentration helps or hinders is a matter about which regional planners argue furiously. Some point to the waste and danger of having all eggs in the same basket, but others reply that where there are few eggs the only way to have an omelette is by putting them all together. Here, arguing from the Western experience is tricky; for the close historical connection in Europe and America since 1800 among urban growth, industrial expansion, and a number of other changes such as the long-run decline in the birth rate make it seem plausible that they are functionally related to one another, yet very difficult to sort out the causes and the effects. In the case of fertility changes, Abu-Lughod shows that much of the news coming in from countries like Egypt confounds the expectations about rural-urban differences—notably higher rural fertility—which Westerners have commonly taken to come close to natural law.[3] These are more than academic questions; the location and size of urban population have turned out to be crucial policy issues for nations undertaking planned industrialization.

The policy problem appears in almost every country. For whether the cities already in existence grew mainly from trade, conquest, or something else, their organization differs from that of large industrial centers. Many sociologists make a fundamental distinction between the industrial and "preindustrial" forms of cities and urbanization. It is not that all nonindustrial cities are alike; but rather, that the industrial/preindustrial distinction makes sense today because the industrial form is practically superseding all others in most parts of the world and because in sheer scale and rapidity it stands out from all the rest. As Davis reminds us in his article, before the industrial city no country ever had much more than a tenth of its people in cities, and no city ever had much more than a million people. Today England has only a tenth of her people left in the country, Italy alone has three or four cities with a population of over a million, and by some definitions Tokyo and New York approach twenty million each. With significant help from the growth of the modern nation-state, industrialization did it.

But just what did industrialization do? The easy part is to point out the effects of new technologies. Large-scale industrial production favors the agglomeration of producers, markets, and middlemen more than ever before, and it produces a material surplus to support complicated specialties and institutions. Scientific agriculture sensationally reduces the number of men in the country needed to support 100 men in the city. Speedy, flexible transport and communication permit a single center to remain in contact with complex activities spread over vast territories. Organized sanitation and medical services reduce the odds that cholera or dysentery will decimate a huge city's population. And the techniques of city-building themselves—steel frames, reinforced concrete, prefabricated housing— increase the possible pace and scale of construction.

New technologies do not automatically and painlessly produce big, modern cities. Almost all industrializing countries extract a large part of their working capital from a more or less reluctant countryside. They do it by means of taxes, corvees, drafts, price controls, and outright seizures. Where the efficiency of agriculture is rising fast and the central government or the entrepreneurs are adept at creating and then seizing the surplus, the extraction may work to the firm advantage of the cities and the industrial establishment. England looks like such a case.

At least as often, however, the mobilization of surplus goes badly, and the hinterland evades central control. Indonesia has such problems much more seriously than England ever did. In any case the process means bitter rural-urban conflict and some form of expanding coercion from the city. One of the powerful undercurrents of conflict during the French Revolution developed from the incessant demand for grain in the primate city of Paris that was placed on the trading towns and villages within its grasp. The civilian "revolutionary armies" which marched out into the provinces from the capital had politics on their minds, but they gave their most persistent attention to assuring the grain supply. Many other countries have discovered the same convergence of the needs of its revolution, the needs of its economic expansion, and the needs of its cities.

The struggle of city versus country occurs in all kinds of urbanization. Industrial urbanization simply exaggerates the process; with industrial urbanization the pace, scale, demands for capital, and pressures for concentration are simply much greater than with trade or conquest. Many of the uniformities in industrial urbanization are of this sort: matters of scale, not peculiarities of the processes by which industrial cities grow.

In some regards, however, in the term "industrial urbanization" the "industrial" is more important than the "urbanization." As the process moves on, the division of labor in a nation's cities clearly becomes more complex; specialists in coordination, communication, and control more numerous; formal organization more prominent; the use of the city's space more differentiated; the rhythm of mobility more frenzied—at least to a point. Sam Bass Warner's portrayal of Philadelphia in 1774, 1860, and 1930 (reprinted in Chapter 4) shows how all these changes appeared in the labor force, geography, and organizational structure of that city as North America industrialized. It is probably also true that in the industrial city the nuclear family of father, mother, and children gains new independence and importance as compared with the clan, the lineage, or other larger kinship groups; that the proportion of all people's lives spent in tight-knit groups of friends, neighbors, and kinsmen goes down; and that impersonal situations and channels of communication assume a larger part in everyday life. These changes, however, are not so great or so simple as old notions of the isolation of urbanites and of the decline of the family used to say. We will look at them more closely in Chapters 3 and 4.

Industrial urbanization, then, differs from other varieties of urbanization mainly in terms of its rapid pace, large scale, and thoroughness. By releasing a majority of the people from work on the land and putting incredible concentrations of energy at the disposal of the nonagricultural population, it permits an extreme division of labor and an extraordinary complexity of organization. The other major city-building activities—political centralization, trade, and the growth of religious cults—each produce characteristically different patterns of urban growth and different kinds of cities without drawing nearly as many people from the land as does industrial urbanization.

The general trends of industrial urbanization do not follow a single, inevitable track. While the experiences of Japan and England have some important general features in common, Japan is not simply recapitulating the history of England. The fact that other nations have already passed along the trail lets the latecomers examine a record and borrow a technology the first ones could not use. Also, the starting situation differs. Most countries now in the earliest stages of industrial urbanization are outside the Western European tradition. Most of them are burdened with critical population pressures, face powerful competition from other wealthier nations, and have adopted substantially different political arrangements from the Western countries which began the process earliest. Deliberate public policy is playing a larger part in the form of industrial urbanization than ever before. Controlled migration, careful land-use planning, the establishment of new cities, and governmental decisions about industrial location all make the developing nations the real laboratories of urbanization. It would not be amazing if the important new ideas in urbanization soon began to come from their experiments, reversing the flow of innovations from highly urban countries to the rest of the world.

CONSEQUENCES FOR SOCIAL LIFE

How deeply and how regularly does urbanization transform everyday social life? There are a number of different connections to consider. We can sum up the most important ones with a new version of an old diagram, Figure 2. This time it does not matter much whether we take a locational, normative, ecological, or interactional approach to urbanization. All of them suggest an independent impact of every one of these changes on everyday social life. They differ, however, in the weights assigned to the different components of urbanization and in the ideas of how these various relationships work. In Rhoads Murphey's mainly locational analysis of changing Asian cities, for instance, the main effects mentioned come directly from the large-scale activities: the trade and manufacturing carried on in

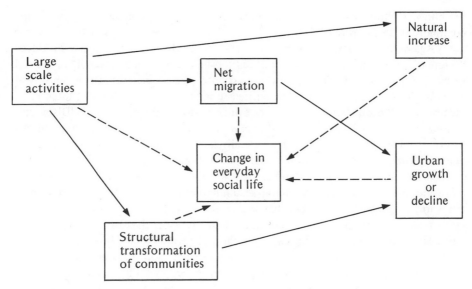

Figure 2. A Simple Model of Connections between Urban Growth and Changes in Social Life

the great coastal cities which were for a long time the main points of contact with world markets. The principal mechanisms by which Murphey suggests Asian urbanization affected social life are forms of diffusion: the spread of ideas, models, goods, and organizational forms. My own analysis of the impact of urbanization on collective violence in nineteenth-century France, "The Chaos of the Living City," on the other hand, stresses interaction. Much of the paper goes into showing that neither migration nor urban growth as such directly stimulated collective violence, but that the structural transformation of communities strongly affected the capacity of different groups of people for collective action, which in turn determined who was ordinarily involved in violence. Janet Abu-Lughod's ecological analysis of rural-urban differentials in Egypt, finally, pays more attention to the implications of migration and natural increase for the character of social life in city and country.

For American sociologists of thirty years ago, who were much taken with Louis Wirth's labeling of "urbanism as a way of life," urban growth as such caused important changes in everyday life; large size and high density in themselves produced a special kind of experience in cities. The mass of research since then has complicated things. It shows that in such highly industrial countries as England, France, and the United States the big cities still contain large patches of presumably traditional social organization—transplanted villages, extended kin groups, and so forth. (In this book, the articles by Abu-Lughod, MacDonald and MacDonald, Michelson, and Fried all consider these features of cities.) More important, it traces the diffusion of the characteristic industrial forms of social organization far beyond the cities and thus makes us wonder how necessary is the connection between the city and the "urban way of life."

Again, it is becoming less and less certain that urbanization regularly produces "disorganization" in the forms of increased criminality, family instability, mental illness, or protest. My articles in this chapter on nineteenth-century political conflicts in France and twentieth-century migration in the United States both center on that big question and present evidence against the old beliefs. "Disorganization" is, of course, a word with slippery handles; if we define it cleverly, we can make urbanization and disorganization equivalent, and the notion of a connection between them true by definition. Leaving definitional tricks aside, the tendency of rapid urban growth to shatter individuals and dissolve groups is much weaker or more indirect than we used to think; accumulating evidence indicates that it even tends to reduce some sorts of conflict and protest.

What we *can* say without too much doubt is, first, that the development of cities on an unprecedented scale is a normal part of industrialization; second, that in the course of industrialization cities became even more crucial stations in the coordination and control of activities going on throughout the society; third, that the characteristic forms of industrial society reach their fullest expression in the larger cities; fourth, that the cities play a special role in exposing people to the ways of industrial life by attracting and assimilating newcomers, by accumulating and displaying innovations, and by spreading the news outside.

The spread and exchange of life styles from city to city and city to country encourage a standardization of some crucial activities throughout the society. The imposition of uniform clock time is one example: things and people running on schedule. Language provides another example. Standard Italian over the last century spread from cities such as Florence and Rome to replace (or at least coexist with) the countless dialects which used to break up the linguistic map of Italy. African linguae francae such as Hausa began first as tribal languages, then became media of communication among different tribal groups in large cities, and finally spread as national and international tongues. The short article on the place of the Guarani language in Paraguay by Garvin and Mathiot in this chapter deals with exactly that process; they find an Indian dialect on its way to becoming a standardized national language. Because the tempo of innovation, the degree of specialization, and the almost inevitable appearance of chinks, cracks, leaks, and contradictions in very complex structures work against it, this standardization of some parts of life usually goes along with diversification of other parts. The diversification confounds critics who see all of urban-industrial life marching toward gray monotony. Yet the standardization is great enough that men can and do easily transport their accumulated experience, as well as themselves, from city to city.

In the early stages of industrial urbanization, when the death rate in the great cities more or less neutralizes their gains through births and there are few other cities to draw on, mass migration from the countryside supplies the new urban population. Some of it is permanent, some of it temporary. Much of it consists of villagers joining people already in the city to whom they are connected by kinship or common origin. The predominance of this sort of migration helps produce the city of tribal, regional, and national enclaves we discussed earlier. The Congo's Kisangani (formerly Stanleyville), with its distinct settlements of Lukele, Bamanga, Bakusu, and other tribes, is a good example; so is the Chicago of fifty years ago, proud to be one of the largest Polish cities as well as one of the largest German cities, not to mention its thousands of Czechs, Greeks, Italians, and Russians. Gradually, the rural sources of migrants diminish while mobility remains high, so that exchanges of population among cities take on greater and greater importance. In modern times three-quarters of the newcomers to American metropolitan areas come from other big cities or their suburbs.

As migration changes character, the rate of transmission of men and of messages from city to city and within big cities rises rapidly. The substitution of the transmission of images for the bodily transport of men, through such devices as telephones and television, is proceeding steadily enough that one might expect the mobility of persons to level off and the volume of messages to accelerate. So far—with jets, trains, and cars covering more and more passenger-miles—no country has yet seen that leveling off. Nevertheless, the most striking effect of the industrial city in the long run probably will be its impact on human communication. Through its massing of people, information, and complex tasks, the industrial city steadily has overworked existing means of communication from the pneumatic tube to the text-reading computer. In the span of a few generations, industrial urbanization has created a new type of man attuned to media of mass communication and has regulated important areas of his life by those media.

Industrial urbanization will continue its work of transforming the world for some time to come. Most likely we will have even bigger cities in store, although it is quite conceivable that a new form of carefully controlled, geographically separate settlements lightning-linked by lines of power, transport, and communication will emerge. Few countries will escape intensive urbanization. Yet the forms will continue to vary.

We have a great deal to learn about the processes of urbanization. So far, we know that industrial urbanization brings some standard changes into a nation's life, that the major activity stimulating urbanization seriously marks its character, and that every country plays its own variation on the common theme. The readings in this chapter show how these large processes work out in practice. They also demonstrate that the differences among the major approaches to urbanization we have discussed are real, but that they are more complicated than the elementary scheme separating territory, activity, and population might make it seem. Lewis Mumford's article in this chapter wraps up a great debate on the origins of cities in the Middle East and adds something uniquely Mumfordian to the debate. It never pretends to anything less than a grand view of urbanization. Abu-Lughod's analysis of rural-urban population differences in Egypt and Davis' general survey of world urbanization both begin with an ecological framework and consider shifts in the location of crucial activities as well as transformations of the pattern of social interaction. My analysis of French urban conflicts in the nineteenth century and the paper by Tilly and Brown on migration to an American city both concentrate on interaction but stray without warning into normative, demographic, and locational changes. Murphey's synthesis of the twentieth-century development of Asian cities adopts a broadly locational orientation but in fact takes up the whole range of problems suggested by urbanization. The apparently narrow focus on linguistic changes in Garvin and Mathiot's discussion of a South American Indian language dissolves into a wide examination of population, activity, and social interaction.

Our jobs as readers, then, are first to decide what we could hope to learn from essays on these topics, second to see what the authors have to say, third to detect what differences their theoretical perspectives make to the way they treat their material, fourth to compare (and, if possible, to synthesize) their conclusions. The reader who does these jobs conscientiously will, I think, begin to get a sense of urbanization as the normal consequence of the expansion of the scale, coordination, and centralization of human activities. He will begin to feel the difference that the kind of activity which is expanding makes to the character of urban growth, and to see the importance of making careful analytical distinctions among the intertwining processes accompanying urbanization in Egypt, France, China, South America, or the world at large.

NOTES

1. Some of the material in this introduction comes from Charles Tilly, "The Forms of Urbanization," in Talcott Parsons, ed., *American Sociology: Perspectives, Problems, Methods* (New York: Basic Books, 1969), pp. 75–89, and is used here by permission of the publisher.
2. Karl Marx, *Capital* (London: Lawrence & Wishart, 1970), I, 352.
3. As a matter of fact, the closer look that European historians have recently been giving their own demographic experience is revealing that the differentials were much more variable than historians and demographers used to assume. See the literature reviewed in E.A. Wrigley, *Population and History* (New York: McGraw-Hill, 1969) and in Richard Tilly and Charles Tilly, "Agenda for European Economic History in the 1970s," *Journal of Economic History* 31 (March, 1971): 184–198.

CITY INVINCIBLE

Lewis Mumford

Lewis Mumford is a great interpreter and critic of cities. His massive book The City in History *places the whole Western experience with urban life in a single perspective. It traces the overgrowth and inhumanity of contemporary industrial cities to tendencies which were inherent in urbanization from the beginning, but which men in most ages have had the luck or the sense to keep under control: self-serving concentrations of technical and political power, domination of decision-making by the market, obsession of the powerful with monumental display. In this essay, written not long before the publication of* The City in History, *we find Mumford formulating a theory about the world's first urbanization: the emergence of cities in the ancient Near East. The essay is the final address of a conference bringing together many of the people who had been studying particular cities, regions, processes, and problems. Mumford's task is to suggest connections. He does it imaginatively and in keeping with his own work. The implicit message is that men invented a particular kind of institution—the city—six or eight thousand years ago; that throughout its history that institution bore the mark of the particular conditions under which it first came into being; that by and large it was a powerful, creative, even successful invention; that the major drawbacks of today's cities result from failing to check tendencies which were always present in city-building; and that unless we check those tendencies we will be unable to save the creativity of cities.*

The central argument Mumford states in this essay is that the city emerged from the synthesis of two institutions which were already well established in the Neolithic world: the warrior-hunter-king and the resource-containing agricultural village. In terms of urban form, the fortress represents the institution of kingship, the wall the institution of containment of re-sources. Mumford puts them together in the hypothesis that "the main function of the ancient city was the containment and control of a large population—perhaps ten to twenty thousand people—for the immediate bene-fit of a ruling class and for the ultimate benefit of a whole community whose capital resources and creative potential had been raised to a higher level by this ruling minority." Compulsion and accumulation were inherent in the city from the start; Mumford goes on to suggest that they were only tolerable when they multiplied human creativity and liveliness, and that the recurrent problem of cities is the overwhelming of creativity by compulsion and accumulation. This is a holistic analysis, considering the city as a crucial arena for the whole range of human potentiality.

I would like to go back to one of the themes that originally prompted this meeting, the part played by the city in development and expansion of cultures. In this field, as in every other, I speak not as a specialist but as a generalist whose special competence is to put the scattered and often arbitrarily separated parts together in meaningful relationships. There are certain rules of the game, of course, that a generalist must keep when he tries to put the pieces together. He must not manufacture any of the pieces himself in order to fill out the pattern. He must be willing to scrap the pieces as soon as one of the specialists discovers that they are

Reprinted by permission from "Concluding Address" by Lewis Mumford in *City Invin-cible* edited by Carl H. Kraeling and Robert M. Adams (Chicago: University of Chicago Press, 1960), pp. 224–242. Copyright © 1960 by the University of Chicago.

inadequate or that they belong to another stratum and are unusable at the particular level under discussion. If there are not enough parts, I cannot give anything like a plausible picture. On the other hand, if my design will not hold all the parts presented to me, then that pattern is a faulty one and will have to be thrown out.

"What is the city?" Dr. Hoselitz asked yesterday. "When does it begin and under what conditions does it take shape?" I purpose to address myself to these questions. I share fully Dr. Jacobsen's timidity about going into the problem of chronology, if only because the beginnings of the city predate the written record; and the stratigraphic record, even if it were more abundant, would still not tell us what we most need to know. To come close to the origins of the city we must, I think, extrapolate backward from the fullest known urban remains to their original components, however remote in time and space from the actual city.

One is tempted too easily to say that the city has come into existence at the moment one finds, either below or above the surface, a visible ruin big enough to resemble a town as defined by the census today. That seems to me an oversimplified solution of the problem; in fact it begs the whole question as to the nature of the city by supplying only a physical, quantitative answer. I submit, as a working hypothesis, that all the essential parts of the city were in existence before the city itself took form and that their mobilization and concentration within an encircling wall helped bring about a radical change in neolithic culture.

Our problem, on these terms, is to find out what forces played a part in this transformation; for the form that it took was widely copied or reinvented in every part of the world and held together right down to the seventeenth century. One of the symbols of the end, I would say, was the building of Versailles. At that moment the original core of the city, the fortified citadel, escaped from the surrounding community and became a suburb of the city it had once dominated; the royal power, instead of being fortified by a masonry wall, was protected for a few generations by a hundred thousand armed men. But that was the beginning of the end. Within a few short centuries the city itself, instead of being an almost impregnable agent of military power, became a military liability, so that we now face a new situation culturally and politically—we must learn to live in an open world.

When I look for the origins of the city, I find myself happily close to the eminent scholar on my left (Albright), for I welcome his suggestion that we must go back to a far earlier stage of human culture than your actual diggings indicate—at least as far back as the earliest paleolithic findings of permanent graves. In the uneasy life of primitive man, the dead were the first to have a permanent dwelling place. And perhaps the first form of the city is the cemetery, the city of the dead, a place to which people returned to keep a sense of family identity and continuity. As a matter of fact, one might write a whole interpretation of the city in this vein. I do not think that Egypt and China were so abnormal in their respect for the dead or that Abraham's concern to get a cave for family burial was not shared by much earlier peoples. In time, when the city at last develops, it serves as a kind of tomb, filled with dead institutions as well as dead bodies, so that, even when it is destroyed as often as Troy, the survivors return to the same spot out of piety to the dead.

If the cemetery was perhaps the first permanent meeting place, the cave, as a center of art and ritual, was another paleolithic contribution. Though these caves were not inhabited, Lascaux and Altamira seem to have been ceremonial centers of some kind, as much so as Nippur or Abydos. Here we encounter for the first time an art whose imaginative quality is not touched again till we reach the temples and palaces of a much later period. And if this art was, as some hold, only an incidental by-product of magic, did it not even at the earliest date exert a special magic of its own which drew men at intervals back to the sacred spot? This brings to mind other venerable shrines that embodied sacred powers: sacred stones, sacred groves, sacred single trees, sacred wells, fixed landmarks and meeting places for those who shared the same religious beliefs. In time these became the core of the city.

One must not, of course, overlook more practical needs that brought people together seasonally even in a collecting or hunting economy. Camp sites near a particularly good yield of water, perhaps medicinal water, or by waters heavily stocked with fish and shellfish seem to have served as bases for mesolithic settlements even before nontuberous plants were domesticated. Eventually we find the hunter's camp in the very heart of the city, next to a sacred shrine, a paleolithic enclave walled off from the neolithic villages at its base. But note that two of these three original aspects of temporary settlement have to do with sacred things: the sacred dead and the sacred ritual caves or shrines. Except where cremation was practiced, these were permanent components of the city.

The point I am making is that the city begins as a meeting place to which people periodically return; it is an object of pilgrimage, and this ceremonial function makes it a natural magnet, which at a later stage greatly facilitates the more practical functions of political organization and control of commercial transactions and industrial specialization. Unlike the village, the city from the beginning draws on a population larger than that which permanently gets a living from the near-by farming area. People come to the city for some special participation in the good life; it is Passover, and they go up to Jerusalem, just as today, for more secular reasons, they stream from every part of the United States to New York to see a popular musical comedy. The purpose is different, but the urban function remains the same. Thus the most typical phrase, the one dropped most often perhaps in the city, in all cities at all times, is "I'm a stranger here myself." That is true, even if the "strangers," like the rustics in Aristophanes, come from a near-by village. This merely emphasizes the fact that from its dimmest beginnings, the city is a meeting place. Meeting, intercourse, intermixture are the very breath of its life and the source of its special dynamism. But even when meeting is on a permanent basis, a year-round affair, it does not by itself bring the city into existence or encompass all its functions. So let us look further.

You are all, of course, sufficiently vigilant to the danger of taking strata too seriously. Respect for strata remains a necessity for archeology as a way of defining time limits and successions. But only material culture ever remains stratified. The nonmaterial culture is fibrous in nature; though the long threads may often be broken, they go through every stratum and, even when they are out of sight, they are continuously present. Thus we must remember, when we deal with the village's contribution to the city, that the mobile, restless, imaginative paleolithic hunter is coming back into the city. He does not disappear at any time; and probably the city would never have taken exactly the form it did but for his special gifts and special interests.

But now let us look at the village. There comes a moment, perhaps in mesolithic times, but certainly in neolithic culture, when the domestication of plants produces a more secure and abundant food supply, since the hard grains can be kept over from season to season; and with this a continuous life in one place becomes possible, with more opportunity for child nurture, greater scope for woman's role, a more rich and varied diet that probably abetted fertility, and with all this a great gain in order and regularity and general stability, if also a greater tolerance of repetition and monotony. As for the last, witness the change from the swift snapping of paleolithic tools to the slow process of grinding neolithic tools. The first characteristically needs skill and luck; the second needs dogged patience.

Here lies the beginning of domestication and permanent settlement. Without getting involved in the controversy over Bachofen's *Das Mutterrecht* we cannot doubt that woman exercised a great influence over neolithic culture, from seed selection and hoe cultivation to coiled pottery; but, above all, she domesticated man and thus contributed a new factor toward the formation of the city—hearth and home. This village element remains an essential part of every city, whether the house nestles under the wall of the citadel or like Rahab's house is part of the outside wall or whether it lies as much as five miles away from the center like the ancient Mayan villages. Without this village element, the ancient city could not be fed; and without its surplus children, it could not remain populated. Subsistence economies, collecting or hunting, do not produce that surplus.

From this village culture the city also gets an essential moral ingredient whose character Robert Redfield did so much to illuminate for us. In the more complex forms of the city, the village becomes disguised as a temple quarter, a parish, a neighborhood unit, sometimes, as in Greek and Moslem examples, a place to which a closely knitted group of families is transplanted, each quarter retaining its identity. What Fustel de Coulanges a century ago discovered about the foundations of the ancient city have now been carried back to a much earlier manifestation in Ur, with a family hearth, a household god, and even a mortuary chapel right at hand. The dead were never closer to the living.

The persistence of the village pattern both within and outside the city explains how people were able to survive the perversions and destructions that have accompanied the growth of great urban centers throughout history. For the neighbor is the new contribution of the village. He is not yet a citizen but one who dwells near by and gives help and succor when they are needed, because he in turn cannot survive without such help in times of stress. Remember what Hesiod says about neighbors?

> Call him who loves you to your feast.
> . . . By no means least
> Invite a man whose house is near,
> For if upon a place comes hurt,
> The neighbors hurry out ungirt,
> But kinsmen dawdle o'er their gear.

The village breaks down to some extent the pure kin grouping and makes the neighbor more important; and in times of stress, in plague or war, the city may return to the undifferentiated state of the village, where rank, wealth, class, and caste cease to be important.

With the village comes a new technology, for the symbolically masculine weapons of the hunter, the spear and the bow and arrow, are supplemented by more feminine forms. In interpreting this contribution, I shall first approach the city itself from the standpoint of technology, though there is much one might add on the reciprocal effect of the city upon technology. I would like to call to your attention the technology of utensils, of utilities, of containers. We have no clue to the development of early cultures—or even of our own complex technology—if we concern ourselves only with tools and the beginnings of the machine. We must remember that the neolithic period is pre-eminently a period of containers, a great age of pottery, of vases, pots, jars, vats, cisterns, bins, barns, granaries, houses, and, not least, inclosed villages and cities.

Wherever a surplus must be preserved and stored, containers are important. Without the container, people could not store beer, wine, oil or carry water any distance. No wonder it is in containers that the neolithic inventors outdid themselves, and so well that we are still using their methods and preserving many of their forms, even though plastics have been invented! With storage there is continuity as well as a surplus to draw on in lean season. The setting-aside of unconsumed seeds for the next year's sowing was the first step toward capital accumulation; and the city derives this from the village. The hunter cannot save; he has to consume his game almost on the spot, for he has only human containers for transport and storage. He has no means of independent capital accumulation. But out of the neolithic village come, directly or by further elaboration of the same habits and function, the granary, the storehouse, the arsenal, the library, the archives, the reservoir. Remember that the irrigation ditch and the canal and the aqueduct are also containers, which enable a community to store and transmit a surplus. Without these inventions the ancient city would not have taken the form that it did, for it was a container of containers.

But I am going too fast. We are still in the village, and, as you know, village life has gone on for thousands of years almost untouched by the rise and fall of cities and empires. Max Sorré, the French geographer, has pointed out that four-fifths of the world's population still live in villages. That will not be true much longer; but it should be chastening for us to realize that we still live in a world supported, physically and morally, by the old neolithic culture, though it is dominated by a late iron-age culture and threatened with premature extinction by an early uranium-age technology, whose lack of life-conserving taboos would disgrace the most primitive folk yet discovered. There must have been a fairly long period when nothing that could be called a city had yet come into existence but during which all the components of the city were already in being, crudely shaped, imperfectly related, waiting for the critical moment that would bring the fully dimensioned city into existence. Perhaps only by its area and the number of its inhabitants could this proto-city be distinguished from a village, though even at an early stage its growth may have been due to its being a special cult center.

But where is the paleolithic hunter? What has happened to him? He has been pushed out of the cultivated areas somewhat. If small game can be found there, it is snared or hunted by villagers probably; big game, though, is pushed back a little as the area of cultivation increases; it remains in the swamps and the highlands. But some of the hunting groups do not go along with the secure, orderly, methodical life of neolithic agriculture; perhaps they feel about it the way Huckleberry Finn felt about the "tarnation tidiness" of the "Widder." Did agriculture push the hunter back permanently, or did the growing scarcity of game make him feel that his own predatory life was becoming too insecure as long as he depended upon killing other predators? Was he perhaps lured by the comforts and sociabilities of the village? Before the city springs into being the hunter's camp turns into a permanent stronghold, held by someone a little too vaguely described as the "local chieftain."

Do I stretch the evidence if I suggest that this chieftain was a hunter who had partly abandoned his roving life for a settled one and a predatory life for what was at best a commensal relationship with the village community, at worst a parasitic-predatory domination? It seems to me that the hunter must have had a function in the early neolithic economy. With his mastery of lethal weapons, he protected the village against the lion, the tiger, the wolf, the rhinoceros, the hippopotamus. He knew how to handle these dangerous beasts, whereas the villager had perhaps lost the skill and probably lacked the weapons or, still more, the adventurous animus needed. Gilgamesh, that permanent chieftain, was a heroic hunter, was he not? And is it an accident that the early culture heroes are hunters? Can we close our eyes either to the fact that kings, their lineal successors throughout history, practice hunting as *the* royal sport and are just as proud of their skill in slaying lions as of their prowess in capturing or slaying men? If the great royal metropolises of modern times have open spaces in their very heart, it is because these spaces were originally royal hunting parks or imitations of such parks and because the hunter insisted on preserving large tracts of open land for game, no matter how much the peasant might want it for cultivation.

And yet there is another side to the hunter's control of dangerous animals: one has to pay for protection. Our Victorian ancestors might not have understood this as well as we do. With one gang chieftain or another controlling an industry or a transportation union in our time, we know that we have to pay for "protection" lest the protector himself show even uglier teeth than the animals he is guarding us against. We began to learn this sad lesson under Prohibition, and we have been paying ever higher prices as the system has spread. Similarly, although the hunter had a function in the village economy, he had to be bought off; and, since he was in a minority, probably the function of his castle or fortress was as a holding point—not a protective retreat *for* the villagers but a means of defense *against* them. Do not your diggings suggest that the wall around the citadel preceded the wall around the city?

This is of course a mythological reconstruction; but, since you have no documents to show me, I have to insert a few suppositious events to make the visible data look plausible. Admittedly, it is easier to spot the hunter in the hills of Palestine or in Greece. Where did he hang out in Mesopotamia and Egypt. . . ? I cannot find him on the map until the city appears; and by that time he has taken on other attributes, and the chieftain has assumed control not only of his own special territory but of the large-scale operations necessary to sustain a more complex life.

The proto-city might exist wherever there was either marginal farming or herding; it would not surprise me to find it on the uplands, away from any good source of transportation or communication. Jericho does not surprise me nor upset me, though what has now come to light in Jericho may still be buried, perhaps irretrievably, in Mesopotamia or the Nile Delta. Such an aggregation of houses might have kept on growing without producing the new forms and institutional activities of the city. For the decisive change that creates the city is not just an increase in numbers but a transformation of its institutions and the creation of a new pattern of life. Thus the city is an emergent in the definite sense that Lloyd Morgan and William Morton Wheeler used that concept. In an emergence, the introduction of a new factor produces an over-all change, not a mere addition, but a change such as we see in the passage of relatively unorganized matter into a crystalline form, or of the small stable molecule into the large complex unstable protein molecule, or of reptiles into birds. On the new plane, all the old components are carried along, but they now have qualities and potentialities that they did not possess in their original state.

In the act of urban emergence other elements—the ritual cave, the holy shrine, the sacred mountain, the hunter's camp or stronghold, the primitive village "agora," the nest of peasants' houses—come together to form a new pattern in which each part is both more highly differentiated and greatly magnified in form or intensified in activity. In a sense, the city marks a real break in the neolithic economy but not a revolution. I do not like Childe's term "urban revolution." Revolution means turning things upside down and leaving the past order behind. But nothing was left behind in the city; on the contrary, more and more things were gathered there and preserved there. It was within the close quarters of the city that the human representatives of paleolithic culture and neolithic culture came together, reacting upon one another and influencing one another.

The dynamic, imaginative, audacious, violent, custom-breaking element we have to attribute mainly to the intruder from the outside, the hunter, and to his successor, the roving herdsman. There is certainly more imagination, a more exquisite aesthetic sense, in a paleolithic cave than there is in any early neolithic pottery or sculpture. A little sadly we must confess that the good, sober, industrious, utilitarian, life-oriented neolithic villagers were probably a little deficient in imagination. But, on the other hand, these docile villagers, with their stable custom-bound routine, had something that the hunter, by the very nature of his occupation, lacked: a tolerance of mechanical order or of repetitive humdrum activities. The marriage of audacity and docility, of competent individual command and collective regimentation, gave the city powers that neither the village nor the proto-city possessed.

Though the proto-city could grow anywhere, the full-grown city could come into existence only on one of the great natural channels of transportation and communication. The old lady who remarked that God was very kind because He always put rivers next to cities said something very profound. That is why the earliest indubitable examples of the city appear in the valleys of the Nile, the Tigris-Euphrates, the Indus, and the Hoang-ho, for the city demands a mobilization of resources and facilities that the immediate agricultural area cannot supply.

What made this mobilization and concentration possible must be our next concern, for it produced not only the city but a change in technology, in religious and political institutions that has colored every subsequent phase of civilization. The plow, the potter's wheel, irrigation, astronomy, abstract mathematics, writing and the permanent record, the permanent division of labor into single lifetime occupations, forced labor, slavery, bureaucratic and military organization, and, if I am correct, war itself as an institution all come into existence at about the same time, give or take a few centuries. In that total change in the pattern, the new urban centers were both agent and product.

What I am going to suggest as a key explanation I would hardly dare bring forward were I not merely carrying a little farther the work of one of your old compeers, whose absence we must all deeply regret. I am speaking of the late Henri Frankfort. Both he and Robert Redfield, from different sides, came very close to this explanation; but my main debt is to the author of *Kingship and the Gods.* Frankfort located the lock and provided the key; my function now is merely to turn the key and open the door. I suggest that the key agent in the foundation of the early city is the king and that one of the attributes of Ptah, that he founded cities, is in fact an all but universal attribute of kings.

Here I am very grateful to Mr. Wilson for using the figure of the cell, with the nucleus of the cell surrounded by the cytoplasm and its "wall." That is a good figure for the new urban unit, almost an exact description. I hesitate sometimes to use it, lest it be taken too literally, but even physicists have had to recognize the existence of a nucleus that seems to hold the charges of the atom in an orderly dynamic system. And because we know that the nucleus of a living cell carries the inheritance of the cell or the organism, the analogy is all the more apt in my definition of the city. The nucleus of the city is the citadel, the walled precinct of the palace and the temple. Frankfort's interpretation seems to me to point to a profound change that took place when secular power and sacred power were brought together permanently within a limited area. At that point the physical force exerted by a mere chieftain was enormously enhanced by close association with the thaumaturgic powers of a priesthood, so that what command and coercion could not do alone and what magic and ritual could not sufficiently effect by persuasion alone the two together could perform with an overwhelming power never before approached in any society. Since this change came before the written record, it cannot be satisfactorily dated. It may have needed only a few generations, it may have slowly accumulated over centuries before its elements reached the critical weight needed for a reaction. By 3000 B.C. the urban results are plainly visible. Here I find myself naturally using the current vocabulary of nuclear physics for perhaps an extra reason, namely that the forces that brought the city into existence were the products of a fusion reaction and, like that reaction, released an enormous amount of energy for collective work.

You know how suddenly, speaking in centuries, the little step pyramid became the overpowering Great Pyramid. But did not such expansion and magnification take place all along the line and would it not explain how a mere chieftain could become not only a king but likewise, in Egypt, a god? You know the magnitude of the physical works that are still visible or detectable—the great temples, the complex irrigation systems, the vast platforms above the flood, built out of the mud by hand, the mighty walls. No council of elders acting on precedent could have deployed vast bodies of men in such efforts; no mere desire for profitable trade could have created such an extravagant setting for life. Only a king identified as a ·god or treated as the human representative of a god, a god inflated to astronomical dimensions, could have brought about this transformation. The new powers often assumed paranoid proportions, with paranoid accompaniments of hostility, suspicion, aggression, delusions of grandeur, which may help explain how war repeatedly brought these great achievements to ruin. But it is more important here to recognize that the city endowed the collectivity with cosmic powers and almost superhuman potentialities. No similar magnification and intensification was achieved again until our own times.

This unification of heaven and earth, symbolized so widely, if not universally, by the man-made sacred mountain, completed ideologically the unification of paleolithic and neolithic modes of life. People were drawn to the city voluntarily, no doubt, to participate in these awe-producing powers that were not visible or viable elsewhere, though such participation might demand acts of submission, abnegation, and sacrifice not required in the meaner environment of the village. All the resources of art and technics were mustered in the city to reinforce the claims of kingship and priesthood with the overpowering symbolic representations of authority. Under these conditions the king gathered to himself and ultimately bestowed upon a favored minority a large part of the surplus of the new economy of abundance; and it is not for nothing that you so often find the royal granary within the citadel, for this monopoly of food gave the king the powers of life and death over the whole community. By the same token, the priesthood and the scribes monopolized the production and the transmission of higher learning; this monopoly was more or less maintained in all cultures until the invention of printing. But in return for heavy tribute and heavy toil, the king undertook large-scale public works, of drainage, irrigation, and river control, which were beyond the scope of any smaller community. Democratic communities notoriously shrink from taxing themselves, even for their own benefit, while the royal power, if extravagant and perverse, often had something to show at the end that exalted the humble and caused them to identify their fate with their master's.

In all this my debt to Frankfort is obvious, though even before I had been put on the trail, without guessing how far it would go, by Herodotus, who gives a much later version of how Deioces was turned from a village councilor into a king. That was a sort of shorthand version, not taking account of the earlier religious change, of the change-over from Jacobsen's Mesopotamian council of village elders to a unifying central agent capable of making quick decisions, meeting unexpected emergencies, breaking with ancient customs, capable of giving commands and exacting obedience not merely within its immediate ambit but at a distance, through his distant civil and military agents. From the earliest stronghold on, the walled city was a *Zwingburg* and played an essential part as an instrument of compulsion and control. Whether the wall was originally a religious or a military feature or, more likely, a combination of both, it lessened the need for coercion. In a cityless culture like that of the Spartans, who for long disdained to build walls, the ruling class was forced to remain alertly under arms at all times, lest it be overthrown by the Helots. But where the religious aspect played a relatively larger part, or was accepted with more docile faith, so that the ruler and his followers had less reason for anxiety and distrust, the physical means of ensuring control by a minority, including the wall itself, may have been less conspicuous and the form of the city a more open one, with the bulk of the population remaining in villages, whose number perhaps increased. This seems to hold for early Mayan culture and would indicate not merely an absence of war but perhaps an absence of class conflicts and resentments within the community. And perhaps the same holds for Egypt; if so, it would perhaps help to ease Mr. Wilson's difficulties in finding archeological evidence of the city to support the documentary references to the city's existence in Egypt. But note that one of Deioces' conditions for assuming rulership was that a city should be built for him and that an inviolable royal precinct should be established.

If there are parallels between the original magnification of power through a fusion of secular functions and sacred purposes and similar changes in our own time, with science substituting for theology, there are also important differences. Ours is an age of explosions; and, as a result of undirected technological advances, the city has burst open and scattered its organs and organizations incoherently over the landscape; even the surviving core of the city seems threatened with disintegration. We are witnessing a sort of devolution of urban power into a state of randomness and unpredictability. But the forces that originally produced the city moved in just the opposite direction; they produced not an explosion but an implosion by which a multitude of diverse and often conflicting and colliding particles were held together within a strong urban container. That very containment was perhaps one of the conditions under which the urban cultural potential was built up.

We must not lose sight of this difference when we try to understand the nature of the earliest cities. Whatever else they were, they were above all containers of religious and royal power; and it was that central nucleus of power, itself contained in the palace and the temple, that called people from a distance and united them in tasks that men had never attempted before. Thus the city became the great reservoir of manpower, available for digging, building, trading, fighting, engaging in the specialized trades and professions, the arts and sciences, no longer needed for agricultural labor. The market is a by-product of this concentration and this surplus; but it is the drawing power of the city that brings the trader, not the trader who creates the city. The trader, in time, appears wherever crowds gather, at festivals, funerals, shrines, games, but he does not by his own activities cause population growth nor does he produce the distant goods that circulate in trade. On this matter, Henri Pirenne's description of the extension of the medieval stronghold to include the merchant's suburb has caused many scholars to misinterpret the whole process; and Max Weber, who also looked at the city through medieval spectacles, colored by early capitalism, unfortunately reinforced him.

The attractive power of the ancient city comes not from its market but from its gods. Perhaps the shortest way to define a city, to distinguish it from any mere massing of buildings in a limited area, as at Kahun, is to describe it as the home of a god. But it is even more than that, as emphasized by Mr. Eliade; it is a replica of the universe or that part of the universe in which cosmic order has prevailed over chaos. This connection with heaven gives the city a sort of extra-territoriality, with special privileges and immunities. People put up with the discomforts and congestions of urban life in order to be at the ordered center of things. The city, then, is a model, so to say, of the real world, the significant world, the world representing a wider cosmic order.

Perhaps instead of making so many flat statements, which I have not the time to elaborate in a convincing manner, I should put what I am getting at in the form of questions; for on all these matters I cannot move farther without asking your assistance and gaining your assent. So let me ask: Was the change from the village or the proto-city possible without the institution of kingship, however feasible it was to dispense with that authority at a much later stage, as in Athens? Do you ever find cities of any size without discovering the castle or palace, along with the temple, in a sacred, usually fortified, precinct? Do you find any early cities in which there is not a dominant minority in control of the instruments of power and culture and a much larger group contained by the city but participating only vicariously in its higher activities?

If all these relationships were in fact present from the beginning of cities, as I suppose, and remained constant beneath various disguises and alleviations, they would perhaps point to the fact that the very form and contents of the city produced a result that has too often been overlooked: it minimized the need for application of external force and coercion to its own population, because its divine services and its sacred buildings did more than any pressure of police to polarize its activities and command obedience to its rulers.

Now I want to come back to the question we started with. What is the city? And first we must distinguish between the functions of the city and the purposes and goals that it embodied or made possible. I would say that the main function of the ancient city was the containment and control of a large population—perhaps ten to twenty thousand people—for the immediate benefit of a ruling class and for the ultimate benefit of a whole community whose capital resources and creative potential had been raised to a higher level by this ruling minority. In time the goods monopolized by the citadel, from immortality to water closets, from the written record to systematic science, would filter down to the rest of the community.

But once the urban container was created, it happily subserved many other functions. The special virtue of the container is that the old unchanging form easily adapts itself to new contents. And first, because the rivers were the main transportation routes of the early cities, cities not merely drew for raw materials, food, and manpower from their surrounding region but drained the whole valley and brought together, within a small area, such an intermixture of people, customs, languages and dialects, and craft skill and technologies as could never have taken place between small isolated villages. The function of the small container is to multiply the opportunity for human contact and intercourse. People who would be lost to each other even a day's journey apart would meet frequently within a walled town and be aware of one another's existence even when they did not meet. The opportunities for cultural cross-fertilization were of many kinds; and even the widening of biological choices in mating may have given the city a special advantage. Without such interactions and transactions, practical and ideological, human cultures tend toward fossilization or toward perverse elaboration on a low level.

So much for the essential urban functions. But the purposes of urban culture transcend these functions to give the city a different role, namely that of adding new forms, values, and significances to the human heritage. In other words, the city is the means of transforming power and productivity into culture and translating culture itself into detachable symbolic forms that can be stored and transmitted. Without the organs and institutions concentrated in the city, it is doubtful whether a complex culture could be transmitted and, still less, continue to develop.

Yet the original form of the city—a self-inclosed container "holding its own"—is in some sense at odds with its function of widening the area of organization and control and bringing into a common center the people and the products of other regions and cultures. Or it might be said that the city is both a container and a magnet and that it plays at once static and dynamic roles, perpetuating its complex past but transforming itself too. This ambivalence seems particularly notable in the central nucleus, and it has some bearing, I submit, upon the whole problem of the expansion of cultures and the expansion of political power in the form of empires. The very form of the city, with its tight encapsulated nucleus, its limited area, its walled periphery, makes it an excellent organ for one-sided control but a poor one for large-scale co-operation on a give-and-take basis. When royal power, by its very successes, began to expand, it came into conflict with similar concentrations of physical and magical force in other cities; and instead of producing a fusion reaction, with an increase in power, the collision would destroy the nucleus of the rival city and repeatedly wipe out all the co-operative institutions it had fostered. This is not, you will recognize, a mere metaphor; the first object of military attack was to destroy the rival city's god. Characteristically, the Aztec symbol for a captured city is a destroyed temple. Thus, at the moment of its expansion, the city tends to be the chief enemy of every rival city. All over the world, the archeologist has been uncovering the same sad picture: one destroyed city on the debris of another destroyed city. If the cemetery is the first sign of a permanent urban settlement, the necropolis is the last. When culture made one step forward, power too often took two steps backward.

The city, with all its advantages and achievements, was the product of a closed system; and the problem of civilization, still unsolved, is that of creating an open system without losing the important qualities that the first urban containers brought into existence. The size and form of the city must always bear some relation to the complexity and density of the culture it embodies. The ancient city, up to perhaps the beginning of the iron age, was capable of holding and transmitting the major elements of its culture, outside the orbit of agriculture. But it could not expand indefinitely without losing its inner coherence and without encroaching on the territory claimed as the sphere of another city. Given the nature of the container, neither federation nor empire solved this problem. The original isolation and confinement of the city, and the tensions, antagonisms, anxieties generated with it, always or almost always led to a destructive solution. If Egypt seems largely an exception, at least until the Hyksos invasion, this may possibly be because the Nile Valley itself was the main container, and desert, mountain, and ocean served as its walls. But even when the wall became the frontier of a great state, the institutional apparatus created by the city stamped the ampler unit. Perhaps that is why the periods of greatest cultural intermixture seem to be those of destruction and confusion.

But if the combination of sacred and secular power, in the institution of kingship, was responsible for the original form of the city, how is it that the city itself was not radically transformed by the weakening of these powers? The answer is, I think, that, even when one or another element dropped out of the original divine pattern or new factors like overseas commerce and specialized industry became important, the pattern as a whole nevertheless held. Perhaps Athens would seem an exception; but it was not. Athens was a pseudodemocracy, not a real democracy. Even when new institutions came into the city, like the gymnasium, the internal divisions remained. There was a rich man's gymnasium and a poor man's gymnasium; you followed Plato or you followed Antisthenes.

Such freedom and democracy as Hellenic culture knew were probably due to the fact that the village component remained stronger in the city and, with a sturdier development of what Mr. Albright calls "empiricological" thinking, the Greeks, as Herodotus remarked, were less given to nonsense than were their Near Eastern predecessors. More than once, through the offices of the Olympic games, the shrines at Delphi and Delos, and even the medical sanatoria of Cos and Cniddus, the Greeks seemed to be on the verge of breaking through the limitations of the old form of the city and its disruptive empire-building alternative. But the new federated pattern, more mobile, flexible, open, never got a hold on their best minds or even entered them for a receptive examination. Both Plato and Aristotle conceived of the ideal city as a closed container, in which all the higher elements of culture are monopolized by a dominant minority.

If this interpretation of the critical change that made the city possible should help account for the almost universal form of the historic city, from Babylon to Peking, it perhaps also throws a little light on something that the historian and the archeologist, seeking for evidences of human progress in the arts and sciences, too easily overlook, namely that the cult of kingship, with its overmagnification of power and absolute control, with its assumption of absolute sovereignty, also released aggressive and destructive tendencies that the sheer feebleness of earlier communities gave no scope to. These anxieties and delusions account for the invention of war as a typically civilized institution, indeed, as Plato remarked, the main business of states. I have not the time here to go into some of the fresh lines of thought that this opens up; it is enough to point out that by the time the record becomes visible, the original magical purposes of war—except among the Aztecs and the Maya—have been obscured by presumably sensible excuses for aggression in conflicts over territory or water rights. But in any event, the city, by its very form and original contents, institutionalized destruction and extermination as a condition for maintaining and perpetuating its (magical) sovereign powers.

As an instrument of culture, the city has proved indispensable; and if our age of explosions should blow all the ancient cities into thin amorphous suburban film, it will, I think, be necessary to reinvent the city if all the higher manifestations of human culture are not to perish. But as an instrument for monopolizing power and extending that monopoly, through a system of tribute, to other communities, the city bears the unfortunate stamp of its origins and has constantly torn down with one hand what the other hand built up. For this reason I regret that Toynbee wrote twelve whole volumes on the rise and expansion and destruction of civilizations without even mentioning the city, except in two incidental passages. If the perversions of urban power have not in the past proved fatal, that is probably because the mass of mankind continued to live outside cities. This factor of safety is disappearing before our eyes; and if mankind is to survive it must invent a new kind of urban container, on an open pattern, based on the realities of human association and development, not on paranoid claims to godlike domination.

I have merely tried to suggest that one of the chief keys to the development of civilization from about 4500 B.C. to about A.D. 1500—at the end rashly risking a few dates—lies in the radical change of pattern that took place through the implosion of many diverse and conflicting forces in a new kind of container, the nucleated city, and that the new institution of kingship by divine right and appointment may lie at the very center of that change even as it still lies at the heart of all the cant about the unlimited sovereignty of purely earthly governments today. Whether my hypothesis is worth examining or not, I hope I have given you the courage to go back and look more closely at the origins of the city—more closely than even Childe, with his somewhat Victorian antireligious bias, permitted himself to look. Whether these speculations hold water is unimportant. But if you look further, we, or at least our successors, may some day meet at another conference and come to grips with some of these difficult but deeply fascinating problems.

URBAN-RURAL DIFFERENCES AS A FUNCTION OF THE DEMOGRAPHIC TRANSITION

Janet Abu-Lughod

Students of population change in Western countries formulated the theory of the "demographic transition" during the 1920's and 1930's. Put very briefly, it stated that in the course of industrialization populations went from high, stable birth rates and high, fluctuating death rates to low, stable birth and death rates; this occurred through a transition in which death rates declined early and fast, followed by a slower decline of birth rates, resulting in very high rates of natural increase (and consequently large increases in total population). Urbanization played an important part in many versions of the theory. This phenomenon was supposed to bring with it the life-saving techniques, comforts, and facilities which brought down the death rate, and eventually to provide the exposure to new expectations and opportunities which encouraged people to have fewer children. The theory seemed to fit with a number of rural-urban differences commonly observed in Western countries—for example, the prevalence of higher birth rates in rural areas.

Some parts of the theory have stayed in place since the 1930's. It is clearer than ever that poor countries have shifted toward extremely rapid population growth because death rates have declined much faster than birth rates, and that highly industrial countries generally have comparatively low birth rates, death rates, and rates of natural increase. However, a number of the supposed facts and a number of the explanations built into theories of the demographic transition have not held at close scrutiny, or meshed with the experience of the world since the 1930's. Janet Abu-Lughod's article on Egypt examines some of the supposed facts and proposes a new stage model. Her model gives considerable stress to long-run changes in the world outside the particular population experiencing the "transition"—for example, the invention of pesticides and efficient contraceptive techniques. As a result, it predicts a different course of population change in today's Third World from the one already passed through by Western industrial countries. She derives from the model a series of statements about the rural-urban differences we might expect to find in different kinds of countries at different stages of the "demographic transition."

Within Western industrialized countries certain differences have been noted in the demographic structures of urban and rural areas. Early in the present century, when these were first being probed, the observed variations were emphasized and urban areas were considered to differ *sui generis* from rural ones. More recently, as urban culture has spread out from the metropolitan centers to encompass more and more of the rural hinterlands, and as rural values, patterns, tastes, and standards tend increasingly to approximate those set in cities, many of the differentials hitherto considered inviolate have begun to blur. The wide spread between urban and rural fertility rates commonly observed several decades ago in the United States has been narrowing precipitously, and further diminution is anticipated. Similarly, differences between urban and rural mortality rates, infant death rates, and longevity have been vanishing.

From the opposite side evidence accumulating on the characteristics of urban and rural populations in underdeveloped regions frequently contradicts the generalizations that have long prevailed in urban-rural sociology. "Expected" differences often fail to materialize and, in some cases, reverse differentials have been observed. This point is clearly illustrated by a comparison between certain generalizations elaborated through the study of industrialized countries, particularly the United States, and data available from one newly industrializing country, Egypt.[1] After identifying the discrepancies we shall consider how these disparate sets of facts might be placed within a common framework of analysis.

PROPOSITION I

Urban fertility is lower than rural fertility, and the typical urban family is smaller than the rural. *Corollary:* The larger the city the lower the fertility. (Differences are decreasing.)[2]

Egyptian Evidence. The association between urban life and low fertility has been observed so frequently that urbanization has seriously been suggested as a "tool" of population control. In addition, an entire theory concerning the "changing functions of the family" has been formulated to explain the decline in fertility associated with urbanization. It is therefore particularly significant that in Egypt *urban and rural fertility patterns are substantially the same.* Nor is this a recent phenomenon. Both Cleland,[3] utilizing data from 1906 to the early 1930's, and Kiser,[4] using the Census of 1937, concluded that there appeared to be no urban-rural fertility differential in Egypt. El-Badry computed the average number of children per married woman in 1947 (3.65 for urban as compared with 3.66 for rural) and concluded that there was no "excess of rural fertility over that of urban areas," even when the metropolis of Cairo was isolated.[5]

Investigation of more recent data fails to identify any basic change in this situation. For at least two generations the crude birth rate of Egypt has remained remarkably constant at about 43/1000. The recorded crude birth rate of Cairo has ranged between 50 and 55/1000 in recent decades while the rate for rural areas

Reprinted by permission of the author and publisher, University of Chicago Press, from "Urban-Rural Differences as a Function of the Demographic Transition: Egyptian Data and an Analytical Model" by Janet Abu-Lughod, *American Journal of Sociology*, 69 (1964), pp. 476–490. Copyright by the University of Chicago, 1964.

served by health bureaus has been in the vicinity of 45/1000.[6] While differential underregistration makes it impossible to compare urban and rural fertility directly through birth rates, Cairo, which benefits from the fullest reporting, has a rate so close to the maximum found anywhere that it is difficult to conceive of the rural rate being higher, even if there were full reporting. Nor do fertility ratios reveal significant differences between urban and rural areas. In 1952, the rural fertility ratio was 599 while urban centers had ratios ranging between 592 and 610.[7] Even more direct evidence is available from a recently completed survey of 2,000 urban, almost 700 semiurban and over 3,000 village women in Egypt, which measured fertility by "children ever born to completed families." While some differences were found between urban and rural Christian families, within the Muslim majority (over 90 per cent of the population) the difference between the number of live children ever born to rural women and the number ever born to urban women was too small to be statistically significant.[8]

Thus far, therefore, the expected relationship between fertility and place of residence has not appeared in Egypt, at least for the Muslim majority. Differences in age, duration of marriage, and religion are sufficient to account for observed variations.

In the absence of a clearly defined difference between urban and rural fertility it is not surprising that an association between fertility and city size should also be conspicuously absent. While certain industrial cities, particularly in the fast-growing Canal region, seem to have higher fertility rates than older, more diversified centers both smaller and larger, these appear to be functions of their youthful populations, a result of high migration rates, rather than of their size.[9]

PROPOSITION II

General death rates are lower in rural than urban areas, although cities have somewhat lower rates of infant mortality. (However, where finer breakdowns have been analyzed in the most recent period, the mortality advantage of rural areas has almost entirely disappeared.)

Egyptian Evidence. While fertility differences have not yet appeared in Egypt there can be little doubt that rather dramatic differences between urban and rural mortality rates have become apparent in recent years. These differences are in the opposite direction from those predicted in Proposition II. *Urban mortality rates in Egypt are now substantially below those in rural areas.* This is a totally new phenomenon dating back little more than a decade and a half.

Cities have always been notoriously unhealthy environments. When the "great killers" were still at large, the urban population, because of its greater density and its removal from subsistence agriculture, was much more vulnerable than the population on the land. Until fairly recently this was still true in Egypt. The first mortality decline of the modern period occurred during the second half of the nineteenth century when Egypt experienced an agricultural revival and a consequent expansion in the carrying capacity of the land. It was the rural areas that benefited most from this decline. Flood and famine, the major Malthusian checks in rural areas, were coming under control; their urban counterparts of epidemics and disease remained rampant.

It was not until the closing years of the century that the major causes of urban mortality were attacked. Smallpox vaccination became mandatory in 1890; the nuclei of municipal water systems were installed in Cairo and Alexandria by 1870 and gradually extended; services such as collection of refuse and night soil were commenced, and food and beverage standards were imposed. By the turn of the century urban mortality rates began to decline, reaching a level comparable to the rural rate by the 1920's. By 1937, mortality rates in urban and rural areas were still substantially the same, although the rates for the largest cities may have been lower.[10] This situation prevailed up to 1946, a date that can be established rather precisely.[11]

Between 1945 and 1947, the Egyptian death rate dropped sharply. In the earlier year the crude death rate, corrected for underreporting, was about 33/1000. Two years later it was about 25/1000 (our corrected estimate). This decrease has persisted steadily since 1947 and we would now estimate Egypt's crude death rate at no more than 18–20/1000.[12] With this drop came a rather marked divergence between urban and rural rates, with the former now substantially below the latter.[13]

The decline in infant deaths has been even more extreme than total mortality. From a recorded infant mortality rate of 174/1000 live births in 1932, the Egyptian rate declined to 118/1000 by 1956, the major change occurring between 1945 and 1947.[14] While corrections for underreporting elevate the earlier figure to over 200, inflate the 1945 rate to perhaps 196, and require an upward adjustment of at least 25 per cent for the 1956 rate,[15] still the magnitude of the decline offers impressive testimony to the efficacy of antibiotics in controlling the devastations of infant enteritis, colitis and respiratory infections, the major causes of death in Egypt's population under one year. The urban infant mortality rate is now significantly below the rural. Despite the tendency for infant deaths (and the births preceding them) never to reach the official registers in rural sections, even the *recorded* urban rates are below the rural. In 1956–57, for example, the Cairo rate was 115/1000. Other urban areas had an uncorrected rate of 117/1000 while, in the grossly underreported rural areas served by health bureaus, the recorded infant mortality rate was 125/1000. Any adjustments in these admittedly inaccurate rates can only serve to increase the observed differential in favor of urban areas.

In summary we may conclude that accompanying the rapid decline in mortality since 1946 has been the emergence of a marked differential between the major cities and the remaining rural areas. The gap between the two has been widening and, for the immediate future, no reversal of this trend can be foreseen. Both crude death rates and infant mortality rates are substantially lower in urban centers.

PROPOSITION III

As a corollary of the first two propositions, the excess of births over deaths is higher in rural than urban areas, with the rate of natural increase declining precipitously with city size. Urban growth must therefore come primarily from migration.

Egyptian Evidence. As we have shown, birth rates in rural and urban Egypt are approximately equal while mortality rates are now significantly lower in the major cities. Therefore, there can be little doubt that the Egyptian urban rate of natural increase is considerably higher than the rural rate. In fact, natural increase has become the major, if still overlooked, source of population growth in the largest cities. Migration has so often attracted the attention of analysts that it is assumed to be, if not the *only* source of growth, at least the most significant one. There are now excellent reasons to suspect that since the 1940's natural increase has accounted for at least half of the growth recorded for Egypt's major cities and for possibly as much as three-fifths in the 1950's. This unprecedented phenomenon deserves careful study since it clearly deviates from all accepted urban theory.

The shift in the relative importance of migration and natural increase for Egypt's urban growth can be illustrated indirectly by comparing Cairo's rate of growth with the natural increase rate of the country.[16] Between 1800 and 1848, the population of Egypt increased by about 35 per cent while Cairo grew by only 20 per cent. Since urban and rural birth rates were roughly comparable and there was no out-migration from the capital, Cairo's lower rate of growth must be attributed to deficient natural increase, that is, higher mortality. Between 1848 and 1897—the opening phase of modern development—Egypt's population increased by 130 per cent while the capital city grew by only 90 per cent. Since this was a period of healthy migration to the capital, the figures suggest an even greater discrepancy between urban and rural rates of natural increase, brought about by a decline in rural mortality rates in the face of stable urban rates.

During the course of the present century this situation was gradually but totally reversed. The installation of a drainage-sewerage system in Cairo during World War I was translated almost immediately into a 5/1000 decrease in the crude death rate, making natural increase rates in the capital and the country comparable for the first time in history. Between the two world wars Egypt's demographic situation seemed to have become stabilized. With birth rates slightly lowered due to an increase in the age at marriage and with death rates apparently on a plateau, the country's rate of increase slowed to little more than 1 per cent per year. During this depressed period, natural increase in Cairo possibly outstripped that of the country but the difference was not substantial. It was not until World War II set in motion the drastic drop in mortality—a drop most precipitous in the largest cities—that the current situation came about in which natural increase in Cairo now amounts to 32/1000/year in contrast to 23–25/1000 in rural areas. For the first time, capital-city growth is coming primarily from an excess of births over deaths.

While this is an unprecedented phenomenon, one cannot believe that Egypt is simply a unique case. A similar change may now be occurring in other overpopulated, underindustrialized countries, although better data than are currently available would be necessary to substantiate this. We would hypothesize that the largest Indian cities, for example, now have higher natural increase rates than prevail in their rural hinterlands, despite arguments to the contrary.[17] If this should prove to be the case, current theories must be revised to take into account the new element that has been introduced in industrializing countries by the postwar tumbling of mortality rates.

PROPOSITION IV

Urban and rural areas differ significantly in the age compositions of their populations. The percentage of population in the "productive years" is highest in the largest cities and declines smoothly with size of place; rural areas, on the other hand, contain concentrations of the very young and the very old. Differential fertility and mortality as well as selective migration create this situation.

Egyptian Evidence. A similar but much less marked gradient is found in Egypt for which migration alone appears to be responsible. Table 1 illustrates this. The magnitude of the observed differences is relatively small, and within the size classes the exceptions are so numerous that one must conclude that the differential is far less developed than in the United States. Only the very largest cities deviate significantly, a fact that must be attributed to the Egyptian pattern of migration which tends to bypass smaller cities and towns and be directed almost exclusively toward the largest cities.[18]

TABLE 1
Average Percentage of Young and Middle-Aged Persons
in Egyptian Communities of Different Sizes, 1947[a]

	Percentage of Total Population (Class Average)	
Size Class	*Under 15 years*	*15–50 years*
Entire country	39.3	45.0
Cities 500,000 plus	37.1	52.1
100,000–499,999	39.2	50.1
50,000–99,999	39.5	49.3
30,000–49,999	40.2	48.8
20,000–29,999	39.5	48.7

[a]Computations based on separate returns of the 1947 Census for the fifty-seven urban places having 20,000 or more inhabitants.

PROPOSITION V

Urban and rural populations are characterized by different sex ratios. Females predominate in cities whereas males outnumber females in rural farm and non-farm areas.

Egyptian Evidence. So accustomed have we become to the female excess in American cities that it shocks us to learn that in rapidly developing countries the reverse is much more common. In Egypt it is the cities that have positive sex ratios while the rural areas have ratios of under 100. This is clearly illustrated in Table 2.

Differences in sex ratios must be traced always to selective migration. Table 3 demonstrates the close relationship between Egyptian patterns of migration and the resultant sex ratios in sending and recipient communities.[19] Note that within the youngest age class—that least likely to be imbalanced by selective migration—males and females are quite evenly matched. Rural-to-urban migration, concentrated after fifteen years of age, produces a major dislocation noticeable particularly in the middle years of life, with the sex ratios highest in the large, fast-growing communities.

TABLE 2
Sex Ratios by Community Size, Egypt, 1947[a]

Size of Place	Males per 100 Females
Country total	98
Cities over 100,000	103
Cities 50,000–99,999	101
Cities 20,000–49,999	97
Villages 10,000–19,999	99
Villages 5,000–9,999	97
Places under 5,000	95

[a]Computations ours from data presented in United Nations *Demographic Yearbook 1955*.

TABLE 3
Average Sex Ratios for Egyptian Urban Communities, by Size, Class, and Regional Location, 1947[a]

Size and Type of Community		Ratio of Males per 100 Females in Ages		
	No.	Under 15	15–49	50 plus
Receiving:				
500,000 plus	2	98.0	105.5	106.6
100,000–499,999	5	98.6	110.6	105.8
50,000–99,999	9	98.0	101.0	104.0
Sending:				
30,000–49,999	15	100.0	97.8	105.0
20,000–29,999	26	99.8	95.4	98.8
Total	57			
All fast-growing	10	100.3	111.8	106.1
Slow-growing in:				
Upper Egypt	24	100.0	91.7	108.0
Lower Egypt	23	98.9	96.6	90.5

[a]Computations ours from special data processed for the fifty-seven Egyptian communities with populations of 20,000 or more in 1947.

As can be seen, fast-growing cities, regardless of location, have the highest ratios. Among the remaining cities, however, regional location is of critical importance, reflecting the cultural differences between Upper and Lower Egyptian migration patterns. When people from the Delta (Lower Egypt) migrate to the cities, they often move as a nuclear family; men migrating alone rarely return to their community of origin once having gone to the city. The reverse is true for the typical Upper Egyptian migrant. First, migration is almost exclusively a male matter, and second, migrants frequently return to their families in the village after decades of only intermittent contact. While these differences have been identified elsewhere, the sex ratio differentials revealed in Table 3 give added credence to them.[20]

Thus, with respect to sex ratios the urban-rural differential is found to be as extreme in Egypt as it is in the United States but in the opposite direction. This is due to differences in selective migration which in turn are related to the types of employment opportunities available in the cities of each and to the cultural determinants of labor-force participation.[21]

PROPOSITION VI

To summarize the rather complex data for the United States, there is a moderate relationship between size of place and the marital status of the population, if age composition is standardized. Larger cities contain greater proportions of single, widowed, and divorced adults. The reverse is true for smaller towns and rural non-farm areas, while farm regions contain more single men and more married women than a standard population.[22]

Egyptian Evidence. The inconclusive data for Egypt indicate that both the married and the divorced states are more common in the larger communities while single status is more frequent in rural communities, although the lack of age standardization throws doubt on some of these conclusions. In 1947, 39 per cent of Cairo's male and an equal per cent of her female population (total) was married, as compared to the national rate of 38 per cent for each sex. The annual marriage rate shows a slightly greater discrepancy. For example, in 1957, the *Quarterly Return* recorded 17.7 marriages per thousand Muslims within the entire country, while the comparable rate in Cairo was 20.2 marriages. Judgment on these points must be reserved, however, since differences in age distribution, age at marriage, and incidence of remarriage make it impossible to interpret these figures in a meaningful way.[23]

While the variations in nuptiality are so slight that they might be dissipated entirely by a more refined analysis, this is hardly true with respect to the incidence of divorce. According to the 1947 Census, some 1.7 per cent of the males sixteen years of age and older and fully 3.1 per cent of the adult females in Cairo were listed as divorced, as compared to 0.9 and 1.3 per cent, respectively, in the country as a whole. Within recent years the annual divorce rate for Cairo Muslims[24] has fluctuated between 9–12/1000, according to various issues of the *Quarterly Return*, although the comparable rate for the entire country has varied between 3.5– 6.5/1000 each year. Thus the Cairo rate has been consistently two to three times higher than the national rate, indicating a significant differential.

We may tentatively suggest that, with the exception of specific industrial centers that recruit an unattached male labor force, urban areas and rural areas in Egypt are roughly comparable in the percentage married. On the other hand, urban life does appear to affect the frequency of divorce. Given the legal ease with which a Muslim union may be dissolved, social and familial sanctions play the major role in minimizing divorce within the closed village society; when these become less effective (although hardly inoperative) in the city and as urban heterogeneity encourages more exogamous matches, divorce rates increase. Cairo's higher rate is due more to these factors than to any selective principles of migration.

THE EGYPTIAN DEVIATIONS—ACCIDENTAL OR SYSTEMATIC?

When six commonly accepted propositions on the demographic differences between urban and rural areas are tested in a country at an entirely different stage of the demographic-industrial revolution, we find that on almost every point the Egyptian data deviate more or less from the "expected." The deviations are not capricious but bear a systematic relation to each other and to the historic and cultural context of their appearance.

Furthermore, Egypt's experience cannot be dismissed merely as a unique or exceptional case. Many of the Egyptian "deviations" are shared by other countries at similar stages of modernization and may even have characterized Western countries several centuries ago. While it remains outside the scope of this article to provide proof for these statements, one can point to suggestive evidence. A recent Indian study indicates an absence of the urban-rural fertility differential in that country.[25] Since many newly modernizing countries experienced the same drastic decline in mortality after World War II[26] that Egypt did and for the same reasons, it is not unlikely that they are experiencing also a divergence between their urban and rural mortality rates by this time. Studies have appeared that indicate the presence in many Asian countries of the same age and sex differences as those identified in urban and rural Egypt.[27] In short, there is congruence to the deviations.

A PROPOSED MODEL FOR ANALYSIS

The theory of the demographic transition offers a useful conceptual framework within which both the generalizations derived from industrialized countries and those applicable to modernizing countries may find their place.[28] On the basis of that theory and the expanding body of knowledge relating to the dynamics of demographic change, it is possible to construct a hypothetical model in which specific urban-rural differentials (or their absence) can be predicted at various stages of the transition.

The model presented below is consciously derived from the Egyptian case, although it has been modified by data from other areas and has wider application and, hopefully, more general value. No model can hope to be equally relevant to all cases. Exceptions and necessary modifications will be discussed in a final section.

Assumptions. Beginning with the simplest proposition, one may state: The demographic transition from a preindustrial equilibrium (a function of high birth, crude death, and infant mortality rates leading to a relatively stable, young, and small population) to a postindustrial equilibrium (a function of relatively low birth rates, very low infant mortality rates, and moderate mortality rates leading to a relatively stable, older, and larger population) takes place over time (X) *in a given and predictable temporal sequence* that affects certain variables before others and certain social and geographic subgroups of the population before others. Therefore, at any particular point in time, *observed differences in the characteristics of urban and rural populations can be explained with reference to the temporal sequence.*

A second proposition must be appended if the remaining variations observed in individual case studies are to be accounted for, namely:

Both (*a*) the *technologies of birth and death control* extant at the historic epoch during which a country's transition is effected and (*b*) the *cultural-social system of the society* undergoing the transition will modify the rates at which specific changes take place and may even, in exceptional cases, lead to minor revisions in the temporal sequence itself. *The temporal sequence of the transition* may be summarized in terms of several non-discrete phases.

PREINDUSTRIAL OR FEUDAL AGRARIAN

1. The economy is based upon subsistence agriculture or, if under colonial administration, an exported agricultural surplus, and the total population is therefore "relatively" small.

2. Crude birth rates are high and fluctuate little from year to year except when unusual circumstances force postponements of marriage or when economic conditions permit a lowering of the average age at marriage. While there may be a relationship between economic status and size of family (due to survivorship), a gross urban-fertility differential is extremely unlikely.

3. Crude death rates are high and are furthermore subject to violent periodic fluctuations in which the small natural increase gains of many years may be totally wiped out. Because of unsanitary conditions, cities will usually have much higher mortality rates than rural areas.

4. Natural increase will be higher in rural than urban areas, and urban growth will depend heavily upon continual replenishment through migration. Selective migration will lead to marked age and sex differences.

5. Only a small percentage of the population can reside in cities[29] which serve chiefly as the locus of concentrations of religious and military power, as central places for a very circumscribed hinterland, and/or as "break-in-bulk" points for wider trade. The urban population consists of a very small elite, a somewhat larger and fairly stable artisan-merchant class, and a massive "floating" population, unskilled and of rural origin, which is culturally undifferentiated from the peasant class except in terms of often temporary place of residence. The rural population is organized along feudal lines.

6. There is little dominance of the city over the hinterlands except in tax and conscription matters. Cultural values of the urban elite—including those affecting fertility and mortality—are transmitted neither to the urban proletariat nor to the peasants.

EARLY TRANSITION

1. The first variable affected when a society begins the demographic transition (which may or may not coincide with economic reorganization) is mortality. Death rates decline but at a rate that has varied significantly during different epochs of "death control technology." At least three major periods must be distinguished:

Prior to about 1850. Very gradual decline in death rates, more pronounced in rural than urban areas. In countries beginning the transition during this epoch—for example, England and Wales—the differential between urban and rural mortality rates inherited from the preindustrial phase not only persisted but became even wider.

1850–1946. Moderately rapid decreases in mortality were achieved chiefly through advances in epidemic control, public health regulations, and environmental sanitation. Both urban and rural mortality rates declined, the latter often earlier but more gradually than the former. The differential inherited from the preceding period usually grew no wider and may actually have decreased. A distinction must be made between indigenous development and imposition of death-control technology. France during the nineteenth century illustrates the first development; Egypt from 1890 provides an example of the second.

After 1946. Mortality rates may fall quite rapidly in response to widespread use of DDT, antibiotics, etc. The decline will probably be even faster in urban than rural areas. Depending upon the preexisting gap between urban and rural rates and upon the extent of urban-to-rural diffusion, the mortality differential may disappear entirely or even be reversed so that the lowest death rates may be found in the largest cities.[30] Most so-called underdeveloped countries are entering the transition stage under conditions of this type.

2. Fertility rates remain constant or may actually increase somewhat if prosperity encourages a lowering of the marriage age.[31] The lack of a noticeable urban-rural fertility differential persists.

3. The "population explosion" experienced at this stage results from the progressively larger gap between stable fertility and declining mortality. Whether this explosion will be more marked in urban or rural areas is totally dependent upon the direction and degree of the mortality differential.

4. The pressures created by the population increase can be relieved through (*a*) emigration, (*b*) premature rural-to-urban migration, or (*c*) land expansion through conquest of reclamation of marginal territory, or some combination of all three. Europe depended primarily on the first; Egypt, Japan, Korea,[32] etc. have depended more upon the second; while Mexico and many South American countries have found the third alternative practicable. The chances that urbanization and industrialization will develop apace are greater where the first and third alternatives are available; where only the second is feasible, the time lag between premature urbanization and commensurate industrial development will be greater.

5. Since much of the pressure is relieved through migration from rural-to-urban areas, rather marked differences between the age and sex compositions of urban and rural areas should appear at this time. Selective migration on a large scale modifies the age and sex structures of both sending and receiving areas, the net effect being a function of (*a*) the degree and consistency of the selection and (*b*) the ratio of migrants to base population. The *specific* differentials that will be found, however, depend upon the cultural patterns of a country and no single model will suffice for predictive purposes. Most countries will develop uniform age differentials since in all countries youth tends to be more mobile than age. With respect to sex ratios, on the other hand, culture will be determinative. Attitudes toward and opportunities for employment of women outside the home are the key variables affecting urban-rural sex ratios.

INDUSTRIALIZATION AND THE TRANSITION PROPER

Once the economy has passed the "taking-off" point and the processes of industrialization have become firmly and irreversibly established, hitherto inert variables begin to change.

1. A decline in fertility appears but is not distributed at random in society. It begins within certain socioeconomic and cultural groups and diffuses according to a fairly predictable sequence, a phenomenon that facilitates prediction of the specific urban-rural differentials that reach maximum visibility during this phase of the transition. As was necessary in the case of mortality, one must distinguish several epochs in the technology of birth control:

Prior to circa 1875. During the eighteenth and much of the nineteenth century fertility could be only imperfectly controlled by inadequate techniques. The very gradual rates at which fertility declined in Western countries undergoing the demographic transition at that time must be attributed in part to inefficiency rather than lack of motivation.

From 1875 to the Present. During this epoch fertility was rendered increasingly subject to human control through the development of improved, though scarcely perfected, methods of contraception. This reduced the time interval required by an industrializing society (for example, Japan) to make the transition from high to low fertility, indicating that faulty techniques rather than values had constituted the major deterrent during the earlier period.

After 1964. A third epoch in the history of fertility control, one that may revolutionize birth rates as dramatically as the advances of the 1940's revolutionized death rates throughout the world, appears to be imminent. A technological breakthrough in the provision of a simple, non-repetitive, inexpensive, and highly effective method of birth control will make it possible for societies now entering the second stage of the demographic transition to transform their fertility rates within a considerably briefer period of time than has ever before been recorded. Again, although motivation must be present, this writer believes that the latent demand for effective birth control is so great that all our current projections will prove to have been overly pessimistic, once this third epoch of fertility control is entered.[33]

2. The rural-urban differences that appear during this stage of the transition, however, result more from the sequence of the fertility decline than from its speed, although the more rapidly over-all fertility declines, the briefer the period during which these differentials will be apparent. The following model of sequence is composite and cultural differences will lead to minor variations.

a) Fertility declines *first* within the newly emerging professional and managerial class that is "created" by industrialization and concentrated in the cities.[34] This class, characterized by upward mobility and possession of skills rather than land, has most of the factors that, in numerous studies, have been linked to family-planning motivation and birth-control effectiveness. It has incorporated most completely the values of "rationalism" and ends-means into its *Weltanschauung;* it tends to experience the greatest discrepancy between its level of expectation and its income; it tends to delay marriage until later in life; and members tend to select wives from higher educational levels. A lower fertility is therefore to be expected.

b) Only after industrialization has begun to undermine the traditional bases of prestige characteristic of the preindustrial phase (such as land, religious role, even "foreignness") will the older aristocracy begin to take its cues from the new upper-middle class. Only then and quite gradually will this group experience a downward trend in fertility.

c) Emulation will lead members of the urban lower-middle class to adjust their fertility patterns next. This group, through its white-collar employment in the government and corporate bureaucracies, is maximally exposed to the new professional-managerial elite with whom it can identify more readily than with the older aristocracy. This makes it likely that they will incorporate the new values, although not without perhaps a lengthy and painful conflict.

d) In descending order of exposure and capacity to "identify" are the urban artisan class, the semirural or migrant city dweller, and finally, the peasant. Declines in group fertility can be anticipated in this order. *Note that the sequence begins with urban subgroups and terminates with rural groups.* Therefore, urban-rural fertility differentials will appear to develop along a U-shaped curve, minor at the point when the fertility transition begins, maximal toward the middle, and negligible at the terminal phases of the transition.

3. The simultaneous urbanization of the country exaggerates the urban-rural differentials created by the sequence of fertility decline. Urbanization serves to increase membership in classes likely to be experiencing a fertility decline while it reduces membership in those classes least affected by the new fertility patterns. At this point significant changes are occurring in (*a*) the role of cities in the national economy; (*b*) the percentage of the population engaged in non-agricultural pursuits; and (*c*) the relationship between cities and their hinterlands. These changes have important implications for urban-rural differentials.

a) During the period of "incipient" industrialization, particularly in densely populated regions, the urban population may expand to include one-fifth or more of the total without any alteration in the role of cities in the economy. Urban growth results more from pressures expelling people from rural areas than from urban opportunities attracting them. Once industrialization becomes established, however, urban growth attains a momentum of its own with a basis in economic viability. If cities can offer sufficient industrial employment opportunities, social mobility and cultural assimilation of migrants will be encouraged, which will lead to a more rapid decline in over-all urban fertility rates.

b) This expansion in the industrial sector, accompanied by the gradual substitution of rational farming methods for the rural horticulture formerly practiced, leads to a shift away from farming in the long run, even if this is temporarily disguised by "underemployment" in densely populated countries such as India and Egypt. The net result is an increase in the percentage of the labor force engaged in urban-type occupations and thus an increase in the number of persons "exposed" to conditions and values favoring lowered fertility.

c) The third change that occurs affects the relationship between cities and their hinterlands. One major morphological difference between Western industrial cities and their counterparts in pre- and semi-industrial areas is that, whereas the former are surrounded by a wide zone of transitional uses, the latter tends to terminate abruptly with almost no density gradient, as if they were surrounded by invisible walls. This physical fact is matched by the less obvious sociological fact that the city's influence ends almost as sharply as its physical plant.[35] This makes it unlikely that urban-nurtured values and patterns will have any impact on rural persons. With industrialization and more particularly with the proliferation of the transport and communication networks prerequisite to industrial growth comes a radical expansion in the city's sphere of influence that is manifested physically in the development of a transitional suburban ring and sociologically in the increased capacity of the city to affect economic conditions, aspirations, and ways of life in an ever widening hinterland.

It is significant that the first two changes in the nature of the city tend to increase the demographic contrast between urban and rural areas while the last tends, in the long run, to destroy it. In the history of Western urbanization the first two operated initially and only at a much later stage did the third factor enter to mitigate their effects. A major difference between the Western model and one appropriate for societies currently undergoing the transition, then, is that in the latter all three processes are occurring simultaneously, *which may prevent the emergence of as extreme an urban-rural contrast as developed in the nineteenth-century West.*

4. Since urbanites still constitute a minority of the population, the over-all birth rate of a country will appear to be declining only very gradually during the first stages of the fertility transformation, although the urban-rural fertility differential will be progressively widening. Once urban patterns diffuse to rural areas the over-all crude birth rate will drop rapidly, but by the time this occurs, the demographic differences between urban and rural populations will have already begun the process of coalescence that terminates within the succeeding (and for the present, terminal) stage of the demographic transition.

5. Differential mortality plays only a minor role during this phase. Its impact is chiefly upon the changing age structure, a phenomenon that becomes critical during the next stage.

POSTINDUSTRIAL SOCIETY: A NEW TAKING-OFF POINT?

The basic characteristic of a postindustrial society is that urbanization and industrialization have become so pervasive that their presence or absence within any given geographic subarea is culturally "irrelevant." Just as preindustrial cities absorbed their dominant ethos from agrarianism, so postindustrial rural enclaves derive theirs from urbanism. In neither instance can simple criteria such as size of community, density of settlement, etc., serve as reliable indices to values or "ways of life." And just as preindustrial societies maintained a relatively stable demographic balance *in the absence of major urban-rural differences*, the postindustrial society appears to develop its own equilibrium despite urban-rural uniformities. This period is characterized by:

1. Relatively stable birth rates comparable in so-called urban and so-called rural areas, with significant intraregional variations due primarily to ecological specialization within the metropolitan complex. From the very limited experience to date it appears that fertility rates may dip dangerously low before stabilizing at a more moderate level.

2. Relatively stable death rates equivalent in urban and rural areas with

regional and intraregional differences due almost exclusively to age, sex, and income differentials. Again from limited experience, it appears that the death rate reaches an abnormal low before the effects of an aging population appear and then rises slightly to a fairly stable level.

3. Moderate population growth rates are dependent upon economic conditions that encourage or inhibit planned fertility. Natural increase, once at the mercy of mortality fluctuations in the preindustrial era, becomes almost solely a function of fertility.

4. Continuance of selective migration not to compensate for urban deficits but to allow for a constantly increasing degree of conurbation. Rapidly growing regions will have younger populations and ostensibly higher birth and lower death rates; declining regions will have older populations, lower birth and higher mortality rates, but these variations will not necessarily be related to the degree of urbanism per se.

5. Relation of existing mortality and fertility differentials more to socioeconomic status than to place of residence. That mortality decreases with higher socioeconomic status has already become apparent; evidence is now accumulating to suggest a future positive association between income and fertility during the postindustrial period. Sweden has recorded such an association for some time, and data from the United States appear to be moving in the same direction.

APPLICATION OF THE MODEL AND SOME LIMITATIONS

Application of the above model to the Egyptian case is relatively simple since the model has, in part, been derived from the data. Briefly, one can summarize it as follows: prior to 1850, Egypt's demographic condition was preindustrial. Toward the end of the nineteenth century she entered the initial stage of the transition, as evidenced by the decline in rural mortality which was translated immediately into rapid population growth more marked in rural than urban areas. The industrialization stimulated during World War II seems to have propelled Egypt into the opening phases of the established transition, since fertility in the limited class of urban professionals and technicians now shows a significant deviation from the high fertility norm. It appears that this norm has already lost ideological support and one can therefore anticipate that an urban-rural fertility differential—conspicuously absent up to the present—will shortly appear in Egypt. As Egypt advanced along the demographic transition, certain urban-rural differentials were found to increase while others decreased or were reversed. Thus the "deviations" of Egypt from the patterns found in industrialized countries and from patterns that previously prevailed within Egypt itself can be accounted for within the framework of the demographic transition.

To what extent can this model be used to analyze the urban-rural differences found in other countries and regions? Only slight modifications would appear to be required to adjust the model to other relatively overpopulated and newly industrializing countries of Southeast Asia and the Middle East. "Horizontal" comparisons, that is, comparisons of observed urban-rural differences within these countries *at the same phase* of the demographic transition, would permit us to develop and refine the generalizations hypothesized in the model and, further, would permit us to trace the *residual* variations due to technology and culture.

The model in its present form would not be applicable either to the African case or, perhaps, to certain parts of Latin America.[36] Since the transition in Africa is basically from tribal to urban organization without a significant intervening period of settled agrarianism, a separate model must be developed. Basic modifications would also be required for the countries of Central and South America, since the ethnic cleavage between urban and non-urban subgroups is so deep and prolonged that observed urban-rural differences there may merely reflect separate cultural strains.

NOTES

1. Efforts to test the generality of these propositions using the comparative statistics assembled in various issues of the United Nations *Demographic Yearbook* appear to this writer highly dubious. Countries whose conditions are most likely to contradict the generalizations have statistics most in need of careful adjustment. In contrast to many other industrializing nations, Egypt has fairly accurate data over a long period of time. Decennial censuses have been taken since 1887 and registration of births and deaths has been mandatory (though not enforceable) since the late nineteenth century. Even so, however, figures have had to be adjusted and interpreted, a procedure possible *only* when the investigator has detailed knowledge of statistical peculiarities and local conditions. For this reason we have advisedly eschewed random and gross comparative statistics.
2. See, for example, O. D. Duncan and A. J. Reiss, Jr., *Social Characteristics of Urban and Rural Communities, 1950* (New York: John Wiley & Sons, 1956); and R. Freedman *et al., Family Planning, Sterility and Population Growth* (New York: McGraw-Hill Book Co., 1959), pp. 309—17.
3. W. W. Cleland, *The Population Problem of Egypt* (Lancaster, Pa.: Science Press, 1936), particularly Table IV, p. 39.
4. Clyde Kiser, "The Demographic Position of Egypt," in *Demographic Studies of Selected Areas of Rapid Growth* (New York: Milbank Memorial Fund, 1944), pp. 97—122.
5. M. el-Badry, "Some Aspects of Fertility in Egypt," *Milbank Memorial Fund Quarterly,* January, 1956, pp. 22—43.
6. Vital rates in areas served by health bureaus are released quarterly by the Egyptian Ministry of Statistics and Census. See various issues of the *Quarterly Return of Births, Deaths, Infectious Diseases, Marriage and Divorce.* Health bureaus now cover all urban and many rural areas, accounting for about one-third of the total population. Underregistration in rural areas served by health bureaus is still serious. Underregistration *outside* health bureau districts is alarmingly high.
7. Computations ours from the Quarterly Return. A ratio of children to women fifteen to forty-five years has been used since the Egyptian Census age categories do not break at twenty and modal and median age at marriage for Muslim females is below twenty.
8. See Hanna Rizk, "Fertility Patterns in Selected Areas in Egypt" (unpublished Ph.D. dissertation, Princeton University, 1959). A summary of findings appears in her "Social and Psychological Factors Affecting Fertility in the United Arab Republic," *Marriage and Family Living,* XXV (February, 1963), 69—73. Other basic sources on Egyptian population are: M. el-Badry, "Some Demographic Measurements for Egypt Based on the Stability of Census Age Distributions," *Milbank Memorial Fund Quarterly,* July, 1955, pp. 268—305; S. H. Abdel-Aty, "Life Table Functions for Egypt Based on Model Life-Tables and Quasi-Stable Population Theory," *Milbank Memorial Fund Quarterly,* April, 1962, pp. 350—77; A. al-Dali, "The Birth Rate and Fertility Trends in Egypt," *Egypie contemporaine,* October, 1953, pp. 1—12; G. Marzouk, "Fertility in the Urban and Rural Population of Egypt," *Egypie contemporaine,* January, 1957, pp. 27—53.
9. An inherent bias introduced by Egyptian methods of estimating postcensal population bases in cities may also be responsible, since the method tends to ignore migration.
10. See Kiser, *op. cit.*

11. Differential underregistration of deaths makes a direct comparison between urban and rural mortality rates ill-advised. For example, Weir found in 1948 that the recorded death rate in a village containing the health bureau office was 32/1000, while two villages only a mile away had rates of 19 and 23 respectively. A third village some three miles from the office had a recorded death rate of only 12. More graphic proof of the need to adjust and correct recorded rates would be difficult to find. See J. Weir, "An Evaluation of Health Sanitation in Egyptian Villages," *Journal of the Egyptian Public Health Association*, Vol. XXVII (1952).

    With this caution in mind, we have taken the liberty of using published rates merely as the starting point of our own estimates, which are as follows: During the nineteenth century the mortality rates in the largest cities ranged between 45 and 50/1000 while the average rural rate was only about 40/1000. For serial data on Cairo and national rates since 1875 see M. Clerget, *Le Caire: Étude de géographie urbaine et d'histoire économique* (Cairo: Schindler, 1934), II, 24.

    During the twentieth century up to 1946, the overall death rate of the country was apparently on a plateau of 30–35/1000. See detailed estimates by M. el-Badry in "Some Demographic Measurements . . . ," *op. cit.*, p. 303. The rural rate had ceased to decline before 1920, although the decline in the urban mortality rate continued steadily. The urban rate was probably somewhat below the rural by the 1940's.

12. Official government statistics suggest a stable death rate between 1920 and 1945 of about 28/1000, a drop to 21/1000 by 1947, and a current rate below 15/1000.

13. Only indirect evidence can be used to show that, at least since the "break" in the 1940's, the mortality situation in the major cities has become increasingly superior to that in rural areas. In order to use the admittedly inaccurate recorded rates certain assumptions must be made: first, that urban underregistration is less extreme than rural underregistration; and second, that while registration has become more complete in recent years, the "difference in degree" of underregistration in urban and rural areas has remained fairly constant. If these assumptions are correct, any decrease in the difference between urban and rural death rates may be interpreted as a change in their relative positions, *even if* the actual values cannot be precisely determined. In the late 1930's uncorrected rural mortality rates were consistently 8–10/1000 below the uncorrected urban rates. By 1956, this difference had almost entirely disappeared (the rural rate was only 1/1000 below the urban). If urban underregistration is between 2–3/1000 and underregistration in rural areas served by health bureaus is about 10–11/1000 (see above), a "guestimate" of 1956 true rates would be 16/1000 in the largest cities, as compared to a rural mortality rate in the vicinity of 22–24/1000.

14. Various issues of the United Nations *Demographic Yearbook* and computations (ours) from the *Quarterly Return . . .* cited earlier.

15. The five-year moving average for health bureau areas declined from 296/1000 live births in 1908 to 216 by 1930. See Cleland, *op. cit.*, p. 54. Kiser suggests 198/1000 for health bureau areas in 1939, but this may be too low. El-Badry, using Weir's formula to correct for underregistration, estimated an infant mortality rate between 200 and 240 for the same period. We would estimate that, by 1957, Egypt had a corrected infant mortality rate of about 150/1000 with the urban rate down to 135–40 and the rural rate above the national one.

16. Because Egypt has peculiarly low rates of in- and out-migration, it is possible to take total population growth as equivalent to natural increase. In the analysis that follows the raw data, the criticisms of them, and the corrections and extrapolations that underlie the conclusions have had to be omitted. Statistical substantiation is available from the author and will appear in a forthcoming volume on the evolution and organization of the city of Cairo.

17. In a recent book on urbanization in India several very reliable demographers concluded, on the basis of census data up to 1951, that it was highly unlikely that urban growth in India could ever come from an excess of births over deaths. See Kingsley Davis, "Urbanization in India," particularly pp. 5–6; and D. Bogue and K. Zachariah, "Urbanization and Migration in India," particularly pp. 27–28, in Roy Turner (ed.), *India's Urban Future* (Berkeley: University of California Press, 1962). The next census may provide an unexpected turn of events.

18. This phenomenon has been identified and substantiated in J. Abu-Lughod, "Urbanization in Egypt: Present State and Future Prospects," forthcoming.
19. The age categories of under 15, 15–49 and 50-plus have been selected because of their sensitivity in Egypt. The majority of Egyptian migrants move by the age of twenty; and only 10 per cent of the Egyptian population is fifty or more years of age.
20. See J. Abu-Lughod, "Migrant Adjustment to City Life: The Egyptian Case," *American Journal of Sociology*, July, 1961, particularly p. 27. Subsequent publication of the preliminary results of the 1960 Census permits an analysis of post-1947 changes. Postwar migration from Upper Egypt differed from earlier movements in that the sexes were quite evenly balanced. The 1947 sex ratio of Upper Egyptians in Cairo was 400; this has been reduced to 129, as computed from the 1960 Census, representing an important departure from a pattern of very long duration.
21. The low rate of participation of Egyptian women in the *urban* labor force is evident from the following figures computed from the unpublished 1957–58 sample Labor Force Survey of Egypt. Only 3 per cent of all females five years of age and older were employed in "urban-type" occupations, i.e., in manufacturing, commerce, government, services, etc. By contrast, almost half of the male active labor force was engaged in "urban-type" occupations.
22. See Duncan and Reiss, *op. cit.*, Table 15, p. 71.
23. The higher nuptial rate of Cairo appears to be due more to age composition than other factors. In addition, remarriage is more common in Cairo than elsewhere in the country, which would serve to inflate the nuptial rate. On the other hand, the median age at marriage is somewhat higher in Cairo than elsewhere (21.6 as contrasted with under 20 for Muslim females); but since these figures include women entering second and third unions as well as first, they are unreliable.
24. Muslim figures are used exclusively in this analysis since the major Christian sect in Egypt prohibits divorce except under very unusual and unlikely circumstances.
25. Edward Driver, in *Differential Fertility in Central India* (Princeton, N.J.: Princeton University Press, 1963), found no significant differences between urban and rural fertility patterns in the sample studied.
26. See George Stolnitz, "The Revolution in Death Control in Non-Industrial Countries," in *Annals of the American Academy*, CCCXVI (March, 1958), 94–101.
27. See, for example, the findings summarized in UNESCO, *Urbanization in Asia and the Far East*, ed. P. Hauser (Calcutta: Research Centre on the Social Implications of Industrialization in Southern Asia, 1957), pp. 123–25.
28. In a field in which theory seems to be converging very rapidly, no claim to originality can be justified. The basic framework provided by P. Sorokin, Amos Hawley, and particularly Frank Notestein has shaped much of the author's thinking. A parallel approach which appeared after this article was framed is found in D. Cowgill, "Transition Theory as a General Population Theory," *Social Forces*, March, 1963, pp. 270–74.
29. See G. Sjoberg, *The Preindustrial City* (Glencoe, Ill.: Free Press, 1960); also E. Lampard, "The History of Cities in the Economically Advanced Areas," *Economic Development and Cultural Change*, III (January, 1955), 81–136.
30. This is because modern techniques of death control are more readily available in urban areas and acceptable to urbanites, while folk techniques persist more vigorously in rural areas.
31. This is suggested by William Petersen in "The Demographic Transition in the Netherlands," *American Sociological Review*, June, 1960, pp. 334–47. Confirmation can be found in the Egyptian data.
32. See, for example, T. O. Wilkinson, "The Pattern of Korean Growth," *Rural Sociology*, XIX (March, 1954), 32–38.
33. The high latent demand for birth control in Egypt's urban areas is confirmed by a recent study conducted by the Alexandria Institute for Social Work, as reported in *Al-Ahram* (Cairo), August 11, 1963, p. 4. Within a relatively poor area of Alexandria, 96 per cent of the wives and 84.5 per cent of the husbands interviewed favored family limitation. The ideal size of family was placed overwhelmingly at three children, which appears to be a developing universal ideology found equally in such places as Puerto Rico and Indianapolis!
34. El-Badry, analyzing differential reproduction in Egypt in 1947 by occupation of father,

found that only one occupational class—comprised of engineers, doctors, officers, and technicians—had fewer children. No other occupational differences were statistically significant. See his "Some Aspects of Fertility in Egypt," *loc. cit.*, pp. 35–39.

35. One of the few studies of this phenomenon is Richard Ellefson, "City-Hinterland Relationships in India," in Roy Turner (ed.), *op. cit.*, pp. 94–115.

36. Several studies of Mexican fertility seem to refute predictions that would follow from our model. The South American situation is well documented in Kingsley Davis and Ana Casis, "Urbanization in Latin America," *Milbank Memorial Fund Quarterly*, XXIV (April, 1946), pp. 186–207.

THE CHAOS OF THE LIVING CITY

Charles Tilly

This study considers some phenomena which urbanization is often said to cause: protest, conflict, and violence. It deals with nineteenth-century France, where plenty of people thought that the rapid growth of Paris and of smaller industrial cities was disrupting traditional forms of social life and thus causing a whole range of disorderly behavior. The argument goes through several stages: (1) an effort to sum up standard theories linking "disorder" to urbanization, criticize them, and state what the evidence concerning collective violence should look like if those theories are correct; (2) a sketch of an alternative argument in which the structure of the community affects the form and intensity of collective action, and violence is mainly a by-product of collective action (by this argument, there should be little connection between urbanization as such and collective violence); (3) a presentation of a variety of evidence, much of it quantitative, concerning patterns of collective violence in nineteenth-century France; (4) an interpretation of the evidence as favoring the collective action argument and casting doubt on the tracing of disorder to urbanization.

The implicit models of community structure, cities, and urbanization in this article are interactional: communities are settings for social interaction, cities are communities in which specialized, complex, and large-scale sets of social relations are relatively prominent, and urbanization consists of the relative growth of such communities. One of the weaknesses of the article, however, is that it makes do with gross, conventional measures of urbanity and urbanization where in principle it should introduce refined descriptions of changes in the communities under study. One of its strengths, I think, is that it employs relatively fine, rich, and differentiated descriptions of the "disorder" which is usually handled crudely.

THE CITY AS CHAOS

As life is disorderly, so is the city. Yet is the city itself the source of disorder? Since the rise of the industrial metropolis, generations of Western men have proclaimed it so. The nineteenth-century sociologists who argued that the mobility, complexity, and scale of the modern city were bound to strip men of social ties, disorient them, and thus to push them toward individual and collective derangement were simply articulating a well-established tradition. The tradition has not yet died.

We find the precise tone in Baudelaire:

Swarming city, city of dreams
Where ghosts grab strollers in broad daylight . . .

How admirable it is, he tells us elsewhere, to join the few who are free of the spectral grasp:

And so you go your way, stoic, uncomplaining
Through the chaos of the living city . . .

"Through the chaos of the living city!" A great motto for the study of urban disorder.

Hauser (1963, p. 212) tells us that:

Another group of serious problems created or augmented by rapid rates of urbanization are those of internal disorder, political unrest, and governmental instability fed by mass misery and frustration in the urban setting. The facts that the differences between the "have" and "have not" nations, and between the "have not" peoples within nations, have become "felt differences", and that we are experiencing a "revolution in expectations", have given huge urban population agglomerations an especially incendiary and explosive character.

In Hauser's view, the breaking of traditional bonds and the conflict of values feed disorder, while the swelling city's combination of misery and heightened hopes nearly guarantees it. Change produces tension, tension breaks out in collective explosions, and a form of action more frenzied than that of stable, developed countries erupts into life. Hauser's analysis, I believe, sums up the predominant sociological position. Seen from the outside, the set of ideas looks solid and

Copyright © 1973 by Charles Tilly. This paper is a top-to-bottom revision of "A travers le chaos des vivantes cités," presented to the Sixth World Congress of Sociology (Evian-les-Bains, France), 1966. The original version was published in Meadows and Mizruchi, 1969 (citations in this form refer to the list of references at the end of the paper). The research reported in the paper received support from the Center of International Studies (Princeton University), the Social Science Research Council, Harvard University, the MIT-Harvard Joint Center for Urban Studies, the Canada Council, and the National Science Foundation. The Institute for Advanced Study gave me much-prized leisure to complete the revision. I am especially grateful for research assistance to Karen Ambush, Lutz Berkner, Judy Carter, Priscilla Cheever, James Doty, Ronald Florence, Judy Kammins, Lynn Lees, A.Q. Lodhi, Ted Margadant, Virginia Perkins, Sue Richardson, James Rule, Ann Shorter, Edward Shorter, Gerald Soliday, Cyrus Stewart, and Sandra Winston.

chinkless. From inside, it seems much less likely to withstand pressure. For one thing, it contains a notion of the equivalence of different types of disorder. Personal malaise, moral deviation, crime, and political upheaval are supposed to flow into each other.

Almost mystically, Louis Chevalier announces that essential unity. Outside the major outbursts, he says,

> The political and social violence which has been studied so often and so minutely is replaced by other forms of violence—more continuous, more complex, harsher, involving greater numbers, taking from the rise and the bulk of the masses their progress, their unity and their force. Here is another form of connection among crises: Private dramas, daily ones, add their weight to the public ones, developing outside them, but accumulating and culminating in them (Chevalier, 1958, pp. 552–553).

Chevalier does not hesitate to call nineteenth-century Paris a sick city, or to consider misery, crime, suicide, street violence, and popular rebellion so many expressions of the same pervasive pathology. That is one side of the standard sociological formulation.

Turn this set of ideas over. On the other side is stamped a complementary set: that there is a sharp disjunction between healthy and pathological social states, between the normal and abnormal, between order and disorder, which justifies treating different specimens of disapproved collective behavior as manifestations of the same general phenomenon—"deviance." The responses which other people give to the disapproved behavior win another general label—"social control."

Collective violence almost automatically receives both the complementary treatments. It is easy to treat as the final expression of a fundamental pathology which also shows up as a crime, delinquency, family instability, or mental illness. It is even easier to treat as radically discontinuous from orderly political life. Long before Taine and Le Bon had dismissed the mass actions of the French Revolution as the work of the demonic guttersnipes, Plato had shuddered over the outbreaks of man's "lawless wild-beast nature, which peers out in sleep," and James Madison had warned of "an unhappy species of the population . . . who, during the calm of regular government, are sunk below the level of men; but who, in the tempestuous scenes of civil violence, may emerge into the human character, and give a superiority of strength to any party with which they may associate themselves."

More recently, Hannah Arendt (1963, pp. 9–10) has argued that "violence is a marginal phenomenon in the political realm . . . ," that "political theory has little to say about the phenomenon of violence and must leave its discussion to the technicians," that "insofar as violence plays a predominant role in wars and revolutions, both occur outside the political realm." The political realm, to Miss Arendt's mind, contains normal social life.

Here two ideas intertwine. One is that violence appeals to the beast in man and to the beasts among men. The other is that men, in becoming violent, step over an abyss which then separates them from coherent rationality.

Despite their devotion to death-dealing automobiles, aggressive detectives, and murderous wars, it is true that men ring round forms of interpersonal violence with extraordinary taboos and anxieties. Yet collective violence is one of the commonest forms of political participation. Why *begin* an inquiry into the effects of urbanization with the presumption that violent politics appear only as a disruption, a deviation or a last resort? Rather than treating collective violence as an unwholesome deviation from normality, we might do better to ask under what conditions (if any) violence disappears from ordinary political life.

That is, however, a mischievous question. The treatment of collective behavior in terms of change: tension: tension-release and the assumption of drastic discontinuity between routine politics and collective violence cling to each other. Most students of large-scale social change cling to both. Challenging either the fit between the two notions or their independent validity therefore smacks of rabble-rousing. Yet there are some alternatives we simply cannot ignore.

First, collective violence often succeeds. Revolutionaries do come to power, machine-breakers do slow the introduction of labor-saving devices, rioters do get public officials removed. The local grain riot, so widespread in Western Europe from the seventeenth through the nineteenth centuries, often produced a temporary reduction of prices, forced stored grain into the market, and stimulated local officials to new efforts at assuring the grain supply (L. Tilly, 1971). I do not mean that, by some universal calculus, violence is more efficient than nonviolence. I simply mean that it works often enough in the short run, by the standards of the participants, not to be automatically dismissed as a flight from rational calculation.

Second, whether or not it succeeds in the short run and by the standards of the participants, collective protest is often a very effective means of entering or remaining in political life, of gaining or retaining an identity as a force to be reckoned with. Eugene Debs boasted that "no strike has ever been lost," and American advocates of Black Power consider their appeal the only means of mobilizing Negroes as an effective political force. Although there are always Revisionists to argue that the dispossessed will gain power more cheaply by circumventing revolution—even though the Revisionists are often right—collective violence does frequently establish the claim to be heard and feared. In that sense, too, it can be a rational extension of peaceful political action.

Third, acts of collective violence often follow a well-defined internal order. The order goes beyond the Freudian logic of dreams or that symbolic correspondence Neil Smelser finds between the beliefs embodied in collective movements and the strains which produce them. In many cases it is sufficiently conscious, explicit, and repetitive to deserve the name "normative." Many Western countries on the eve of intensive industrialization, for example, have seen a recurrent sort of redressing action against what the people of a locality consider to be violations of justice: mythical avenging figures like Rebecca or Ned Ludd, threats posted in their names, outlandish costumes (women and Indians being favorite masquerades), routine, focussed, roughly appropriate punishments inflicted on the presumed violators of popular rights (see Hobsbawm and Rudé, 1968; Hobsbawm, 1969; C. Tilly, 1969). Disorder displays a normative order.

Fourth, the participants in collective violence are frequently rather ordinary people. Recent studies of popular disturbances in France, England and elsewhere have shifted the burden of proof to those who wish to claim that mass actions recruit from the lunatic fringe. Not that these studies portray the recruitment as a kind of random sampling; real grievances, local economic conditions, established paths of communication, the character of local politics all help determine who take part. Yet the rioters and local machine-breakers commonly turn out to be fairly ordinary people acting on important but commonplace grievances. The "dangerous classes" stay out of sight.

Finally, the large-scale structural changes of societies which transform everyday politics through their effects on the organization, communication, and common consciousness of different segments of the population also transform the character and loci of collective violence. As the scale at which men organize their peaceful political actions expands, so does the scale at which they organize their violence. As workers in mechanized industries become a coherent political force, they also become a source of disorder. The correlations are obviously complex and imperfect; that is precisely why they are interesting. Yet they are correlations rather than antitheses.

So there are five reasons for hesitating to assume that collective violence is a sort of witless release of tension divorced from workaday politics: its frequent success as a tactic, its effectiveness in establishing or maintaining a group's political identity, its normative order, its frequent recruitment of ordinary people, and its tendency to evolve in cadence with peaceful political action. The five points are debatable and worthy of debate—not to mention empirical investigation. To the extent that they are valid, they lead to somewhat different expectations from the usual ones concerning the development of political disturbances in the course of urbanization.

RELATING COLLECTIVE VIOLENCE TO URBANIZATION

Urbanization *could* affect collective violence in three main ways: by disrupting existing social ties and controls, by exposing more individuals and groups to urban institutions and living conditions, and by changing relations between city and country. In fact, an abundant (if largely theoretical and anecdotal) literature asserts the disturbing effects of each of these changes. The disruption of ties and controls is commonly supposed to incite disorder either by removing restraints to impulses which would under normal circumstances be muffled or by inducing anxiety in individuals detached from stable, orderly surroundings. (Mass migration to cities is the standard example.) Exposure to urban institutions and. living conditions is usually considered to promote collective violence in two respects: (1) by imposing intolerable privations in the form of material misery and unfamiliar disciplines, or (2) by communicating new goals via heightened communication within large groups sharing common fates and interests, and via the diffusion of higher standards of comfort and welfare from the existing urban population to the newcomers. Thus rapid urban growth is said to exacerbate the "revolution of rising expectations." The changing relations between city and country are often thought to engender disturbance in the country itself as cities expand their claims for goods, men, taxes, and subordination, while rural communities resist those claims. Thus regions of distinct tribal character presumably become ripe for rebellion.

If the disruption of existing ties and controls, the exposure of individuals and groups to urban institutions and living conditions, and the changing relations between city and country all uniformly encourage collective violence, then matters are delightfully simple: the pace and location of upheaval should be closely correlated with the pace and location of urban growth. That hypothesis easily lends itself to testing. The surprising thing is that it has not yet been truly tested.

Even in the absence of good data on either side of the relationship, however, we may legally doubt whether it is so splendidly straightforward. In no Western European country have the peak years of urban growth since 1800 also been the peak years of political upheaval. Such quantitative international studies as we have of the twentieth century give relatively little weight to the sheer pace of change in the explanation of the frequency of protest and violence; instead, they tend to substantiate the importance of political structure and of short-term deprivation. So a global connection of upheaval to urban growth seems unlikely.

Happily, the various components of urbanization also lend themselves to separate analysis. We can, to some extent, isolate the political correlates of rapid migration from rural areas to large cities, of miserable urban living conditions, or of the expansion of central control into the rural backland. Rather than the amassing of case studies of violence or the statistical manipulation of general indices drawn from samples of whole countries, two strategies getting at differentials within countries seem particularly suitable. The first is to compare segments of the country—communities, regions, classes, as well as periods—in terms of the frequency and intensity of collective violence, of the forms violence takes, of the participants in it. Whereas international comparisons ordinarily make it tough to disentangle the correlates of urban poverty from those of rapid migration to cities, and case studies usually hide the significance of negative instances, systematic comparisons within countries promise the opportunity to examine the differences between turbulent and placid periods or settings in meaningful detail, with reasonable controls.

The second strategy is to separate—and, where possible, to index—the appearance of different *forms* of collective violence. This means eschewing summary indices of "turbulence" or "instability." It also means paying as much attention to variations in the form of collective outbursts as to shifts from calm to fury and back again. Here the illuminating work of George Rudé and Eric Hobsbawm, who have depicted the characteristic preindustrial disturbances and stressed their replacement by other kinds of disturbances with the advent of industrialization, offers questions and hypotheses galore.

The power to close in on such hypotheses gives these two strategies their attraction. The ideas about urbanization and collective violence I earlier characterized as the standard sociological treatment immediately suggest predictions: those periods and regions in which the intensest urban growth goes on should be the richest in disturbances; misery, mobility, and cultural diversity will have separate and roughly additive effects; collective violence and other forms of "deviance" will be positively correlated in gross and will recruit in the same parts of the population, while at a given level of urban concentration or a given pace of urbanization they will be negatively correlated since they are alternative expressions of the same tensions; collective violence will recede as new groups become formally organized, integrated into the nation's political life.

There is surely something to all these hypotheses. They deserve checking. Yet the second thoughts on the nature of collective violence we encountered earlier suggest some different predictions: a weak connection of political disturbances with crime, misery, or personal disorder; a corresponding rarity of the criminal, miserable or deranged in their ranks; a strong connection with more peaceful forms of political contention; a significant continuity and internal order to collective violence where it does occur; a long lag between urban growth and collective outbursts due to the time required for socialization; organization and formation of a common consciousness on the part of the newcomers; a tendency for disturbances to cluster where there is a conflict between the principal holders of power in a locality and more or less organized groups moving into or out of a modus vivendi with those holders of power, a marked variation of the form of the disturbance with the social organization of its setting. On the whole these hunches are harder to verify than those deducible from the standard sociological treatment. Still they can be tested, and should be.

For some years now, a group of sociologists and historians at several different universities in Europe and North America has been working on the relevant comparisons for Germany, France, Italy, and a few other European countries since around 1830. The work on France is at present further along than the studies of the other countries, so we are not yet in a good position to make systematic comparisons *among* the countries. But we do have over a century of French experience well documented, and enough information about the other countries to give some sense which features of France's experience are peculiar, and which commonplace. This paper deals exclusively with the French evidence.

THE EXPERIENCE OF MODERN FRANCE

France of the last century and a half is a good starting point. Its territory is fairly constant, the general lines of its political history well known, its violent incidents abundant. The period 1830–1960—the main one under examination here—contains several important surges of industrial expansion and urban growth. The records are remarkably rich—often richer, contrary to our sociological prejudices, for the earlier years than for the later ones.

The raw materials come from French archives, newspapers, political yearbooks, government reports and statistical publications, occasional memoirs, and specialized historical works. For information on collective violence, our basic procedures are (1) to enumerate as many as possible of the violent conflicts above a certain scale occurring in France each year and code them all in a summary, standard way; (2) to select a systematic sample of them for intensive analysis, gathering as much additional information about them as possible from the archival sources and historical works, coding them in a very detailed fashion according to a regular scheme; (3) to organize special studies of especially informative periods or conflicts.

The basic unit in the analysis of collective violence is the "disturbance"—any event occurring within the country in which at least one group of fifty or more persons took part, and in which some person or property was seized or damaged over resistance. The disturbances in the general sample are all such events trained readers encountered in scanning two national newspapers from 1830–1860 and 1930–1969, plus three randomly-selected months per year from 1861–1929. There are about 2,000 disturbances in the general sample, 500-odd in the intensive one, and a dozen disturbances singled out for special analysis.

A good deal of general information about the social setting of disturbances, of course, enters the analysis in the form of observations on the disturbances themselves. But that way of accumulating information slights the settings with few disturbances, or none. We have tried to get around that difficulty by assembling comparable information on major social changes—for example, urban population, net migration, labor force shifts—year by year for France as a whole, for its eighty to ninety departments, and for the larger cities.

We have also begun to deal with other forms of collective conflict by putting together roughly comparable information on most of the strikes (some 100,000 of them) reported in France from 1830–1960. The two sets of conflicts overlap usefully, since a small proportion of the strikes turned into violent encounters. Despite this extensive standardization of the sources, however, the sorts of questions this research raises often drive us back to other materials in order to account for contrasts in violent propensities between different years, areas and segments of the French population. In short, the data collected offer the possibility of moderately firm tests of existing hunches concerning differentials in collective violence, plus some good leads for further investigation; they cannot conceivably provide a total explanation of France's turbulent political history.

Figure 1 presents our count of the number of disturbances per year in France from 1830–1960, smoothed to five-year moving averages.[1] Despite the considerable smoothing, the curve reveals the tremendous bunching of violent events in time. That bunching in itself rules out many of the interpretations of collective violence as a response to structural change, which lead us to expect more gradual crescendos and decrescendos of violence. Collective violence is unlike crime, suicide, fertility, marriage, or migration, all of which the pace of industrialization or urban growth does affect directly, and all of which display large but very gradual long-run swings. It resembles strike activity more closely, since strikes come in sudden surges superimposed on massive long-run trends. That is more or less what we should expect of a form of action clearly dependent on slow processes like unionization, industrialization of the labor force, and changes in the organization of firms, but also responsive to short-run economic and political crises affecting the position of organized labor (see Shorter and Tilly, 1971). But the fluctuations of collective violence correspond most directly with the ebb and flow of political conflict at the national level. The periods of the Revolution of 1848 and of the Popular Front—both times of massive popular mobilization—dominate the curve.

The swings of collective violence, on the other hand, do not correspond to the pace of urban growth, which was most rapid in the 1850's, the 1920's, and the 1950's. If anything, the correlation runs the other way: rapid urban growth, less collective violence. I expect, in fact, that more detailed studies will reveal a general tendency for collective violence to *decline* when and where urbanization is most rapid, because rapid urbanization means both (1) that many people are leaving the countryside where they are embedded in communities which are organized for collective action, and (2) that many people are arriving in cities where it takes a long time for them to acquire the means of collective action, or to be drawn into the ones which already exist. My premise, obviously, is that violence flows directly from organized collective action instead of being an alternative to it.

A Closer Look at 1830–1860. Let us close in on the first thirty years of the period 1830–1860. The three decades lead us through several major upheavals and

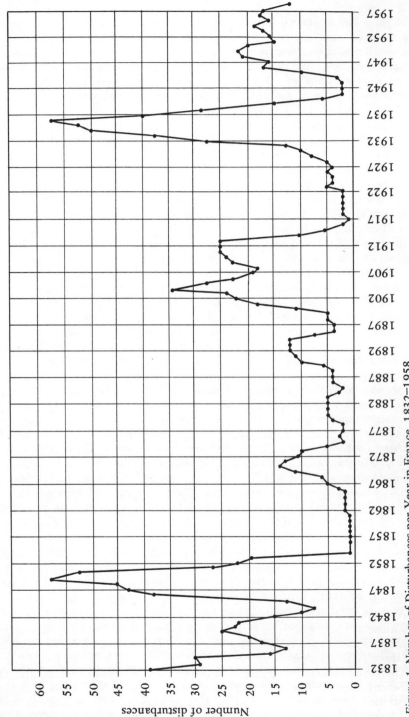

Figure 1. Number of Disturbances per Year in France, 1832–1958
(Five-Year Moving Average Centering on Year Shown)

changes of regime in France: from the Restoration to the July Monarchy via the Revolution of 1830, through the Monarchy with its insurrections in Lyon and Paris, from the July Monarchy into the Second Republic via the Revolution of 1848 and its turbulent aftermath, to the Second Empire through Louis Napoleon's coup d'état.

The thirty years also bracket an unprecedented push of economic expansion and urban growth. The expansion was slow in the 1830's, punctuated by depression in the 1840's, and extraordinarily vigorous in the 1850's. During that third decade the railroads proliferated and modern industry got under way. Correspondingly the growth of big cities accelerated from moderate in the 1830's and 1840's to fast in the 1850's. While at the beginning of the period the leaders were mainly the old regional capitals—Toulouse, Strasbourg, Marseille, Lyon, Paris, with St. Etienne and Roubaix-Tourcoing starting to represent the newer industrial centers—by the 1850's the entire region of Paris and all the industrializing Northeast were full of spurting cities.

On this smaller stage, we still do not see collective violence dancing to the rhythm of urban growth. The turbulent years of this period, even leaving the major revolutions aside, were 1830, 1832, 1848, and 1851. Roughly two-thirds of all the disturbances we have enumerated in the entire three decades from 1830–1860 occurred in the seven years from 1830–1832 and 1848–1851. The later 1850's, those peak years for urban growth, were practically empty of violent disturbances; so were most of the 1860's. Again the correlation over time is inverse: rapid growth, little disturbance.

This does not mean, however, that the cities were calm and the countryside turbulent. The pattern was much more complicated than that. It is true that short-lived disturbances flourished in the smaller towns and rural areas of France in the 1830's and 1840's. Three types of events recur again and again: food riots, violent resistance to taxation, and collective invasions of forests, fields, and other rural property. (A fourth frequent form of collective violence of the mid-nineteenth century—the smashing of machines by unemployed or fearful workers—did not reach its stride in France until the Revolution of 1848.) Here we have the recurrent, and somehow coherent, "preindustrial" forms of disturbance described by Edward Thompson or Eric Hobsbawm. The food riot, with its regular combination of grumbling against price rises, massing in markets, seizure of grains being shipped or held in storage, and forced public sale at a price locally determined to be just, sums up their character.

Even in the 1830's, however, the larger conflicts and the ones which most seriously affected the distribution of power in France clustered in and around the great cities. Paris usually led the way; Lille, Lyon, Rouen, Marseille, and Nantes rarely stayed out of the action. During any substantial block of time, therefore, we see three broad classes of disturbance: major conflicts centered on the great cities; ramifications of those major conflicts in smaller cities and in the hinterlands of the great cities; smaller-scale events, only indirectly linked to nationwide conflicts, spread through the rest of the country.

The Revolution of 1830 and its aftermath display this pattern clearly. The central events were no doubt Paris' Three Glorious Days of July, 1830: with large demonstrations and extensive street fighting across barricades, a coalition of work- ers and bourgeois brought down the Bourbon monarchy of Charles X and installed the house of Orleans with Louis Philippe as king. Yet much happened outside of Paris. Almost immediately, struggles for power broke into violence in Dijon, Nantes, Amiens, Bordeaux, Lille, and Toulouse and went on without public confrontation in most other big cities. As the new government attempted to reestablish its control over the provinces, resistance to taxation and to other actions from the center produced clashes through large regions of France. The struggles continued into 1831 and 1832. Figure 2 reveals the considerable spread of involvement in violent conflict. The map, which shows estimated participants in each department per 100,000 population, singles out Paris as a small spot of intense participation in the midst of a region where conflict was under control. It also shows the high involvement in collective violence of the Rhône (which is essentially

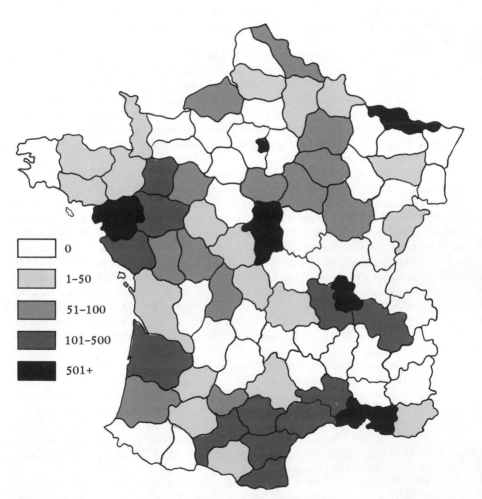

Figure 2. Participants in Collective Violence per 100,000 Population, 1830–1832 (Corrected to Annual Rate)

that of Lyon), the influence of several major conflicts over taxes in Bourges and elsewhere in the Cher, a long series of food riots in Moselle, the repeated conflicts in the West, and the widespread resistance to central power in a whole band of departments running across southern France from Bordeaux to Marseille.

Let us summarize the pattern statistically. Suppose we calculate rates of participation per 100,000 population for the revolutionary months of July and August, 1830, for the period of consolidation during the remainder of 1830, and for the period 1830–1832 as a whole. The breakdown by urbanity of department is found in Table 1. In general, the more urban the department, the heavier its involvement in collective violence. Yet even the rural departments produced significant numbers of participants, especially during the last months of 1830.

TABLE 1
Participants in Collective Violence per 100,000 Population
by Urbanity of Department, 1830–1832

Percentage of Population in Cities of 10,000 or More	*Revolution*	*Post-Revolution*	*1830–1832*
0.0	19	54	20
0.1–5.0	43	84	34
5.1–10.0	92	218	66
10.1–15.0	720	136	135
15.1+	2904	412	727
Total	573	175	158

Collective violence, then, clustered around the cities but not exclusively in them. Big cities like Lyon and Marseilles stand out, as do their surrounding areas. Paris and its department, the Seine, tower over all the rest. Yet very rural departments like Ariège remain in their company. Furthermore, despite the example of Paris, there is not an obvious tendency for the fastest growing cities or the most rapidly urbanizing departments to produce more collective violence than the rest.

To make that fact clearer, we may turn to correlational analysis of the same data concerning 1830–1832. Table 2 presents correlations of various indicators of crime, malaise, and collective violence with three different measures of urbanism and urbanization: (a) the population in cities of 10,000 or more in 1831, (b) the *change* in that population from 1821–1831, (c) the net migration into the department from 1826–1831. In general, the measures of crime, malaise, and collective violence are most highly correlated with urban population and least highly correlated with net migration; urban increase regularly occupies the middle position. All the correlations are positive, and some are substantial. As a consequence, a first reading of the table may well produce the impression that crime, individual malaise, and collective violence do, after all, spring from urban growth, and in similar ways. That would be hasty.

TABLE 2
Correlations between Indicators of Urbanization and Indicators of Crime,
Individual Malaise, and Collective Violence, Partialed for Total Population,
for Departments of France, 1830–1832

	Indicators of Urbanization		
	Population in cities of 10,000 or more	Increase in urban pop. 1821–1831	Net migration into department 1826–1831
Incidence of crime (1831)			
Rebellion	.837	.613	.255
Crimes against persons	.246	.122	.236
Crimes against property	.823	.626	.259
Vagrancy	.771	.581	.265
(1831) Incidence of individual malaise			
Illegitimate births	.771	.502	.290
Suicides	.839	.693	.425
(1830–1832) Incidence of collective violence			
Disturbances	.671	.673	.328
Participants	.913	.878	.526
Killed and wounded	.925	.840	.406

Sources: Compte de l'administration de la justice criminelle en France, 1831; Censuses
of 1821, 1826, 1831; general sample of disturbances; partial correlations among indicators of
urbanization: urban population × urban increase .777; urban population × net migration .465;
urban increase × net migration .511.

Note: Partial correlations of absolute numbers in each category, total population
partialed out.

The problem, of course, is that urban population, urban increase, and net
migration are sufficiently correlated with one another (even when the relationships
are partialed for the total population of the department, as they are here) that their
separate effects are hard to distinguish. A multiple regression of the same data
separates them more sharply. Table 3 presents the multiple correlation coefficients
and standardized regression coefficients for four different indicators of the magnitude of collective violence within a multiple regression incorporating the number of
persons in the department charged with "rebellion" (which covered all sorts of
resistance to the law) in 1831, the number of suicides, the total population,
population in cities of 10,000 or more, increase in urban population 1821–1831,
and net migration 1826–1831. The pattern is the same as we saw with the
correlation coefficients, but the differences among the three urbanization variables
are now far greater. It now appears there was no relationship at all between the
volume of recent migration into a department and the extent of collective violence.
Whatever the effect of urban increase on collective violence, therefore, it does not
operate through the unsettling arrival of uprooted migrants. What is more, the

TABLE 3

Multiple Regression Analysis of Correlates of Collective Violence, 1830–1832

Dependent Variable	Multiple Correlation	Standardized Regression Coefficient		
		Urban population	Urban increase	Net migration
Number of disturbances	.785	.757	.440	−.075
Participants	.960	.714	.420	.042
Killed and wounded	.959	.677	.333	−.093
Arrested	.928	.665	.307	−.141

effect of urban population as such appears to be about twice as great as the effect of urban *increase*. The presence of cities made the big difference; their expansion mattered much less.

The Effects of Urbanity. When looked at more concretely, the distinction is perfectly plausible, and easy to grasp. The segments of the population with sufficient organization to carry on collective action at a scale large enough to bother the authorities—and therefore to lead to violent encounters with troops, police, and others—were concentrated in the larger cities and their vicinities. This is emphatically true of organized workers, and one of the chief reasons for two features of the strike activity of the 1830's and 1840's which our analyses confirm: (a) the considerable correspondence between the geography of strikes and the geography of collective violence; (b) the tendency of strike activity to come disproportionately from the older, established trades rather than from the expanding factory-based industries. In Aguet's careful enumeration the most strike-prone departments are (in descending order) Seine, Rhône, Seine-Inférieure, Loire, and Bouches-du-Rhône—which is to say the departments of Paris, Lyon, Rouen, St. Etienne, and Marseille. These same departments ordinarily rank high in tallies of disturbances. In short, strikes and collective violence went together.

It is not that they were the same thing. I have already pointed out how many of this period's smaller disturbances were food riots, conflicts with tax collectors, and forcible invasions of rural property. Practically none of them began as strikes. Yet a significant number of the minor disturbances were simply the violent parts of series of actions pitting workers against employers: demonstrations, political agitation, threats, property damage, strikes as well. They grew from the same basic conflicts. Some of the great outbursts (the insurrections of Lyon being the best-known examples) flashed in direct response to strikes.

George Rudé considers the working-class disturbances of the 1830's to have started a great new phase. "For the first time," he concludes, "we find the same workers being engaged in successive political demonstrations, wage demands being put forward at a time of economic depression, and wage earners participating as readily in political as in economic movements" (Rudé, 1964, p. 165). He might have added that the wage earners still came from the older crafts and established industries rather than the swelling modern factories. To return to Aguet's enumeration of French strikes, the number of strikes reported by industry for five-year intervals are shown in Table 4. The figures drastically underestimate the total number of strikes and give far too much weight to Paris, but they are the best we have so far.

TABLE 4
Number of Strikes in France by Industry, 1830–1844

Industry	Years			Estimated Labor Force in 1840–45 (in thousands)
	1830–34	*1835–39*	*1840–44*	
Agriculture, forestry, fishing	0	0	1	7,000
Mining and extraction	3	3	8	108
Food products	3	1	3	256
Chemical products	1	0	1	20
Paper and printing	9	2	12	47
Leather products	2	3	3	235
Textiles	32	26	30	1,560
Wood products	10	6	8	502
Metal products	8	2	6	305
Construction	13	6	21	474
Services and professions	0	0	2	3,000
Total	81	49	95	13,507

Sources: Toutain 1963, Aguet 1954.

By sheer bulk, the textile industry dominated both the industrial labor force and the strike scene. For their size, however, construction mining and, especially, printing seem to have produced exceptional numbers of strikes. As the century wore on, textiles and construction held their own, the mines grew in importance as sources of strikes, the printers lost their force, and the metal-working industries with their factory production came into prominence. The great Parisian series of strikes in 1840 brought out the tailors, papermakers, nailmakers, carters, wainwrights, masons, stonecutters, locksmiths, turners, carpenters, shoemakers, spinners, bookbinders, and bakers—mostly men from the skilled, established crafts.

The same occupations and industries led the Parisian working class political activity and fed the city's violent confrontations. The city's prefects of police were aware enough of the connection to always have their spies circulating through the workmen's cafes and hiring areas around the Place de Grève and the Place du Châtelet. A prefect's report from July, 1831 read like this:

The painters who gathered yesterday at Châtelet said that since the authorities were tolerating recruitment of Legitimist forces for the Vendée, they would take justice into their own hands; and they stated their intention to break into the houses of the Swiss living in the area around Paris and to wreck them.

Those gathered at the Place de Grève started to grumble yesterday; they complained about their poverty, praised the reign of Napoleon and said that in his day there was no shortage of jobs, but since then the working class had always been in bad shape (Archives Nationales $F^{1c}133$, 22 July 1831).

Now, the workers of Grève and Châtelet talked more than they acted politically, and acted peacefully more than they rebelled. But the spies were in the right place, listening to the right things. For the working-class neighborhoods behind those squares were the breeding grounds of rebellion after rebellion. The men who took part were by and large politically alert, organized, integrated into the life of the city—that is, not the uprooted, outcast, dangerous classes.

The studies which have been done of participants in diverse outbreaks of collective violence in Paris between 1830–1860 point in the same direction. For the Revolution of 1830, Adeline Daumard observes that "artisans on the border between the common people and the bourgeoisie were at the core of the insurgents" (Daumard, 1963, p. 578); David Pinkney's careful enumerations agree (Pinkney, 1964). The violent days of April, 1834 brought into action such men as:

> 36-year-old Louis Bertembois, a shoemaker born in St. Frambourg (Oise); François Soubrebois, 29, a typographer, originally from Perpignan; the wagon-painter, J. P. Etienne, 17 years old, a Parisian; caterer Jean Pouchin, 32, from a small town in Calvados, reputed to be a member of the Society of the Rights of Man; 22-year-old Jean Hallot, a cabinet-maker from Paris, labeled in the police reports as an "instigator" (Archives de la Préfecture de Police, Paris, Aa 422).

In the revolution of February, 1848, George Rudé points out, the city's wage earners "left their workshops with their masters and, with them, jointly manned the barricades; radical journalists, students, *polytechniciens,* and National Guards had also played their part; and on the lists of those decorated for their part in the February events the names of wage earners appear alongside those of shopkeepers, master craftsmen, and members of the liberal professions" (Rudé, 1964, pp. 168–169).

There is one more Parisian case of special interest: the June Days of 1848. That bloody disturbance deserves our attention both because it had the most proletarian appearance of any up to its time, and because it left remarkably detailed evidence concerning who took part. Table 5 summarizes the available information on the origins and occupation of more than 11,000 persons of the probable 15,000 arrested for participation in the June Days. (In order to give a general sense of their relation to the labor force of the time, it also presents the number of workers in each group of industrial establishments reported by employers to the Chamber of Commerce in 1847 and 1848, and relates the arrests to the industries as a series of rates per 10,000 workers.) While comparisons within the sample display a slight tendency for construction workers to have been arrested on suspicion, then released, and a significantly greater tendency for arrested soldiers and persons born in Paris to finally be convicted, this tabulation represents the men and women actually implicated in the rebellion fairly faithfully.[2]

TABLE 5
Persons Arrested for Taking Part in June Days of 1848 by Industry and Birthplace

Industry	Birthplace					No. of Workmen Reported in 1848 Survey	Arrests per 10,000 Workers
	Seine	Other France	Foreign	Unknown	Total		
Food	53	348	21	42	464	10,428	445
Construction	363	1511	70	133	2077	41,603	499
Furniture	214	352	70	44	680	36,184	188
Clothing	160	724	87	74	1045	90,064	116
Textiles	71	246	11	18	346	36,685	94
Leather	36	113	9	11	169	4,573	370
Carriagemaking, saddlery, etc.	39	135	12	9	195	13,754	142
Chemicals and ceramics	44	76	11	17	148	9,737	152
Ordinary metals	323	886	45	80	1334	24,894	536
Fine metals	99	109	8	23	239	16,819	142
Basketry	32	93	4	6	135	5,405	250
Novelties, toys, etc.	67	126	12	9	214	35,679	60
Printing	167	217	21	42	447	16,705	268
Transportation	132	336	25	41	534	—	
Services	67	321	30	43	461	—	
Retail Trade	168	518	36	69	791	—	
Military	111	272	15	103	501	—	
Liberal professions	81	193	17	37	328	—	
Other	264	770	60	96	1190	—	
Not Reported	65	169	15	197	446	—	
Total	2556	7515	579	1094	11,744		

Sources: Archives Nationales F⁷ 2586, *Liste générale en ordre alphabétique des inculpés de juin 1848*; Chambre de Commerce de Paris, *statistique de l'industrie à Paris résultant de l'enquête faite par la Chambre de Commerce pour les années 1847–8* (Paris, 1851).

It does not show a simple cross-section of the Parisian population, but it does show a wide spread across its various categories. The largest single occupational group were the 699 day laborers, who were in the company of 576 stonemasons, 485 cabinetmakers, and 447 shoemakers. Construction, metalworking, and the clothing trades had the largest shares in absolute numbers. Compared with their parts in the working population of the time, men from construction, food production, and metalworking industries seem to have played an exceptional role. Their arrests run around 5 percent of all the men reported in each industry. Mechanics (especially from the railroads), leatherworkers, and printers also appear to have contributed more than their share to the rebellion. Textile workers, it seems fair to say, were underrepresented.

Georges Duveau's sketch of the June Days has as its principal characters a mechanic of La Chapelle, a hosier of the faubourg Saint-Denis, and an *ébéniste* from the faubourg Saint-Antoine (Duveau, 1965). If he had added a stonemason from the Hotel de Ville, a day laborer from Popincourt, and a tanner from Saint-Marcel, his cast would have been representative.

The distribution we find is remarkably like the strike activity of the time: an amalgam of the old, politically active trades with a few sections of modern industry. By comparison with previous disturbances, the center of gravity was shifting toward the mass-production industries, gradually, in step with other forms of contention and political activity, not in such a way as to call the miserable outsiders into the streets.

The bulk of the rebels had originally come from outside of Paris. That is most true of construction, as one might expect, and least true of printing. Just under a quarter of those arrested and a little less than a third of those convicted were natives of the Seine. But as it happens, Louis Chevalier's data indicate that about 40 percent of Paris' population of the time, including children, were natives (Chevalier 1950:45). The adult working population was surely well below that proportion. So there is no clear sign that outsiders were overrepresented. Furthermore, the distribution of departments of origin follows Chevalier's estimates for the Paris of 1833 quite faithfully. In addition to the 2,556 born in the Seine, we find 516 from Seine-et-Oise, 335 from Seine-et-Marne, 362 from Moselle, 276 from Nord, 236 from Creuse, 222 from Somme, 220 from Aisne, and so on through the list of regular suppliers of migrants to Paris. While these data do not make the point, Rémi Gossez, who knows the histories of the individual rebels of June far better than anyone else, remarks, "The typical insurgent was an individual who, if a native of the provinces, came to Paris to settle or at least to complete his training and who in general was moving up in the world, a move blocked by economic change and crisis" (1956, p. 449). Again the violent masses turn out to be those integrated into the setting rather than those at the margins of society.

The findings therefore cast doubt on theories which trace a main link between cities and protest through a process of disorganization. On the contrary, the whole array of evidence we have been examining suggests a positive connection between *organization* and conflict. The moderate relationship discovered earlier between collective violence in 1830–1832 and urban growth from 1821–1831, for instance, probably represents the appearance of new contenders for power in the largest industrial centers over the whole decade rather than individual disorientation or malaise from exposure to the modern city.

THE LONG-RUN PATTERNS

We are not, in any case, dealing with a constant pattern. Over the long run of the nineteenth and twentieth centuries, collective violence in France drifted away from the countryside and toward the cities faster than the population itself did, as the power and resources which mattered most politically concentrated in the great cities. In the short run, the extent of urban concentration of collective violence depended on the nature of the unresolved political issues at hand. Food riots formed a more dispersed pattern than violent strikes; strikes were more scattered than major struggles for control of the national political apparatus. Since food riots, strikes, and major struggles for control followed different rhythms, the geographic pattern fluctuated. Perhaps the largest alternation went from battles for power at the center (which produced a high urban concentration of collective violence) and resistance to pressures from the center (which produced more disturbances at the periphery). In the period we are examining here, the revolutionary years 1830 and 1848 concentrated their violence in cities, while years of consolidation of central power like 1832 and 1851—both very turbulent times—spread their violence farther and more evenly.

Some of this alternation comes out in Table 6, which chops up the entire period from 1830–1860 into five-year blocks. The table shows the striking contrast in overall participation between a revolutionary period like 1830–1834 and a nonrevolutionary one like 1835–1839. It also shows how much steeper the gradient of collective violence from rural to urban departments was in years of fundamental struggle for control of the state than in years of consolidation of state power; a comparison of 1845–1849 (which includes, of course, the revolution of 1848) with 1850–1854 (whose biggest violent conflict was the resistance to Louis Napoleon's

TABLE 6
Participants in Collective Violence per 100,000 Population
by Urbanity of Department, 1830–1859,
Corrected to Annual Rates

Percentage of Population in Cities of 10,000 or More	1830–34	1835–39	1840–44	1845–49	1850–54	1855–59
0.6	17	4	40	25	152	0
0.1–5.0	23	22	16	70	70	0
5.1–10.0	53	22	48	68	43	9
10.1–15.0	104	19	10	81	15	2
15.1+	731	57	64	689	86	0
Total	147	22	37	210	56	3
Total participants (thousands)	240	41	64	371	101	5

1851 coup, which eventually permitted him to move from elected president to emperor) makes that point dramatically.

The long trend and the short-term fluctuations both followed the same principle: nationalization of political conflict produces urbanization of collective violence. The principle has nothing to do with the disorganizing effects of urban life; it has a great deal to do with the location of groups of people mobilized to join different kinds of struggles for power. Explaining the actions of the participants in collective violence as responses to the chaos of the city discounts the reality of their struggle.

That is the general conclusion toward which all our explorations point. The absence of the uprooted, the continuity of different forms of conflict, their gradual change in response to shifts in the collective conditions of work and community life, the sheer lack of correlation between rapid urban growth or extensive in-migration and mass violence all challenge the cataclysmic theories of urbanization. Yet our evidence confirms that the distinctive social organization of cities—their hospitality to formal associations, the complexity of their communication systems, their widespread external relations, their gross patterns of segregation—strongly affects the character of the collective conflicts which occur within them. In that sense, urbanization, over the long run, transforms collective violence.

Through the chaos of living cities, what do we see? Certainly neither the lawless disorder advertised by a romantic notion of urbanization, nor bucolic bliss. We see men held to their routines by commitments and controls, often dismayed by their routines, sometimes articulating and acting on their dismay, mostly singly, and in nonviolent ways. Occasionally these men are trained in another way of understanding to combat the evils of their present situation by joining with other men to strike out against the situation itself. There is a kind of order to the city's collective disorders, if not the one the forces of order would like to see prevailing.

Christopher Fry, the poet, states the theme properly: "There's no loosening, since men with men are like the knotted sea. Lift him down from the stone to the grass again, and, even so free, yet he will find the angry cities hold him." Angry cities, but not mad; violent cities, but not pathological; living cities, in the last analysis not nearly so chaotic as widespread sociological ideas imply.

NOTES

1. The estimates for 1861 to 1929 are based on a 25% sample of the months in that interval and have not been verified as carefully as those for 1830–1860 and 1930–1960; they are therefore subject to considerably greater error. Both general knowledge of the government's treatment of the press and close study of our own data lead me to conclude that censorship probably reduced the number of disturbances reported in the newspapers on which we relied during the postwar periods of 1870–1874, 1918–1921, and 1944–1954. On the other hand, such detailed comparisons as we have been able to make with other full sources (e.g., with all disturbances mentioned in the inventories of the major national series of police reports in Archives Nationales BB 18 and BB 30) indicate that the sharp drops in disturbances during the two world wars and after Louis Napoleon's assumption of power in 1851 are real. For control of the press, see Bellanger, Godechot, Guiral & Terrou, 1969; Collins, 1959; Hatin, 1859–1861; Kayser, 1958 and 1963; Manevy, 1955; Mottin, 1949; Weill, 1934.

2. The source of quantitative data is a huge register (Archives Nationales F^7 2586) containing uniform descriptions of about 12,000 persons arrested for taking part in the June Days; a duplicate of the register resides in the Archives Historiques de l'Armée, as do the individual dossiers of the arrestees. Lynn Lees and I have examined a 1 percent sample of the individual dossiers, which establishes that the registers accurately represent the general characteristics of those apprehended for taking part in the insurrection, but omit a large part of the information actually available concerning the average individual. The register has been drawn on before by Rémi Gossez (1956), George Rudé (1964), and very likely Georges Duveau (1948); see also Gossez, 1967 for background. However, no one has so far reported the sorts of detailed counts and comparisons presented here.

REFERENCES

Aguet, Jean-Pierre. *Contribution à l'histoire du mouvement ouvrier français: les grèves sous la Monarchie de Juillet (1830–1847)*. Geneva: Droz, 1954.

Arendt, Hannah. *On Revolution*. London: Faber & Faber, 1963.

Arendt, Hannah. *On Violence*. New York: Harcourt, Brace & World, 1970.

Bellanger, Claude, Jacques Godechot, Pierre Guiral, Fernand Terrou, eds. *Histoire générale de la presse périodique. II. De 1815 à 1871*. Paris: Presses Universitaires de France, 1969.

Belvèze, Claude. "L'Insurrection des 5 et 6 juin 1832." Unpublished Diplôme d'Etudes Supérieures, History, Paris, 1959.

Bezucha, Robert J. "Association and Insurrection: The Republican Party and the Worker Movement in Lyon, 1831–1835." Unpublished doctoral dissertation in History, University of Michigan, 1968.

Bienen, Henry. *Violence and Social Change: A Review of Current Literature*. Chicago: University of Chicago Press, 1968.

Bouvier, Jean. "Mouvement ouvrier et conjonctures économiques." *Mouvement social* 48 (1964): 3–28

Brode, John. *The Process of Modernization: An Annotated Bibliography on the Sociocultural Aspects of Development*. Cambridge, Mass.: Harvard University Press, 1969.

Chevalier, Louis. *La formation de la population parisienne*. Paris: Presses Universitaires de France, 1950.

Chevalier, Louis. *Classes laborieuses et classes dangereuses*. Paris: Plon, 1958.

Cobb, Richard. *Les armées révolutionnaires, instrument de la Terreur dans les départements*. 2 vols. Paris: Mouton, 1961–63.

Cobb, Richard. *Terreur et subsistances, 1793–1795*. Paris: Clavreuil, 1964.

Cobb, Richard. *The Police and the People*. Oxford: Clarendon Press, 1970.

Collins, Irene. *The Government and the Newspaper Press in France*. Oxford: Oxford University Press, 1959.

Conant, Ralph W., and Molly Apple Levin, eds. *Problems in Research on Community Violence*. New York: Praeger, 1969.

Connery, Donald., ed. "Urban Riots: Violence and Social Change." *Proceedings of the Academy of Political Science*, (1968) 29, entire issue; also published separately.

Cornelius, Wayne A., Jr. "The Political Sociology of Cityward Migration in Latin America: Toward Empirical Theory." In *Latin American Urban Annual*, edited by Francine F. Rabinowitz and Felicity M. Trueblood. Beverly Hills, Calif.: Sage Publications, 1970.

Daumard, Adeline. *La bourgeoisie parisienne de 1815 à 1848*. Paris: SEVPEN, 1963.

Davies, C. S. L. "Révoltes populaires en Angleterre (1500–1700)." *Annales; Economies, Sociétés, Civilisations* 24 (1969): 24–60.

Duveau, Georges. "L'ouvrier de 1848." *Revue socialiste*, n.s. nos. 17–18 (1948): 73–79.

Duveau, Georges. *1848*. Paris: Gallimard, 1965.

Fischer, Wolfram. "Social Tensions at Early Stages of Industrialization." *Comparative Studies in Society and History* 9 (1966): 64–83.

Fogelson, Robert N., and Robert B. Hill. "Who Riots? A Study of Participation in the 1967 Riots." *Supplemental Studies for the National Advisory Commission on Civil Disorders*. Washington: U.S. Government Printing Office, 1968.

Furet, François, Claude Mazauric, and Louis Bergeron. "Les sans-culottes et la Révolution Française." *Annales, Economies, Sociétés, Civilisations* 18 (1963): 1098–1127.

Godechot, Jacques. *The Taking of the Bastille.* New York: Scribner's, 1970.
Gossez, Rémi. "Diversité des antagonismes sociaux vers le milieu du XIXe siècle." *Revue économique* (1956), 439–457
Gossez, Rémi. *Les Ouvriers de Paris. I. L'Organisation, 1848–1851.* La Roche sur-Yon: Imprimerie Centrale de l'Ouest, 1967.
Graham, Hugh Davis, and Ted Robert Gurr, eds. *Violence in America: Historical and Comparative Perspectives.* Washington: U.S. Government Printing Office, 1969. Several other paperback editions.
Gurr, Ted Robert. *Why Men Rebel.* Princeton, N.J.: Princeton University Press, 1969.
Hatin, Eugène. *Histoire politique et littéraire de la presse en France.* 8 vols. Paris: Poulet-Malassis & de Broise, 1859–61.
Hauser, Philip. "The Social, Economic and Technological Problems of Rapid Urbanization." In *Industrialization and Society,* edited by Bert Hoselitz and Wilbert Moore. The Hague: Mouton for UNESCO, 1963.
Hobsbawm, E. J. *Bandits.* New York: Delacorte, 1969.
Hobsbawm, E. J., and George Rudé. *Captain Swing: A Social History of the Great Agrarian Uprising of 1830.* New York: Pantheon, 1968.
Hofstadter, Richard. "Reflections on Violence in the United States." In *American Violence: A Documentary History,* edited by Richard Hofstadter and Michael Wallace. New York: Knopf, 1970.
Huntington, Samuel P. *Political Order in Changing Societies.* New Haven, Conn.: Yale University Press, 1968.
Kayser, Jacques. *La presse de province sous la Troisième République.* Paris: Colin; Cahiers de la Fondation Nationale des Sciences Politiques, 92, 1958.
Kayser, Jacques. *Le quotidien français.* Paris: Colin; Cahiers de la Fondation Nationale des Sciences Politiques, 122, 1963.
Kirkham, James F., Sheldon G. Levy, and William J. Crotty. *Assassination and Political Violence.* Washington: U.S. Government Printing Office, 1970. Also published separately.
Manevy, Raymond. *La presse de la IIIe République.* Paris: Foret, 1955.
Masotti, Louis H., and Don R. Bowen, eds. *Civil Violence in the Urban Community.* Beverly Hills, Calif.: Sage Publications, 1968.
Mazauric, Claude. *Sur la Révolution française.* Paris: Editions Sociales, 1970.
Meadows, Paul, and Ephraim Mizruchi, eds. *Urbanism, Urbanization and Change.* Reading, Mass.: Addison-Wesley, 1961.
Mottin, J. *Histoire politique de la presse, 1944–49.* Paris: Bilans Hebdomadaires, 1949.
Mumford, Lewis. *The City in History.* New York: Harcourt, Brace & World, 1961.
Nelson, Joan. "The Urban Poor: Disruption or Political Integration in Third World Cities?" *World Politics,* 22 (1970): 393–414.
Peacock, A. J. *Bread or Blood: The Agrarian Riots in East Anglia: 1816.* London: Gollancz, 1965.
Pinkney, David. "The Crowd in the French Revolution of 1830." *American Historical Review* 70 (1964): 1–17.
Rudé, George. *The Crowd in the French Revolution.* Oxford: Oxford University Press, 1958.
Rudé, George. *The Crowd in History.* New York: Wiley, 1964.
Rudé, George. *Paris and London in the 18th Century.* London: Collins, 1970.
Rule, James, and Charles Tilly. "1830 and the Unnatural History of Revolution." *Journal of Social Issues* 28 (1972): 49–76.
Sewell, William. "La classe ouvrière de Marseille sous la Seconde République: structure sociale et comportement politique." *Mouvement social* 76 (1971): 27–66.
Shorter, Edward, and Charles Tilly. "The Shape of Strikes in France, 1930–1960." *Comparative Studies in Society and History* 13 (1971): 60–86.
Skolnick, Jerome H. *The Politics of Protest.* Washington: U.S. Government Printing Office, 1969. Also published separately in paperback.
Smelser, Neil J. *Theory of Collective Behavior.* New York: Free Press, 1963.
Soboul, Albert. *Les sans-culottes parisiens en l'an II.* La Roche-sur-Yon: Potier, 1958.
Thompson, E. P. *The Making of the English Working Class.* London: Gollancz, 1963.
Tilly, Charles. "Reflections on the Revolutions of Paris." *Social Problems* 12 (1964): 99–121.
Tilly, Charles. "Collective Violence in European Perspective." in Graham & Gurr, 1969.

Tilly, Louise. "The Food Riot as a Form of Political Conflict in France." *Journal of Interdisciplinary History* 2 (1971): 23–58.

Tilly, Richard. "Popular Disorders in Nineteenth Century Germany: A Preliminary Survey." *Journal of Social History* 4 (1970): 1–140.

Tønnesson, Kåre. *La défaite des sans-culottes.* Oslo: University Press, 1959; and Paris: Calvreuil, 1959.

Toutain, J.-C. *La population de la France de 1700 à 1959.* Paris: Institut de Science Economique Appliquée; Cahiers de l'ISEA, AF 3, 1963.

Vidalou, Huguette. "Les mouvements révolutionnaires d'avril 1834 à Paris." Unpublished Diplôme d'Etudes Supérieures, History, Paris, 1959.

Vovelle, M. "From Beggary to Brigandage: The Wanderers in the Beauce during the French Revolution." In *New Perspectives on the French Revolution* edited by Jeffry Kaplow. New York: Wiley, 1965.

Weill, Georges. *Le journal. Origines, évolution et rôle de la presse periodique.* Paris: Albin Michel, 1934.

Williams, Gwynn. *Artisans and Sans-Culottes.* Oxford: Oxford University Press, 1968.

ON UPROOTING, KINSHIP, AND THE AUSPICES OF MIGRATION

Charles Tilly and C. Harold Brown

"On Uprooting, Kinship, and the Auspices of Migration" takes up some of the same issues as the previous article, "The Chaos of the Living City," but in a very different setting and with very different kinds of evidence. The study of collective violence in France took me into archives, libraries, and the world of the historian. The study of migration to Wilmington, Delaware took me into private homes and the world of the survey researcher. The worlds are not the same; in the historian's world you can look at plenty of variation over space and time, but there are many questions you simply cannot go back and ask your sources. In the survey researcher's world the time is the present and the recent past, and it is much easier to make comparisons among individuals than to get hold of long processes of change. In the first article, I am not able to be as precise as I would want about the particular individuals and groups affected by urbanization or involved in collective violence. In the second article, Harold Brown and I have to infer changes in behavior from our respondents' retrospective reports and from differences among sets of people who have been in the city varying lengths of time. There are ways of doing better on both these scores, but only within limits. That is why I undertook such different investigations of such similar problems.

"The Chaos of the Living City" asks how closely the patterns of collective violence in nineteenth-century France correspond to standard ideas concerning the links of disorder to urbanization, and how closely they correspond to my alternative argument concerning the city as a shaper of collective action. "Uprooting" focuses on a prior question: To what extent

does migration to cities create the isolation and helplessness which is commonly supposed to be a prelude to social disorder? Again we contrast a classic view (originating this time from the work of Robert Park, one of the founders of urban sociology) with a counter-argument. This time the argument says that most migrants come to the city already well linked to it by one or several structures (professions, kins groups, and so on), that the structures under whose auspices they come vary systematically by social origin, that the auspices under which they come make a significant difference to their subsequent involvement in the city, and that as a result migration itself produces little of the isolation and disorganization which exists in cities. These themes will reappear in Chapters 3 and 4. For not only is migration one of the prime city-building processes, and therefore worth studying in its own right; migration is also a process in which the everyday routines and supports of social life change for a while or permanently; the routines and supports become visible and challenge our conventional ideas of how they work.

The ghost of Robert Ezra Park will not be silent. Turn to the study of urban spatial arrangements; there is his idea that the city's landscape records its pattern of social mobility. Turn to the writings on ethnic relations; there is his metaphor of social distance. Turn to the analysis of migration; there is the theory of the marginal man. The essence of that justly famous theory is not so hard to state: migration detaches individuals and groups from traditional restraints and supports, casts them into a marginal position full of personal turmoil and potential social disorganization, and eventually leads to their simultaneous socialization and reintegration into the receiving population, the pace of the reintegration depending on the cultural gap between newcomers and the receiving population. Meanwhile, as Park and Burgess put it:

> Disorganization of attitudes and conduct is almost invariably the lot of the newcomer to the city; and the discarding of the habitual and of what has been called the moral is not infrequently accompanied by sharp mental conflict and sense of personal loss.[1]

Migration uproots, and replanting takes time.

The curious thing about the theory is not that many people have found it plausible, but that it has passed into sociological writing as an explanatory principle with very little elaboration and precious little testing. If there is a general correlation between the mobility of an area's population and some measure of social

Reprinted by permission from "On Uprooting, Kinship, and the Auspices of Migration" by Charles Tilly and C. Harold Brown, *International Journal of Comparative Sociology*, 7 (September 1967), pp. 139–164. This is a revised version of a paper presented to the Faculty Seminar on "Human Processes of Adaptation to Increasing Complexity" of the Boston College Institute of Human Sciences, which in turn included some fragments of "Kinship and Migration," presented to the Society for the Study of Social Problems. The Economic Research Service of the United States Department of Agriculture and the School of Agriculture, University of Delaware, supported the research. Footnotes renumbered.

disorganization, it hardly seems worth determining whether the most mobile inhabitants contribute most vigorously to that disorganization. If cities in rapidly industrializing countries are often politically turbulent, it seems natural to attribute some of the turbulence to the disruptive effects of large-scale migration. If new arrivals to American cities pose problems of public welfare, it goes almost without saying that they are personally maladjusted. Yet these connections among mobility, personal maladjustment and social disorganization are in fact neither firmly established nor well understood.

The underlying theory gains much of its credibility from its excellent fit with another fundamental conception: the city as an impersonal mechanism. Park's restless mind refused to be contained in any one metaphor, but this metaphor shaped his idea of migration and marginality. Behind it stands its near-corollary, the conception of a more traditional form of social integration based on small scale, like-minded and intense communication. The city presumably draws its newcomers from that kind of setting. Hence the strength of the conclusion that urban migration ordinarily disorganizes the individual and, thereby, his society by destroying at once his restraints and his emotional supports.

To be sure, the same line of thought leads to the idea that urbanites eventually become so skilled at dealing with the strains and the apparatus of urbanism that they drift from setting to setting with impunity. But even there we commonly assume that the immediate consequences of mobility are detachment and disorganization.

In a useful return to earlier wisdom, students of urban life have recently been declaring that its social relations are not so impersonal as they seem. Following a path cleared by William F. Whyte's *Street Corner Society,* they have found ostensibly disorganized areas with high levels of internal organization, and everyday urban contacts rich with kinship, friendship and neighborliness.[2]

This rediscovery of personal relations makes a difference in the analysis of mobility's consequences. If we suppose that extensive personal relations are actually common in cities, and that such relations often ease the pain of abrupt shifts in social position, we can conclude that the sequence going from migration to personal disorganization to social disorganization will in fact be fairly rare. We can expect the maintenance of social networks already in existence to reduce the shock of transfer for some individuals, and the rapid establishment of new personal relations to do the same for others. (The absorption of emigrant villagers by their Toronto *paesani* and the frantic sociability of suburban newcomers illustrate the extreme forms of these two alternatives.)

Indeed, the reappraisal of supposed connections between mobility and disorganization has already begun. It does look as though American long-distance migrants have higher rates of detected major mental disorder. Yet this does not seem to be true for countries such as Norway and Canada; H. B. M. Murphy's careful review of the literature suggests that the varying ways different groups of migrants respond to the peculiarities of their members, rather than any general disturbing effects of mobility, may account for the differentials.[3] With respect to crime and delinquency, the evidence is beginning to point in a new direction: migrants less likely than the general population to be apprehended for violations of the law, and only slowly acquiring the criminal patterns of their new communities.[4] For some reason the old idea that mobility and marital instability go together has not yet received the same reappraisal, but even there it does not take long to discover that the relationship, although rarely challenged, remains unproven.

Instead of one big variable—how much mobility—we are probably dealing with three of them. Migrants vary in the extent to which they are involved in shallow, fleeting, specialized, impersonal social relations. They vary in the extent to which they transfer memberships in groups of the "traditional" type, in ascriptive solidarities. They vary in the means and the rapidity with which they establish new personal relations. All of these ought to affect the amount of disruption mobility causes.

These are large problems and fundamental processes. We can do no more here than to seize one of their implications. Let us present some ideas about the role of kin groups in migration to cities, and examine them in the light of information about migration to a particular city.

We may well begin with kinship, because a good deal of the recent reformulation we have mentioned has attacked the idea that urban society and extended kinship are incompatible, and a good deal of recent research has uncovered vigorous relations with kinsmen among deeply urbane populations.[5]

Here are three basic questions:

First, what part does kinship play among the major auspices of migration to cities?

Second, what forms do relations with kinsmen take during the process of migration itself?

Third, what happens to relations with kin during the assimilation of the migrating group to the new community?

Anyone who tries to answer these questions in general for all types of migrants and all types of migration will soon find himself reduced to useless platitudes or utter frustration. But there are some systematic variations in these respects well worth considering.

AUSPICES

By the auspices of migration, we mean the social structures which establish relationships between the migrant and the receiving community before he moves. We may say that an individual migrates under the auspices of kinship when his principal connections with the city of destination are through kinsmen, even if he comes desperately seeking a job. Likewise, we may say that he migrates under the auspices of work when the labor market or a particular firm provides the main organized relationship to the new community, even if he also has kinfolk there. Of course, he may migrate under several auspices at once, or under none at all.[6]

Although they have not used exactly this language, other researchers have found kinship playing a powerful part among the auspices of American migration. They have found, for example, that migrants from rural areas tend to go to cities where their kinfolk are already established. Chain-migration is simply the most extreme expression of this tendency.[7] In fact, migration under the auspices of kinship seems to be most common among groups which have the least skill in dealing with impersonal urban institutions like markets, bureaucracies, and communication systems, or the most uncertain relationships to those institutions. The support and protection of their kinfolk balances their weakness in these other respects.

If this is generally true, we might expect the tendency to migrate under the auspices of kinship to decline with rising rank, increasing urban experience, and greater previous mobility, to be greater for groups more likely to meet discrimination in the new community, and to be highest at the extremes of age. And we ought also to find that within the categories particularly inclined to migrate under the auspices of kinship, individuals who do *not* do so more commonly suffer personal disruption when they move.

RELATIONS WITH KINSMEN DURING MIGRATION

The general designation of auspices does not tell us exactly how kinfolk take part in the process of migration. The recent explorations of urban life already mentioned reveal a lush undergrowth of kinship in what had been charted as an urban desert. Kin groups gather not only on ritual occasions, but also for emergencies and for ordinary sociability. The vigor of kinship relations prevails in both lower-class and middle-class populations, and offers a means of extraordinary support during crises. If this is true, it ought to be all the truer of the crisis of migration. Among a number of the groups that have been studied, kinfolk do offer a wide range of aid and encouragement during migration and immediately after it.[8]

However, there are some differences among groups. On the whole, the same groups we have tagged as likely to migrate under the auspices of kinship rely more heavily and more exclusively on kinsmen for everyday aid and moral support.[9] Lower-ranking migrants, those with little urban experience, those at the extremes of age, and those suffering greater discrimination might therefore be expected to receive a wider variety of aid and more of it from kinsmen during migration. Having migrated under the auspices of kinship should simply accentuate this tendency.

Kin groups specialize in certain kinds of aid. They rarely have jobs in their gift. They can more often offer housing, at least temporarily. They vary greatly in how much information and how much skill in dealing with major urban institutions they can lend to a newcomer. Their enduring specialty lies in the internal operation of the household rather than its external relations. So we might expect to find kin groups most regularly offering domestic forms of aid at migration—lodging, personal care, food, emotional support, short-term cash. We might also expect to find this specialization in domesticity greatest among those groups relying least on their kinsmen during migration, on the supposition that they develop specialized means for meeting each of their significant problems at migration.

RELATIONS WITH KIN AFTER MIGRATION

The next phase, relations with kin *after* migration, brings us into contact with a much longer span of time and with the very large problem of assimilation. Relations of kinship provide functional alternatives to personal skill, knowledge and power in dealing with the receiving community. That is clearly true of relatively formal relations within the community, like entering the housing market: some groups commonly find housing through word passed along kinfolk, while others commonly find it through such impersonal channels as newspapers and real estate agencies. It is also true in a subtler way of informal relations; most urbanites spend part of their leisure in the company of people from outside their households, but members of some groups spend it almost exclusively with kinfolk and individuals first encountered through kinfolk, while others spend it almost exclusively with individuals first encountered in formal settings. In each case, effective dealing with the impersonal setting requires a good measure of skill, knowledge and power.

Let us assume, for convenience' sake, that all groups of migrants face the same general problems in the receiving community—assuring a source of income, finding shelter, acquiring commodities, establishing supplies of advice, information and emotional support, and so on. Those rupturing closeknit networks of kinship at migration presumably undergo a much greater change in their ways of facing these problems than those not rupturing them, and often register the cost of the change in personal discontent and disorganization.[10] But the cost, the consequent upset, the time and energy required to establish new means of meeting these problems are greatest for those who bring with them the least transferable skill, knowledge and power. When migration does cut kinship ties, we might therefore expect it to cause greater disruption among lower-ranking migrants, those with little urban experience, those suffering discrimination, and those at the extremes of age.

Among those who do maintain or establish bonds with kinfolk in the receiving community at migration, we should expect to find a continuation of intensive contact with them well beyond the first throes of adjustment. But, as experience with the community accumulates, we should also expect to find migrants developing individual skill and alternative sources of aid in meeting problems; the shift should be fastest among those who transfer the most experience from the previous community. Even if the norms concerning obligations to kinsmen were fairly constant from one segment of the population to another, this effect plus the effect of varying conditions of migration to a community would produce substantial internal differences (by age, rank, color and residential background) in the extent of reliance on kin.[11]

Actually, the relationship between individual skill and dependence on kin is two-way. Those who become skilled in dealing with the community's institutions make themselves independent. But those who have no kin at hand to rely on surely have a strong incentive to acquire skills and alternative sources of aid, and more energy to spend in other forms of social relationship. Let us assume that there is a standard package of skill, style and social relationship which most members of a community eventually possess. Then migrants actively involved with kinfolk in the community will be slower to gain that standard package than others will. To state it more narrowly and manageably: migrants who come under the auspices of kinship will increase their direct, formal participation in the city's impersonal institutions more slowly and over a longer period than others.[12]

We began with general questions about the effects of mobility on social integration, and have arrived at fairly specific questions about the role of kinsmen in the process of migration. The discussion has produced several general hypotheses:

1. Reliance on kinfolk, on the one hand, and transfer of skill, knowledge and power appropriate for dealing with major urban institutions, on the

other, are two alternative patterns of migration, and reliance on kinfolk is more common among those handicapped with respect to those institutions by low rank, little urban experience, extreme youth or age, and discrimination.

2. Either one works to mitigate the disruption caused by migration.

3. Kin groups specialize in domestic forms of aid, and the specialization is greatest in those groups relying least on kinfolk.

4. Migration under the auspices of kinship promotes continuing intense involvement in kin groups, and thereby slows down assimilation to the formal structures of the city.

None of these is an undoubted truth. All are worth testing.

A STUDY OF MIGRATION

A study of migrants to Wilmington, Delaware done in 1961 dealt with these general questions.[13] Using a standard one-hour questionnaire which mainly treated residential history, conditions of migration to Wilmington and present social participation, interviewers collected information from the heads of 244 families with children in the city's public elementary schools. Rather than forming a random miniature of Wilmington's population, the sample consisted of quotas for each of the twelve categories created by simultaneously distinguishing white collar from blue collar, white from nonwhite, and natives, migrants arriving before 1953 and migrants arriving in 1953 or later from each other. The sample consists of adults living in families, heavily concentrated in their thirties and forties, most of them in the labor force. This plan greatly increases the meaningful comparisons among different types of migrants possible within a small sample.

The plan also homogenizes the composition of the households. Since the composition of the household and its involvement in more extensive networks of kinship are surely closely related, this homogenization most likely minimizes the amount of variation in involvement with kinfolk from one part of the population to another. Nevertheless, as we shall see, such involvement does vary systematically within the sample. And there are still some differences in household composition within the sample. Blue collar households average a little larger, contain non-members of the primary family a bit more often, and are more frequently broken by separation, divorce or death, than the white collar households. Broken families are also more common among migrants in the city at least eight years than among others, more common among whites than nonwhites, more common among migrants from rural origins than among those from urban origins. No doubt these variations make a difference in relations to kinfolk outside the household. Nevertheless, almost 90 percent of the heads of sample households are married with spouses present, and 75 percent of the households consist of a man, his wife, their children, and no others. Differences in composition of households are not likely to account for any major variation in relationships to larger kin groups.

This relative homogeneity at the time of the interview, however, does not mean homogeneity at the time of migration to Wilmington. The average respondent had been in the city about eight years at the interview. The *size* of the groups with which the migrants came, for example, was larger for rural than for urban, larger for white collar than for blue collar; the essential contrast is between individuals migrating alone and primary families coming together.

Altogether, about 30 percent of the heads of households in the sample came to the city alone, and 60 percent came with their own primary families. "Irregular" arrangements, such as a married man migrating alone, or a group of non-relatives migrating together, appeared more often among blue-collar workers. Primary families were rarer for urban migrants, nonwhites, and those from close to Wilmington. The proportion of all migrants who were unmarried and alone, unsurprisingly, declined regularly with the age of the migrant, at least up to 40 years of age. [See below.] Two variables, in fact, appear to override all the rest: the rank of the migrant (at least as indicated by his being white collar or blue collar) and his age. The youngest and the oldest blue collar migrants are the most likely to come to the city on their own, apart from their primary families.

Age at Migration	Percent Unmarried Individuals	Percent Primary Families	Percent Other
21 or less	65.5	31.0	3.5
22 to 28	30.9	50.9	18.2
29 to 34	13.2	67.9	18.9
35 to 39	6.5	83.8	9.7
40 and over	13.6	68.2	18.2
Total (N = 190)	25.3	60.0	14.7

A closer look at the migrants who were already married at the time of coming to Wilmington adds something to this conclusion. How many of their primary families did migration tear apart for any considerable period? Just under 30 percent of those primary families did not re-form until at least the month following the departure of the head of the household: over half that 30 percent were apart three months or more. Blue collar families and older heads of households had to wait especially long to bring their families back together, while nonwhite and rural migrants lagged a little longer than white and urban migrants. On the whole, lags increased with the distance migrated, but blue collar migrants from the state of Delaware often left their families behind for a while.

So far, the information suggests that migration more often disrupted family life for blue collar migrants and those at the extremes of age (although the word "extremes" exaggerates the range of ages actually under consideration); nonwhites also seemed to feel that disruption a little more often, but there were no consistent differences between migrants of rural and urban origins. The data on lags in re-forming primary families fit the notion that lags and chain-migration go together, although they are far from proving it. If so, "disruption" may be a misleading term, for more distant kinsmen may be playing a strong role in precisely those groups in which migration commonly separates individuals from their primary families.

This idea returns us to two of our general hypotheses:

1. Reliance on kinfolk, on the one hand, and transfer of skill, knowledge and power appropriate for dealing with major urban institutions, on the other, are two alternative patterns of migration; reliance on kinfolk is more common among those handicapped with respect to those institutions by low rank, little urban experience, extreme youth or age, and discrimination.

2. Either one works to mitigate the disruption caused by migration.

We shall bring little direct evidence to bear on the second hypothesis. An examination of the auspices of migration, however, will give some idea of the validity of the first.

AUSPICES OF MIGRATION TO WILMINGTON

Establishing which social structures linked the migrant with his city of destination—identifying, that is, the auspices of his migration—is no light task. The use of restrospective accounts of migration makes it all the heavier. The migrant's report of his sources of aid, information or encouragement in making the move provides some of the essential information, in one of its more reliable forms.

The respondents in Wilmington reported on their sources of information about jobs, housing and living conditions in the city. They also answered a series of questions like this:

13. Did anyone help you or encourage you to come to Wilmington?

a. If YES, will you tell me who encouraged or helped you and what relationship they were to you, or if not related exactly who they were? You need not give their names if you don't want to.

FOR EACH PERSON OR GROUP NAMED: How did they help or encourage you?

A number of people named more than one source of aid, encouragement or information, and more than one type of source. We have simplified the classification of auspices by combining the responses to all these questions and sorting all migrants naming more than one *type* of source (except for the combination of kin and friends, which was too common and too interesting to neglect) into the category "other". In addition to these combinations, "other" also includes social agencies, religious or political officials and such specialists in mobility as real estate agents.

Let us illustrate the sorting. If the migrant named friends only, regardless of how many friends he named, he received the classification "friends". If, on the other hand, he named friends three times and his place of employment once, he fell into the category "other". The procedure, in short, discards some of the finer information available in order to arrive at relatively distinct types.

This sorting produced the following breakdown of the 190 migrants.[14] [See below.] The distribution is interesting in itself, because of the weight it gives to kinfolk and because of the challenge it lays down to the common assumption of the overwhelming importance of work to migration.

Auspices	Number
None	31
Kin	51
Friends	23
Kin and friends	14
Work	19
"Other"	52

What about group differences? Our general hypothesis leads us to expect a) blue collar workers, b) migrants from rural origins, c) nonwhite migrants and d) the youngest and the oldest migrants, to name kinfolk more often. In the present sample, the gross comparisons for occupation and age come out as expected, the differences by origin are in the expected direction but relatively weak, and the differences by color contradict the hypothesis.

Tables 1 to 4 present the data. Table 1 shows auspices by occupation. The blue collar migrants relied on kinfolk distinctly more often than the white collar migrants did. They also got aid, encouragement or information from friends more often. The white collar migrants more frequently claimed no aid at all, or fell into the "other" category. Eliminating "none" and "other", which brings the table down to perilously small numbers, yields a comparison like [the one below]. The reduced table raises a small, not entirely false, alarm. Let us combine our knowledge that the category "other" mainly contains *combinations* of auspices with the plausible assumption that "none" hides a variety of subtle, generalized relations with the city of destination which do not occur to a respondent asked specifically about aid, information and encouragement. We might better interpret the findings to mean that while blue collar workers are more likely to be linked to the city of destination primarily through kinfolk, white collar workers more often have multiple links with the city, and these links often include kinship. The alternatives, that is, are not nearly so mutually exclusive as our original statement of the hypothesis implies. With this modification the conclusion stands: the blue collar workers in this sample migrated under the auspices of kinship considerably more often than the white collar workers did.

	Percent	
Auspices	*White* (N = 28)	*Blue* (N = 79)
Kin	46.5	48.2
Friends	17.8	22.8
Kin and friends	14.2	12.6
Work	21.5	16.4
	100.0	100.1

Turning to the comparison of migrants from urban and rural origins[15] (Table 2), we find a pattern of differences rather like that between white collar and blue collar migrants, but not so pronounced. Part of the similarity, indeed, is due to the fact that 77 percent of the rural migrants are blue collar. But even within the occupational groups the pattern persists. Since the differences are not large enough to reach statistical significance, the comparison leaves this segment of the basic hypothesis doubtful.

The differences by color (Table 3) clearly do not conform to expectations. If anything, they indicate that nonwhites are less likely than whites to migrate under the auspices of kinship, and more likely to migrate under the auspices of work. We

TABLE 1
Auspices at Migration by Occupational Status

	Occupational Status		
Auspices	*White collar* (N = 70)	*Blue collar* (N = 120)	*Total* (N = 190)
None	24.3%	11.7%	16.3%
Kin	18.6	31.7	26.8
Friends	7.1	15.0	12.1
Kin and friends	5.7	8.3	7.4
Work	8.6	10.8	10.0
Other and combination	35.7	22.5	27.4
Total	100.0	100.0	100.0

Chi-square (5 d.f.) = 12.90, $P < .05 > .02$

TABLE 2
Auspices by Urbanity of Background

	Urbanity		
Auspices	*Urban* (N = 88)	*Rural* (N = 102)	*Total* (N = 190)
None	19.3%	13.7%	16.3%
Kin	19.3	33.3	26.8
Friends	12.5	11.8	12.1
Kin and friends	6.8	7.8	7.4
Work	10.2	9.8	10.0
Other	31.8	23.5	27.4
Total	99.9	99.9	100.0

Chi-square (5 d.f.) = 5.59, $P > .30$

had reasoned that discrimination would handicap nonwhites with respect to relatively impersonal auspices, and turn them back on ascriptive solidarities, especially kinship. Many *ad hoc* "explanations" of the failure of the present data to support that reasoning come to mind, but prudence dictates their being laid aside for further investigation.

Age at migration has powerful links with a number of other characteristics of migrants, both at the time of their coming to the city and later.[16] Up to the late thirties, the skill in dealing with impersonal institutions, the mobility, the urbanity of this group of migrants tends to rise with their age at migration to Wilmington. Not only do older people face a different social situation at migration, but also those people who are still on the move at 40 belong to a different type from those

TABLE 3
Auspices by Color of Migrating Household

| | Color | | |
| | White | Nonwhite | Total |
Auspices	*(N = 120)*	*(N = 70)*	*(N = 190)*
None	20.0%	10.0%	16.3%
Kin	28.3	24.3	26.8
Friends	11.7	12.9	12.1
Kin and friends	5.8	10.0	7.4
Work	6.7	15.7	10.0
Other	27.5	27.1	27.4
Total	100.0	100.0	100.0

Chi-square (5 d.f.) = 7.62, P < .20 > .10

who make their last big change at 21. The variation in the auspices of migration (Table 4) reflects the first part of this difference. As expected, the proportion of migrants coming to Wilmington under the auspices of kinship declines with age at migration up to 40, and then rises again somewhat. The proportion migrating under "other" auspices describes an opposite curve. The variations in other respects are more irregular and less pronounced.

The rise and fall of "other" auspices recalls our speculations on the comparison of white collar and blue collar workers. Since the "other" auspices are mainly combinations of two or three forms of relationship to the city, the data suggest that the range of statuses, experience and relationships that migrants transfer on coming to the new city expand with age—up to a certain point. The proportion describing

TABLE 4
Auspices by Age of Head of Household at Time of Migration

| | Age of Head of Household | | | | | |
| | 21 or less | 22–28 | 29–34 | 35–39 | 40 and over | Total |
Auspices	*(N = 29)*	*(N = 55)*	*(N = 53)*	*(N = 31)*	*(N = 22)*	*(N = 190)*
None	27.6%	14.5%	15.1%	19.4%	4.5%	16.3%
Kin	37.9	32.7	26.4	12.9	18.2	26.8
Friends	10.3	14.5	15.1	3.2	13.6	12.1
Kin and friends	6.9	10.9	1.9	3.2	18.2	7.4
Work	–	9.1	15.1	9.7	13.6	10.0
Other	17.2	18.2	26.4	51.6	31.8	27.4
Total	99.9	99.9	100.0	100.0	99.9	100.0

Chi-square (20 d.f.) = 33.74, P < .05 > .02

their coming to Wilmington as an orderly change of job (as opposed to looking for work) rises steadily and remarkably to a peak in the age range 35 to 39. The seeking of aid from mobility specialists follows the same sequence, although the curve is flatter. We already know that the share of migrants coming with their primary families traces the same trajectory. Up to a point, rising age at migration seems increasingly to sort out experienced, skilled, urbane, integrated, mobile persons, like the chemists or the automobile workers who play such a prominent part in migration to Wilmington.

But only up to a point. The older migrant sometimes belongs to this type. As age continues to rise, however, it begins to select more and more persons whom the labor market has shunted aside. Displaced coal miners from West Virginia and retired parents of Wilmington residents typify such persons in the migration to Wilmington. The proportion of migrants who said they were "looking for work" when they came to the city varies remarkably. [See below.] The youngest and the oldest migrants, in short, tend to have the most uncertain connection with the labor market, and to migrate under the auspices of kinship. The variation follows our general hypothesis.

Age at Migration	*Percent "Looking for Work"*
21 or less	60.0
22 to 28	33.3
29 to 34	24.4
35 to 39	24.0
40 and over	41.2
Total	30.6

Fairly emphatically in the case of occupation and age, rather doubtfully in the case of urbanity of background, if not at all in the case of color, the data from Wilmington display the expected variation in the auspices of migration from one group to another. If the auspices really matter, two things should follow: (1) there should be a systematic relationship between auspices and other conditions of migration which do not enter into their definition, (2) the initial difference should affect the form and degree of the migrant's later integration into the life of the city. To gauge the influence of auspices in these respects, let us first look at some of the correlates of auspices, then examine the components of auspices in somewhat greater detail and then, finally, review some indications of their further consequences.

CORRELATES OF AUSPICES

Since the distribution of auspices varies with the status of the migrants, and other characteristics of migrating groups do as well, we should not be overly surprised to find a relationship between the auspices of migration and these other characteristics. Precisely because auspices and status vary together, the small number of cases in the present analysis forbids any really adequate simultaneous examination of the effects of status and auspices. Nevertheless, it is worth knowing whether the correlates do come out as expected. Roughly speaking, they do (Table 5). Unmarried individuals migrate under the auspices of kinship more frequently than other categories do; exactly half of them fall under the headings "kin" or "kin and friends". Intact primary families most often come under "other" auspices. Yet rather few of the irregular groups of migrants, such as sets of friends coming together, are under the auspices of kinship. And the differences among the other categories are not very great.

The reasons the migrants offer for their moves to Wilmington also shed some light on the correlates of auspices. We doubt that such statements are *explanations* in any reliable sense of the word, but they do indicate something of the social setting of the decision to move. Here are the most common reasons given, in terms of the percentage of all persons in the specified category of auspices making the reply. [See below.] These responses vary markedly with the auspices of migration as determined by sources of aid, information and encouragement; on the whole they reinforce the value of the distinctions of auspices. Migrants under the auspices of kinship rarely report coming because of a transfer or a new job, while migrants under the auspices of work almost always do. Family reasons—typically such statements as "We want to be closer to the folks"—loom much larger for migrants under the auspices of kinship. And those who come under work or other auspices less often describe themselves as coming to *look* for work. Of course, the logical contents of the two classifications overlap. To some extent, they simply measure the same thing twice, so the discovery of their correlation is an illusion. To exactly that extent, nevertheless, the discovery of the correlation clarifies the concept of auspices and verifies its identification of phenomena worth singling out.

Auspices (Percent)

	None	Kin	Friends or kin and friends	Work	Other
Transfer or new job	50.0	12.4	13.6	93.3	36.1
Looking for work	33.3	31.3	50.0	6.7	25.0
Family reasons	0.0	25.0	4.5	0.0	11.1

The explanations the migrants give of any trips to the city before actually migrating also illuminate their relations to it at the time of the move. Another informal table [below] presents the most common responses. This tabulation exposes some inadequacies in the classification of auspices. Considering what a large number of them had been in Wilmington before, many of the migrants under the heading "none" surely had well-defined relations with the city at the time of migration. Furthermore, some members of every category had visited friends and relatives in Wilmington before migrating, which raises the suspicion that the questions about aid, information and encouragement missed some established and important contacts with the city.

Auspices (Percent)

	None	Kin	Friends or kin and friends	Work	Other
No trips before actual migration	19.3	33.3	18.9	52.6	21.1
Preparation for the move only	32.3	9.8	2.43	21.1	2.38
Visiting friends and relatives	22.6	45.1	40.5	10.5	23.1

The tabulation, on the other hand, does show the relationship between migration under the auspices of kinship and prior contact with the city through kin and friends. The auspices of friendship, or a combination of friendship and kinship, come out similarly. Migrants coming under "other" auspices, or those of work, report prior visiting with kin or friends in the city much less often. Fewer than half of the migrants coming under the auspices of work (who included a large share of people making job transfers and coming considerable distances) had ever made trips to the city before actually moving there; maybe this category, rather than that of displaced rural migrants, is the one to inspect for acute consequences of mobility. If our earlier interpretation of "other" auspices as implying multiple relations with the new city is correct, then those who have only the new job to link them with the city may be the group who most often face personal isolation after the move. Those who migrate under the auspices of kinship have ready-made sets of personal relations already at their disposal.

TABLE 5
Composition of Migrating Group by Auspices

Composition of Migrating Group

Auspices	Unmarried individual only (N = 48)	Married head of house- hold only (N = 10)	Primary family only (N = 114)	Other (N = 18)	Total (N = 190)
None	12.5%	10.0%	20.2%	5.6%	16.3%
Kin	35.4	30.0	25.4	11.1	26.8
Friends	10.4	40.0	8.8	22.2	12.1
Kin and friends	14.6	—	5.3	5.6	7.4
Work	6.3	20.0	7.9	27.8	10.0
Other	20.8	—	32.5	27.8	27.4
Total	100.0	100.0	100.1	100.1	100.0

HOW MUCH HELP FROM KINFOLK, AND WHAT KIND?

The means of identifying auspices of migration employed in this study forces most combinations into the single category "other". While it classifies the sources of aid, information and encouragement, it does not include their amount or the nature of their action. For these reasons, we still have something to learn from a closer examination of aid, information and encouragement. (Let us save words by calling these "help" collectively from now on.)

An earlier tabulation showed that all but 31 (about 16 percent) of the respondents named at least one source of help. Table 6 lays out the major sources of help by occupation and origin. About 38 percent of all migrants got help from relatives, 34 percent from friends (there were, in fact, almost no neighbors mentioned), 20 percent from work-related persons or groups, 17 percent from specialists in mobility. We find the white collar workers leaning more heavily on work and specialists, blue collar workers relying on friends and, especially, relatives. We also find the rural-urban differences varying with occupation, with blue collar migrants from rural backgrounds getting help from kinfolk more than half the time.[17] In short, the statistics simply produce a slightly more textured version of the comparisons already made among auspices. A strong occupational difference and a weak rural-urban difference confirm the relationship between reliance on kinfolk and low rank or little urban experience. There is another way to analyze the same responses.

TABLE 6
Sources of Aid or Information at Migration by Origin
and Occupational Class

| | *Occupational Class and Origin* | | | | |
Source	White collar urban origin (N = 46)	White collar rural origin (N = 24)	Blue collar urban origin (N = 42)	Blue collar rural origin (N = 78)	Total (N = 190)
None	21.7%	27.2%	16.7%	9.0%	16.3%
Relatives	28.3	20.8	38.1	51.3	38.9
Friends and neighbors	34.8	29.2	33.3	34.6	33.7
Social agencies, religious or political officials	4.3	—	11.9	3.8	5.3
Mobility specialists	26.1	20.8	11.9	14.1	17.4
Employer, union, work associates	21.7	37.5	19.0	14.1	20.0

Note: Percents do not total to 100.0, since more than one source of aid or information could be mentioned.
Chi-square (5 d.f.) for occupation = 15.79, P < .01
Chi-square (5 d.f.) for origin = 5.00, P > .30

There were four different points at which the migrant interviewed could name sources of help. They were when he was asked where he got:

1. information concerning housing;
2. information concerning jobs;
3. information concerning living conditions;
4. other aid or encouragement.

Although these are not by any means equally important, we have some right to conclude that a migrant naming a particular source for three or four of these got more help from that source than a migrant naming the source only once, or not at all. Calling the number of these respects in which migrants name kinfolk the Aid Index, we can examine how the index varies from one group to another.

The results do not differ substantially from those already presented. Taking the mean Aid Index by color and occupational class, for example, yields this small table [below]. There may be, that is, some tendency for whites at a given occupational level to rely on kinfolk more than nonwhites do (the apparent discrepancy between the marginals and the body of the table is due to the small number of white collar nonwhites), but the strong difference is by occupation. The urban mean, again, is 0.72, the rural 1.06. The means fluctuate by age at migration as follows. [See below.] The curve is already very familiar. Likewise, the index is particularly high for those who came unmarried and alone, for migrants from Delaware and the South, for those explaining their coming to Wilmington through "family reasons" and—to insert two variables not discussed before—for migrants making major changes in type of job and migrants coming directly from rural areas. All these are quite consistent with the earlier findings.

	White Collar	*Blue Collar*	*Total*
White	0.65	1.20	0.92
Nonwhite	0.60	0.92	0.88
Total	0.64	1.06	0.91

Age at Migration

21 or under	*22 to 28*	*29 to 34*	*35 to 39*	*40 and over*
1.21	1.11	0.72	0.58	0.91

What *kinds* of help do kin groups give? The responses to the separate questions concerning sources of information about jobs, housing and living conditions touch the hypothetical specialization of kin groups in domestic forms of help. In each case, the respondent not only enumerated his sources of information, but also identified the most important one. By the hypothesis, kin groups should play a larger part in housing and living condition than in jobs, and this specialization should be greater for the types of migrants relying least on their kinfolk.

In fact, the data on sources of information do not confirm the hypothesis. A small table [below] summarizes the findings, in terms of the percentage of all migrants naming the particular source. Considering the variation in the proportion naming any source of information at all—high for jobs, low for living conditions—the proportion naming kinfolk is relatively constant. In all three respects, kinfolk are the most commonly named source. That confirms their importance in migration, but does not confirm the hypothesis of specialization. Of course, if we calculate the proportion of those actually naming a source of information who name relatives, we get a progression of this sort: jobs 28%, housing 38%, living conditions 40%. Yet that way of "saving" the hypothesis does not allow for the possibility that *not* getting a certain kind of information from available kinfolk is just as significant as getting it.

	Percent		
Source	*Jobs*	*Housing*	*Living conditions*
None	27.9	35.8	52.1
Relatives	20.5	24.2	19.1
Friends and neighbors	16.3	15.3	11.6
Social agencies, religious and political officials	2.6	3.2	3.2
Employer, work associates, union	17.4	7.9	6.3
Mobility specialists	7.4	7.9	1.1
Other	7.9	5.8	6.3
Total	100.0	100.1	99.7

The pattern of variation by status generally follows familiar lines, but it does not support the hypothesis of specialization either. The following figures [below] rapidly summarize the percentages naming kinfolk as their most important sources

	Percent		
Status	*Jobs*	*Housing*	*Living conditions*
White collar	14.5	15.7	12.9
Blue collar	24.2	29.2	23.3
White	18.5	25.0	20.0
Nonwhite	24.3	22.7	18.6
Urban	19.5	20.5	11.4
Rural	21.6	27.5	26.5
Age at Migration			
21 and under	27.6	24.1	27.6
22 to 28	39.0	29.1	16.4
29 to 34	17.0	18.9	17.0
35 to 39	3.2	22.6	19.4
40 and over	18.2	27.3	22.7

of information. The differentials are essentially those we have already discussed at length, with the variation by age a bit more irregular than in previous comparisons, and nonwhite-white differences inconsistent.

The hypothesis of specialization takes this form:

Kin groups specialize in domestic forms of aid, and the specialization is greatest in those groups relying least on kinfolk.

If this is true, there should be a greater difference between the proportions getting "domestic" and "non-domestic" forms of aid within groups relying little on kinfolk than within groups relying much on kinfolk. It seems reasonable to consider the giving of information about housing and living conditions "domestic" and the giving of information about jobs less so. The groups relying more heavily on kinfolk at migration are blue collar workers, rural migrants and the extremes of age.

In general, the differences between the proportions getting one kind of information from kinfolk and those getting another kind are small. Nor is there any detectable tendency for the differentials to be smaller among blue collar workers, rural migrants or those at the extremes of age. Once the overall variation in how much information migrants get from relatives is taken into account, the kind of information gained from them does not seem to vary systematically with status.

Before taking this as the final conclusion, perhaps we should examine what the migrants said when asked exactly what kind of aid they received from those who "helped or encouraged" them. For the sample as a whole, the breakdown was as follows:

	Percent
No one helped or encouraged	47.4
Helped in finding a job	27.9
Material assistance	7.9
General encouragement	11.6
Other	5.3
	100.1

Differences by color or origin in these regards were slight (although blue collar nonwhites from rural backgrounds reported an exceptional amount of "material assistance": temporary housing, loans, gifts, and so on). Occupational and age groups varied more: blue collar workers more often got material assistance and less often got help in finding a job, while general encouragement and material assistance were both high, and help in finding a job low, at the extremes of age.[18]

Such comparisons do not get at the specialization of help, since they lump all sources of help together. Table 7 cross-classifies type of aid received by source of aid, with white collar and blue collar workers separated. (This fractionation of the sample brings the analysis down to tiny numbers, but in this one case it is worth it.) The table records a degree of specialization among the various sources of help. Work-related persons and groups give help in finding jobs; friends are particularly likely to give general encouragement; relatives most often give material assistance (to blue collar workers) or general encouragement (to white collar workers). Yet relatives and friends alike often help in finding jobs. None of these emphases constitutes a monopoly. As for the hypothetical greater specialization of kin groups

TABLE 7

Type of Aid Received from Principal Source by Source of Aid and Occupation

Source and Occupation

Type of Aid	None		Relatives		Friends	
	White collar (N = 31)	*Blue collar* (N = 59)	*White collar* (N = 15)	*Blue collar* (N = 32)	*White collar* (N = 5)	*Blue collar* (N = 12)
None	100.0	100.0	—	—	—	—
Help in finding a job	—	—	26.7	28.1	40.0	41.7
General en- couragement	—	—	46.7	18.8	60.0	50.0
Material assistance	—	—	—	37.5	—	8.3
Other	—	—	26.7	15.6	—	—
Total	100.0	100.0	100.1	100.0	100.0	100.0

Type of Aid	Work associates		Other		Total	
	White collar (N = 19)	*Blue collar* (N = 15)	*White collar* (N = 0)	*Blue collar* (N = 2)	*White collar* (N = 70)	*Blue collar* (N = 120)
None	—	—	—	—	44.3	49.2
Help in finding a job	94.7	93.3	—	50.0	34.3	24.2
General en- couragement	—	—	—	—	14.3	10.0
Material assistance	5.3	—	—	50.0	1.4	11.7
Other	—	6.7	—	—	5.7	5.0
Total	100.0	100.0	100.0	100.0	100.0	100.1

in "domestic" forms of help in groups relying less on kinfolk—in this case, among white collar workers—it simply does not appear. The hypothesis of specialization gains little support from these data.

Why? Maybe it is just the peculiarities of the sample or the crudity of the measurement. But if the specialization we expected to find really does not exist, that conclusion raises two intriguing possibilities: (1) status differentials in relationship to kinfolk found in previous research largely reflect the *availability* of kinfolk, rather than substantial variations in the form of relationship with those who are actually available,[19] (2) because of relative homogeneity of status within kin groups, the skills and influence available within kin groups vary sufficiently with the migrant's status and the claims for aid the migrant can make on them are strong enough that—when present at all—they are usually among the most effective intermediaries between the migrant and the new community.

If the first were true, it would cast a new light on the whole analysis. For it would bring a quite different problem than we have been considering into prominence: how the availability of kinfolk comes to differ from one status to another. There are several fascinating factors which surely affect that availability: the sheer size of coherent kin groups, the extent to which the presence or absence of kin at possible destinations affects both the direction and the selectivity of migration, the effects of the presence or absence of kin on the probability of departure from a given locality. Analyses of aggregate patterns of migration and the assimilation of migrants have ground on in splendid insulation from each other; practically no one, for example, has ever systematically allowed for the influence of kinship networks in studies of selective migration. In a field flooded with facts, there are few assembled facts on this crucial matter.

If the second alternative—systematic variation by status in the ways in which kin groups mediate between new arrivals and the community—were the valid one, it would not raise such serious questions about our general line of argument. Finer instruments than the crude classifications we have used here, but similar in principle, ought in that case to disclose the nature of that variation. This alternative, too, offers a splendid invitation to further research.[20]

We should make one thing clear. The findings (or non-findings) concerning the specialization of different kinds of aid do not challenge the general conclusion that the auspices of migration vary systematically with the status of the migrant. The speculations those negative findings have suggested could affect the *explanation* of that systematic variation as well as the analysis of its consequences. Let us turn briefly to those consequences.

AUSPICES IN THE LONGER RUN

Any information concerning systematic changes over fairly substantial periods of time which a study like that of Wilmington yields has to come from one of two sources: (a) the comparison of segments of the sample presumably at different stages in a continuous process, (b) the retrospective accounts of the respondents. The first not only raises painful logical problems, but also requires meticulous control of powerful variables which may be correlated with the sorting into stages. The second becomes suspect on precisely the points which interest the student of assimilation most directly: changes in involvement with different groups in the community, changes in skill, changes in attitudes. On the basis of the data from Wilmington, we can do little more than suggest some possible lasting consequences of coming to the city under one set of auspices or another.

Table 8 presents some characteristics of the migrants at the time of the interview. That was on the average about eight years after migration to Wilmington. The characteristics are indicators of assimilation into different aspects of the life of the city; all the indicators rise to some extent with length of residence in the city, and all vary systematically with status.[21] The table arrays them by the auspices under which the respondents originally migrated to Wilmington.

In most of these respects, those who migrated under "other" auspices score highest. Migrants under the auspices of work are generally close to them. Those

TABLE 8

Various Indicators of Assimilation by Auspices of Migration to Wilmington

Auspices	Percent Voting in the Last Election	Percent Owning Their Homes	Median Organizational Participation Score	Median Neighboring Score	Mean Information Level
None	67.7	41.9	12.2	11.0	8.5
Kin	76.5	49.0	12.4	9.0	7.7
Friends	69.6	52.2	5.9	9.0	6.5
Kin and friends	71.4	21.4	6.0	7.0	7.0
Work	84.2	47.4	17.0	10.0	7.2
Other	80.8	51.9	17.6	12.0	8.1
Total	74.7	46.8	12.2	10.0	7.7

who came under the auspices of kinship participate less actively in voluntary associations, neighbor somewhat less and are a little less likely to vote, but they are home owners about as often as the others, and their level of information on city affairs averages about as high. In fact, the least assimilated by these criteria tend to be migrants who came under the auspices of friendship or a combination of kinship + friendship.

In principle, such differences could result from differences in length of time in the city. In fact, largely because of the study design, the various categories of auspices are similar in length of residence. The differences could also result from variations in status, which we already know very well to be correlated with the auspices of migration. That is hard to check out. But let us look at the one indicator of those presented here which has been most used as a measure of assimilation in other studies: the intensity of participation in voluntary association. We can at least learn how controlling for occupation affects the figures in Table 8.

Here are the figures for median organizational participation score [below]. The main discrepancy (since the high median for white collar kin + friends is based on only four cases) is the low participation of blue collar migrants who came under "other" auspices. That discrepancy is large enough to recommend caution. We may continue to speculate that auspices affect long-run integration into the life of the city, but these data certainly do not establish the speculation as a fact.

Auspices	White Collar	Blue Collar	Total
None	14.6	5.8	12.2
Kin	19.0	11.4	12.4
Friends	13.0	5.6	5.9
Kin and friends	32.7	5.5	6.0
Work	18.0	17.0	17.0
Other	30.3	9.2	17.6
Total	23.7	7.8	12.2

CONCLUSIONS

After a bold beginning, we have had to do a lot of qualifying. It will take much more investigation to answer our general questions about the role of kinship in migration and assimilation. The four hypotheses concerning the auspices of migration emerge partly untested, partly shaken and partly confirmed. We have not really brought any data to bear on the question of how much disruption of social life occurs under various auspices of migration. The data we have offered concerning the longer-range effects of various auspices give no more than hints, and contradictory hints at that.

Our hypotheses concerning (a) variations in auspices according to the status of migrants and (b) specialization of the help kin groups give at migration brought more profit, although we certainly cannot claim clear-cut confirmation in either case. Indeed, the data do not show any strong specialization of kin groups in particular forms of aid; they tend to disconfirm the hypothesis. But they do show the considerable amount of aid that kin groups give at migration, and suggest that more of the variation by status in this regard than is ordinarily realized may be due to variations in the sheer availability of kinfolk.

The results concerning variation in auspices with status are the most definite. The data from Wilmington produce a moderately consistent picture of strong differences by rank and age at migration, weak differences by urbanity of origins, no real differences by color. Except for the puzzling absence of marked differences in auspices between nonwhites and whites, the findings conform to the general hypothesis. Even here, however, two *caveats* are in order: (1) the crudity of the present classification of auspices makes it urgent to carry on further investigations with finer, theoretically more apposite, measures of auspices, (2) our hidden initial assumption that the various auspices were more or less mutually exclusive did some violence to the facts of overlap and combination.

If, in this ordinary industrial city, such elaborate and systematic variations in patterns of migration exist, if kin groups play such a large part in the reception of newcomers, then the facts raise questions about the theory of uprooting, marginality and disorganization. Everywhere we find more persistence and proliferation of personal relations than should be there. The very groups one would expect to find disrupted by migration, for lack of security, experience or skill in city life, show extensive contacts among kinfolk. Perhaps the kin groups do eventually break down, before their members have managed to become full-fledged urbanites; but nothing in the evidence from Wilmington suggests that it happens.

Of course, mobility often distresses people, old attachments disappear, many city-dwellers lead disorganized lives. The question is how these and other facts of urban life fit together. The meager evidence so far accumulated does not justify the conclusion that genuine uprooting is widespread in cities, or that its occurrence inevitably brings on individual malaise and social disintegration.

NOTES

1. Robert E. Park and Ernest W. Burgess, *The City* (Chicago: University of Chicago, 1925), p. 54; see also Robert E. Park, "Human Migration and the Marginal Man," *American Journal of Sociology*, 33 (May, 1928), 881–893.
2. Marc Fried, "Transitional Functions of Working-Class Communities: Implications for Forced

Relocation," in Mildred B. Kantor, ed., *Mobility and Mental Health* (Springfield, Illinois: Charles C. Thomas, 1965), plus extensive references there, and other papers in the same volume; Herbert Gans, *The Urban Villagers* (New York: Free Press, 1963); Philippe Garigue, *La Vie familiale des canadiens français* (Montreal: Presses de l'Université, 1962); Scott Greer, *The Emerging City* (New York: Free Press, 1962); Madeline Kerr, *The People of Ship Street* (London: Routledge and Kegan Paul, 1958); Peter Marris, "The Social Implications of Urban Redevelopment," *Journal of the American Institute of Planners*, 28 (1962), 180–186; Harold Wilensky and Charles Lebeaux, *Industrial Society and Social Welfare* (New York: Russell Sage Foundation, 1958); Michael Young and Peter Willmott, *Family and Kinship in East London* (London: Routledge and Kegan Paul, 1957).

3. H. B. M. Murphy, "Migration and the Major Mental Disorders," in Kantor, *op. cit.*

4. Leonard Savitz, *Delinquency and Migration* (Philadelphia: Commission on Human Relations, 1960); Judith L. Kinman and Everett S. Lee, "Migration and Crime," *International Migration Digest*, 3 (1966), 7–14.

5. Morris Axelrod, "Urban Structure and Social Participation," *American Sociological Review*, 21 (1956), 14–18; Wendell Bell and Marion Boat, "Urban Neighborhoods and Informal Social Relations," *American Journal of Sociology*, 62 (1957), 391–398; Paul-Henry Chombart de Lauwe and others, "L'Intégration du citadin à sa ville et à son quartier," four mimeographed volumes, Centre d'Etudes des Groupes Sociaux, 1961–62; Allan Coult and Robert Habenstein, "The Study of Extended Kinship in Urban Society," *Sociological Quarterly*, 1962: 141–145; Oscar Lewis, "Further Observations on the Folk-Urban Continuum and Urbanization with Special Reference to Mexico City," in Philip M. Hauser and Leo F. Schnore, eds., *The Study of Urbanization* (New York: Wiley, 1965).

6. Work and kinship are simply the two special cases which are most prominent in migration to American cities. Elsewhere, other formal structures than work and other ascriptive solidarities than kin play a much larger part. See, for example, Peter C. W. Gutkind, "African Urbanism, Mobility and the Social Network," *International Journal of Comparative Sociology*, 6 (1965), 48–60; Joseph H. Greenberg, "Urbanism, Migration and Language," in Hilda Kuper, ed., *Urbanization and Migration in West Africa* (Berkeley and Los Angeles: University of California Press, 1965); W. T. Morrill, "Immigrants and Associations: the Ibo in Twentieth Century Calabar," *Comparative Studies in Society and History*, 5 (1963), 424–448.

7. Leonard Blumberg, *A Pilot Study of Recent Negro Migrants into Philadelphia* (Philadelphia: The Urban League, 1958); James S. Brown, Harry K. Schwarzweller and Joseph J. Mangalam, "Kentucky Mountain Migration and the Stem-Family: An American Variation on a Theme by Le Play," *Rural Sociology*, 28 (1963), 48–69; John S. MacDonald and Leatrice MacDonald, "Chain Migration, Ethnic Neighborhood Formation, and Social Networks," *Milbank Memorial Fund Quarterly*, 42 (1964), 82–97; Morton Rubin, "Migration Patterns of Negroes from a Rural Northeastern Mississippi Community," *Social Forces*, 39 (1960), 59–66; Eldon Dee Smith, "Migration and Adjustment Experiences of Rural Migrant Workers in Indianapolis," unpublished Ph.D. dissertation, University of Wisconsin, 1953. If this is the case, the great missing variable in analyses of selective migration may be the presence or absence of kinsmen at points of opportunity for new migrants. Cf. Frank W. Young and Ruth C. Young, "Individual Commitment to Industrialization in Rural Mexico," *American Journal of Sociology*, 71 (1966), 373–383.

8. Leonard Blumberg and Robert Bell, "Urban Migration and Kinship Ties," *Social Problems*, 6 (1959), 328–333; Lewis Killian, "The Adjustment of Southern White Migrants to Northern Urban Norms," *Social Forces*, 32 (1953), 66–69; Eugene Litwak, "Geographic Mobility and Extended Family Cohesion," *American Sociological Review*, 25 (1960), 385–394; Smith, *op. cit.*; Ralph H. Turner, "Migration to a Medium Size American City: Attitudes, Motives and Personal Characteristics Revealed by Open-Ended Interview Methodology," *Journal of Social Psychology*, 80 (1949), 229–249.

9. Caution: what is unclear about previous findings on this subject is how much may be due to group differences in reliance on those kin who are present, and how much to the sheer presence or absence of kin. It could be, for example, that mobile middle-class people are just as ready as anyone else to seek aid from their kin, but less often have any kin at hand. It could also be (as Everett Hughes suggested to us in criticism of an earlier draft of this paper) that middle-class people who cut themselves off geographically from actual

kinsmen acquire sets of sponsors, advisers and other quasi-kinsmen toward whom they behave in kinlike ways.

10. Albert K. Cohen and Harold M. Hodges, "Characteristics of the Lower-Blue-Collar-Class," *Social Problems,* 10 (1963), 303–334; Marc Fried, "Grieving for a Lost Home," in Leonard J. Duhl, ed., *The Urban Condition* (New York: Basic Books, 1963); Peter Morris, *Family and Social Change in an African City* (London: Routledge and Kegan Paul, 1962); Harry Schwarzweller, *Family Ties, Migration, and Transitional Adjustment of Young Men from Eastern Kentucky* (Lexington: Kentucky Agricultural Experiment Station, 1964).

11. The matter is even more complicated than this. Not only are there genuine variations in norms (for example, by national background), but the cycle of migration which prevails within a given category of rank, color or residential background also makes a difference in the sheer availability of kin. Suppose that a) the presence of kin in a city makes it more attractive to a migrant than other destinations; b) the presence of kin in a city makes the potential out-migrant less willing to leave; c) both of these effects increase with age; d) the distribution over a lifetime of incentives to move varies systematically by rank, color and residential background. Then citydwellers of all types will tend to join kin and be joined by them as years go on, but the timing will vary. And the timing will produce both a (partly spurious) rise in involvement with kin as years in the city increase, and systematic average differences among groups. Moral: distrust simple cross-sectional comparisons of involvement with kinfolk. For evidence of persistent class differences in involvement with kin at migration, see Jane Hubert, "Kinship and Geographical Mobility in a Sample from a London Middle-Class Area," *International Journal of Comparative Sociology,* 6 (1965), 61–80. For a promising attempt to get around the weaknesses of cross-sectional comparison, see Robert C. Hanson and Ozzie G. Simmons, "The Role Path: A Concept and Procedure for Studying Migration to Urban Communities," unpublished paper presented to the American Sociological Association, 1966.

12. Cf. Janet Abu-Lughod, "Migrant Adjustment to City Life: The Egyptian Case," *American Journal of Sociology,* 67 (1961), 22–32; Raymond Breton, "Institutional Completeness of Ethnic Communities and the Personal Relations of Immigrants," *American Journal of Sociology,* 70 (1964), 193–205; Oscar Handlin, *The Uprooted* (Boston: Little, Brown, 1951); Arnold Rose and Leon Warshay, "The Adjustment of Migrants to Cities," *Social Forces,* 36 (1957), 72–76.

13. A general description of the study appears in Charles Tilly, *Migration to an American City* (Newark, Delaware: Division of Urban Affairs and School of Agriculture, University of Delaware, 1965).

14. Fifty-four of the respondents were "natives"—individuals born in the city who had always lived there, or individuals who had come before their thirteenth birthdays—and therefore do not appear in these tabulations. "Kin" includes anyone outside the primary family the respondent identified as a "relative" or by specific kinship terminology; "work" includes place of employment, union, and work associates.

15. "Urban" migrants spent the greater part of their first 18 years in cities or suburbs, "rural" migrants the greater part of their first 18 years in small towns, villages or open country. There is, as one might expect, a relationship between origin and occupation; this little table states it:

	White collar	*Blue collar*	*Total*
Urban	46	42	88
Rural	24	78	102
Total	70	120	190

16. The sample design produced subgroups similar in present age distribution, except that this homogenization of present age introduced a negative correlation between years in the city and age at migration. Some samples of the correlates of age at migration: number of memberships in voluntary associations, intensity of various types of formal participation,

level of information about the city and (as we shall see) isolation from kinfolk all rise with age at migration up to around 40, while those who were younger at migration make distinctly more local changes of job than those who were older. We should emphasize that by design the categories of age at migration do not differ greatly in proportion to white collar or blue collar, a fact which makes it less likely that age at migration simply marks a variation in social rank.

17. Other tabulations show relatives particularly important for the youngest and oldest migrants as well as those from nearby (as many as two-thirds of the blue-collar migrants from the South received some help from relatives) and suggest a tendency for nonwhites to rely on friends for help.

18. Caution: as will be clearer later on, the differences in job-finding do not reflect differences in the *kind* of help given by any particular source, but differences in which sources of help people relied on.

19. Cf. Alan F. Blum, "Social Structure, Social Class, and Participation in Primary Relationships," in Arthur B. Shostak and William Gomberg, eds., *Blue-Collar World* (Englewood Cliffs: Prentice-Hall, 1964).

20. There are some promising leads in current work on French-Canadian kinship and migration, e.g. Helgi Osterreich, "Geographical Mobility and Kinship: A Canadian Example," *International Journal of Comparative Sociology,* 6 (1965), 131–144; Ralph Piddington, "The Kinship Network among French Canadians," *International Journal of Comparative Sociology,* 6 (1965), 145–165; Marcel Rioux, *Kinship Recognition and Urbanization in French Canada* (Ottawa: Bulletin of the National Museum of Canada, No. 173, 1959).

21. The *organizational participation score* gives 1 point for membership, 2 points for regular attendance, 3 for financial contribution, 4 for committee membership and 5 for holding office in each voluntary association; the *neighboring score* compounds a) the varieties of contact with neighbors, b) frequency of visits to their homes, c) knowledge of neighbors' names; the *information level* grades the respondent's knowledge of two major public issues in the city at the time of the interview.

TRADITIONALISM AND COLONIALISM: CHANGING URBAN ROLES IN ASIA

Rhoads Murphey

Europeans and Americans find it easy to forget that the city first emerged in Asia, and that in terms of the sheer number of man-years lived in cities, Asians have had more urban experience than the rest of the world put together. The Chinese, in particular, have belonged continuously to a city-dominated civilization for more than two thousand years. Rhoads Murphey's survey recalls the long urban history of Asia and sweeps across the last few hundred years of that development. The fundamental contrast to which Murphey calls our attention sets the traditional inland capital against the colonial ports through which Westerners gained access to the markets, goods, and raw materials of the Asian interior. The inland capitals coordinated vast markets and sprawling political systems long before the Westerners had any significant impact. But the ports, in Murphey's analysis, became crucial entry points for outside goods, ideas, models, and political pressures. What is more,

*Western colonial strategies were similar throughout Asia, as were the extrac-
tive port cities produced by those strategies. By the end of the colonial
period, Murphey points out, the dominant city in almost every Asian country
was a port founded, or at least developed, by Westerners.*

*Murphey is a geographer. More so than the other articles in this chapter,
his essay calls attention to the characteristics of the sites on which the great
port cities grew up: their frequent physical unattractiveness, the initial
impracticability of their harbors, their situation at the confluence of major
ocean routes. His approach to the subject is locational; it emphasizes distributions of activities over territory and employs an implicit model of urbanization as the diffusion of different kinds of influence from cities to the regions
around them. At that point, however, he avoids the temptation to adopt a
strictly mechanical analogy to energy spreading from a single location—sound
waves from a source of noise or iron filings around a magnet. Instead,
Murphey insists on the contrast between the limited short-run influence of
the colonial ports on the routine lives of most Asians and the deep penetration of those lives by the traditional capitals. The colonial ports worked their
profound effects indirectly and over the long run, by acting "as the spearheads and the catalysts of Asia's modernization."*

The subject of this essay—better so labeled than as a research paper—is too
broad to permit more than a sweeping as well as selective treatment in the short
space of a journal article. It may nevertheless be worth presenting in those terms,
painting with an overly broad brush on too large a canvas perhaps, but attempting
through its scope to relate as parts of a common phenomenon events and patterns
in separate areas. Such an effort may help to throw light on an aspect of the grand
design of European colonialism in Asia and on some of its consequences. These
were different in each area and some of the differences, notably between China and
the rest of Asia, may be instructive as they can help us better to understand
idiosyncratic aspects of the diverse history of modern Asia. But the similarities in
events, patterns, and consequences which such a gross comparison can also illustrate
may be equally instructive, and often overlooked. India's modern history and
China's, Japan's, and Southeast Asia's, are for good reasons commonly examined
separately by separate specialists. Many politically conscious Asians of the colonial
or semi-colonial period, and most of the colonialists themselves, did not see Asia
that way but more nearly as a single system, for all its regional variety, on which
the overt and implicit force of the modern West as an alien system was attempting
to impinge.

Such an image of the colonial period can especially clearly be seen through
the essentially uniform character and at least intended roles which were shared by
all of the many port cities established or controlled by Westerners in every Asian
area or country which touched the sea. The setting, the local circumstances, the

Reprinted by permission from "Traditionalism and Colonialism: Changing Urban Roles
in Asia" by Rhoads Murphey, *Journal of Asian Studies*, 29 (1969), pp. 67–84. Copyright ©
1969 by the Association for Asian Studies, Inc.

physical appearance, the institutions, the iconography, and the ambitions of colonial Calcutta and Batavia were widely duplicated in two or three score foreign-dominated ports like them throughout coastal South and East Asia. A Westerner could feel, to some degree, at home in any of these cities, and could also feel that only a few superficial aspects changed as he moved from one to another of them, across national or colonial boundaries and from one major Asian culture area to another fundamentally different one. Each of the ports symbolized and articulated the supreme self-satisfaction and confidence of the Victorian West. It was the same set of foreigners in each successive period, occasionally the same individuals, who helped to plant these cities, to dominate their commercial life, and to shape their ambitions. The Western dream—the grand colonial design—was essentially uniform from one part of Asia to another, as were its immediate instruments, the colonial ports.[1] If the results were far from uniform, that should have something to tell us about Asian regional differences, as the uniformity of design and ambition should tell us something about the nature of Western imperialism.

Traditional Asia,[2] before the eighteenth century, was composed primarily of inward-facing states and empires. The great cities, and indeed nearly all of the important urban centers, were inland, related to internal rather than external concerns. Without exception in any of the traditional states, the largest city was the political capital. These capitals were intended as cosmic creations, substantive and symbolic pinnacles of and resplendent thrones for the Great Tradition, enshriners as well as administrators of a relatively homogeneous and particularistic culture, to which the market towns and the peasant villages of the Little Tradition also belonged.[3] Their planned, monumental urban forms reaffirmed their role as the head pieces of unitary civilizations centered on their own cultural worlds. They were predominantly political and cultural rather than economic phenomena, functioning as microcosms of the national polity, symbols of authority, legitimacy, and power, creators and molders of literate culture, and seats of the dominant ideology. Commercial functions, both in the capitals and in the other traditional Asian cities, were for the most part secondary, and were in any case under varying degrees of control or manipulation by the state, whose chief monument was the city itself.

Except for insular Japan (where productive and, hence, populous level land hugs the sea) and parts of insular Southeast Asia, traditional Asian cities as a whole were sited inland where they could best administer and control the territory of the state or best ensure its defense against incursion across what was regarded as the chief exposed frontier. Ch'ang An, Peking, and Delhi are classic examples of the latter, Loyang, Nanking, Pataliputra, Ava, Ayuthia, Ankor, Polonnaruwa, and Jogjakarta of the former. It is worth noting, however, that even in insular Ceylon and Java, as in thalassic Burma and Siam with their long seacoasts where the main centers of population were close to the sea, the political capitals and most of the other important cities remained consistently inland until the European colonial period. In Japan as well, for all its striking apparent maritime configuration, the capital was not shifted from inland Kyoto to coastal Edo (Tokyo) until 1869. Traditional Asian cities were both sited and planned so as to ensure an appropriate symbolization of legitimate authority. In China without exception, and periodically in India, cities were walled (indeed the common Chinese word for *city* meant and still means *wall*), not primarily for protection (the Chinese city's military role was not its own defense but the defense of its entire administrative area[4]), but as a mark of imperial or administrative sanction. City morphology was in turn shaped by the great gates, one at each of the four cardinal points of the compass, from which major avenues led to a center where some piece of monumental building—a temple, a drum tower, an array of government offices or troop barracks—further reinforced the symbol of authority.

Commerce and manufacturing there certainly were, but although their absolute amounts were large, their relative importance rarely rivaled that of administration and other noneconomic enterprises as the chief urban function, including the administration of trade. In China, for example, the major center of external trade, Canton, was nevertheless far more involved with administrative functions on behalf of the province as a whole, while foreign trade itself was a state monopoly and hence, most important merchants were also necessarily officials. The relatively few urban centers in the traditional system which one may classify as industrial, for example Chingtechen, the site of the Imperial Potteries, were without exception of very minor rank in size. The pattern in India appears to have been less consistent over time, given India's troubled and fragmented political history, but in general there too the hand of the state (local or national) seems to have been strong and nearly all cities are described by the early Europeans of the seventeenth century as ceremonial and administrative phenomena in which merchants and artisans also happened for convenience to carry on their activities.[5] In Japan, where cities were not walled, and in Southeast Asia, where walling was at best inconsistent, the traditional city, nevertheless, functioned primarily as an administrative, ceremonial, cosmic, symbolic center rather than as a base for trade or manufacturing.[6]

Cities of this sort contrast forcibly with the urban type which has been dominant in the West for most of the past two or three millennia. At the beginning of the Western tradition, the cities of classical Greece were sea-oriented and trade-centered, as were the city colonies which the Greeks founded elsewhere on the shores of the Mediterranean. Even Rome, although it became the capital of a huge empire and thus came to play both a real and a symbolic role as a center of authority and administration, was at best a hybrid in that trade remained one of its most important functions through its maritime link with the port of Ostia and its incorporation of the commerce-centered Greek Mediterranean. But even in medieval Europe the greatest cities were not the cathedral towns or the seats of royal power but the centers of trade—Venice, Genoa, Florence, Hamburg, Bruges—and London and Paris as commercial foci rather than as political capitals. The distinction has been preserved to the present in the case of London, where the "City," until the eighteenth century a geographically separate entity, is at least symbolically still set off from the seat of political authority at Westminster. With the Age of the Discoveries, the accelerated revival of trade, and the coming of technological revolutions in agriculture, transport, and manufacturing, the Western city became and remains predominantly an economic phenomenon and with overwhelmingly economic functions.[7]

Although most of the traditional Asian states did conduct some trade by sea, this was with few exceptions a minor note in a series of largely self-contained systems. Where oceanic ports existed, they were by comparison small, and, in the traditional perspective, remote, on the fringes of the ecumene, minor dots on the periphery of a greater whole whose life centered elsewhere. But with the coming of colonialism, what was clearly a Western kind of city was in effect imported by the expanding Europeans as they constructed trade bases on the maritime fringes of the Asian empires. There is indeed some irony in the ultimate confrontation between sea-oriented West and land-oriented East, a confrontation for which the Europeans were far better prepared than the Asians. European mastery of the sea, in both commercial and naval terms, gave them the advantage they needed to establish themselves on the coasts of Asia, on sites hitherto little valued by Asians, and in time to transform these settlements into the port cities which by the end of the nineteenth century had reoriented the entire domestic system of each country. The port cities founded or largely developed by Westerners became the nuclei of a modernizing Asia, as well as its gates to the modern world; through them came nearly all of the influences and elements which have shaped Asia in the last two or three centuries. In present terms, virtually all of the largest coastal or near-coastal cities in Asia owe the bulk of their growth, most of their essential nature, and in many cases even their origin to Western traders since the seventeenth century. European attention to the maritime fringes of each country was rewarded by the discovery of plentiful opportunities for a commercially minded and vigorously expanding West to establish trade centers on its own models, responding to situational advantages for trade which until then had been largely neglected. It was the seaman and the merchant (usually in the same person) who sought out, from the deck of a ship, the most promising places for the establishment of settlements best calculated to serve the interests of external trade. Those of them which eventually supported the dominant port cities combined maximum access to and from the sea for deep-draft carriers with maximum internal access to and from those parts of each country which were actually or potentially (with the help of Western capital and management) productive of goods for export. This was urban development from the point of view of the commercial entrepreneur, in sharp contrast to the urban patterns of the Great Asian Traditions.

By the end of the period of colonial control,[8] the "Age of daGama" as the Indian historian K. M. Panikkar has labeled it,[9] the overwhelmingly largest city in each country (with the qualified exception of Japan) was a Western-founded or largely Western-developed port.[10] Japan is a qualified exception in the sense that Tokyo became, after it was made the national capital in 1869, a major port whose boom development, albeit in Japanese hands, resulted more than anything else from Japan's new economic and institutional integration with the West; in effect, the Japanese acted as their own Westernizers, and Tokyo (with Yokohama as its adjunct, a city which, like Kobe, started life as a treaty port) became a more uncompromisingly Western city than any in Asia. Bangkok, it is true, became the Thai capital, by historical coincidence, on the eve of the major nineteenth century Western drive in Asia, but its growth from small and inauspicious beginnings in 1782 as a refuge for the defeated court on the deltaic fringe of the country to its modern primacy as the nerve center of Thailand took place under Western dominance and was fueled primarily by Western entrepreneurial efforts to stimulate external trade. The same historical pattern fits the growth of Rangoon, although there the Western hand was, of course, far stronger.[11] These new port cities were not only far larger than the traditional capitals; they had preempted their functions as new national centers, institutionally and ideologically as well as economically. The mechanized transport nets which spread within each country after about 1850, almost entirely as a result of Western enterprise, focused on the port cities and further cemented their primacy while completing the abrupt about-face of each national order, toward the gates of sea and land.

In the larger countries such as India and Indonesia, port cities founded *de novo* by Westerners occupied the first several places in the urban size hierarchy. In India, Calcutta, Bombay, and Madras remained, in that order, the big three until after independence, as they had been since at least 1850, despite the shift of the colonial capital from Calcutta to Delhi in 1911 in an effort to legitimize the British imperium. The Indonesian hierarchy at independence was led, in order, by Batavia (now Djakarta), Surabaja, and Semarang.[12] All of these Indian and Indonesian port cities had arisen on sites either empty until the planting of the first Western fort, or occupied by insignificant villages. In the smaller countries, the one major city which dominated the urban hierarchy in multiple primacy was the Western-colonial port: Colombo, Rangoon, Bangkok, Singapore, Cholon–Saigon, Hanoi–Haiphong, and Manila. The position of these cities as ports was even stronger. Over 90 percent of India's foreign trade in the 1930's passed through Calcutta, Bombay, Karachi, and Madras, in that order,[13] none of them in existence before the seventeenth century and all developed with the impetus provided by Western entrepreneurs. A similar proportion of China's foreign trade in the same period passed through the foreign-dominated treaty-ports of Shanghai, Tientsin, Dairen, Hankow, and Hong Kong-Canton.[14] In the smaller countries, foreign trade was to the same or to a greater degree concentrated in one port which owed most of its development to Western initiative.[15]

The coming of independence has brought a predictable paradox: In most of these countries, there has been little rational alternative to adopting as the national capital an originally alien city. The national life had come to center on the Western-developed ports to an irreversible degree, quite apart from their simple primacy. All lines of internal communication focused on them, and in nonmaterial terms they had also become the leading bases of Asian nationalism and intellectual renaissance.[16] As each Asian country had responded to Western stimuli and altered its own outlook, its world had been refocused on its seaward gates, originally the funnels for export and the vestibules for Western manipulators, but ultimately also the breeding grounds and the apexes of a new Asia. Westerners were only a tiny minority in all of these cities; they were numerically dominated by Asians, but in a cosmopolitan mixture which included large numbers of people attracted by the expanding economic opportunity in the ports from distant provinces or other countries: Gujeratis and Marwaris in Calcutta, Tamils in Colombo, Chinese in all the Southeast Asian port cities (not only in Singapore and Bangkok, where Chinese were a majority of the total population), Indians in Rangoon, Cantonese and Szechuanese in Shanghai, as well as the variety of European nationalities and entrepreneurial groups such as Armenians and Parsees who operated in almost all of the ports.[17]

The cosmopolitan or hybrid nature of these cities called attention to the new role which they played, as the meeting grounds for the long-delayed confrontation between Asia and the West through the medium primarily of maritime trade, and as the new foci for the development of national unity in each country. They were also the seats of colonial or semi-colonial bureaucracies, concerned both with political/financial administration and with the management of new commercial and industrial enterprises. The bureaucracies were staffed by Asians as well as by Europeans; they represented an important vehicle of Westernization, and a school of Asian nationalism. Although the number of Asians employed in the Indian Civil Service, the Chinese Maritime Customs Service, or their equivalents elsewhere was never very large, many were involved in lower-status posts associated with these organizations, and the model which they offered of integration and organization was important. In wider terms, the colonial cities represented or had themselves created most of the new economic opportunity in each country, and their mushrooming populations were a clear reflection of this fact. Only in the two great continental empires, India and China, was the capital retained in the traditional inland seat, but in both cases the largest cities and the primary centers of modernization remained the originally colonial or semi-colonial ports—Calcutta, Bombay, Shanghai.[18] The urban pattern inherited from colonialism has not been significantly altered, nor does it seem likely to be while Asia remains intent on modernization and the consequent emphasis on relations with the rest of the world, through the gates of its coastal cities.

The evolution of the final pattern was, however, spread over a long period. It is too easily forgotten that for nearly three centuries after daGama's voyage to Calicut in 1498, Westerners remained confined in most of Asia to precarious and tiny footholds on the oceanic margins. The period of relative Western insignificance in Asia, from 1498 to the end of the eighteenth century in broad terms, lasted a good deal longer than the period of Western dominance, which came to an effective end in 1941, or at the latest in the 1950's. Europe in the sixteenth, seventeenth, and eighteenth centuries was not the Europe of the nineteenth, nor was the relative ineffectiveness of the Asian orders after about 1750 a reasonable guide to their ability to keep the Europeans at arms' length in the earlier period. To begin with, Western traders attempted to establish their warehouses, in the form of the late medieval "factory," in or beside the small existing Asian trade centers on the coast, on the fringes of a system still dominated by indigenous entrepreneurs and political powers. There they competed not only with local traders in each place and with one another but with the Arab, Malay, Chinese, Gujerati, and other Asian groups who had for centuries manipulated maritime commerce among the countries of Asia, a competition in which the Europeans were by no means completely successful even into the nineteenth century. The innovation which they represented was the beginning of direct trade by sea with the West.

Before the end of the sixteenth century, it became apparent that Western traders represented a new kind of power. Although their ships were at the beginning of the confrontation little if any more efficient as traditional trade carriers than those with which they competed, they were significantly better armed, with guns specifically adapted for use at sea; they progressively reduced the Asian naval fleets to impotence while at the same time enjoying greater security against the perennial problem of piracy. With the experience of the long sea route around Africa, their ships also became better long-distance carriers than any Asian ships, adjusted to a different set of conditions. They were faster on long hauls, increasingly larger, and better provided with the growing set of navigational aids whose development had been accelerated especially in fifteenth-century Portugal.[19] In these respects there was already presaged the ultimate overwhelming of Asia by superior Western

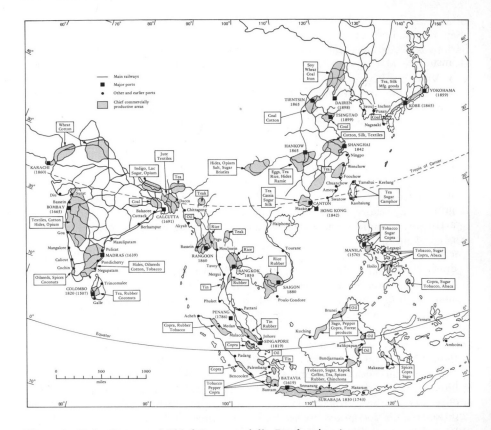

Figure 1. Major Ports and Chief Commercially Productive Areas
in East Asia 1600–1940

Names in capitals are the major ports. Those in lower case are the most important of the
lesser ports, most of them in existence before the arrival of the Europeans, some early
European trading bases, but all eclipsed in the course of the nineteenth and twentieth centuries
by the rise of the dominant ports. Dates for the major ports indicate the beginning of
significant development under foreign influence or control; dates in parentheses show the year
of actual founding where this was wholly or partially a foreign initiative. Note the wide and
more or less even dispersal of the smaller (and generally earlier) ports, and the locational
advantages suggested by the map for each of those shown in capitals, which dominated the
trade of each area by the end of the nineteenth century.

Singapore, as a strategically located island free port, handled a large share of the trade of
what is now Indonesia plus North Borneo-Sarawak, as Raffles intended that it should, and also
of later-developed Malaya. In the twentieth century, Singapore has been consistently the fifth
or sixth largest port in the world in shipping tonnage handled.

Canton is left here without a date, since it was a major port for many centuries before
the Europeans arrived; unlike Shanghai, Tientsin, and Hankow, which had also been important
ports traditionally, Canton's size and functions were not fundamentally altered by the European impact.

Rivers shown are only those on which power-driven vessels carried a significant volume
of traffic.

An effort is made to indicate the most important goods produced in each shaded area for
export over the period covered (i.e., not all of them were produced simultaneously), but not to

technology. But the full force of that superiority was neither real nor apparent until the nineteenth century. Until then, Europeans were, as indicated, limited for the most part to isolated spots on the Asian coasts, and it was only with the age of steamships, railways, plantations, mines, and the Suez Canal that a few of these early trading factories were transformed into national funnels for the growing stream of goods exported to industrializing Europe and into service centers for the new commercial areas which fed them. Thus, it was only with the deterioration or collapse of the traditional orders and the penetration of Western commercial enterprise inland that these cities could become the *points d'appui* between the whole of Asia and the West, the "head links," as O. H. K. Spate has called them,[20] between a booming, aggressive West and an Asia increasingly caught up in a world economy and finally bent on its own modernization. Three centuries of trial and error, and of slowly increasing Western effectiveness to match the corresponding progressive decrease in Asian effectiveness, lie between daGama and the emergence of a triumphant Europe as the molder of modern Asia, through the medium of a score or so of great port cities developed by Westerners. In terms of both size and function, but in order from west to east, these include Karachi, Bombay, Colombo, Madras, Calcutta, Rangoon, Bangkok, Singapore, Saigon, Batavia, Manila, Hong Kong, Shanghai, Dairen, Kobe, and Yokohama. Canton, Tientsin, and Hankow became similar centers under Western stimulation and domination, but had existed as major port cities earlier—the China case is a special one and is discussed below. The development of Seoul-Inchon, Pusan, Taipei-Keelung, and Kaohsiung [see Figure 1] as the same kind of phenomena was, of course, the result of Japanese colonialism.

In the simplest terms, what happened was the same process of concentration as has taken place everywhere else where the transport and commercial revolutions have spread. The literally hundreds of tiny ports which shared the fragmented traditional trade of Asia and the early period of Asia's direct trade with the West were increasingly overshadowed and in the end virtually extinguished by the mushroom growth of a few giants. It would be tedious to name and locate all of these earlier maritime centers of inter-Asian and East–West trade,[21] but the most important of them are shown on the map. The map's principal purpose, however, is to show how commercialized Asia, as it had developed by the high tide of colonialism in the first half of the present century, was related to the great ports, each of which was situated so as best to serve what had by then become the major areas productive of export goods and the major markets for foreign imports. The key to their success was not, of course, merely physical nearness, but as with the growth of cities elsewhere, access. Until the nineteenth century, access from the sea was more or less equally possible at a great variety of small ports, each with its own restricted hinterland to landward, although some of them, especially in the East Indian archipelago (notably Acheh, Malacca, Makassar, Bantam) also served a wider "foreland" by sea, as entrepots. With the nineteenth century increase in the size of

---

suggest the importance of those and other areas as markets for imported goods, to which the best and simplest single guide is probably a population map. Production for local consumption is not considered here. It is of course extremely difficult to select and show appropriately on this basis both the chief commercially productive areas and the most important commodities. The solution adopted here is necessarily gross and arbitrary, but is based on detailed analysis of trade figures and on more general economic history for each country and for each major port.

ships, and particularly with the coming of steel and steam, the great majority of these earlier ports were no longer physically adequate, nor could they provide cargoes or markets for imports on a level to take full advantage of the economies of scale which larger ship capacities made possible. At the same time, the rapidly rising production of goods for export became in the course of the nineteenth century increasingly concentrated in certain areas, a process which was related to accessibility, measured in terms of transport costs. Plantations, mines, and other forms of Western investment in the production process were naturally developed first and most extensively in the areas from which goods could economically be brought out for export by sea, via the port which could handle contemporary ocean shipping. Where exploitable minerals or physically favorable areas for the growing of export crops existed far from the sea—for example, oil in central Burma, tea land in Assam, or cotton land on the Bombay Deccan—railway or mechanized river transport connections were provided, all focused on the one port best situated to serve as the outlet for exports and to provide commercial services, including imports, to the most rapidly expanding economic areas.

With a few exceptions, however, these ports had wretched harbors and prospered despite physical sites which are still notably deficient. Only Bombay, Singapore, Manila, Hong Kong, and Dairen (Tsingtao might be added as a lesser and later case, plus Kobe and Yokohama in their rather different context), blessed with excellent natural harbors, escaped this handicap, although they substituted other problems for it, including the relative difficulty of landward access in several areas. Calcutta probably still deserves the title of the world's worst harbor among major world ports,[22] but it has many close rivals among the originally colonial or semi-colonial port cities of Asia. A great many of them were deltaic—Karachi, Calcutta, Rangoon, Bangkok, Saigon, Canton, Shanghai, Tientsin (and to a lesser degree, Madras, Colombo, and Batavia)—and presented formidable problems both for sailing vessels and for the increasingly larger steamships.[23]

Another set of problems common to a great many of the colonial port cities in East Asia was associated with the disadvantages of most of their local sites. Extollers of the benefits of the Western presence in the East, and of the model which European action presented to "backward" Asia (Shanghai, for example, was known to its Western residents as "the Model Settlement"), were particularly fond of pointing to the cities which had arisen under Western management along the swampy foreshores of tidal rivers or on rocky or jungly coasts, previously little more than "haunts of coot and tern," which now supported flourishing metropolises, the very embodiment of progress, Western style. But despite the filling of swampy ground and the bunding (embanking) of the streams, flooding has remained chronic at all of the deltaic sites, ground water levels are high, drainage difficult to manage, and building an awkward and expensive problem. Western health has also suffered, although overindulgence in food and drink, in the high-living atmosphere of the colonial ports, was probably also a factor and can to a degree be documented from mess records, memoirs, and import figures. Calcutta acquired a notorious reputation for morbidity, especially in the early days when the mortality rate among Europeans was indeed shockingly high,[24] but it was little if any worse than most of the other ports. C. N. Parkinson estimates,[25] on a variety of evidence, that probably less than 25 percent of those who went out from

England to the East India Company's stations in India, Ceylon, Southeast Asia, and China between 1765 and 1820 survived to return—and it was consistently their aim to return as quickly as possible after "shaking the pagoda tree"—i.e., making a fast fortune. The French and Dutch records were little better. No doubt it was in part this situation which helped to explain the attitude which Adam Smith found hard to accept on the part of East India Company servants:

> It is a very singular government in which every member of the administration wishes to get out of the country . . . as soon as he can, and to whose interest, the day after he has left it and carried his whole fortune with him, it is perfectly indifferent, though the whole country was swallowed up by an earthquake.[26]

Such attitudes were common to Western traders as well and were at least as prominent in semi-colonial China and East Asia as in India. Foreign Shanghai was probably more notorious in this respect than Calcutta. It may in some ways seem surprising that Europeans accomplished some change in Asia under these circumstances. But the commercial motives which primarily drove them led to activities with powerful catalytic effects, far beyond their own port settlements and despite the relatively brief Asian careers of most individuals. The planting of tiny islands of modern commercial development in the new ports on the fringes of each country eventually set in motion changes which have spread over East Asia like ripples covering a pond from the casting of a single stone. This happened, however, in the face of local site problems inevitably resulting from the choice of spots whose advantages for trade were accompanied by serious disadvantages for the physical welfare of traders:

> It has been observed that of all the European nations who have planted distant settlements, the English have invariably shewn the least regard for the proper selection of localities for the sites of their colonial cities; and this I think must in general be ascribed to the commercial spirit taking the lead . . . the embouchures of great rivers were the first objects of desire.[27]

This puts the point neatly, but is hardly fair in suggesting that the French or Dutch settlements were notably different. Low-lying Batavia, for example, with its creeks and artificial canals clogged with refuse and breeding disease and its vectors, was as ill-favored as Calcutta. The choice of Hong Kong a few years after the above was written was a fortuitous exception, as an elevated island off the delta of the West River where it combined both a magnificent natural harbor and a healthful (albeit somewhat cramped) site with excellent access to a major productive area. But Hong Kong was indeed exceptional, as was Bombay, although to a much lesser extent, and port cities on sites as favorable as Hong Kong's—Tsingtao and Dairen—were not developed until the twentieth century.

The great port cities in Asia, as elsewhere, arose where navigable water and productive land met and where internal lines of access were concentrated. The major river mouths were obvious places of this sort; in the island countries, strategically located coastal sites could develop similar access to the most productive areas by coastal shipping. As the map shows, the great majority of the commercially developed zones, especially in the insular and peninsular areas, were close to the sea, a pattern which reflects the concentration of Western investment where access was easiest and which goes far to explain the success of Southeast Asian tin and plantation production in competition with other tropical areas where transport costs were heavier. Given this sea-oriented pattern, Singapore could easily serve the whole of the tin and rubber belt along the west coast of Malaya, as Colombo could for the quite compact plantation area of Ceylon, Manila for the Philippines as a whole, and Batavia for Indonesia, where commercial production was heavily concentrated in Java and along the east coast of Sumatra. In wider terms, Singapore and Batavia especially stood at or near focal points on the major sea lanes, through the Straits of Malacca and Sunda, respectively, and thus served as entrepots for much larger areas. To a somewhat lesser degree, Colombo and Manila also profitted from location on longer-distance routes, Colombo on the main track to both Europe and Australia, and Manila lying conveniently on routes between China–Japan and both South and Southeast Asia.

Thalassic as these ports all were, connected with their commercial hinterlands and service areas largely by sea, they did not suffer from the local absence of navigable rivers. But they illustrate as clearly as do the deltaic or riverine ports the early dependence of Westerners in Asia on water defenses for their settlements. Whatever the nature of their sites in other respects, the colonial and semi-colonial Asian ports were so situated as to have water on two, three, or even four sides, if possible navigable, a pattern to which there are exceedingly few exceptions among the ports with which this essay deals. In several cases, existing waterways were deepened for this purpose, or artificial canals dug. Shanghai, where one such waterway was called "Defense Creek," and Batavia, with its network of canals, provide two prominent examples. The original objective of defense is a reminder of the foreigners' precarious position, until the latter part of the eighteenth century in India, considerably later in many parts of Southeast Asia, and in China really until the end of the period with which we are concerned here. But beyond its defensive function, the water which encircled these ports highlighted their alien nature and their external, maritime orientation. The presence of ships was a symbol not merely of the nature and function of these cities, as "head-link" windows on a world across the sea, but of the particular capabilities which made the Western position in Asia possible. As George Balfour, the first British consul at the water-surrounded foreign settlement of Shanghai, put it in 1843: "By our ships our power can be seen, and if necessary felt."[28] In China, foreign naval forces, conspicuously displayed in the treaty-ports, continued to be used for the protection of foreign lives and property into the 1930's, but elsewhere in Asia as well it was indeed by their ships that the power of the Westerners could be seen, not merely in terms of force but as the symbol of the commercial and technical revolution which had made the West the arbiter and guide of so much of modern Asia's development.

These port cities had their great period of growth only as Western enterprise became free to develop mechanized transport routes internally and commercial production for export along them; imports and services flowed inland from the ports in return. The maintenance of internal order, which the colonial governments came to provide, was a further necessary condition. Karachi grew to major rank as a port only with the British-directed spread of irrigation in the Indus Valley and Punjab after 1860, the growing of wheat and cotton for export, and the provision of railway connections. Bombay's big growth, beginning only slightly earlier, was similarly dependent on railways to bring to it the greatly increased cotton produc-tion of Gujerat and the Deccan, the latter especially a commercially underdevel-oped area before the mid-nineteenth century.[29] Colombo's rise was a direct result of the boom growth of tea, coconut, and rubber production and its linking by rail to the port. The somewhat later growth of Rangoon and Bangkok as important ports awaited the equally massive development especially of deltaic rice production for export, from areas earlier neglected. Batavia and Singapore[30] became major centers only with the spread of the "culture system" in Java after 1830, the beginnings of large-scale plantation production (sugar, coffee, tea, rubber, chin-chona, kapok, tobacco, and other crops in Java and Sumatra, rubber in Malaya) and mining (oil and tin), and the development of steamship networks. The same pattern is clear, on slightly varying time scales and with differing commodities, in the growth of Madras (oil seeds, tobacco, sugar, tea, hides in South India), Calcutta (jute, indigo, lac, opium, sugar in the lower Ganges valley, tea in Assam), Saigon (rice and rubber in the delta), Manila (sugar, tobacco, copra, and abaca in Luzon, Cebu, Samar, and Mindanao), and Dairen (soy beans, wheat, coal, and iron in the Liao Valley). Kobe and Yokohama grew more in response to Japanese industrial-ization than to changes in primary production for export, but there is a reasonable parallel.

In China, however, no government during the semi-colonial period from 1842 to 1940 was able to establish adequate or consistent civil order; its absence was perhaps the critical factor in limiting or aborting the modern development of the Chinese economy. Foreigners were not permitted to own land or make investments in property outside the treaty-ports,[31] and their impact on the nature and volume of Chinese production as a whole was in part for this reason minimal. Chinese resistance to foreign pressures for railway building gave way after the first few main lines were completed by the first decade of the twentieth century to chronic civil war following the revolution of 1911. Traffic on both railways and waterways was continually and seriously disrupted up to the time of the Japanese invasion, and production suffered as well. China was exposed to the same West and through the same kinds of oceanic entrances as was the rest of Asia, but for a variety of reasons, the Chinese response was different, as was the Chinese content. The mere size of the country, plus continued Chinese obstruction and simple xenophobia, kept Western influence at a far lower level than elsewhere in Asia, and combined with Great Power rivalry to prevent any full-scale colonial control. The traditional Chinese economy and its entrepreneurs were also significantly more effective, especially in competition with Westerners, than was the case in any of the other Asian countries except for Japan; foreigners and their domestic allies, the "running dogs," found it impossible to sweep the commercial field, as to a greater extent they did in India and Southeast Asia. Most commercial goods continued to come from traditional domestic producers and to move by traditional means—junk, pack animal, human porter. Most marketing continued to take place through traditional centers, including the periodic market fairs whose honeycombed structure domi-nated the economic and social landscape of the great bulk of the country even into the 1940's.[32] China's urban world remained for the most part as it always had been, even in many of the larger cities to which a foreign concession had been attached. Nearly all Chinese cities remained walled, closed their gates at sundown, displayed the heads of executed criminals on poles, and preserved their traditional internal morphology and functions essentially unchanged. The China treaty-ports set up according to the treaties of 1842 and 1858–60 remained until the end tiny and isolated Western islands in an alien and resistant Chinese sea. The demonstration effect they represented was of paramount importance, but as compared with the record of the colonial ports elsewhere in Asia, it was more negative than positive, a goad which goes far toward explaining the ultimate bitter and total rejection by China of the treaty-port legacy even while the Communist government has pursued its own road to wealth and power through the modernization and industrialization of the Chinese economy.[33]

It is far from coincidental that all of the mainland China treaty-ports, with the late and unrepresentative exceptions of Tsingtao and Dairen[34]—there were perhaps twenty-five of major importance all told—were established not on new sites but purposely at existing major trade centers, places which had been important ports for centuries. In the absence of colonial control and of freedom to manipulate the production process outside the treaty-ports through investment, the foreigners had to be content with attempting to tap a commercial system already there, at nuclei which it had already developed. The foreign stimulus which was the primary cause of the spectacular post-1860 growth of Shanghai, Tientsin, and Hankow especially was accompanied by some deflection of traditional trade flows (helped by the expansion of steamship and railway lines), and certainly a significant increase in external trade. But the Chinese economy, and the urban and port hierarchy, were only partially altered, let alone transformed, as they so strikingly were in South and Southeast Asia. There was no marriage of East and West in China of the sort which did take place in colonial Asia, or in Japan, where Westernization and modernization spread in successive waves from the new port cities over each country and remade its economy and polity. The China treaty-ports remained by comparison, as the Communists have called them, excrescences on the fringes of a generally hostile system which in the end rejected them. In some ways, the foreigners' role in China suggests the even more limited role of the Portuguese during their period of Asian prominence in the sixteenth century. Both groups controlled only a few scattered outposts, waystations on the sea routes, and in the absence of any extensive territorial sovereignty, neither produced substantial changes in the economies of the areas with which they traded, as one more in a long succession of traders, manipulating but not transforming.[35]

Such a necessarily simplified and foreshortened analysis may not be entirely fair to Shanghai, for example, which under foreign domination became by far the largest Chinese city, having risen since 1842 from the position of a second-rank regional center, or to Hong Kong, a genuinely new and first-rank port city built by the foreigners and serving external trade. Indeed, it is difficult to exaggerate the ultimate importance of the treaty-port impact on the Chinese *mind*, or the role which the ports played, as secure havens and as working models of the modern West, in fostering institutional and ideological revolution as well as eventual political change. China's early industrialization was also overwhelmingly centered in the treaty-ports, as well as what modernization in other respects China achieved until 1949. But there is an obvious and sharp contrast between China and the rest of Asia—including Manchuria (see note 34 . . .)—in the degree to which the Western planting of new port cities was followed by the transformation of each city's hinterland, and the eventual reshaping of each country as a whole around the port cities as the new vital centers.

But all of the ports with which this essay deals were beachheads of an exogenous system, planted by Westerners in a variety of Asian contexts, peripheral but nevertheless revolutionary.[36] The similarities among them, including the objectives pursued by their Western builders, make an obvious pattern despite the differing quality and degree of results especially as between China and the rest of Asia. Even their physical appearance was similar, a jumble of hybrid architecture clustered around the waterfront and its bund, combining local and Western models and materials adapted to a warm, humid climate, although the style was carried also to Tientsin. It was not only in terms of size that these cities stood out; in nearly all of the countries they also had a semi-monopoly of extra-local trade, of machine manufacturing, of banking, insurance, and capital markets, of long-distance transport nuclei, of the beginnings of technical and university education, of a national press, intellectual ferment, and the stirrings or open manifestations of Asian nationalism. In all of this, and in the goals and attitudes which lay behind such developments, these cities were transplants of the new urban–commercial–industrial order which had arisen in Europe since the decline of the Middle Ages. It was a yeasty mixture which was set down on a series of oceanic doorsteps, and it is not surprising that its ramifications spread far beyond the original points of entry. The spread and effectiveness were greatest where colonial control made foreign investment in production, transport, and civil order easiest, but the port cities also drew to them and remolded a new group of Asians, committed to and involved in the process of modernization. A whole new set of national structures emerged as a result, outward-facing as they had never traditionally been, centered on the originally foreign ports which had started the process and which were connected to a supra-national external world of modernization and change at least as much as they were to the particular country whose periphery they occupied.

In each country, albeit to differing degrees, the new port cities set in train processes which resulted in the rearrangement of spatial patterns of settlement, movement, and resource use. This was accomplished, from the outside in, through the use of new, largely imported techniques which could manipulate factors of time and cost—mechanized transport, extraction, production, and communication—and management/organizational skills focused on the preservation of order and the furthering of commercial development. Outside China, the foreigners sought very early to establish their own factories and settlements independent of traditional ports and local authority—this was the reason for the foundation of Batavia, Madras, Calcutta, and Bombay, for example—and by whatever means they could to attract trade and production to them. Early factory records, both English and Dutch, are full of references to the importance of inducing Asian craftsmen and merchants to settle in the new European bases. At Bombay, for example, the East India Company's agents were urged "to use all just means possible to invite and encourage weavers of all sorts to inhabit on the island."[37] Nearly a century later they were still being assured that " . . . by the exercise of a mild good government people from other parts may be induced to come and reside under our protection. Let there be entire justice to all persons without distinction, and open trade to all."[38] In the end, Bombay, like all other colonial ports, created or remade its own hinterland, and ensured that trade would flow to the port which had so largely brought it into being.

The influence of these developments on Asian welfare has long been debated, and it is understandable that many Asians have seen them as a drain of Asian wealth to Western profit.[39] The port cities discussed here were clearly enough funnels through which primary production and treasure were drained out to the West and manufactured goods were brought in, to the frequent detriment of domestic producers. Increases in commercial crops were usually accompanied by at least relative decreases in food crops, and in several cases (Bengal, Ceylon, Malaya, the Philippines) by rising food deficits and a precariously balanced economy overly dependent on Western prices for two or three primary products as exports. The colonial ports were not merely part of this pattern; in a basic sense, they had created it. But in so doing, they also acted as both the spearheads and the catalysts of Asia's modernization. The demonstration and backwash effects from even their crassest commercial manipulations, and still more from the investments in production, transport, and administration which flowed from them, generated the changes which are still remaking the whole of Asia. The colonial ports have rightly been reclaimed by an awakened Asian nationalism, but only after they had first brought Asia into the wider modern world.

NOTES

1. Such an analysis, of course, glosses over basic differences in the Western impact from one period to another, and in any one period between its different components. But in every Asian country touched by the West, missionaries, traders, and consuls/administrators played similar roles at similar times.

2. Throughout this essay "Asia" refers to the area between the Khyber Pass and Hokkaido and from Indonesia to the present Afghan and Soviet borders.

3. For an excellent discussion of the traditional Chinese city as a cosmic creation and of the extent to which it represented and served a homogeneous culture largely lacking the urban–rural dichotomy more familiar in the Western experience, see F. W. Mote, "The Transformation of Nanking, 1350–1400," forthcoming as part of a volume on the pre-modern Chinese city edited by G. W. Skinner and J. W. Lewis, to be published by Stanford University Press in 1970.

4. See S. D. Chang, "Some Aspects of the Urban Geography of the Chinese Hsien Capital," *Annals American Geographers*, II (1961), 23–45.

5. Travellers' descriptions of seventeenth-century India are numerous. Two convenient collections may be cited here: J. N. das Gupta, ed., *India in the Seventeenth Century*, (Calcutta: 1916); and Wm. Foster, ed., *Early Travels in India*, (London: 1921).

6. See, for example, J. W. Hall, "The Traditional Japanese City," forthcoming as part of a volume on the pre-modern Chinese city edited by G. W. Skinner and J. W. Lewis, to be published by Stanford University Press in 1970, and "The Castle Town and Japan's Modern Urbanization," *Far Eastern Quarterly*, XIV (1955), 37–56; Paul Wheatley, "What the Greatness of the City is Said to Be," *Pacific Viewpoint*, IV (1963), 163–88; T. G. McGee, *The Southeast Asian City*, (London: 1967).

7. For an essay contrasting urban roles in western Europe and traditional China, see R. Murphey, "The City as a Centre of Change: Western Europe and China," *Annals of the Association of American Geographers*, XLIV (1954), 349–62.

8. Only Japan remained fully independent, although even there extraterritoriality and other special rights for Westerners stemming from a set of "unequal treaties" as in China,

especially in the treaty-ports of Kanagawa–Yokohama, Shimoda, Hakodate, Nagasaki, Niigata, and Kobe (Hyogo), remained in force from the 1850's to 1899; Japanese tariff autonomy was not regained until 1911. A more thoroughgoing and long-lasting semi-colonial system was imposed on China and Thailand.

9. *Asia and Western Dominance,* (London: 1953).

10. Population statistics available for the countries and cities in question, now or at the time of independence, are of widely varying reliability and usability. In most cases, urban population figures are also ambiguous in terms of the extent of the conurbation they include, and are seldom reliably comparable within any one country or between different census periods. A variety of population totals can readily be obtained, from different and often conflicting sources, for all of the cities considered here, but in very few cases can they be used with confidence except as indicating a general order of magnitude. For this reason, I have not attempted to list exact populations for any of these cities at any period, but their ranking within each country, including the period 1870–1940, is perfectly clear.

11. For more detail on Bangkok, see D. G. E. Hall, *A History of Southeast Asia,* (London: 1955), pp. 389–402; for Rangoon, see B. R. Pearn, *A History of Rangoon,* (Rangoon: 1939).

12. Census figures are available for India from 1872, and although there are numerous and continued ambiguities and inconsistencies in the urban count, the ranking is unmistakable. For Indonesia there is much less statistical material, but the census of 1930 shows a marked pattern of urban concentration which is at least generally valid.

13. The *Statistical Abstract of India,* an annual publication, lists total trade values and shipping tonnages for all important ports from 1909; earlier all-India figures refer only to states or presidencies and do not distinguish individual ports, although they do suggest a closely similar pattern. See also footnote 15.

14. Hong Kong and Canton are best regarded for trade statistical purposes as a single unit. The *Annual Returns of Trade* published each year from 1864 for all of the "open" ports by the foreign-administered Maritime Customs Service until its dissolution include figures for the total value of trade at each port and for the country as a whole, plus tonnages of shipping entered and cleared, by ports and in grand total. See also footnote 15.

15. It is even more difficult in Asia than in most of the rest of the world to obtain accurate, meaningful, or comparable figures showing the volume of trade through the various ports, especially before about 1950. The only widely (though by no means uniformly) available data, generally between about 1880 and 1938, are those listing gross registered tons of shipping entered and cleared (sometimes, especially in earlier years, only the total number of ships). This does not, of course, have any necessary relationship to actual cargo passing in or out, and in any case tends misleadingly to exaggerate the importance of ports of call, for example, Colombo, where a great deal of the shipping using the port was in fact carrying cargo to and from elsewhere and might do minimal loading or unloading. For this reason, no attempt is made here to show any but the most general ranking, where the data permit, or to measure the quantitative importance of the ports.

16. Two recent studies have made this especially clear in the Indian case: J. H. Broomfield, *Elite Conflict in a Plural Society: Twentieth Century Bengal,* (Berkeley: 1968); and Anil Seal, *The Emergence of Indian Nationalism: Competition and Collaboration in the Later Nineteenth Century,* (New York: 1968). The China experience and context were different, but there too the treaty ports acted as both goad and model for the development of Chinese nationalism. This is effectively portrayed in J. R. Levenson's magistral work *Confucian China and its Modern Fate,* 3 vols., (Berkeley: 1958–65), but see also Lloyd Eastman, "Political Reformism in China Before the Sino-Japanese War," *Journal of Asian Studies,* XXVII (1968), 695–710, and Chien Po-tsan et al., eds., *Wu-hsu pien-fa* (The reform movement of 1898), 4 vols., (Shanghai: 1957), especially Vol. IV.

17. The mixing in these cities of people and cultures previously isolated from each other, and their growth largely as a result of in-migration in response to new economic opportunity and greater physical security, contributed to their closely similar character in every Asian country. For a study of a typical and early-developed example, see N. K. Bose, "Calcutta: A Premature Metropolis," *Scientific American,* CXIII (Sept. 1965), 91–102.

18. For a more detailed discussion of the capital issue, see R. Murphey, "New Capitals of Asia," *Economic Development and Cultural Change,* V (1957), 216–43, and references cited therein.

19. For two readable and reliable surveys of this period and its shipping, see C. M. Cipolla, *Guns and Sails in the Early Phase of European Expansion: 1400 to 1700* (London: 1965) and J. H. Parry, *The Age of Reconaissance,* (London: 1963); two summary studies are by C. R. Boxer: *Four Centuries of Portuguese Expansion,* (Johannesburg: 1961), and *The Dutch Seaborne Empire,* (London: 1965). C. N. Parkinson in his *Trade in The Eastern Seas* (Cambridge: 1937), deals with some of these matters as well as describing (pp. 320 ff.) the practice among Asian shipbuilders, especially along the west coast of India after the first Portuguese impact, of adopting a Western-looking rig in the hope of scaring off pirates; dummy gun ports were also often added.

20. "Factors in the Development of Capital Cities," *The Geographical Review,* XXXII (1942), 622–31.

21. Sources dealing with this period and with the great variety of smaller ports which were then important are numerous, and make fascinating reading. Two examples may be given here: Thomas Bowrey, *Countries Round the Bay of Bengal, 1669–1679,* ed. R. C. Temple, (Cambridge: 1905), and Alexander Hamilton, *A New Account of the East Indies* (first published London: 1727), ed. W. Foster, 2 vols., (London: 1930). Some of this material is summarized in (among a great number of other secondary sources) V. T. Harlow, *The Founding of the Second British Empire, 1763–93,* 2 vols., (London: 1952); Harlow in turn draws heavily on the account of Alexander Dalrymple, *A Plan for Extending the Commerce of this Kingdom and of the East India Company,* (London: 1769).

22. For an account of Calcutta's harbor problems during the colonial period, see R. Murphey, "The City in the Swamp: Aspects of the Site and Early Growth of Calcutta," *The Geographical Journal,* CXXX (1964), 241–56. P. B. Mitra, "The Port of Calcutta," *Calcutta Municipal Gazette,* L (Sept. 17, 1949), 494–96, provides a more recent but very brief survey. K. Bagchi, *The Ganges Delta,* (Calcutta: 1944), is a book-length study primarily of the geological and hydrographic aspects of the area. M. Logan, "The Port of Calcutta," PhD thesis, University of Chicago, 1949, is a useful economic study.

23. Coastal sites for cities had also been avoided in the past partly because of piracy, which was endemic in the Bay of Bengal, along most of the coasts of Malaysia and its adjacent areas, and along the south China coast. O. K. Nambiar, *Portuguese Pirates and Indian Seamen,* (Mysore: 1955), and Grace Fox, *British Admirals and Chinese Pirates,* (London: 1940), provide two accounts. In Ming and Ch'ing China the problem was severe enough during the height of Japanese pirate depredations that the government attempted to evacuate all settlements from the coastal zone—see Hsieh Kuochen, "Ch'ing-ch'u tung-nan yen-hai ch'ien" (The evacuation of the south-east coast in early Ch'ing), *Kuohsueh chi-k'an,* II (Dec. 1930), 797–826. On Japanese piracy in the Ming more generally, see Ch'en Mao-heng, "Ming-tai wo-k'ou k'ao-lueh" (Japanese pirate attacks during the Ming), *Yenching hsüeh-pao,* Monograph Series No. 6, (Peking: 1934).

24. I have given a summary account of this problem in "The City in the Swamp . . . ," *The Geographical Journal,* CXXX (1964), 241–56.

25. *Trade in the Eastern Seas,* (Cambridge: 1937), pp. 71–74.

26. *The Wealth of Nations,* (London: 1776), p. 605.

27. J. R. Martin, *Notes on the Medical Topography of Calcutta,* (Calcutta: 1837), printed in Appendix XVI of the *Census of India,* 1951, Vol. I, Part II, 37–53.

28. Quoted in George Lanning, *A History of Shanghai,* (Shanghai: 1923), p. 134.

29. Before about 1800 Bombay was, in fact, inconveniently isolated, easily defended as a chain of seven originally separate islands but cut off from the main streams of trade, although prominent as a center for ship-building and repair. The most detailed account of Bombay's early history is given in P. M. Malabari, *Bombay in the Making, 1661–1726,* (London: 1910); but see also S. M. Edwardes, *The Rise of Bombay,* (Bombay: 1902). On the development of the shipyards in the eighteenth century, see R. A. Wadia, *The Bombay Dockyards and the Wadia Master Builders,* (2nd ed., Bombay: 1957). S. Leacock and D. G. Mandelbaum, "A Nineteenth Century Development Project in India: The Cotton Improvement Program," *Economic Development and Cultural Change,* III,

(1955), 334–51, gives an account of the development of cotton production for export from the Deccan, Gujerat, and the Indus Valley.

30. The earlier trading city of Sinhapura—the "lion city"—from which Raffles, with his keen sense of history and his interest in the old sea-based empire of Majapahit, took the name, had ceased to exist long before 1819.

31. Later in the nineteenth century missionaries were permitted by treaty provision to negotiate long-term leases of land and to build mission stations, although even these activities were periodically contested locally—see Paul Cohen, *China and Christianity: The Missionary Movement and the Growth of Chinese Anti-Foreignism, 1860–1870*, (Cambridge, Mass.: 1963).

32. For a detailed study of this system, and its implications in helping both to describe and to explain how and why traditional China managed so successfully to resist Western-style commercialization and institutional change, see G. W. Skinner, "Marketing and Social Structural in Rural China," *Journal of Asian Studies*, XXIV (1964–65) 3–43, 195–228, and 369–99.

33. I develop the foregoing and following arguments in considerably greater detail in "The Treaty Ports and China's Modernization: What Went Wrong?" forthcoming as part of a volume on Chinese urbanization edited by G. W. Skinner and J. W. Lewis, to be published by Stanford University Press in 1970.

34. Dairen is especially unrepresentative, since it served the Manchurian economy, increasingly after 1905 a piece of outright colonial property, as China Proper never was, where Japanese investment in agriculture, mining, and railways was very great and where the entire economy was remade under Japanese colonial control. The Manchurian experience pointedly contrasts with that of the rest of China, and calls attention to the importance of effective territorial control and investment as a condition of economic development and modernization. Hong Kong has, of course, been since its establishment foreign territory, not part of China.

35. For assessments of the Portuguese impact, see G. Masselman, *The Cradle of Colonialism*, (New Haven: 1962), p. 220 ff.; M. A. P. Meilink-Roelofsz, *Asian Trade and European Influence in the Indonesian Archipelago*, (The Hague: 1962), pp. 134 ff., 178 ff.; and J. C. Van Leur, *Indonesian Trade and Society*, (The Hague: 1955), pp. 162 ff.

36. The pattern of interaction between center and periphery has common features in many historical settings; transformation of the center through changes initiated at the periphery, and often of alien origin, has, in fact, been widespread in many parts of the world. For a provocative discussion of this (among other matters), see E. R. Wolf, "Understanding Civilizations: A Review Article," *Comparative Studies in Society and History*, IX (1967), 446–65, and the several studies cited therein.

37. Letter dated Nov. 4, 1676, from the factors at Surat to those at Bombay, quoted in Holden Furber, *Bombay Presidency in the Mid-Eighteenth Century*, (London: 1965), p. 176.

38. Letter from the East India Company directors in London to the Company's Government in Bombay, dated March 15, 1748, quoted in S. M. Edwardes, *The Rise of Bombay*, (Bombay: 1902), p. 172.

39. For an interesting general discussion which includes a typology of colonial cities as "parasitic," see B. F. Hoselitz, "Generative and Parasitic Cities," *Economic Development and Cultural Change*, III (1954), 278–94. Colonial cities are considered in a somewhat different context, as being "heterogenetic" as opposed to "orthogenetic" by Robert Redfield and Milton Singer in "The Cultural Role of the Cities," *loc. cit.*, III (1954) 53–73, and are specifically contrasted with the "orthogenetic" capitals of the Great Traditions.

THE URBANIZATION OF THE GUARANÍ LANGUAGE

Paul L. Garvin and Madeline Mathiot

With Garvin and Mathiot we come to one of the more exotic titles on our list. Only two or three million people in the world speak Guaraní, but that includes practically the entire population of Paraguay. Paraguayans tend to be bilingual in Spanish and Guaraní, with Guaraní predominant in the rural areas and Spanish more important in the capital region of Asunción. Guaraní is gaining in Asunción as well. The question Garvin and Mathiot pose is simple and telling: As Guaraní gains in the metropolis and in the country as a whole, is the language undergoing changes in form and content which scholars have commonly noticed in the emergence of "standard languages" elsewhere? If it is, they suggest, then the linguistic shift is probably part of a larger movement from folk to urban culture in Paraguay. If it is, furthermore, it should be possible to gauge to what extent different segments of the population have moved into the urban culture by observing how close their version of Guaraní comes to the standard language. They conclude that the answer is "yes" right down the line: the Guaraní language is standardizing, that standardization is part of a larger urbanization of Guaraní culture, and the speaking of standard Guaraní is a good index of the overall urbanization of different segments of the population.

This little gem of an article is a rare find—a precise and pure use of a normative approach to urbanization. Hundreds of essays treat orientation to a common set of norms as the touchstone for the existence of a community, view orientation to "urban" norms as the distinction between cities and other kinds of communities, and consider urbanization as the diffusion of "urban" norms to new segments of the population. They are almost always vague about the criteria for those urban norms and the appropriate ways to trace their spread. This essay comes as a refreshing change, for it shows how that sort of reasoning can be applied to an important class of norms—linguistic norms—and suggests the possibility of carrying out similar analyses of dress, life style, and perhaps even patterns of social relations.

This paper is based on the assumption that Redfield's concepts of folk and urban[1] are applicable to language as well as culture. The linguistic equivalent of the distinction between folk cultures and urban cultures is the differentiation made by the scholars of the Linguistic Circle of Prague and others between folk speech and

Reprinted by permission from "The Urbanization of the Guaraní Language—A Problem in Language and Culture" by Paul L. Garvin and Madeline Mathiot in *Men and Cultures:*

the standard language,[2] which we here tentatively define as a codified form of a language, accepted by and serving as a model to, a larger speech community. The Prague School has formulated a set of criteria for differentiating a standard language from folk speech, the latter of which, conversely, is characterized by the absence of these criteria.

These criteria are such that they presuppose the existence of an urban culture in the speech community using, or aspiring to use, a standard language. Consequently, we may consider a standard language a major linguistic correlate of an urban culture, and we may furthermore consider the degree of language standardization in this technical sense a measure of the urbanization of the culture of the speakers.

Conversely, since folk speech has been defined negatively, a low degree of standardization or its absence, is here proposed as one possible diagnostic criterion of a near-folk or completely folk culture.

There are two possible scales of language standardization that can be applied here. In cross-cultural terms, different standard languages can be compared as to the degree to which they meet the formulated criteria, and one language can then be rated as more or less highly standardized than another, just as one culture can be called more urban or more folk than another. In intra-cultural terms, different segments of a speech community can be compared as to the degree to which the standard language has penetrated them, just as different subcultures of the same culture can be compared in terms of different degrees of penetration by urban elements.

This paper will be concerned with a concrete case of language standardization. The authors believe that by presenting some of the differential criteria for a standard language and applying them to their case, they can contribute to a further specification of the concept of urban, that is, non-folk culture.

We have chosen the recent ethnolinguistic development of Guaraní in Paraguay as our test case.

Two languages are spoken in Paraguay : Guaraní and Spanish. In rural areas, Guaraní is spoken almost exclusively. In the Asunción metropolitan area which includes a large percentage of the country's population, both Guaraní and Spanish are used. Traditionally, Spanish has been the official language and the language taught in the schools, but in recent years there has been a developing movement in the metropolitan area to give Guaraní equal status with Spanish, which Paraguayans call the Guaraní renascence. This movement exhibits certain significant parallels with the nationalistic movements of the post-Enlightenment period of Europe (late 18th and early 19th centuries) to put some of the "lesser" languages on a par with the "great" languages. Unlike much of the European development, however, the desire in Paraguay is not to eliminate the "great" language, Spanish, as a competitor, but to have Guaraní and Spanish coexist as equals.

In view of the parallelism referred to above, the criteria developed by the Prague School in discussing the formation of the modern Czech standard language

Selected Papers of the Fifth International Congress of Anthropological and Ethnological Sciences edited by Anthony F. C. Wallace (Philadelphia: University of Pennsylvania Press, 1956), pp. 783–790. Copyright © 1960 by the Trustees of the University of Pennsylvania. Footnotes renumbered. The conceptual framework of this paper has been the major responsibility of the senior author; the Guaraní data and their systematization have been the major responsibility of the junior author.

in competition with German, supplemented by some more recent thinking,[3] are considered by the authors to be applicable to the recent development of Guaraní in competition with Spanish, and we propose the hypothesis that there is now in the process of formation a Guaraní standard language as part of an emergent bilingual urban culture.

To formulate our hypothesis in detail, and to prepare the ground for a procedure for its verification, we shall set forth the criteria for a standard language, and relate them to Guaraní data to the extent allowed by preliminary research at a distance.

We are proposing three sets of differentiative criteria for a standard language: (1) the intrinsic properties of a standard language, (2) the functions of a standard language within the culture of the speech community, (3) the attitudes of the speech community towards the standard language.

PROPERTIES OF A STANDARD LANGUAGE

We shall here consider two differential properties of a standard language: flexible stability as originally stated by Vilém Mathesius,[4] and intellectualization as originally stated by Bohuslav Havránek.[5] Both of these properties are gradual and allow quantitative comparison.

Flexible Stability. This is by Mathesius discussed as an ideal property: a standard language, in order to function efficiently, must be stabilized by appropriate codification; it must at the same time be flexible enough in its codification to allow for modification in line with culture change.

There are two things involved in codification: (1) the construction of a codified norm, contained in formal grammars and dictionaries; (2) the enforcement of the norm by control over speech and writing habits through orthoepy and orthography. The construction of the norm is entrusted to a codifying agency or agencies, the enforcement of the norm is achieved through the schools.

The flexibility of the norm is achieved by including in the normative code the necessary apparatus for modification and expansion, which includes provisions both for a systematic expansion of the lexicon, and an equally systematic expansion of stylistic and syntactic possibilities. This is the responsibility of the codifying agency or agencies.

In the case of Guaraní, the codifying agency is the recently founded Academía de Cultura Guaraní. Urban Paraguayans look upon the Academy as the final authority in language matters, to whom the language problem has been entrusted. The Paraguayan government has recently recognized the status of the Academy and accorded it a subsidy. The Academy is at present engaged in the preparation of normative orthographic, grammatical and lexical materials preparatory to an expected and hoped-for introduction of the teaching of Guaraní in the schools.

In these efforts, the Academía de Cultura Guaraní is continuing a normative tradition established by the Jesuit fathers of the 16th century (in their work on Língua Geral), and resumed informally during the Chaco War, when a military terminology was evolved to allow the use of Guaraní for communications understood by Paraguayans only.

In terms of the requirement of flexible stability, the revival of the interest in the normalization of Guaraní has not yet led to the achievement of this objective.

But the conditions have been created for ultimately meeting this requirement, and there is a strong desire and expectation among Paraguayans to see it met.

Intellectualization. Havránek defines the intellectualization of a standard language as "its adaptation to the goal of making possible precise and rigorous, if necessary abstract, statements,"[6] in other words, a tendency towards increasingly more definite and accurate expression. This tendency "affects primarily the lexical, and in part the grammatical, structure."[7]

In the lexicon, intellectualization manifests itself by increased terminological precision achieved by the development of more clearly differentiated terms, as well as an increase in abstract and generic terms.

In grammar, intellectualization manifests itself by the development of word formation techniques and of syntactic devices allowing for the construction of elaborate, yet tightly knit, compound sentences, as well as the tendency to eliminate elliptic modes of expression by requiring complete constructions.

In essence, then, intellectualization consists in a tendency towards greater relational systematization and explicitness of statement. This is by Havránek summarized in a three-step scale of intellectualization, leading from simple intelligibility via definiteness to accuracy, to which correspond a conversational, workaday technical, and scientific functional dialects, respectively.[8]

Whereas folk speech is limited to the conversational and some phases of the workaday technical dialects, all three functional dialects are represented, at least as an ideal, in a standard language.

The degree of intellectualization of Guaraní remains to be tested. While there is a strong awareness on the part of our informants of the requirement of flexible stability, there is no comparable awareness of the requirement of intellectualization, beyond the expectation that Guaraní should develop into a language in which anything can be expressed adequately.

Our informants have made emphatic claims as to the precision and abundance of Guaraní terminology in certain limited areas. These claims will have to be checked. The work of the Guaraní Academy in reference to both terminology and syntax will have to be investigated and evaluated. No conclusions in this respect can be reached without a detailed linguistic analysis of Guaraní.

The entire question is thus still wide open.

FUNCTIONS OF A STANDARD LANGUAGE

We shall discuss three symbolic functions and one objective function of the standard language. The three symbolic functions are: (1) the unifying function, (2) the separatist function, (3) the prestige function; the objective function is (4) the frame-of-reference function.

Unifying Function. A standard language serves as a link between speakers of different dialects of the same language, and thus contributes to uniting them into a single speech community. A consequence of this is an identification of the individual speaker with the larger language community, in addition to or instead of, the smaller dialect community.

In the case of Guaraní, not enough is known about the dialect situation to evaluate whether the Asunción form of speech serves as an interdialectal lingua franca or not. In terms of the group identification under the unifying function the situation is, however, clearcut: Paraguayans think of themselves as speakers of Guaraní, and not as speakers of any of its dialects; they even go as far as to deny the existence of dialect differences within Paraguayan Guaraní.

Separatist Function. Whereas the unifying function opposes the standard language to the dialects, the separatist function opposes a standard language to other languages as a separate entity rather than a subdivision of a larger entity. It thus can serve as a powerful symbol of separate national identity, and the individual's identification with his language community is then no longer a matter of course but becomes highly emotionally charged.

This is the case with Paraguayans. Guaraní is what makes them into a distinct Paraguayan nation, rather than just another group of South Americans. To all of them, those who speak Guaraní are fellow Paraguayans, those who speak only Spanish—although they may live in Paraguay—are not; they are foreigners and they are called "gringos." Even Paraguayans who speak mainly Spanish at home will speak Guaraní to each other when they meet abroad because, as one of our informants put it, "nos acerca más de nuestra tierra."

The identification is with the language and not with Indian ancestry. Immigrants, in order to be accepted as Paraguayans, will learn Guaraní. As Justo Pastor Peníttez, a leading Paraguayan historian and writer, puts it: "La iniciación se realiza por el idioma guaraní, vehículo de la identificación nacional,"[9] because "hablar guaraní es ser dos veces paraguayo."[10] Thus the President of the Republic, in spite of his German name, is "paraguayo," because he speaks Guaraní.

Prestige Function. There is prestige attached to the possession of a standard language; one of the ways of achieving equality with an admired high-prestige nationality is to make one's own language "as good as theirs," which in our terms means bringing it closer to the ideal properties of a standard language.

Making of Guaraní a "lengua de cultura" like Spanish is one of the major motivations of the work of the Academía de Cultura Guaraní. Although the achievement of a Guaraní lengua de cultura is so far only an ideal, Paraguayans take great national pride in being the only American nation possessing a language all of their own that is capable of such a development, and they think of themselves as a model for the other South American nations in their quest for national individualization. "La misión histórica que el Paraguay está destinado a cumplir en América . . . ," says Benítez, "es de dar algo propiamente americano, un destello del alma del Nuevo Mundo."[11]

The prestige function has thus been transferred from the possession of a functioning standard language to the possession of a potential standard language. This transfer of the prestige function has become possible because the functioning standard languages of South America, Spanish and Portuguese, are shared by several national units and thus are not capable of carrying the separatist function and serving as a vehicle of nationalist symbolism.

Frame-of-Reference Function. The standard language serves as a frame of reference for speech usage in general by providing a codified norm that constitutes a yardstick for correctness. Individual speakers and groups of speakers are then judged by their fellows in terms of their observance of this yardstick.

The standard language furthermore serves as a frame of reference for the manifestation of the esthetic function in language,[12] which by the Prague School is defined as the property of speech forms to attract attention primarily to themselves rather than to the message they convey. The esthetic function so conceived appears not only in literature and poetry, but also in humor, advertising, and any conspicuous linguistic usage in general. In a standard language community, routine standard usage is the culturally expected, and deviations from this usage have esthetic function in the above sense, since their cultural unexpectedness attracts attention irrespective of content. Thus, the standard language is a frame of reference for the esthetic function.

In the case of Guaraní, the desirability of a frame of reference for correct speech is strongly felt, but the frame-of-reference function in this regard exists as yet only potentially.

The situation with regard to the esthetic frame-of-reference function is not clear-cut at all. On the one hand, Paraguayans claim that Guaraní is "marvelous for poetry and humor," which would indicate a strong occurrence of the esthetic function. On the other hand, whether this esthetic function manifests itself against the background of the incipient codified norm, against the background of informal folk usage, or even against the background of Spanish, is as yet an open question.

The only known factor in this problem is that present-day Guaraní poetry, of which there is a good deal, follows a European rather than a folkloric Indian esthetic canon as to its form, although the motifs are often aboriginal folkloric.

ATTITUDES TOWARDS A STANDARD LANGUAGE

The functions of a standard language discussed above give rise to a set of cultural attitudes towards the standard: the unifying and separatist functions lead to an attitude of language loyalty, the prestige function arouses an attitude of pride, and the frame-of-reference function brings about an attitude of awareness of the norm.

Language loyalty and pride are closely similar positive attitudes; we differentiate between them by assigning the intellectual and nationalistic attitudes to language loyalty, and the personal emotional attachments to pride.

Language Loyalty. This is the name given by Uriel Weinreich[13] to the desire of a speech community to retain its language and, if necessary, to defend it against foreign encroachment. Although language loyalty may be given to a form of folk speech, it becomes highly organized and articulate when it is given to a standard language, especially one that has not yet become sufficiently stabilized and generally recognized. Then language loyalty commonly manifests itself in attempts to justify the incipient standard language and to prove its worth.

This is dramatically true in Paraguay, as illustrated by Guillermo Tell Bertoni's comments quoted by Robustiano Vera in *La Defensa de la Lengua Guaraní*:[14] "La rica lengua del Paraguay puede disputar un puesto entre las lenguas cultas y dignas de un país civilizado." Guaraní is worthy of preservation and improvement because, as Justo Pastor Benítez says, "el guaraní tiene tradición viva," it expresses "toda la gama del alma de una raza que vivía en contacto íntimo con la naturaleza."[15] Robustiano Vera attempts to prove the worth of Guaraní by attributing a high-prestige ancestry to it: "Hay muchas voces guaraníes que no sólo son analógas, sino idénticas a sus similares egipcia, griega y sanscrita . . . gracias a la filología comparada . . . quizás hallemos una primitiva lengua hablada por nuestra especie en una edad ignota."[16] Eloy Farina Nuñez in *El Idioma Guarani*[17] sees the value of Guaraní in the understanding which its aboriginal character gives us of ancient cultures, including the Greek, and "un instrumento que, como el guaraní, en vez de alejarnos, nos aproxima mas de la intimidad de la cultura helénica, hasta ponernos en contacto con el misterio de sus mitos y el milagro de su sensibilidad poética, bien merece la atención de los estudiosos del Nuevo Mundo."

Guaraní is, however, not merely worthy of improvement but capable of it. In Moisés S. Bertoni's words, "es un sistema filológico mas único que raro, que posee en potencialidad miles de palabras jamás consignadas en ningún léxico, y probabilidades infinitas de formar cuantas se necesitan, aún para expresar lo que jamás se ha expresado, y siempre de una manera tan precisa y clara que todos han de comprender."[18]

Throughout our interviews with Paraguayans runs a current of appreciation and love for Guaraní. They love to speak Guaraní because, as one informant put it, "uno se siente mas dueño de sí mismo," or as another put it, "one has the feeling of having *said* something."

Guaraní finally plays an important part as an ingredient in Paraguayan patriotism. According to our informants, Paraguayan troops during the Chaco War, who would have reacted lethargically to Spanish commands, obeyed commands in Guaraní with enthusiasm and contempt for death.

Pride. As in the case of language loyalty, the possession of a form of folk speech as well as that of a standard language may be a source of pride for the speakers. Some positive attitude such as pride is a prerequisite for the desire to develop one's language into a standard. This attitude of pride will usually be focused on one or the other real or alleged property of the language. As with language loyalty, pride is often the more militant, the less recognized the status of one's language is by others.

There is no question but that the Paraguayans are proud of having Guaraní. We have already discussed the significance they attribute to it under the prestige function further above.

Only a very small segment of the population, the nouveaux riches of Asunción and some of the immigrants—so our informants tell us—show a contrary attitude: they look down on or are ashamed of Guaraní because it is an Indian language. But even in this group the negative attitude is not always permanent: one of our informants told us that his mother, a German immigrant, did not want him to learn this Indian language. Nevertheless, he could not help learning it, and his adult attitude is one of pleasure and pride in knowing it. It is, he says, not a mere dialect but a real language, and the more educated Paraguayans become, the more they appreciate Guaraní and make a conscious effort to improve their command of it.

What the Paraguayans appreciate most about Guaraní is that it is "la lengua del corazón." It is better suited, they say, for expressing emotions than Spanish—or, as one informant put it, than any other language he knows.

In Benitez' words, "son verdaderamente asombroses el número como del donaire de sus modismos; giros que hablan de una honda penetración; equivocos que se prestan a una sutil ironía; palabras que resumen todo un estado de alma; suaves y delicadas voces para el amor; expresiones de energía y afirmación como un grito de guerra . . . "[19] The flavor of Guaraní, they feel, is untranslatable—hence, even Paraguayan Spanish is studded with Guaraní loans.

Awareness of the Norm. This is an attitude more specifically limited to a standard language, since it is essentially a positive attitude towards codification. The codified norm is considered good and necessary.

In Guaraní, this attitude manifests itself primarily in a feeling for the desirability of a norm. Hence the high regard of literate Paraguayans for the work of the Academía de Cultura Guaraní which is expected to produce one.

The Paraguayan conception of a desirable norm for Guaraní is highly puristic. This purism is a correlate of their pride in Guaraní which we have discussed above. Many Paraguayans are bilingual and would like to speak both Spanish and Guaraní elegantly; they feel that mixing them, especially introducing unnecessary Spanish loans into Guaraní, is sloppy. We have already mentioned the conscious efforts to expand Guaraní vocabulary from native resources, which can be related to this puristic attitude.

Our preliminary survey of the Guaraní situation indicates that the conceptual framework which we have formulated is applicable to it at least in broad outline. As we see it, the descriptive aspect of the problem involves a multitude of questions of detail, some of them technical linguistic, some of them ethnopsychological, some technical ethnographic. The broader ramifications of the problem—the relation of this linguistic phase of the culture to other phases of present-day urban Paraguayan culture—touch upon the core problem of the interpretation of modern cultures: what is a modern culture, as opposed to an aboriginal one? Even if one rejects the many proposed dichotomies of civilized versus primitive, Kulturvolk versus Naturvolk, or folk versus urban, there remains a strong impressionistic awareness that there is some difference.

We feel that a language-and-culture problem such as ours, which allows the introduction of certain quantitative technical criteria, constitutes a useful point of departure to throw further light upon the folk-urban problem.

NOTES

1. Cf. R. Redfield, *The Folk Cultures of Yucatán,* passim. Chicago, 1941.
2. See Bohuslav Havránek, "Úkoly spisovného jazyka a jeho kultura" (= "The Functions of the Standard Language and its Cultivation"), in *Cercle Linguistique de Prague, Spisovná čeština a jazyková kultura* (*Standard Czech and the Cultivation of Good Language*), Prague, 1932, pp. 32 ff. A portion translated as *The Functional Differentiation of the Standard Language in a Prague School Reader on Esthetics, Literary Structure, and Style,* Paul L. Garvin, Transl. (Publ. of the Washington Linguistic Club, No. 1, Washington, D.C., 1955), pp. 1–18.
3. Cf. Uriel Weinreich, *Languages in Contact,* Publication of the Linguistic Circle of New York, No. 1, New York, 1953.
4. Vilém Mathesius, *op. cit.* in fn. 2, pp. 14 ff.
5. B. Havránek, *loc. cit.*
6. *Op. cit.* in fn. 2, p. 45; transl. *op. cit.* in fn. 2, p. 5.
7. *Op. cit.,* p. 46; transl. *op. cit., ibid.*
8. *Op. cit.,* p. 67 ff.; transl. *op. cit.* p. 15 ff.
9. *El Paraguay y su Ciudadanía,* América (Buenos Aires), May–June 1954.

10. *El Solar Guaraní* (n.p., 1947).
11. *Op. cit.* in fn. 10.
12. Jan Mukařovský, *Jazyk spisovný a jazyk básnický* (*Standard Language and Poetic Language*), *op. cit.* in fn. 2, pp. 123 ff., transl. *op. cit.* in fn. 2, pp. 19 ff.
13. *Op. cit.* in fn. 3, pp. 99 ff.
14. *Paraguay en Marcha,* Vol. II, núm. 13 (January, 1949).
15. *Op. cit.* in fn. 14.
16. *Ibid.*
17. *Revista del Turismo* (Asunción), May, 1945.
18. *Op. cit.* in fn. 14.
19. *Ibid.*

THE URBANIZATION OF THE HUMAN POPULATION

Kingsley Davis

"The Urbanization of the Human Population" is one of the best-known essays in this book. It first appeared in a widely read magazine and has been reprinted a number of times since then. A quick reading will tell you why the essay has been popular: it is a straightforward, sure-handed, and comprehensive presentation of the major trends in the urbanization of today's world. It touches deftly on a number of the issues I raised in this chapter's introduction: problems of definition and measurement, components of urban growth and urbanization, differences between the historical Western pattern of urbanization and Third World patterns today, and several others. Davis also emphasizes three issues that the introduction does not:

> *1. the typical S-curve of urbanization—first accelerating, then decelerating, to describe a flattened S with its top at the maximum proportion in cities—which in its last manifestation is likely to leave the whole world predominantly urban by the end of the twentieth century;*
> *2. the impact of extremely high rates of natural increase on the patterns of urban growth and urbanization in the poorer countries of today's world;*
> *3. the resulting demographic pressure on the major cities of the Third World, which raises the possibility of enormous urban concentrations by the end of the century.*

Davis sees national rates of population growth, rather than excessively rapid urbanization, as lying behind the major urban problems of the Third World.

One other observation Davis makes will reappear later in this book. He points out that in the course of urbanization rural-to-urban migration eventually exhausts its own source of supply, the rural population. Like the overall path of urbanization, it ordinarily describes an S-curve: first accelerat-

ing, then decelerating. But neither urban growth nor migration to cities necessarily cease with the slowing of the rural-urban flow. Urban growth, long dependent mainly on net migration from the rural sector, comes to depend increasingly on natural increase in the urban population itself. In urban-industrial countries the pace of migration has so far remained high because people move from city to city. Rather than a transition from one form of immobility to another, the urbanization of the world brings a shift from large movements of people out of the countryside to large exchanges of people among existing metropolises.

Urbanized societies, in which a majority of the people live crowded together in towns and cities, represent a new and fundamental step in man's social evolution. Although cities themselves first appeared some 5,500 years ago, they were small and surrounded by an overwhelming majority of rural people; moreover, they relapsed easily to village or small-town status. The urbanized societies of today, in contrast, not only have urban agglomerations of a size never before attained but also have a high proportion of their population concentrated in such agglomerations. In 1960, for example, nearly 52 million Americans lived in only 16 urbanized areas. Together these areas covered less land than one of the smaller counties (Cochise) of Arizona. According to one definition used by the U.S. Bureau of the Census, 96 million people—53 percent of the nation's population—were concentrated in 213 urbanized areas that together occupied only .7 percent of the nation's land. Another definition used by the bureau puts the urban population at about 70 percent. The large and dense agglomerations comprising the urban population involve a degree of human contact and of social complexity never before known. They exceed in size the communities of any other large animal; they suggest the behavior of communal insects rather than of mammals.

Neither the recency nor the speed of this evolutionary development is widely appreciated. Before 1850 no society could be described as predominantly urbanized, and by 1900 only one—Great Britain—could be so regarded. Today, only 65 years later, all industrial nations are highly urbanized, and in the world as a whole the process of urbanization is accelerating rapidly.

Some years ago my associates and I at Columbia University undertook to document the progress of urbanization by compiling data on the world's cities and the proportion of human beings living in them; in recent years the work has been continued in our center—International Population and Urban Research—at the University of California at Berkeley. The data obtained in these investigations can be used to show the historical trend in terms of one index of urbanization: the proportion of the population living in cities of 100,000 or larger. Statistics of this kind are only approximations of reality, but they are accurate enough to demonstrate how urbanization has accelerated. Between 1850 and 1950 the index changed at a much higher rate than from 1800 to 1850, but the rate of change from 1950 to 1960 was twice that of the preceding 50 years! If the pace of increase that obtained between 1950 and 1960 were to remain the same, by 1990 the fraction of the world's people living in cities of 100,000 or larger would be more than half. Using another index of urbanization—the proportion of the world's population living in urban places of all sizes—we found that by 1960 the figure had already reached 33 percent.

Clearly the world as a whole is not fully urbanized, but it soon will be. This change in human life is so recent that even the most urbanized countries still exhibit the rural origins of their institutions. Its full implications for man's organic and social evolution can only be surmised.

In discussing the trend—and its implications insofar as they can be perceived—I shall use the term "urbanization" in a particular way. It refers here to the proportion of the total population concentrated in urban settlements, or else to a rise in this proportion. A common mistake is to think of urbanization as simply the growth of cities. Since the total population is composed of both the urban population and the rural, however, the "proportion urban" is a function of both of them. Accordingly cities can grow without any urbanization, provided that the rural population grows at an equal or a greater rate.

Historically urbanization and the growth of cities have occurred together, which accounts for the confusion. As the reader will soon see, it is necessary to distinguish the two trends. In the most advanced countries today, for example, urban populations are still growing, but their proportion of the total population is tending to remain stable or to diminish. In other words, the process of urbanization—the switch from a spread-out pattern of human settlement to one of concentration in urban centers—is a change that has a beginning and an end, but the growth of cities has no inherent limit. Such growth could continue even after everyone was living in cities, through sheer excess of births over deaths.

The difference between a rural village and an urban community is of course one of degree; a precise operational distinction is somewhat arbitrary, and it varies from one nation to another. Since data are available for communities of various sizes, a dividing line can be chosen at will. One convenient index of urbanization, for example, is the proportion of people living in places of 100,000 or more. In the following analysis I shall depend on two indexes: the one just mentioned and the proportion of population classed as "urban" in the official statistics of each country. In practice the two indexes are highly correlated; therefore either one can be used as an index of urbanization.

Actually the hardest problem is not that of determining the "floor" of the urban category but of ascertaining the boundary of places that are clearly urban by any definition. How far east is the boundary of Los Angeles? Where along the Hooghly River does Calcutta leave off and the countryside begin? In the past the population of cities and towns has usually been given as the number of people living within the political boundaries. Thus the population of New York is frequently given as around eight million, this being the population of the city proper. The error in such a figure was not large before World War I, but since then, particularly in the advanced countries, urban populations have been spilling over the narrow political boundaries at a tremendous rate. In 1960 the New York–Northeastern New Jersey urbanized area, as delineated by the Bureau of the Census, had more than 14 million people. That delineation showed it to be the largest city in the world and nearly twice as large as New York City proper.

As a result of the outward spread of urbanites, counts made on the basis of political boundaries alone underestimate the city populations and exaggerate the rural. For this reason our office delineated the metropolitan areas of as many countries as possible for dates around 1950. These areas included the central, or political, cities and the zones around them that are receiving the spill-over.

This reassessment raised the estimated proportion of the world's population in cities of 100,000 or larger from 15.1 percent to 16.7 percent. As of 1960 we have used wherever possible the "urban agglomeration" data now furnished to the United Nations by many countries. The U.S., for example, provides data for "urbanized areas," meaning cities of 50,000 or larger and the built-up agglomerations around them.

. . . .My concern is with the degree of urbanization in whole societies. It is curious that thousands of years elapsed between the first appearance of small cities and the emergence of urbanized societies in the 19th century. It is also curious that the region where urbanized societies arose—northwestern Europe—was not the one that had given rise to the major cities of the past; on the contrary, it was a region where urbanization had been at an extremely low ebb. Indeed, the societies of northwestern Europe in medieval times were so rural that it is hard for modern minds to comprehend them. Perhaps it was the nonurban character of these societies that erased the parasitic nature of towns and eventually provided a new basis for a revolutionary degree of urbanization.

At any rate, two seemingly adverse conditions may have presaged the age to come: one the low productivity of medieval agriculture in both per-acre and per-man terms, the other the feudal social system. The first meant that towns could not prosper on the basis of local agriculture alone but had to trade and to manufacture something to trade. The second meant that they could not gain political dominance over their hinterlands and thus become warring city-states. Hence they specialized in commerce and manufacture and evolved local institutions suited to this role. Craftsmen were housed in the towns, because there the merchants could regulate quality and cost. Competition among towns stimulated specialization and technological innovation. The need for literacy, accounting skills and geographical knowledge caused the towns to invest in secular education.

Although the medieval towns remained small and never embraced more than a minor fraction of each region's population, the close connection between industry and commerce that they fostered, together with their emphasis on technique, set the stage for the ultimate breakthrough in urbanization. This breakthrough came only with the enormous growth in productivity caused by the use of inanimate energy and machinery. How difficult it was to achieve the transition is agonizingly apparent from statistics showing that even with the conquest of the New World the growth of urbanization during three postmedieval centuries in Europe was barely perceptible. I have assembled population estimates at two or more dates for 33 towns and cities in the 16th century, 46 in the 17th and 61 in the 18th. The average rate of growth during the three centuries was less than .6 percent per year. Estimates of the growth of Europe's population as a whole between 1650 and 1800 work out to slightly more than .4 percent. The advantage of the towns was evidently very slight. Taking only the cities of 100,000 or more inhabitants, one finds that in 1600 their combined population was 1.6 percent of the estimated population of Europe; in 1700, 1.9 percent, and in 1800, 2.2 percent. On the eve of the industrial revolution Europe was still an overwhelmingly agrarian region.

With industrialization, however, the transformation was striking. By 1801

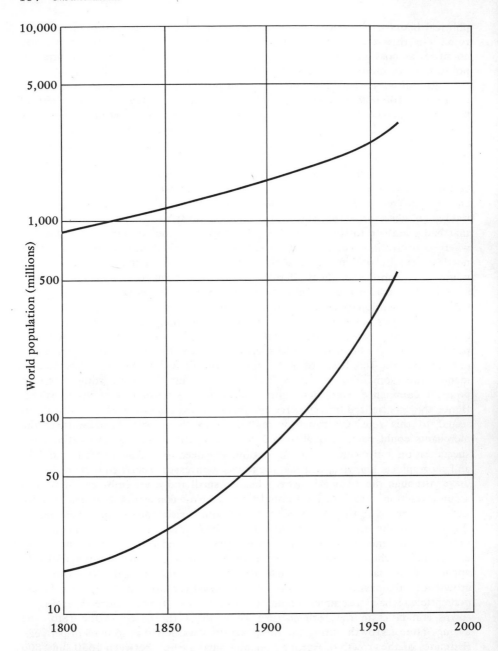

Figure 1. Rapid urbanization of the world's population is evident in this comparison of total population (upper curve) with the population in cities of more than 100,000 inhabitants (lower curve) over more than a century and a half. The use of cities of 100,000 or larger to define an urban population shows a close correlation with other definitions of urbanism.

nearly a tenth of the people of England and Wales were living in cities of 100,000 or larger. This proportion doubled in 40 years and doubled again in another 60 years. By 1900 Britain was an urbanized society. In general, the later each country became industrialized, the faster was its urbanization. The change from a population with 10 percent of its members in cities of 100,000 or larger to one in which 30 percent lived in such cities took about 79 years in England and Wales, 66 in the U.S., 48 in Germany, 36 in Japan and 26 in Australia. The close association between economic development and urbanization has persisted; in 199 countries around 1960 the proportion of the population living in cities varied sharply with per capita income.

Clearly modern urbanization is best understood in terms of its connection with economic growth, and its implications are best perceived in its latest manifestations in advanced countries. What becomes apparent as one examines the trend in these countries is that urbanization is a finite process, a cycle through which nations go in their transition from agrarian to industrial society. The intensive urbanization of most of the advanced countries began within the past 100 years; in the underdeveloped countries it got under way more recently. In some of the advanced countries its end is now in sight. The fact that it will end, however, does not mean that either economic development or the growth of cities will necessarily end.

The typical cycle of urbanization can be represented by a curve in the shape of an attenuated *S*. Starting from the bottom of the *S*, the first bend tends to come early and to be followed by a long attenuation. In the United Kingdom, for instance, the swiftest rise in the proportion of people living in cities of 100,000 or larger occurred from 1811 to 1851. In the U.S. it occurred from 1820 to 1890, in Greece from 1879 to 1921. As the proportion climbs above 50 percent the curve begins to flatten out; it falters, or even declines, when the proportion urban has reached about 75 percent. In the United Kingdom, one of the world's most urban countries, the proportion was slightly higher in 1926 (78.7 percent) than in 1961 (78.3 percent).

At the end of the curve some ambiguity appears. As a society becomes advanced enough to be highly urbanized it can also afford considerable suburbanization and fringe development. In a sense the slowing down of urbanization is thus more apparent than real: an increasing proportion of urbanites simply live in the country and are classified as rural. Many countries now try to compensate for this ambiguity by enlarging the boundaries of urban places; they did so in numerous censuses taken around 1960. Whether in these cases the old classification of urban or the new one is erroneous depends on how one looks at it; at a very advanced stage the entire concept of urbanization becomes ambiguous.

The end of urbanization cannot be unraveled without going into the ways in which economic development governs urbanization. Here the first question is: Where do the urbanites come from? The possible answers are few: The proportion of people in cities can rise because rural settlements grow larger and are reclassified as towns or cities; because the excess of births over deaths is greater in the city than in the country, or because people move from the country to the city.

The first factor has usually had only slight influence. The second has apparently never been the case. Indeed, a chief obstacle to the growth of cities in the past has been their excessive mortality. London's water in the middle of the 19th

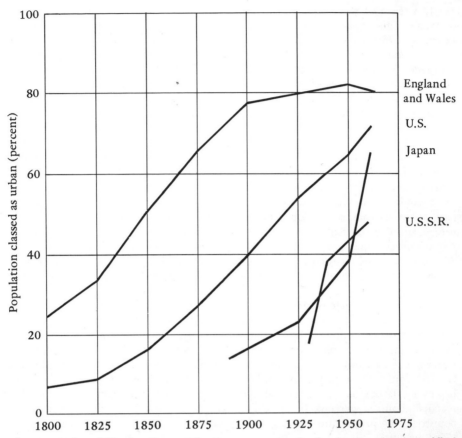

Figure 2. Industrialized nations underwent a process of urbanization that is typified by the curves shown here for four countries. It was closely related to economic development. The figures for 1950 and 1960 are based on a classification that counts as urban the fringe residents of urbanized areas; that classification was not used for the earlier years shown.

century came mainly from wells and rivers that drained cesspools, graveyards and tidal areas. The city was regularly ravaged by cholera. Tables for 1841 show an expectation of life of about 36 years for London and 26 for Liverpool and Manchester, as compared to 41 for England and Wales as a whole. After 1850, mainly as a result of sanitary measures and some improvement in nutrition and housing, city health improved, but as late as the period 1901–1910 the death rate of the urban counties in England and Wales, as modified to make the age structure comparable, was 33 percent higher than the death rate of the rural counties. As Bernard Benjamin, a chief statistician of the British General Register Office, has remarked: "Living in the town involved not only a higher risk of epidemic and crowd diseases . . . but also a higher risk of degenerative disease—the harder wear

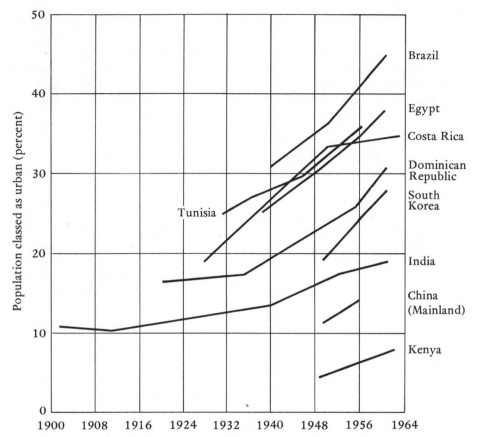

Figure 3. Nonindustrial nations are undergoing a process of urbanization that is typified by these curves. The process started much later than in the industrialized nations, as can be seen by comparing this chart with . . . [Figure 2], and is attributable more to the rapid rise of total population in these countries than to economic development.

and tear of factory employment and urban discomfort." By 1950, however, virtually the entire differential had been wiped out.

As for birth rates, during rapid urbanization in the past they were notably lower in cities than in rural areas. In fact, the gap tended to widen somewhat as urbanization proceeded in the latter half of the 19th century and the first quarter of the 20th. In 1800 urban women in the U.S. had 36 percent fewer children than rural women did; in 1840, 38 percent and in 1930, 41 percent. Thereafter the difference diminished.

With mortality in the cities higher and birth rates lower, and with reclassification a minor factor, the only real source for the growth in the proportion of people in urban areas during the industrial transition was rural-urban migration. This source had to be plentiful enough not only to overcome the substantial disadvantage of the cities in natural increase but also, above that, to furnish a big margin of growth in their populations. If, for example, the cities had a death rate a third higher and a birth rate a third lower than the rural rates (as was typical in the latter half of the 19th century), they would require each year perhaps 40 to 45 migrants from elsewhere per 1,000 of their population to maintain a growth rate of 3 percent per year. Such a rate of migration could easily be maintained as long as the rural portion of the population was large, but when this condition ceased to obtain, the maintenance of the same urban rate meant an increasing drain on the countryside.

Why did the rural-urban migration occur? The reason was that the rise in technological enhancement of human productivity, together with certain constant factors, rewarded urban concentration. One of the constant factors was that agriculture uses land as its prime instrument of production and hence spreads out people who are engaged in it, whereas manufacturing, commerce and services use land only as a site. Moreover, the demand for agricultural products is less elastic than the demand for services and manufactures. As productivity grows, services and manufactures can absorb more manpower by paying higher wages. Since non-agricultural activities can use land simply as a site, they can locate near one another (in towns and cities) and thus minimize the friction of space inevitably involved in the division of labor. At the same time, as agricultural technology is improved, capital costs in farming rise and manpower becomes not only less needed but also economically more burdensome. A substantial portion of the agricultural population is therefore sufficiently disadvantaged, in relative terms, to be attracted by higher wages in other sectors.

In this light one sees why a large flow of people from farms to cities was generated in every country that passed through the industrial revolution. One also sees why, with an even higher proportion of people already in cities and with the inability of city people to replace themselves by reproduction, the drain eventually became so heavy that in many nations the rural population began to decline in absolute as well as relative terms. In Sweden it declined after 1920, in England and Wales after 1861, in Belgium after 1910.

Realizing that urbanization is transitional and finite, one comes on another fact—a fact that throws light on the circumstances in which urbanization comes to an end. A basic feature of the transition is the profound switch from agricultural to nonagricultural employment. This change is associated with urbanization but not identical with it. The difference emerges particularly in the later stages. Then the availability of automobiles, radios, motion pictures and electricity, as well as the reduction of the workweek and the workday, mitigate the disadvantages of living in the country. Concurrently the expanding size of cities makes them more difficult to live in. The population classed as "rural" is accordingly enlarged, both from cities and from true farms.

For these reasons the "rural" population in some industrial countries never did fall in absolute size. In all the industrial countries, however, the population dependent on agriculture—which the reader will recognize as a more functional definition of the non-urban population than mere rural residence—decreased in absolute as well as relative terms. In the U.S., for example, the net migration from farms totaled more than 27 million between 1920 and 1959 and thus averaged approximately 700,000 a year. As a result the farm population declined from 32.5 million in 1916 to 20.5 million in 1960, in spite of the large excess of births in farm families. In 1964, by a stricter American definition classifying as "farm families" only those families actually earning their living from agriculture, the farm population was down to 12.9 million. This number represented 6.8 percent of the nation's population; the comparable figure for 1880 was 44 percent. In Great Britain the number of males occupied in agriculture was at its peak, 1.8 million, in 1851; by 1961 it had fallen to .5 million.

In the later stages of the cycle, then, urbanization in the industrial countries tends to cease. Hence the connection between economic development and the growth of cities also ceases. The change is explained by two circumstances. First, there is no longer enough farm population to furnish a significant migration to the cities. (What can 12.9 million American farmers contribute to the growth of the 100 million people already in urbanized areas?) Second, the rural nonfarm population, nourished by refugees from the expanding cities, begins to increase as fast as the city population. The effort of census bureaus to count fringe residents as urban simply pushes the definition of "urban" away from the notion of dense settlement and in the direction of the term "nonfarm." As the urban population becomes more "rural," which is to say less densely settled, the advanced industrial peoples are for a time able to enjoy the amenities of urban life without the excessive crowding of the past.

Here, however, one again encounters the fact that a cessation of urbanization does not necessarily mean a cessation of city growth. An example is provided by New Zealand. Between 1945 and 1961 the proportion of New Zealand's population classed as urban—that is, the ratio between urban and rural residents—changed hardly at all (from 61.3 percent to 63.6 percent) but the urban population increased by 50 percent. In Japan between 1940 and 1950 urbanization actually decreased slightly, but the urban population increased by 13 percent.

The point to be kept in mind is that once urbanization ceases, city growth becomes a function of general population growth. Enough farm-to-city migration may still occur to redress the difference in natural increase. The reproductive rate of urbanites tends, however, to increase when they live at lower densities, and the reproductive rate of "urbanized" farmers tends to decrease; hence little migration is required to make the urban increase equal the national increase.

I now turn to the currently underdeveloped countries. With the advanced nations having slackened their rate of urbanization, it is the others—representing three-fourths of humanity—that are mainly responsible for the rapid urbanization now characterizing the world as a whole. In fact, between 1950 and 1960 the proportion of the population in cities of 100,000 or more rose about a third faster in the underdeveloped regions than in the developed ones. Among the underdeveloped regions the pace was slow in eastern and southern Europe, but in the rest of the underdeveloped world the proportion in cities rose twice as fast as it did in the industrialized countries, even though the latter countries in many cases broadened their definitions of urban places to include more suburban and fringe residents.

Because of the characteristic pattern of urbanization, the current rates of urbanization in underdeveloped countries could be expected to exceed those now exisiting in countries far advanced in the cycle. On discovering that this is the case one is tempted to say that the underdeveloped regions are now in the typical stage of urbanization associated with early economic development. This notion, however, is erroneous. In their urbanization the underdeveloped countries are definitely not repeating past history. Indeed, the best grasp of their present situation comes from analyzing how their course differs from the previous pattern of development.

The first thing to note is that today's underdeveloped countries are urbanizing not only more rapidly than the industrial nations are now but also more rapidly than the industrial nations did in the heyday of their urban growth. The difference, however, is not large. In 40 underdeveloped countries for which we have data in recent decades, the average gain in the proportion of the population urban was 20 percent per decade; in 16 industrial countries, during the decades of their most rapid urbanization (mainly in the 19th century), the average gain per decade was 15 percent.

This finding that urbanization is proceeding only a little faster in underdeveloped countries than it did historically in the advanced nations may be questioned by the reader. It seemingly belies the widespread impression that cities throughout the non-industrial parts of the world are bursting with people. There is, however, no contradiction. One must recall the basic distinction between a change in the proportion of the population urban, which is a ratio, and the absolute growth of cities. The popular impression is correct: the cities in underdeveloped areas are growing at a disconcerting rate. They are far outstripping the city boom of the industrializing era in the 19th century. If they continue their recent rate of growth, they will double their population every 15 years.

In 34 underdeveloped countries for which we have data relating to the 1940's and 1950's, the average annual gain in the urban population was 4.5 percent. The figure is remarkably similar for the various regions: 4.7 percent in seven countries of Africa, 4.7 percent in 15 countries of Asia and 4.3 percent in 12 countries of Latin America. In contrast, in nine European countries during their period of fastest urban population growth (mostly in the latter half of the 19th century) the average gain per year was 2.1 percent. Even the frontier industrial countries—the U.S., Australia–New Zealand, Canada and Argentina—which received huge numbers of immigrants, had a smaller population growth in towns and cities: 4.2 percent per year. In Japan and the U.S.S.R. the rate was respectively 5.4 and 4.3 percent per year, but their economic growth began only recently.

How is it possible that the contrast in growth between today's underdeveloped countries and yesterday's industrializing countries is sharper with respect to the absolute urban population than with respect to the urban share of the total population? The answer lies in another profound difference between the two sets of countries—a difference in total population growth, rural as well as urban. Contemporary underdeveloped populations have been growing since 1940 more than twice as fast as industrialized populations, and their increase far exceeds the growth of the latter at the peak of their expansion. The only rivals in an earlier day were the frontier nations, which had the help of great streams of immigrants. Today the underdeveloped nations—already densely settled, tragically impoverished and with gloomy economic prospects—are multiplying their people by sheer biological increase at a rate that is unprecedented. It is this population boom that is overwhelmingly responsible for the rapid inflation of city populations in such countries. Contrary to popular opinion both inside and outside those countries, the main factor is not rural-urban migration.

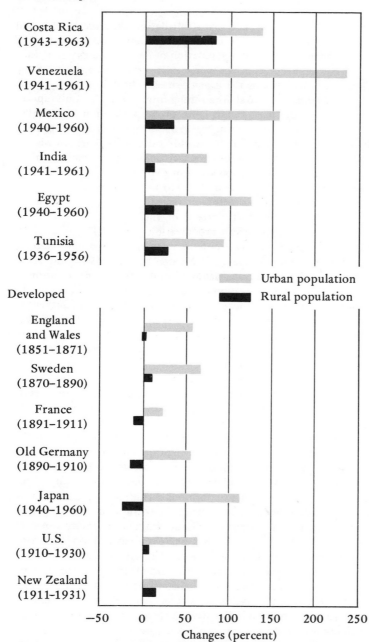

Underdeveloped

Costa Rica
(1943–1963)

Venezuela
(1941–1961)

Mexico
(1940–1960)

India
(1941–1961)

Egypt
(1940–1960)

Tunisia
(1936–1956)

Urban population
Rural population

Developed

England
and Wales
(1851–1871)

Sweden
(1870–1890)

France
(1891–1911)

Old Germany
(1890–1910)

Japan
(1940–1960)

U.S.
(1910–1930)

New Zealand
(1911–1931)

−50   0   50   100   150   200   250

Changes (percent)

Figure 4. Rural and urban populations of several undeveloped countries are compared with those in the currently developed countries at a time when they were undergoing rapid urbanization. It is evident that in the underdeveloped countries the rural population is rising in spite of urbanization, whereas in the earlier period it rose slightly or dropped.

This point can be demonstrated easily by a calculation that has the effect of eliminating the influence of general population growth on urban growth. The calculation involves assuming that the total population of a given country remained constant over a period of time but that the percentage urban changed as it did historically. In this manner one obtains the growth of the absolute urban population that would have occurred if rural-urban migration were the only factor affecting it. As an example, Costa Rica had in 1927 a total population of 471,500, of which 88,600, or 18.8 percent, was urban. By 1963 the country's total population was 1,325,200 and the urban population was 456,600, or 34.5 percent. If the total population had remained at 471,500 but the percentage urban had still risen from 18.8 to 34.5, the absolute urban population in 1963 would have been only 162,700. That is the growth that would have occurred in the urban population if rural-urban migration had been the only factor. In actuality the urban population rose to 456,600. In other words, only 20 percent of the rapid growth of Costa Rica's towns and cities was attributable to urbanization per se; 44 percent was attributable solely to the country's general population increase, the remainder to the joint operation of both factors. Similarly, in Mexico between 1940 and 1960, 50 percent of the urban population increase was attributable to national multiplication alone and only 22 percent to urbanization alone.

The past performance of the advanced countries presents a sharp contrast. In Switzerland between 1850 and 1888, when the proportion urban resembled that in Costa Rica recently, general population growth alone accounted for only 19 percent of the increase of town and city people, and rural-urban migration alone accounted for 69 percent. In France between 1846 and 1911 only 21 percent of the growth in the absolute urban population was due to general growth alone.

The conclusion to which this contrast points is that one anxiety of governments in the underdeveloped nations is misplaced. Impressed by the mushrooming in their cities of shantytowns filled with ragged peasants, they attribute the fantastically fast city growth to rural-urban migration. Actually this migration now does little more than make up for the small difference in the birth rate between city and countryside. In the history of the industrial nations, as we have seen, the sizable difference between urban and rural birth rates and death rates required that cities, if they were to grow, had to have an enormous influx of people from farms and villages. Today in the underdeveloped countries the towns and cities have only a slight disadvantage in fertility, and their old disadvantage in mortality not only has been wiped out but also in many cases has been reversed. During the 19th century the urbanizing nations were learning how to keep crowded populations in cities from dying like flies. Now the lesson has been learned, and it is being applied to cities even in countries just emerging from tribalism. In fact, a disproportionate share of public health funds goes into cities. As a result throughout the nonindustrial world people in cities are multiplying as never before, and rural-urban migration is playing a much lesser role.

The trends just described have an important implication for the rural population. Given the explosive overall population growth in underdeveloped countries, it follows that if the rural population is not to pile up on the land and reach an economically absurd density, a high rate of rural-urban migration must be maintained. Indeed, the exodus from rural areas should be higher than in the past. But this high rate of internal movement is not taking place, and there is some doubt that it could conceivably do so.

To elaborate I shall return to my earlier point that in the evolution of industrialized countries the rural citizenry often declined in absolute as well as relative terms. The rural population of France—26.8 million in 1846—was down to 20.8 million by 1926 and 17.2 million by 1962, notwithstanding a gain in the nation's total population during this period. Sweden's rural population dropped from 4.3 million in 1910 to 3.5 million in 1960. Since the category "rural" includes an increasing portion of urbanites living in fringe areas, the historical drop was more drastic and consistent specifically in the farm population. In the U.S., although the "rural" population never quite ceased to grow, the farm contingent began its long descent shortly after the turn of the century; today it is less than two-fifths of what it was in 1910.

This transformation is not occurring in contemporary underdeveloped countries. In spite of the enormous growth of their cities, their rural populations—and their more narrowly defined agricultural populations—are growing at a rate that in many cases exceeds the rise of even the urban population during the evolution of the now advanced countries. The poor countries thus confront a grave dilemma. If they do not substantially step up the exodus from rural areas, these areas will be swamped with underemployed farmers. If they do step up the exodus, the cities will grow at a disastrous rate.

The rapid growth of cities in the advanced countries, painful though it was, had the effect of solving a problem—the problem of the rural population. The growth of cities enabled agricultural holdings to be consolidated, allowed increased capitalization and in general resulted in greater efficiency. Now, however, the underdeveloped countries are experiencing an even more rapid urban growth—and are suffering from urban problems—but urbanization is not solving their rural ills.

A case in point is Venezuela. Its capital, Caracas, jumped from a population of 359,000 in 1941 to 1,507,000 in 1963; other Venezuelan towns and cities equaled or exceeded this growth. Is this rapid rise denuding the countryside of people? No, the Venezuelan farm population increased in the decade 1951–1961 by 11 percent. The only thing that declined was the amount of cultivated land. As a result the agricultural population density became worse. In 1950 there were some 64 males engaged in agriculture per square mile of cultivated land; in 1961 there were 78. (Compare this with 4.8 males occupied in agriculture per square mile of cultivated land in Canada, 6.8 in the U.S. and 15.6 in Argentina.) With each male occupied in agriculture there are of course dependents. Approximately 225 persons in Venezuela are trying to live from each square mile of cultivated land. Most of the growth of cities in Venezuela is attributable to overall population growth. If the general population had not grown at all, and internal migration had been large enough to produce the actual shift in the proportion in cities, the increase in urban population would have been only 28 percent of what it was and the rural population would have been reduced by 57 percent.

The story of Venezuela is being repeated virtually everywhere in the underdeveloped world. It is not only Caracas that has thousands of squatters living in self-constructed junk houses on land that does not belong to them. By whatever name they are called, the squatters are to be found in all major cities in the poorer countries. They live in broad gullies beneath the main plain in San Salvador and on the hillsides of Rio de Janeiro and Bogotá. They tend to occupy with implacable determination parks, school grounds and vacant lots. Amman, the capital of Jordan, grew from 12,000 in 1958 to 247,000 in 1961. A good part of it is slums, and urban amenities are lacking most of the time for most of the people. Greater Baghdad now has an estimated 850,000 people; its slums, like those in many other underdeveloped countries, are in two zones—the central part of the city and the outlying areas. Here are the *sarifa* areas, characterized by self-built reed huts; these areas account for about 45 percent of the housing in the entire city and are devoid of amenities, including even latrines. In addition to such urban problems, all the countries struggling for higher living levels find their rural population growing too and piling up on already crowded land.

I have characterized urbanization as a transformation that, unlike economic development, is finally accomplished and comes to an end. At the 1950–1960 rate the term "urbanized world" will be applicable well before the end of the century. One should scarcely expect, however, that mankind will complete its urbanization without major complications. One sign of trouble ahead turns on the distinction I made at the start between urbanization and city growth per se. Around the globe today city growth is disproportionate to urbanization. The discrepancy is paradoxical in the industrial nations and worse than paradoxical in the nonindustrial.

It is in this respect that the nonindustrial nations, which still make up the great majority of nations, are far from repeating past history. In the 19th and early 20th centuries the growth of cities arose from and contributed to economic advancement. Cities took surplus manpower from the countryside and put it to work producing goods and services that in turn helped to modernize agriculture. But today in underdeveloped countries, as in present-day advanced nations, city growth has become increasingly unhinged from economic development and hence from rural-urban migration. It derives in greater degree from overall population growth, and this growth in nonindustrial lands has become unprecedented because of modern health techniques combined with high birth rates.

The speed of world population growth is twice what it was before 1940, and the swiftest increase has shifted from the advanced to the backward nations. In the latter countries, consequently, it is virtually impossible to create city services fast enough to take care of the huge, never-ending cohorts of babies and peasants swelling the urban masses. It is even harder to expand agricultural land and capital fast enough to accommodate the enormous natural increase on farms. The problem is not urbanization, not rural-urban migration, but human multiplication. It is a problem that is new in both its scale and its setting, and runaway city growth is only one of its painful expressions.

As long as the human population expands, cities will expand too, regardless of whether urbanization increases or declines. This means that some individual cities will reach a size that will make 19th-century metropolises look like small towns. If the New York urbanized area should continue to grow only as fast as the nation's population (according to medium projections of the latter by the Bureau of the Census), it would reach 21 million by 1985 and 30 million by 2010. I have calculated that if India's population should grow as the UN projections indicate it will, the largest city in India in the year 2000 will have between 36 and 66 million inhabitants.

What is the implication of such giant agglomerations for human destiny? In 1950 the New York–Northeastern New Jersey urbanized area had an average density of 9,810 persons per square mile. With 30 million people in the year 2010, the density would be 24,000 per square mile. Although this level is exceeded now in parts of New York City (which averages about 25,000 per square mile) and many other cities, it is a high density to be spread over such a big area; it would cover, remember, the suburban areas to which people moved to escape high density. Actually, however, the density of the New York urbanized region is dropping, not increasing, as the population grows. The reason is that the territory covered by the urban agglomeration is growing faster than the population: it grew by 51 percent from 1950 to 1960, whereas the population rose by 15 percent.

If, then, one projects the rise in population and the rise in territory for the New York urbanized region, one finds the density problem solved. It is not solved for long, though, because New York is not the only city in the region that is expanding. So are Philadelphia, Trenton, Hartford, New Haven and so on. By 1960 a huge stretch of territory about 600 miles long and 30 to 100 miles wide along the Eastern seaboard contained some 37 million people (I am speaking of a longer section of the seaboard than the Boston-to-Washington conurbation referred to by some other authors in this book). Since the whole area is becoming one big polynucleated city, its population cannot long expand without a rise in density. Thus persistent human multiplication promises to frustrate the ceaseless search for space—for ample residential lots, wide-open suburban school grounds, sprawling shopping centers, one-floor factories, broad freeways.

How people feel about giant agglomerations is best indicated by their head-long effort to escape them. The bigger the city, the higher the cost of space; yet, the more the level of living rises, the more people are willing to pay for low-density living. Nevertheless, as urbanized areas expand and collide, it seems probable that life in low-density surroundings will become too dear for the great majority.

One can of course imagine that cities may cease to grow and may even shrink in size while the population in general continues to multiply. Even this dream, however, would not permanently solve the problem of space. It would eventually obliterate the distinction between urban and rural, but at the expense of the rural.

It seems plain that the only way to stop urban crowding and to solve most of the urban problems besetting both the developed and the underdeveloped nations is to reduce the overall rate of population growth. Policies designed to do this have as yet little intelligence and power behind them. Urban planners continue to treat population growth as something to be planned for, not something to be itself planned. Any talk about applying brakes to city growth is therefore purely speculative, overshadowed as it is by the reality of uncontrolled population increase.

Selected Readings on Urbanization

Abu-Lughod, Janet. "Urbanization in Egypt: Present State and Future Prospects." *Economic Development and Cultural Change* 13 (April 1965), 313–343.

Adams, Robert M. *The Evolution of Urban Society.* Chicago: Aldine, 1966. A splendid historical comparison of the ancient Near East and Middle America.

Ahmad, Qazi. *Indian Cities: Characteristics and Correlates.* Chicago: Department of Geography, University of Chicago, 1965. Research papers, No. 102.

Becker, Marvin. *Florence in Transition.* Vol. II. Johns Hopkins University Press, 1968. Studies in the rise of the territorial state.

Benet, Francisco. "Sociology Uncertain: The Ideology of Rural-Urban Continuum." *Comparative Studies in Society and History* 6 (1963): 1–23.

176 *Urbanization*

Boserup, Ester. *The Conditions of Agricultural Growth*. London: George Allen & Unwin, 1965. An analysis which attributes an extraordinary role to population growth, and indirectly to urban demand.

Braidwood, Robert J., and Gordon R. Willey, eds. *Courses toward Urban Life*. Chicago: Aldine, 1962. Expert archaeological appraisals of the antecedents of urban development in numerous world areas.

Breese, Gerald. *Urbanization in Newly Developing Countries*. Englewood Cliffs, N.J.: Prentice-Hall, 1966. A quick, competent survey.

Calderon, Luis. *Problemas de urbanización en America Latina*. Bogotá: Oficina International de Investigaciones sociales de FERES, 1963.

Cipolla, Carlo M. *The Economic History of World Population*. Harmondsworth, England: Penguin, 1962. Brief, dense, competent summary, without much explicit discussion of cities.

Cottrell, Fred. *Energy and Society*. New York: McGraw-Hill, 1955.

Dénis, Jacques. *Le Phénomène urbain en Afrique centrale*. Brussels: Academie royale des sciences coloniales, 1958.

Durand, John D. "The Modern Expansion of World Population." *Proceedings of the American Philosophical Society*, III, no. 3 (1967), 136–159. Reasoned estimates of the numbers involved.

Dyos, H. J., ed. *The Study of Urban History*. London: Arnold, 1968. A wide selection of papers with much information on techniques of research.

Ennen, Edith. *Frühgeschichte der europäischen Stadt*. Bonn: Rohrscheid, 1953. An extension of Max Weber's work and argument.

Epstein, A.L. "Urbanization and Social Change in Africa." *Current Anthropology*, October 1967, 275–296.

Forde, Daryll, ed. *Social Implications of Industrialization and Urbanization in Africa South of the Sahara*. Paris: UNESCO, 1956. A bulky collection of fragments: theories, methods, case studies.

Francastel, Pierre. *Les origines des villes polonaises*. Paris: Ecole Pratique des Hautes Etudes, 1961.

Gamst, Frederick C. "Peasantries and Elites without Urbanism: The Civilization of Ethiopia." *Comparative Studies in Society and History*, 12 (October, 1970), 373–392.

Geertz, Clifford. *Peddlers and Princes: Social Change and Economic Modernization in Two Indonesian Towns*. Chicago: University of Chicago Press, 1963.

Germani, Gino. "Algunos aspectos de la familia en transicion en Argentina." In *Economic Development and its Social Implications* edited by Georges Balanchier. Paris: Presses Universitaires de France, 1962.

Gibbs, Jack P. "Measures of Urbanization." *Social Forces* 45, No. 2 (December, 1966), pp. 170–177.

Glaab, Charles N., and Theodore A. Brown. *A History of Urban America*. New York: Macmillan, 1967. Compact, emphasizing changes in form and social life.

Goldrich, Daniel. "Peasants' Sons in City Schools: An Inquiry into the Politics of Urbanization in Panama and Costa Rica." *Human Organization* 23 (1964): 328–333.

Green, Constance McLaughlin. *The Rise of Urban America*. London: Hutchinson University Library, 1965. A compact no-nonsense history.

Greer, Scott, et al. *The New Urbanization*. New York: St. Martins, 1968. Studies concentrating on the internal organization of cities in modernizing countries.

Habakkuk, H. J. "La disparition du paysan anglais." *Annales; Economies, Sociétés, Civilisations*, 20 (1965), 649–663.

Hall, John W. "The Castle Town and Japan's Modern Urbanization." *Far Eastern Quarterly* 15 (1955): 37–56.

Hauser, Philip M., ed. *Urbanization in Asia and the Far East*. Calcutta: UNESCO Research Centre, 1957.

Herlihy, David. *Pisa in the Early Renaissance*. New Haven, Conn.: Yale University Press, 1958.

Herrick, Bruce H. *Urban Migration and Economic Development in Chile*. Cambridge, Mass.: MIT Press, 1966.

Jackson, J. A., ed. *Migration*. Cambridge, England: Cambridge University Press, 1969. About half deals with migration to cities. About half of that and half of the rest deals with non-Western migration.

Jacobs, Jane. *The Economy of Cities.* New York: Random House, 1969. A general examination of the conditions for the rise and fall of cities, by an outstanding critic of the ways we run and plan those we have.

Köllmann, Wolfgang. "The Process of Urbanization in Germany at the Height of the Industrialization Period." *Journal of Contemporary History* 4 (1969), 59–76. One of a series in a special issue on urbanism.

Kraeling, Carl H., and Robert M. Adams, eds. *City Invincible.* Chicago: University of Chicago Press, 1960. Symposium dealing with the origins of urban civilization in the Near East. Includes some mind-stretching essays.

Lerner, Daniel. *The Passing of Traditional Society.* Glencoe, Ill.: Free Press, 1958.

Little, Kenneth. *West African Urbanization.* Cambridge, England: Cambridge University Press, 1965. A study of voluntary associations in social change.

McKelvey, Blake. *The Emergence of Metropolitan America.* New Brunswick, N.J.: Rutgers University Press, 1968.

McKelvey, Blake. *The Urbanization of America.* New Brunswick, N.J.: Rutgers University Press, 1963.

Mauersberg, Hans. *Wirtschafts-und Sozialgeschichte zentral-europäischer Städte in neurer Zeit.* Gottingen, Germany: Vandenhoeck & Ruprecht, 1960.

Meier, Richard L. *A Communications Theory of Urban Growth.* Cambridge, Mass.: MIT Press, 1962.

Mukherjee, Ramkrishna. "Urbanization and Social Transformation in India." *International Journal of Comparative Sociology* 4 (1963), 178–210.

Murphy, H. B. M. "Social Change and Mental Health." *Milbank Memorial Fund Quarterly* 39 (1961): 385–445.

Nadal, Jorge. *La población española* (siglos XVI a XX). Barcelona: Ariel, 1966. Comprehensive demographic history of modern Spain, with ample information about cities.

Pulgram, Ernest. *The Tongues of Italy.* Cambridge, Mass.: Harvard University Press, 1958. Linguistic history with great sensitivity to social change.

Redford, Arthur. *Labor Migration in England.* 2d ed. Edited by W. H. Chaloner. Manchester: Manchester University Press, 1964.

Robinson, Warren C. "Urbanization and Fertility: the Non-Western Experience." *Milbank Memorial Fund Quarterly* 41(1963): 291–308.

Rörig, Fritz. *Die europäische Stadt und die Kultur des Burgertums im Mittelalter.* 2d ed. Göttingen: Vandenhoeck & Ruprecht, 1955.

Sjoberg, Gideon. *The Preindustrial City.* Glencoe, Ill.: Free Press, 1960.

Sovani, N. V. *Urbanization and Urban India.* New York: Toplinger, 1966. A collection of essays including some interesting arguments on the idea of "over-urbanization."

Stone, Leroy O. *Urban Development in Canada.* Ottawa: Dominion Bureau of Statistics, 1967.

Textor, R. B., et al. *The Social Implications of Industrialization and Urbanization.* Calcutta: UNESCO Research Centre, 1956. Asian case studies, emphasizing migration to major cities.

Tilly, Charles. *The Vendée.* Cambridge, Mass.: Harvard University Press, 1964. Relates major eighteenth-century conflicts in western France to the pattern of urbanization.

Troedsson, Carl. *The Growth of the Western City during the Middle Ages.* Goteborg, Germany: Gumpert, 1959.

Wade, Richard C. *The Urban Frontier.* Cambridge, Mass.: Harvard University Press, 1959. The development of cities in the western United States, 1790–1830.

Weber, Max. *The City.* Glencoe, Ill.: Free Press, 1958.

Wilkinson, Thomas O. *The Urbanization of Japanese Labor, 1886–1955.* Amherst: University of Massachusetts, 1966. Primarily demographic.

Wolf, Eric R. *Sons of the Shaking Earth.* Chicago: University of Chicago Press, 1959. Review of Central American cultural history with ample attention to changes in settlement pattern and community organization.

Wrigley, E. A. "A Simple Model of London's Importance in Changing English Society and Economy 1650–1750." *Past and Present* 37 (July 1967), 44–70.

Wrigley, E. A. *Population and History.* New York: McGraw-Hill, 1969. Demographic history, mainly European, with careful detail and attractive illustrations.

Chapter

3

Communities

INTRODUCTION

The male song sparrow begins to mark out his own place within the flock's breeding ground as the first warm days break into waning winter. His song asserts a claim to one location within a well-defined territorial system. No other bird can settle himself without challenge inside a distance indicated by the loudness of the song. If a bird does not successfully lay claim to one of the places within the breeding ground, he will not mate. Since the density of places within the breeding ground is a function of the normal food supply, the sparrow's singing helps assure that the size of the whole flock will remain fairly constant. Among song sparrows and many other birds, in fact, the arrangement works so that the population stays at a level somewhat below the maximum which could survive on the normal food supply.

Beneath its surface spontaneity, birdsong follows some marvelous regularities. As V. C. Wynne-Edwards (from whom I have borrowed the news about song sparrows) describes:

In character and content it is generally quite specific, and often if not always identifies the individual singer. It is usually a seasonal phenomenon, reaching a peak at the time of maximum dispersive activity, just before the breeding season. It is normally produced by adult males, and is a declamation directed primarily at other adult males, supplying the characteristic cohesive-antagonistic bond between them. It is of a loudness consistent with the distance (related to the territory-size) over which it needs to carry. It frequently shows a characteristic diurnal pattern of production, as well as an annual one, beginning at a precisely determined hour at dawn and then, after a short intensive period during which it is usually the principal occupation of all the singers, gradually declining, its function being for the time sufficiently discharged. It commonly reaches a secondary peak at dusk. It is emulative, and can often be stimulated to greater intensity by the sound of rival voices. Thus, in the still hour before dawn, the farmyard cocks of our youth used one at a time to answer back to each other's crowing far across the parish; or again, in quite different surroundings, silent nightingales can often be stirred into action by human whistling. In many species the first and most spirited singing of the day comes into the dawn chorus at the peak season of territorial competition, just about the time that nesting begins.[1]

What is more, the song of the birds turns out to have a lot in common with the drumming of the cicada, the croaking of the tree frog, the scraping of the katydid, or the roaring of the howler monkey. All of these displays—and thousands of other sounds, sights, and smells produced by the whole range of animals—have the effect of maintaining a territorial order which is crucial to the survival of the population as a whole.

The percolation of biological findings of this sort into the public domain has brought with it the notion of a territorial *instinct:* something deep in the nature of many species, including man, propelling the individual to attach himself to a particular niche and defend it against all comers. Frustrate that propulsion, goes the argument, and the social order begins to crumble. Overpopulation, the abolition of private property, or the breakdown of the national state, some people have speculated, might all have that effect.

Personally, I doubt the existence of a territorial instinct in anything like that sense. The animal behavior reported by Wynne-Edwards and other biologists probably has a genetic base. But the actual subdivision of territory and the allocation of individuals to subdivisions vary enormously among species; the same species, furthermore, makes new adjustments with changes in the food supply, the threat from predators, and other conditions governing collective survival change. The striking thing about these varied territorial orders is that they are *collective;* the whole population creates them. Furthermore, the fit among the food supply, the territorial arrangements and the ways of mating, feeding, and protecting offspring determines not so much whether any particular individual survives, but whether the population as a whole survives. Finally, the usual effect of an imbalance of these elements is not a disintegration of the "social order" but a disturbance of the population's size. The population may well disappear with its standard ways of behaving persisting up to the end, like the fabled captain going down with his ship. That is how the dodo went: by *not* changing its behavior when man began the slaughter.

The other primates—the animals most closely related to man—ordinarily organize their social lives in well-defined territorial patterns. Some of the most fascinating work now going on in biology, psychology, and anthropology now consists of field studies of primates in Africa, South America, or elsewhere. The results of the field work are rapidly changing our understanding of the regularities in primate social organization, so that any synthesis now has to be highly provisional. As of 1970, John Crook summed up the tendencies of the accumulating literature on the ecology and spatial dispersion of primates in the following outline:

a. The home range size of terrestrial open-country primates is a function of food availability in relation to population density.

b. In arboreal forest primates, spacing behavior is a function of high density relative to high environmental productivity in more or less stable habitats. It involves the maintenance of group dispersion by social communication patterns with or without the defense of topographically defined territories.

c. In addition to the effect of food availability in relation to density, open country traditions of social structuring are a function of past or present predation upon individuals. Coherent groups with organized deployment occur in areas with greatest predation pressure. The nightly dispersion of groups into sleeping parties arises where protective sleeping sites are limited in frequency and effectiveness. The distribution of secure sleeping sites may therefore also affect density.

d. Populations divided into one-male groups and all-male groups . . . tend to show greater dispersion of social units under conditions of poor food availability and to congregate when food becomes superabundant.

e. The integration of social units, particularly large bisexual troops . . . varies inversely with the density of vegetation and the dispersion of food resources.[2]

Obviously, the ethologists (the systematic students of animal behavior) are not discovering a "territorial instinct" among the primates. They are discovering that even the tendency to defend a particular fixed territory against outsiders only occurs in some primates under some conditions. Their findings, on the other hand, are making it clearer than ever that each primate group develops a well-defined way of spacing itself through the territory it occupies, somehow tunes the pattern to the threats and opportunities the whole group faces, and expresses its internal bonds and divisions in its spatial pattern.

MAN AND TERRITORY

The fact that other primates maintain powerful and elaborate territorial systems makes it seem likely that man himself has some genetic predisposition toward territoriality. Whatever genetic base man's territorial behavior has, however, lies deep beneath an overlay of custom, technology, symbolism, and psychic experience. All we can observe directly is that men organize much of their lives territorially; and the organizational rules they follow are often so pervasive as to pass unnoticed until someone breaks them, much as no one notices the aroma of the air until the gasworks spring a leak.

This curious combination of compulsion and invisibility shows up at the smallest scale in the way men define and manage their individual space. Each of us, as Edward Hall puts it, carries an "invisible bubble" which defines his personal space. Inside that space (which might extend, for example, as much as twenty inches in front of the person's face, but only six inches from his side) the individual tries to maintain control. Anyone who enters without invitation is intruding; voluntarily bringing someone else within that range implies a degree of intimacy. Hall offers a ladder correlating conversational distance, appropriate subject matter, and proper voice.[3] (See table below.)

	Distance in Feet	Subject Matter	Voices
Very close	.25–.50	Top secret	Soft whisper
Close	.75–1.0	Very confidential	Audible whisper
Near	1–1.75	Confidential	Indoors soft voice; outdoors soft voice
Neutral 1	1.75–3	Personal	Soft voice, low volume
Neutral 2	4.5–5	Nonpersonal information	Full voice
Public distance	5.5–8	Public information	Full voice, slightly overloud
Across the room	8–20	Talking to a group	Loud voice
Stretching the limits of distance	20–24 indoors; up to 100 outdoors	Hailing distance, departures	Shouting

Source: From *The Silent Language* by Edward T. Hall, copyright © 1959 by Edward T. Hall. Reprinted by permission of the author and Doubleday Company, Inc.

On the whole, Americans—true to their expansive reputation—maintain rather large personal spaces. The corresponding distances are slighter for Latin Americans and Mediterraneans. As a result, an Italian who positions himself for a casual conversation with an American often finds the American retreating in puzzlement, while the American who establishes the initial distance is likely to find the Italian closing in.

That is what makes the maintenance of personal space interesting—the fact that it is attached to a cultural system of communication. The size and shape of the invisible bubble vary from culture to culture and with the position of the individual within the culture. Any particular group of people tend to have similar bubbles. The individual only modifies his bubble very gradually and has to negotiate implicit new agreements with others as he does so. Personal space is not really an individual phenomenon at all, but a social product parallel to a language.

In fact, we have only to look around carefully at a gathering to see how each person's maintenance of his own space compounds into complicated patterns which themselves communicate some news about the occasion to each participant. Watch what happens to the spatial pattern when half a dozen conversational groups turn into a single audience at the sound of a guitar. Just as important, the social definition of the occasion silently sets the rules for personal space; compare riding on a subway, reading in a library, drinking in a bar. (If you doubt that the rules are all that well-defined, try adopting subway reading distances in a library sometime.)

At the scale of the village, city, or region, regularities in the human organization of space are just as striking, although they are much less open to explanation in terms of genetics or small-group dynamics. Each people has its own pattern of settlement. Within North America alone, traditional village arrangements run to a great variety, including the French-Canadian line village with its streets parallel to the river and its farms perpendicular to both; the New England town centered on the green and meeting places; the clustered Spanish-Mexican settlement; the ideologically prescribed Mormon spatial plan; a hundred variants of Indian and Eskimo village patterns. Each bears the stamp of the people's routines and preoccupations.

The overt symbolism of spatial arrangements varies from culture to culture and from activity to activity. The Javanese, according to Justus Van der Kroef, forcefully impress their conceptions of the universe on the space they occupy:

> Even in its outward structures the community of men conforms to cosmic precept: the partitions of the traditional Javanese house no less than the architectural plan of *kraton* (court) or urban square, or the concentric structure of temple shrine and monument, show the existence of the ancient classification system, the divisions according to the wind directions, each indicating an appropriate human function or ritualistic obligation. . . .[4]

Most people, however, live within spatial arrangements whose order is both less obvious and less overtly symbolic than that of the Javanese town. The standard grid pattern of American towns results to an important degree from a certain kind of real estate speculation, but its builders neither conformed self-consciously to sacred precept nor deliberately undertook to lay out a memorial to real estate.

Many other determinants besides conscious symbolic intentions shape human spatial patterns. The normative approach to community analysis may emphasize symbolic intentions, but it also covers those patterns arising as a by-product of behavior which follows certain rules and orientations. For example, Orthodox Jews who reject mechanical transportation on the Sabbath will cluster near Orthodox synagogues even in the absence of an injunction to settle together. Interactional theorists often have called attention to the ways in which a class system based on selection and exclusion produces residential segregation where residence itself is an important base for personal interaction. Locational arguments tend to concentrate on the ways that economizing on time-distance for the carrying out of critical activities such as marketing and manufacturing leads to regular spatial distributions of those activities. Ecological analyses tend to give the greatest weight to relations between human populations and specific features of their nonhuman environment: obstacles, natural resources, climate, and so on. As the review article by Otis Dudley Duncan in this chapter suggests, the most general, systematic theories we have of these relations between large-scale patterns of human activity tend to stress the economizing of time, space, effort, and resources. That may be because the basic spatial regularities are essentially economic; I think it is because economic geographers and their allies have put more effort into spatial analysis than anyone else, and because they began the work with more comprehensive theories.

WHICH AFFECTS WHAT?

The connection between spatial arrangements and social life offers the hope that we can read one from the other. Since large-scale spatial patterns are publicly visible, perhaps we can use them to learn about the stratification system or the operation of the economy. Several of the studies reported by Duncan make that sort of effort—for example, using the spatial distribution of residences of different occupational groups within American cities to get at the nature of the occupational hierarchy. My report on Boston's social structure applies the same kind of procedure to comparisons among racial, ethnic, and occupational segregation within the metropolitan area. The segregation pattern is in itself a social fact which influences the lives of city-dwellers, for example by determining the length and character of their daily journeys to work. Most students of segregation patterns, however, attempt to do more than specify their effects; they aim to grasp the systems of discrimination and stratification which lie behind them.

Actually, the effects of spatial arrangements are hard to track down. We do not really know, for instance, at what point densities of settlement themselves begin to disrupt established patterns of social life—if only because rising densities also *result* from changes in established patterns. How do we separate cause and effect? Calhoun did some famous laboratory experiments with Norway rats in which, beyond a critical threshold, rising numbers brought a switch to erratic behavior even when the food supply was adequate. There he separated cause and effect by deliberately manipulating density while holding other major factors constant. We would not want any experimenter to have that much power over human living conditions. So we have to search for "natural experiments," where densities change while other things remain fairly constant or change in a way which is easy to allow for. Natural experiments are rare. As a result, no one can be sure that the conditions we often find with high density have any causal connection with it.

In a similar vein, many Americans think that location in a high-rise apartment, a row house, or a single-family dwelling (with a yard) in itself makes a big difference to the character of family life. It is easy to establish that different kinds of families do actually live in each; it is possible to try out alternative explanations of why they do. Yet above and beyond the sorting process, does placement in one kind of dwelling or another significantly affect the family's social life? Imagine the sort of "natural experiment" that requires: similar families, similarly observed, in dissimilar dwellings but under similar general conditions—an unlikely set of conditions, to say the least.

What is more, the most careful studies done so far indicate that the independent effect of housing (as compared with class, national origin, and so on) on such central matters as health, school performance, or family stability is weak and complex. So it is with most direct effects of spatial arrangements on social life. Since community planning bears mainly on the arrangements and use of space, this means reliable conclusions concerning the effects of alternative designs for planning the environment are hard to obtain. For that reason, even the modest and tentative insights concerning housing design offered by Michelson's article in Chapter 5 required a great deal of sifting among ambiguous and conflicting findings. As the articles in this book illustrate, the relations we know well are correlations but not necessarily causes.

Obviously, all social activities take place in space. Only some activities have strong ties to particular spaces or to particular arrangements of space. Religious ceremonies often draw an important part of their impact from their location in holy places: the spring pilgrimage to the shrine at the head of the valley, the temple wedding, the rites of Artemis' sacred grove. Games often depend on a standardized spatial order, but the players usually can recreate the order in a variety of locations. The game of checkers takes a checkerboard, yet one can make his own board and play the game almost anywhere. I have played baseball where the bases were a few old boards and a street corner. Still, without some sort of diamond the game is not baseball.

Some complicated social activities, such as group singing, have neither a compelling spatial order nor a strong attachment to any particular location. (Yet the ease with which we recognize the "proper" arrangement and location of a choir tells us that nothing about singing makes it *intrinsically* incompatible with ritualized spatial order; we are dealing with powerful cultural conventions, not necessary connections.) Both spatial order and localization are variables. They vary somewhat independently of each other.

TERRITORIAL GROUPS

Spatial order and localization vary for groups as well as for activities. That should surprise hardly anyone, for one of the main ways of identifying a population as a "group" is by tracing its involvement in a common set of activities. A corporation has a home office, but (as compared, say, with a household or a state) corporations float in space. On the other hand, a special way of sharing a private space defines a household, and a special relationship to a particular, substantial, continuous territory defines a state. By and large, the groups to which men acquire primordial attachments and obligations have well-established territorial bases. For the most part, groups which are not localized and which have little spatial order exert only weak, fleeting, and specialized control over the lives of their members— although exceptions like the modern corporation make it clear that this is a trend and not an iron law. The generally stronger ties of members to groups which have well-defined locations and/or spatial orders probably result from the greater ease of monitoring and controlling performance under those circumstances, and from a tendency of nonspatial groups which accumulate coercive power and loyalty also to acquire control over distinct territories. As Stinchcombe puts it in his article in this chapter, significant "small social systems" almost invariably acquire their own private spaces and succeed in having their prior rights to those spaces recognized by other interested parties.

The community, then, is but one of several groups distinguished by a well-defined attachment to a particular territory and a well-defined arrangement of population and activities within the territory. The state, the province, the clan, the neighborhood (where it exists), some kinds of bands, some kinds of gangs, and the household all belong to the same general class as the community.

Conflicting definitions of community abound. Fabricators of definitions all tend to begin from the notion of a localized group with strong ties and a well-defined spatial order; they begin to take rather different tacks when considering groups with strong ties, weak localization, and little spatial order (as in, say, a "professional community"), or weak ties with strong localization and extensive spatial order (as in, say, a "metropolitan community"). The way to arrive at a consistent and useful definition is to use only one of the major theoretical alternatives—locational, interactional, ecological, or normative—and follow it through. Yet for the moment what matters is the central picture of a localized population with well-defined spatial organization, strong ties of coercion, and/or loyalty binding the individual to the group. The great bulk of the world's population, present and past, have lived most of their lives within groups which easily fit such a picture.

THE CHIMERA OF COMMUNITY

In thinking about the communities in which most people have lived, however, we should guard against assuming that they were ordinarily tight, happy, and unified. When people today complain about the "loss of community," they usually have more than territorial coexistence in mind. They mean loss of solidarity, which they suppose happened recently with the rise of industrial organization. The same theme preoccupied moral and political writers of the nineteenth century. In his *Sybil,* one of the best-known novels of nineteenth-century social life, the statesman Benjamin Disraeli inserted the following dialogue:

> "As for community," said a voice which proceeded neither from Egremont nor the stranger, "with the monasteries expired the only type that we ever had in England of such an intercourse. There is no community in England; there is aggregation, but aggregation under circumstances which make it rather a dissociating than a uniting principle. . . ."
> "It is a community of purpose that constitutes society," continued the younger stranger, "without that, men may be drawn into contiguity, but they still continue virtually isolated."
> "And is that their condition in cities?"
> "It is their condition everywhere; but in cities that condition is aggravated.

A density of population implies a severer struggle for existence, and a subsequent repulsion of elements brought into too close contact. In great cities, men are brought together by the desire of gain. They are not in a state of co-operation, but of isolation, as to the making of fortunes; and for all the rest they are careless of neighbors. Christianity teaches us to love our neighbor as oneself; modern society acknowledges no neighbors."[5]

Strip away the Victorian language and you find an argument which is current today. Disraeli's line of thought took root in a discipline—sociology—which was just forming as he wrote. The sociologists have kept alive the idea of an antithesis between large scale and solidarity, between self-interest and interdependence, between urbanization and community, up to our own day.

Time and time again, students of local life in the industrial world try to determine whether "the community" still exists, or has disintegrated. Is the urban neighborhood a real community? Is the rural market area a community? What would it take to remake cities into genuine communities?

For the most part, these questions are misleading. A number of real changes have occurred in human communities with the advance of industrial organization. They have grown larger, more complicated, more interdependent. Yet none of these transformations guarantees a loss of solidarity. When we look at smaller, simpler, more independent communities in which men used to live, we find them divided, stratified, oppressive—not always, by any means, but often enough to make us realize that the picture of the old rural community with which people commonly compare today's cities and suburbs is a myth. In his article on a French village in this chapter, Pitt-Rivers describes a small peasant community with a relatively simple structure and a fair degree of autonomy. He also describes the mutual contempt and structural division between the factions of villagers and farmers. The changes Pitt-Rivers observes as his village is drawn increasingly into French national life are certainly making it a different sort of place: more completely French-speaking, more attuned to the national ranking of occupations or styles of life, and so on. The changes are not, however, destroying the reality of a unified, solidary community.

The historical myth of disappearing solidarity expresses a moral sense that men *ought* to live in solidary communities. It belongs to a whole set of cherished historical myths: the declining functions of the family, the increasing rootlessness of mankind, the dissolution of religious faith, the rise of criminality. Every one of these is false as a simple, general statement about modern experience; they serve mainly as a device for comparing (unfavorably, without exception) present reality against a moral ideal. These myths therefore figure frequently in utopian thinking of both the reactionary and the radical variety; they have been built into standard schemes for the analysis of social change which treat them as regular consequences of something called "modernization." And every one of them points, in a confused way, to transformations which really have occurred.

The chimera of community brings together two elements: the moral longing for solidarity and an awareness that the rise of the industrial community has changed the likely bases of solidarity. The great bulk of the world's people still live, as they always have, in relatively small households composed mainly of close kinsmen. But in industrial countries households are now relatively less important as containers of the whole round of social life, as holders of property, as basic political units within communities. Associations, firms, parties, unions, and other large, formally organized groups have gained in importance. To some extent they claim loyalty and provide the bases of solidarity.

The change is only relative. As the review of migration patterns by Mac-Donald and MacDonald in this chapter shows, even in great industrial cities networks based on kinship and common origin play an enormous part in tying people into local social life. The authors describe the widespread practice of "chain migration," in which one person or household migrates from a community without losing contact with it, establishes a foothold in a new community, sends back information, funds, and other resources, assists the migration of other members of the sending community, and so on until a regular chain of migrants exists. Chain migration acts to create durable clusters of Italians in American cities.

Variants of this migratory pattern operate throughout the world. The general pattern sometimes has the paradoxical effect of making attachments to kinsmen and fellow countrymen more salient in the big city than they ever were back in the village. (Janet Abu-Lughod's analysis in Chapter 2 of rural-urban differences in Egypt mentions migration patterns from village to city which have some important parallels with the American situation.) The result is not just a big village within the city, or a more tightly knit community, but a new kind of structure. These are real changes, although they do not amount to the dissolution of community.

The bases of solidarity matter. Kin groups behave differently from labor unions. If the acting units within communities shift from kin groups to labor unions, the communities themselves will behave differently. The trouble with treating such a shift a priori as a "loss of community" is precisely that it hampers any serious analysis of the conditions under which communities or their subdivisions can act together, develop orientations to common goals, provide their members with a sense of belonging, and so on. That task will be easier if we start from a strictly locational, strictly interactional, strictly ecological, or strictly normative conception of the community, and then proceed to treat the degrees and forms of solidarity as variable features of communities, as variables to be explained.

Norton Long's provocative article "The Local Community as an Ecology of Games" (see the bibliography to this chapter) illustrates what I have in mind. Long begins by identifying a community as nothing more than all the groups interacting within a particular territory. He goes on to point out that sets of the groups interact with particular intensity and carry on the joint activities he labels *games:* the banking game, the communications game, and so forth. The games themselves interact—hence the analogy to a set of organisms interacting within the same niche, an ecology—and produce collective effects such as the flow of traffic or the distribution of wealth. Finally, he begins to sketch the conditions under which the players are likely to coordinate their efforts deliberately, to orient themselves to the common territory as such, and to respond somehow to the collective welfare (or "ill-fare") of the groups within the territory. His sketch is tentative and controversial; but it is a vast improvement over debating whether the city, suburb, or metropolitan area really *is* a community.

ARTICLES IN THIS CHAPTER

None of the authors in this chapter troubles himself much whether certain places really are communities. The objects of their study range from very small communities to very large, and their actual means of delineating communities vary over the whole range of normative, ecological, interactional, and locational ideas. The authors tend to be matter-of-fact rather than agonizing about whether they really are studying communities. Otis Dudley Duncan's review of a variety of findings concerning the spatial distributions of human populations stays close to an ecological perspective and demonstrates the advantages of its clarity. Duncan does not state general principles of community structure or territorial organization. He does show that there are some persistent and intriguing regularities in the way men occupy their territories and that the regularities lend themselves to analysis by simple quantitative procedures. The article by Julian Pitt-Rivers is very different: the anthropologist's discussion of a general problem in social organization through the careful analysis of a single place he knows by direct experience. The general problem is the relationship between the external involvements of a community and the character of the divisions within it. Pitt-Rivers has some valuable things to tell us about the intersection of social class, linguistic practice, and lines of solidarity and division within his community. For our purposes, his study is valuable for the glimpse it gives us of a time-honored method, the intense study of a single small community by a participant. John and Leatrice MacDonald obviously have some particular cities like New York in mind as they write about chain migration, but they, too, attempt to identify the regular features of a process which is very widespread.

Arthur Stinchcombe provides the most deliberately comparative paper in the chapter. Like Pitt-Rivers, he is searching for the answers to a fairly narrow set of questions: the explanation of the major differences in police practice between cities and rural communities. Also like Pitt-Rivers, the set of explanatory principles he brings into play will serve for a much wider range of phenomena. Stinchcombe systematically considers how the various divisions of different kinds of communities into public and private spaces (the public spaces being the ones police can patrol easily) affect the aspects of social life which occur in view of strangers. My treatment of metropolitan Boston's social structure has something in common with Stinchcombe's article, in that every metropolitan resident develops some sort of mental map of the metropolis, yet few can grasp the whole pattern without the help of specialized tools like land-use maps or tabulations of population distribution. The essay consists mainly of crude descriptions of population distribution using some simple devices and some common sources of data. I have included it in this chapter because (1) it presents a schematic picture of a whole community (and a big one, at that), (2) the procedures it uses are widely applicable elsewhere, (3) it gives a sense of the complexities and special features of metropolitan communities, and (4) it shows the analytic approach based on territory: activity: population in action instead of in the abstract formulation with which this book began.

NOTES

1. V. C. Wynne-Edwards *Animal Dispersion in Relation to Social Behavior* (New York: Hafner, 1962), pp. 45–46.
2. Reprinted by permission from John Hurrell Crook, "The Socio-ecology of Primates," in J. H. Crook, ed., *Social Behavior in Birds and Mammals* (New York and London: Academic Press, 1970), p. 125.
3. See also Edward T. Hall, *The Hidden Dimension* (Garden City: Doubleday Anchor, 1969); Robert Sommer, "The Distance for Comfortable Conversation," *Sociometry* 25 (1962): 111–116; Sommer, *Personal Space: The Behavioral Basis of Design* (Englewood Cliffs, N.J.: Prentice-Hall, 1969).
4. Justus M. Van der Kroef, "Javanese Messianic Expectations: Their Origin and Cultural Context," *Comparative Studies in Society and History* 1 (June 1959): 302.
5. Benjamin Disraeli, Earl of Beaconsfield, *Sybil, or the Two Nations* (London: Longmans, Green and Co., 1907), pp. 74–76.

POPULATION DISTRIBUTION AND COMMUNITY STRUCTURE

Otis Dudley Duncan

In this essay, O. D. Duncan makes a deliberate effort to link the study of human communities to plant and animal ecology. Many people write essays restating the old truths: that man is part of nature, too; that organisms which destroy their environments eventually destroy themselves; that the unrestrained growth of any element of an ecosystem upsets all other parts of the ecosystem. Duncan does not deny the old truths. Yet his essay stands out from most other writings on the subject in two regards. First, he wrote it ten or fifteen years before ecology became a popular watchword. Second, he lays out specific findings concerning the distribution of human populations without making quick and risky analogies to animal behavior. (No "territorial instinct" here.)

Instead, Duncan calls attention to a series of regularities in the spatial distributions of human populations: density gradients in cities, divisions of labor between major cities and their hinterlands, occupational differences by size of place, "population potential" as a predictor of densities and of economic activity. In each case, he identifies the problem, sketches the kinds of models people have used to deal with the problem, mentions some of the findings, and pinpoints difficulties in the models or the findings. He gives, for instance, a lucid summary of research showing how the geography of economic activity in a region orients itself to the location of the region's major cities. Duncan offers no grand synthesis or "supertheory." He wants to show simply that the distribution of human population displays a number of important and intriguing regularities, that the regularities are open to systematic analysis, and that we have available a few models which help make sense of the regularities.

The essay does not consider the process of urbanization explicitly, but it does deal with communities and with cities as special types of communities. Within Duncan's ecological framework, neither the solidarity of the community nor the extent to which it is clearly distinguishable from other communities poses much of a problem. Boundaries present practical problems, such as distinguishing metropolitan areas from the rest of the country; but a variety of solutions to the problems will work so long as they are clear and consistent. Any permanent local population counts as a community. Cities, then, are large, dense, nucleated, nonagricultural communities. Both definitions fall well within the ecological tradition. From the definition, Duncan proceeds to a simple theory: as a consequence of being large, dense, nucleated, and nonagricultural, cities (1) exert strong influence over their own supply and market areas, (2) develop an extensive division of labor "on both a territorial and a social basis." The article follows up the theory with supporting evidence. Some of the evidence concerns the interactions between cities and their hinterlands; some of it concerns the internal differentiation of cities; all of it serves to demonstrate the utility and flexibility of an ecological approach to social organization.

I doubt that the fundamental principles of zoological, botanical, and economic location theory differ very greatly.—August Lösch (1954, p. 185)

The thesis of this paper is that population ecology and community ecology are, or should be, closely related branches of human ecology. For purposes of illustration the paper focuses on the linkages between the study of population distribution—sometimes regarded as a demographic problem—and the analysis of community structure. The concept of community structure is given a somewhat more inclusive meaning than it sometimes has in human ecology, in that it is conceived here to embrace not only the organization of localized populations, but also the interrelations among local communities.

Substantively, the paper presents examples of data supporting various empirical propositions about community structure. These propositions are more or less plausible in terms of generalized notions about the nature of the human community. However, they could not be said to represent careful deductions from a body

Reprinted by permission from "Population Distribution and Community Structure" by Otis Dudley Duncan, *Cold Spring Harbor Symposia*, XXII (1957), pp. 357–371.

of rigorously organized theory. Nor can it be claimed that the verification of these propositions is satisfactory as yet, in the absence of extensive comparative studies. But at least they will illustrate some of the approaches and methods of contemporary human ecology. It is left for the reader to judge whether Lösch's remark affords a basis for interaction between students of the human community and investigators dealing with plant or animal populations and the biotic community.

The paper comprises four major parts, taking up in turn the city, the metropolitan center and its hinterland, the hierarchy of cities, and demographic gravitation, each considered as a framework for the study of population distribution.

1. THE CITY

The ecological conception of the city regards it as a permanent nucleated settlement of population within a circumscribed territory whose inhabitants are too numerous and closely spaced to grow or appropriate directly their own food supply. The essential features of the city are, then, its permanence, its size, its density (Wirth, 1938), and its nonagricultural subsistence base (Sorokin and Zimmerman, 1929, Chap. 1). To these must be added the necessity of a social organization functionally adapted to this mode of existence. The most important organizational considerations are (1) interdependence between the city and its supply and market areas, (2) differentiation and specialization in the activities of units of the urban community, and (3) the allocation of space to these units within the community area—in short, a division of labor on both a territorial and a social basis. We are entitled to regard nucleation as a basic aspect of the city because relationships among units of the urban community are not spatially randomized, but rather tend to be focused or concentrated at one or a few points. The concept of nucleation is broad enough to admit of multiple nucleation, although it is often true that multi-centered cities have a single, more or less distinct, predominant center. A somewhat different aspect of nucleation is brought out by the observation that the city as a whole may serve as a center or node for a more or less extended trade or service area; this phenomenon is examined subsequently.

If nucleation is fundamental to urban community organization, one would naturally begin the study of population distribution within the city by examining its pattern with respect to the city's center or centers. Surprisingly little systematic study has been devoted to the pattern of variation of population density from one part of the city to another. Stewart (1947b) and Clark (1951) have suggested that residential density tends to fall off exponentially with increasing distance from the principal center of the city. Table 1 presents, for several American cities, Clark's estimates of the parameters of the function, $y = Ae^{-bx}$, where y is number of inhabitants (in 1,000's) per square mile and x is distance in miles from the center of the city (in the "downtown" or central business district). The parameter, A, represents the density in the immediate (infinitesimal) vicinity of the center, but it is a purely hypothetical quantity, for two reasons: first, because density at a point has no strict mathematical meaning, even as a limit; and second, because the central area is essentially a non-residential district whose resident population density usually is far below that of the contiguous areas. The parameter, A, does, however, give some notion of the peak level of density encountered in areas near the center.

TABLE 1

Estimated Parameters of the Function $y = Ae^{-bx}$, for y = Population
(in 1000's) per Square Mile and x = Distance (in miles) from Center of City,
for Selected Cities in the United States: 1900 and 1940

City	1900			1940		
	A	b	Range, x = 0 to	A	b	Range, x = 0 to
Boston	160	.85	5	50	.30	17
Chicago	110	.45	7	120	.30	18
Cleveland	—	—	—	90	.45	11
Los Angeles	—	—	—	30	.25	17
New York	250	.55	8	120	.20	25
Philadelphia	120	.65	6	60	.40	12
St. Louis	70	.75	5	40	.45	10

Source: Clark (1951)

The parameter, *b*, appearing in the equation with a minus sign, indicates how rapidly density falls off with distance: the greater the absolute magnitude of *b*, the steeper the density gradient.

Clark's estimates indicate considerable variation among cities and over time in the height and slope of the density gradient. One hypothesis that comes to mind immediately is that the timing of changes in the technology of local transportation is responsible for certain of these variations. In all five cities for which comparative figures are given, the density gradient became much less steep over the forty-year period. It was around the middle of this period that the automobile was becoming a major element in the system of local movements, permitting rapid access over more widely dispersed parts of the community area than had been true under earlier technologies. The low densities and gentle gradient observed in Los Angeles no doubt are related to the fact that a major portion of that city's growth occurred in the "automobile age," as contrasted with some of the older cities whose residential patterns were well established under an earlier regime of technology (see section 3 of this paper). Of course, other factors are relevant—for example, the obstacles to constructing multi-story buildings presented by the substratum of the city's site. Inasmuch as all these cities expanded in both areal and population size during the last several decades, one can infer from the figures that more recent growth has been at lower densities, on the whole, than earlier growth, as expected from the improvement in accessibility. On the other hand, the developments in construction technology have influenced the change in the opposite direction. With a larger sample of cities it would be pertinent to compare cities having equal population sizes at different dates, to bring out the effect of technological changes and the timing of expansion.

Blumenfeld (1949) presents residential density figures with three degrees of "net-ness" in the measurement of land area. (See Table 2.) These figures make it

TABLE 2
Gradients in Density of Residential Population
and Manufacturing Employment, Philadelphia: 1940

| Miles from Center of City | *Resident Population per Acre of—* | | | *Manufacturing Employment per Acre of All Land (1943)* |
	All land	*Land in "residential area"*	*Land in residential parcels*	
City, total	22.6	55.2	102.5	3.9
0–1	47.4	99.2	173.3	28.4
1–2	74.2	101.0	196.1	8.2
2–3	54.4	93.7	177.4	7.1
3–4	29.9	72.5	138.3	5.3
4–5	20.2	47.7	85.6	5.5
5–6	18.8	35.7	67.9	2.3
6–7	17.3	32.0	58.3	1.2
7–8	8.5	20.4	36.0	1.1
8–9	6.7	17.2	33.1	0.7
9 and over	0.8	5.1	8.5	0.4

Source: Blumenfeld (1949).

plain that the exponential decrease of density with distance characterizes not only gross population density, but also densities calculated on the basis of area devoted to residential uses. The following (graphic) estimates of the parameters in the function, $y = Ae^{-bx}$, with y = density in persons per acre and x = distance from center, are obtained for the three series in Table 2: gross density (calculated on the basis of all land), $A = 110$, $-b = .33$; net density, based on "residential area," $A = 160$, $-b = .26$; net density, based on land in residential parcels, $A = 320$, $-b = .27$. These equations were calculated from the data for areas between one and 9 miles from the center, because the first interval is not expected to conform to the equation and the last interval is given in open-end form.

(The figures given by Blumenfeld for gross density are not quite consistent with Clark's 1940 equation for Philadelphia, as will be seen from transforming Clark's equation to a persons-per-acre basis. Apparently there is a systematic error in Clark's figures on land area, and/or his estimates are heavily weighted by the data for distance intervals beyond 9 miles.)

The declining gradient of residential density with increasing distance from the center no doubt is produced by two factors: the closer spacing of residential structures toward the center of the city, and the tendency of multiple-unit structures to be concentrated toward the center. In Chicago in 1939, the number of dwelling units per residential structure varied as follows from the center of the city outward: 3.7, 3.0, 2.9, 2.8, 2.3, 1.5, 1.3, and 1.4 (by two-mile intervals, running from 0 to 2 miles to 14 to 16 miles from the center of the city).

The more intensive use of residential land toward the center of the city reflects both the competition among residential units (households) for accessible sites and the competition among residential and non-residential units for such sites. Blumenfeld's data, cited in the last column of Table 2, indicate that there is a declining gradient in the density of manufacturing employment with increasing distance from the center of the city. Not only industrial, but also commercial establishments are more effective than residential units in acquiring control of accessible sites. Hence the proportion of land in residential use tends to be lowest at the center of the city and to increase as one moves outward from the center. In Chicago in 1939, only 2.3 per cent of the land within one mile of the center was in residential use, as compared with 33 per cent at a distance of 7 to 9 miles (B. Duncan, 1957).

But non-residential units compete effectively for accessible sites only by using land more intensively. Table 3 shows that the number of persons working in manufacturing establishments per unit of land occupied by such establishments declines rapidly with distance from the center of the city. The data in the first column of Table 3 suggest that the gradient is approximated by the exponential formula, $y = 8.0\ e^{-.19x}$, where y is number of employees in manufacturing per 1,000 square feet of land occupied by manufacturing establishments and x is distance in miles from the center of the city. As a consequence of the more intensive industrial land use near the center, typically only small establishments can occupy sites in this vicinity. Thus the data in the second and third columns of Table 3 indicate that establishment size, either in terms of employment or in terms of land area occupied, decreases toward the center of the city. (The survey on which Table 3 is based was not entirely complete; it is estimated that about 3/10 of all

TABLE 3
Gradients in Industrial Land Use, Chicago: 1951

Miles from Center of City	Manufacturing Employees per 1000 Sq. Ft. of Land Occupied	Manufacturing Employees per Establishment	Land Occupied per Establishment (in 1000 sq. ft.)
City, total	2.5	85.7	34.1
0–2	7.1	63.6	9.0
2–4	3.1	70.5	22.7
4–6	3.4	107.0	31.9
6–8	2.7	99.2	36.9
8–10	1.3	61.0	47.0
10–12	1.4	257.5	181.4
12–14	0.6	220.4	371.9
14–16	0.4	200.2	561.0

Source: Unpublished tabulations of the 1951 Industrial Survey of the Chicago Plan Commission.

establishments were omitted, but that the employment count and land area measurement were only 1/10 incomplete. This may account, in part, for the fact that the gradient in column two is not so regular as that in column one.) Consequently, establishments requiring a large labor force or an extensive area tend to locate toward the periphery of the city. This produces a differentiation among parts of the community area in terms of kind of industry.

In confirmation of the last point, total manufacturing can be broken down by kind of industry, yielding 25 industry groups. A measure of the degree to which each group is concentrated toward the center of the city—the "index of centralization"—exhibits strong relationships with indexes of establishment size and propensity to use land intensively. The rank correlation, over the 25 industry groups, between the index of centralization and the average number of employees per unit of land occupied for establishments in the industry is .63, while the rank correlation between centralization and land area per establishment is −.69. Moreover, industries tending to be "decentralized" within the city are, by and large, the same ones that tend, in disproportionate numbers, to find "suburban" locations beyond the city limits. The rank correlation, over the 25 industry groups, between the per cent of city employment located in the "inner zone" of the city (approximately a five-mile radius from the center) and the per cent of the total metropolitan area employment located within the city limits is .73. This correlation rises to .84 if one omits the most deviant single industry, which happens also to be the smallest one in the metropolitan area in terms of employment.

(The "index of centralization" referred to in the preceding paragraph is a generalization of Gini's "concentration ratio" obtained as follows: Compute the percent of an industry's employment in each distance zone, and cumulate the percentages from the center outward. Compute, similarly, the cumulated percentages for a suitable base quantity to which to relate employment. In this case, resident population was used as the base quantity, but similar results are obtained by using, say, land area. The index is obtained from the formula,

$$\sum_{i=1}^{k} X_{i-1} Y_i - \sum_{i=1}^{k} X_i Y_{i-1},$$

where X_i is the cumulated proportion of employment through the ith zone, Y_i is the corresponding cumulated proportion of the base quantity, and k is the number of distance zones. This index varies between −1.0 for complete decentralization, through zero for even distribution by zones, to +1.0 for complete centralization. For details regarding computation and interpretation, see Hauser, Duncan, and Duncan, 1956.)

In Chicago, one finds such industries as printing and publishing, apparel and related products, and the manufacture of instruments and related products highly concentrated toward the center of the city, whereas industries like blast furnaces and steel mills, processing of petroleum and coal products, and the fabrication of heavy transportation equipment are peripherally located, on the whole. One would expect to observe similar differences by type of industry in other manufacturing centers, though, of course, the specific locational patterns would vary from city to city.

Thus far, we have considered only two (households and industrial establishments) among the many kinds of units whose spatial disposition reflects the territorial structure of the urban community. Similar kinds of analysis can and should be carried out for others, of course. Letting these results serve as illustrations, we may consider two significant global measures of the pattern of nucleation—the distribution of daytime population and aggregate land values.

Units, other than households, typically are distributed in accordance with the sites at which the population carries on its daytime activities, work, shopping, education, and so on. The distribution of daytime population, therefore, is closely related to the over-all intensiveness of nonresidential land use. Unfortunately, we have no accurate counts of daytime population by small areas of the city, but rough estimates indicate that the gradient of daytime population density by distance from the center is much steeper than that of resident population. Foley (1954) gives the following estimates, for a composite of five large cities, of the ratio of daytime to resident population, by distance zones in half-mile intervals from the center of the city: 23.84, 7.41, 2.33, 1.53, 1.15, 0.93, 0.95, and 0.94, with a ratio of 0.82 for the entire area outside a four-mile radius. For the aggregate of all areas in the five cities, the ratio is 1.24, implying a considerable movement of population into the city during the day from beyond the city limits, in addition to the pronounced shift of the city's own residents toward the center during the day. (These estimates may be somewhat too high, but there is no doubt as to the general direction of the diurnal population movement.) The daytime population distribution, of course, is not a fixed pattern: It is more realistic to think in terms of daily and weekly cycles of daytime population *movement*. The figures just cited reflect the peak of the movement away from residential locations, which is generally observed around 12 noon to 3:00 P.M.

The consequence of intensive land use toward the city center and the competition among units for central sites is that land values are inflated at the center, diminishing toward the periphery of the city. Hawley (1955) gives data on mean assessed land value by distance from the center of Okayama, Japan, in 1952 which suggest that the gradient is roughly exponential in form, and may be approximately described by the equation, $y = 76e^{-.74x}$, where y is value in yen (adjusted to the 1940 value of the yen) per tsubo (3.4 square meters) and x is distance from the point of highest value in kilometers. The curve fits the data moderately well over the range from 0.5 to 5.0 kilometers, but the average land value, 114 yen, in the zone within half a kilometer of the center is considerably higher than would be estimated from the equation. The land value data, therefore, like the statistics on daytime population, indicate that the importance of the central area is disproportionate to that of the immediately contiguous zones. A remarkable feature of Hawley's study is that the land-value pattern observed in 1952 bore a strong resemblance to that of 1940, despite the fact that about two-thirds of the city's built-up section was destroyed by aerial bombardment during World War II and rebuilt subsequently. The re-establishment of the pattern points strongly to the conclusion that the land-value gradient is no mere historical accident, but reflects the influence of powerful forces determining the structure of the city. The land-value pattern of Okayama resembles that of many American cities, although the writer is not familiar with any data depicting the distance gradient for an American city in as convenient a fashion as Hawley's data for Okayama.

Thus far, households or residential units have been considered as one type of unit in the organization of the urban community. But it is necessary to recognize as well numerous categoric distinctions among kinds of households. Among the important categoric groups are households of similar social status and those of common ethnic background. Two propositions will be illustrated: (1) Variation among status groups in ability to pay for more or less desirable residential sites and structures leads to a spatial segregation of these groups, such that the degree of spatial separation of two groups is a direct function of the discrepancy between their socio-economic levels. (2) When increments to the population of a city occur by successive waves of ethnically distinct groups, there develops a pattern of segregation among these groups reflecting the length of time they have been in the community (and, in all likelihood, their socio-economic status, which, in turn, is related to time of arrival).

Table 4 presents indexes of dissimilarity in spatial distribution of the eight major occupation groups in Chicago and averages of such indexes for a group of selected smaller cities. (The index of dissimilarity is computed as the sum of the positive differences between two per cent distributions. In this case the distributions are calculated to show the percentage of all persons employed in a given

TABLE 4
Indexes of Dissimilarity in Residential Distribution among Major Occupation
Groups, for Employed Males, Chicago Metropolitan District
and Average for Eight Medium-Sized Cities: 1950
(Distributions computed for census tracts)

	Major Occupation Group							
Major Occupation Group	*1*	*2*	*3*	*4*	*5*	*6*	*7*	*8*
1. Professional, technical, and kindred workers	—	13	15	28	35	44	41	54
2. Managers, officials, and proprietors, except farm	13	—	13	28	33	41	40	52
3. Sales workers	15	12	—	27	35	42	38	54
4. Clerical and kindred workers	25	21	16	—	16	21	24	38
5. Craftsmen, foremen, and kindred workers	36	31	28	16	—	17	35	35
6. Operatives and kindred workers	46	41	39	28	17	—	26	25
7. Service workers, except private household	48	45	42	35	31	22	—	28
8. Laborers, except farm and mine	58	54	53	44	38	25	20	—

Source: Chicago data: Duncan and Duncan (1955); eight-city data: Wilkins (1956).
Note: Above diagonal, figures for Chicago; below diagonal, figures are averages for the cities (urbanized areas) of Hartford, Syracuse, Columbus, Indianapolis, Richmond, Atlanta, Memphis, Fort Worth.

occupation group who reside in each census tract in the city. A census tract is a small statistical area containing, on the average, about 3,000 to 5,000 inhabitants. The index thus indicates the proportion of one group who would have to move to a different tract to make its spatial distribution the same as that of the other group. The index of dissimilarity permits only pair-wise comparisons of distributions, but it is possible, as in Table 4, to study variations in these comparisons.)

The order in which the occupation groups are listed in Table 4 is approximately the order in which they would appear in a ranking by income, level of living, or social prestige, although there are minor variations among these alternative bases of ranking. If this order is accepted as an indicator of the "social distance" among the groups, we would expect the measure of spatial separation (the index of dissimilarity in residential distribution) to increase, reading either horizontally or vertically from the diagonal of the table. The data for the aggregate of eight medium-sized cities confirm this expectation without exception. The dissimilarity in residential distribution for such closely related groups as the managerial and the sales occupations is only 12 per cent, as compared with an index of dissimilarity of 58 per cent between such widely different occupations as the professional and manual labor jobs. The pattern for Chicago, though conforming in general to the hypothesized pattern, is not quite so regular; the same could be said for each of the eight other cities studied separately. This suggests that each community may exhibit more or less idiosyncratic features in its spatial organization, perhaps related to peculiarities of its social structure. Variations in pattern from one city to another are, of course, of considerable interest, but are beyond the scope of the present paper. (For full discussion of several pertinent hypotheses see the sources from which the data in Table 4 were drawn.)

Table 5 presents data in support of the second proposition on residential differentiation of categoric groups. Several relationships are noted: First, the residential separation of groups representing the "new" immigration (countries whose emigrants came to the United States in large numbers from about 1890 to the first World War) from the native white population is much greater than that of the "old" immigrant groups (countries sending the bulk of the emigrants before 1890). Second, the greatest degree of residential separation is observed for the Negro population. Although Negroes are not immigrants, in the sense of coming from a foreign country, the Negro migration to the North began in large volume during and after World War I, and served in many respects as a substitute for the "new" immigration, which was effectively closed off. The "newest immigrant," then, experiences the greatest spatial isolation. Third, each immigrant group is more highly separated from the remaining immigrant groups than it is from the native white population. This indicates the tendency for the formation and persistence of more or less distinct "ethnic colonies." As these colonies dissolve in the course of assimilation, their erstwhile residents tend to be absorbed into neighborhoods inhabited by the general or native population, rather than to intermingle with other particular ethnic groups. However, the tendency toward mutual separation is more apparent among the "new" immigrant groups than among the "old" immigrant groups. The former are separated as much from each other as they are from the "old" immigrant groups, which, in turn, have become spatially intermixed to a degree.

A number of the temporal changes in spatial relationships among older

TABLE 5
Indexes of Dissimilarity in Residential Distribution among
Selected Race-Nativity Groups, Chicago, 1950
(Distributions computed on the basis of the 75 community areas of Chicago)

Race or Nativity	Dissimilarity to Native White	Average Index of Dissimilarity with Respect to—		Dissimilarity to Negro
		"Old" immigrants	"New" immigrants	
Native white	—	26	46	80
Foreign-born white				
"Old" immigrants:				
Austria	18	31[a]	48	82
England and Wales	19	28[a]	51	78
Germany	27	38[a]	52	85
Ireland (Eire)	32	38[a]	59	81
Sweden	33	41[a]	63	86
"New" immigrants:				
Italy	40	52	57[a]	70
U.S.S.R.	44	48	61[a]	87
Poland	45	59	51[a]	91
Czechoslovakia	49	56	53[a]	89
Lithuania	52	58	58[a]	85
Negro	80	82	84	—

Source: Duncan and Duncan (1956).
[a]Average index of dissimilarity with respect to the other four countries in this group.

residents and in-migrating groups, inferred from the data in Table 5, are confirmed and elaborated in longitudinal studies of residential succession (Cressey, 1938; Duncan and Duncan, 1957). There is no room to summarize this body of evidence here. It should be observed, however, that each of the distributional aspects of urban structure may be studied in terms of the processes by which it develops as well as the pattern it assumes at any given moment of time.

2. METROPOLIS AND HINTERLAND

The very definition of a city, as a community which is not self-sufficient from the standpoint of sustenance, implies that there must be a territory with which it maintains regular relationships. Such a territory has come to be called the "hinterland" of the city, and its population is sometimes said to be under the "dominance" of the city. The latter concept is subject to some misunderstanding, for it is not the case that the city is less dependent on the hinterland than the hinterland is on the city (though it is perhaps true that a city can find new market and supply areas, leaving portions of its old hinterland "stranded"). The important point is that the units which mediate and control the relationships between the center and the periphery tend to be localized within the center itself. The joint localization of many such units in the city gives rise to the notion of the city as a center of dominance. Under modern conditions of cheap long distance transportation (Gilmore, 1953) and interregional trade in large volume (Gras, 1922), certain cities come to exercise "dominance" functions not only with respect to their own immediate hinterland, but also with respect to other, subordinate, centers (Vance and Smith, 1954). Such a city, typically having a comparatively large population, may be termed a metropolis. Because the relationships involved in metropolitan organization are complex and ramified, human ecologists have made only a beginning in delineating its major features and the processes by which it develops. The discussion here is confined to certain aspects of population distribution related to the structure of the metropolitan unit—the center with its tributary area.

By its very nature the concept of a metropolitan hinterland is somewhat indefinite. It is not surprising, then, that different investigators have devised different schemes for identifying metropolitan centers and for setting boundaries to their tributary areas (see, for example, Park, 1952, Chap. 16; Vance and Smith, 1954). Official statistics now frequently make use of the concepts, "standard metropolitan area," and "metropolitan State economic area." Two other concepts, proposed by private research workers, are illustrated in Table 6. Hawley's (1956) concept of "extended metropolitan area" pertains essentially to a central city of 50,000 inhabitants or more with the surrounding territory lying within a radius of approximately 45 or 50 miles. Bogue's (1949) "metropolitan communities," on the other hand, are so delineated as to exhaust the territory of the United States, on the assumption that every part of the country falls into the hinterland of one or another of the major metropolitan centers. Bogue employs somewhat more stringent criteria of metropolitan status than does Hawley, and consequently recognizes fewer metropolitan centers. There are differences between the two concepts, even for sets of identical centers: certain of the metropolitan centers recognized by Hawley are regarded by Bogue as subordinate to his centers and are assigned the status of "subdominant" cities; and Bogue's areas are much larger than Hawley's. (Compare the third and fourth columns of Table 6.) An incidental difference is that Hawley's data were obtained by aggregating statistics for minor civil divisions of counties, whereas Bogue's were secured by summing figures for whole counties.

Whichever of the two concepts of metropolitan area is employed, the data in Table 6 make it plain that there is a rather regular gradient of population density extending from the metropolitan center into the periphery of its hinterland. This finding is *prima facie* evidence of a division of labor between the central and the outlying parts, on the assumption that population density is correlated with type of economic activity. The data also suggest the hypothesis that the forms of dominance vary with size of center, inasmuch as the density gradients lie at a higher level for the largest centers than for all centers combined, both at the center and throughout the extent of the hinterland.

The density gradients shown in Table 6 cannot be fitted closely with the exponential equation used for intra-city densities in the previous section. The rate of decrease in density near the center is too great in relation to that observed at the greater distances to make the gradient linear in the logarithm of density. It would

TABLE 6
Density Gradients (population per square mile) in the Metropolitan Hinterland, Defined in Two Ways, for the United States, 1940

Distance Zone (miles)	157 Extended Metropolitan Areas	67 Metropolitan Communities	Central Cities 1,000,000 +	
			5 Extended metro. areas	5 Metro. communities
Central cities	7,862	9,047	13,846	13,053
Outside central cities				
0–5	681		11,143	
5–10	281		3,915	
10–15	137	215	1,977	957
15–20	91		841	
20–25	64		458	
25–30	63	93	297	292
30–35	58		194	
35–45	42	61	94	228
45–65	—	63	—	156
65–115	—	42	—	63
115–165	—	29	—	—
165–265	—	15	—	—
265–465	—	5	—	—
465 and over	—	4	—	—

Source: Data for "extended metropolitan areas" from Hawley (1956), Tables 3 and 11 and Appendix Table 2; data for "metropolitan communities" from Bogue (1949), Tables 3–1, 4–3, 6–1, and 6–4.

no doubt be possible to find another function to fit the data, but its value for other than purely descriptive purposes would be questionable, inasmuch as the kind of gradient observed depends a good deal on how the metropolitan areas are delineated.

Direct evidence on the division of labor between metropolis and hinterland is available in economic statistics. For example, data for 1948 show that median per capita retail sales in central cities of standard metropolitan areas amounted to $1,239, as compared with $952 in metropolitan suburbs (cities and towns of 10,000 inhabitants or more within standard metropolitan areas, but outside their central cities), and $1,243 in all other cities and towns of 10,000 to 50,000 inhabitants. These data indicate that the metropolitan center performs a considerable part of the retailing function for its suburbs, but probably only a very small part of that for cities in the more remote hinterland. The differences are not explained by purchasing power, for by and large the suburbs have higher incomes than the central cities. That the per capita sales of the more remote hinterland cities equal those of the metropolitan centers is partly explained by the fact that each such city has its own local trade territory. By contrast, the 1948 figures for median per capita wholesale sales are $1,529 for metropolitan centers, $367 for suburbs, and $701 for the remaining hinterland cities. Thus the metropolis performs wholesaling services for the entire hinterland, not for suburbs alone. The outlying cities and towns, though equalling metropolitan centers in per capita retail volume, have less than half their wholesale volume (Duncan and Reiss, 1956, pp. 229–30).

Figures on a more detailed areal basis, for the 67 metropolitan communities identified by Bogue, are given in Table 7. These data suggest that suburbs within 25 miles of the metropolitan center are dependent upon the center for certain retail services, whereas the entire hinterland depends on the center for an appreciable part of its wholesale services. Both the retail and wholesale series indicate that cities in the more remote parts of the hinterland are less dependent on the central cities than are the suburban and satellite places near the center. By contrast, the data for manufacturing reveal a concentration of manufacturing activity in a belt roughly 0 to 65 miles in radius surrounding the center. Both the central cities and the peripheral areas beyond 65 miles have a smaller relative volume of production than this intermediate zone.

The data just given demonstrate that the territorial pattern of the division of labor varies according to the kind of activity or function examined. As broad categories of economic activity are subclassified, the actual complexity of central-peripheral differentiation and specialization becomes more apparent. For example, Isard and Whitney (1949) have shown that the relative importance of the retailing function of central cities varies considerably by kind of business. Taking per capita retail sales in central cities as a base (= 100), total per capita sales in the cities of 10,000 inhabitants or more in a zone 1 to 10 miles from the central city had an index value of 75, as compared with an index of 118 for cities located 51 to 70

TABLE 7
Per Capita Value of Retail Sales, Wholesale Sales, and Value Added
by Manufacture, for Cities of 10,000 Inhabitants or More,
by Distance from Metropolitan Centers, United States, 1939–40

Distance from Nearest Metropolis (miles)	Retail Sales	Wholesale Sales	Value Added by Manufacture
All cities	$466	$331	$303
Metropolitan centers	471	1,172	284
0–24	397	239	351
25–44	483	273	380
45–64	511	325	347
65–164	502	443	225
165 and over	563	534	103

Source: Bogue (1949), Table 3–4.

miles away. Individual kinds of business, however, showed a variety of patterns of relative retail volume. The corresponding figures for food stores were 111 and 129; for general merchandise stores (primarily department stores) the indexes were 30 and 80; for all apparel stores, 58 and 105; for women's ready-to-wear stores, 31 and 110; for automotive stores, 99 and 196; for furniture, household goods, and radio stores, 99 and 129; for lumber and building supply stores, 144 and 199; for drug stores, 82 and 107; and for jewelry stores, 78 and 102. Apparently the drawing power of central cities is greatest for department stores, women's clothing stores, and apparel stores in general. By contrast, even the immediate suburbs, and especially the more distant satellite cities, had higher relative levels of trade volume in such kinds of business as food merchandising and lumber and building supply stores. (These figures, for 1940, pertain to ten major metropolitan centers and their surrounding areas; they were extracted from the complete distributions given by Isard and Whitney (1949) for all ten-mile zones up to 70 miles and reexpressed in index form.)

Some caution must be exercised in interpreting such figures in the absence of data on the actual flow of trade. It seems unlikely, for example, that any significant numbers of automobile purchases by residents of metropolitan centers are made in satellite cities over 50 miles from the center. The more probable situation is that such satellites compete more successfully with the central city for the automotive trade of small towns and rural areas in the hinterland than they do for, say, the apparel trade.

Thus far, metropolitan-hinterland relationships have been illustrated primarily in terms of comparisons of levels of economic activity in the central city and the outlying urban places. However, the dominance of the metropolis is indicated as well by differentiation in patterns of rural economic activity. For example, of all employed males living on farms in 1950, 42 per cent of those residing in metropolitan counties were engaged in nonfarm occupations, as compared with 29 per cent in submetropolitan counties, and only 22 per cent in nonmetropolitan counties. (In this analysis, "metropolitan" counties are those contained in the "standard metropolitan areas" of the U. S. Bureau of the Census, "submetropolitan" counties are those containing a city of 25,000–50,000 inhabitants, and "nonmetropolitan" counties are all other counties.) Moreover, of all farms in metropolitan counties, 41 per cent were operated as "part-time and residential" farms, as compared with 33 per cent in submetropolitan counties, and 30 per cent in nonmetropolitan counties. In metropolitan counties, only 11 per cent of farms were operated by tenants, in contrast to 23 per cent in submetropolitan counties, and 28 per cent in nonmetropolitan counties (Duncan and Reiss, 1956, Chapter 13).

3. THE URBAN HIERARCHY

The classification of population agglomerations as "metropolitan" or "nonmetropolitan" is a somewhat artificial dichotomy. It is perhaps more natural to think of cities as varying in size, pattern of economic specialization, and degree to which central or "dominance" functions are exercised. A convenient approach to the development of a conception of the urban hierarchy is the study of correlates of community size (Ogburn, 1937; Duncan, 1951; Schnore and Varley, 1955; Duncan and Reiss, 1956).

An interesting feature of population distribution relating to community size is the positive correlation between size of community and density of population. The relationship is somewhat loose, owing, in part, to the difficulty of measuring precisely the residential area of a community. However, the data in Table 8 suggest that multiplication of community size by a factor of 10 produces an increase in over-all density of about 1,900 persons per square mile. The breakdown by age of city reveals significant differences between old and new cities. Older cities have somewhat higher average densities, and their densities respond more to increases in size than is the case for cities a major portion of whose growth has taken place since the inception of the "automobile age." According to the observed regression relationships, an urbanized area of 1,000,000 inhabitants over half of whose central city population growth occurred in the 19th century will have a density of 6,370 persons per square mile, as compared with only 4,063 persons per square mile in an urbanized area of the same size where the bulk of central city growth occurred since 1930. The data indicate, therefore, that changes in the technology of local transportation (McKenzie, 1927; Ogburn, 1946) are causing a profound alteration in the pattern of urban settlement, though the effects are manifested after a considerable time lag in cities whose residential patterns were established before the advent of the automobile.

A number of investigators—of whom Lotka (1925) was one of the earliest—have noted that the frequency distribution of local communities according to population size is highly skewed. Moreover, if one takes as a territorial universe a relatively large and self-sufficient national economy, the cumulative size distribution tends to take on the form of the so-called Pareto curve, that is, $y = Ax^{-a}$, where x is the size (number of inhabitants) of a community, y is the number of communities of size x or larger, and A and a are parameters estimated from the data. It frequently is the case that a has a value close to unity, although fairly wide

TABLE 8

Summary of Regression of Density on Population Size, for Urbanized Areas of 100,000 Inhabitants of More, by Age of Central City, for the United States, 1950

Age of Central City[a]	Number of Ur-banized Areas	Constants[b] for $D = a + b \log P$		Computed Density for P =	
		a	b	100,000	1,000,000
All urbanized areas	119	−5,453	1,876	3,927	5,803
1900 or earlier	28	−5,096	1,911	4,459	6,370
1910	34	−6,834	2,140	3,866	6,006
1920	25	−5,435	1,902	4,075	5,977
1930 or later	32	2,203	310	3,753	4,063

Source: Computed from data in the 1950 Census.

[a]Census date at which population first attained half of its size in 1950.

[b]D = Density, persons per square mile; P = Population, number of inhabitants.

departures from this value are observed in some countries. If a is exactly unity, the equation simplifies to $xy = A$, A becomes the estimated size of the largest community, and the estimated size of the nth ranking community is A/n (the so-called "rank-size rule").

The generality of the Pareto distribution is not definitely established, either as to the number of countries or regions for which it holds, the time periods for which it is relatively accurate, or the minimum community size for which the formula is valid. However, Allen (1954) shows that it applies, at least to a rough approximation, in a large number of modern countries, and that it often is fairly accurate down to a size that one would regard as a small town. Madden (1956) presents evidence that the form of the distribution and the parameter, a, have been relatively constant (with changing values of A, of course) in the United States during the last century and a half.

Table 9 exhibits the fit of the Pareto curve to the city-size distribution in the contemporary United States. The example chosen is one that is presumed to be favorable for a close fit. The "cities" whose size distribution is shown are actually "urbanized areas," more or less natural agglomerations of population, whose boundaries were carefully delimited in the field by the census geography staff—rather than municipalities whose political boundaries and, consequently, population sizes may reflect historical accidents of incorporation and annexation. With the exponent, a, slightly below unity, the fit is observed to be quite good. As is indicated by Duncan and Reiss (1956, Chap. 2), the same equation does not work equally well for smaller places, in part, it is supposed, because the "urbanized area" concept was not applied to places with fewer than 50,000 inhabitants.

In discussing the size-frequency distribution, Lotka (1925, p. 307) stated "It may be left an open question how much significance is to be attached to this empirical formula." Subsequent writers, trying to resolve the question, have produced a good deal of dubious speculation, along with some interesting suggestions.

TABLE 9
Pareto Curve Fitted to Size Distribution of Urbanized Areas
of 100,000 Inhabitants or More, for the United States, 1950

x = Size of Urbanized Area	*y = Cumulative Frequency of Places with Size $\geq x$*	
	Calculated[a]	*Actual*
1,000,000	12.5	12
500,000	24.6	25
300,000	39.9	42
200,000	60.7	60
150,000	80.5	82
125,000	96.4	98
100,000	120.0	119

Source: Computed from data in the 1950 Census.
[a] From formula, log y = 6.99356 − .98356 log x, computed graphically from the data.

Recently, Simon (1957, Chap. 9) has described a stochastic process that produces the Pareto distribution, and gives a rather cursory rationalization for accepting it as a model of the evolution of the community-size distribution. Irrespective of the goodness of fit of such a formal probabilistic scheme, human ecologists are likely to prefer a structural-functional "explanation" of the size distribution. Lösch (1954) and Hoover (1955) have noted a connection between the community-size distribution and the hierarchical system of central places that is deduced on the basis of abstract location theory. The central place scheme postulates a gradation of functions such that some, relatively ubiquitous, functions have small market and supply areas and are found in centers of all sizes, whereas other functions serve progressively larger areas and are localized in progressively larger centers. With appropriate simplification of the determinants of urban location, function, and size it is possible to generate the Pareto distribution of sizes, approximately, from this hypothetical scheme.

There is, however, an empirical difficulty in using the Lösch-Hoover approach to the explanation of the Pareto size distribution. So-called central-place functions form but one major class of urban locational determinants, the other two, as identified by Harris and Ullman (1945), being break-of-bulk services, and "specialized" services (mining, manufacturing, resort, and the like, often associated with resource localization). Whereas the tendency of central places is toward even or uniform spacing (apart from topographic distortions), the other two categories of cities tend toward regional concentration and eccentric localization. Now it is plausible that the likelihood of a city having important functions other than central-place functions is directly related to its size. At any rate, large cities are prone to have non-central locations. Schnore and Varley (1955, Table 1) have tabulated metropolitan centers by size and type of location, with the following results: Of the 19 metropolitan centers with populations exceeding 500,000, 12 (63%) are located on the sea or lake coasts with access to deep water transport routes, and 7 (37%) are located on rivers. Of the 75 centers with populations in the 100,000 to 500,000 range, 25 per cent have coastal locations, 28 per cent river locations, and 47 per cent other locations. Corresponding figures for the 74 centers of 50,000 to 100,000 inhabitants are 12 per cent coastal locations, 22 per cent river locations, and 66 per cent other locations. But it is precisely the largest cities that tend to follow the Pareto distribution most closely. The Pareto formula is clearly inadequate for the smallest towns and villages, which, in all likelihood, serve primarily as central places for small trade and service areas, and which conform most closely to the expectation of uniform spatial distribution. Hence the Pareto size distribution cannot be regarded as a simple consequence of the central-place hierarchy. However, it is still useful to hypothesize that size variation is accompanied by functional differentiation, though probably not in the simple fashion suggested by the central-place theory (compare Stolper, 1955).

Tables 10–12 present data concerning the functional specialization of communities in relation to size. It is obvious that specialization in one major industry category—the extractive industries—will be inversely related to size of community (first column, Table 10). However, there is no pronounced relationship between size of place and the proportion of the labor force engaged in either of the other two broad industry sectors, the processing and fabricating industries, and the service industries (second and third columns of Table 10). More significant than the

TABLE 10
Selected Characteristics of the Employed Labor Force, by Size of Community,
for the United States, 1950

	Per Cent Employed in—			
Size Class	Extractive industries[a]	Processing and fabricating industries[b]	Service industries[c]	Clerical and kindred oc-cupations[d]
Urbanized areas				
1. 3,000,000 or more	0.7	36.8	61.1	17.8
2. 1,000,000 to 3,000,000	0.6	38.0	60.1	17.8
3. 250,000 to 1,000,000	1.4	34.1	63.3	16.7
4. 50,000 to 250,000	1.6	37.0	60.2	14.6
Other urban places				
5. 25,000 or more[e]	2.3	34.0	62.5	13.6
6. 10,000 to 25,000	4.2	33.4	61.2	12.0
7. 2,500 to 10,000	6.9	31.5	60.1	10.6
Rural territory				
8. Rural nonfarm	14.4	34.0	49.6	7.5
9. Rural farm	72.3	12.5	13.4	2.4

Source: Computed from data in the 1950 Census.
[a]Agriculture, forestry, fisheries, and mining.
[b]Manufacturing and construction.
[c]Transportation, trade, finance, administration, personal, professional, and business services. Note: sum of industry categories is less than 100 per cent because of nonreporting.
[d]Includes clerical occupations in all industries.
[e]Includes a few places with slightly more than 50,000 inhabitants.

figures for these broad categories are the figures (fourth column of Table 10) showing that, irrespective of industry structure, a much higher proportion of workers in large places are engaged in clerical and similar jobs. This finding accords with the supposition that large cities are focal points for administrative and coordinating functions, requiring a sizable complement of personnel to keep records and channel communications. The pronounced size gradient in proportion of clerical workers is, therefore, presumptive evidence of a "dominance" gradient by city size.

(Additional details on occupational structure are presented in Duncan and Reiss, 1956, and will not be reviewed here since the information is readily available. The industry statistics by size of community have not, however, been published previously.)

If industry statistics are to reveal evidence of functional hierarchy in relation to community size, it will evidently be necessary to examine fairly detailed industry classifications. Unfortunately, the census industry distributions—though based on a less detailed classification than is desirable for this purpose—require too much space for extensive presentation, and the relationships revealed by them are too complex to summarize industry by industry. Therefore, an expedient for summarizing the data has been adopted. The industry distribution for each size class is compared with that of each other size class by computing the index of dissimilarity between the two distributions (see section 1 for a definition of this index). If there is, indeed, a tendency toward hierarchy in the industry distributions, one would expect the magnitude of the indexes to vary directly with the difference in size of community—specifically, in Tables 11 and 12, one would expect the indexes to increase reading vertically and horizontally away from the diagonal.

TABLE 11
Indexes of Dissimilarity among Community-Size Classes in Industry Composition for the United States, 1950

| | Size Class | | | | | | | | |
Size Class	1	2	3	4	5	6	7	8	9
1	—	11.9	10.9	15.2	16.9	18.6	22.8	28.1	73.7
2	10.7	—	9.9	11.6	15.5	19.1	22.9	27.8	74.3
3	8.0	5.9	—	6.4	8.7	12.1	16.9	24.4	73.0
4	14.2	10.4	3.4	—	6.3	9.6	14.2	22.0	72.7
5	13.8	11.3	7.8	3.3	—	5.6	10.4	20.1	71.4
6	15.0	14.4	9.2	6.0	3.6	—	6.7	17.3	69.6
7	16.4	16.3	11.1	8.6	5.4	3.8	—	14.1	67.7
8 (RNF)	14.8	13.3	10.7	8.4	7.2	5.8	3.6	—	61.9
9 (RF)	1.6	2.0	1.4	1.3	0.7	0.9	1.9	4.1	—

Source: Computed from data in the 1950 Census.
Note: Above diagonal, for all industries; below diagonal, indexes for all industries less indexes for 4 broad groups (extractive, fabricating-processing, service, and industry not reported). See Table 10 for identification of size classes.

The upper right section of Table 11 shows indexes of dissimilarity computed from per cent distributions for all 41 industry groups. The expected hierarchical pattern is clearly evident, with only a few minor inversions in comparisons of adjacent size classes. The indexes below the diagonal have been computed so as to eliminate the effect of different proportions of extractive workers and to check the hypothesis that the hierarchical pattern is produced by variations in proportions employed in individual industry groups. That is, the index of dissimilarity based on four broad industry groups was subtracted from the index based on all industry groups. The hierarchical tendency still remains, but within the urban category of communities only, and with the variation in the indexes considerably damped.

Table 12 exhibits the hierarchical pattern of specialization within the manufacturing and the service sectors, respectively. In both cases the pattern of differences is generally as hypothesized, though with certain irregularities. For example, as far as manufacturing industries are concerned, almost all the major inversions of the expected pattern involve size class 2 (urbanized areas of 1,000,000 to

TABLE 12
Indexes of Dissimilarity among Community-Size Classes in Composition
of Manufacturing Industries and Service Industries,
for the United States, 1950

					Size Class				
Size Class	*1*	*2*	*3*	*4*	*5*	*6*	*7*	*8*	*9*
1	—	21.6	16.7	24.3	23.2	24.0	28.2	28.8	35.1
2	7.9	—	17.6	18.0	22.4	28.6	33.5	31.3	36.9
3	10.1	8.3	—	10.4	11.8	17.2	24.0	23.6	32.4
4	11.1	8.3	7.5	—	8.9	15.0	20.4	20.0	27.5
5	13.6	11.7	11.0	4.3	—	9.8	15.7	15.3	24.2
6	15.0	13.4	13.0	6.3	3.2	—	10.0	13.4	22.4
7	16.4	14.9	14.5	8.0	5.1	2.8	—	12.0	18.3
8 (RNF)	16.2	14.8	14.0	8.7	8.3	7.6	6.4	—	10.6
9 (RF)	23.8	20.3	22.2	17.0	16.9	15.3	13.8	10.9	—

Source: Computed from data in the 1950 Census.
Note: Above diagonal, based on manufacturing industries (15 industry groups); below diagonal based on service industries (21 industry groups). See Table 10 for identification of size classes.

3,000,000 inhabitants). This size class includes the city of Detroit, with its great concentration of workers in automobile manufacturing. This disturbance of the pattern does not, however, appear in the data for service industries.

It is perhaps significant that the indexes of dissimilarity are much higher for the manufacturing industries than for the service industries. This happens despite the fact that the latter sector has a larger number of categories, the mathematical effect of which is to increase the index of dissimilarity. This result suggests that cities are more uniform in their service structure than in their manufacturing structure. Some caution is required, however, because the result may also be, in part, an artifact of the particular classification system being used. In any case, the hierarchical pattern occurs for the service as well as for the manufacturing sector, even though the variation in the index of dissimilarity is smaller for service than for manufacturing industries.

4. DEMOGRAPHIC GRAVITATION

If one were assigned the task of describing the distribution of population over a region or other extensive territory, he would have various techniques at his disposal: the computation of population densities for areal subdivisions of the territory, cartographic presentation of the location of centers of population concentration, calculation of density gradients, and so on (O. D. Duncan, 1957). It would be a convenience, to say the least, to have a means of summarizing the entire complex pattern of population distribution in such a fashion that population distribution could be entered into an explanatory model as a single independent variable. There are good reasons for supposing that no satisfactory, all-purpose, single index of distribution can be devised. But there is a method of summarizing the major features of a pattern of distribution that appears to have great heuristic significance. The concept of "population potential," suggested by Stewart (1947a) has been applied by several investigators, notably Harris (1954), and now appears to be on its way to adoption as a standard part of demographic-ecological method.

The potential of population at any given point, L_0, in a territory is a function of the disposition of each population unit over that territory. Theoretically, one would compute potential at L_0 by measuring the distance of each person from that point and summing the reciprocals of these distances. Potential, therefore, is expressed in person-mile units. If potential at L_0 figures out at 350,000, this means that, "on the average," a person at L_0 is within a mile of 350,000 other persons. The general rationale of such a computation is the assumption that the influence of persons at a distance is inverse to their distance—a proposition that finds support in a wide variety of empirical findings. In practice, of course, the computation of potential is accomplished by measuring the distance from L_0 of each of a manageable number of areal subdivisions, assuming, in effect, that every person in an areal subdivision is located at its center, and calculating the quantity, $\Sigma P_i/D_i$, where P_i is the population of area i, and D_i is its distance from L_0. A special formula is used for calculating the potential of the area containing L_0 "on itself" (Stewart, 1947a). The precision of the results is, of course, generally in direct proportion to the number of areal subdivisions employed in the calculation.

After computing potential for a number of points, it is possible to interpolate graphically for other points, and to construct a map of isopotential lines, that is, lines which are the loci of points having equal population potentials. Figure 1 shows

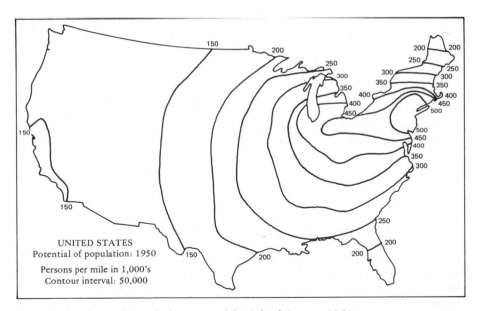

Figure 1. Isolines of Population Potential, United States: 1950

such a map for the United States in 1950. This map is a small-scale or coarse-grained version of the map which would show numerous local "peaks" and "eddies" of potential if calculated in detail. However, it serves to bring out the salient features of population distribution in the country: The massive concentration of population in the New York–Philadelphia area, the westward pull of the high densities along the lower Great Lakes, and the sparse and dispersed settlement of much of the western part of the United States.

To indicate some uses of potential measurement, two results of correlating potential with ecologically significant variables will be indicated. The first computation was suggested by Harris' (1954) observation that manufacturing is concentrated in those parts of the country where proximity to large populations offers a readily accessible market for manufactured products. Considering the 149 cities of 25,000 to 50,000 inhabitants located outside metropolitan areas (standard metropolitan areas and metropolitan State economic areas), one finds a correlation of .62 between per cent of the employed labor force engaged in manufacturing (Y) and the population potential (X) of the State economic area in which the city is located. The observed regression relationship is approximately $Y = 0.8\ X - 1.0$, with X in 10,000's. Outside metropolitan areas and apart from local peaks, potential varies from about 120,000 to about 550,000 person-miles. Consequently, the proportion engaged in manufacturing in these cities varies, on the average, from about 8.5 per cent in areas with the lowest potential to about 43 per cent in the areas with the highest potential (based on 1950 census data). The results would differ if one considered specific manufacturing industries. In particular, the correlation with potential would probably be higher than that mentioned for market-oriented industries (*e.g.,* apparel manufacturing) and lower for most resource-oriented industries (*e.g.,* blast furnaces and steel mills).

The second example concerns the density of the rural population, observed by Stewart (1947b) to be positively related to potential. For nonmetropolitan State economic areas a correlation of .54 was found between rural-farm population per 1,000 acres of land in farms (Y) and population potential (X_1). It is interesting to see what happens when other variables representing influences on farm population density are included in a regression equation along with potential. The variables considered here are X_2, log of mile distance of the nonmetropolitan State economic area to nearest metropolis; X_3, an index of urbanization of the area's population; and X_4, an index of ground conductivity, suggested by Albrecht (1956) as a rough measure of soil quality for agricultural purposes. The multiple correlation of Y on the combination of these four variables is .68, and the partial regression coefficients, in standard form, are as follows: $B_1 = .39$, $B_2 = -.07$, $B_3 = -.24$, and $B_4 = -.36$. (These results, based on 1950 census materials, were obtained by Beverly Duncan in a current project under the writer's direction.)

These results are for a sample of only 100 nonmetropolitan areas, and are not highly reliable. However, taken at face value with some allowance for sampling fluctuation, they have some important implications: First, the influence of potential on farm population density is not explained away when other relevant variables are considered. Second, the effect of potential is, at least in part, independent of the effect of proximity to a given metropolitan center and of the effect of local population concentrations. Third, the "pull" of potential appears to be sufficient to draw a significant part of the farm population away from the best farm land, even to the extent of making the net relationship between farm population density and soil quality a negative one. Finally, this application of multiple regression analysis suggests the feasibility of developing models treating simultaneously several aspects of population ordinarily examined separately, that is, the location of cities, variations in population density, and orientation to metropolitan centers. The concept of population potential, therefore, appears to be a promising technique in studies aimed at explaining the structure and development of communities and regions (Anderson, 1956).

5. CONCLUDING OBSERVATIONS

Research on population distribution—one of the principal subdivisions of demography—has been shown to be a fruitful approach to the study of community structure. It is possible to exhibit various empirical regularities of distribution and its correlates that provide an outline of some of the major structural features of contemporary human communities. No doubt several, if not all, of these alleged regularities will require qualification and modification as a result of further research. One is especially aware of the limits to generalization imposed by restricting the universe of observation to the contemporary United States. There is, then, a need for comparative studies of community structure in a large number of regions to ascertain the empirical limits of the propositions set forth and to increase our knowledge of the conditions under which they may be expected to prove valid. It can be anticipated, too, that many empirical results will come to be viewed in a somewhat different light as a result of revisions and elaborations of theoretical formulations. At present, as was indicated, the relationships described in this paper have greater or lesser "plausibility" in terms of a general conception of the nature of the community. But discrimination among alternative, equally plausible explanations of findings requires, in part, a sharpening of concepts and systematization of assumptions.

It should be clear that the problems treated here, though considered important for human ecology, by no means exhaust the preoccupations of that discipline (Hawley, 1950; Duncan, 1959). The study of distributive and structural aspects of the human community needs to be supplemented with at least four other kinds of investigation:

(1) The study of flows, movements, and interchanges among units of the community is essential to a fuller understanding of structural features and patterns of distribution. Promising beginnings in this field are represented by investigations of the diurnal flow of population within the city (Schnore, 1954), the movements of people among communities (Anderson, 1955), and economic relations among metropolitan regions (Isard and Kavesh, 1954), among others.

(2) The explanation of distributive patterns is incomplete until they are analyzed in terms of the processes—growth, expansion, concentration, deconcentration, and the like—which produce them. Recent studies of differential growth (*e.g.*, Hawley, 1956; Bogue and Harris, 1954) offer one methodological prototype of research in this field.

(3) It is necessary for the human ecologist to think of community structure as being subject to evolution, albeit an evolution whose time scale is that of human

history rather than that of genetic systems. Incidental reference was made earlier in this paper to pronounced trends in patterns of population distribution (and, by inference, community structure) observed over a period as brief as half a century (see also McKenzie, 1927). The appearance of the city as a stable form of human settlement is approximately coterminous with the initiation of the historical record some six millennia ago, and, in an important sense, the phenomenon of large-scale urbanization is unique to the last couple centuries (Davis, 1955). Fortunately, it appears that the human ecologist concerned with the recent phases of this evolution may expect some cooperation in developing the whole evolutionary picture from anthropologists and others investigating the origins and development of the kind of communities we know today (Steward, 1955; Childe, 1942).

(4) Finally, the human ecologist who takes as his starting point the analysis of population distribution quickly comes to realize the necessity of recognizing a wider range of environmental variables than just sheer geometric space. There has unquestionably been a tendency for students of the human community with a background of training in the social sciences to accept too readily the proposition that human culture and social structure develop in independence of the environmental setting (Steward, 1955; Meggers, 1954). That this partiality is about to be overcome is suggested by the human ecologist's renewed, sophisticated interest in regional analysis (Bogue, 1950). In these regional studies, aspects of the environment are investigated as part of the configuration of factors—demographic, environmental, technological, and organizational—that has been termed the "ecological complex" (Duncan, 1959). The study of population distribution reduces this complex to perhaps its simplest terms. It is, therefore, only a starting point, but an excellent starting point, for developing a theory of community structure.

REFERENCES

Albrecht, William A., 1956, Physical, chemical, and biochemical changes in the soil community. In: Man's Role in Changing the Face of the Earth, edited by William L. Thomas, pp. 648–673. Chicago, University of Chicago Press.

Allen, G. R., 1954, The 'courbe des populations': a further analysis. Bull. Oxf. Univ. Inst. Stat. 16: 179–189.

Anderson, Theodore R., 1955, Intermetropolitan migration: a comparison of the hypotheses of Zipf and Stouffer. Amer. Soc. Rev. 20: 287–291.

    1956, Potential models and the spatial distribution of population. Pap. Proc. Regional Sci. Assoc. 2: 175–182.

Blumenfeld, Hans, 1949, On the concentric-circle theory of urban growth. Land Econ. 25: 209–212.

Bogue, Donald J., 1949, The Structure of the Metropolitan Community. Ann Arbor, University of Michigan Press.

    1950, Economic areas as a tool for research and planning. Amer. Soc. Rev. 15: 409–416.

Bogue, Donald J., and Harris, Dorothy L., 1954, Comparative Population and Urban Research via Multiple Regression and Covariance Analysis, Studies in Population Distribution, Number 8. Oxford, Ohio, Scripps Foundation.

Childe, V. Gordon, 1942, What Happened in History. Harmondsworth, Middlesex, Penguin Books.

Clark, Colin, 1951, Urban population densities. J. Roy. Statist. Soc., Ser. A 114: 490–496.

Cressey, Paul F., 1938, Population succession in Chicago: 1898–1930. Amer. J. Sociol. 44: 59–69.

Davis, Kingsley, 1955, The origin and growth of urbanization in the world. Amer. J. Sociol. 60: 429–437.

Duncan, Beverly, 1957, Intra-urban population movement. In: A Reader in Urban Sociology, edited by Paul K. Hatt and Albert J. Reiss, Jr. Rev. ed. Glencoe, Ill., The Free Press.
Duncan, Otis Dudley, 1951, Optimum size of cities. In: A Reader in Urban Sociology, edited by Paul K. Hatt and Albert J. Reiss, Jr. Glencoe, Ill., The Free Press.
1957, The measurement of population distribution. Popul. Stud.
1959, Human ecology and population studies. In: The Study of Population: An Inventory and Appraisal, edited by Philip Hauser and Otis Dudley Duncan. Chicago, University of Chicago Press.
Duncan, Otis Dudley, and Duncan, Beverly, 1955, Residential distribution and occupational stratification. Amer. J. Sociol. 60: 493–503.
1956, Chicago's Negro Population: Characteristics and Trends. Chicago, Office of the Housing and Redevelopment Coordinator and the Chicago Plan Commission.
1957, The Negro Population of Chicago: A Study of Residential Succession. Chicago, University of Chicago Press.
Duncan, Otis Dudley, and Reiss, Albert J., Jr., 1956, Social Characteristics of Urban and Rural Communities, 1950. New York, John Wiley & Sons.
Foley, Donald L., 1954, Urban daytime population: a field for demographic-ecological analysis. Social Forces 32: 323–330.
Gilmore, Harlan W., 1953, Transportation and the Growth of Cities, Glencoe, Ill., The Free Press.
Gras, N. S. B., 1922, An Introduction to Economic History. New York, Harper and Bros.
Harris, Chauncy D., 1954. The market as a factor in the localization of industry in the United States. Ann. Ass. Amer. Geogr. 44:315–348.
Harris, Chauncy D., and Ullman, Edward L., 1945, The nature of cities. Ann. Amer. Acad. Pol. Soc. Sci. 242: 7–17.
Hauser, Philip M., Duncan, Otis Dudley, and Duncan, Beverly Davis, 1956, Methods of Urban Analysis: A Summary Report. San Antonio, Texas, Air Force Personnel & Training Research Center.
Hawley, Amos H., 1950, Human Ecology. New York, Ronald Press.
1955, Land value patterns in Okayama, Japan, 1940 and 1952. Amer. J. Social. 60: 487–492.
1956, The Changing Shape of Metropolitan America: Deconcentration since 1920. Glencoe, Ill., The Free Press.
Hoover, Edgar M., 1955, The concept of a system of cities: a comment on Rutledge Vining's paper. Economic Development and Cultural Change 3: 196–198.
Isard, Walter, and Kavesh, Robert, 1954, Economic structural interrelations of metropolitan regions. Amer. J. Sociol. 60: 152–162.
Isard, Walter, and Whitney, Vincent, 1949, Metropolitan site selection. Social Forces 27: 263–269.
Lösch, August, 1954, The Economics of Location, translated by William H. Woglom with the assistance of Wolfgang F. Stolper. New Haven, Yale University Press.
Lotka, Alfred J., 1925, Elements of Physical Biology. Baltimore, Williams & Wilkins.
Madden, Carl H., 1956, On some indications of stability in the growth of cities in the United States. Economic Development and Cultural Change 4: 236–252.
McKenzie, R. D., 1927, Spatial distance and community organization pattern. Social Forces 5: 623–627.
Meggers, Betty J., 1954, Environmental limitation on the development of culture. Amer. Anthrop. 56: 801–824.
Ogburn, William F., 1937, Social Characteristics of Cities. Chicago, International City Managers' Association.
1946, Inventions of local transportation and the patterns of cities. Social Forces 25: 313–319.
Park, Robert Ezra, 1952, Human Communities: The City and Human Ecology. Glencoe, Ill., The Free Press.
Schnore, Leo F., 1954, The separation of home and work: a problem for human ecology. Social Forces 32: 336–343.
Schnore, Leo F., and Varley, David W., 1955, Some concomitants of metropolitan size. Amer. Soc. Rev. 20: 408–414.
Simon, Herbert A., 1957, Models of Man. New York, John Wiley & Sons.

Sorokin, Pitirim, and Zimmerman, Carle C., 1929, Principles of Rural-Urban Sociology. New York, Henry Holt & Co.

Steward, Julian H., 1955, Theory of Culture Change. Urbana, University of Illinois Press.

Stewart, John Q., 1947a, Empirical mathematical rules concerning the distribution and equilibrium of population. Geogr. Rev. *37*: 461–485.

1947b, Suggested principles of 'social physics'. Science *106*: 179–180.

Stolper, Wolfgang, 1955, Spatial order and the economic growth of cities. Economic Development and Cultural Change *3*: 137–146.

Vance, Rupert B., and Smith, Sara, 1954, Metropolitan dominance and integration, in The Urban South, edited by Rupert B. Vance and Nicholas J. Demerath. Chapel Hill, University of North Carolina Press.

Wilkins, Arthur H., 1956, The residential distribution of occupation groups in eight middle-sized cities of the United States in 1950. Unpublished Ph.D. dissertation, Department of Sociology, University of Chicago.

Wirth, Louis, 1938, Urbanism as a way of life. Amer. J. Sociol. *44*: 1–24.

SOCIAL CLASS IN A FRENCH VILLAGE

Julian Pitt-Rivers

On first reading, the treatment of community structure in Duncan's article and the treatment in this essay on a French village seem to come from different worlds. Duncan's analyses are large in scale, quantitative in style, abstract in formulation. Pitt-Rivers' analyses confine themselves to a single village, attach no numerical values to the variables involved, and contain a good deal of concrete description. One takes a characteristic sociological approach to the study of communities; the other, a characteristic anthropological approach. Yet the two essays have in common a central concern with the relationship between territorial organization and relations among people. Reading the two essays together makes one wonder how precisely the spatial divisions within the French village reflect the class divisions which Pitt-Rivers identifies. It also raises another question: Pitt-Rivers stresses the village/hinterland distinction. How generally does the line between village and hinterland separate communities according to the variables Duncan emphasizes— density, wealth, occupational distribution, and so on?

Anthropologists have made small, self-contained communities their particular province. They have developed their own style of work: becoming immersed in the day-to-day life of the community, carrying on extended discussions with key informants, accumulating copious field notes. (These are not, by any means, the only things anthropologists do, but they distinguish anthropological work from sociological, psychological, geographic, or economic investigations more than the other procedures anthropologists employ.) In many anthropological studies, the community is simply a setting for the observation of some social process or way of life; the anthropologist is not trying to make statements about the organization of communities as

such. In others, the community itself is the object of study. Pitt-Rivers'
investigation falls into the second category.

After living in a Spanish town (about which he wrote The People of the
Sierra*), Pitt-Rivers settled down in a village in southwestern France. In this*
essay, he puts together his observations on the interplay among several
principles of division within the community: the world of French versus the
world of patois, *the central settlement versus the dispersed farms, the nation-*
al orientation versus the local orientation, the property holders versus those
without property. He makes four essential points:

> *1. These divisions make a real difference in the allocation of pres-*
> *tige, the formation of factions, and the routines of social interaction.*
> *2. They coincide to an important degree: the characteristics of*
> *speaking French, living in a central settlement, having a national orien-*
> *tation and little property go together.*
> *3. The discrepancy between the high prestige of French, central*
> *location, and national orientation, on the one hand, and the weakness*
> *resulting from lack of property occasions much tension and bitterness.*
> *4. The superior position of the farmers and of the "local" sphere is*
> *eroding, as the community becomes more vulnerable to the influence of*
> *the national market and the farmers' children escape to the world*
> *outside.*

The concept of social class is central to the discussion of the structure of any
modern European community, for it concerns the differentiation of its members in
terms of superiority and inferiority, the ties of reciprocity between them and the
bond of solidarity based upon equality. Yet there is little agreement as to the status
or proper usage of the term among social scientists and where there is it tends to lie
in the acceptance of a set of simple assumptions regarding "stratification" which
nevertheless remain highly questionable in certain social contexts. Most writers
today appear to prefer as the criteria by which they define social classes or "strata"
the standards of differentiation of the people themselves—the ethnographical view
of class, so that the word is used as a descriptive term referring only to the ways in
which people view themselves as differentiated. It tends, nonetheless, to be assumed
that, even though the picture of the persons within the system varies according to
the position within it of the viewer, it can at least be viewed by the social scientist
as a single system, in the sense that the same criteria of inferiority or superiority are
accepted by the whole society; that it is unnecessary to delineate the society within
which the system operates; and that there is only one system of class in any one
society, that the same values pertain to a class system throughout. It is thought thus
to be possible to establish a single system of stratification by asking the inhabitants

Reprinted from "Social Class in a French Village" by Julian Pitt-Rivers, *Anthropological Quarterly*, 33: 1 (1960), pp. 1–13, by permission of the author and the *Anthropological Quarterly*. An early version of this paper was offered at the American Anthropological Association Meeting in Chicago, December 1958.

to rate their neighbours in terms of class or prestige without always examining what are the perceptual categories by which they will do this, nor whether they are the same in every instance, nor whether this is asking them to perform an operation which they find necessary and natural in the process of their normal lives or an exotic sociological quiz.

I have already shown, in the instance of a Spanish town (Pitt-Rivers, 1954) how the nature of social class may change according to the position of the individual community-member within the national structure and according to the social context, but there was at any rate, in spite of the different connotations given to class relations by the different participants, a rough general agreement in that society as to who was superior socially to whom. In this instance of a French village even this basic agreement is missing and the implications of this for a discussion of social class are far-reaching. In the case of the Spanish town the divergent social norms were related to the closely integrated plebeian community on the one hand and to the structure of the region on the other. The same kind of distinction can be made here: the class system relating to the traditional structure of the village is not the same system as that relating to the outside world of the modern national urban society.

Yet, while it was possible to interpret the data from the Spanish town in terms of the function of the upper class within both the system of local patronage and the structure of the state, the "national-culture" element within the French village exercises no patronage and so far from representing the leadership of the community constitutes for its leaders a despised element. It fulfills no function in terms of the village community and in order to explain its presence it is necessary to look for connections wider and more complex than those contained within the social structure of the local community.

The cultural distinction between the two elements, a concomitant of the different values of the two systems, is underscored by a linguistic distinction which enables us to see the problem with greater clarity, though it is not suggested that the fortuities of linguistic history could be put forward as a cause of such a situation. On the contrary, it is suggested that comparable structural situations may well be found where only much less obvious linguistic markers exist.

France is, or rather once was, divided into two distinct linguistic halves: the land of the *langue d'oïl* and the land of the *langue d'oc*, and to these two languages there corresponded two distinct cultures. The *langue d'oc* blossomed earlier than the *langue d'oïl* and gave us the literature of the troubadours but it was the people of the latter who won the political hegemony of France, and their language became French; the capital of the country Paris and not Toulouse nor Avignon.

Since then, the language frontier of the *langue d'oc* has receded not only geographically, but "vertically" as the sociologists would put it. That is to say, in the later Middle Ages and up till the mid-fifteenth century the upper class spoke *langue d'oc* ordinarily and for formal purposes Latin, while the population spoke only *langue d'oc* which was taught as a written language in the schools. (Pansier, 1925, I, p. 38.) By the mid-twentieth century the upper and urban classes speak only French, the only language taught in school, and the peasants are bilingual. At the same time the *langue d'oc* has been lost in the large towns and centres of communication which speak only French. Rather than view the matter in terms of class, it is better to view it in terms of community and function. The function of government was the first to be taken over by the *langue d'oïl* and the hegemony of the French crown corresponded to the imposition of the French language as the language of the ruler. Subsequently, where Latin is eliminated, it gives way to French, not to *langue d'oc,* in the context of the law or of religion and education. Local administrations and legal proceedings move from *langue d'oc* to French though not without a considerable variation according to area. For example, in spite of an ordinance of the crown of 1539 that notaries should keep their minutes in French, one finds notarial acts in the archives of Cahors written in *langue d'oc* as late as the end of the sixteenth century. (Dobelman, 1940, p. 3.)

Langue d'oc continued to be spoken by the educated after they had ceased to write it but once it ceased to be taught in the schools its orthography was lost. At the same time a quantity of gallicisms were introduced which result in the eighteenth century in the formation of the bastard language known as *"patois"* which remained the spoken language of the population. Down to the mid-nineteenth century French was not much spoken even in the towns. (Arnaud et Morin, 1920, xxii.) However, the great increase in the number of public servants and the tendency not to post them to their native regions, increased emigration and reimmigration, compulsory military service and a constant campaign against the *patois* in the schools, brought about a further change. The industry and commerce of the nineteenth century grew up speaking French, while agriculture remained the sphere of *patois,* with the result that the language dichotomy came to approximate to the dichotomy between town and country, and since langued'oc-speaking France is above all a land of small peasant farmers, in many social situations between rich and poor. Social superiority was accorded to the modern, the urban, the French, and the attempt to revive the language and culture of the langued'oc, the "félibrige," remained a purely literary movement without influence over the populace.

Though the decline of the *patois* has continued steadily since the mid-nineteenth century and the urban and bourgeois have virtually lost their knowledge of it, it is still spoken in rural areas in the appropriate context. The entire population is French-speaking with the exception of certain ancient persons living on isolated farms whose frailty has confined them for years to the company of their family and who have forgotten it. At the other end of the scale, the younger members of the professional classes know virtually none, though the older tradespeople in the market towns can usually manage a smattering of it. Even so they can barely be considered bilingual. Yet *patois* is still the language of agriculture and of the market and in the *forail* (the agricultural fairground) scarcely a word of French is spoken save by the occasional dealer from the North. For the peasants it is the language of the local, as opposed to national tradition, of proverbs and invective, of merrymaking and salty jokes whose humour, it is asserted, is lost if translated into French, of intimacy and the family. Old men can still remember how they felt lost when they went into the army and had to speak French all the time, and how, if they spoke *patois,* the other soldiers, northerners or city folk, jeered at them, shouting "en voilà encore un qui mange de la paille!" ("here's another straweater!") and so forth. In contrast to the spontaneous world of the patois, the world of French is that of formal relations, and a striking difference in demeanour is often observable between the two contexts.

Magnac is a village of 450 inhabitants, situated in largely fertile but rather broken country between the limestone plateau of the Quercy and the Massif Central. It had a larger population fifty years ago like most of the villages of this region and earlier still, before the phylloxera killed the vines, it was much larger again. In consequence of the decline in numbers, the size of land-holdings has increased and the average family holding is somewhere around 60 acres. The largest is 140 acres and the smallest entirely supporting a family is 30. In addition, there are many smaller properties which only partially support a household. These belong to artisans, retired people and people who work elsewhere and rent them out in anticipation of their own retirement or who supplement their pension by keeping a flock of sheep.

The village lies in a valley overlooked by its church, a fortified romanesque edifice once part of the defenses, and by the chateau which was inhabited by a noble family of the region down to the first world war. They were one of the last of the local nobility to disappear from the scene.

The southwest of France has an ancient tradition of emigration dating from before the time when modern conditions accentuated the impoverishment of its agriculture. The younger sons of noble families were traditionally military adventurers. The small and arid department where Magnac is situated furnished two of Napoleon's marshals. The culinary art of its inhabitants has made it famous and has provided a profitable living for a number of its sons in the restaurant business in Paris. Other than as waiters, café and restaurant-keepers, they also go to Paris and Toulouse in search of a more generous wage than local employers can afford to pay. They are frequently employed in the Paris Metro (subway). These emigrants do not willingly sever their connections with the village as a rule. In this, they are similar to their neighbours of the Auvergne and the newspaper *"Auvergnat de Paris"* covers the area of Magnac, giving a weekly account of every recent event of social importance, village by village, for the benefit of the metropolitan exiles. They frequently come to spend their summer vacations with relatives in the village and some maintain a house there for the purpose, to which they will perhaps return when they receive their pension and retire. Others whom ill-health has forced to retire early have returned prematurely to their birth-place.

In addition to these retired persons there are others who have come to spend their years of retirement here because the climate is agreeable and because houses in this depopulated area can be bought for very little, and life is not expensive. Furthermore, there are persons who fled to this area in front of the German invasion in 1940 and, having no reason to go elsewhere, they remained. Pensions and part-time agriculture supply the livelihood of these people, but there is also a small number of persons living here who work in a brick factory four miles away.

All these people live in the village of Magnac and its immediate environs. They constitute something of a group, or perhaps one should say "faction." In opposition to them are those who have never left the soil of their fathers, the farmers.

The farms, very ancient and picturesque buildings surrounded by their out-houses and vegetable garden, are scattered over the territory of the *commune*. They are inhabited, in the majority of cases by their owners who work from dawn till dusk and go to the village only on Sunday mornings for Mass and shopping, or during the week to visit the blacksmith with an animal. Their children, however, go down daily to school. There are two grocery stores though there is barely enough business for one, for the farmers make many of their purchases in the local towns where they attend the markets. The market is no longer held at Magnac, though the building remains and serves as a covered parking lot for hay-carts in summer and for the still in autumn.

Each farm is a family exploitation, but families are small and occasional labour scarce. The difference between wages which the farmers here consider that they can afford to pay and the wages paid in richer areas or in industry is very considerable, so that those who intend to seek permanent employment go elsewhere. The labour force of each farm consists of a potential elderly couple in semi-retirement, the farmer and his wife, and their children of whom only one will remain to marry and inherit, an occasional transient semi-skilled employee or exceptionally, a permanent employee in the shape of an elderly bachelor or widower who has preferred to remain upon his native land. Wage-labour by the day is performed irregularly by one or two retired persons and occasionally by one of the minor members of a poorer farming household.

The inhabitants of the farms are sometimes referred to as "les estrangers," the people who live outside, but they do not constitute a group as such and they are certainly not outsiders in any but the geographical sense. As a social group they are "les propriétaires," a group of whom one lives in the village. They are the guardians of tradition, very conservative in their ways. A few of them still wear the black peasant smock and black felt hat when they come to the village on Sundays. Their wives wear the traditional black straw hat.

Their lives are entirely ordered by the business of making a living from the land and the tradition of polyculture dies hard. "Produce it yourself, then you don't have to pay for it" was once their guiding economic principle and remains their preference. Economically, farming is a hard fight. Prices have been going steadily against the farmer since the war, while taxes, social insurance and the cost of industrial products have been going up. They pay out as little as possible, make their own wine in many cases and all of them make their own alcohol. They work on Sundays during the rush season and save every penny. Their relaxations are few: they go rarely to the entertainments offered in the towns; they attend the "FÊTE" of Magnac but only the young go to the FÊTES of other villages. The threshing on different farms provides a day of work which ends in a feast, and visiting is done largely in connection with agricultural affairs and in particular with the arrangements of reciprocal services. People visit their kin and friends on Sundays if they live near by, but only the life crises of close kin take them further afield. Among neighbours there exists, or rather existed, a traditional reunion for the long winter's evenings when friends would be invited to come to a "dénoisillage," the shelling and peeling of walnuts, at which food and drink were offered and traditional stories were told. Otherwise, Sundays, feastdays and funerals gather the village community together. The visit, monthly or more often, to the market in the local towns ranks as an important social event and an occasion—the only one—where this society unites on a more than local basis in the context of its dominant value, agriculture.

A clearly defined notion of ranking exists among these people which relates to the size and prosperity of their farms. The symbols of this system are all in terms of production, not of consumption: first of all, the value of the property; and secondly, the value of the *cheptel*, that is the equipment and stock, are significant, but the ability to produce of the individual farmer, to produce quality and quantity, is also a title to prestige. Since the market is where the produce is compared and admired, it has, in addition to its function as a meeting-place, that of a testing-ground of a man's worth. Prestige does not attach to consumption patterns, and the differences noticeable here such as washing machines and station-wagon automobiles which are undoubted signs of affluence, are, considering their utility in terms of time and labour saving, more properly classed as part of the *cheptel*. Apart from their pure utility they enjoy the same kind of prestige-value as a new tractor.

Between farmers there exists a network of reciprocal services which are never admitted to be reciprocal but are couched in the idiom of disinterested neighbourly duty. These concern the loan of animals and machinery as well as services, and of reciprocal gifts of produce. A certain number of share-cropping arrangements are made, mainly between the farmers and the agricultural members of the village who take on the labour of weeding and harvesting a root crop in return for a third of the produce.

Until recently these people held a virtual monopoly of political power. All the municipal councillors came from among their number. The mayor was quite simply the largest landowner, and the councillors were all *propriétaires*, even though the land of one was so unproductive that he lived miserably. The village-dwellers lumped them together under the title of "les gros," the men of substance. Another characteristic of the councillors was that they were all elderly. The mayor was over seventy, the youngest was a grandfather. This was the traditional system, a gerontocracy.

It may seem curious that these old men were able to dominate the political scene so completely, for their families outnumber the village-dwellers only by 2:1. However, in municipal and syndical elections there are no party politics; no one stands as anything but himself, and there are normally only the same number of candidates as there are seats. The gerontocrats decide among themselves who is to stand and no one else thinks it worth while to stand uninvited and in opposition. He would be certain to be outvoted and would be much criticized by the majority as one who wished to sow discord in village affairs.

In national politics the division between the two elements is clearly marked; 20% of the suffrage goes to the Communist candidate and this is known to be the village vote less certain elements, mainly female. The strongest party was tradition-ally the M.R.P., but it is not a vote which is profoundly attached nor is there any party organization in the commune. At the election in January, 1956 Magnac's figures showed a landslide to the left and the SFIO candidate gained an absolute majority. This was not on account of any change in Magnac's way of thinking regarding either politics or religion but simply because a doctor known for his devotion to his patients among the farmers and for his capacity in the politics of the region presented himself on an SFIO ticket. Other than the expression of his belief in the greatness of France in which he recalled the sacrifice made by his electors in two world wars, and his determination that the war in Algeria must be stopped (he did not suggest how), his speech to the electors of Magnac dealt uniquely with local issues concerning the welfare of the commune. The doctor's success reflected his clear understanding of social realities.

Let us take a look at the village element. They do not speak *patois*, either because they come from further north (retired people) or because, having gone to work as young men, they have forgotten how to speak it. The farmers who are bilingual have fairly clearly defined contexts where one language or the other is spoken, but the language for the matters which they value and the contexts where they amuse themselves, is *patois*. For them French is the language of national affairs, not community affairs.

The values of the village-dwellers are urban values. They are accustomed to the notion of fixed incomes, and their prestige rating is done in terms of consumption not production. They buy things, they do not produce them, and they look to the city and urban life for their ideals. It is very difficult to speak of "they" for they are much less homogeneous than the farmers. All who live in the village do not sympathise with "the village element," while some of the younger members of the poorer farming families do so. These are in many cases in the process of detaching themselves from the land and are seen a year or two later to have left altogether for permanent employment elsewhere. The young of the village-dwellers work in the local town to which they go on low-powered motorcycles.

There is one type among the village dwellers whom one could describe as belonging to both factions: the artisans. Though they are no more than a few households they are important as the only group which belongs to both factions. They speak *patois* freely with their clients from outside the village, and they are born and bred in the commune. Indeed they are among the most traditional people in some ways for they are all that remains of a once prosperous and numerous element whose economic role has been usurped to a large extent by the shops and workshops of the market-town. Their sympathies and aspirations are with the village faction, however.

I speak of faction because, in spite of a number of kinship ties between the two elements, a deep distrust and even hatred exists, which cannot be understood without looking outside the village at its place within the nation.

France is governed from Paris and the laws are made there which rule the whole country. The leadership in commerce and the arts, in fashions and in the intellectual world is centered in Paris. The ambitious young man must leave his natal village and go to town if he wishes to escape from the slowly increasing apathy of an impoverished countryside. Success more than the acquisition of a few extra acres means success in the national world of France. This is so in any social class.

Such of the traditional country gentry and ancient bourgeoisie as remain live mostly elsewhere and come to their properties only for the summer or in old age. Their occupations oblige them to live in Paris or Toulouse where many have entered the liberal professions. The summer visitor is always socially superior to a person of the locality who follows the same calling, or pretends to the same rank. The aristocrat who lives in Paris refers to his noble country-dwelling neighbour as *un petit genre amusant que produit la province française* (an amusing little product of the French provinces). The doctor's wife who lives in Toulouse is at pains to correct the impression that she is the wife of a local doctor. The urban classes all regard the peasants with a patronising and amused superiority.

Within the area there are to be found two or three men who have made good in Paris in the café business and have retired to buy a farm in their native land. They have spent money making modernised exploitations which local farmers admire while at the same time asserting that they are quite uneconomical and require to be supported by the receipts of the café. This is almost certainly untrue, though the owners have no interest in disputing it. These returned natives are few in number and none lives within the commune of Magnac. The farming population is the element of the community which elected to remain from earliest youth. They are aware that they are rough, that they have little verbal facility in French, that they are thought backward by the urban population, that urban people have a higher standard of living and are more sophisticated. They admire those who make good in the capital but they distrust urban people. This is the basis of their ambivalence towards national as opposed to local culture. Politically they show the same ambivalence: they are patriotic, are proud to have served their country in war. But the French nation for which they fought is one thing and the French state is another. (Cf. Wylie, 1957, chap. X.) They believe in defending themselves from interference and interference means interference from Paris.

Therefore the village faction presents something of an anomaly to them. They are sophisticated, know about national politics, do not speak "patois" and aspire to represent "national" culture. But they are only there because they tried to make good upon the national scene and failed. Their presence in Magnac is the badge of their failure. The feeling of the farmers towards them is one of distrust and contempt.

But this contempt is reciprocated. The villagers despise the farmers for their backwardness, their speech, their way of life, their reluctance to spend money. They believe themselves superior to peasants on account of their national culture and their knowledge of the world. Their lack of money is a fortuitous factor in their eyes. It makes them keenly conscious of any sign of prosperity upon the farms, but it does not make them feel inferior, only jealous. If they had the money they would know what to do with it better than those who have it.

Moreover the farmers do nothing to help them. The system of informal reciprocal services is important to the agriculture and much stress is laid on the virtue of the neighbourly "coup de main" (helping hand). But the village-dwellers are mostly unable to reciprocate—and it is nevertheless essential to reciprocate—in the only way which the farmers would accept, that is, with labour on the farm. Therefore with the exception of the artisans there is little cooperation between the two groups. This fact gives occasion for the village faction to criticise the farmers as uncooperative and mean.

How should we explain this situation? Much has been made since Marx of the difference between rural and urban classes. (Cf. Friedmann, 1951, chap. IV.) But is one justified in speaking of an urban class which lives in the country? Should we reject altogether the concept of social class to interpret a social scene where the inhabitants nevertheless evaluate their relations in terms of superiority and inferiority, choosing the same cultural and economic criteria as the definitions of the classical theorists? Should we call in other factors; the difference in economic level between country and capital which is responsible in the first place for the presence of the village faction, the traditional xenophobia of the French peasant community, the historical enmity between the *langue d'oc* and the *langue d'oïl*? Should we indulge in the tempting comparison to a "poor white" situation?

It has been observed in a number of cases that the revolutionary rank-and-file in nineteenth century urban society was provided by the rural element which had abandoned the countryside in order to go to town to work. Here the contrary is true; it is the urban element retired from the towns which forms the rebellious force in a country village. The lack of a cultural norm for the whole community may be invoked in both instances to explain the rebellion of a nonintegrated minority. So one might argue on the local plane. But looking at the situation on a grander scale I think it is helpful to envisage the tension as one between two systems of social class, two value systems, rather than between two classes. I think this becomes clear if one considers what are the values attaching to social superiority in the case of:

(a) the farmers: they expect to find as social superiors, not Parisians, but local persons in touch with Paris, successful and wealthy on the local plane thanks to which they represent the interests of the community on a wider scale, but whose values are nevertheless in large measure those of the country. The village-dwellers appear to them pretentious, affecting a culture to which they have no right and they represent a threat both to traditional values and also to the political unity of the commune.

(b) the village faction: they are accustomed to tolerate the existence of a superior class which embodies their cultural ideals, but does not impinge on their daily life, and to political leaders who share their values. The farmers do none of these things and yet they possess the power.

It is the clash between the expected association of cultural values with superiority—and the reality in each case, which causes the bitterness between these groups who have little, materially, to quarrel over.

But this situation is the product of time. The economic, technological and demographic impetus of the age will carry us past this moment. Under modern conditions of transportation the villages themselves are anachronistic and are disappearing in favour of the larger unit, the market-town. The gerontocrats are already a thing of the past, not on account of their age but on account of their ideas. Their children have different views. Already some of them speak only in French to their children.

REFERENCES

Arnaud, F. and Morin. G. 1920. Le language de la Vallée de Barcelonnette. Paris.

Dobelmann, Suzanne. 1940. La langue de Cahors des origines à la fin du XVI siècle. Paris.

Friedmann, Georges (editor). 1951. Villes et Campagnes. Symposium organised by the Centre d'Etudes Sociologiques. Armand Colin. Paris.

Pansier, Dr. P. 1925. Histoire de la langue provençale à Avignon du XII au XIX siècle. Avignon, 3 t.

Pitt-Rivers, J. A. 1954. The People of the Sierra. New York.

Wylie, Laurence. 1957. Village in the Vaucluse. Harvard University Press.

CHAIN MIGRATION, ETHNIC NEIGHBORHOOD FORMATION, AND SOCIAL NETWORKS

John S. MacDonald and Leatrice D. MacDonald

In our paper on migration in the previous chapter, Harold Brown and I took the structures of the communities sending and receiving migrants more or less for granted, and concentrated on the experiences of the people making the move. In this paper, MacDonald and MacDonald turn the tables; they discuss how the pattern of migration affects the structure of the receiving community. They show that "chain migration" feeds on itself and builds self-contained ethnic communities within big cities. Their analysis fits with what Brown and I determine to be the individual consequences of migration under the auspices of kinship, friendship, and common origin; but it goes beyond the individual consequences to group structure. They show that chain migration is "that movement in which prospective migrants learn of opportunities, are provided with transportation, and have initial accommodation and employment arranged by means of primary social relationships with previous migrants." Most likely the great majority of long-distance migrants throughout the world of the last century have made their moves through chain migration; surely the majority of migrants to North America did. The Mac-Donalds focus on Italian migration to the United States, but much of what they say applies to the Chinese in Indonesia or the Irish in Argentina—to name but two large international movements of the last century. They find kinship ties and patron-client relationships behind the bulk of Italian-American migration. Contrary to myth, they do not find villages migrating together, or even serving as the structures through which migration occurs. Instead, they conclude that the "Little Italies" of North America are by-products of the operation of overlapping chains of kinship and patron-client relations.

Here they are contradicting or minimizing several other common explanations of the formation of ethnic neighborhoods in big cities. One is that ethnic segregation results from discrimination and self-defense. Another is that it is a by-product of differences in income among ethnic groups. A third explanation is that people from the same background share preferences for the same sorts of location and housing, even when they are indifferent about the ethnic origins of their neighbors, and therefore end up clustered together. These different theories matter because some of them suggest that ethnic neighborhoods will break up almost automatically as the people involved adapt to American life, while others make ethnic segregation tough and durable. Which theories are right also matters because essentially the same competing explanations have been offered for racial segregation in cities—and the effectiveness of different housing policies depends on the correctness of one or another of them. Of course, they could all contain part of the truth.

To the extent that the MacDonalds' analysis catches the principal origins of ethnic neighborhoods, however, we should expect these neighborhoods to be self-perpetuating.

Migration is patently more complex than that merely mechanical reshuffling of heads which is assumed by crude economic "push-pull" models. Numerous contemporary studies in Africa, Asia and Latin America pay attention to the sociological factors involved in induction of manpower into growing economies. This paper draws attention to the possibilities of illuminating current problems by historical studies. The vast documentary material on the sociology of migration and labor force reorganization in the past in Europe and North America is largely neglected by current studies.

From the standpoint of organization, migration may occur in several ways. Among these are two contrasting extremes: "chain migration" and "impersonally organized migration."[1] Chain migration can be defined as that movement in which prospective migrants learn of opportunities, are provided with transportation, and have initial accommodation and employment arranged *by means of primary social relationships with previous migrants.*

Chain migration is thus distinct from impersonally organized migration which is conceived as movement based on impersonal recruitment and assistance. In the postwar period, impersonally organized migration is exemplified by the arrangements for selection, transportation, reception, instruction and placement made by the International Refugee Organization; other clear examples are the century-old sequence of schemes for officially assisted migration from the United Kingdom to her colonies and dominions, and also from southern Europe to Argentina and Brazil.[2]

In the postwar period, chain migration is exemplified in the various forms of sponsorship of close relatives permitted by countries of large European settlement. The quota system of the United States is an outstanding case. These arrangements are subject in many cases to severe screening, however, so that having helpful close relatives in the receiving country is only a necessary condition, but may be far less than sufficient qualification. Thus recent chain migration across international borders has taken place within an elaborate framework of administrative hurdles.

European migration to the United States before the First World War was politically free by comparison. Moreover, from 1885, the impersonal organization of immigration by foreign governments, domestic employers, shipping companies, land companies and other large enterprises was banned. In effect, only chain migration was permitted for continental Europeans.[3] They did not know English and, in any case, they were rarely prepared to enter America simply on their own initiative and resources. At the same time, the United States' restrictions on chain migration were minimal.

Reprinted by permission from "Chain Migration, Ethnic Neighborhood Formation, and Social Networks" by John S. MacDonald and Leatrice D. MacDonald, *Milbank Memorial Fund Quarterly*, 42 (1964), pp. 82–97.

In the nineteenth century, the Italian authorities took only perfunctory steps to restrain the worst excesses of the shipping companies, hotel-keepers, ticket sellers and miscellaneous racketeers attracted to the migration business. The Catholic Church did not shepherd the emigrants' worldly interests, while the emigrants, for their part, did not seek help, being among Italy's most unobservant anti-clerics.

In 1901, the Italian government set up its General Emigration Commission to take special care of the outwardbound emigrant. It is hard to say how effective this Commission was. In order not to conflict with United States law, it could not promote emigration positively. Its competence was limited to inhibiting those who preyed upon the emigrant, and to enforcing higher standards of accommodation until he reached foreign territory. The Commission had only one weapon for fighting abuses within foreign territory, the discretion to ban emigration toward that destination. This power was never invoked against emigration to the northern United States.[4]

Consequently the period 1885–1914 is especially germane to an analysis of chain migration. The "internal" organization of migration, whether of the chain or impersonal type, has a strong bearing on the results of movement. The kinds of people caught up in chain migration, as well as the ways in which they land and settle or repatriate, depend in part on inconspicuous sociological developments which are not commonly recognized by the policy-maker, legislator or administrator.

The main purpose of this paper is to examine the bonds between successive Southern Italian immigrants in this period, and also some of the consequences of this social structure.

Migration from Southern Italy[5] to the Northern cities of the United States can be explained in terms of political freedom of movement and economic "push" and "pull." The settlement of Southern Italians in the slums of the Northern cities can be explained in terms of the ecology of the American urban class and caste structure. Neither of these valid explanations, however, answers the question: Why did immigrants from certain towns[6] in Southern Italy settle together in certain localities in the United States? These immigrants were not distributed among the "Little Italies" by chance (see Appendix II). Prospective immigrants needed passage money, as well as assistance in finding initial employment and accommodation. These were generally provided by earlier immigrants from their hometowns. Immigration from Southern Italy consequently occurred in interdependent waves. There were two distinctive movements: the ebb and flow of lone working males, and delayed family migration.

The chain relationships which linked old and new immigrants can be classified in three broad types. First, some established immigrants encouraged and assisted prospective male immigrants of working age in order to profit from them. These *padroni* (bosses) exploited the new immigrants directly, or were paid a commission by American employers for providing labor. Second, there was serial migration of breadwinners. Before deciding to settle permanently in the United States and bring out their wives and families, lone males often assisted other breadwinners to come to the country and get established. Third, there was delayed family migration. Lone male immigrants eventually brought out their wives and children.

In the early days of Southern Italian immigration, *padroni* brought young boys to the United States for shoeshine and other juvenile menial work. By the

1890's, this type of indenture had been virtually eliminated by the Italian and American authorities (Foerster, p. 324, see Appendix I).

Before the First World War, the great majority of Southern Italian immigrants were males of working age who intended to save money in the United States and return home. Among them were many married men, but very few were accompanied by their wives and children on their first voyage. At first, they were usually "birds of passage." It was only after some years in the United States, and one or more return voyages to their home towns, that they decided to become permanent American residents. This pattern was dictated in part by the motives which led them to leave home and also by the instability of the work which was generally open to them in the United States.

They left Italy, for the most part, in order to return to their birthplace with money to buy land and a better house and to raise their social status. They did not intend, at first, to enter American society and raise themselves in its terms. They had little contact, other than impersonal service relationships, with the host society, and it was many years before they were assimilated into it.

They were inferior in the eyes of the "Old" Americans and earlier immigrant groups, such as the Irish and the Germans. They entered the American class structure at the bottom, and they ran up against job and housing discrimination, open hostility, and even violence.

New arrivals from Southern Italy generally could find only temporary employment, usually on a seasonal basis. Most had no skills useful in urban America. Therefore, most of these immigrants spent at least their first few months as common laborers in open air work, which stopped each winter, or at other temporary jobs, such as construction laboring. The Southern Italian fruit vendor and storekeeper were familiar figures in the American street scene, but only a small proportion of the immigrants were engaged in petty commerce. Southern Italians were not outstandingly successful in commerce or other business enterprises, except in the limited number of establishments which arose to serve the "Little Italies." During the slack periods in the American labor market, a large proportion returned to their homeland.

They had little desire to learn English and become acquainted with the American scene. Remaining in great ignorance of the larger economy and society around them, they were able to find work through better established, more knowledgeable compatriots who functioned as middlemen between new arrivals and American employers.

MIGRATION THROUGH PADRONI

In addition to financing immigration, the *padrone* provided employment and numerous other services which isolated new arrivals from American society and kept them dependent. For example, a *padrone* might act as banker, landlord, foreman, scribe, interpreter, legal adviser, or ward boss. Moreover, his clients were buying continuing protection from a public figure who was somewhat subject to community pressure and dependent on its good will. It was therefore better to travel under his auspices than to rely on any stranger encountered along the way.

Most important of the *padrone's* functions, from our standpoint, was that he kept his *paesani* together. The continuing dependence of his wards was sanctioned by Southern Italian custom. Before serial migration and delayed family migration assumed large proportions, the *padrone* system took the place of the traditional family and kinship system.[7] *Padroni* were often god-fathers to the immigrants whom they assisted; god-parenthood in Southern Italy was perhaps as important as the rural Spanish *compadrazgo* (see Bibliography: 42, p. 43; 44, p. 482).

The *padrone* system was not self-perpetuating. As the immigrants who had been dependent on them became better acquainted with American conditions and learned English, they were able to fend for themselves and also help later immigrants. Thus the *padroni* gradually lost their monopolistic powers as the cluster of roles with which they had been vested were taken over by the close relatives and friends of prospective immigrants.

Although many new arrivals first worked on railroad gangs in rural areas, they tended sooner or later to settle in cities. They were eventually able to move into factory work from temporary or seasonal employment as common laborers. This broadening and stabilizing of employment, which was particularly marked at the beginning of this century, decreased the power of the *padroni*. Many American industries did have Southern Italian foremen who functioned as middlemen, but factories did not offer as many opportunities for exploitation of dependency as the sub-contracting and "straw boss" systems in railroad and construction work.

In any case, in 1906, the major railroads curtailed the powers of their *padroni* by taking direct responsibility for engaging labor, by paying unskilled workers' wages without intermediaries, and by regulating conditions in their camps. Furthermore, a few years before the First World War, labor unions began to organize successfully among Southern Italian immigrants. American labor unions were slow to organize among unskilled laborers and in those occupations which were largely filled by recent immigrants. However, they were active among the large numbers of Southern Italian barbers employed in America's cities. Moreover, Southern Italians organized their own unions in semi-skilled and unskilled occupations such as construction laboring, mining, stonecutting and bricklaying in some areas. The labor unions diminished the importance of the *padroni* in these fields by negotiating directly with employers, opposing exploitation and informing ignorant new arrivals of better opportunities. The Italian General Emigration Commission, founded in 1901, may also have usurped some of the *padroni's* functions, but its effect cannot have been great.

SERIAL MIGRATION OF WORKERS

Serial migration, like the *padrone* system, kept Southern Italian neighborhoods relatively homogeneous because, in their homeland, kinship and friendship ties did not extend beyond the immigrants' districts of origin. Indeed, marriage, friendship and other close ties rarely linked adjacent towns.[6]

Before settling permanently and bringing out their wives and children, lone males often assisted male relatives and friends of working age to immigrate. This chain migration in series apparently accounted for a large part of adult male immigration from Southern Italy, even before the beginning of this century, because the *padroni* never had absolute control of Southern Italian immigration. New arrivals usually went directly to the relatives and friends who had financed their passage, and relied on them to find their first lodgings and employment. Their guardians usually lodged them in their own quarters or found a room in the neighborhood, and found them work close by, since the "Little Italies" were conveniently located near the principal markets of unskilled labor.

Campanilismo (hometown loyalty) was not a basis for chain migration. The "Little Italies" abounded in mutual benefit societies with membership limited to fellow townsmen. These clubs did not organize immigration, however. Furthermore, there were no associations or bodies organizing emigration in Southern Italy. Indeed there were no associations or bodies which *could* organize emigration, with the possible exception of the Mafia in western Sicily. The social structure of this section of Italy is still extremely individualistic and familistic. Bonds outside the nuclear family household were almost exclusively along a dyadic patron-client axis. Corporate organizations are still inconceivable in most of Southern Italy, except when they are forced upon it by the centralized State.[7]

DELAYED FAMILY MIGRATION

It was only by delayed family migration that the Southern Italian sex ratio in the United States tended toward equality. An unmarried female travelling alone was inconceivable in a culture which took extremely restrictive precautions to safeguard family honor.[7]

Immigrants were rarely able to take home the fortunes of which they had dreamed. Also, mass emigration brought about rapid inflation in Southern Italy as money flowed back from America to its stagnant economy. Moreover, it was cheaper for immigrants to bring out their families and put them to work in the United States, than leave them in Italy and return home periodically; and, in America, they could put their women to work more profitably.

Women in Southern Italy rarely took individual employment outside the home or family enterprises. In the United States, they avoided work as domestic servants, which was regarded as a threat to their chastity. However, a large percentage broke with tradition by working in factories, especially as garment workers and textile factory operatives.

The stresses and conflicts to which traditional family life was subjected by wives' and daughters' new economic roles outside the family were minimized by adapting the family to the factory situation. A study of Southern Italian textile workers in Norristown shows in detail how wives and daughters chaperoned each other at work; how these immigrant women chose industries where they did not have to work with men; how kinship reciprocity continued as a means of getting jobs, skills and better pay; how parental authority was used by the factory as a form of sub-management whereby young girls were put to work under their mothers or aunts (see Bibliography: 18).

They could increase the family's earnings in less disruptive ways, by taking in home work from the garment, textile, embroidery, hat and glove industries, by boarding lone males or relatives' families, or by running the family store while their men worked out for wages. Boarding and lodging with families were practically unheard of in Southern Italy, but in the United States it was a common device for profiting from the great excess of lone males in the Southern Italian population while keeping wives and daughters in the house.

There was very little intermarriage between Southern Italians and "Old"

Americans or other nationality groups in the United States (see Bibliography: 16 among others). They definitely preferred to marry Southern Italian women. Paradoxically, their insistence on a bride who had never been kissed was the very reason for the shortage of marriageable Southern Italian women in the United States. The number of marriageable women very slowly increased as unmarried daughters accompanied their mothers to join their fathers. Consequently, most bachelors had to return home to marry, or bring out proxy wives.

SUMMARY AND CONCLUSIONS

The clustering of fellow townsmen from Southern Italy in the cities of the northern States cannot be adequately understood without analysis of chain migration. In this case, chain migration was an adaptation of the familism and dyadic patronage which were the crucial forms of the contributing society, providing a "feedback" of information and assistance from immigrants in the United States to prospective emigrants in their home towns.

Chain migration not only led to the growth of "Little Italies," but also produced "chain occupations," particular niches in the American employment structure to which successive immigrants directed their fellows on the basis of their own experience. The evolution of ethnic succession in this country is a reflection of this "chain occupation" process.

If we study chain migration, we must also study its logical opposite, that is, when chains do not operate. Banfield[8] reports on a town in Basilicata where prospective emigrants could not leave because their numerous fellow townsmen abroad had severed all ties with home. The social organization of this town was extremely atomistic—even more so than is the rule in Southern Italy—making chain migration impossible. Associations, community organizations, clans or other forms of segmental solidarity are conspicuous by their absence in Southern Italy. Moreover, the nuclear family household, the multilateral kinship system, and dyadic patronage—the basic forms of social organization in this part of Italy—are precarious. Chain migration based on a hometown society of the Southern Italian type necessarily runs the risk of leaving some prospective emigrants out on a limb. A potential sponsor abroad may desert his family, friends and clients when he assimilates to his host society, or when the frequent conflicts in this kind of society rupture bonds. Another possibility: a sponsor may fulfill his obligations to those few fellow townsmen who are close relatives, friends or clients, and not give any thought to the majority to whom he has no customary obligations. We have found such cases of "broken" chain migration among Southern Italians in Australia. The information available for the United States provides only positive instances of chain migration.

A further approach to understanding chain migration would be to study contrasting societies where reciprocal obligations and corporate solidarity have a different scope. We might examine the role of the Southern Slav and Albanian *Zadruga* and clan in emigration. Chain migration derived from clans and extended families is certainly crucial to an explanation of ethnic group formation and chain occupations among the Chinese in South East Asia and the United States.[9]

APPENDIX I

This paper is based on a survey of American secondary sources on Italian immigration in the period 1880–1914, undertaken with a Population Council Fellowship. The principal sources are R. F. Foerster, *The Italian Emigration of Our Times,* (Cambridge, 1919), and U.S. Immigration Commission, *Reports* (Washington, 41 vols., 1911), which are referred to simply as Foerster and Im. Com. The sources cited in the text and the references are subsidiary, except on those particular points. Some of the same material is discussed from a different standpoint in our "Urbanization, Ethnic Groups and Social Segmentation," *Social Research,* 29(4). Winter, 1962.

APPENDIX II

Definitive Examples of Chains and Neighborhoods (Numbers in parentheses refer to the Bibliography following). In Manhattan, Sicilians from the town of Cinisi were concentrated in Midtown (31). Immigrants from Avigliano (Basilicata) clustered in East Harlem (14, 15). Park and Miller found separate enclaves from different towns and districts in the "Little Italy" near New York's Bowery, where the blocks were heterogeneous but each building housed distinctive clusters (31). Jacob Riis also found Calabrians on Mulberry Street grouped according to their town of origin (37). In Utica the great majority of the Southern Italians came from Laurenzana and adjacent towns in Basilicata (43). Southern Italians from different towns settled in different parts of New Jersey (8). Most Southern Italians in Norristown (Pennsylvania) came from the town of Sciacca in Girgenti province, Sicily. They were highly concentrated within Norristown's Italian section (18, 20). In New Haven immigrants from the Salerno coast of Campania were concentrated in one neighborhood. They were drawn in the main from the towns of Amalfi and Scafati Atrani. Those from the mountain provinces of Campania settled in a second "Little Italy" (7, 22, 29, 33). In Middletown (Connecticut), the greater part of the large Italian population came from the Sicilian town of Melilli in Syracuse province, and concentrated in one neighborhood (40). Most of the Italians of Stamford (Connecticut) were drawn from Avigliano (Potenza) and S. Mango sul Calore (Campania) (10). In Cleveland there was a large concentration of Sicilians from Termini Imerense, in Palermo province (13). The largest Southern Italian neighborhoods in Chicago derived from the Sicilian towns of Altavilla Milicia, Bagheria Vicari, Monreale and Termini Imerense, in Palermo province (31). Milwaukee's "Little Italies" were peopled by immigrants from the coastal towns of northern Sicily, between Palermo and Milazzo (23). "The Bagnolese migration (from Abruzzi-Molise) to Detroit is a typical chain effect. . . . The Detroit cluster sprang from a single migrant (and his family) who persuaded others to follow."[10]

There are many more cases of "Little Italies" which were not cross-sections of the total Italian or Southern Italian movement to the United States. Presumably their peculiar provenance was due to chain migration. But the information on the composition of these neighborhoods is given only by region or province, not by district or hometown of origin.

No indication of the genesis of chains was found except in two cases. The Southern Italians of Utica stemmed originally from itinerant street musicians who simply happened to settle there. The ubiquitous street musicians of Basilicata planted numerous colonies around the world. The Southern Italians of Middletown can be traced back to a sailor and a circus act. Presumably all the chains derived from such fortuitous occurrences. Chance, however, cannot explain the continuance or discontinuance of chains.

NOTES

1. We hesitate to hypothesize two polar ideal types and an intervening unilinear continuum.
2. Analytically purer examples of impersonally organized migration would be the transatlantic slave trade, the deportation of convicts from Europe to penal colonies, and the Nazi "extermination-through-work" programme.
3. Im. Com., "Contract labor and induced and assisted migration," vol. II, pp. 14–15; "Emigration conditions in Europe," vol. IV, p. 61.
4. For appraisals of the General Emigration Commission and earlier sanctions on Italian emigration, see Bibliography: 26, 52.
5. In this paper, Southern Italy comprises the regions of Abruzzi-Molise, Campania, Apulia, Basilicata, Calabria and Sicily, a basically agricultural area with few cities, negligible manufacturing and mining, and fairly homogeneous traditions and social structure. The definition of Southern Italy by the U. S. Immigration Commission of 1907 is based on arbitrary racial grounds, and includes the regions of Liguria, Tuscany, Umbria, the Marches and Latium (Rome). These regions are commonly classified together as Central Italy, because of their distinctive traditions and economic and social structure. In any case, the very great majority of Southern Italian immigrants, as defined by the U. S. Immigration Commission, did come from Southern Italy in the sense used in this paper; very few immigrants came from Central Italy.
6. "Town," not "village," is used here because the rural population of Southern Italy resided almost entirely in agglomerations of 1,500 or more inhabitants.
7. For an introduction in English to Southern Italian society and culture, see Bibliography: 2, 4, 24, 26, 33.
8. *op. cit.*
9. See Bibliography: 6, 45.
10. Personal Communication from Leonard W. Moss.

BIBLIOGRAPHY

1. Ascoli, M., The Italian-Americans, in *Group Relations and Group Antagonisms*. Robert M. MacIver (ed.), New York, 1944.
2. Banfield, E. C., *The Moral Basis of a Backward Society*, Glencoe, 1958.
3. Campisi, P. J., The Adjustment of Italian-Americans to the War Crisis. Unpublished M.A. dissertation, University of Chicago, 1942.
4. Cappannari, S. C. and Moss, L. W., A Sociological and Anthropological Investigation of an Italian Rural Community. Paper read at IVth World Congress of Sociology, International Sociological Association, Milan, September, 1959.
5. Carlson-Smith, W. *Americans in the Making; The Natural History of the Assimilation of Immigrants*. New York, 1939.
6. Cattell, S. H., *Health, Welfare and Social Organization in Chinatown, New York City*. Community Service Society, New York, August, 1962.
7. Child, I. L. *Italian or American? The Second-Generation in Conflict*. New Haven, 1943.
8. Churchill, C. W., The Italians of Newark. Unpublished Ph.D. dissertation, New York University, 1942.

9. Clark, R. E., *Our Italian Fellow Citizens in Their Old Homes and Their New.* Boston, 1919.
10. Comitato Coloniale per il Congresso degl'Italiani all'Estero, Stato del Connecticut. Stamford, 1908.
11. Concistre, M. J., Adult Education in a Local Community; A Study of a Decade in the Life and Education of the Adult Italian Immigrant in East Harlem. Unpublished Ph.D. dissertation, New York University, 1943.
12. Corsi, E., Italian Immigrants and Their Children. *The Annals,* (September, 1942), Vol. 223.
13. Coulter, C. W., *The Italians of Cleveland.* Cleveland, 1919.
14. Covello, L., The Social Background of the Italian-American School Child. Unpublished Ph.D. dissertation, Columbia University, 1941.
15. _____: *The Heart is the Teacher.* New York, 1958.
16. Drachsler, J., *Intermarriage in New York City; A Statistical Study of the Amalgamation of European Peoples.* New York, 1921.
17. Fairchild, H. P., *Immigration; A World Movement and Its American Significance.* New York, 1928.
18. Huganir, G. H., The Hosiery Looper in the Twentieth Century; A Study of Family Process and Adaptation to Factory and Community Change. Unpublished Ph.D. dissertation, University of Pennsylvania, 1958.
19. Hutchinson, E. P., *Immigrants and Their Children, 1850–1950.* New York, 1956.
20. Ianni, F. A., The Acculturation of the Italo-Americans in Norristown, Pennsylvania: 1900 to 1950. Unpublished Ph.D. dissertation, Pennsylvania State College, 1952.
21. Jerome, H., *Migration and Business Cycles.* New York, 1926.
22. Koenig, S., *The Immigrant Settlements in Connecticut; Their Growth and Characteristics.* W.P.A., Federal Writers' Project, Connecticut. Hartford, Connecticut State Department of Education, 1938.
23. La Piana, G., *The Italians of Milwaukee.* Milwaukee, 1915.
24. Lopreato, J., Interpersonal Relations: The Peasant's View. *Human Organization,* (Spring 1962), 21(1).
25. Lord, E., Trenor, J. D. and Barrows, S. J., *The Italians in America.* New York, 1905.
26. MacDonald, J. S., Migration from Italy to Australia. Unpublished Ph.D. dissertation, Australian National University, 1958. Chaps. I–V.
27. MacDonald, J. S. and MacDonald, L. D., Agricultural Organization, Migration and Labour Militancy in Rural Italy. *Economic History Review.* (1963), 16:1.
28. Mangano, A., *Sons of Italy; A Social and Religious Study of the Italians in America.* Boston, 1917.
29. Myers, J. K., The Differential Time Factor in Assimilation; A Study of Aspects and Processes of Assimilation Among the Italians of New Haven. Unpublished Ph.D. dissertation, Yale University, 1949.
30. Odencrantz, L. C., *Italian Women in Industry; A Study of Conditions in New York City.* New York, 1919.
31. Park, R. E. and Miller, H. M., *Old World Traits Transplanted.* New York, 1921.
32. Pesaturo, U. M., *Italo-Americans of Rhode Island; An Historical and Biographical Survey of the Origin, Rise and Progress of Rhode Islanders of Italian Birth or Descent.* Providence, 1940.
33. Pisani, L. F., *The Italian in America.* New York, 1957.
34. Pitkin D. S., The Intermediate Society. American Ethnological Society Annual Spring Meeting 1959, *Intermediate Societies, Social Mobility and Communication.* Seattle, 1959.
35. Ratti, A. M., Italian Migration Movements, 1876 to 1926: W. F. Willcox and I. Ferenczi (eds.), *International Migrations.* New York, 1929.
36. Riis, J., *How the Other Half Lives.* Scribner's, New York, 1890.
37. _____: *Out of Mulberry Street; Stories of Tenement Life in New York City.* The Century, New York, 1898.
38. Rose, P. M., *The Italians in America.* Doran, New York, 1922.
39. Rubin, V. D., *Fifty Years in Rootville; A Study in the Dynamics of Acculturation.* Boston, 1951.
40. Sangree, W. H., Mel Hyblaeum; A Study of the People of Middletown of Sicilian Origin. Unpublished M.A. dissertation, Wesleyan University, 1952.

41. Sartorio, H. C., *The Social and Religious Life of Italians in America*. Christopher, Boston, 1918.
42. Schiavo, G. E., *The Italians of Chicago*. Italian American Publishing Co., Chicago, 1928.
43. Schiro, G., *Americans by Choice (History of the Italians in Utica)*. Griffiths, Utica, 1940.
44. Sheridan, F. J., Italian, Slavic and Hungarian Unskilled Laborers in the United States. *Bulletin of the U.S. Bureau of Labor*, (September 1907), Vol. 15, No. 72.
45. Taft, D. R. and Robbins, R., *International Migration*. Ronald Press, New York, 1955.
46. T'ien, J. K., *The Chinese of Sarawak*. London, 1953.
47. Tomanio, A. and Lamacchia, L. N., *The Italians of Bridgeport*. University of Bridgeport, Bridgeport, 1950.
48. U.S. Commissioner of Labor, The Italians of Chicago. *Ninth special report*, (Washington, 1897).
49. Ware, C. F., *Greenwich Village, 1920–1930*. Houghton Mifflin, Boston, 1935.
50. Williams, P. H., *Southern Italian Folkways in Europe and America*. Yale University Press, New Haven, 1938.
51. Winsemius, A., *Economische Aspecten der Internationale Migratie*. Haarlem, 1939.
52. Wittke, C., *We Who Built America; The Saga of the Immigrant*. Prentice-Hall, New York, 1939.
53. Woog, C., *La Politique d'Emigration d'Italie*. Paris, 1930.
54. Writers' Program, New York, *The Italians of New York*. W.P.A., New York, 1938.

INSTITUTIONS OF PRIVACY IN THE DETERMINATION OF POLICE ADMINISTRATIVE PRACTICE

Arthur L. Stinchcombe

Here is another article that hides fascinating content behind a forbidding title. Stinchcombe's analysis is mainly locational; it treats the community as a set of activities distributed over a territory. The analysis has three components tightly connected to one another. First, Stinchcombe points out that urban and rural areas differ in the distribution of public and private spaces; most important, cities have a much higher proportion of their total area in public spaces. Second, he notices that crimes differ sharply in their allocation between public and private spaces: murder occurs almost exclusively in private spaces; for some crimes, such as public drunkenness, the location is part of the very definition of the action as criminal. Third, he shows what the combination of the first two factors means: the spatial pattern of crime is quite different in urban and rural areas, the patterns of surveillance open to the police in urban and rural areas also differ greatly, and as a consequence the entire routine of policing follows contrasting patterns in city and country. Some of the difference in rates of reported crime between city and country undoubtedly results from the contrasting administrative practices.

Those are the main arguments. Some of the secondary observations are also quite illuminating. Stinchcombe points out the intimate connection between the survival of small social systems and their control of private

*spaces in which they can carry on their own affairs. (On reading Stinch-
combe, we begin to see why gangs might want to control their own corners
and candy stores.) Developing that line of thought, he gives us a provocative
definition of the modern liberal state: "... it uses the monopoly of violence
(which all modern industrial states have) to guarantee the boundaries of
small, autonomous social systems." He suggests that the central meaning of
vagrancy and related offenses is being found without legal access to a private
space. As a practical demonstration of the impact of spatial organization on
everyday life, the article is powerful.*

*Stinchcombe's essay makes another less obvious contribution. It helps
to show how much order underlies the supposed disorder of the city. Other
articles in this book (including Marc Fried's discussion of the working-class
communities and my study of urbanization and collective violence in France)
make similar observations, but none in so fine and precise a manner as
Stinchcombe's. To be sure, people do murder each other in cities, although
not with notably greater frequency than in the countryside. Public drunkenness really occurs. Rape happens. Stinchcombe's contribution is to show how
much the disapproved behavior and its detection depend on the way the
community organizes its space. In doing so, he counters the old notion of the
city as a place where rules and routines dissolve.*

Legal institutions in general depend on rare events, such as arrests or civil
court cases, to structure the field in which frequent events take place. This makes
the operation of legal institutions very difficult to study, except when fairly
comparable types of frequent events operate in strikingly different legally structured fields. The institutions of liberty generally, and of legally protected privacy in
particular, have the characteristic that rare events, such as a case being thrown out
of court because the law of search and seizure has been violated, structure the field
in which the everyday activity of police is carried out. The many types of crimes
that police deal with are very differently situated with respect to the legal institutions of privacy, as we shall try to demonstrate in the first part of this paper.

Certain statistics on the arrest and conviction rates for different types of
crimes as well as pieces of common knowledge can be used to explore the different
characteristics of police administrative practice in these different legally structured
fields. We will then try to show that police administrative practice with respect to
different types of crime varies strikingly and systematically with the relation of the
crimes to the legal institutions of privacy. This paper then tries to conduct an
empirical study of that kind of "structural effect" on which the regulatory power
of the law depends, namely, an effect on the behavior of many of an action by the
courts that specifically applies only to the action of a few.

The order of presentation will be as follows: first I shall outline some
well-known characteristics of the legal institutions by which "private places" are
defined, and the effects of the growth of large cities on the social structure of

Reprinted by permission of the author and publisher, University of Chicago Press, from
"Institutions of Privacy in the Determination of Police Administrative Practice" by Arthur L.
Stinchcombe, *American Journal of Sociology*, 69 (1963), pp. 150–160. Copyright © University
of Chicago, 1963.

"public places." Then I shall outline the relation of certain types of crime to these legal institutions and show how the location of crimes with respect to private and public places affects the organized activities of the police in handling these crimes. Since the police "organization" is made up of organized activities with respect to crime, this is really an indirect approach to studying the effect of social structure on organizational structure. To show this more clearly, in the final part of the section I shall summarize the way that the socially determined activities of police for particular types of crime are organized into police subsections with different characteristics.

LEGAL RELATIONS OF POLICE POWER TO PRIVACY

Most of our daily life is lived in a number of small, bounded social systems, such as families, schools, factories, clubs, etc., that have their own norms, goals, and facilities. The maintenance of the boundaries of these systems is necessary to their free and autonomous development. If agents of the state or strange private citizens could enter these systems arbitrarily and interfere with interaction within them, they cannot develop freely.

The central practical boundaries are such mundane things as walls, doors, window shades, and locks. But in modern society few of these are made to withstand a concerted effort by a group of men to breach them (in contrast to feudal societies, for example). Yet these fragile doors and windows effectively prevent police or private citizens from interfering with our sleep, our classrooms, our toolbenches, or our bars, at least most of the time. This is because a door is a legal entity of great importance: legitimate concerted social efforts to break down a door may only take place on legally defined occasions. These occasions are defined in the law of arrest[1] and the law of search and seizure,[2] and therefore, derivatively, in the criminal law.

The legal defense of doors and walls and windows means that small social systems which have legal possession of a place can maintain *continuous, discretionary* control over who crosses their boundaries. And this discretion may be enforced against agents of the state unless they have legal cause to penetrate the system or are invited in. Whenever such continuous discretionary control is maintained, the law speaks of "private places." The legal existence of "private places," then, is the main source of the capacity of small social systems to maintain their boundaries and determine their own interaction without interference from the outside. The distinctive feature of a modern *liberal* state is that it uses the monopoly of violence (which all modern industrial states have) to guarantee the boundaries of small, autonomous social systems.

The central importance in our society of the private places created in this way is indicated by two facts. First, in Maryland, a state not much less free than others, a man entirely without access to private places is legally unfree:

> Every person, not insane, who wanders about in this state and lodges in market houses, market places, or in other public buildings [note that some of these "public buildings" are "private property"] or in barns, outhouses, barracks, or in the open air, without having any lawful occupation in the city, town, or county in which he may so wander, and without having any visible

means of support, shall be deemed to be a tramp, and to be guilty of a misdemeanor, and shall be subject to imprisonment, at the discretion of the Court or Justice of the Peace hearing the charge, for a period of not less than thirty days nor more than one year. This section not to apply to Allegany County.[3]

That is, if a man is not a member of some organization or family or other group that has control over a "private place" (which may, of course, be "public property," as for instance a county hospital), then he has to *satisfy a policeman* that his occupation in the area is lawful, and has to make visible his means of support (except in Allegany County). Access to private places is itself sufficient evidence that a man has a legitimate relation to the social structure; without that evidence, special evidence of legitimate occupation has to be provided. "Occupation" here means any legitimate activity, not specifically a job.

The second fact indicating the importance of the legal definition of private places is that unless continuous discretionary control of access to a piece of property is maintained (creating a "private place"), police may freely enter and supervise interaction and arrest without a warrant:

An officer in uniform or in citizen's clothes, may enter any public house, if open, as other people enter, for the purpose of detecting or suppressing crime, and having peaceably entered, may arrest for any offense committed in his presence. [Apparently a common law rule, as cases are cited for authority rather than statutes.][4]

A man's affairs are never, then, legally free of police supervision except within private places. Police may not legally, of course, forbid actions in public places that are not prohibited by law. But there is a fundamental difference between conducting the affairs of a small social system in such a manner that no crimes committed shall *come to the attention* of the police, and conducting them so that a physically present policeman will approve. In the first case, the problem is to prevent complaints, perhaps by agreement; in the second, the problem is to satisfy the police, rather than other members of the system, that all is as it should be. Few of us ever see a policeman in those places where we spend most of our time; a "tramp" sees one wherever he goes, and the policeman has the discretionary power to "run him in."

DISTRIBUTION OF PRIVATE PLACES AND
URBAN-RURAL POLICE PRACTICE

The concentration of the population into cities concentrates intensively used "public places" within a small geographical area, thus greatly reducing the amount of "public" area per person and making professional control of public places much more economical. At the same time the size and anonymity of the city decrease the chance of small social systems to control the behavior of their members in public. In a small village, activity in public places easily comes to the attention of the family, the priest, the employer, and the peers of the offender. Further, in large cities there are much stronger norms about "deliberately not noticing" the behavior of other people. This means that in cities, much more behavior is *only* inquired into by the police.

That is, in cities it is economically possible to patrol public places, and at the same time it is functionally necessary. City police can therefore depend much more on their own presence and information for the detection of crime (especially certain types of crime) than can a rural police force. To a large degree (except for the patrol of main highways) rural police depend on complaints from people who are injured or know of a crime rather than on their own patrol.

Besides leading to different structural conditions of police practice, intensively used public places pose new problems. The most important are, of course, traffic jams and accidents. But also, extensive traffic creates opportunities for the use of public places for private profit in ways that create a "nuisance." Soliciting for prostitution, begging, street vending, speech-making, all become profitable uses of public places when the traffic gets heavy enough. The control of these "nuisances" is easily done without access to private places, along with other patrol duties.

The increasing predominance of patrol of public places means that policemen act much more on their own initiative. Much or all of the evidence that justifies arrest will be collected by the policeman on the spot. The arrest often need not involve any invasion at all of private places. Consequently these arrests are much more likely than are those in rural areas to be arrests without a warrant, and therefore without prior check by the judiciary, or to be a direct summons to appear in court (as in traffic cases).

ARRESTS INVOLVING ENTRY INTO PRIVATE PLACES

Private autonomy alone cannot guarantee liberty in the sense in which we understand it today. Feudal manors or plantations in the ante bellum South were much more autonomous and free of state interference than modern factories and business places. But this private autonomy did not create liberty in the modern sense because the police power was privately appropriated and consequently not exercised according to "due process of law." The practical implication of this is that besides *not* entering small systems *except* on legally defined occasions, *entering* them *on* those occasions is a duty of the police in liberal societies. A primary function of the criminal law is the limitation of coercion within small social systems.

But once the small systems are entered by the state, "due process of law" means mainly a set of procedures which guarantee that the autonomy of individuals and small social systems will be restored as quickly as possible if a crime has not in fact been committed. And it means that the process of investigating and legally establishing the existence of a crime shall not so far damage the small social system that they cannot function after they have been found innocent.

Due process thus involves a grading of coercion applied by the police, into arrest and the seizure of evidence, coerced appearance in court, and coerced paying of the penalty of crime. Each of these grades of coercion changes the legal status of the presumed offender. Each of these changes of the legal condition of the presumed offender must be justified by evidence of a probability that a crime has been committed and probability that the defendant committed the crime. The probabilities increase with the increase in severity of coercion. The probability required to justify arrest (by a police officer at least) is not as high as that required to coerce an appearance in court (a "prima facie case"). To justify conviction the commission of a crime must be established "beyond reasonable doubt." We now have sufficient background to discuss the structural location of different types of crime with respect to the institutions of privacy and the effect of this structural distribution on police practice.

THE EFFECT OF THE SOCIAL LOCATION OF DIFFERENT CRIMES ON POLICE PRACTICE

It is immediately evident that different types of crime will be distributed differently with respect to the institutions of privacy. For instance, wife-beating rarely goes on in public places. Soliciting for prostitution requires some systematic contact with an anonymous public through a pimping apparatus. Except for call girls and prostitutes in well-known houses, this requires soliciting (often by the woman herself) in some public places. But prostitution takes place in private places. Burglary consists in the invasion of the private place of another, generally in secret, which results in a complaint against an unknown person. The person's identity has to be established by the police. Murder generally takes place within small social systems, behind doors. Riots take place in streets and other public places.

Of course these variations in the social location of crimes imply differences in police practice. Information relevant to each stage of the criminal process comes to the police in different ways, different degrees and kinds of coercion have to be applied for different purposes, different things have to be proved with the evidence. There are differences in the number and types of private places that have to be penetrated, and in the amount of preparation of the case previous to this penetration. The kinds of people who commit different types of crime have different stability of social ties, which makes due process work differently.[5] We may distinguish the following types of crime.

a) Coercion in Private Life. The application of force or other coercion in private life is either controlled and adjusted within the small social system (as when a wife puts up with a beating), or it is not. When it is not, the crimes are, generally speaking, "crimes of passion." Probably the legally defined crimes with the highest proportion originating in this way are incest and murder,[6] but some unknown proportion of other crimes against persons (rape, aggravated assault) originate the same way.

Such crimes generally either result in complaint to the police or in such heinous crimes that access to private places is hardly a difficulty, at least for investigation. Because the people who participate in small social systems are highly visible once the system is penetrated, and because often the complainant knows perfectly well who coerced whom, arrests are fairly easy to make. Crimes against persons generally have a high proportion of "crimes known to the police" that are "cleared by arrest" (see Table 1).

But the same conditions that produce easy arrests create another characteristic of enforcement against these crimes, namely, that arrests quite often do not result in conviction. Legal responsibility of the assailant must be established. His intentions are not immediately obvious from the nature of the act (as they are, for example, in burglary). The kind of passionate conflicts that lead to murders rarely

242   *Communities*

TABLE 1
Proportion of Crimes Known to the Police "Cleared by Arrest," and Proportion
of Those Charged Who Are Convicted, for Various Crimes[a]

Crime	Percentage Cleared by Arrest	Percentage Convicted
Crimes indicating coercion in private life:		
Murder, including non-negligent manslaughter	92.7	59.4
Forcible rape	73.6	43.0
Aggravated assault	64.7	43.9
Crimes indicating coercion in public places:		
Robbery	42.5	64.8
Crimes indicating invasion of private places of another:		
Burglary	30.7	71.4
Larceny (over $50)	20.9	72.6
Auto theft	26.2	67.5
Crimes indicating individual public disorder:		
Vagrancy	N.a.	77.5
Drunkenness	N.a.	86.5
Disorderly conduct	N.a.	69.7

[a]Computed from Federal Bureau of Investigation, *Uniform Crime Reports—1959* (Washington, D.C.: Government Printing Office, 1960), Tables 12 and 14.

make the motives of the crime absolutely clear. In the highly intensive interaction between the presumed offender and the victim the crime may have been provoked, for example, by requiring self-defense, or by consent before the presumed rape of a woman.

In addition, conviction before a jury generally requires that the defendant be judged not only legally but also morally responsible for the crime. In spite of the legal tradition, rape of a prostitute or murder of a really oppressive husband, seems to be a lesser crime. Evidence of moral responsibility is much harder to produce in crimes of passion. Finally, complaint to the police is something of a betrayal of those to whom we have close personal ties. Once the complaint is made, and the immediate danger and anger past, the personal ties or embarrassment of the complainant quite often reassert themselves, and the main source of evidence refuses to testify further.

The processing of the presumed offender then typically takes the following form: the arrest may be made on a warrant after preliminary investigation, but fairly often the offender is still at the scene and is arrested without a warrant; after the arrest supporting evidence must be collected by skilled investigation, both questioning and examination of physical clues; this is generally challenged very carefully and fully in court. A fairly general administrative pattern then is for uniformed patrol police to be called first; they come and take control of the scene and of the relevant evidence, and perhaps make arrests. Then the work passes to the detective force, which tries to establish the case (and generally takes credit for the conviction or blame for the poor case).

Crimes against persons in public places tend to depart from this pattern in several respects. In the first place, the officer is much more likely to happen on the scene, so that his own information is sufficient to justify arrest. Second, the assailant is generally unknown and not intimately tied to the victim. Consequently the location of the assailant may be more of a problem. In the case of strange assailants, however, the establishment of legal and moral responsibility is easier if they are located, and there is less motivation for the complainant to drop the case. The only crime for which statistics are given that uniformly falls in this category is robbery. As expected, the proportion cleared by arrest is somewhat smaller (42.5 per cent) and the proportion of charges leading to conviction considerably higher (64.8 per cent). ("Robbery" refers to taking things from persons, generally strangers, by violence or threat of violence.)

Crimes against persons, then, normally take place within the boundaries of morally dense small social systems. They come to the attention of the police typically through complaint, and arrests are usually easy to make. But conviction is very problematic, and requires detailed investigation of high skill.

b) Illegitimate Businesses and "Dangerous" Organizations. Illegitimate businesses such as prostitution, the illegal narcotics trade, and gambling in most of the United States, use the institutions of privacy to cloak activities that the society chooses to suppress. "Dangerous" organizations such as revolutionary or conspiratorial political parties stand in approximately the same relation to the institutions of privacy. These types of crime do not have "victims" in the same sense as do theft or murder. Instead the "victim" is an active participant in the system, either as a customer or party member. Consequently complaints do not come from within the system to the same degree that they do with crimes against persons. On the other hand, illegitimate businesses do not generally (directly) create disorder in public places. This means that patrol alone does not produce evidence justifying arrest or conviction. And although revolutionary political organizations must produce speech in public places, the speech is generally tempered enough (or if not tempered, ineffective enough) not to threaten the peace.

These conditions set the stage for the characteristic police practices in this field: "undercover" work, harassment, and regulation of the (relatively epiphenomenal) public aspects of the business. The prevalence of "undercover" work follows directly from the nature of the offense: the fact that it does not produce complaints, and that it takes place behind the barriers that protect privacy. Secret police activity is more prevalent *in societies* where the government routinely invades and distorts the functioning of small social systems; it is more prevalent *within* liberal societies when the suppression of illegitimate business or "dangerous" organizations is demanded by law and police policy.

By harassment I mean periodic or continuous enforcement of laws not normally enforced against the general public against people in illegitimate businesses or "dangerous" organizations. For instance, street soliciting of various kinds may be held to be a nuisance, but this is more likely to be enforced against prostitutes than against the Salvation Army, and the quality of evidence required to arrest prostitutes may be negligible.[7] Or a license required for "street vendors" may be required of the salesman of radical newspapers, though no other news vendors have been required to have licenses.

Harassment is easy to carry out because the participants are quite often infamous, without many friends who will appear in public in their defense, and personally demoralized, without a conviction of their own innocence. This is, of course, more true of people who run illegitimate businesses than of those who belong to "dangerous" organizations. The pattern of harassment produces a degree of discretionary power over illegitimate business by police. This discretion may be privately appropriated by the officer or by a political machine and used to "tax" illegitimate business.

The third pattern of law enforcement activity often produced by illegitimate business or "dangerous" organizations is tight regulation of public manifestations. In Baltimore, for example, the set of bars in which solicitation for prostitution goes on is concentrated in a relatively small area, and during the evening hours this area is very heavily patrolled. This prevents street soliciting and obnoxious forms of "barking" of the strip shows (prevalent, at least several years ago, in San Francisco), prevents the bars from serving minors, keeps bars closed after hours, and generally maintains public decorum without substantially disturbing the business. The same pattern is found in many large cities in the area set aside for "lunatic fringe" speakers. Heavy patrol helps prevent speakers being attacked, prevents potential riots from getting very far, prevents audiences from interrupting traffic, and so forth.

The general problem presented to police by illegitimate business or "dangerous" organizations, then, is that "crimes" do not become "known to the police."[8] When they do become known, conviction is generally relatively easy for the demoralized employees of illegitimate businesses, and for "dangerous" organizations depends on the public temper and the mood of the Supreme Court. In liberal societies, activity by secret police posing as customers of illegitimate businesses or as members of "dangerous" organizations tends to be concentrated in this field. The barriers of privacy require that the police get permission to enter where the "crime" is being carried on, and they have difficulty getting that permission if they are openly policemen. Harassment and corruption are both latent consequences of the legal suppression of systems that function behind barriers of privacy.

c) Invasion of Private Places by Criminals. Burglary, much larceny, and trespass involve the invasion of the private place of another without permission, generally in secret. These crimes present distinctive enforcement problems because they very often result in complaint to the police, yet the secrecy of the act makes it difficult to locate offenders. Relatively few of the "crimes known to the police" are "cleared by arrest." The proportion is lower than that of crimes against persons, either in public (robbery) or in private (see Table 1 above).

Unless they are caught in the act (which is the main way complaints of trespass originate), the offenders can generally be caught only by physical evidence (e.g., possession of contraband), by informers, or by confession. Confession quite generally happens only when the offender is arrested on some other charge or illegally arrested "on suspicion," and some informing takes place under the same conditions.

If enough evidence has been collected to connect a particular person with the crime to justify arrest, there is generally enough evidence to justify conviction. Contraband does not change its testimony out of love or pity. The act itself communicates its intention much better than does, say, the act of killing someone.

The establishment of legal and moral responsibility is therefore not so difficult, and most arrests result in convictions.

These are crimes, then, where both arrest and preparation of evidence are generally the job of specialized investigative police. These police must be highly trained in scientific analysis of physical evidence, must have contacts in the underworld for information, and may find a period of questioning arrested people "under pressure" very useful. Although relatively few arrests are made, generally on the basis of carefully collected evidence and therefore on a warrant, a large share of these result in conviction. These are the crimes, and not the murders that figure so heavily in detective stories, which produce the ideal typical pattern of "detective" activity. A latent consequence of this type of crime is the "third degree."

d) Disorder and Nuisance in Public Places. The regulation of public places is the central responsibility of patrol police. We may distinguish three main types of public disorder: individual, collective, and structural. Perhaps the ideal type of individual disorder is "drunk and disorderly." By "collective disorder" I refer primarily to riot, parades that get out of hand, and other types of collective behavior, though in unusual circumstances private military groups may create collective disorder. By "structural disorder" I refer especially to the modern phenomenon of the traffic jam. No crowd or individual "wills" a traffic jam.

1. Individual disorder in public places consists mainly of doing things that would be entirely legitimate if done in private, such as getting too drunk to stand up, or sleeping on park benches. Other individual disorder, such as soliciting for prostitution, or begging, may be illegal even if done in private, but is in fact relatively safe there.

This means first of all that there is a good deal of difference in the "commission" of these "crimes" according to the degree of access people have to private places. Homeless men are obviously more likely to commit the crime of vagrancy, which is the crime of being a homeless man. And if they get drunk, homeless men are more likely to have to sleep it off in the street. Since there is a rough correlation between social class and access to private places (particularly *enough* private places to cover most of one's social life), individual public disorder is related to social class even if the behavior of all classes is the same.

The fact that the "commission" of individual disorder is an index of the lack of connection to small social systems results in a main characteristic of these offenders, that they have not the will, the money, the friends, or the reputation to make good use of their legal right to defend themselves. For will depends on social support of intimates; money for defense often comes from the collective resources (or credit) of a small system; friends are products of intimate interaction; and reputation is generally dependent on a guaranty of good behavior by a small system. Those whose ties to small systems are weak are at a disadvantage in all these ways. Hearings before a police court magistrate in these cases are generally purely formalities; it is assumed by all concerned, including the defendant, that the presumed offender is guilty. The only question that remains to be decided is how much *noblesse oblige* the magistrate should show. As Table 1 shows, the conviction rates for these crimes are quite high, and this is not the result of the sterling qualities of the evidence.

The information on which arrest is based is generally collected entirely by the patrolman, and he has a relatively wide degree of discretion about whether behavior constitutes "disorder." Arrests are almost entirely without a warrant. The fact that police information rather than complaint starts the proceedings means that there are no "crimes known to the police" that have not been solved. The FBI has the good sense not to try to report how many people were drunk or disorderly on the streets of the nation during the year. Investigative police are hardly ever involved.

In summary, the substitution of police for small bounded social systems in the government of the streets produces discretionary power in the hands of the police, particularly over population groups that are unlikely to defend themselves vigorously and effectively in court. The arrest is rarely justified to a judicial officer before it takes place, nor afterward except by the word of the policeman. When convictions do not follow on arrest, it is generally due to *noblesse oblige* rather than to defense by the presumed offender.

2. Collective public disturbances are quite often the immediate stimulus to the formation of quasi-military uniformed police forces. The London Metropolitan Police were partly an answer to the impending Chartist agitation; many state police forces in the United States were originally designed as a more controllable and delicately adjusted mechanism than the National Guard for dealing with industrial disturbances. Since police forces are almost always in a minority in a riot, their military organization is essential in this field.

Collective public disturbances by their nature involve questions of political legitimacy, the channels of political expression, the nature and role of the military, and other very complex topics. These are beyond the scope of this paper. Briefly, however, police are appropriate tools only for temporary control of acting crowds and are rarely competent to defeat an organized military effort by a social movement (unless they have much more military organization than American police do, as the Spanish *Guardia Civil*), and rarely have much to do with the basically political process of channeling the discontent that results in riot. Their competence does extend to expressive crowds that get out of hand, but, as the reams of material on the collective disturbances surrounding the House Un-American Activities Committee hearings in San Francisco in the Spring of 1960 show, the ultimate questions are not police questions.

3. Structural disorder in public places, as opposed to collective disorder, arises from the disorderly effects of individual "innocent" actions. A traffic jam, or a smog problem, is at most attributable to "negligence" of individuals, that is, to *their* not taking account of the structural effects of their actions. More often, the traffic jam could not have been avoided by people as individuals, even if they tried. Traffic control then consists in the regulation of otherwise innocent action that would have unfortunate consequences if not regulated.

Since the "offenses" do not offend the moral sensibilities of the population, being convicted is not much of a defamation. There are few reasons to protest innocence except to avoid the penalty, but the penalty for "minor" infractions cannot be very great. Though generally preserved in fiction, the whole adversary procedure is generally dispensed with, and all the complicated changes of status of due process are done away with. Patrolmen have factual discretionary power to levy penalties for traffic infractions. The police here play the peculiar role of administrators of the anonymous masses, rather than the role of detectors and punishers of crime.

DETERMINATION OF DIVISION OF LABOR
IN POLICE PRACTICE

We may briefly group these socially determined activities into the functional divisions they normally have in police departments:

1. Traffic patrol and other patrol of structural disorder, which enforce regulations not involving moral turpitude of those who break the law. Typically due process of law is irrelevant to the processing of offenders, arrests are uncommon, and when made are made without a warrant. Enforcement does not involve the invasion of private places.

2. Street patrol (including radio cars), especially in downtown areas, to control individual offenses in public places and to be quickly available in cases of coercion within small social systems. The offenses generally involve some degree of moral disapproval, but the friendlessness and lack of resources of the defendants largely eliminates due process of law. Information is obtained primarily by the patrolman's observation, on which both arrest and conviction are based. Arrests are generally without a warrant.

3. Investigative work, generally involving complaint from a small social system, which has to be turned into acceptable evidence of crime. The crimes may be against people within these small systems, in which case arrest is easy (often done by patrolmen) but conviction difficult. Or it may involve the invasion of private places by criminals, in which case arrest is difficult but conviction easy. Most arrests made on warrants and focus on due process derive from this area. But these kinds of offenses create pressures toward the "third degree," toward illegal search and seizure. It is police activity in this area that makes the police force a heroic and newsworthy enterprise, rather than merely a technical device for administering the streets of a city. And much police ideology about "hardened criminals" derives from work in this area. Many of the differences between federal police and local police, generally attributed to the federal agents' greater competence or the greater control by federal courts (e.g., the fact that federal police generally arrest on a warrant), are attributable instead to their work being almost entirely investigative.

4. Undercover work, in which fraud is used to get inside social systems otherwise protected by the institutions of privacy. Subversion and illegitimate business are the main offenses dealt with.

5. Quasi-military action, in which the problem is to apply coercion to control the public riot of some social movement. There quite often are few arrests. Perhaps most of the military trappings of police departments derive from their historical origin in the control of rioting.

CONCLUSIONS

The argument of this paper is that differences in police practice with respect to different types of crimes are closely related to the social location of these types of crime vis-à-vis the institutions of privacy. We would be on more solid ground if direct classifications of crimes of one type (such as murder) were made by social location, rather than depending on the known correlation of murder with private places. Then we could determine whether murders that took place between mutually anonymous people showed a systematically different administrative pattern than murders among kin, eliminating the possibility that other features of murder explain the differences in administration noted. Or people arrested for a crime could be systematically classified by the solidity of their connection to small social structures, to see how much of the variation in the operation of due process of law in criminal matters really derives from differences in the strength of the social ties of the offender.

Second, the indexes of differences between administrative practices for different types of crime used here are extraordinarily crude. While this may convince us that there must have been a strong difference in reality to create a difference in such crude measures, and hence indicate that further research is worthwhile, many of the more interesting hypothesized relations cannot be tested by these data. For instance, the proportion of witnesses changing their testimony or refusing to testify further for different types of crime (either the crude types we have used here, or refined social-location types as suggested above) could be computed, to see whether this indeed explains any of the variation between the conviction rates of murder and burglary. Likewise, the proportion of times the complainant named a suspected offender, the length of time between complaint and arrest, the official status of the officer making an arrest, the proportions of arrests where a warrant was previously obtained, the number of entries into private places by police officers in the course of enforcement, and so on, could be precisely computed.

From knowledge of the characteristic social location of different types of crime, we can make predictions about the structural changes that are likely to take place in a subsection of a police department when a new crime is added to its responsibility. If the crime has a fundamentally different social location than the crimes that have traditionally been the responsibility of the subsection, then we would predict that new specialized roles will be developed in the subsection to deal with the new crime. On the other hand, if the new crime is fundamentally similar in social location to the crimes previously dealt with, responsibility for it will probably be added to the role obligations of old roles. For instance, if the control of the narcotics trade (an illegitimate business) is newly added to a police subsection which has previously dealt with burglary, murder, and other crimes of a different kind, we would predict that narcotics law enforcement will quite quickly become the responsibility of specially designated officers. If a newly serious narcotics problem is made the responsibility of a police subsection that already handles illegitimate businesses, such as a vice squad, we would expect much less pressure toward specialization. Any actual study would have to take account of other forces that help determine the degree of specialization, such as the size of police departments. Both the establishment of such a phenomenon, and an exploration of the dynamics of role differentiation under these circumstances, would increase our knowledge of the causes of the division of labor in organizations.

As for the general problem of studying the causal relations between rare events and frequent events, which is in some ways the foundation of the problem of studying authority, we have less to say. It is commonly alleged in police circles that Supreme Court cases on admissible evidence (e.g., whether evidence will be admitted that is collected in an "unreasonably long" period between arrest and appearance before a magistrate) will have a large effect on the efficiency of police practice. I am less hopeful. It seems that with our present research technology, the connection between such rare events and the frequent events on which we can collect statistics must remain a qualitative step in the research process. The definition of private and public places in the law and its application to the situations in which different types of crime are committed is an example of such a qualitative step in this paper. Presumably there is a long chain of events on a large scale, structuring rewards and constraints in police practice, and structuring criminal behavior of different types with respect to the norms established and continually enforced in a few court cases. This chain of events should, in theory, be amenable to study. But it is often a matter of historical time and of rather subtle readjustments of other rare events (such as promotions of policemen) to the new situation, so that in practice such studies are extremely difficult to carry out. It seems to me that if sociology is to enter in a systematic way into the empirical study of the sociology of law, the technique of combining qualitative judgments of which norms apply to which behavior, with statistical study of that behavior, is going to need substantial development. I hope that the strong relations among variables derived in this qualitative way, found in Table 1, help to provide motivation for more attention to this problem.

NOTES

1. A good summary of the law of arrest is R. M. Perkins, "The Law of Arrest," *Iowa Law Review*, XXV (1940), 201–89.
2. See E. W. Machen, Jr., *The Law of Search and Seizure* (Chapel Hill: University of North Carolina Press, 1950).
3. H. E. Flack (ed.), *The Annotated Code . . . of Maryland, 1951.* Art. 27, Sec. 666.
4. *Instructions . . . and Digest of the Statutes, Ordinances and Decisions* (Baltimore: Baltimore Police Department, 1939), p. 13.
5. A statistical reflection of this could be obtained by computing the proportion of appeals to higher courts of convictions for those types of crime that indicate weak connection to the social structure, such as vagrancy, and comparing this with the rate of appeals for other types of crimes with approximately the same penalties.
6. For instance, in a study in Denmark, 57.0 per cent of murder victims were relatives, 30.8 per cent acquaintances (ranging from "close" to "met the day before"), and only 12.2 per cent strangers (see K. Svalastoga, "Homicide and Social Contact in Denmark," *American Journal of Sociology*, LXII [1956], 37–41).
7. For the situation in London, see Anonymous, *Women of the Streets* (London: British Social Biology Council, Secker and Warburg, 1955), pp. 18–23.
8. Statistics on "crimes known to the police" are not given for these offenses in the *Uniform Crime Reports*, probably for the reasons given above.

METROPOLITAN BOSTON'S SOCIAL STRUCTURE

Charles Tilly

This essay adopts a simple but broad conception of community structure: the durable patterns relating activities and population to the territory and to each other. I deliberately adopted a broad conception because the paper was supposed to serve as a background to research on the whole range of social phenomena relevant to planning in the Boston metropolitan area. That aspiration was hopelessly grand. Yet the paper does, I think, lay out some elementary but useful ways of getting at important features of a community's structure.

The general outline corresponds to the scheme I used to distinguish ecological, normative, interactional, and locational approaches in the introduction to this book. Step by step, it moves around the ecological triangle: activity to population, population to territory, territory back to activity, then around again. The largest part of the discussion treats the territorial distribution of the metropolitan population, especially its segregation by occupation, race, and national origin. Boston turns out to be a highly segregated metropolis. The segregation by occupation is fairly strong, and its internal rank order is quite well defined. Segregation by race and national origin is very strong, although (1) some groups, such as people of Canadian origin, are dispersed through the metropolitan area; (2) the rank order among ethnic and racial groups has less consistency than among occupations—each one simply tends to have its own areas of concentration. (In addition to the remarks I make in this paper, you will find partial explanations of these segregation patterns in Duncan, "Population Distribution and Community Structure"; MacDonald and MacDonald, "Chain Migration"; Alonso, "Historical and Structural Theories of Urban Form"; and Fried, "Functions of the Working-Class Community.") The metropolitan community thus consists of hundreds of distinct social worlds: subcommunities. The subcommunities are only weakly linked to each other, but they influence each other through the big structures: the labor market, the housing market, networks of political power, the mass media, school systems, and so on. This paper helps to identify the broad spatial patterns formed by Boston's subcommunities. However, it only touches on the ways they are connected to each other through conflict, cooperation, and mutual influence.

THE ELEMENTS OF SOCIAL STRUCTURE

One fairly simple way to think of social structure is to consider how a territory, a population and a set of activities fit together. Although a mapmaker can

Slightly edited version of an article which first appeared in Richard Bolan, ed., *Social Structure and Human Problems in the Boston Metropolitan Area* (Cambridge, Mass.: Joint always get himself a fight over the exact placement of a metropolitan boundary, he can almost always identify an unambiguous core along with the debatable periphery; there is the territory. The population is the set of persons who enter the territory; we tend to pay the greatest attention to those who spend the greatest share of their time in it, or who have the strongest attachments to it. The activities are the ways the population spends its time in the territory; we tend to pay the greatest attention to those which endure or recur. Describing a city's social structure may begin with separate sketches of territory, population and activities, but it ends with a picture of their interdependence. How we affect one affects all.

We might diagram that interdependence with a simple triangle.

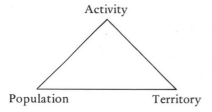

Activity

Population   Territory

Let us call it the *ecological triangle,* in order to keep in mind the analogy with the main elements in the ecological analysis of plant and animal communities. The various disciplines treating the city differ in the parts of the ecological triangle they single out: geographers (and, to a lesser extent, planners) basing themselves in the territorial corner of the triangle, demographers in the population corner, economists in the activity corner, sociologists and political scientists along the side from population to activity. Most of the meaningful statements about urban social structure we are now in a position to make deal with one side of the triangle only—not with a single element, but not with the interaction of all three elements either. For example, we know quite a bit about the location of various kinds of industrial activity within the metropolitan territory, and quite a bit about the division of the population among those kinds of activity, but rather little about the connections between industrial location and the demographic traits of different industries' work forces, and even less about the collective effects of these factors on the general distribution of the population over the metropolitan territory.

Students of cities have a number of standard devices for characterizing the points of the triangle describing any particular metropolis. Perhaps the purest treatments of territory without reference to activity or population are topographic maps or the featureless outlines which grace census tract bulletins. Population comes out in age-sex distributions and classifications of color or national origin.

Center for Urban Studies of the Massachusetts Institute of Technology and Harvard University, 1965), pp. 1–31. Reprinted by permission of the Metropolitan Area Planning Council and the Joint Center for Urban Studies. I am grateful to Joe Feagin, Nancy Howell, Ellen Snyder, and Patricia Turner for research assistance; financial assistance for this study was provided by the Housing and Home Finance Agency.

Activity appears especially in the form of aggregate economic characteristics such as value added by major industries.

The most important descriptive devices, however, deal with the sides of the triangle rather than its points. The land use map (and its special cases, the map of transport lines and the map of industrial or commercial locations) spreads predominant activities through the metropolitan territory; spot maps of crime, illness or voting take a similar tack. Maps of the residential distributions of different types of persons, classifications of personal characteristics by type of residential area, and combinations of the two of them like Social Area Analysis treat the territorial arrangements of the population.[1] There is a wider range of devices for bringing together population and activity: the usual classifications of the metropolis' members by occupation, industry, income, religious or political affiliation, marital status and mobility, the now-flourishing techniques for identifying elites and influentials, the less common sociometric identification of clusters of individuals linked by kinship, friendship or acquaintance, and the still rarer time budget for different categories of city-dwellers.

A complicated version of the earlier diagram brings together these various devices for the description of urban social structure. (See Figure 1.) One can identify or imagine other ways of portraying the interaction of population, territory and activity, but these are the main ones now in use.

Urban sociologists have played all the angles of this triangle, but they have less to say about the relations of activity to territory than about the relations of population to activity and to territory. They have devoted a very large part of their total effort to relatively simple description of one or the other of these relations. In fact, "urban structure," when it appears in the writings of sociologists, commonly means a persistent spatial pattern of population distribution. When seeking to explain a uniformity on a given side of the triangle, sociologists have commonly sought to link it with another uniformity on either the same side or one other side via statements about a point they have in common. For example, many students of urban problems have tried to account for the spatial distribution of juvenile delinquency by linking it to the spatial distribution of poor families via statements about the local effects of poverty, thus going from activity:territory to territory: population via territory. Others, staying on a single side, have accounted for the more active formal participation of higher-ranking residents of cities by pointing to differences in the social skills various occupations demand of or impart to their holders, thus connecting two observations concerning activity:population via statements about the intersection of activities.

In short, sociologists have kept their sensitivity to the interactions in the ecological triangle, and have been properly skeptical of one-factor explanations. They have not been very successful, on the other hand, at taking all three elements into account at once. As a result one can count on the students of urban social structure for good descriptions of internal variation, one can count on them for advice on what variables to take into consideration when dealing with a particular urban phenomenon, one can count on them for an abundant supply of two-variable uniformities which may allow a limited sort of prediction or intervention, but one cannot count on them for anything as complicated as, say, predicting the effects of a heavy expenditure for metropolitan mass transit on the occupational composition of the central city's population.

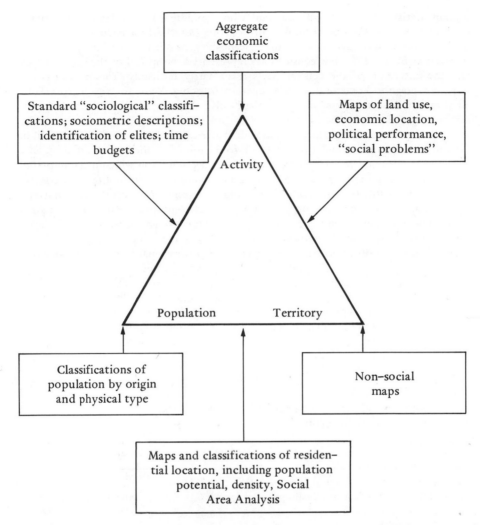

Figure 1. Devices for Describing Urban Social Structure

THE ELEMENTS OF METROPOLITAN BOSTON

This discussion will deal with less complicated things. After a quick identification of the points of the triangle which sums up metropolitan Boston's social structure, I shall turn to comments on major features of its three sides. While some of metropolitan Boston's unmistakable uniqueness will surely creep in, I shall not make an extraordinary effort to distinguish local peculiarities from urban commonplaces. The important thing is to search out traits of the city's social structure which force serious decisions on those who hope to shape the future.

For a *territory*, we may settle on Boston's Census-defined Standard Metropolitan Statistical Area, a half-doughnut whose middle is Boston Harbor. We might quibble over the Census' trimming off of the Lowell, Lawrence and Brockton SMSA's, but would have to agree that the pushing out of the official metropolitan boundaries over the last few censuses has represented the spread of the built-up area and the extension of the central city's reach fairly faithfully. This Boston is the northern neighborhood of the rich supercity running down to Washington, D.C. The smaller Boston recognized by politics holds a declining share of the metropolis' territory, people, and riches.

Even among the prosperous cities of America's Atlantic coast, metropolitan Boston has a favored population. In 1960, for example, its median reported income of 6,687 dollars and the 53.4 percent of its adult population which had completed high school placed it near the top of the list of American metropolitan areas. Here, however, the distinction between metropolitan Boston and the central city matters. An extraordinarily small proportion—about a quarter—of metropolitan Boston's 2.5 to 3 million people live in the central city. As is true elsewhere, the more privileged tend to live outside, in the metropolitan ring. Table 1, a simple comparison of the proportion for 1960 of all employed persons in professional and technical occupations, makes the contrast clear, and also displays the Boston area's exceptional concentration of these specialized workers. Although Boston's ring has a substantially higher share of professional and technical workers than the central city, both of them stand high compared with other metropolitan areas. Education gives a similar picture, with the 11.2 percent of metropolitan Boston's adults who were college graduates rising above the metropolitan United States' 8.8 percent, New England's 8.9, and New York's 9.5.

TABLE 1
Percentage Employed in Professional and Technical Work,
U.S. Metropolitan Areas, 1960.

	Total SMSA	Central Cities	Rings
All SMSAs of the continental U.S.	12.3%	11.4%	13.3%
All SMSAs from Boston to Washington	12.7	10.7	14.9
New England SMSAs	12.5	10.5	14.2
New York SMSA	12.4	11.1	16.2
Boston SMSA	14.6	11.6	15.8

The population stands out in other ways. As American metropolitan areas go, Boston has a relatively high proportion of people over 65, a low proportion of Negroes, many individuals born outside the United States, but a less mobile population than the average.

The population is not immobile, however. Many of Boston's newcomers, of course, come from elsewhere in Massachusetts and adjoining states. Between 1955 and 1960, the state of New York made by far the largest outside contribution to metropolitan Boston's population. More generally, migration to metropolitan Boston is coming from two sets of states: the coastal band from Maine to Florida (including sizable contingents from Maryland, Virginia, and Florida) and populous, urban states all over the country (including many from Ohio, Michigan, Illinois and California). Boston, once a great port of entry for overseas migrants of the diversest origins, now draws mainly on areas with which it has a great deal in common.

The word "migration" often conjures up a picture of poor people arriving in the central city. In fact, migration affects all parts of the metropolis. The people migrating from outside into any particular section of the metropolitan area generally have quite a bit in common with those already there. On the average, the migrants are better educated and more highly skilled than the receiving population. And long-distance migrants actually come to such outlying areas as Acton, Bedford, Stoughton or Topsfield more often than to the central city. Suburbanites know the sight of the cross-country moving van very well. A great deal of the so-called flight to the suburbs is much less a movement of families from central Boston to the edge of the metropolitan area than shuffling of families *among* metropolitan areas.

Yet some flight has occurred within metropolitan Boston; it has left the central sections of the metropolitan area to receive the migrants with the smallest resources and the greatest disadvantages. Most of them, even today, are whites. But the most evident group of migrants to that central area are Negroes.

Migration from states to the south is expanding Boston's Negro population; from 1950 to 1960 the metropolitan area's total went from about 50,000 to about 75,000 Negroes. The central city absorbed more than nine-tenths of that increase, at the same time as it was losing some 130,000 whites. The same pattern of Negro increase and white decrease in the central city—amounting to substantial rises in the proportion of the central city population Negro, but only slight increases in the proportion for the metropolitan area as a whole—has surely continued since 1960. At that time, Negro migrants were coming mainly from the coastal band we have already noticed, especially New York. Virginia, North Carolina, South Carolina and Georgia. But Boston is receiving a very small share of the migrants now moving up the coast; Negroes form less than five percent of the metropolitan population. Only their extreme segregation in one part of the central city makes them the most conspicuous minority.

As for *activity*, what there is to say is already familiar to Bostonians; the manipulation of symbols is the city's particular specialty. The 65,000 workers in education are an exceptionally large stock for an American metropolis of any size. Schools and colleges stand everywhere one turns. Institutions even more devoted than schools to the preservation of the past, like museums, abound in the Boston area. But so do institutions devoted to the forming of the future, like the famous belt of science-based firms along Route 128. Add hospitals and other direct consumers of advanced teaching and research. The unmistakable conclusion is that Boston's work is brainwork.

Activity and Population. So far we have leaped from point to point on our ecological triangle without passing along the sides. We have seen an expanding territory, a prosperous population, a good deal of intellectual activity. But how do they fit together?

One obvious but important thing is the uneven distribution of major categories of the population among the principal activities. The division of occupation and industry by sex, for instance. Almost exactly a third of the metropolitan area's million workers are women. But over nine-tenths of the domestic workers are women, two-thirds of the clerical workers are, two-fifths of the service workers are, and only an eighth of the managers and proprietors, one-thirtieth of the unskilled laborers, one-thirtieth of the craftsmen and foremen. Likewise, women are everywhere in retail trade, finance and insurance, education, personal services and (especially) hospitals, virtually absent from construction and mining.

Clearly women are distributed among the occupations very unequally. The same is true of the distribution by race. In 1960, nonwhites (a census category which in metropolitan Boston contains very few people who are not Negroes) comprised the following percentages of the major occupational categories among males:

professional and technical	1.7%
managers and proprietors	0.8
farmers and farm managers	3.0
sales workers	0.6
clerical workers	2.3
craftsmen and foremen	1.8
operatives	4.4
private household workers	24.9
service workers	7.1
laborers	5.0
farm labor	2.0

If we use the proportion of all male workers who are Negroes—about three percent—as a standard of even distribution, then we find both the notorious under-representation of Negroes in occupations giving higher rewards, and some further inconsistencies. Practically no Negroes in Boston are sales workers, managers or proprietors of their own businesses. They are better represented, in fact, in the professions. The largest concentrations of Negroes are not among unskilled laborers, but among private household workers and other service occupations. The occupational system does not seem to block Negroes from jobs where they are in contact with whites, so much as to keep them from positions as equals or bosses. Nor have Negroes been able to take the path of small business and private entrepreneurship, by which many European migrants of a half-century ago made their way.

This concentration of Negroes in service activities shows up in the industrial classification as well, in great contrast to the virtual absence of Negroes from finance, insurance, real estate or construction. It raises some puzzling questions. How do these proportions compare with those for ethnic groups such as Italians or Jews? What kind of discrimination, and how much of it? What keeps Negroes from entrepreneurship? What part does inferior education play? What about the simple fact that the service industries were the ones expanding most rapidly during the time when the most Negroes were migrating to Boston? The answers make a tremendous difference to our choice of means to equalize opportunity. Unfortunately, we have no more than glimmers of answers.

Some related puzzles come even closer to the hearts of planners. Considering that service activities (as compared, say, with manufacturing) spread rather widely across the metropolis, and that Negroes live in a very few sections of metropolitan Boston but work in service, do these facts put an exceptional strain on transportation facilities, and on them? John Kain (1964) has suggested that residential segregation itself cuts down the range of jobs available to Negroes. Is that happening here? We do not really know, but we certainly ought to find out.

Population and Territory. Of the many ways of spreading the population across the territory, let us concentrate on where people live.[2] Boston, with over 2,500 persons per square mile, has one of the most densely packed populations of any American metropolitan area. The outsider can sense some of that density by touring the residential sections of Somerville and Cambridge, or fighting his way down midtown Washington Street on a shopping tour. Yet if he does any more touring, he will also notice enormous variations: 23,000 persons per square mile in Somerville, well over 10,000 in such places as Cambridge, Chelsea or Malden, around 1,000 in Cohasset or Scituate, closer to 100 in areas like Dover or Lincoln. The high average density gives Boston some of its liveliness. The variation adds to its pleasurable diversity. The high density poses problems, but may also offer great advantages to mass transportation, preservation of open space or provision of public facilities. So far the ungainly sprawl of other American metropolitan areas has not overcome the Boston area. But with plenty of cars, highways and demands for space it is easier to spread than to contain. Metropolitan Boston's planners should consider the control of density their special opportunity and challenge.

The high average density does not mean crowding within dwellings; the metropolitan average of about 0.6 persons per room is rather low. Again we find large variations: from a section of Cambridge where hardly a house has more persons than rooms, to a section of South Boston where a quarter of the dwellings do. And the variations in density or crowding lead us to variations in the social characteristics of the local population.

Frank Sweetser's handy maps of social characteristics in the Boston area for 1950 and 1960 provide a good starting point for any survey of local variations in population. They show, for example, the larger proportions of young children at the edge of the metropolitan area and the concentrations of older people near the core. They show the rarity of the foreign born at the edge and the concentration of families of Italian stock near the core. They display the particularly high fertility of the western and northwestern suburbs and the larger proportions of working women in the city of Boston and its immediate vicinity. And one of the most interesting maps shows the general rise in "social rank" (combining the education and occupations of the population) as one goes out in almost any direction from central Boston, with the greatest mass of high-ranking people due west from the center. Most Bostonians know some of these things in a fragmentary way; that is how they use addresses to place other people socially. Few people are aware of the whole pattern, or able to articulate it as such maps of the population do.

Maps do not do such a good job of showing how groups of characteristics of the population vary together. There are other, less graphic, ways of handling that interesting problem. We may take another look at social rank, for example, by asking not just which sections of metropolitan Boston have many high-ranking people, but which occupational groups tend to live together. Table 2 answers this question by presenting rank-order correlation coefficients for each pair of major occupational categories—theoretically varying from −1.0 to +1.0—and measuring the extent to which the percentages of the two occupational groups tend to rise and fall together from one census tract to another. The correlation of +.58 tells us that the proportions of managers and proprietors, on the one hand, and the proportions

TABLE 2
Rank-Order Correlation Coefficients (TAU) for Percentages
of Employed Males in Major Occupational Categories,
over All Census Tracts in the Boston SMSA, 1960

	Professional and Technical Workers	Managers, Proprietors, etc.	Sales Workers	Clerical, etc.	Craftsmen, Foremen, etc.	Operatives, etc.	Service Workers	Nonfarm Laborers
Professional and technical workers	—							
Managers, proprietors, etc.	+.58	—						
Sales workers	+.48	+.59	—					
Clerical, etc.	-.14	-.15	-.09	—				
Craftsmen, foremen, etc.	-.15	-.07	-.03	+.15	—			
Operatives, etc.	-.60	-.50	-.41	+.18	+.18	—		
Service workers	-.30	-.40	-.37	+.22	-.05	+.22	—	
Nonfarm laborers	-.48	-.46	-.43	+.09	+.13	+.48	+.31	—
Private household workers	+.19	+.16	+.11	-.15	-.20	-.20	-.10	-.11
Median income, 1959	6741	7420	5345	4598	5378	4501	3864	3543

TABLE 3

Rank-Order Correlation Coefficients (TAU) for Percentages of Total Population in Major Ethnic and Racial Categories, over All Census Tracts in the Boston SMSA, 1960

	Swedish	British	Canadian	Irish	Polish	Italian	Russian	"Other Races"	Negro
British	+.37	—							
Canadian	+.25	+.22	—						
Irish	+.02	+.07	+.15	—					
Polish	-.11	-.03	-.08	+.03	—				
Italian	+.01	-.13	+.06	+.05	-.12	—			
Russian	.00	+.11	-.04	-.04	+.37	-.10	—		
"Other Races"	-.07	-.04	-.05	-.05	+.01	-.23	+.12	—	
Negro	-.12	-.14	-.08	-.10	+.03	-.16	+.08	+.39	—
Native Stock	+.29	+.27	+.07	-.09	-.12	-.13	-.16	-.18	-.23
Foreign Born	-.24	-.17	-.01	+.15	+.17	+.17	+.19	+.12	+.07
Median Education	+.38	+.36	.00	-.08	-.03	-.20	+.13	-.06	-.17
Median Income	+.35	+.25	+.09	-.04	-.05	+.05	+.01	-.34	-.33

Note: Both the headings across the top (the columns) and those down the side (the rows) refer to characteristics of all Census tracts in the SMSA: either the percentage of the total population in the category named or, in the last two cases, the median for the tract. To find the relationship of any pair of characteristics, locate the column for one and the row for the other, then look at their junction in the table. The proportions of persons of British and of Swedish stock, for example, show a moderately strong (+.37) tendency to vary together, those of Polish and Swedish stock a slight (−.11) tendency to vary in opposite directions, the proportions of Swedish and Russian stock no relation at all (.00) to each other. The bottom two rows can be read a little differently: persons of Swedish stock are a little more concentrated (+.35) than are persons of British stock (+.25) in tracts with higher levels of income. Or: there is a weak (−.20) tendency for level of education to decline as the proportion of persons of Italian stock rises. The table gives no direct information on the characteristics of the categories of the population themselves.

of professionals, on the other, fluctuate together; the −.50 indicates that where there are many operatives there are few managers and proprietors, and vice versa.

I have placed the occupational categories in the order a well-known scheme for assessing occupational prestige gives them. The table expresses a definite rank order. Occupations similar in prestige have high positive correlations; dissimilar occupations, high negative correlations. The private household (that is, domestic) workers, service workers and the clerical workers keep the order from being neat, surely because the domestic workers often live in, perhaps because many service workers are Negroes and because clerical workers have relatively low incomes. Ability to pay does not account for the general pattern, although it has something to do with it. Metropolitan Boston has sorted out its population into a distinct rank order, in which occupation plays an important part.

We can ask the same kind of question about race and national background. All Bostonians know that the North End has many Italians, Charlestown many Irishmen, Roxbury many Negroes. Do we find something like the occupational rank order when we look at the distribution of these groups over the metropolitan area? Do we find an order that corresponds to the sequence in which the largest numbers of these various groups arrived in Boston (cf., Lieberson 1963)? Table 3 indicates a mixed reply: a rough rank order of education, income, and residential similarity to the native stock[3] which follows the sequence of migration to some extent, but not nearly the clear internal rank order which appears among the occupational groups. The table takes pairs of the largest categories of race and national background and summarizes their tendency to covary over all tracts of the Boston area. (The position of a group in the table follows the closeness of its relationship to the native stock.) The correlations average much lower than those for occupation. Swedes and Britons seem to gather to some extent; so do Poles and Russians, Negroes and members of other nonwhite races. Otherwise, there are no strong pairs. Nor is the internal ranking consistent.

Such findings could mean that race and national origin do not matter much in the over-all sorting of Bostonians into residential areas, or that each racial or ethnic group has its own residential pattern, more or less independent of the others. Which is it?

To get a clearer idea on that question, we must turn to another method. Imagine taking all tracts of the Boston area and ranking them in terms of the share that group X has in their populations (cf. Beshers, Laumann and Bradshaw 1964). At one end of the rank order for Polish stock, for example, we would find the 14 tracts where 19 percent of the population is Polish. If group X is spread evenly, there will be little progression: few tracts with very low percentages, few tracts with very high percentages. We can graph that pattern like this.

SPREAD

Average percent for all tracts

Lowest   Highest

If group X congregates in some areas, but as a whole is not isolated from the rest of the population, there will still be few tracts with very low percentages of group X, but there will now be some with very high percentages. We can graph that *congregated* pattern like this.

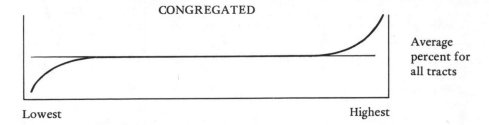

CONGREGATED

Average percent for all tracts

Lowest   Highest

Finally, if the group is genuinely isolated from the rest of the population, there will be many tracts with tiny proportions of group X, and a few with very high proportions. That *segregated* pattern looks like this.

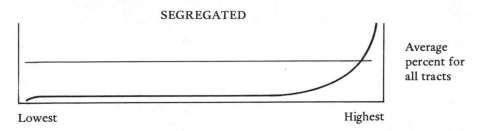

SEGREGATED

Average percent for all tracts

Lowest   Highest

Figure 2 gives the actual curves for the major ethnic and racial groups of the Boston area in 1960 (the coordinates of the graph make all the curves less like the segregated pattern than they actually are, in order to make them easier to read). The answer to our earlier question seems to be that ethnicity and race do matter. Some of the categories simply congregate, but some are highly segregated.

The British are at one extreme; their curve looks very much like the ideal "congregation" curve I have sketched. The Irish, despite local mythology, are not much more concentrated. Negroes, on the other hand, are highly segregated. More than a third of metropolitan Boston's tracts have no Negroes at all, four-fifths of the tracts have fewer than two Negroes out of every hundred persons, and yet there are six tracts with over 80 percent of their populations Negro, one of them reaching 95 percent. That is segregation. People of Italian and Russian stock are segregated to quite a degree, but not like Negroes. And the numerous Canadians—the area's largest "ethnic group"—are spread fairly evenly through the metropolitan area, except for a few tracts with Canadian concentrations, very likely French Canadian sections.

Metropolitan Boston's ethnic geography has obviously changed a great deal over the last half-century. The descendants of Irish immigrants have moved out to all sections of the metropolis. Occasional clusters of families of Greek, Lithuanian or Armenian origin hold only small minorities of the total populations in these

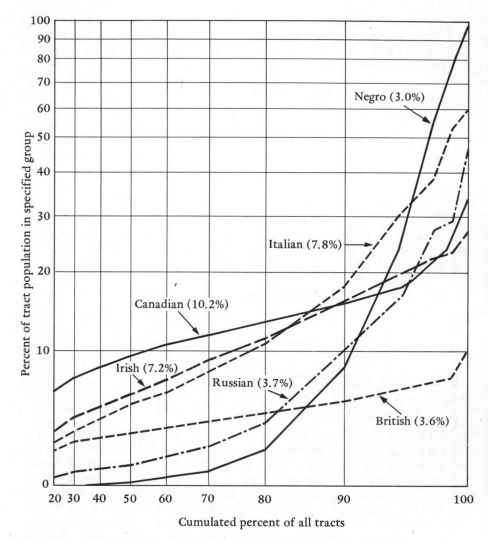

Note: The proportion of any group relative to the entire SMSA is given in the parentheses.

Figure 2. Segregation Curves for the Largest Categories of Race and Foreign Stock in the Boston SMSA, 1960

categories. Some neighborhoods have changed ethnic character two or three times, and many have lost all ethnic identity. The melting pot has done at least some melting in metropolitan Boston. If anything, the metropolis seems to have substituted segregation by class for segregation by national background.

Or has it? For the majority who are more than a generation away from other national origins, ethnic ties to a particular neighborhood may not matter so much.

The sorting process does bring together neighbors who are similar in occupation, education and income. Yet ethnic divisions survive. Immigrants and their children still cluster. The segregation curves set off metropolitan Boston's Poles, Italians and Russians from the rest of the population. For members of these groups, congregation, or even segregation, by national background may be more significant than division by social class.[4]

The graphs for occupational groups strengthen that impression. (See Figures 3 and 4.) All the occupational curves resemble the "congregation" model more than the "segregation" model. The small category Private Household Workers is the greatest exception; aside from it, service workers, laborers and professionals have the more remarkable concentrations at the curve's high end. But none of these look

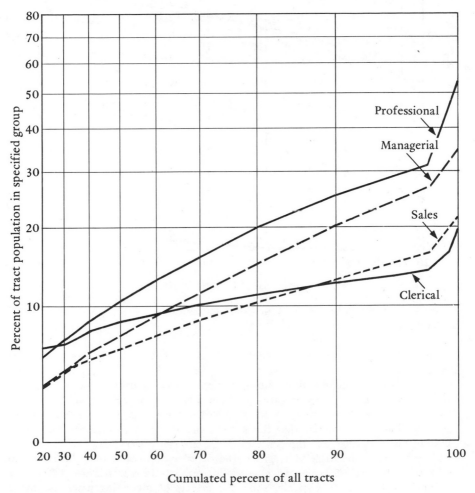

Figure 3. Segregation Curves for White Collar Categories in the Boston SMSA, 1960

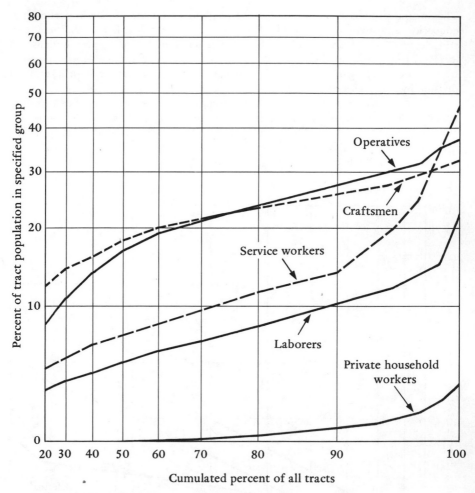

Figure 4. Segregation Curves for Blue Collar Categories
in the Boston SMSA, 1960

like the steeply rising curves for Negroes, persons of Russian stock or persons of
Italian stock.

One last look at this kind of information will add another important conclusion. Figure 5 presents the segregation curves for Negroes in the Boston SMSA from
1940 to 1960.[5] It shows unmistakably that Negroes were highly segregated over the
entire period. It also shows that the pattern changed somewhat as more Negroes
came and more whites left the central city. From 1940 to 1950 we see a definite
increase in the segregation of Negroes—the decisive formation of a ghetto. From
1950 to 1960 we find instead a consolidation of the ghetto; the differences
between the two curves basically show the effects of increasing numbers, rather
than any important shift in the spatial pattern. Today, Boston is a very segregated
metropolis.

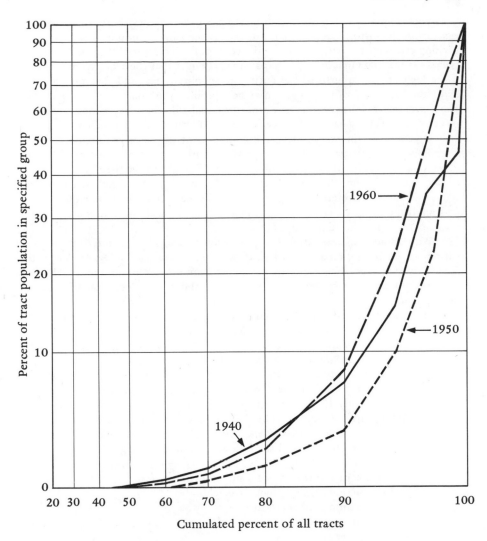

Figure 5. Segregation Curves for Negroes
in the Boston SMSA, 1940–1960

   This segregation shows up vividly on the map of census tracts as well as on
their curves. While Negroes moved into parts of Dorchester and Jamaica Plain
between 1950 and 1960, and a few Negroes found homes in far-off suburbs
(especially in the northwestern sector of the metropolitan area), what happened
mainly was consolidation in the old ghetto. Since 1950, various public actions have
displaced many Negroes, but have not shaken segregation. While the whites displaced from the old West End, for example, scattered all over the metropolitan
area, the Negroes displaced from the South End moved practically *en bloc* to
Roxbury and North Dorchester.

Such a movement is doubly interesting. First, it shows the tenacity of racial segregation in Boston. Second, it illustrates the continuing importance of a sector reaching out west to southwest from the center of the city—with Washington Street its axis—as the main line of Negro expansion. The fact that the sector contains some of the highest-rent suburbs in the entire metropolitan area, and that the axis soon leaves the city of Boston, suggest that new problems are on their way. Suburban school systems, suburban housing authorities, and suburban city officials will have to face decisions they have so far been content to leave to the central city.

Of course, I am exaggerating the containment of the Negro population (and of problems of segregation and integration) within the central city. Within the sector I have been discussing, Newton and Brookline both have their concentrations of Negroes, and some looming problems of race relations. Besides, Cambridge, Lynn, Malden and Everett, among other suburbs, have contained miniature ghettos for some time. In any case, the Negro neighborhoods near the center are products of the metropolitan housing market as a whole.

Why? Some answers come easily: discrimination, low income, lack of information, self-selection, reliance on friends in seeking housing, and so on. Yet listing likely factors is one thing, and weighing their importance quite another. Beyond what everybody knows, we know very little about the operation of Boston's housing market.

We could learn a certain amount from scattered data already collected for other purposes. For example, the first 90 interviews in a study of Roxbury families now underway yield some interesting information about housing. Of this group of 90 families (by no means a cross-section of the Boston population, or even of Roxbury's), only 34 had been in their homes two years or more, and 30 had been in less than three months; the median family had made about three moves in the previous six years. Only 12 definitely expected to be in the same dwelling five years later, and 58 definitely expected to be elsewhere. This is a population on the move.

When the interviewers asked these people how they had found their present dwellings, their first replies formed the following pattern:

Just heard about it, saw a sign, accidental, etc.	21
Information from a friend or neighbor	16
Information from a relative	12
Real estate agent	24
Newspaper ad	6
Other	11

Only a third of these families found the dwelling through a newspaper or a real estate agent, the two most likely sources of information about housing outside their immediate neighborhood. The largest number depended on chance and personal contacts. Any segment of the population which takes this sort of approach to the housing market is likely to remain concentrated near its starting point. We obviously need to know much more about how different parts of metropolitan Boston's population now find their housing, in order to intervene intelligently in the market, or to anticipate the effects of new planning measures. In addition, we need better information on the present role of the real estate and mortgage finance industries in forming Boston's residential patterns.

We also need increased knowledge of present and future shifts in those patterns. Another fragment from the interviews just examined illustrates a type of information which would be useful on a larger scale. The interviewers asked the families what kinds of housing and which locations in the Boston area they would prefer if they could freely choose. Fifty-four of the 90 said they would like to have a single family house in the suburbs (some of the same people, however, also said they would like a new apartment in Roxbury). Of a larger list which the respondents ranked, the favorite suburbs turned out to be, in order, Brookline, Cambridge, Jamaica Plain and Newton. But Jamaica Plain also got the most negative votes; it divided the people more than the other locations did. It looks as though these Roxbury residents, when they think of the suburbs, are mainly interested in the communities which are close at hand.[6]

We have already noticed, of course, that the segregation of Negroes is simply the most acute form of a more general phenomenon. Even though its history is longer, we actually have less information about the segregation of families of Italian and Russian stock. In both cases, the segregation curves look more like the curve for Negroes than, say, the curve for the British. In both cases, a religious element— Italians being largely Catholic, Russians being predominantly Jewish—enters in. In both cases, finally, the classification is not so certain to correspond with the way the person identifies himself or the way others identify him as does the classification "Negro," since the grandparents' place of birth determines it; some families retain identification with the ethnic group longer than two generations, while others lose it in one.

The metropolitan map shows a clustered movement of the two ethnic groups away from the center of Boston, in different directions. The largest group of Italian families have moved from an immigrant base in the North End toward the northern suburbs. In fact, a number of northern suburbs have felt the political influence of Italian voters, after long Irish supremacy, during the last couple of decades. The *en bloc* displacement of Italians is not nearly so marked as in the case of Negroes (I have already mentioned the scattering of the West End's predominantly Italian population), but it is still considerable.

In the city of Boston and in the metropolitan area as a whole, people of Russian stock make up about a tenth of all the foreign stock, and from four to five percent of the total population. But the proportion varies sharply: from the fifteen tracts with no one of Russian origin to a few tracts in Newton and Brookline where a quarter or a third of the entire population is of Russian origin, to sections of South Dorchester where close to half the population falls into that category. The greatest concentrations of Russian stock are in the same west-to-southwest sector leading away from the center of the city that contains the main movement of Negroes. In fact, more than one neighborhood in that sector has seen a succession of populations from Yankee to Irish to Russian to Negro. One of the most interesting questions about metropolitan Boston is how regular such sequences have been in the recent past, and how likely they are in the near future.

It is hard to be sure how much of a religious identity the label "Russian" covers. Remember the fairly strong tendency for the proportions of Russian and Polish stock to vary together throughout metropolitan Boston. The residential affinity of the two groups for each other showed up in Boston as far back as 1880 (Lieberson 1963: 79). It could be mainly a covariation of Jewish population, with national origins rather unimportant. But common origin in Slavic countries, or similarity of the original timing and conditions of migration from these countries, might also have set the two categories in parallel channels. Mapping the locations of synagogues and kosher markets over the last fifty years would help in gauging the specifically religious element in this residential clustering. So far we know little about it. Considering Boston's great role in the European migration, the splendid books (like those of Oscar Handlin) which have treated the first years of the migrants in Boston, and the other remarkable works (like those of William Foote Whyte and Herbert Gans) which have described particular ethnic neighborhoods in Boston, scholars have devoted surprisingly little attention to the persistence, displacement or decline of the metropolitan area's ethnic neighborhoods.

We know such neighborhoods have not died completely. Members of a Lithuanian parish played an important part in resistance to Cambridge's plans for urban renewal a few years ago. Many observers feel that the concentration of families of Irish background in Charlestown makes a great difference in that area's response to any plans for renewal. Herbert Gans' remarkable study of the West End before renewal—appropriately called *The Urban Villagers*—portrays a vigorous local life based especially on common Italian origin. Gans warns that a neighborhood which looks from outside like a lifeless slum sometimes has great internal vitality. He insists that the inability of local residents to take a public, collective position tells us little about their local attachments; some neighborhoods, like some peasant villages, turn all their energies inward, rather than outward. Marc Fried's West End respondent, Mrs. Figella, called the area "a wonderful place, the people are friendly." After relocation, her main complaint with her new place was that "It's in Arlington and I want to be in the West End" (Fried 1963: 161-2).

I certainly do not want to suggest that one should simply leave all ethnic and racial neighborhoods as they are. The average West Ender, for example, moved into better housing than he had before (at the expense of a considerable increase in rent: Hartman, 1964). Some of the people in the area were glad to get out. Inferior ethnic status and inferior housing or public facilities often go together. Remember that four-fifths of the metropolitan area's dwellers in sub-standard housing are white; many of them live in ethnic neighborhoods. The point is that we know far too little about the distribution or organization of ethnic groups in the Boston metropolitan area to anticipate the effects on them of attempts to reshape the metropolis. Just as we have forgotten to investigate possible motives for self-segregation on the part of the Negro community, we have neglected research on the nature of today's ethnic groups in metropolitan Boston.

That neglect could cause planners trouble. The metropolitan area's patterns of ethnic, racial and occupational segregation may reinforce each other more than anyone realizes. If they do, their interaction may thwart planners' attempts at residential rearrangement. Here are three questions to keep in mind:

1. How regular is the succession of occupational, ethnic and racial groups in metropolitan Boston's neighborhoods, what determines it, and what does it indicate for the next areas of settlement of Boston's most segregated groups?

2. How much of the residential pattern of the racial and ethnic groups really shows the incidental effects of their differences in occupation or income, rather

than the direct effects of exclusion or self-selection on the basis of race or ethnic background?

3. How regularly does the self-selection of one group fortify the segregation of other, less privileged, groups?

We have already glanced at the first question. The answer to the second makes a difference in the effectiveness of such measures as income redistribution in reshaping the pattern of residence in the metropolis. We have some chunks of that answer (for example, further analyses of the tract data already presented indicate that variations in education and income account for a good part of the occupational pattern of residence, but only a much smaller part of the ethnic and racial pattern). But planners and urban researchers will have to put more of the chunks into place before being able to anticipate with any confidence the results of different kinds of intervention in the housing market on the ethnic and racial pattern.

The third question has not gotten enough attention. In their varicolored essay on New York, *Beyond the Melting Pot,* Nathan Glazer and Daniel Patrick Moynihan often find themselves torn between admiring an ethnic group for the way its self-help moved it ahead, and recognizing that the banding together that self-help involves sometimes means the exclusion of less fortunate outsiders. Sometimes this happens in housing. What shall we do if the dwellings best suited to the needs of the ill-housed are in areas dominated by other ethnic and racial groups? If we adopt a policy of preserving the ethnic "urban villages" Herbert Gans has described, do we in effect exclude Negroes, Puerto Ricans and other recent arrivals in the city from spaces they need? A metropolitan planning agency could profitably commission a good deal of research on these issues.

We have seen that ethnic and racial barriers still matter much in metropolitan Boston's dwelling areas. Maybe the aging of metropolitan Boston's foreign-born population forecasts the rapid depletion of ethnic areas in the central city; yet ethnic and racial divisions seem to be persisting well beyond the immigrant generation. How much do they depend on each other? These problems deserve the concern of those who wish to shape the city's future.

In the present state of our knowledge, we cannot accurately predict the effects of a change, say in the incomes of Negroes, or even state how one could most effectively change the pattern. So far programs like those of the Massachusetts Commission Against Discrimination or Fair Housing, Incorporated have not made much difference, relocation officers of the Boston Redevelopment Authority have certainly gotten no more than a draw in their battle with segregation, and even Boston's public housing is decisively segregated. Planners need both to recognize the extent and nature of residential segregation in the Boston area, and to start much deeper inquiries into the way it operates.

Directions for Research on Territory and Population. One way to grip these problems more firmly is to assemble better data on local movements in population and local shifts in land use. Except in the central city, metropolitan Boston's planners and researchers have virtually ignored a resource which could give them an edge over their colleagues in other metropolitan areas: the annual police census. That annual listing of the adult population of every town by name, address, age, place of birth, previous residence, occupation, and so on, constitutes an incomparable account of population characteristics and movements within the metropolis. There it is, year by year, street by street, person by person. Some people doubt the completeness and accuracy of the enumeration. Even if the rate of error were as high as five percent, however, the listing could provide a valuable continuous account of residential mobility for the metropolitan area. Furthermore, a check of completeness and accuracy would probably produce ideas on how to make the census better. The police lists (or, better, the cards from which they are printed) form the logical point of departure for a metropolitan data bank. One can easily imagine, for example, bringing together the data they contain with building permits and assessment records. With the techniques for computer mapping and assembly of data banks now being developed at Boston's universities, these sources would increase incredibly both the amount of current information on the state of the metropolitan area available to the planner, and the rapidity with which he could put it in usable form.

I recognize that data alone do not solve all the planner's problems. Good data do not in themselves provide an understanding of how the city works, knowledge of which parts of the process are open to intervention, a vision of what should be, or the power to bring the vision into being. Yet the data we have reviewed raise some acute issues for the planners of metropolitan Boston.

The first: how should planners deal with residential segregation and sorting of the population? Every plan somehow affects the pattern of segregation by class, race or national background, if only by fortifying the status quo. The recently announced General Plan for Boston—while announcing a policy of making the central city's population more like that of the whole metropolitan area—seems on the whole to accept the existing neighborhood divisions within the city. And individual renewal plans commonly take as an objective the local rehousing of the population already on the site. What difference does that make? How deliberately should metropolitan planners seek to obliterate ghettos and disperse their members? Should they approach "urban villages" in the same way? Should they accept some kinds of sorting of the population (e.g. by occupation, age, or income) but not others? Hard questions, and crucial ones. Planners cannot shrug them off.

The second: how much should planners intervene in the general operation of the housing market? For example, to the extent that the real estate industry, by guiding different parts of the population to different parts of the city, influences the location of the poor, or the aged, or the recently arrived, should planners seek to regulate that industry? What if a general plan for renewal rests on the assumption of a housing market free from discrimination? Is antidiscriminatory legislation the planner's business? What about housing those who are too poor to make their way in the existing market? Consider this declaration:

> Lack of housing accommodations for workers at a reasonable rental is still a serious problem; and while theoretically it would be an ideal situation to have the city erect homes to be sold at cost to the people, as a practical proposition it is neither feasible nor good business. Through experience with such properties as the city owns and which come largely into possession as a consequence of taking for school and other municipal purposes, it has been found that as a collector of rents the city is an absolute failure. Consequently, it is necessary to seek some other method of solving a most distressing and

difficult problem. . . . Self-reliance, which is but another name for optimism, was the cornerstone of the greatness and prosperity of early New England.

The tone is familiar, and the problem evidently enduring—for the year is 1924, the writer Boston's Mayor James Michael Curley. The difference is that nowadays, the housing of the poor is a problem not just for Boston's mayor, but for the entire metropolis.

Activity and Territory. The distribution of Boston's population across its territory both affects and reflects the distribution of its activities. There is so much to say about it that I shall say almost nothing. And the first observation is obvious: to the extent that activities are based on homes, residential segregation creates segregation in those activities. That is the nub of *de facto* segregation. Where a family lives affects which parks it uses, which library its members borrow from, which school its children attend. The planner faces all the elements of *de facto* segregation: in laying out residential locations, in locating centers of activity, and in proposing means of transit between them. These are not simply matters of convenience; they are grave problems of public policy.

If the planner is dealing with such grave matters, he should consider how to consult those whom his plans affect. "Planning with people" is already a cliché, but a cliché risky to ignore. In Boston—Charlestown, Mission Hill, Roxbury, the South End, and elsewhere—some groups are trying to organize the inarticulate and dispossessed at the scale of the building, the block or the neighborhood. There are signs of the same sort of move in such suburbs as Cambridge. More than anything else, such local organizations will concern themselves with housing, planning and renewal. If local organizations form and flourish, planners will have some interesting political choices to make. For such organizations are likely to make it hard to ignore the political implications of any new plan, and may well choose the announcement of renewal plans as occasions for more general political offensives. That could make it all the more difficult to "plan with people" without getting directly involved in political negotiations with local leaders. Of course, it would not be the first time that the area's neighborhoods were well organized to influence public decisions. A well-organized Lower Roxbury gave Curley his political base, and Lynn, Quincy, Revere, Cambridge and other large towns of metropolitan Boston have all seen plenty of neighborhood-based politics in their time. But now such a circumstance would divide the planner between his professional expertise and his sense of the possible.

The possible depends in part on the scale at which planning is undertaken. It may be useless, for example, to attempt to deal with employment problems at the level of the municipality, because the labor market extends throughout the metropolitan area. It may be hopeless, on the other hand, to undertake renewal plans at the level of the metropolitan area so long as each proposal becomes a local political issue. The number of features of social structure which seem to disregard political boundaries tempts many sociologists, including me, to conclude that it is better to plan for whole metropolitan areas than for the individual municipalities within them. But the best units for analysis are not always the strategic ones for intervention. Any family doctor knows that.

The identification of the appropriate units for intervention ought to fascinate any metropolitan planning agency. The Boston area gave one of the earliest examples of intervention and control at the metropolitan scale: its Metropolitan District Commission. But now—because of the very large part of its population outside the limits of its central city—it faces the common consequences of metropolitan fragmentation in an acute form. The problems of housing and segregation we have reviewed take on added difficulty because they affect the entire metropolis, while housing authorities and other agencies designed to deal with these problems can only act on fragments of the metropolis. Renewal programs often look like hunting hippopotami with popguns, because what there is to renew spreads across the boundaries of any particular municipality. Urban orators often curse the central city's combination of service to the metropolis, heavy welfare responsibilities, diminishing population, and dwindling sources of revenue. Federal urban programs have usually fortified the very municipal boundaries which limit their effectiveness. Setting up authorities to deal with urban problems within each municipality seems to reward non-cooperation, to encourage parochial planning, and reinforce local vested interests. So many municipalities may prosper while the metropolis suffers the pains. We should expect the pains to become more painful as current efforts to diminish poverty encourage individual municipalities to "do something" about unemployment by treating the metropolitan labor market as if it respected political boundaries. A metropolitan area planning organization should earnestly consider other ways of bringing together such efforts.

I am not ready to whisper the magic phrase, "metropolitan government," even less ready to declare it politically feasible. Perhaps separate agencies carrying on specialized functions throughout the metropolis can do the job; but their weakness shows up in their inability to deal at once with interdependent facts like segregation in housing and segregation in schools. Perhaps compacts among local governments or statewide administrative entities will serve some planning purposes better, despite their unwieldiness. The conclusion remains: metropolitan Boston has the opportunity—indeed, the necessity—to design new means of intervening in urban processes on the scale at which something can actually be done about them. For most purposes, that means a scale larger than any municipality.

NOTES

1. There are of course other significant locations for the population than their homes, but the American obsession with residential location and the practice of enumerating people at their dwellings have held back any comparable mapping of population by workplace, locus of entertainment, and so on. Current studies of traffic flow come closest to breaking with this tradition.
2. In doing so, we make up a fictitious population, since there is never a time at which all the people are in the places we assign them to. But this fiction, like many others, is more useful than the reality.
3. Stock essentially classifies the birthplace of the person's grandparents.
4. A very simple measure of segregation—essentially stating how far to the right of the graph the curve for the particular group crosses the line representing its share of the entire metropolitan population—puts the categories we have been working with in the following order:

Negro	84.5
Russian	79.5
Other Races	78.4

Polish	71.5
Italian	70.4
Swedish	65.4
Irish	59.7
British	59.5
Canadian	56.0

For comparison, here are corresponding figures for the major occupational categories:

Private Household	82.2
Managers, etc.	73.6
Sales	72.4
Professional, etc.	68.8
Craftsmen, etc.	67.0
Clerical, etc.	65.6
Service	61.3
Labor	57.9
Operatives, etc.	54.0

Even this simple measure shows the greater segregation by race and ethnicity than by occupation in metropolitan Boston.

5. Unfortunately, the census data do not permit the construction of similar curves for the major categories of national background for 1940 and 1950. It would be fascinating to trace the changes for some of the other groups we have discussed.

6. The excellent recent work of a group based at Brandeis University (Watts and others, 1965) also illustrates the utility of current social research for planning purposes. That study of middle-income Negro families in the Washington Park urban renewal area helps indicate both the sorts of families that find it easiest to move out of the ghetto, and the nature of the ties holding them and others to the Negro community. And it sharply presents the dilemma: desegregate by encouraging the very people best prepared for local leadership to move out of the ghetto vs. consolidate the Negro community. The fact that the great majority of these families remained in Roxbury, despite an earlier interest in departing and despite housing opportunities outside, tells us that changing the balance of segregation is more complicated than simply manipulating the stock of housing.

REFERENCES

Beshers, James, Edward O. Laumann and Benjamin S. Bradshaw, "Ethnic Congregation-Segregation, Assimilation, and Stratification," *Social Forces*, 42 (May, 1964), 482–490.

Fried, Marc, "Grieving for a Lost Home," in Leonard J. Duhl, ed., *The Urban Condition* (New York: Basic Books, 1963), 151–171.

Gans, Herbert J., *The Urban Villagers* (New York: Free Press, 1962).

Handlin, Oscar, *Boston's Immigrants* (Cambridge: Harvard University Press, 1959, revised edition).

Hartman, Chester, "The Housing of Relocated Families," *Journal of the American Institute of Planners*, 30 (November, 1964), 266–286.

Kain, John F., "The Effect of the Ghetto on the Distribution and Level of Non-white Employment in Urban Areas," unpublished paper presented to the American Statistical Association, 1964.

Lieberson, Stanley, *Ethnic Patterns in American Cities* (New York: Free Press, 1963).

Watts, Lewis G., and others, *The Middle-Income Negro Family Faces Urban Renewal* (Waltham: Florence Heller Graduate School, Brandeis University, 1964).

Whyte, William F., *Street Corner Society* (Chicago: University of Chicago Press, 1943).

Selected Readings on Communities and Territorial Organization

Banfield, Edward C. *The Moral Basis of a Backward Society.* Glencoe, Ill.: Free Press, 1958. Southern Italy—"amoral familism," says Banfield.

Barker, R. G. *Ecological Psychology.* Evanston, Ill.: Row, Peterson, 1967.

Barton, Allen H. *Communities in Disaster: A Sociological Analysis of Collective Stress Situations.* Garden City, N.Y.: Doubleday, 1969. Synthesis of a wide range of studies.

Beardsley, Richard K., John W. Hall, and Robert E. Ward. *Village Japan.* Chicago: University of Chicago Press, 1959.

Bennett, John W. *Hutterian Brethren: The Agricultural Economy and Social Organization of a Communal People.* Stanford, Calif.: Stanford University Press, 1967. Detailed examination of six colonies in southwestern Saskatchewan.

Berque, Jacques. *Histoire sociale d'un village egyptien au XXe siècle.* Paris and the Hague: Mouton, 1957.

Blythe, Ronald. *Akenfield: Portrait of an English Village.* London: Allen Lane, The Penquin Press, 1969. Portraits of individuals, adding up to portraits of a community.

Breton, Raymond. "Institutional Completeness of Ethnic Communities and the Personal Relations of Immigrants." *American Journal of Sociology* 70 (September, 1964), 193–205.

Buder, Stanley. *Pullman: An Experiment in Industrial Order and Community Planning, 1880–1930.* New York: Oxford U.P., 1967. The quintessence of the paternalistic company town.

Calhoun, John C. "Population Density and Social Pathology." *Scientific American* 206 (February, 1962). A general report of some famous experiments with overcrowded rats.

Chisholm, Michael. *Rural Settlement and Land Use.* London: Hutchinson University Library, 1962. A wide-ranging review in terms of location theory.

Dice, Lee R. *Man's Nature and Nature's Man: The Ecology of Human Communities.* Ann Arbor: Michigan University Press, 1955.

Duncan, Otis Dudley. "Social Organization and the Ecosystem." In *Handbook of Modern Sociology* edited by Robert E. L. Faris. Chicago: Rand-McNally, 1964. Pp. 36–82.

Ecole Pratique des Hautes Etudes, VIe Section. *Villages désertés et histoire économique, XIe–XVIIIe siècle.* Paris: SEVPEN, 1965. A huge compendium of reviews of the various ways villages disappeared from the European map during the Medieval, Renaissance, and Early Modern periods.

Frankenberg, Ronald. *Communities in Britain.* Hammondsworth, England: Penguin, 1966. An extremely competent summary of English community studies.

Geertz, Clifford. *Agricultural Involution.* Berkeley and Los Angeles: University of California Press, 1963. The process of ecological change in Indonesia.

Goffman, Erving. *Behavior in Public Places: Notes on the Social Organization of Gatherings.* New York: Free Press, 1963. Many discussions in passing of how people use spatial relations to communicate and control.

Haggett, Peter. *Locational Analysis in Human Geography.* London: Seward Arnold, 1965.

Hall, Edward T. *The Hidden Dimension.* Garden City: Doubleday Anchor, 1966. An anthropologist's exploration of the ways men define, defend, and organize their personal space and their implications for crowding.

Halpern, Joel M. *The Changing Village Community.* Englewood Cliffs, N.J.: Prentice-Hall, 1967. A convenient anthropological summary.

Halpern, Joel. *A Serbian Village.* New York: Columbia University Press, 1958.

Hawley, Amos H. *Human Ecology, A Theory of Community Structure.* New York: Ronald Press, 1950. In its time, an important synthesis.

Johnson, E. A. J. *The Organization of Space in Developing Countries.* Cambridge, Mass.: Harvard University Press, 1970.

Ledrut, Raymond. *L'espace social de la ville.* Paris: Anthropos, 1968. Sociology for planning in Toulouse.

Long, Norton. "The Local Community as an Ecology of Games." *American Journal of Sociology* 64 (1958), 251–261.

Lyford, Joseph P. *The Talk in Vandalia.* New York: Harper Colophon, 1965. Just that: a naturalistic account of what people talk about in Vandalia, Illinois.

Meier, Richard L., and Ikumi Hoshino. "Adjustments to Metropolitan Growth in an Inner Tokyo Ward." *Journal of the American Institute of Planners* 34 (July, 1968), 210–222.

Miner, Horace. *The Primitive City of Timbuctoo.* Princeton, N.J.: Princeton University Press, 1953.

Morin, Edgar. *Commune en France—La métamorphose de Plodémet.* Paris: Fayard, 1967. Published in English as *The Red and the White;* in either language, a sensitive study of change in a Breton town.

Olson, Philip. "Rural American Community Studies: The Survival of Public Ideology." *Human Organization* 23 (1964): 342–350.

Parsons, Talcott. "The Principal Structures of Community." In *Structure and Process in Modern Societies.* Glencoe, Ill.: Free Press, 1960.

Pitt-Rivers, Julian, ed. *Mediterranean Countrymen: Essays in the Social Anthropology of the Mediterranean.* Paris and The Hague: Mouton, 1963.

Pred, Alan. *Behavior and Location: Foundations for a Geographic and Dynamic Location Theory.* Lund: C.W.K. Gleerup, 1967; Lund Studies in Geography, Series B, Human Geography, No. 27. A clear and rather rigorous statement with an extensive review of the literature.

Redfield, Robert. *The Little Community.* Chicago: University of Chicago Press, 1955. A brief crystal-clear series of reflections on ways of studying communities.

Sheppard, Thomas F. *Lourmarin in the Eighteenth Century: A Study of a French Village.* Baltimore: Johns Hopkins Press, 1971. Old Regime social structure in the South of France, seen up close.

Skinner, G. William. "Marketing and Social Structure in Rural China." *Journal of Asian Studies* 24 (November, 1964), 3–43, and later issues.

Sommer, Robert. *Personal Space: The Behavioral Basis of Design.* Englewood Cliffs, N.J.: Prentice-Hall, 1969. Psychologists' studies of the organization of personal space and its applications to architecture.

Sorre, Maximilien. *Rencontres de la Géographie et de la Sociologie.* Paris: Rivière, 1957.

Stein, Maurice R. *The Eclipse of Community.* Princeton, N.J.: Princeton University Press, 1960. Review and interpretation of American community studies.

Tilly, Charles, Barry Kay, and Wagner Jackson. *Race and Residence in Wilmington, Delaware.* New York: Teachers College, 1965. Longer on description than explanation; concentrates on segregation and housing discrimination from 1940 to the early 1960's.

Vayda, Andrew P., ed. *Environment and Cultural Behavior.* Garden City, N.Y.: Natural History Press, 1969. Human ecology, especially as studied by anthropologists.

Vidich, Arthur J., Joseph Bensman, and Maurice R. Stein, eds. *Reflections on Community Studies.* New York: Wiley, 1964. Retrospect by writers of well-known studies.

Willmott, Donald E. *The Chinese of Semarang.* Ithaca, N.Y.: Cornell University Press, 1960. A sophisticated study of an important minority in an Indonesian city.

Wolf, Eric R. *Peasants.* Englewood Cliffs, N.J.: Prentice-Hall, 1966. A brilliant synthesis of materials on diverse peasant communities.

Wylie, Laurence, et al. *Chanzeaux.* Cambridge, Mass.: Harvard University Press, 1966. A remarkable series of essays on a French village.

Wylie, Laurence. *Village in the Vaucluse.* Cambridge, Mass.: Harvard University Press, 1957. A loving, sensitive reconstruction.

Zuckerman, Michael. *Peaceable Kingdoms: New England Towns in the Eighteenth Century.* New York: Knopf, 1970. How the good citizens kept each other in line before the Revolution.

THE DIVERSITY OF CITIES

In his *Tristes Tropiques,* anthropologist Claude Levi-Strauss tells us that when he first saw South America after spending his youth in Europe, he felt disturbed. "The scale of man and the scale of things had been stretched so far apart that a common standard was no longer possible."[1] The buildings, streets, and cities were just too big. American visitors regularly have the converse experience: they find European towns, even the great ones, quaint, crowded, and contained.

Part of this effect comes from the sheer scale of structures and spaces. Another part comes from variations in population density. Even in the United States the density of very large cities ranges from 900 residents per square kilometer (about 2,500 per square mile) in Dallas to 9,000 residents per square kilometer in New York City (30,000 per square kilometer in Manhattan). If you ever fly from New York to Dallas, be sure to look out the window as you take off and land; the difference between the two densities shows up clearly from 2,000 feet in the air: cramp versus sprawl. The effective range of densities in American cities is even greater. The intensity of contact among the people using the city also depends upon the volume of daily movements in and out of the center, the extent to which people are stacked vertically as well as spread horizontally over the city's surface, the amount of activity which goes on in public places rather than indoors, and the sheer pace of movement in the city. The experience of being in one city or another varies accordingly.

On the average, North American cities of a given size operate at lower densities than cities in most other parts of the world. One of the most important reasons is that they have grown up with means of transportation—especially the automobile—encouraging dispersion of the population and consuming a great deal of central city space. Even compared with New York's 9,000 residents per square kilometer—a high density for the United States—the 14,000 residents per square kilometer of Moscow, the 28,000 of Paris, or the 50,000 of Old Delhi give a different texture to daily experience. Since devices like subways and skyscrapers extend New York and Moscow far above and below the surface, while high-density cities such as Delhi, Singapore, or Cairo hug the ground, the statistics greatly understate the variety of density, and therefore of life, at street level.

The statistics also average out what are actually complicated variations within each city. Densities normally peak in the center, fall off toward the periphery, cluster along transport lines, pulse with the city's daily rhythm, and fade out in irregular blocks of little-used land or water. Furthermore, the whole pattern varies systematically by type of city—South American cities have higher densities in the new settlements at their rims than comparable North American cities do. The decline of density with increasing distance from the center is more drastic in compact Asian cities than in sprawling American ones. Industrial cities produce a distinctly nodal pattern of densities and fluctuations, while the older West African cities break into relatively homogeneous fragments, each one containing a distinctive national or regional population plus a dense off-center nucleus of commerce and industry. Finally, in Western countries recent urbanization commonly has produced a sequence consisting of rapid rises in the densities at the centers of cities, followed by long declines as the cities spread out; while Asian cities, much more often cramped for space, have commonly experienced continuous increases in central density. The difference shows up in the sense of unused space an Asian sometimes feels in the middle of an American city. The urban density map is like a thumbprint: unmistakably the imprint of a city, varying systematically with the type of city, yet in many particulars representing a single, unique community.

The same blend of uniqueness and uniformity appears in the pattern of land use or in the residential locations of different parts of the population. The geographic site shapes land use and dwelling areas. Rio de Janeiro embraces a spectacular harbor. Tokyo expands around a great bay. Princely Buda and mercantile Pest were long divided then finally united into Budapest by the Danube. Because particular societies and special types of cities develop affinities for certain kinds of sites and standard ways of dealing with them, even the terrain can help produce uniformity amid the diversity of cities. North American lakeside cities such as Toronto, Cleveland, and Chicago, for example, have in common the following patterns: rectilinear streets leading to the port, expansion first along the lake and then at right angles to it, and remarkably regular, rank-ordered, movements of population toward areas of higher prestige at increasing distances from the center.

This chapter considers the uniformity in cities without losing sight of the diversity. First of all, we face problems of definition. Every one has his own sense of what makes a community a city. The distinction of locational, interactional, normative, and ecological perspectives sorts out the main alternatives fairly well, although it is far from catching every nuance. In a locational perspective, a city is the focal point of a field of activities, the place where the coordination of diverse and widespread activities goes on. By an interactional criterion, a city is a community in which specialized and large-scale structures of social relationship (as opposed

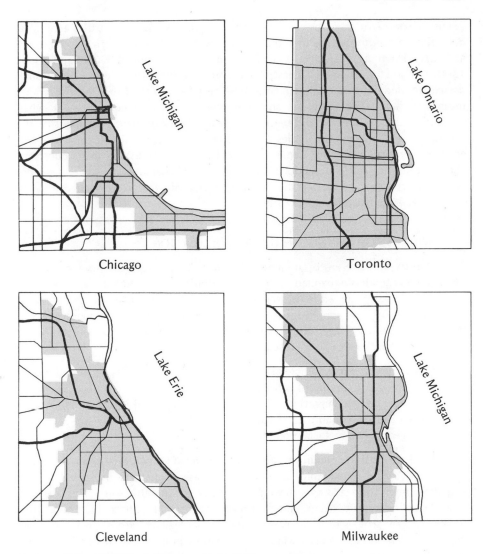

Chicago

Toronto

Cleveland

Milwaukee

Source: © Rand McNally & Company, R. L., 1969.

Figure 1. Major Street Patterns of Some North American Lakeside Cities

to diffuse and localized social relations) prevail. A normative criterion leads us to look for communities whose inhabitants display an "urbane" style of life: secular, mobile, widely knowledgeable, and so on. From an ecological point of view, any large, dense aggregate of population is likely to qualify as a city.

Large cities such as Tokyo and New York are on our list of cities no matter which of these standards we employ. Yet the different perspectives yield very different results when we consider more marginal cases. The big, dense agricultural towns of southern Italy, for example, tend to qualify if we use a strict ecological definition, but not if we use the others. Important Renaissance trading centers such as Danzig, Hamburg, Marseille, or Toledo had no more than 20,000 inhabitants in 1500. On a strict numerical test, they were hardly cities; yet by locational, normative, and interactional standards they certainly were. These inconsistencies mean that we cannot rely on common sense or established agreement when comparing the "cities" of different times and places or trying to identify the general effects of living in "cities." So let us begin with a simple demographic-ecological criterion: any big, dense settlement is a city. Then we can ask questions about the locational, interactional, and normative characteristics of big, dense settlements, not to mention the other demographic features which ordinarily accompany large size and high density.

SOURCES OF CHANGE IN URBAN POPULATION

Density and size are by no means the same thing. As an American motor city like Albuquerque has expanded by annexing suburban areas to the central city, its population has shot up while its overall density has gone down. Yet in the broadest sense the same general conditions affect size and density. Only three conditions can make a community bigger and denser than those around it; these are the basic conditions for urban growth we discussed before:

1. Its rate of natural increase (the difference between its birth and death rates) can be higher than that of other places.
2. Its rate of net migration (the difference between migration in and migration out) can be higher than that of other places.
3. Its geographic or social boundaries can change.

All three of these conditions are more complicated than they seem at first. A community can, for example, have a higher rate of natural increase than its neighbors simply by standing still while the others decline; that sometimes happens in a plague or a war. Again, net migration can rise through an increase in the number of new arrivals or a decrease in the number leaving, or both; net migration from San Juan to New York swings from positive in one year to negative in the next, for both reasons, depending on the relation between current opportunities in the two cities. The change of boundary is, of course, only one kind of structural transformation of a community. If size and density are our only criteria for the city, the change in boundary is the only one that counts. If we begin adding other requirements for a community to qualify as a city, they will begin to affect the movement of communities in and out of our categories as well. So simple an additional standard as Duncan's requirement that the labor force be predominantly nonagricultural opens up the possibility that shifts in the labor force will make a community a city, or remove it from that category, without a change in size or density. And the *reasons* for changes in birth rates, death rates, in-migration, out-migration, and boundary changes are, of course, even more complicated.

Let us consider natural increase. Over the past century or so, the people of cities in Western countries have, on the average, produced children at a lower rate than the people of rural areas in the same countries. Some of the difference has been due to the relatively high proportions of unmarried persons in cities; some of it, the result of a tendency in urban families to have fewer children. The evidence on mortality is much more mixed: there are some signs that the early phases of industrialization pushed up the death rates in cities and that the improvement of urban medical facilities eventually brought them down to below rural levels. But the fact that cities have relatively few infants and relatively few old people—the two age groups with high risk of death—makes the comparison difficult. .

In any case, relatively high mortality plus relatively low fertility means low or even negative natural increase. So for Western countries over the last century, we may squeeze out a cautious generalization: natural increase within the city has not been an important source of urban growth. This contrasts with the situation of contemporary India (see the article by Davis, in Chapter 2); there, despite high mortality, urban fertility is high enough to produce huge urban growth without any migration at all. Nevertheless, even in India it is net migration that is the great urbanizing force; a high rate of natural increase which is no higher in the city than in the country simply keeps city and country at a constant ratio.

In the West in recent decades, the usual combination has been small natural increase and large net migration. Explaining this combination involves explaining the whole system of population movement which links cities with the countryside, and covering the whole range of migrations: irreversible mass displacements of the peasantry; drifting young people in search of adventure; chain migration with its large flow of migrants back home; periodic shifts of executives or professionals following careers in which getting ahead means moving.

Our earlier discussions of urbanization neglected boundary changes while mentioning natural increase and net migration. At a national scale, boundary changes are not usually very important. For a particular community, however, they sometimes make a tremendous difference: the population of Paris exploded from 1.2 million at the census of 1856 to 1.7 million at the census of 1861, but about four-fifths of the great increase came from the annexation of nearby suburbs. Most cities grow outward, developing new settlements around their rims; the new settlements eventually become incorporated in the city itself.

How large a component of growth boundary changes will be depends very much on the conventions used to set boundaries: if we were to set the limit of the "real" New York at the point where population densities dropped below 1,000 persons per square mile, for instance, we would run the city most of the way from New Haven to Philadelphia. A minimum of 100 would create a New York running from around Boston to Washington, containing some 50 million people and gaining the largest part of its annual population growth from the addition of new areas to its domain. By the strict political criterion commonly used in the United States, New York's boundaries have remained the same since around the beginning of the twentieth century; perhaps half its growth from 3.4 million to 1900 to 7.8 million

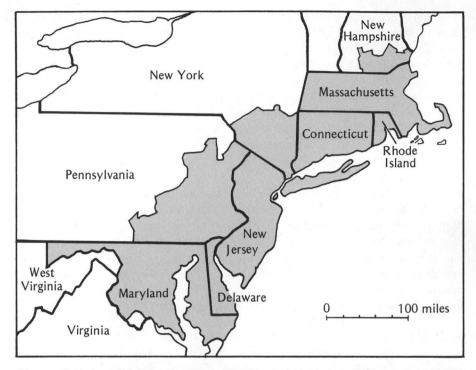

Source: From Jean Gottmann, Megalopolis: The Urbanized Northeastern Seaboard of the United States. © 1961 by The Twentieth Century Fund, New York. Adapted by permission.

Figure 2. Megalopolis: Metropolitan Counties along the U.S. East Coast in 1960

in 1960 was attributable to net migration. From 1960 to 1970 the region's population was still growing fast. New York City, however, only grew by about 86,000—and that was due to the overbalancing of a net *loss* through migration of more than 500,000 by a natural increase on the order of 600,000.

The grand totals summarize widely different experiences on the part of major segments of the population. If we separate the whites from the rest of the New York population in the figures just quoted, we can make the account of changes from 1960 to 1970 shown in Table 1. The white population sustained a large net loss—almost a million—through migration but compensated for about a third of the loss through natural increase. Blacks and other minority races increased in both ways, but net migration was the larger component. Obviously migration is still playing a fundamental part in shaping New York's population.

SPECIAL FEATURES OF URBAN POPULATIONS

The patterns of net migration and natural increase which distinguish cities from other communities lead directly to other demographic differences. It is

TABLE 1

Components of Change in New York City's Population, 1960–1970.

	1960 Population	*1970 Population*	*Change*	*Natural Increase*	*Net Migration*
Whites	6,640,662	6,023,535	−617,127	+338,392	−955,519
Blacks and other minority races	1,141,322	1,844,225	+702,903	+267,063	+435,840
Total	7,781,944	7,867,760	+ 85,776	+605,455	−519,679

common for cities in the early phases of extensive long-distance migration to have high sex ratios: significantly more than 100 men for each 100 women. In the mining cities of Central Africa, the high sex ratio results largely from the frequency with which men come into cities alone to work for a few years, remit their savings home, and then return to their villages to live out their lives. But sex ratios also ran high in American industrial cities during the first phases of mass migration from Europe; there, too, the men came first, and many returned home. Under routine, short-distance migration it is common for sex ratios to run well below 100 (fewer than 100 men per 100 women) as young women leave rural areas more eagerly than young men—or, to put it another way, as the opportunities and attractions of work in the countryside decline faster for women than for men. Under those circumstances, young women tend to take up jobs in the expanding administrative and service industries of the city.

These are strong tendencies but not immutable laws. In the case of modern Egypt, Janet Abu-Lughod shows (Chapter 2) that the migration of whole families into village-type settlements within the great city of Cairo not only means that urban fertility patterns remain quite similar to rural ones, but also that the urban sex ratio does not differ much from the rural sex ratio. The variation in sex ratio matters, because a very high or a very low sex ratio ordinarily means a high proportion of unmarried people and consequently a low level of fertility.

From all this it should be obvious that rural-urban migration also draws young adults more heavily than other age groups. As a result, cities experiencing heavy in-migration commonly have more than their share of people in their twenties but less than their share of children and old folks. A simple graph shows the impact of migration clearly. The "population pyramid" places two histograms— one for males, one for females—back to back along a vertical axis representing age. A closed population with stable birth and death rates forms a regular pyramid; the higher the ratio of birth rates to death rates, the wider the base relative to the whole pyramid. Figure 3 puts together three population pyramids for the great Italian industrial city of Milan during 1881–1911, its first important period of factory-based industrialization.[2] The city was expanding from 314,000 to 623,000

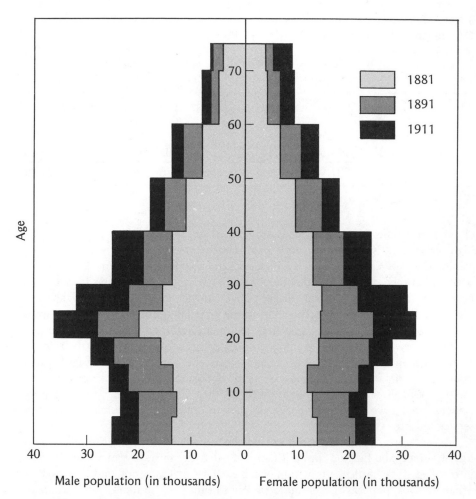

Figure 3. Three Population Pyramids for Milan, Italy, 1881–1911

people in those thirty years. Out of that increase of 309,000 about 256,000 came from net migration. One can easily see the effects of the massive migration on the age-sex distribution of the population. The concentration of migrants in the age range from 15 to 30 puts a great bulge in that part of the graph; it leaves the city with relatively few people under 15 and over 40. The bulge grows larger as time goes on, although it is already noticeable in the graph for 1881. The age band from 20 to 24 has a slight excess of males, due to the presence of a garrison averaging around 6,000 men. The other age bands have roughly equal numbers of males and females with the proportions of females rising in the older categories.

The relatively equal numbers of males and females contrast with the situation in J.A. Banks' discussion of the English city during early industrialization. There

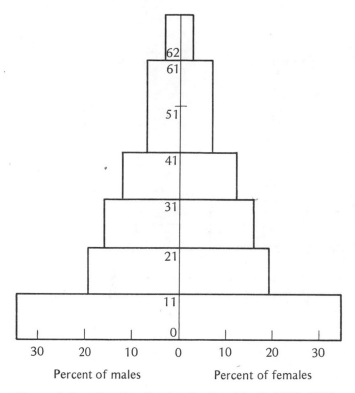

Figure 4. Age–Sex Distribution for Rural India 1953–1954

the short-distance migration of women produced low sex ratios, as it does in most European cities today. But the English cities were like Milan in having great concentrations of their population in the young adult age range. Nineteenth-century England and Italy were still industrializing, but they were already more urban and wealthier than the majority of the world's countries are today. Two population pyramids from India illustrate a common situation in relatively poor and rural countries of our own time.[3] Figure 4 presents the age–sex distribution of India's rural areas in 1953–1954. Figure 5 gives the distribution for India's largest cities at the same time. The figures do not come from a complete census but from sample surveys totaling about 50,000 people; some of the irregularities in the big-city pyramid are undoubtedly due to the difficulty of sampling the enormous, often drifting and homeless population of cities such as Bombay and Calcutta. Despite the irregularities, a comparison of the two pyramids brings out the pre-dominance of males in the large Indian cities. It is a result of the prevalence of temporary long-distance migration by young men; many of those men return home in their thirties or forties. The pyramids show that the big cities have much higher proportions of their populations in the ages from 22 to 41 than do the rural areas. But they also show that the effects of the high birth rates, relatively high death

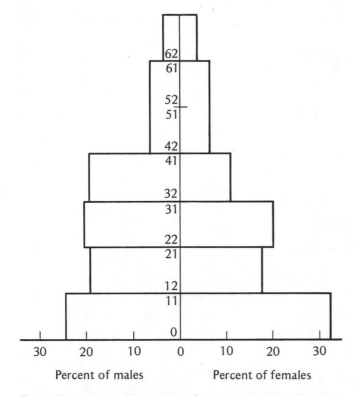

Figure 5. Age—Sex Distribution for Indian Cities 1953—1954

rates, and natural increase are so rapid that the cities would grow fast even if no migration occurred at all.

The sex ratios and the exact age distributions in cities, then, vary a good deal with the pattern of migration and the structure of employment. Yet almost everywhere the dependence of cities on migration and the concentration of migrants in the young adult range produces an urban population with disproportionate numbers of young adults. As my essay in this chapter on migration to American cities points out, the youth of new arrivals helps to create an urban population with a higher proportion of potential wage earners—and a lower proportion of persons who are dependent on others because of their age—than in other communities.

The heavy welfare burdens of big American cities may make their low proportion of dependents (due to age) hard to believe. In fact, those burdens are huge *despite* a favorable age distribution. The American metropolitan pattern of residential segregation by class and color concentrates the households which are too poor to survive without public assistance in the central cities—too poor because they have bad jobs or no jobs at all. Periodically, especially in times of rising unemployment, city politicians go through the motions of "tightening up" eligibility requirements or increasing the minimum period of residence for welfare benefits in hopes of discouraging the in-migration of the poor. The general tightening of requirements may well reduce the city's welfare budget, although only a small proportion of those denied assistance are likely to be freeloaders with readily available alternative sources of support.

The migration argument is entirely misconceived, both because there is no evidence that a city's level of welfare benefits affects its volume of in-migration and because the net effect of blocking in-migration would be to depress the overall educational and occupational qualifications of the city's population. To be sure, if a city could find a formula which admitted the highly employable and excluded everyone else (which is one of the main objectives of the extensive controls over movement in the Soviet Union, Poland, and other East European countries) it could prosper in both regards. Leaving aside the many political objections to such a policy, the selective recruitment would be very unlikely to work without a fundamental alternation in the means by which workers outside the exalted world of executives and professionals get information about urban job opportunities. Too much now depends on family, friends, and neighbors.

If we concentrate on the narrowly defined central city, we may also find it hard to understand that, in general, cities differ from other kinds of communities by having a more diverse and yet more highly qualified labor force. Without making any explicit comparisons with other communities, Sam Warner's description of Philadelphia at three widely different periods (reprinted in this chapter) shows how much that city remained at the leading edge of occupational change in the United States. He describes the city in 1755 as heavily engaged in manufacturing and shipping; by 1860 there develops an increasing administrative sector; by 1930 the labor force is increasingly involved in communication, coordination, symbol-manipulation, and record-keeping. At all three points, the population of Philadelphia as a whole was richer, better educated, and more skilled occupationally than the American average. That is usually true of cities, despite the different impression given by the sheer size and visibility of slums and poor populations in big cities throughout the world.

AN URBAN WAY OF LIFE?

Yet do big, dense communities have a distinctive quality of life, an "urbane" way of living? With that question the real difficulties begin. The main difficulties, I suppose, are four:

1. the existence of a myth concerning the impersonality, individuality, mobility, instrumentality of urban social life which is so persuasive that it prevents the cool comparison of different kinds of communities;
2. the great variability of different cities and different segments of the same city along any dimension of quality of life;
3. the confusion between ways of living associated with youth, bureaucracy, high levels of education, and other characteristics of people and organizations

which happen to be concentrated in cities, on the one hand, and features of social life which have some direct connection with large size and high density;

4. the sheer difficulty of observing, measuring, and comparing "ways of life."

A. J. Reiss' careful analysis of the time-budgets of different groups of men in the Nashville metropolitan area makes an interesting start at resolving some of these difficulties. Reiss' findings do not confirm the old picture of lonely city-dwellers and sociable countrymen; on the contrary, they show the rural-farm men spending more time alone than anyone else. But they do indicate that the city men spend significantly more of their time in businesslike "client" relationships. And they suggest that the big differences in social life among city, small town, and country-side are mainly associated with occupational routines and population mixtures, not with some general difference in the quality of life.

More debunking comes from Gutkind's essay in this chapter on urban African social life. Although Gutkind's comparison of kin-based and association-based networks of relationship suggests real differences in the structure of social life in city and country, he finds bonds of kinship and tribal origin at the very core of urban social relations. This observation—which by now has become a standard outcome of African urban studies—has led African urbanists first to reject the old European and American models of rural-urban differences as guides to the study of Africa and then to question whether they even apply in their countries of origin.

SOCIAL NETWORKS IN CITIES

Over the past decade or so, students of American working-class areas have seriously challenged the old notions of the impersonality and atomization of urban life. They have established that many low-income urban families maintain extensive daily contacts with kinsmen and friends of the same origins. Why this is so remains a matter of lively controversy, but the fact shows up in city after city throughout the Western world. Relocation through urban renewal, highway construction, and so on has received particular attention because it regularly breaks up these local networks.

Many people find this breakup acutely distressing. Marc Fried has described their "grief" at the loss of a home and has attributed that grief mainly to the severing of crucial social relations.[4] Depending on the character of their local social relations before the move, the nature of the areas to which they move, and the ease with which the earlier social relations can be transplanted or replaced, some families experience relocation as a routine change, some as a transformation of their way of life, and some as the destruction of their most meaningful attachments.

In Fried's view (which comes out of a great tradition of analyses of urban working-class life in England and America), the great questions about social relations before the move are how much they are localized and how much they are "close-knit." Localization is fairly easy to understand; the idea of "knit" needs more explanation. One of the earliest influential statements of the notion came from the anthropologist J.A. Barnes. In studying a Norwegian island community he found it useful to turn away from traditional concerns with the *content* of local social relations, with the *common properties* of people linked by them, and with *sentiments of attachment* to the group as a whole. Instead, he fixed his attention on their *structure*. A set of relations among pairs of persons treating each other as approximate equals he called a *network*. Barnes noted that

> ... one of the principal formal differences between simple, primitive, rural or small-scale societies as against modern, civilized, urban or mass societies is that in the former the mesh of the social network is small, in the latter it is large. By mesh I mean simply the distance round a hole in the network. In modern society, I think we may say that in general people do not have as many friends in common as they do in small-scale societies.[5]

Having mutual friends matters for more than one reason. It means having third parties to observe, to control, and often to stabilize each relationship. It reduces the individual's opportunity to behave in incompatible ways in different contexts. It often provides the newcomer who enters the network at any point with a ready-made, fairly extensive set of friends. These circumstances differ a great deal from the situation in which a person joins different sets of friends for each activity or context. They also differ from having few friends, or none. Another way to make Barnes' point is therefore to distinguish three structural arrangements: (1) many isolated individuals or isolated pairs, which we might call "atomized"; (2) long chains of pairs, which we might call "specialized"; (3) many interlocking sets of three or more mutual friends, which we might call "close-knit": The point is that even though any particular pair of friends may treat each other in pretty much the same way, the shape of the larger network significantly affects the impact of friendship on the individuals involved.

Of course, there is no need to restrict the idea of "knit" to friendship alone. The same formal notions apply to any other social tie. In fact, most students of social networks are more inclined to call them close-knit when several different kinds of ties—especially ties of kinship, friendship, and geographic proximity— coexist. The test for an extremely close-knit population would be this: every time we find that (1) X is a friend, a relative, or a neighbor of Y and (2) Y is a friend, a relative, or a neighbor of Z; we also find that (3) X and Z have at least one of the three ties between them.

This idea has proved useful in describing differences among societies and communities. It also has entered into accounts of differences in social relations *within* the communities. Elizabeth Bott, for example, explains the decided segregation of husbands' and wives' roles in English working-class families as a consequence of the involvement of men and women in close-knit networks of geographically clustered relatives and friends who impede their forming a fully independent pair, maintain their attachments to the same-sex peer groups they belonged to before marriage, and reinforce traditional definitions of male and female responsibilities.[6] The more frequent "partnership" arrangements of middle-class families, according

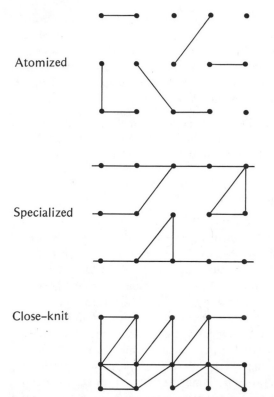

Atomized

Specialized

Close–knit

Figure 6. Atomized, Specialized, and Close-Knit Networks

to Bott, are made possible by the loose knit of middle-class social networks. It follows that as mobility breaks up geographic clustering and married couples find their friends and relatives dividing into insulated sets, the relations of husbands and wives to each other change as well.

NETWORKS AND MOBILITY

If we start from the frequent assumption that the close-knit network is the traditional form of social organization, while the specialized and atomized networks are the integrated and disintegrated versions of the modern form of social organization, we can arrive easily at two interesting conclusions: (1) the more traditional segments of the urban population—especially those recently transplanted from highly traditional settings—will be more frequently organized in close-knit networks; (2) with steady exposure to urban life, each traditional group arriving in the city will eventually acquire the desire and the means to move up occupationally, will thus be drawn into the kinds of social relationships demanded by complicated occupational structures, and will therefore move gradually from close-knit to loose-knit social relations.

In his article in Chapter 5, Marc Fried gives each of these hypotheses a sophisticated formulation. He insists that the members and the activities involved in close-knit networks matter less than the *form* of the networks. He stresses the recent common origin of much of the urban working class in rural communities which share the same collective, local, and ascriptive orientations as ordinarily appear in close-knit networks. Fried also describes the conflict between attachment to the working-class community and attraction to the rewards of occupational mobility. In the long run, the pressures for mobility prevail.

To his reformulation of the two standard hypotheses, Fried adds two further conclusions: (3) since the working-class communities of big cities are constantly receiving infusions of rural people, since the support received from close-knit social networks is essential and the shift to loose-knit networks demanding if inevitable, and since different types of working-class people vary considerably in their psychological and cultural readiness for participation in loose-knit ways, the working-class community operates as a protective, processing mechanism which at any given time includes a wide range of people at different stages of a common process; (4) the forced displacement of an entire working-class community will affect its members differently, depending mainly on the stage in the process they have reached; the least advanced will be hardest hit. Forced relocation will ravage the most recent arrivals, those from the most alien origins, and those with the greatest personal dependence on reassurance by destroying the close-knit networks which give them sustenance.

Marvin Lipman's research on relocation in Toronto, which follows Fried's ideas and procedures closely, identifies one uncertainty in that argument.[7] Within a diverse population displaced from a downtown slum, Lipman found that the group of the most recent arrivals (the Portuguese) did indeed have the closest-knit ties of friendship and kinship but that they accepted relocation most easily.

However, his findings do not contradict Fried's reasoning as flatly as it seems. Much more than their native Canadian neighbors, the Portuguese families managed to reconstitute—and even to consolidate—their close-knit networks in the course of moving. Two conditions made this possible: (1) there were areas of low-cost housing nearby within the range of search feasible with the personal-contact, word-of-mouth procedures characteristic of close-knit networks; (2) the Portuguese actually relied heavily on those networks in their housing search.

Their behavior was perfectly consistent with what we know of the residential mobility patterns of poor families. It was the same search pattern that produces frequent short-distance moves in low-income areas and contributes to the "voluntary" segregation of Negroes and Mexican-Americans. The conclusions we draw are: (1) that close-knit networks significantly affect the mobility patterns of low-income families, and (2) that forced relocation tends to produce the dire effects Fried describes if the persons displaced have no means of retaining, using, or reconstituting their networks.

Fried's explanation of the prevalence of close-knit networks in urban working-class areas is more or less a functional one: that kind of network comes into being as a defensive organization. It makes the adjustment to the city easier, or at least it persists because it serves that purpose.

There are at least two important alternatives to the functional line of argument. One is the old idea of a direct transplantation of rural ways into the city—rural communities are organized on close-knit principles, and rural people grow up attached to that sort of social arrangement. When rural people move to the city, they bring their culture and social arrangements with them. Only gradually do they adopt cosmopolitan ways. It is a matter of culture but not necessarily of self-defense. Thus Marcel Rioux argues that the scope of the recognized kin group in French Canada shrinks with urban residence but is still greater for the rural-born than for the urban; Lewis Killian sees the mountaineer migrant to Chicago as carrying his community life with him in the same way that he carries his accent and his taste for country music.[8]

An important variant of the idea of transplantation shows more promise of dealing with Fried's problem. Instead of being content with a flat contrast of "rural" and "urban" social arrangements, some anthropologically aware investigators insist on the variability of rural cultures and point to corresponding variability in the whole process of migration. Ray Birdwhistell's close examination of two nearly adjacent communities in rural Kentucky led him to identify two substantially different types of social organization, which he styled "segmental" and "interdependent."[9] People from "interdependent" Green Valley, involved in extensive networks of mutual obligation, were unlikely to migrate from the land to the city; if they did, they tended to remain within their own small capsules of friends and relatives, to stay in contact with the folks at home, and to avoid occupational and residential mobility. People in "segmental" Dry Ridge, although personally almost indistinguishable from Green Valleyites, sharply distinguish their strong obligations to members of their own households from their weak obligations to persons outside it. They migrate fairly frequently. Once in town, they often move up in occupation and on to other cities. Birdwhistell implies that the rural migrants still transplant their culture, but which culture they transplant fundamentally affects both their mode of migration and their subsequent involvement in urban life.

Still another possibility is that the social arrangements by which migration occurs determine the local involvements of the migrant in the city. The migrant who comes to the city through contact with relatives or friends living there commonly finds a close-knit network ready to absorb him on arrival, he has little choice but to remain in it. Since working-class and rural migrants to North American cities come through such contacts much more often than do middle-class and urban migrants, the persistent differences in networks by class and origin might very well result from the social arrangement of migration. In their article in Chapter 3 John and Leatrice MacDonald point out how the chain migration of Southern Italian immigrants to the United States has created dense, localistic Italian neighborhoods in big American cities. Raymond Breton has found that in Montreal the availability of ethnic churches, clubs, and other institutions largely determines how much of their lives the members of an ethnic group spend within its boundaries.[10]

This availability is itself strongly affected by the social arrangements of migration. If the conditions of migration deeply affect the involvement of different urban groups in close-knit networks, there is little reason to assume that close-knit networks are somehow *necessary* to the psychological and social welfare of working-class families in general.

CHOOSING AMONG ALTERNATIVE THEORIES

No doubt each of the three arguments has something to it: the social arrangements of migration do promote or inhibit the formation of close-knit networks; rural migrants do bring with them a propensity to form, join, or cling to close-knit groups; and existing close-knit networks do serve defensive purposes which reinforce them. That leaves unanswered, however, how important each of these factors is and how they interact.

The weighting of the factors matters for theoretical reasons, since students of cities search eagerly for explanations of the formations of different kinds of subcommunities within cities. It also matters practically, since the consequences of any public program spurring people in close-knit networks to move from position to position or place to place depend on the way these factors fit together. If close-knit networks meet deep needs in irreplaceable ways, then rapid desegregation, forced relocation, or accelerated occupational mobility will hurt many working-class people. If close-knit networks are carry-overs from rural culture or products of the particular conditions of migration, most likely they can be replaced with less pain.

Fortunately, we have ways of investigating these alternatives. We can compare the experiences of migrants from different cultural origins or of migrants from similar origins who face different social situations in the city. The comparison of the social networks of working-class members of different ethnic and racial groups in the city will help us sort out the proper explanations; it is surprising, for example, to discover how little evidence anyone has assembled so far on the social networks of black urbanites. We can examine what happens to networks when people move voluntarily or involuntarily; such "natural experiments" are happening all the time.

Studies on these questions already have ruled out some bad answers, such as the old assumption that slums create and preserve social disorganization, while good housing guarantees satisfactory social life. Studies have documented the widespread existence of close-knit networks, especially those built around kinship, in urban working-class areas. They have made much clearer what the promising alternative explanations are and how to test them. Yet they certainly have not produced solid answers so far.

CONSEQUENCES OF URBAN SOCIAL TIES

This review of social ties in cities has dwelt on working-class communities and on residential mobility, because those are the topics in which notions of interpersonal networks have been most widely used. Clearly this set of ideas has a wider scope. Scott Greer is reaching for a network account of urban political participation when he extends the general logic of the cosmopolitan/local dichotomy to a distinction among isolates, local actors, and community actors and then analyzes the impact of residential segregation and "parapolitical" organization on the prevalence, political knowledge, and political behavior of these three types of actors in different parts of the metropolis.[11]

Studies of urban rebellions in Europe and America are piling up more and more evidence against the old idea that marginal, atomized urbanites have a special propensity to extremism and violence. Recent work tends to portray the ordinary rebels as very much tied into local life, collectively aggrieved, and organized for action in common. On the whole, the populations most capable of collective political action seem to be grouped in relatively small, tight networks which are in turn linked to each other via a few crucial and effective intermediaries. Corner gangs in American ghettoes and workshops in nineteenth-century European cities resemble each other in sharing these characteristics.

Now it is a little easier to see what separates cities from other kinds of communities. There are real differences which contrasts between "personal" and "impersonal" social relations and similar distinctions do not capture. We are dealing not so much with contrasts in the quality of the bond connecting any particular person with another as with contrasts in structure: in the scale, the pattern, the mix, the ramifications of social relations. Richard Meier pushes toward a general explanation of the existence of cities in his analysis of the "civic bond," which describes the significant advantages of populations which build fairly complex and efficient systems of communication and control. In Meier's view there may be some small tendency for large, dense populations to form such complex systems. The main relationship, he thinks, probably runs the other way: the existence of efficient systems of communication and control encourages populations to pile up at the central locations of those systems.

Meier's essay contains a number of important clues. A city has a large number of subcommunities, each with its own organization with only weak direct links to each other, but which are tied together by a few large structures: a labor market, a housing market, an interdependent set of firms, a network of political relations, a few big formal organizations such as a city government, and a complex structure of communications. The subcommunities group together people of similar characteristics and people engaged in closely related activities: ethnic groups, sects, neighborhoods, professions, and some other self-selected nonoccupational groups (such as opera buffs, drug addicts, cyclists, and political activists). Most people's strong ties concentrate within one or two of these subcommunities. But the interdependence of the subcommunities—even when they are fighting with each other—and their common dependence on the large structures create an operating system without any strong central direction.

The major causal connections in this way of analyzing the city appear in Figure 7. All cities are segregated into subcommunities of one kind or another, as indicated in the diagram, but what kinds of subcommunities prevail in a particular

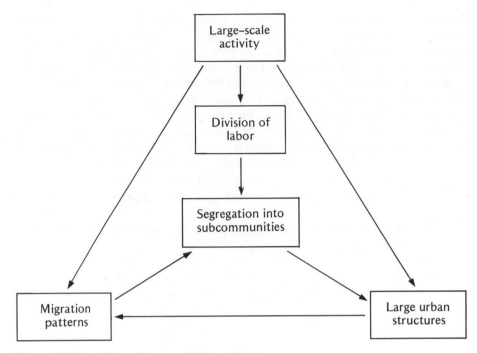

Figure 7. Major Determinants of Urban Structure

city depend on the division of labor created by the city's dominant activity and on the most important patterns of migration to and from the city. It also indicates that the chief migration patterns depend on the character of the dominant activity and on the nature of the large urban structures. A city devoted to manufacturing in which one of the major structures is an efficient and centralized labor market, for example, tends to recruit a large share of its migrants through the operation of that labor market.

This is, obviously, a great simplification of the reality, of the implications of the articles in this chapter, and of the observations I made earlier about social ties in cities. It identifies the main relationships and leaves the refinements aside. Let us try one more simplification along the same line. We can imagine the migration patterns discussed here or there in this chapter as forming a continuum running from short-run circular migration, in which everyone leaves a village, spends some time working in the city, then returns to the village; to chain migration, in which a network of friends, relatives, or tribesmen partly established in the city organize migration and involvement in the city—many migrants return home after awhile, but there is a net flow into the city; to career migration, in which organizations and labor markets provide the essential means and incentives for migration, and migrants tend to pursue occupational careers. Every real city has a mixture of all three, with other types falling in between, but we can place the city on the continuum by the predominance of one type or another. We can imagine a second continuum running from (1) the city segregated into subcommunities of a small, relatively permanent group of bosses and their staffs, on the one hand, and a series of labor camps, on the other; to (2) the city containing a cosmospolitan cluster and a number of urban villages; to (3) the city segregated by social class. Finally, we might arrange the chief urban structures relating the subcommunities to each other and to the city as a whole from (1) brokers who act on behalf of an entire subcommunity and thus provide links between subcommunities; (2) networks of patron-client relationships, with a limited number of important patrons but with each person involved in a somewhat different network; (3) large organizations and markets. Again, we do not expect to see pure types anywhere in the world, but we are able to say that one or another of these structures is prominent in a particular city.

The three continua are related to each other. Here is the general relationship:

Migration	circular	chain	career
Subcommunities	bosses & labor camps	cosmopolitans, urban villages	class clusters
Large structures	group brokers	patron—client networks	organizations and markets

The first type includes an interesting range of cities: mining centers, military outposts, and others often with high proportions of males to females and enormous concentrations in the young adult age range. The second type has been dominant over most of urban history and is still visible through much of the world. The third we see slowly growing out of the second in the richest and most industrial countries of the world.

ARTICLES IN THIS CHAPTER

The reports in this chapter provide the means of refining and correcting this first approximation. Kevin Lynch's essay on the "pattern of the metropolis" deals mainly with the spatial arrangement of structures, activities, and people. Its whole point, however, is to show how different spatial arrangements imply different social priorities, different social costs, and different structures of social relationship. In a sense, Sam Warner's description of Philadelphia in the eighteenth, nineteenth, and twentieth centuries makes the very same point. For Warner shows us how the changing distribution of population and activities within the city reflected the shifts in Philadelphia's position in the world economy and shifts in the character of the world economy itself. Warner's discussion has the additional advantage of demonstrating the amount to be learned from very simple statistical information.

The analysis of personal relations in different parts of a metropolis by Albert J. Reiss deals more directly with the distinctive qualities of urban life. The research he reports is methodologically interesting, both because of the care he takes to distinguish the effects of location from those of occupation and because he makes successful use of a device—the time-budget—which has great promise for the study of life in big cities.[12] He draws cautious, mixed conclusions which nevertheless confirm the existence of real differences in the structure of social relations in urban, rural-nonfarm, and rural-farm areas.

My essay on migration to American cities considers two general topics: (1) the overall pattern of American urban migration and its principal variants; (2) the impact of migration on some features of American cities which their residents commonly consider to be "problems" caused or aggravated by migration to the city. On the whole, the evidence reviewed there contradicts the idea of migration as a major cause of urban hardship or disorganization; instead, it brings out the ways in which migration rejuvenates cities and feeds them talent. J. A. Banks' analysis of the nineteenth-century English city picks up some of the same themes, placing a greater emphasis on the demographic dimensions of migration to the new industrial centers. He wants to "explore the possibility that the movement into the towns was a direct response to some feature of town life which was attractive to the rural population of the nineteenth century" and eventually singles out the potential liberation from the burdens of country living which young women saw in the city. He concludes that, for all the hardships of the industrial work to which the young women were moving, they were not entirely wrong.

P. C. W. Gutkind, too, is portraying young people finding a new world in the city. But his young people are Africans, mainly male. Gutkind is concerned to show what kinds of structures rural Ugandans join, form, and use in finding work, housing, and friendship in the city. He shows a considerable use of ties which are broader than the city, existing before the migrant's arrival in the city; yet he also shows that the structures formed by these ties are new ones, peculiar to the city, and by no means simple transfers from a "traditional" countryside.

Finally, Richard Meier's analysis of the "civic bond," is a stimulating attempt to isolate the central structural conditions behind urban agglomeration. Meier draws more ideas from communications theory than from anywhere else; he provides one of the most coherent statements of an interactional approach to communities, cities, and urbanization that we have.

NOTES

1. Claude Levi-Strauss, *Tristes Tropiques* (Paris: Plon, 1955), p. 62.
2. Prepared from Comune di Milano, *Dati statistici*, 1884, 1905, 1912, and from *La popolazione di Milano secondo il censimento eseguito il 10 giugno 1911.*
3. Prepared from data in table 1 of N. V. Sovani, *Urbanization and Urban India* (London: Asia Publishing House, 1966), p. 43.
4. Marc Fried, "Grieving for a Lost Home," in Leonard J. Duhl, ed., *The Urban Condition* (New York: Basic Books, 1963), pp. 151–171.
5. J. A. Barnes, "Class and Committees in a Norwegian Island Parish," *Human Relations* 7 (1954): 44; see also his "Networks and Political Process," in Marc J. Swartz, ed., *Local-Level Politics* (Chicago: Aldine, 1969), pp. 107–130.

6. Elizabeth Bott, *Family and Social Network* (London: Tavistock, 1957).
7. Marvin Lipman, "Relocation and Family Life: A Study of the Social and Psychological Consequences of Urban Renewal" (unpublished doctoral dissertation, School of Social Work, University of Toronto, 1968).
8. Marcel Rioux, *Kinship Recognition and Urbanization in French Canada* (Ottawa: Bulletin of the National Museum of Canada, no. 173, 1959); Lewis M. Killian, "The Adjustment of Southern White Migrants to Northern Urban Norms," *Social Forces*, 32 (1953): 66–69.
9. Ray Lee Birdwhistell, "Border County: A Study of Socialization and Mobility Potential" (unpublished doctoral dissertation, Department of Anthropology, University of Chicago, 1951).
10. Raymond Breton, "Institutional Completeness of Ethnic Communities and Personal Relations of Immigrants," *American Journal of Sociology* 70 (1964): 193–205.
11. Scott Greer, *The Emerging City* (New York: Free Press, 1962).
12. See J. P. Robinson and P. E. Converse, "Social Change Reflected in the Use of Time," in Angus Campbell and Philip Converse, eds., *The Human Meaning of Social Change* (New York: Russell Sage Foundation, 1972); Alexander Szalai, "Differential Evaluation of Time Budgets for Comparative Purposes," in Richard Merritt and Stein Rokkan, eds., *Comparing Nations* (New Haven, Conn.: Yale University Press, 1966).

THE PATTERN OF THE METROPOLIS

Kevin Lynch

Kevin Lynch scans the city with a planner's eye. The scheme he presents in this article serves two purposes: (1) to sum up economically the principal ways in which urban form varies from place to place and time to time; (2) to set out rules for planning that form in order to accomplish human purposes. For a sociologist, the form of a city often consists mainly of the distribution of population within it: the division into working-class and middle-class areas, the location of the ghetto, and so on. (My article on "Metropolitan Boston's Social Structure" generally takes that point of view.) Lynch, the planner, emphasizes physical structures much more heavily. In essence, he offers us a 3 X 3 grid for the analysis of form, as shown in Figure 1.

	Structural Density and Condition	Circulation Facilities	Fixed Service Activities
Grain			
Focal Organization			
Accessibility			

Figure 1. Lynch's Scheme for Analysis of Urban Form

"Structural density" means the ratio of floor space in buildings to total land area, while "condition" ranges from very sound to dilapidated. "Circulation facilities" include all sorts of structures and spaces devoted to the movement of persons and goods. "Fixed service activities" are major general-use facilities such as hospitals, theaters, and seats of government. "Grain" refers to the extent to which different structural elements are mixed or segregated: a coarse-grained city has large areas of low-density housing, large areas of high-density commercial activity, and few mixtures of the two. "Focal organization" refers to the extent to which all the elements are oriented to the same point or points; it is roughly equivalent to what people studying the distribution of activities or population would call "centralization." "Accessibility" refers to the time required to get from peripheral to central locations; "concentration" is the word commonly applied to similar characteristics of populations and activities.

Rough Equivalents in Terminology

Planner	Sociologist
Grain	Segregation
Focal Organization	Centralization
Accessibility	Concentration

In Lynch's scheme, then, structures, circulation facilities, and fixed services activities are the elements out of which the city's form is built. Grain, focal organization, and accessibility are aspects of the arrangement of those elements. The scheme makes it easy to pin down the differences in form between Randstad (Holland) and London, New York, and Los Angeles.

The more interesting use to which Lynch puts it, however, is the sketching of alternative general plans for the city of the future. The sheet, galaxy, core, star, and ring represent the chief possibilities, depending on how we assign priorities among grain, accessibility, and focus. After considering the implications of the alternative plans for the accomplishment of different human values, Lynch sketches a more complex urban form which would give residents a choice among different values. The complex plan is an effort to retain the liveliness of cities while recognizing the strong contemporary pressures toward metropolitan dispersion.

The pattern of urban development critically affects a surprising number of problems, by reason of the spacing of buildings, the location of activities, the disposition of the lines of circulation. Some of these problems might be eliminated if only we would begin to coordinate metropolitan development so as to balance services and growth, prevent premature abandonment or inefficient use, and see

Reprinted by permission from "The Pattern of the Metropolis" by Kevin Lynch, *Daedalus*, Journal of the American Academy of Arts and Sciences, Boston, Massachusetts, Winter 1961, pages 79–98.

that decisions do not negate one another. In such cases, the form of the urban area, whether concentrated or dispersed, becomes of relatively minor importance.

There are other problems, however, that are subtler and go deeper. Their degree of seriousness seems to be related to the particular pattern of development which has arisen. To cope with such difficulties, one must begin by evaluating the range of possible alternatives of form, on the arbitrary assumption that the metropolis can be molded as desired. For it is as necessary to learn what is desirable as to study what is possible; realistic action without purpose can be as useless as idealism without power. Even the range of what is possible may sometimes be extended by fresh knowledge of what is desirable.

Let us, therefore, consider the form of the metropolis as if it existed in a world free of pressures or special interests and on the assumption that massive forces can be harnessed for reshaping the metropolis for the common good—provided this good can be discovered. The question then is, how should such power be applied? We must begin by deciding which aspects of the metropolitan pattern are crucial. We can then review the commonly recognized alternative patterns, as well as the criteria that might persuade us to choose one over another. Finally, we may hope to see the question as a whole. Then we will be ready to suggest new alternatives and will have the means of choosing the best one for any particular purpose.

THE CRITICAL ASPECTS OF METROPOLITAN FORM

There are at least three vital factors in our judging the adequacy of the form of the metropolis, once its total size is known. The first of all is the magnitude and pattern of both the structural density (the ratio of floor space in buildings to the area of the site) and the structural condition (the state of obsolescence or repair). These aspects can be illustrated on a map by plotting the locations of the various classes of density ranging from high concentration to wide dispersion, and the various classes of structural condition ranging from poor to excellent. Density and condition provide a fundamental index of the physical resources an urban region possesses.

A second factor is the capacity, type, and pattern of the facilities for the circulation of persons, roads, railways, airlines, transit systems, and pathways of all sorts. Circulation and intercommunication perhaps constitute the most essential function of a city, and the free movement of persons happens to be the most difficult kind of circulation to achieve, the service most susceptible to malfunction in large urban areas.

The third factor that makes up the spatial pattern of a city is the location of fixed activities that draw on or serve large portions of the population, such as large department stores, factories, office and government buildings, warehouses, colleges, hospitals, theatres, parks, and museums. The spatial pattern of a city is made up of the location of fixed activities as well as the patterns of circulation and physical structure. However, the distribution of locally based activities, such as residence, local shopping, neighborhood services, elementary and high schools, is for our purpose sufficiently indicated by mapping the density of people or of buildings. Hence, if we have already specified structural density and the circulation system, the remaining critical fact at the metropolitan scale is the location of the city-wide activities which interact with large portions of the whole.

When we come to analyze any one of these three elements of spatial pattern, we find that the most significant features of such patterns are the grain (the degree of intimacy with which the various elements such as stores and residences are related), the focal organization (the interrelation of the nodes of concentration and interchange as contrasted with the general background), and the accessibility (the general proximity in terms of time of all points in the region to a given kind of activity or facility). In this sense, one might judge that from every point the accessibility to drugstores was low, uneven, or uniformly high, or that it varied in some regular way, for example, high at the center and low at the periphery of the region. All three aspects of pattern (focal organization, grain, and accessibility) can be mapped, and the latter two can be treated quantitatively if desired.

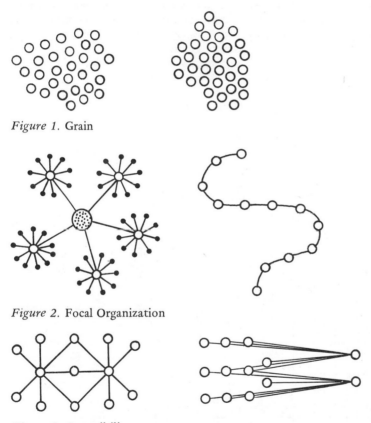

Figure 1. Grain

Figure 2. Focal Organization

Figure 3. Accessibility

It is often said that the metropolis today is deficient as a living environment. It has suffered from uncontrolled development, from too rapid growth and change, from obsolescence and instability. Circulation is congested, requiring substantial time and a major effort. Accessibility is uneven, particularly to open rural land. The use of facilities is unbalanced, and they become increasingly obsolete. Residential segregation according to social groups seems to be growing, while the choice of residence for the individual remains restricted and unsatisfactory. The pattern of activities is unstable, and running costs are high. Visually, the city is characterless and confused, as well as noisy and uncomfortable.

Yet the metropolis has tremendous economic and social advantages that override its problems and induce millions to bear with the discomforts. Rather than dwindle or collapse, it is more likely to become the normal human habitat. If so, the question then is, what particular patterns can best realize the potential of metropolitan life?

THE DISPERSED SHEET

One alternative is to allow the present growth at the periphery to proceed to its logical conclusion but at a more rapid pace. Let new growth occur at the lowest densities practicable, with substantial interstices of open land kept in reserve. Let older sections be rebuilt at much lower densities, so that the metropolitan region would rapidly spread over a vast continuous tract, perhaps coextensive with adjacent metropolitan regions. At the low densities of the outer suburbs, a metropolis of twenty million might require a circle of land one hundred miles in diameter.

The old center and most subcenters could be dissolved, allowing city-wide activities to disperse throughout the region, with a fine grain. Factories, offices, museums, universities, hospitals would appear everywhere in the suburban landscape. The low density and the dispersion of activities would depend on and allow circulation in individual vehicles, as well as a substantial use of distant symbolic

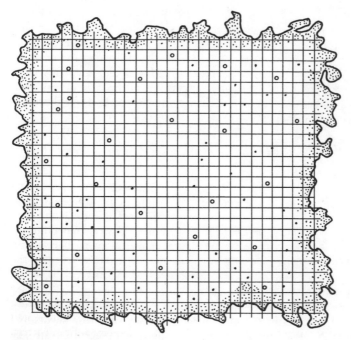

Figure 4. The Dispersed Sheet

communication such as telephone, television, mail, coded messages. Accessibility to rural land would become unnecessary, since outdoor recreational facilities would be plentiful and close at hand. The permanent low-density residence would displace the summer cottage.

The system of flow, concerned solely with individual land (and perhaps air) vehicles, should be highly dispersed in a continuous grid designed for an even movement in all directions. There would be no outstanding nodal points, no major terminals. Since different densities or activities would therefore be associated in a very fine grain, the physical pattern similarly might encourage a balanced cross-section of the population at any given point. Work place and residence might be adjacent or miles apart. Automatic factories and intensive food production might be dispersed throughout the region.

Frank Lloyd Wright dreamed of such a world in his Broadacre City.[1] It is this pattern toward which cities like Los Angeles appear to be moving, although they are hampered and corrupted by the vestiges of older city forms. Such a pattern might not only raise flexibility, local participation, personal comfort, and independence to a maximum, but also go far toward solving traffic congestion through the total dispersion and balancing of loads. Its cost would be high, however, and distances remain long. Accessibility would be good, given high speeds of travel and low terminal times (convenient parking, rapid starting); at the very least it would be evenly distributed. Thus communication in the sense of purposeful trips ("I am going out to buy a fur coat") might not be hindred, but spontaneous or accidental communication ("Oh, look at that fur coat in the window!"), which is one of the advantages of present city life, might be impaired by the lack of concentration.

Although such a pattern would require massive movements of the population and the extensive abandonment of equipment at the beginning, in the end it might promote population stability and the conservation of resources, since all areas would be favored alike. It gives no promise, however, of heightening the sense of political identity in the metropolitan community nor of producing a visually vivid and well-knit image of environment. Moreover, the choice of the type of residence would be restricted, although the choice of facility to be patronized (churches, stores, etc.) might be sufficiently wide.

THE GALAXY OF SETTLEMENTS

We might follow a slightly different tack while at the same time encouraging dispersion. Instead of guiding growth into an even distribution, let development be bunched into relatively small units, each with an internal peak of density and each separated from the next by a zone of low or zero structural density. Depending on the transport system, this separation might be as great as several miles. The ground occupied by the whole metropolis would increase proportionately; even if the interspaces were of minimum size, the linear dimensions of the metropolis would increase from thirty to fifty percent.

City-wide activities could also be concentrated at the density peak within each urban cluster, thus forming an over-all system of centers, each of which would be relatively equal in importance to any of the others. Such a metropolitan pattern may be called an "urban galaxy." The centers might be balanced in composition or

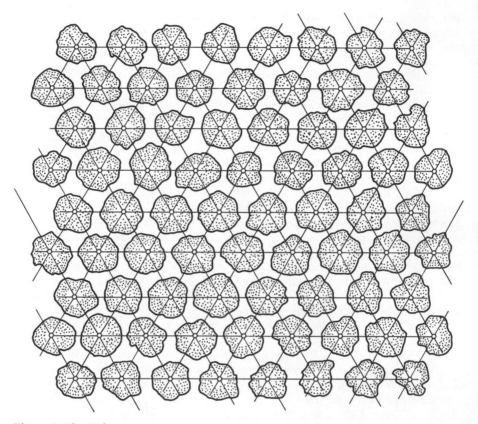

Figure 5. The Galaxy

they might vary by specializing in a type of activity, so that one might be a cultural center, another a financial center.

The system of flow would also be dispersed but would converge locally at the center of each cluster. It might be organized in a triangular grid, which provides such a series of foci while maintaining an easy flow in all directions over the total area. Since median densities remain low, while the centers of activity are divided into relatively small units, the individual vehicle must be the major mode of transportation, but some supplementary public transportation such as buses or aircraft running from center to center would now be feasible.

While it retains many of the advantages of the dispersed sheet, such as comfort, independence, and stability, this scheme probably enhances general communication, and certainly spontaneous communication, through creating centers of activity. It would presumably encourage participation in local affairs by favoring the organization of small communities, though this might equally work against participation and coordination on the metropolitan scale. In the same sense, the visual image at the local level would be sharpened, though the metropolitan image might be only slightly improved. Flexibility might be lost, since local clusters would of necessity have relatively fixed boundaries, if interstitial spaces were preserved, and the city-wide activities would be confined to one kind of location.

The factor of time-distance might remain rather high, unless people could be persuaded to work and shop within their own cluster, which would then become relatively independent with regard to commutation. Such independent communities, of course, would largely negate many metropolitan advantages: choice of work for the employee, choice of social contacts, of services, and so on. If the transportation system were very good, then "independence" would be difficult to enforce.

This pattern, however, can be considered without assuming such local independence. It is essentially the proposal advocated by the proponents of satellite towns, pushed to a more radical conclusion, as in Clarence Stein's diagram.[2] Some of its features would appear to have been incorporated into the contemporary development of Stockholm.

The pattern of an urban galaxy provides a wider range of choice than does pure dispersion, and a greater accessibility to open country, of the kind that can be maintained between clusters. This pattern has a somewhat parochial complexion and lacks the opportunities for intensive, spontaneous communication and for the very specialized activities that might exist in larger centers. Local centers, too, might develop a monotonous similarity, unless they were given some specific individuality. That might not be easy, however, since central activities tend to support and depend on one another (wholesaling and entertainment, government and business services, headquarters offices and shopping). A compromise would be the satellite proposal proper: a swarm of such unit clusters around an older metropolitan mass.

THE CORE CITY

There are those who, enamored with the advantages of concentration, favor a completely opposite policy that would set median structural densities fairly high, perhaps at 1.0 instead of 0.1; in other words, let there be as much interior floor space in buildings as there is total ground area in the city, instead of only one-tenth as much. If we consider the open land that must be set aside for streets, parks, and other such uses, this means in practice the construction of elevator apartments instead of one-family houses. The metropolis would then be packed into one continuous body, with a very intensive peak of density and activity at its center. A metropolis of twenty million could be put within a circle ten miles in radius, under the building practice normal today.

Parts of the city might even become "solid," with a continuous occupation of space in three dimensions and a cubical grid of transportation lines. (The full application of this plan could cram a metropolis within a surprisingly small compass: twenty million people, with generous spacing, could be accommodated within a cube less than three miles on a side.) Most probably there would be a fine grain of specialized activities, all at high intensity, so that apartments would occur over factories, or there might also be stores on upper levels. The system of flow would necessarily be highly specialized, sorting each kind of traffic into its own channel. Such a city would depend almost entirely on public transport, rather than individual vehicles, or on devices that facilitated pedestrian movement, such as

Figure 6. The Core

moving sidewalks or flying belts. Accessibility would be very high, both to special activities and to the open country at the edges of the city. Each family might have a second house for weekends; these would be widely dispersed throughout the countryside and used regularly three or four days during the week, or even longer, by mothers and their young children. The city itself, then, would evolve into a place for periodic gathering. Some of the great European cities, such as Paris or Moscow, which are currently building large numbers of high-density housing as compact extensions to their peripheries, are approximating this pattern without its more radical features.

Such a pattern would have an effect on living quite different from that of the previous solutions. Spontaneous communication would be high, so high that it might become necessary to impede it so as to preserve privacy. Accessibility would be excellent and time-distance low, although the channels might be crowded. The high density might increase discomfort because of noise or poor climate, although these problems could perhaps be met by the invention of new technical devices. As with the previous patterns, the choice of habitat would be restricted to a single general type within the city proper, although the population could enjoy a strong contrast on weekends or holidays. The nearness of open country and the many kinds of special services should on the whole extend individual choice. Once established, the pattern should be stable, since each point would be a highly favored location. However, a very great dislocation of people and equipment, in this country, at least, would be required to achieve this pattern.

Such a metropolis would indeed produce a vivid image and would contribute to a strong sense of the community as a whole. Individual participation, on the other hand, might be very difficult. It is not clear how running costs would be affected; perhaps they would be lower because of the more efficient use of services and transportation, but initial costs would undoubtedly be very high. The segregation of social groups, as far as physical disposition can influence it, might be discouraged, although there is a level of density above which intercommunication among people begins to decline again. Certainly this solution is a highly rigid and unadaptable one in which change of function could be brought about only by a costly rearrangement.

THE URBAN STAR

A fourth proposal would retain the dominant core without so drastic a reversion to the compact city. Present densities would be kept, or perhaps revised upward a little, while low-density development at the outer fringe would no longer be allowed. Tongues of open land would be incorporated into the metropolitan area to produce a density pattern that is star-shaped in the central region and linear at the fringes. These lines of dense development along the radials might in time extend to other metropolitan centers, thus becoming linear cities between the main centers. The dominant core, however, would remain, surrounded by a series of secondary centers distributed along the main radials. At moderate densities (less than the core pattern, and more than the sheet), the radial arms of a metropolis of comparable size might extend for fifty miles from its own center.

The metropolitan center of the star pattern would again contain the most intensive types of city-wide activity. Elsewhere, either in the subcenters or in linear formations along the main radials—whichever proved the more suitable—these activities would be carried on at a less intense level. The system of flow would logically be organized on the same radial pattern, with supplementary concentric rings. An efficient public transportation system of high capacity could operate along the main radials, whereas the ring roads could accommodate public transit of lower intensity. To some degree, travel by individual vehicles, although discouraged for centrally bound flows, would be practicable in other directions.

This pattern is a rationalization of the manner in which metropolitan areas were developing till the individual vehicle became the usual means of travel. It is the form the city of Copenhagen has adopted as its pattern for future growth;[3] Blumenfeld has discussed it at length.[4] This form retains the central core with its advantages of rapid communication and specialized services yet permits the location of other kinds of major activities. Lower residential densities are also possible. Individual choice should be fairly wide, both in regard to living habitat, access to

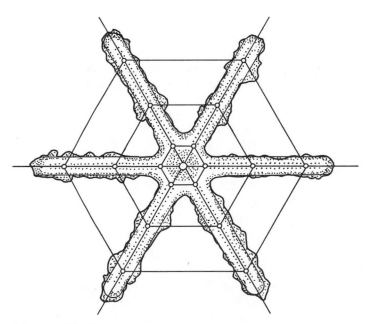

Figure 7. The Star

services, and access to open land—this land lies directly behind each tongue of development, even at the core, and leads continuously outward to rural land.

Movement along a sector would be fairly fast and efficient, although terminals at the core might continue to be congested and, with continued growth, the main radials might become overloaded. Movement between sectors, however, would be less favored, especially in the outer regions; there distances are great, transit hard to maintain, and channels costly, since they would span long distances over land they do not directly serve. Accessibility to services would be unequal as between inner and outer locations.

The visual image is potentially a strong one and should be conducive to a sense of the metropolis as a whole, or at least to the sense of one unified sector leading up to a common center. Growth could occur radially outward, and future change could be accomplished with less difficulty than in the compact pattern, since densities would be lower and open land would back up each strip of development. The principal problems with this form are probably those of circumferential movement, of potential congestion at the core and along the main radials, and of the wide dispersion of the pattern as it recedes from the original center.

THE RING

In the foregoing, the most discussed alternatives for metropolitan growth have been given in a highly simplified form. Other possibilities certainly exist—e.g., the compact high-density core pattern might be turned inside out, producing a doughnut-like form. In this case the center would be kept open, or at very low density, while high densities and special activities surround it, like the rim of a wheel. The principal channels of the flow system would then be a series of annular rings serving the high-intensity rim, supplemented by a set of feeder radials that would converge at the empty center. In fact, this is essentially a linear system, but one that circles back on itself and is bypassed by the "spokes" crossing the "hub." This system is well-adapted to public transportation, both on the ring roads and the cross radials, while individual vehicles might be used for circulation outside the rim.

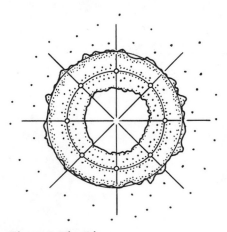

Figure 8. The Ring

Densities within the rim would have to be rather high, while those beyond the rim could be low. A system of weekend houses might also be effectively employed here. The central area could either be kept quite open or devoted to special uses at low densities. City-wide activities could be spotted round the rim in a series of intense centers, supplemented by linear patterns along the annular roadways. There would be no single dominant center but rather a limited number of strong centers (an aristocracy rather than a monarchy). These centers might also be specialized in regard to activity—finance, government, culture, etc.

This pseudo-linear form, like the radial tongues of the star plan, has the linear advantages: a high accessibility, both to services and to open land; a wide choice of habitat and location of activities; and a good foundation for efficient public transit. Congestion at any single center is avoided, yet there is a high concentration. In contrast to the galaxy or satellite form, the variety and strong character inherent in the specialized centers would have some hope of survival because of the relatively close proximity of these centers.

The visual image would be strong (though perhaps a little confusing because of its circularity), producing a particularly clear impression of the centers around the rim, in contrast to the central openness, and of their successive interconnections. The whole metropolis would seem more nearly like one community. One of the most difficult problems would be that of growth, since much development beyond the rim would soon blur the contour and require a new transportation system. A second concentric ring might be developed beyond the first, but it would negate some of the advantages of the first ring and would demand massive initiative by the central government to undertake its development. Another difficulty would be that of control. How can the belts of open land or the accessible center be kept free of building? Even if this problem were solved satisfactorily, a dilemma is also likely to arise in regard to the size of the ring: should it be small enough for the major centers to be in close proximity to one another or big enough to allow all the residences and other local activities to be related to it?

One classic example of this form exists, although on a very large scale—the ring of specialized Dutch cities that surround a central area of agricultural land, Haarlem, Amsterdam, Utrecht, Rotterdam, The Hague, and Leiden. This general pattern is now being rationalized and preserved as a matter of national policy in the Netherlands. In our own country, the San Francisco Bay region appears to be developing in this same direction.

The ring tends to be rather rigid and unadaptable as a form. It would require an extreme reshaping of the present metropolis, particularly with regard to transportation and the central business district; but it might dovetail with an observable trend toward emptying and abandoning the central areas. The plan could be modified by retaining a single major center, separated by a wide belt of open space from all other city-wide activities to be disposed along the rim. It may be noted that this use of open land in concentric belts ("green belts") is exactly opposite to its use as radial tongues in the star form.

THE OBJECTIVES OF METROPOLITAN ARRANGEMENT

Many other metropolitan forms are hypothetically possible, but the five patterns described (the sheet, the galaxy, the core, the star, and the ring) indicate the variation possible. One of the interesting results of the discussion is to see the appearance of a particular set of values as criteria for evaluating these forms. It begins to be clear that some human objectives are intimately connected with the physical pattern of a city, while others are very little affected by it. For example, there has been little discussion of the healthfulness of the environment or of its safety. Although these factors are influenced by the detailed design of the environment, such as the spacing of buildings or the provision for utilities, it is not obvious that the specific metropolitan pattern has any significant effect on them so long as we keep well ahead of the problems of pollution and supply. Psychological well-being, on the other hand, may be affected by the shape of the urban environment. But again, we are too ignorant of this aspect at present to discuss it further.

We have not referred to the efficiency of the environment in regard to production and distribution. This represents another basic criterion that probably is substantially affected by metropolitan pattern, but unfortunately no one seems to know what the effect is. "Pleasure" and "beauty" have not been mentioned, but these terms are nebulous and hard to apply accurately. A number of criteria have appeared, however, and it may well be worth while to summarize them. They might be considered the goals of metropolitan form, its fundamental objectives, either facilitated or frustrated in some significant way by the physical pattern of the metropolis.

The criterion of choice heads the list. As far as possible, the individual should have the greatest variety of goods, services, and facilities readily accessible to him. He should be able to choose the kind of habitat he prefers; he should be able to enter many kinds of environment at will, including the open country; he should have the maximum of personal control over his world. These advantages appear in an environment of great variety and of fine grain, one in which transportation and communication are as quick and effortless as possible. There may very likely be some eventual limit to the desirable increase of choice, since people can be overloaded by too many alternatives, but we do not as yet operate near that limit for most people. In practice, of course, to maximize one choice may entail minimizing another, and compromises will have to be made.

The ideal of personal interaction ranks as high as choice, although it is not quite so clear how the optimum should be defined. We often say that we want the greatest number of social contacts, so as to promote neighborliness and community organization, minimize segregation and social isolation, increase the velocity and decrease the effort of social exchange. And yet, while the evils of isolation are known, we are nevertheless beginning to see problems at the other end of the scale as well. Too much personal communication may cause breakdown, just as surely as too little. Even in moderate quantities, constant "neighborliness" can interfere with other valuable activities such as reflection, independent thought, or creative work. A high level of local community organization may mean civic indifference or intergovernmental rivalry when the large community is involved.

In this dilemma, a compromise could be found in saying that potential interaction between people should be as high as possible, as long as the individual can control it and shield himself whenever desired. His front door, figuratively speaking, should open on a bustling square, and his back door on a secluded park. Thus this ideal is seen as related to the ideal of choice.

Put differently, individuals require a rhythmical alternation of stimulus and rest—periods when personal interchange is high and to some degree is forced upon them, to be followed by other periods when stimulus is low and individually controlled. A potentially high level of interaction, individually controlled, is not the whole story; we also need some degree of spontaneous or unpremeditated exchange, of the kind that is so often useful in making new associations.

The goal of interaction, therefore, is forwarded by many of the same physical features as the goal of choice: variety, fine grain, efficient communication; but it puts special emphasis on the oscillation between stimulus and repose (centers of high activity versus quiet parks), and requires that communication be controllable. In addition, it calls for situations conducive to spontaneous exchange. Storehouses of communication, such as libraries or museums, should be highly accessible and inviting, their exterior forms clearly articulated and expressive of their function.

These two objectives of choice and interaction may be the most important goals of metropolitan form, but there are others of major importance, such as minimum first cost and minimum operating cost. These seem to depend particularly on continuous occupation along the major transportation channels, on a balanced use of the flow system, both in regard to time and direction of flow, a moderately high structural density, and a maximum reliance on collective transport.

Objectives of comfort, on the other hand, related principally to a good climate, the absence of distracting noise, and adequate indoor and outdoor space, may point either toward generally lower densities or toward expensive ameliorative works, such as sound barriers, air conditioning, and roof-top play areas. The important goal of individual participation may also indicate lower densities and an environment that promotes an active relation between an individual and his social and physical milieu, thus giving him a world that to some extent he can manage and modify by his own initiative.

We must also consider that the urban pattern will necessarily shift and expand, and therefore it is important to ask whether the adjustment to new functions will be relatively easy, and whether growth, as well as the initial state, is achievable with a minimum of control and central initiative and intervention. Adaptability to change seems to be greater at lower densities, since scattered small structures are readily demolished or converted. Both an efficient transport system and some form of separation of one kind of activity from another are also conducive to flexibility. Discontinuous forms like the galaxy or the ring require special efforts to control growth, for these patterns raise problems such as the appearance of squatters and the preservation and use of intervening open land.

Stability is a somewhat contradictory goal; it takes into account the critical social and economic costs of obsolescence, movement of population, and change of function. It is very possible that stability in the modern world will be impossible to maintain, and it runs counter to many of the values cited above. Yet stability may be qualified in this light: if change is inevitable, then it should be moderated and controlled so as to prevent violent dislocations and preserve a maximum of continuity with the past. This criterion would have important implications as to how the metropolis should grow and change.

Finally, there are many esthetic goals the metropolis can satisfy. The most clear-cut is that the metropolis should be "imageable," that is, it should be visually vivid and well structured; its component parts should be easily recognized and easily interrelated. This objective would encourage the use of intensive centers, variety, sharp grain (clear outlines between parts), and a differentiated but well-patterned flow system.

THE RELATION OF FORMS TO GOALS

We have now treated a number of objectives that are crucial, that are on the whole rather generally accepted, and that seem to be significantly affected by the pattern of the metropolis: the goals of choice, interaction, cost, comfort, participation, growth and adaptability, continuity, and imageability. Other goals may develop as we increase our knowledge of city form. What even these few imply for city form is not yet obvious; moreover, they often conflict, as when interaction and cost appear to call for higher densities, while comfort, participation, and adaptability achieve optimal realization at lower levels. Nevertheless, we have immediate decisions to make regarding the growth of urban areas, and if we marshall our goals and our alternatives as best we can, we can the better make these decisions.

The clarifying of alternatives and objectives has an obvious value, for this will permit public debate and the speculative analysis of the probable results of policy as related to any given form. Yet this kind of approach will soon reach a limit of usefulness unless it is supported by experimental data. Such experimentation is peculiarly difficult in regard to so large and complex an organism as a metropolis. To some degree we can form judgments drawn from such different urban regions as Los Angeles, Stockholm, and Paris, but these judgments are necessarily distorted by various cultural and environmental disparities. Possibly we can study certain partial aspects of city form, such as the effects of varying density or the varying composition of centers, but the key questions pertain to the metropolitan pattern as an operating whole. Since we cannot build a metropolis purely for experimental purposes, we can only build and test models, with some simplified code to designate pattern. By simulating basic urban functions in these models, tests might be run for such criteria as cost, accessibility, imageability, or adaptability. Such tests will be hard to relate to the real situation, and it is difficult to see how certain objectives (such as interaction or participation) can be tested, yet this technique is our best current hope for experimental data on the implications of the total metropolitan pattern.

DYNAMIC AND COMPLEX FORMS

Until we have such experimental data, what can we conclude from our imaginary juxtaposition of metropolitan form and human goals? Each of the alternatives proposed has its drawbacks, its failures in meeting some basic objectives. A radical, consistent dispersion of the metropolis appears to restrict choice, impair spontaneous interaction, entail high cost, and inhibit a vivid metropolitan image. A galaxy of small communities promises better, but would still be substandard as regards choice, interaction, and cost, besides being harder to realize. A recentralization of the metropolis in an intensive core appears to entail almost fatal disadvantages in cost, comfort, individual participation, and adaptability. The rationalization of the old metropolis in a star would work better if central congestion could be avoided and free accessibility maintained, but this form is less and less usable as size increases. The ring has many special advantages but raises great difficulties in cost, adaptability, and continuity with present form.

Of course, these are all "pure" types that make no concessions to the complications of reality and they have been described as though they were states of perfection to be maintained forever. In actuality, a plan for a metropolis is more likely to be a complex and mixed one, to be realized as an episode in some continuous process, whose form involves rate and direction of change as well as a momentary pattern.

For example, let us consider, on the basis of the little we know, a form that might better satisfy our aspirations, if we accept the fact of metropolitan agglomeration: this form is in essence a variant of the dispersed urban sheet. Imagine a metropolis in which the flow system becomes more specialized and complex, assuming a triangular grid pattern that grows at the edges and becomes more specialized in the interior. Many types of flow would be provided for. Densities would have a wide range and a fine grain, with intensive peaks at junctions in the circulation system and with linear concentrations along major channels, but with extensive regions of low density inside the grid. Through the interstices of this network belts and tongues of open land would form another kind of grid. Thus the general pattern would resemble a fisherman's net, with a system of dispersed centers and intervening spaces.

City-wide activities would concentrate in these knots of density, which would be graded in size. In the smaller centers the activities would not be specialized but the larger centers would be increasingly dominated by some special activity.

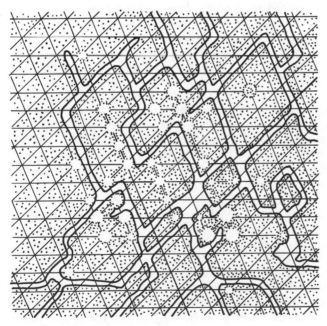

Figure 9. The Polycentered Net

Therefore the major centers would be highly specialized—although never complete-ly "pure"—and would be arranged in a loose central cluster, each highly accessible to another.

A metropolis of twenty million might have, not one such cluster, but two or three whose spheres of influence would overlap. These clusters might be so dense as to be served by transportation grids organized in three dimensions, like a skeletal framework in space. Elsewhere, the network would thin out and adapt itself to local configurations of topography. This general pattern would continue to special-ize and to grow, perhaps in a rhythmically pulsating fashion. With growth and decay, parts of the whole would undergo periodic renewal. Such a form might satisfy many of the general criteria, but each particular metropolis is likely to encounter special problems. Even so, the description illustrates the complexity, the indeterminacy, and the dynamic nature of city form that are inherent in any such generalization.

Perhaps we can make such a proposal more concrete by stating it as a set of actions rather than as a static pattern. If this were the form desired, then the agencies of control would adopt certain definite policies. First, they would encour-age continued metropolitan agglomeration. Second, they would begin to construct a generalized triangular grid of channels for transportation, adapting its interspacing and alignment to circumstances, but aiming at raising accessibility throughout the area as a whole. This grid would provide for many different kinds of flow and would have a hierarchy of its own—that is, the lines of circulation would be differentiated with respect to the intensity and speed of their traffic. Third, peaks of activity and density would be encouraged, but in sharply defined areas, not in rings whose density gradually declines from the center. The present metropolitan center would be encouraged to specialize and thus loosen into a cluster, while one or two major rival centers might develop elsewhere in the network, rather than allowing a general dispersal of city-wide activities. Such major specialized centers might be given even greater local intensity, with multi-level circulation, perhaps as a three-dimensional system of public rights-of-way.

Fourth, every effort would be made to retain, acquire, or clear a system of linked open spaces of generous size that pervaded the network. Fifth, a wide variety of activities, of accommodation and structural character, dispersed in a fine-grained pattern, would be encouraged. Once the concentration of special activities and the arrangement of higher densities in centers and along major channels had been provided for, then zoning and other controls would be employed only to maintain the minimum grain needed to preserve the character and efficiency of the various types of use and density, and large single-purpose areas would be avoided. Sixth, the form of centers, transportation channels, and major open spaces would be controlled so as to give as vivid a visual image as possible. Seventh, the agency would be committed to continuous rebuilding and reorganization of successive parts of the pattern.

Such a set of policies would mean a radical redirection of metropolitan growth. Whether this plan is feasible or worth the cost would require serious consideration. Even if this pattern were chosen, there would still be many crucial questions of relative emphasis and timing to be weighed. If life in the future metropolis is to be worthy of the massive effort necessary to build it, the physical pattern must satisfy human values. The coordination of metropolitan development, however obligatory, will not of itself ensure this happy result. Coordination must be directed toward some desired general pattern, and to define this, we must clarify our alternatives and the goals they are meant to serve.

NOTES

1. Frank Lloyd Wright, "Broadacre City," in *Taliesin*, October 1940, vol. 1, no. 1.
2. Clarence Stein, "City Patterns, Past and Future," *Pencil Points*, June 1942.
3. *Skitseforslag til egnsplan for Storkobenhaven:* Copenhagen regional plan. Summary of the preliminary proposal, 1948–1949, with list of contents and notes explaining all illustrations of the preliminary proposal, translated into English.
4. Hans Blumenfeld, "A Theory of City Form," *Society of Architectural Historians Journal*, July 1949.

IF ALL THE WORLD WERE PHILADELPHIA: A SCAFFOLDING FOR URBAN HISTORY, 1774-1930

Sam Bass Warner, Jr.

Philadelphia was North America's largest city until the end of the eighteenth century and has remained among the top few since then. Nevertheless, as Warner points out, its 24,000 inhabitants at the time of the American Revolution put it in the same size class as a great many other regional centers in the Western world; it did not approach the 400,000 of Naples, the 500,000 of Paris, the 600,000 of Constantinople, or the 900,000 of London. The energetic growth of the United States in the nineteenth-century brought its major cities, including Philadelphia, into the ranks of the world's largest. Warner traces for us the increase of Philadelphia, to nearly 600,000 in 1860, nearly 2 million in 1930. But he is less concerned to show us how the numbers changed than to show us how the city's structure evolved.

Warner uses a few handy devices (similar to the ones in my "Metropolitan Boston's Social Structure" in Chapter 3) to pin down the changes in Philadelphia. He compares the composition of the work force in 1775, 1860, and 1930, showing, among other things, the continuing importance of manufacturing and the rising significance of central-office functions. He gives a rough breakdown of populations and structures between the "core" and the "ring" of the city in 1860 and 1930; it shows, among other things, the way the black population became concentrated in the center as the city expanded outward. He uses an "index of dissimilarity" to show how populations and industries were segregated from each other at the three points in time; the general message is the greatly increasing segregation of the city. Finally, he compares the average sizes of establishments in different industries for 1860

and 1930, discovering a large and general increase in scale. Important seg-
ments of the whole American urban experience show up in this simple but
systematic tracing of change in one city. The work he does here invites
comparison with the many other American cities for which the same sort of
information is available.

From the moment American historians began writing self-conscious urban history they assumed the city was a particular kind of place, an environment, or set of environments, that called for special historical investigation. In his pioneering *Rise of the City, 1878–1898* (New York, 1933), Arthur M. Schlesinger, Sr., took the common-sense view that the crowding in slums, the intense social and economic interactions of the downtown, and the diurnal rhythms of the suburbs, all forced men to learn new styles of life if they were to prosper, indeed if they were to survive. Subsequent urban historians, whether their subject was immigrants, industrial cities, or colonial towns, repeatedly asserted that the city, either as a whole or by its parts, bore uniquely upon the lives of the men and women whose stories they told. Thus far, however, historians have failed to study the sources of this uniqueness in any systematic way.

Perhaps because the idea of a city as a special place, or a cluster of special places, seemed such a truism, it appeared not to be worthy of investigation in its own right. Perhaps because the demands for environmental history forced historians to labor so long to master the detail of a locale, few of them would contemplate a comparative study or a survey of a long time period. Or, perhaps the tradition of local history that has long stressed the distinctiveness of each urban portrait has prevented historians from considering the comparative and sequential aspects of urban environments. Whatever the cause of the lack of system, now thirty-five years after Schlesinger began the speciality, urban history still lacks a study of the succession of urban environments for any major city and the custom of research that would allow a reader to compare the history of one city to the history of any other.

This failure to examine the environment of cities in any systematic way has had serious consequences for the specialty. Teachers of urban history courses in American colleges must patch together chronological series out of books that do not treat comparable events, although the entire selection purports to deal with urbanization. A common sequence touching some of the important areas in American urban history might leap, for example, from Carl Bridenbaugh's description of colonial towns, to Oscar Handlin's analysis of Boston from 1830 to 1880, to Jacob Riis' account of New York's Lower East Side, to Lincoln Steffens' survey of municipal corruption, to Gilbert Osofsky's history of Harlem.[1] There is analysis of urban environments in Handlin, Riis, and Osofsky, although the data presented do not allow strict comparison without much outside knowledge. There is no concept of environment in Bridenbaugh and Steffens. The latter's argument rests on an

Reprinted by permission from "If All the World Were Philadelphia: A Scaffolding for Urban History, 1774–1930" by Sam Bass Warner, Jr., *American Historical Review*, 74 (1968), pp. 182–195. Footnotes renumbered.

interpretation of the structure of urban industry in the early twentieth century, but none of the other books give information on the earlier or later industrial structure. There are immigrants in Bridenbaugh's towns, but no information on acculturation. Just as frustrating to teacher and student as this lack of consistent information from book to book is the fact that no outline of the process of urbanization can be elicited from a chronological reading of our major urban histories. Except to the most imaginative reader, the usual shelf of urban history books looks like a line of disconnected local histories.

From time to time more systematic methods of viewing change in urban environments have been proposed. Soon after Schlesinger's work appeared, Lewis Mumford wrote his wide-ranging urban history of Europe and America, *The Culture of Cities* (New York, 1938). In it he divided urban history according to technological periods, arguing that urban environments responded to a regular sequence of technological events.[2] Economic historians have also worked with the concept of a process of development, and their periods complement the technological periods that Mumford derived intuitively. The economists have related the size of cities to economic functions and thereby tied urban history directly to the history of industrialization.[3] By extension of their reasoning, it is possible to relate internal environments to general economic change by regarding these environments as products of the developing scale and complexity of local, national, and international markets. Thus, the colonial American town becomes a product of an Atlantic system for the exchange of staples and manufactured goods; the big city to which the immigrants came in the early nineteenth century becomes a product of increased interregional commerce; the modern metropolis becomes a product of highly specialized regional and interregional exchanges in which services of all kinds have grown to supplant in significance older manufacturing and commercial functions. The idea of such urban sequences is as old as the concept of industrialization. What is new is the growing ability of economic historians to specify the relationships that determine urban growth and change.

Today it is possible to arrange the kind of basic facts that urban historians tend to gather in the course of their studies in such a way as to reveal the sequences suggested by Mumford and the economic historians. Such an arrangement gives the writer, and later his readers, a measure by which to judge the typicality of the subject; it also enables the writer and his readers to get some idea of where the particular events under discussion fit within the process of Atlantic urbanization. An orderly presentation of a few facts can, in short, provide a kind of intellectual scaffolding for urban history.

This article will demonstrate a systematic arrangement of a few facts about the population of Philadelphia during the years 1774, 1860, and 1930. It will discuss, in order, the growth of the population, the course of industrialization, the changing locations of workplaces and homes, the shifting intensity of residential clusters, and the group organization of work. Philadelphia has special merit for such a demonstration because it became a big city early in our history and because it industrialized early.

By the best current estimate the population of urban Philadelphia in 1775 (Philadelphia, Northern Liberties, and Southwark) was 24,000.[4] Such a size did not make it the rival of Edinburgh and Dublin, as it has often been described,[5] but rather an ordinary provincial town comparable to many towns throughout Europe and Latin America. Though a new town, its physical, social, and economic environments must have been long familiar to the European world. This very typicality of Philadelphia suggests that comparative studies of contemporary European and Latin American provincial cities would reveal important dimensions of the preindustrial world.

In 1860 the consolidated city of Philadelphia (consolidated in 1854 to include all of Philadelphia County) held a population of 566,000, second only to New York in numbers of inhabitants.[6] So rapid had been its growth that it had become one of the great cities of the world, about the same size as the old cities of Vienna and Moscow or the new city of Liverpool. As in the case of Liverpool, industrialization, immigration, and boomtown conditions were its hallmarks.

In 1930 Philadelphia's population (within the same boundaries as in 1860) had risen to 1,951,000. It was then, as it has remained, one of the nation's "big five," grouped with New York, Chicago, Los Angeles, and Detroit. In comparison to other cities of the world it ranked twelfth, behind Osaka, Paris, Leningrad, and Buenos Aires.[7] In this period the key social issue was the manner in which a city of such unprecedented size structured its masses of people and its heavy volume of economic activities.

It is impossible to classify with precision the occupations of city dwellers over a century and a half of modern history. Crude listings can, nevertheless, give useful perspectives on the nature of urban economic life. The statistics for Philadelphia suggest two quite different perspectives: a view of continuity and a view of change.

In terms of continuity, differences of a few percentage points may be read both to suggest the stability of urban life and to point to fundamental change. Note, for example, in Table 1 the move in the Manufacturing category from 52.4 per cent to 45.3 per cent, in the professions from 3.1 per cent to 6.3 per cent, or in the building trades from 7.6 per cent to 8.1 per cent. Although the span from 1774 to 1930 is generally treated by historians as a time of major revolutions, over the entire 150 years the city fulfilled a basic set of functions: it provided clothing, food, and housing for its residents, and professional services, markets, and manufactures for its residents and its trading region. From such a placid viewpoint, even a sharp decline, such as that of the transportworkers, or an equally sharp rise, such as that of the clerks, can be regarded as merely a shift in the nature of the city's commerce, not a departure from its historic functions. This perspective of continuity is especially useful to political history since it helps to explain the enduring power of urban businessmen, the commercialism of urban leadership, and the perseverance of business ideology at all levels of city politics.

The grouping of occupational statistics can also be used to place a city's history in a perspective of change. One can, for instance, interpret the shifts in the percentage of persons engaged in manufacturing and mechanical industries in the three years we are using (1774, 52.4 per cent; 1860, 54.9 per cent; 1930, 45.3 per cent) to suggest a steady decline in the proportions of Philadelphians engaged in manufactures from a peak in 1774. This interpretation seems proper because the 1774 percentage radically understates manufacturing activity. Colonial tax lists did not report the contribution of female domestic labor although such labor constituted an important fraction of the city's output. Indeed, one economic historian

TABLE 1
A Comparison of Some Elements of the Work Structure
of Philadelphia, 1774–1930[a]

	1774	*1860*	*1930*
Occupation:			
Laborers, all industrial categories	13.3	8.1	8.7
Clerks of all kinds, office, and sales	0.8	3.4	13.9
All other occupations	85.9	88.5	77.4
	100.0%	100.0%	100.0%
Workers by industrial categories:			
Manufacturing and mechanical industries	52.4	54.9	45.3
Building	7.6	8.3	8.1
Clothing	7.6	11.7	4.5
Bakeries	3.3	0.9	1.2
Iron, steel, and shipbuilding except autos and blast furnaces	6.2	4.5	4.7
Metalworking except iron and steel	2.0	2.4	0.6
Paper and printing	0.8	3.2	2.9
Miscellaneous textiles except wool and knitting	1.8	4.8	3.8
Balance of manufacturing	23.1	19.1	19.5
Nonmanufacturing	47.6	45.1	54.7
Wholesale and retail except autos	21.1	11.2	15.3
Transportation except railroads and transit	12.3	3.6	2.6
Professional and semiprofessional except entertainment	3.1	4.3	6.3
Hotels, laundries, and domestic service except slaves and indentured servants	5.9	21.8	12.8
Other nonmanufacturing industries	5.2	4.2	17.7
	100.0%	100.0%	100.0%
Total classified	3,654	3,012	864,926

[a]The classification of the Philadelphia work force of this table is that of the 1930 US Census, *Fifteenth Census, Classified Index of Occupations* (Washington, D.C., 1930), and *Alphabetical Index of Occupations* (Washington, D.C., 1930). One exception only has been made: wooden shipbuilding trades have been placed with the iron, steel, and shipbuilding categories for 1774 and 1860. The categories chosen for this table are those showing some specificity and continuity through all three periods and did not, like banking, contain so many unspecified clerks, or, like cotton mills, contain so many unspecified operatives as to defy 1774 or 1860 restoration. Occupations that could not be distributed by industry, like gentleman, widow, clerk, agent, operative, laborer, foreman, and helper, have been omitted from the industrial categorization of 1774 and 1860 and therefore do not enter into the percentage distributions of those years. These variations in classification between 1774, 1860, and 1930 probably account for small fluctuations in the Index of Dissimilarity of Table 3. In a few cases the census names of some industrial categories have been altered for clarity. The census' Other

has estimated that on the eve of the Revolution four thousand Philadelphia women were spinning and weaving.[8] If this interpretation is correct, then the course of urban industrialization takes on a special character. Not only did successive changes in industrial organization and machine processes free men and women from manufacturing for other occupations, but urban industrialization was a progressive sequence, ever lessening the commitment of the urban work force to manufacturing. Such a long trend differs from our common-sense impression that manufacturing occupied more and more city workers from President Jackson's time to the Hoover era.

More detailed comparisons of occupational and industrial groupings can also be made. Such groupings reflect changes in the structure of Philadelphia's economy that accompanied changes in the city's role in the Atlantic and American economy. During the first wave of industrialization, from 1774 to 1860, the proportions of unskilled laborers fell rapidly while the numbers of office and sales clerks multiplied. General wholesaling and retailing, however, declined with the differentiation of the old importing merchant's and general storekeeper's functions into distinct specialities. The labor force tied to marine transport and drayage declined sharply, while new industries like clothing, paper, and printing and some lines of textiles rose to great importance.

In the second wave of industrialization, during the interval 1860–1930, office and sales clerks again multiplied, but unskilled laborers remained a more or less steady proportion of the working population. Clothing, printing, baking, and textiles declined in relative importance, though they remained heavy users of Philadelphia's labor force. New industries, especially electrical machinery and auto parts, surged into prominence.[9] Such changes in manufacturing went forward within the context of a general decline in the proportion of Philadelphians engaged in manufactures and a strong rise in professions, government, commerce, and some services.

In sum, even such a crude table (Table 4) shows that Philadelphia, despite its unique historical mixture of manufacturing, banking, and transportation, participated in the general trend of American and European industrialization suggested by Colin Clark.[10] Philadelphians' economic effort shifted steadily from an early concentration on manufactures and commerce toward a modern emphasis on services, education, and government.

As in the case of all large American cities, Philadelphia's growth was propelled in heavy in-migrations of rural native and foreign immigrants. The successive waves

---

Iron and Steel category appears in the table as Iron, steel, and shipbuilding except autos and blast furnaces; the census' Other Textiles appears as Miscellaneous textiles except wool and knitting; the census' Other Professional appears as Professional and semiprofessional except entertainment. The table's category Hotels, laundries, and domestic service except slaves and indentured servants is a grouping of three census categories: Hotels, Restaurants, and Boarding Houses; Laundries and Cleaning Shops; Other Domestic Services. The 1774 list of occupations was drawn up from a careful comparison of names given on the 1774 Provincial Property Tax List for Philadelphia County with the 1775 Constable's Return for Philadelphia. The tax list is deposited in the Pennsylvania Historical and Museum Commission, Harrisburg; the Constable's Return is in the Archives of the City of Philadelphia, City Hall, Philadelphia. The 1860 material was drawn from a random sample of 3,666 persons taken from the original Eighth Census schedules for Philadelphia County now deposited in the National Archives. The 1930 data were transcribed from unpublished schedules of the Fifteenth Census now in my possession.

of foreign migration have been well documented, and now recent internal migrations have been estimated in state-by-state detail.[11] Today's practical concern with the social and political problems of black core cities and white metropolitan rings has obscured some of the history of urban settlement. The modern core of poverty and ring of affluence date from the late nineteenth century and were not characteristic of the first wave of urban growth.[12]

A kind of core and ring distribution of city dwellers manifested itself from the beginning, but it was much weaker and the reverse of the later distribution. In 1774, the poor seemed to have been pushed to the fringes of the city by the high cost of land near the Delaware River wharves. Then, during the early nineteenth century, Philadelphia grew so rapidly, and from such small beginnings, that no large stock of old housing existed to absorb or to ghettoize the waves of poor people flooding into the city.

Like inhabitants of a booming Latin American city today, Philadelphians of all income levels had to locate in new construction. Shanties, shacks, backyard houses, and alley tenements, as well as the monstrous conversions of the early nineteenth century, all so movingly reported by the nation's first sanitary inspectors, testify to the unpleasant clash of low incomes with the costs of new construction.[13] Under these conditions the poor tended to settle in backyards everywhere, in any old, decaying street that was not being seized by business, and especially at the outer edge of the city where land was cheapest, or could be squatted on.

If laborers are taken as proxies for low-income families, then Table 2 shows the tendency of poverty to concentrate at the ring of the city in 1860, not at the core; clerks concentrated next to the downtown. Such commonplace occupations as carpenters, machinists, shoemakers, and tailors settled in reasonably even proportions in both parts of the city. By 1930 the large stocks of old, cheap housing in the core of the city had completely reversed this pattern; low rents concentrated in the core, homeowners and middle-income rentpayers ($50.00–$99.00) at the ring.

Complementary patterns can be observed in the location of immigrants. In 1860, except for the British who clustered in the ring to be near the city's outer textile mills, immigrants were rather evenly distributed between core and ring. In 1930 the major immigrant groups, the Italians, Poles, and Russians, and the incoming Negroes concentrated in the cheap housing in the core. By the twentieth century, income, ethnic, and racial segregation had become as characteristic of the giant industrial metropolis as jumble and huggermugger had characterized the earlier big city.

As significant to the social geography and social history of the city as the general placement of income, ethnic, and racial groups by core and ring is the question of the intensity of residential clustering.[14] For example, are the shops and houses of the printers so tightly clustered together in one neighborhood that they encourage the establishment of benevolent societies and unions somewhat in the manner of the medieval city with its guilds? Or are the printers' homes so dispersed that only the conditions in the shops themselves contribute to association? Are the immigrants of a given period so tightly clustered that they experience American culture only through the strong filter of an ethnic ghetto? Or are the immigrants mixed in with large proportions of other poor people so that their assimilation is a process of adapting to some more general culture of the American poor? Variations

TABLE 2
Location of Foreign-Born, Negroes, and Selected Occupations, Tenures, and Rents, by Per Cent in Core or Ring, 1860, 1930[a]

1860

	Negro	Foreign-Born	Britain	Germany	Ireland	Total Population
Ring	34.9	62.1	73.7	60.4	60.8	61.9
Core	65.1	37.9	26.3	39.6	39.2	38.1
Total number	22,185	168,556	22,398	43,833	94,989	565,529

	Laborer	Clerk	Carpenter	Machinist	Shoemaker	Tailor	Sample
Ring	75.5	40.6	61.7	69.5	66.9	68.9	58.9
Core	24.5	59.4	38.3	30.5	33.1	31.1	41.1
Number in sample	442	283	149	82	181	122	4,740

1930

	Negro	Britain	Germany	Ireland	Italy	Poland	Russia	Total Population
Ring	19.7	52.6	43.8	52.0	29.5	27.4	30.0	70.4
Core	80.3	47.4	56.2	48.0	70.5	72.6	70.0	29.6
Total number	222,504	36,593	38,066	31,359	68,156	30,582	80,959	1,950,961

	Own Their Home	Rent under $15	Rent $15–$29	Rent $30–$49	Rent $50–$99	Rent $100+	Total Families
Ring	52.4	10.9	16.8	40.3	60.5	44.2	44.2
Core	47.6ᶜ	89.1	83.2	59.7	29.5	55.8	55.8
Number of families	232,591	10,142	63,432	96,026	36,427	6,538	448,653

[a]The core is the original municipality of Philadelphia, 1860, Wards 5–10; the ring is the eighteen outer wards. The location of the Negroes was given in *U.S. Ninth Census: 1860, I, Population*, 254; the location of the foreign-born was determined by transcribing the original eighth census schedules at the National Archives. The error in the transcription was less than 1.0 per cent. The location of the occupations was determined from a sample of *McElroy's Street Directory* for 1860. The ring wards are northeast 23, 35, 41; south 48; west 34, 46, 40; northwest 38, 21, 22, 42; the core is the thirty-seven inner wards of the city. All figures calculated from unpublished tract statistics of the fifteenth census, 1930. The owning families plus the renting families do not quite add to 100 per cent because there were 3,497 families who were listed as renting, but did not specify their rental group. (*U.S. Fifteenth Census: 1930, Population, Families*, IV, 1162–63.)

in the intensity of clustering will also affect the historian's evaluation of the functions of political bosses and their ward machines and of the services of city institutions like hospitals, schools, theaters, and saloons. By noting the ward location of the workers classified according to their industrial groups for Table 1, and by adding information on the foreign-born and on rents, as it became available, one can compare the intensity of residential clustering in 1774, 1860, and 1930.

In the history of Philadelphia, the general trend in concentrations of settlement was striking. Between 1774 and 1860 necessity and convenience caused the members of some industries to cluster their homes. Then, with the improvement in intracity transportation and the creation of large business organizations, the necessity to hive faded away. As this industrial cause of clustering lapsed, intense segregation based on income, race, foreign birth, and class rose to prominence as the organizing principle of the metropolis. (See Table 3.)

A value of twenty-five on the accompanying Index of Dissimilarity (Table 3) makes a convenient boundary between strong and weak clustering.[14] Some groupings of industry like the building trades, wholesaling, and retailing never established strong residential clusters. In 1774 the laborers' homes clustered most intensely at the outer fringe of town; the other strong gatherings were the printers; the shipbuilders near the port; blacksmiths, tinsmiths, and coppersmiths (these occupations are included within the US census categories of Table 3, namely, Metalworking except iron and steel; Iron, steel, and shipbuilding; Paper and printing).

The big city of 1860 continued some of these tendencies toward industrial concentration: professionals such as lawyers and doctors lived and practiced near the downtown; bakers lived and worked there, too, and also clustered near the city's eleven public markets. The strongest industrial cluster of this era, and remaining so in 1930, was the textile workers. Another sign of the future, visible from the tabulation for 1860, was the concentration of the hotel, laundry, and domestic workers. In this case their stronghold lay on the south side of the downtown, the site in 1930 of Philadelphia's sin and slum district. The evidence of the free Negroes also tells of the longstanding caste rules against that race. Theirs was the most intense segregation. The foreign-born Germans had created a strong cluster on the north side of town, but the largest immigrant group of all, the Irish, were evenly distributed throughout the city. They lived in basements, alleys, and attics on every block.[15]

In 1930, except for the textile group, well-paid skilled workers were scattered through the city's wards without much regard as to their industries. The new clusters of industry groupings shown in Table 3 were those who lacked skills and were not well paid: truckers, expressmen, sailors, clothingworkers, and workers in hotels, laundries, and domestic service. These were also the trades of the Negroes and the new immigrants. The index for 1930, then, shows the modern metropolitan pattern: high concentration of low skills and low rents. All the disfavored groups did not live in the same place, to be sure, but these groups divided up what was available wherever cheap old housing prevailed. In Philadelphia in the 1920's these conditions could be found especially in the core and in the old industrial sections of the north side. The rich, of course, huddled together, as segregated in their way as the poorest Negro.

These trends nicely match the general trend in the building of the American

TABLE 3

Index of Dissimilarity, Philadelphia, Southwark, and Northern Liberties, 1774; Philadelphia, 1860; 1930[a]

1774	Index No.	1860	Index No.	1930	Index No.
				Rental under $15 per month	56.0
				Italy, foreign-born	50.7
				Negro, native and foreign	50.7
				Rental $100+	50.2
		Negro, free, native-born	47.3	Russia, foreign-born	44.4
				Poland, foreign-born	44.0
				Miscellaneous textiles	42.3
		Miscellaneous textiles	40.3		
Laborers	37.2				
				Rental $15–$29	35.3
		Germany, foreign-born	34.1		
Metalworking except iron and steel	32.5			Germany, foreign-born	32.4
				Rental $50–$99	31.5
				Hotels, laundries, and domestic	30.8
		Bakeries	30.7		
Iron, steel, and shipbuilding	29.4	Iron, steel, and shipbuilding	29.0		
Paper and printing	29.4			Clothing	27.7
				Transportation except railroads and transit	27.2
				Britain, except Northern Ireland, foreign-born	26.6
		Hotels, laundries, and domestics	25.9		
		Metalworking except iron and steel	25.6		
		Professional except entertainment	25.4		
Transportation except railroads and transit	24.7				
Miscellaneous textiles	24.3				
				Professional except entertainment	23.1
				Owned occupied home	22.6

Clothing 22.3	Laborers 21.9	Ireland, Northern and Southern, foreign-born 21.5
	Clothing 21.8	
Building trades 21.2		Iron, steel, and shipbuilding 20.8
Wholesale and retail 20.5		
	Ireland, Northern and Southern, foreign-born 19.8	
German patronyms 19.7		
Professional except entertainment 19.7		
	Transportation except railroads and transit 19.6	
	Paper and printing 19.0	
		Rental $30–$49 (the median) 17.7
Bakeries 16.7		Metalworking except iron and steel 16
	Building trades 16.4	
		Bakeries 15.2
Hotels, laundries, and domestics 15.1		
		Paper and printing 11.4
		Building 10.4
	Pennsylvania, native-born 10.1	
	Wholesale and retail 9.6	
Homeowners 6.1		
		Wholesale and retail 5.3

ᵃThis Index of Dissimilarity should give the reader some measure by which we can compare the intensity of residential clustering in Philadelphia in 1774 to clustering in 1860 and clustering in 1930. The index has been frequently used by sociologists to discuss segregation in modern American cities. The values of the index in this table are lower than for modern studies because all the tabulations had to be based upon ward data, the ward being the only subdivision of the city for which material was available in all three periods. To construct the index, proportions of each group (laborers, foreign-born Irish, and so forth) to the total population of each ward were calculated. Next the proportion of the group to the total population of the city was calculated. Then the index was computed. The index measures the degree to which the group in question clustered in some wards in higher proportions than its proportion to the total population of the city. It is a measure of the variation of the ward-by-ward distribution of one group as compared to all others in the city. If the index number were 0, then in each ward of the city the group in question would be distributed in precisely its proportion to the entire city's population. If the index number were 100, the group would be entirely concentrated in its ward, or wards, and present in no others. A full explanation of the index and other methods of measuring clustering appears in Tacuber and Tacuber, *Negroes in Cities*, 203–204, 223–38. The sources for the occupations and origins of this table were the same as those mentioned in the note to Table 1. For a more complete description of the archival research behind the data for 1774, see Sam Bass Warner, Jr., *The Private City: Philadelphia in Three Periods of Its Growth* (Philadelphia, 1968), 225–28.

metropolis and the aging of its structures. They also reflect the strong early twentieth-century prejudice against foreigners and the intense caste feeling against Negroes. In this sense, the history of Philadelphia seems to conform to the general national history of urban growth, immigration, and industrialization.[16]

Because most of our social historians who are interested in big cities have been concerned with immigrants, and because our labor historians have not been concerned with cities, American history has failed to deal with the interaction between urban environments and the social organization of work. The simplest statistical computation shows that we have ignored a series of events of wide implication and enormous magnitude. The arrangement of most of the economic activities of a city into work groups is as much of a revolution in the environments of cities as the introduction of the automobile or electricity. In this important dimension of social structure, the town of 1774, the big city of 1860, and the industrial metropolis of 1930 all differed markedly from each other.

In eighteenth-century Philadelphia, with but very few exceptions, most people labored alone, with their family, or with a partner or a helper or two.[17] The first wave of industrialization brought a large fraction of the city's manufacturing workers into a group organization of work. (See Table 4.) The technique of rationalizing tasks so that they could be performed by groups of men and women working within one shop, rather than as individuals laboring in a neighborhood of households, was to my mind the largest component in the first wave of urban industrialization. The early increases in productivity in most lines of urban manufacture came from the work of groups, not from the new machines. The violent strikes and the anti-Catholic and anti-Negro riots of the 1830's and 1840's testify to the painful and revolutionary effect of this social change.[18] By 1930 three-quarters of Philadelphia's work force—in office, factory, store, and government—labored in groups.[19]

In the simplest sense this transformation of the organization of work had the effect of creating a new lattice of loyalties and social relationships in the city. If factoryworkers may be taken as indicative of the behavior of clerical and retail help, then the University of Pennsylvania's Wharton School studies show that most city dwellers in the 1920's settled down to more or less permanent jobs after four or five years of shopping around.[20] It seems fair to reason that in time the men and women of his work group must have become important members of a worker's social life and that the group must have become a source of discipline, loyalty, and culture in its own right. These were some of the positive results of removing a large fraction of the city's work force from entrepreneurial roles.[21]

Research on the historical interactions between the group organization of work and urban residential environments is not yet fairly begun, yet such research seems to hold great promise for extending our comprehension of the processes of urban history. In my own study of Philadelphia I have found that even such simple information as the average size of establishment by industry adds significantly to the understanding of such important events as the rise and decline of unions and strikes, epidemics of street violence, and the development of an isolated mill-town culture in one quarter of Philadelphia as opposed to the suburban-downtown white-collar culture of another quarter.[22]

TABLE 4
Average Size of Establishments in Major Lines of Manufacture,
Philadelphia, 1860, 1930[a]

Total Persons Employed	1860	Average No. Persons per Establishment
98,397	All lines of manufacture	15.6
1,255	Locomotives	627.5
4,793	Cotton goods	94.0
1,131	Gas fixtures	75.4
3,258	Cotton and woolen goods	63.9
1,021	Umbrellas and parasols	48.6
3,290	Shirts, collars, etc.	45.7
14,387	Clothing, men's and boys'	40.9
1,219	Silk fringes and trimmings	39.3
1,876	Bricks	38.3
2,285	Hosiery, woolen	32.2
1,613	Machinery, general, of iron	26.4
2,680	Carpets	21.6
1,190	Bookbinders	20.0
1,038	Carriages and coaches	20.0
1,326	Leather	15.8
8,434	Boots and shoes	12.0
1,627	Furniture and cabinetmakers' wares	10.1
1,290	Cigars	5.6
1,138	Millinery, laces, etc.	4.9
54,851		

	1930	
292,616	All lines of manufacture	52.6
1,986	Sugar refining	662.0
3,103	Iron and steel mills	443.3
20,280	Electrical machinery	375.6
1,535	Paper	307.0
5,105	Leather	204.2
8,321	Worsted goods	180.9
8,564	Cigars and cigarettes	161.6
26,693	Knit goods	134.1
1,861	Chemicals	124.1
1,245	Dental goods and equipment	113.2
13,806	Printing and publishing, newspaper and magazine	99.3
3,479	Silk and rayon manufacture	94.0
2,219	Cotton, small wares	92.5

TABLE 4 (*continued*)

Total Persons Employed	1930	Average No. Persons per Establishment
1,829	Druggists' preparations	91.5
5,692	Cotton goods	79.1
3,002	Woolen goods	73.2
3,327	Shirts	72.3
1,840	Meat packing, wholesale	59.4
13,083	Foundary and machine-shop production	59.2
3,227	Boxes, paper	50.4
4,056	Dyeing and finishing textiles	41.4
4,676	Furniture, including store fixtures	41.0
11,680	Clothing, men's and boys'	39.6
3,884	Confectionery	39.2
2,070	Paints and varnishes	37.6
1,432	Ice cream	36.7
1,114	Structural and ornamental iron	35.9
9,304	Clothing, women's	31.3
1,464	Fancy and miscellaneous articles	30.5
1,463	Planing mill products	28.7
1,513	Nonferrous metals	28.0
1,293	Copper, tin, sheet ironwork	21.9
8,413	Bread and bakery products	16.5
7,319	Printing and publishing, book and job	15.2
189,878		

[a]A major line of manufacturing is one that employed one thousand or more persons in the city of Philadelphia. Office help is included with the mill hands, supervisors, owners, and employers. Many children are omitted in 1860 in those lines, like cigar making, that were dominated by small shops. (Philadelphia Board of Trade, *Manufacturers of Philadelphia* [Philadelphia, 1861], 5–18; *U.S. Fifteenth Census: 1930, Manufacturers*, III, 466–67.)

To sum up, what in the way of intellectual scaffolding for urban history does this survey of Philadelphia offer? It provides a descriptive framework relating changes in scale to changes in structure.

First, at each period of Philadelphia's history (1774, 1860, 1930) the city had grown to a radically different size, from 24,000 to 566,000 to 1,951,000. The proportions of the social elements of the city were thoroughly altered by such shifts, as were all the city's environments. The basic distribution of the city's jobs and houses according to core and ring varied with each period, and the variations depended directly upon rapid urban growth. The implications of such changes in social geography for political institutions, communications within the city, municipal institutions, and informal associations have yet to be explored with any thoroughness. Here is a great opportunity for studies of small areas that would reinterpret the materials of local history.

Second, the occupational history of the city changed according to the sequences suggested by current generalizations of economic history. The very conformity of Philadelphia to these generalizations suggests that the city responded to advances in transportation, business organization, and technology as a member of a large Atlantic economy and society.

Third, the social geography of industrialization appears to have been one of complex changes. The interaction of the events of industrialization with those of rapid growth seems to have shifted residential segregation away from clustering by occupations toward clustering by classes, ethnicity, and race. Studies of these events are just beginning.[23]

Fourth, industrialization populated the city with a new set of social units: work groups. The nature of these groups, their number, and their impact upon other events in the history of large cities changed significantly over time. Again, the subject is unexplored and calls for research that combines local and institutional history.

Altogether the Philadelphia data confirm the utility of Mumford's descriptive sociotechnical categories and the economic historians' developmental sequences as a useful basis for analysis of the history of any large modern city, or for the comparison of different cities. The unities of scale, social structure, economic institutions, and technology at various stages in the modern process of industrialization and urbanization are inescapable.

This article is offered as the first attempt to discover and arrange the data for one large modern city in such a way that historians may find evidence of the processes they have long speculated upon. It is hoped, further, that the data concerning Philadelphia will give urban historians a scaffolding on which to build the studies of small areas that are required for the history of changing urban environments. Since the data are simple, moreover, their systematic arrangement should encourage historians of other cities to make comparisons that will enable us to say if all the world really was Philadelphia.

NOTES

1. Carl Bridenbaugh, *Cities in the Wilderness: The First Century of Urban Life in America, 1625–1742* (New York, 1938), and *Cities in Revolt: Urban Life in America, 1743–1776* (New York, 1955); Oscar Handlin, *Boston's Immigrants: A Study in Acculturation* (Cambridge, Mass., 1941); Jacob Riis, *How the Other Half Lives: Studies among the Tenements of New York* (New York, 1890); Lincoln Steffens, *The Shame of the Cities* (New York, 1904); Gilbert Osofsky, *Harlem: The Making of a Ghetto. Negro New York, 1890–1930* (New York, 1966).
2. In this work and its predecessor, *Technics and Civilization* (New York, 1934), Mumford elaborated a scheme first proposed by the Scottish biologist and city planner, Patrick Geddes, in his *Cities in Evolution* (London, 1915).
3. Eric E. Lampard, "History of Cities in Economically Advanced Areas," *Economic Development and Cultural Change*, III (Jan. 1955), 81–136; Eugene Smolensky and Donald Ratajczak, "The Conception of Cities," *Explorations in Entrepreneurial History*, 2d Ser., II (Winter 1965), 90–131; and a useful survey of various systematic methods of urban study, Philip M. Hauser and Leo F. Schnore, *The Study of Urbanization* (New York, 1965).
4. This figure is calculated from manuscript tax lists and constables' returns. Other colonial statistics in this paper are from 1774. This size of population is of the same magnitude as

that used by Everett S. Lee, "Population," in *The Growth of Seaport Cities, 1790–1825,* ed. David T. Gilchrist (Charlottesville, Va., 1967), 28.

5. Bridenbaugh, *Cities in Revolt,* 217.

6. New York's population was 805,651, Brooklyn's 266,661, giving a combined urban population of 1,072,312. (*U. S. Eighth Census: 1860, Population,* I, xxxi–xxxii.) Baltimore was third with 212,418.

7. The 1860 and 1930 world population data are from Vladimir S. Woytinsky and Emma S. Woytinsky, *World Population and Production* (New York, 1953), 120–22. The population of all cities is according to their political boundaries, not their metropolitan regions.

8. Anne Bezanson, *Prices and Inflation during the American Revolution: Pennsylvania, 1770–1790* (Philadelphia, 1951), 129.

9. See Table 4; and Gladys L. Palmer, *Philadelphia Workers in a Changing Economy* (Philadelphia, 1956), 20–52.

10. Colin Clark, *The Conditions of Economic Progress* (2d ed., London, 1951), Chap. ix.

11. Conrad Taeuber and Irene B. Taeuber, *The Changing Population of the United States* (New York, 1958); Simon Kuznets *et al., Population Redistribution and Economic Growth, United States, 1870–1950* (3 vols., Philadelphia, 1957–64).

12. Sam Bass Warner, Jr., *Streetcar Suburbs: The Process of Growth in Boston, 1870–1900* (Cambridge, Mass., 1962), gives a detailed account of the development of this core and ring pattern in Boston; Leo F. Schnore, *The Urban Scene, Human Ecology and Demography* (New York, 1965), demonstrates three quite different patterns for race, education, and income in large American metropolitan regions, 1950–1960.

13. *Transactions of the American Medical Association,* II (1849); John H. Griscom, *The Sanitary Condition of the Laboring Population of New York* (New York, 1845).

14. Karl E. Taeuber and Alma F. Taeuber, *Negroes in Cities: Residential Segregation and Neighborhood Change* (Chicago, 1965), 43–62.

15. I have compared these Philadelphia Index of Dissimilarity values for foreign-born in 1860 with those of Boston at about the same period. The results are similar: they indicate that the Irish assimilation in Boston also took place in mixed poor neighborhoods of both foreign-born and native poor as well as in heterogeneous wards of all classes and backgrounds. The Index of Dissimilarity values for Boston (twelve wards, 1855) were: foreign-born Irish, 8.0; foreign-born Canadians, 13.9; foreign-born Germans and Dutch, 33.8. (*Census of Massachusetts: 1855* [Boston, 1856], 124–27.)

16. Students in my seminar at Washington University did some computations of the Index of Dissimilarity for 1910 and 1950 and arrived at values consistent with those given here for Philadelphia in 1930 for Baltimore, Boston, Chicago, Cincinnati, Houston, Kansas City, Los Angeles, Louisville, Manhattan and Brooklyn, St. Louis, and San Francisco. Stanley Lieberson did a careful study of ethnic group patterns in Boston, Buffalo, Chicago, Cincinnati, Cleveland, Columbus, Philadelphia, Pittsburgh, St. Louis, and Syracuse, using similar methods. His results also fit with my values for Philadelphia. (Stanley Lieberson, *Ethnic Patterns in American Cities* [New York, 1963], 209–18.)

17. The exceptions were shipyards, ropewalks, and distilleries in the city. In the country the plantation for manufacture or agriculture was the setting for group work. The only other common cases were ships and the army. (Richard B. Morris, *Government and Labor in Early America* [New York, 1946], 38–40; Carl Bridenbaugh, *The Colonial Craftsman* [New York, 1950], 126–29, 136–39, 141–43.)

18. *History of Labour in the United States,* ed. John R. Commons (4 vols., New York, 1918–35), I, 185–230.

19. It seems reasonable to estimate that conditions of work in groups prevailed in all lines of activity where the average size of the establishment was fifteen or more. (William M. Hench, *Trends in the Size of Industrial Companies in Philadelphia for 1915–1930* [Philadelphia, 1948], 7–8, 21–23; *U. S. Fourteenth Census: 1920,* IX, *Manufactures,* 1277; *U. S. Fifteenth Census: 1930, Manufactures,* III, 444, *Wholesale Distribution,* II, 1262–67; Pennsylvania Department of Labor and Industry, "Employment Fluctuations in Pennsylvania 1921–1927," *Special Bulletin 24* [Harrisburg, 1928], 30.)

20. Anne Bezanson *et al., Four Years of Labor Mobility: A Study of Labor Turnover from a Group of Selected Plants in Philadelphia, 1921–1924* (Philadelphia, 1925), 70–96.

21. A good way to get some feeling for the issues of urban work groups would be to look at the

data in *The Pittsburgh Survey*, ed. Paul U. Kellogg (6 vols., New York, 1909–14), in the light of the suggestions of Robert Blauner, *Alienation and Freedom: The Factory Worker and His Industry* (Chicago, 1964); and Marc Fried, "The Role of Work in a Mobile Society," *Planning for a Nation of Cities*, ed. Sam Bass Warner, Jr. (Cambridge, Mass., 1966), 81–104.

22. *Id., The Private City.*
23. There is a suggestive study of Manhattan in 1840 that unfortunately suffers from the incompleteness of street directory data: Allan R. Pred, *Annals of the Association of American Geographers*, LVI (June 1966), 307–38.

RURAL-URBAN AND STATUS DIFFERENCES IN INTERPERSONAL CONTACTS

Albert J. Reiss, Jr.

The basic idea of the time-budget is not very complicated. It consists of dividing up the things a person does in the 1,400 minutes he has in a day among a limited number of categories of activity: eating, sleeping, traveling, and so on. The time-budget is potentially one of our finest sources of information about the ebb and flow of activity within big cities, about differences among urban subcommunities, and about the personal impact of big changes such as the construction of major highways through residential areas. Some practical difficulties stand in the way of the widespread use of time-budgets for these purposes. Complex human activities do not fall neatly into simple categories such as "housework," "child care," "personal care," and "recreation." People neither remember the detailed sequences of activity very reliably nor record them very consistently when asked to keep current diaries. The sheer volume of information mounts up at astonishing speed: if you made a separate observation for each of 100 persons for each minute in a week, you would have just over a million observations to analyze.

Because of these and other practical obstacles, most collectors of urban time-budgets have settled for describing the gross distribution of activities (percent of time spent watching TV, at work, sleeping, and so on) for the entire population and a few subdivisions of it. Reiss' study of Nashville and its metropolitan area is one of the most informative American studies. Instead of collecting time-budgets for a random sample of the entire metropolitan population, Reiss drew six samples in the following design:

		Residence	
Status	*Urban*	*Rural nonfarm*	*Rural farm*
High	*1*	*2*	*3*
Low	*4*	*5*	*6*

The point of this division was to make sure he would have enough people in each of the categories that should have distinctly different patterns of interpersonal relations, according to a standard set of ideas about the isolation of urbanites and the impersonality of social relations in cities. Reiss classified the different kinds of people which the persons interviewed reported interacting with during a day, and counted up the total time spent alone and with each type of companion. He did find, as most of us would expect, that the high-status and nonfarm people reported a higher proportion of their total interactions with "clients" and others only distantly connected to them. But the category of persons who spent the most time alone in the day were low-status farm-dwellers. The mean minutes per day reported in contact with close relatives, intimate friends, and close associates breaks down like this:

	Residence		
Status	*Urban*	*Rural nonfarm*	*Rural farm*
High	*622*	*498*	*507*
Low	*634*	*485*	*488*

This table certainly casts doubt on the isolation and impersonality of life in the city. The rural nonfarm and farm populations hardly differ at all, but the urban population spends distinctly more of its time in close relationships. Reiss' article contains a number of other observations which are just as interesting. In general, they confirm that social relations in cities are different from social relations in small towns and on the farm—but not in the way the old notion of the impersonal city would lead us to expect.

Sociologists customarily describe the ideal type of personal contacts in cities as anonymous, segmental, and impersonal and contrast them with the intimate and personal type in rural areas.[1] A large number of studies offer general support for this description, but most give data for only a rural *or* an urban setting.[2] Comparisons between the two settings are therefore made by inferring the characteristics for one of them.

This paper reports the results of a pilot study to test several hypotheses about differences in types of interpersonal contacts among urban, rural–non-farm and rural-farm residents, the time-budget being used in gathering data. Sorokin and Zimmerman, who provide the most precise statement of supposed differences in the quality and quantity of social contact or interaction of rural and urban residents,[3] state a single hypothesis as to quantitative aspects: "the number of contacts per

Reprinted by permission of the author and publisher, the University of Chicago Press, from "Rural-Urban and Status Differences in Interpersonal Contacts" by Albert J. Reiss, Jr., *American Journal of Sociology*, 65 (1959), pp. 182–195. Copyright © University of Chicago, 1959. Footnotes renumbered.

individual in a given unit of time is greater in urban than rural life." Qualitative differences are described in five hypotheses:

1. The area of the contact system of a member of a rural community, as well as that of the rural community as a whole, is spatially more narrow and limited than the area of a member of an urban community and of the urban community as a whole.

2. . . . Face to face relations occupy a less [*sic*] proportion of the whole interaction system of an urbanite than of a rural individual.

3. . . . The interaction system of an urbanite is woven, to a greater proportion than in the case of a rural individual, out of impersonal and to a less degree out of personal relations.

4. . . . In the totality of relations which compose the network of the interaction system of an urban individual, the part composed of casual, superficial and short-lived relations, in contrast to permanent, strong, and durable relations, occupies a much more conspicuous place than in the interaction system of a rural dweller.

5. . . . The relations are more flexible, less durable, and more impersonal; the whole network of this system of interaction is to be marked by greater complexity, greater plasticity, differentiation, manifoldness, and, at the same time by greater superficiality, "standardization," and mechanization than the network of the interaction system of a rural dweller.

The data from this pilot study permit only a partial test of the first four hypotheses. A sixth hypothesis, which follows from several of the postulates underlying these hypotheses, is also tested. Since agricultural work is less often organized on the basis of personal contacts than is non-agricultural and since in rural areas contacts are relatively fewer in frequency than in non-rural, the rural person is expected to spend a greater part of his time in isolation.

A growing body of evidence shows that the quantity and quality of social interaction is a function of socio-economic status, as well as of residential location. The major hypothesis advanced in sociological literature is that the amount of impersonal contact varies directly with socio-economic status. A corollary is that formal group participation varies more or less directly with socio-economic status, while informal varies inversely among the urban.[4] This paper also examines status, within each residential category, as a further test of the hypotheses.

Residents of high and low socio-economic status classified as rural-farm (RF), rural—non-farm (RNF), and urban residential, comprise the six populations.[5] They were not selected by uniform sampling criteria.

The urban population of the Nashville, Tennessee, Standard Metropolitan Area (SMA) was classified into white-collar and manual-worker census tracts and four white-collar and three manual-worker tracts were randomly selected. A 25 per cent random sample of dwelling units was selected in each of these tracts and a respondent twenty years old and over was interviewed. The RNF and RF respondents were selected from a county south of the Nashville SMA. Two village communities located at maximum distance from the city center were selected, the rural area within a four-mile radius of them, and the major traffic artery from the central city to the areas. A respondent twenty years old or over in every fourth dwelling unit with a male head of household was then interviewed. The place of work of RNF respondents was not held constant. Some worked in the SMA, while others were employed in the villages or in rural locations, such as motel and dam sites, and so on. The population for which comparisons are made is white married males, age twenty to sixty-five, with a regular full-time job. These criteria were imposed to eliminate known sources of variation by sex, marital status, age, and employment status.

TIME-BUDGETS

The allocation of an individual's time during a single day was chosen as the measure of the amount and kind of personal contact. A budget of time was obtained for the nearest previous workday and the last full day off. This paper reports the data for only the workday.

The time-budget opened with the statement: "Now, we would like to know how you spent your time yesterday. We want to know just how much time you spent doing different things during the day and whom you spent it with. Suppose we begin with the time you got up yesterday: what time did you get up?" This was followed by, "What did you do when you first got up? Did you spend the time with anyone, or were you more or less alone? Whom were you with? and, how close are they to you?" Each new activity or block of time was similarly explored until the person said he went to sleep. Interviewers were specifically instructed to get the information so that it could be coded into one of the following mutually exclusive categories:

1. *Intimate kinship,* such as nuclear family members and extended kin members.
2. *Close intimate friends,* friends defined as "very close," "my best friend," etc.
3. *Close associate or client,* a close friend deriving from a work context, whether or not actually seen at work.
4. *Good friend,* a friend defined as "close," "just a good friend," etc.
5. *Distant associate or casual acquaintance,* either a fellow worker who is not defined as a friend or a person with whom one has a "speaking acquaintance."
6. *Cordial recognition,* defined as a person whom one recognizes in address, or "just someone to whom I say, 'hello.' "
7. *Pure client,* defined as a person whom one doesn't know personally, but one with whom contact is made, or with whom interaction takes place in a client relationship.

For analytical purposes, Nos. 1–4 are defined as "primary contacts"; Nos. 5–7 as "secondary contacts"; Nos. 6 and 7 as "impersonal contacts." As the total time awake was obtained, most persons also had some time with "no personal contact."

Part of the daily activity was also allocated to one of three contexts: time spent at work on a job; time spent in exposure to mass media; and time spent where secondary contacts are probable. Persons need not have experienced any personal contact to be coded active in that situation. Classification into these three situations is independent of the classification for interpersonal contacts. The same period of time, therefore, may be coded in both the contact and the situation class.

There are, of course, many problems of classification in allocating time to social situations and types of contact. Several types of contact may occur at a single time, for example, or the situation may include more than one type of activity. This problem was met by asking each respondent to allocate the time among the various types of persons with whom contemporaneous contact was made. It is clear from the time-budgets that urban dwellers spend more time in situations with more than one type of contact than do rural dwellers; the criterion adopted here masks this difference. Similarly, social contact among persons with whom the most intimate relationships are maintained may vary from mingling to copulation. In a strict sense, this study simply allocates daily contact time to persons with whom one has a particular *qualitative* relationship and to types of social situations, given certain *structural* characteristics. The quality and content of the interaction are not usually known.[6]

The time at which a time-budget is obtained affects the allocation of daily time. Seasonal and weekly differences in work influence both the amount of time spent at it, the situation, and the kind of daily contacts. The allocation of time also varies for individual households, owing to such circumstances as the temporary presence of guests or the temporary absence of a member. Such shifts in the daily round cannot be considered atypical and deserve analysis in themselves. They are not controlled in this study, except insofar as the interviewing of all urban respondents in April or May and of all RNF and RF respondents in May or in July allows gross seasonal variations.

Structural characteristics of the society likewise affect the social allocation of time. Age, sex, marital and occupational status are roughly controlled in this study either by selection of respondents or by statistical procedure. Others, such as the size of the family, the presence of preschool children, religious affiliation, the availability of mass media, and type of work are not controlled. A partial listing of some forty structural correlates of time-allocation was made for this study. Obviously, it would take simultaneous study of a very large population of respondents to control variation from all these sources.

TESTING PROCEDURES

The time-budget was recorded in minutes for the waking hours of the day. Respondents erred sometimes in the allocation of minutes spent in a particular activity or relationship, since each was asked to recall the previous day. The error is readily apparent in their frequent "rounding" of numbers of minutes to figures ending in 0 and 5. The allocation of time is perhaps more reliable for activities represented in the "daily round" than for others. Pretests showed that the procedure of having respondents "follow the clock" with their report of daily activity provides a more reliable estimate of time than is obtained if the respondent is simply asked to "recall his day."

The mean and standard deviation were chosen as the measures of central tendency and dispersion for each group, and the null hypothesis of differences in means and variances was tested. The comparison of variances of rural and urban residential contexts is open to question on the grounds that one might logically expect greater variation within urban than rural contexts, since the urban is more heterogeneous in occupational composition. Ideally, occupational composition should be more satisfactorily controlled in comparisons than it is in this study, but our sample size does not permit a more detailed occupational classification. The difference between means was tested by the conventional T-test, which assumes that the populations do not differ significantly with respect to their variances. When the variances differed significantly, unless n_1 was equal to n_2, the standard error of the difference between means was calculated by using the estimates of the two population variances rather than a common estimate of the population variances. A two-tailed test of significance was used only when direction was not predicted.

There are 225 comparisons of types of interpersonal contact and contact situation for high- and low-status urban RNF and RF categories in Tables 2 and 4 involving tests of significance for proportions, for means, and for variances. For purposes of testing the hypotheses in this study, however, attention is directed to the *pattern* of significant differences among the comparisons by residence and status for a type of interpersonal contact or contact situation rather than on each significant comparison.

Tables 1–4 in this paper provide data and statistical tests for fifteen residential area–status group comparisons, but the tests of particular hypotheses do not refer to all comparisons. Zero-order comparisons of either status or residential categories with respect to type of interpersonal contact or situation can be made by recombining information in the tables.

The present study relies solely on a cross-section comparison to test the hypotheses, and historical inferences, therefore, should be drawn only with extreme caution. Conclusions from a comparison of an urban community of today with an ideal typical description of a rural or urban community of a century ago may be highly misleading. Differences in personal contacts among urbanites of one hundred years ago and today could be greater, in fact, than the difference between residents of rural and urban areas at either time, for variation over time in some types of contact may be greater than that between categories at a particular time.

Sorokin and Zimmerman's first hypothesis states that the urban individual and the urban area have a more extensive spatial contact system than do rural persons and rural areas. The distance between workplace and residence is one rough measure, assuming that the greater the distance between the two, the greater the territory over which contact obtains. Using this rough measure of spatial contact, the three residential settings are ranked thus: RNF, urban, and RF; and the hypothesis is not accepted. It seems likely that urban inhabitants may have a larger spatial area of contact if all modes of communication are mapped in territorial space. If this is true, then we might say that city people spread their daily symbolic contacts but not their direct physical contacts over a larger territory than do RNF inhabitants.

If we postulate that contacts with mass media are a measure of an extensive spatial contact system, we have a second test of the hypothesis. Every household in the study had either a radio or a television set and often a telephone and a daily newspaper. Every male, therefore, was potentially exposed to the mass media. The data show a higher proportion of urban than of RNF or RF males exposed to mass-media situations, irrespective of status. Mean exposure time was significantly greater for urban males than for RF males or RNF males of low status. But there are no significant differences by status either in the proportion of males who spend some time in daily contact with mass media or in mean amount of contact with media within the RNF and RF residence categories (see Tables 1–4). This result is consistent with the expectation that urban persons would have a greater range of contact than rural persons, except that RNF males of high status are more like urban than rural males in their exposure time to mass media.

Significantly more of the urban and RNF than RF males, regardless of status, had some exposure to secondary situations (line 16 in Tables 1 and 2). Urban and RNF males, likewise, have a higher mean exposure and variance in exposure to secondary situations than do RF males, but no significant differences of this kind are found between urban and RNF males (line 16, Tables 3 and 4). If we postulate

TABLE 1
Per Cent Reporting Some Workday Contact or Situations,
by Residence and Status

Type of Interpersonal Contact or Contact Situation	Urban		RNF		RF	
	High	Low	High	Low	High	Low
No. of cases	176	75	27	24	28	21
Per cent reporting any contact with:						
1. Intimate kinship	97	99	90	100	100	100
2. Close intimate friend	33	39	80	42	36	24
3. Close associate or client	71	59	25	13	14	a
4. Good friend	32	37	30	38	18	10
5. Distant associate or client	43	44	65	38	46	33
6. Cordial recognition	10	12	a	4	4	a
7. Pure client	45	33	40	29	4	19
Per cent reporting workday time in:						
8. No interpersonal contact	86	81	90	92	82	71
9. Primary contact (1–4)	100	100	100	100	100	100
10. Secondary contact (5–7)	76	68	95	58	50	43
11. All impersonal contact (6–7)	51	41	40	33	7	19
12. All interpersonal contact (1–7)	100	100	100	100	100	100
13. Total waking time	100	100	100	100	100	100
Per cent of total waking time in:						
14. Job situations	100	100	100	100	100	100
15. Mass-media situations	87	88	55	45	61	53
16. Secondary situations	95	87	90	79	36	24

[a]No time reported for any respondent.

TABLE 2

Significant Residence and Status Group Differences in Proportions of Respondents Reporting Contact for Types of Interpersonal Contacts and Situations (P Values)[a]

Type of Interpersonal Contact or Contact Situations	Urban High Status versus					Urban Low Status versus				RNF High Status versus			RNF Low Status versus		RF High Status versus
	Urban low	RNF high	RNF low	RF high	RF low	RNF high	RNF low	RF high	RF low	RNF low	RF high	RF low	RF high	RF low	RF low
1. Intimate kin	−	+	−	−	−	+	−	−	−	+[c]	−	−	−	=	=
2. Close intimate friend	−	−[b]	−	−	+	−[b]	−	+	+[b]	+[b]	+	+[b]	+	+	+
3. Close associate or client	+	+[b]	+[b]	+[b]	+[c]	+[b]	+[b]	+[b]	+[b]	+	+	+[b]	−	+[c]	+[c]
4. Good friend	−	+	−	+	+[c]	+	−	+	+[c]	−	+	+[b]	+	+	+
5. Distant associate or client	−	−	+	−	+	+[b]	+	−	+[b]	+	+	+[b]	−	+	+
6. Cordial recognition	−	+[b]	+	+[b]	+[c]	+	+	+[b]	+[b]	−	−	=	+[c]	+	+
7. Pure client	+	+	+	+[c]	+[c]	+	+	+	+	−	+[b]	+	+[c]	+	−
8. No interpersonal contact	+	−	−	−	−	−	−	−	−	−	+	+	+	+	+
9. Primary contact (1–4)	=	=	=	=	=	=	=	=	=	+	−[b]	−[b]	=	=	=
10. Secondary contact (5–7)	+	−[c]	+	+[c]	+[b]	−[b]	+	+	+[c]	+[b]	+[b]	+[b]	+	+	+
11. All impersonal contacts (6–7)	+	+	+	+[c]	+[b]	+	+	+[b]	+[c]	+	+[c]	+	+[c]	+	−
12. All interpersonal contacts (1–7)	=	=	=	=	=	=	=	=	=	=	=	=	=	=	=
13. Total time awake (1–8)	=	=	=	=	=	=	=	=	=	=	=	=	+[c]	=	=
14. Total time in job situation	=	=	=	=	=	=	=	=	=	=	=	=	=	=	=
15. Total time in mass-media situations	−	+[b]	+[c]	+[b]	+[b]	+[c]	+	+[c]	+[b]	−	+	+	−	−	=
16. Total time in secondary situations	+	+	+[c]	+[b]	+[b]	+	+[b]	+[b]	+[b]	+	+[b]	+[b]	+[b]	+[b]	+

[a] The significance of the difference between proportions was determined from nomographs (Joseph Lubin, "Nomographs for Determining the Significance of the Differences between the Frequencies of Events in Two Contrasted Series or Groups," *Journal of the American Statistical Association*, XXXIV (September, 1939), 540–41. The nomographs report P levels for only a critical ratio of 2 (0.0455) and of 3 (0.0027); levels are reported as 0.05 and 0.003, respectively, in the body of the table. The +, −, and = signs refer to the direction of the difference in each comparison.

[b] 0.003 level of significance.

[c] 0.05 level of significance.

TABLE 3
Mean and Standard Deviation of Time Spent in Specified Types of Interpersonal Contact Situations by Residence and Status

Type of Interpersonal Contact or Contact Situation	Means (in minutes)						Standard Deviations (in minutes)					
	Urban		RNF		RF		Urban		RNF		RF	
	High	Low	High	Low	High	Low	High	Low	High	Low	High	Low
1. Intimate kinship	322	355	282	285	334	401	125	102	176	158	222	255
2. Close intimate friend	43	35	117	93	72	79	108	86	134	140	141	195
3. Close associate or client	223	191	54	21	33	a	215	224	125	66	109	a
4. Good friend	34	54	51	89	64	8	82	114	112	155	173	25
5. Distant associate or client	113	134	215	140	155	123	181	193	239	220	204	201
6. Cordial recognition	8	20	a	27	2	a	31	81	a	120	11	a
7. Pure client	111	48	87	53	1	7	190	117	135	89	4	16
8. No interpersonal contact	119	133	181	241	297	311	140	167	168	234	286	291
9. Primary contact (1–4)	622	634	498	485	507	488	256	251	226	266	281	271
10. Secondary contact (5–7)	233	202	308	222	158	130	225	219	205	222	207	202
11. All impersonal contact (6–7)	120	68	87	81	3	7	193	140	135	139	12	16
12. All interpersonal contact (1–7)	855	836	806	707	665	618	156	181	182	244	291	293
13. Total time awake	974	968	985	948	962	928	92	76	64	76	86	70
14. Total time in job situations	498	491	539	514	641	640	131	77	155	98	138	142
15. Total time in mass media situations	121	125	71	70	62	44	85	89	111	87	65	53
16. Total time in secondary situations	367	324	378	269	71	20	197	242	227	259	111	48

[a] No time reported for any respondent.

TABLE 4
Significant Residence and Status Group Differences in Interpersonal Contacts and Situations (*P* Values)[a]

Type of Interpersonal Contact or Situation	Urban High Status versus					Urban Low Status versus				RNF High Status versus			Low Status versus		RF High Status versus
	Urban low	RNF high	RNF low	RF high	RF low	RNF high	RNF low	RF high	RF low	RNF low	RF high	RF low	RF high	RF low	RF low
1. Intimate kinship	−	+	+	(−)	(−)	(+)	(+)	(−)	(−)	(−)	−	−	−	−	−
2. Close intimate friend	(+)	−b	−	−	(−)	−b	(−)	(−)	(−)	+	+	−	+	+	−
3. Close associate or client	+	(+)c	(+)c	d	d	(+)c	(+)c	(−)	d	+	+	a	−	d	d
4. Good friend	(−)	−b	−	(−)	(+)b	−	−	(−)	(+)b	+	−	(+)	+	(+)b	(+)
5. Distant associate or client	−	d	−	d	+	−	−	+	+	+	+	+	+	+	d
6. Cordial recognition	(−)	d	(−)	(−)	d	−	(+)	(+)	d	d	+	d	d	d	d
7. Pure client	(+)b	+	(+)b	(+)c	(+)c	−	(+)b	(+)b	(+)b	+	(+)b	(+)b	(+)b	(+)b	−
8. No interpersonal contact	+	−	(−)b	(−)b	(−)b	−	(−)b	(−)b	(−)b	−	(−)	(−)c	−	(−)c	−
9. All primary contact (1–4)	+	+b	+b	+b	+b	−b	+b	+b	+b	+	+	+b	−	−	+
10. All secondary contact (5–7)	+	−	+	+	+	−	+	+	+	+	+b	+b	+	+	+
11. All impersonal contact (6–7)	(+)b	+	+	(+)c	(+)b	−	(+)c	(+)b	(+)b	+	(+)b	(+)b	(+)b	(+)b	−
12. All interpersonal contact (1–7)	+	−	(+)	(+)b	(+)b	+b	(+)b	(+)b	(+)b	+	+b	+b	+	+	+
13. Total time awake (1–8)	+	−	+	+	+b	+	+	+b	+b	+	+b	+b	+	+	+
14. Total time in job situation	(+)	−	−	−c	−c	−	−	−c	−c	+	−b	−b	−c	−b	+
15. Total time in mass media situations	−	+	+b	+c	(+)c	+b	+c	(+)c	(+)c	+	(+)	(+)	+	+	+
16. Total time in secondary situations	+	+	+	(+)c	(+)c	+	(+)c	(+)c	(+)c	+	(+)c	(+)c	(+)c	(+)c	(+)

[a] The + and − signs refer to the direction of the difference in each comparison. Parentheses indicate that the variances differ significantly at the 0.02 level.
[b] Means differ significantly at the 0.05 level.
[c] Means differ significantly at the 0.001 level.
[d] No time is reported for any respondent in at least one of the groups; the mean difference, therefore, is not calculated.

that secondary contacts are generally spatially more diffuse than primary ones—a questionable postulate—it appears that non-agricultural workers have a more extensive spatial contact system than do those in agriculture.

These tests of our first hypothesis suggest that residential setting may be less important than occupational situs in determining the range of social contact. Men with nonagricultural employment, even when they reside in village or open country, more often are exposed to secondary contact situations than are males in agriculture. There are probably two main reasons for this: the nature of their job situations and their movement to and from places of work.

Primary social relations are said to be involved in a smaller proportion of the total interaction system of an urban than of a rural individual. There are a number of ways to test this second hypothesis, and much depends upon the definition of an "indirect interaction system" as part of the total system of social interaction. Sorokin and Zimmerman argue, by deduction, that the interaction system of an urbanite consists of a larger network of indirect contacts—persons whom one never sees—than does that of the typical rural person; hence the actual face-to-face, or primary, relations of an urbanite are a smaller proportion of the total interaction system. No data are available on the amount of indirect interaction contacts, since no satisfactory operational definition of them was developed when the study was designed. It is difficult to say, for example, whether a rural dweller's indirect contact with a state or federal authority is greater or less than that of an urban resident, in view of agricultural subsidies, flood-control programs, and the like. The tests of the hypothesis, therefore, were limited to measures based on the actual amount of time spent in interaction.

All the respondents had some primary contact on the workday as shown by line 9 of Tables 1 and 2. This follows from the fact that all respondents were married males. While all men had some exposure to primary contacts during the day, the average urban male reported a significantly greater number of minutes of primary contact than did the average RNF or RF person, regardless of status (see Tables 3 and 4). There are no significant differences between RNF and RF males in total time spent in primary contacts. Table 4 also shows that there are no significant differences between any of the groups in variances in amount of daily primary contacts, despite differences in mean contact. Urban males, on the whole, exhibited no greater variability in this respect than did the RNF or RF. On the average, an urban employed, married male spends over 10 hours a day in primary interaction as compared with, roughly, 8 hours for the low-status RNF or RF male. Urban males, therefore, spend more actual time in primary contacts than do the RNF or RF. But urban males also spend more time on *all* personal contacts than do the low-status RNF and all RF. If one computes a ratio of the average time in primary contact to the average time in all personal contact (ratio of line 9 to line 12 in Table 3) for each residence-status group, the ratios for high- and low-status groups, respectively, are 0.73 and 0.76 for urban, 0.62 and 0.68 for RNF, and 0.76 and 0.79 for RF males. The differences are not particularly large. Certainly, the average urban male does not spend considerably less of his total time in interaction in primary contacts than does the average rural male. It appears that RNF males spend the least part of the total time in interaction in primary contacts, but this difference cannot be attributed to any single type of primary contact.

The third hypothesis—that the interaction system of the urban as compared with the rural individual is, to a greater degree, made up of impersonal relations—is a corollary of hypothesis 2. The types of impersonal relations defined for this study were those of cordial recognition and pure-client relations. The major finding is that urban and RNF males have a higher average amount of impersonal contact than do RF males (line 11, Tables 3 and 4). Only about one-tenth or fewer of the men in any residential setting or status group had contacts of cordial recognition on their workday, as Table 1 shows. It is not surprising, therefore, that there are no sizable significant differences in mean duration of contact in cordial relationships.

The pure-client relationship, however, is clearly not rural. The RF males have pure-client contacts much less often than do urban and RNF males, although the results are not statistically significant for all status categories (line 7 of Table 2). A separate tabulation also shows that no RF male had a pure-client relationship on the job, in contrast to at least two-fifths of the high-status and one-fifth of the low-status urban and RNF males. Urban and RNF males, regardless of status, have a significantly higher mean duration of pure-client contacts than do RF males (line 7 of Tables 3 and 4). The high-status urban male, as expected, has the greatest average contact in a client role, averaging almost 2 hours a day. This average, in fact, is significantly and appreciably above that of all categories except RNF persons of high status. There is also a significantly higher variance for pure-client contacts for urban and RNF than for RF males. High-status urban and RNF males, in fact, tend to have significantly greater variance in pure-client contacts than do the other residence-status groups, although the comparisons are not always statistically significant (line 7 of Tables 3 and 4). This apparently higher variance for high-status urban and RNF males is probably accounted for largely by differences in occupational role composition and job context. Some white-collar jobs—particularly professional and sales occupations—require almost exclusive contact with clients, while others require little, if any.

Sorokin and Zimmerman's fourth hypothesis also is closely related to the second and third hypotheses: that casual, superficial, and short-lived relationships comprise a greater proportion of the total of interaction relations than do the permanent, strong, and durable relationships. Lines 1–7 in all the tables provide comparisons for four types of primary and three types of secondary relationships which permit a partial test; they lend only partial support to it. RF males may have a somewhat greater proportion of their total contact in a primary interaction relationship than RNF males and perhaps urban males of high status, but the differences are small and certainly do not warrant a conclusion that the hypothesis is sustained. The findings on amount of time actually spent in primary and secondary situations tend to support the hypothesis. Urbanites increase their primary contact time over that of their rural counterparts by having primary contacts at their work—an opportunity usually denied to rural males on small farms. Moreover, urban males make more personal contacts of the distinctly impersonal type—the pure-client relationship—than do the rural. These two types of relationships, then, are the major differentia. Yet, lest these differences be interpreted out of context, it must be remembered that the average urban person of high status—the extreme type—spends less than 2 hours a day in a pure-client relationship and only about 4 hours in all secondary contacts, while he spends over 10 hours in all types of primary interaction. His interaction time, therefore, is spent predominantly in primary relationships. These two types of relationships also appear clearly to reflect differences in opportunity for contact at work. Both the differences in primary contact with associates or clients and in the secondary pure-client type occur primarily at work. Non-agricultural work often provides opportunities for both types of contact—a primary friendship relation with a fellow or co-worker at the same or adjacent status levels and a secondary relationship with a member of the public or a client.

The final hypothesis is that the RF male spends a greater part of his waking time without any personal contact, given less opportunity for group contact in both work and non-work situations. There are no significant residence differences in the percentage of persons who spent some time in isolation (line 8 of Tables 1 and 2); however, RF males spend significantly more time in isolation and show greater variance than do urban (but not RNF) males, regardless of status (line 8, Tables 3 and 4).

The mean time spent in social isolation by the several residence-status groups can be expressed as a proportion of the mean time awake. These proportions, for high and low status, respectively, are 12.2 and 13.6 for urban, 18.4 and 25.4 for RNF, and 30.9 and 32.5 for RF males. It is readily seen that the average RF employed married male spends about a third of his day without any personal contact, as compared with only one-seventh of the waking time of urban employed married males, regardless of status; the RNF proportions are in between. It may be true that for single persons the urban environment is more conducive to living in almost complete isolation from social contact, but the typical urban married male in this study is less likely to spend part of his day isolated from social contact than is the typical RF married male. The average urban married male has more of primary contact and less of isolation than does the average married RNF or RF. The variance in amount of time spent without personal contact also is greater for RF than for urban married males. This at least suggests that the extremes of isolation (other than with intimate kin) are approached more closely by the RF than by the urban married male.

The modern period of Western society is often referred to as an age of potential leisure. This is attributed to the historical change in the amount of time spent at work by both agricultural and non-agricultural workers. The average time spent on the job was significantly longer for RF males than for RNF or urban males, regardless of status (line 14 of Tables 3 and 4). The average agricultural worker spent between 8 and 9 hours a day at work. The fact that the lowest variance for time spent on the job (line 14, Table 4) occurs for the non-agricultural worker of low status follows from the prevalence of a workday and week standardized by contract. The variance in length of workday for urban workers of low status, in fact, is significantly below that of urban and RNF workers of high status and all RF workers.

The reduction in working hours provides considerable opportunity for persons to divide their waking hours among other activities (line 13 of Tables 3 and 4). There are a few significant differences between residence-status groups in the average duration of waking hours and no significant differences in variance. The mean waking interval is a little over 16 hours a day, with a standard deviation of 60–90 minutes, except for low-status RF persons. If one takes as a very crude measure of potential leisure the ratio of working hours to total hours awake, almost half the waking time of urban and RNF married males is spent outside the work context. These ratios for high- and low-status groups, respectively, are 51 and 51 for urban, 55 and 54 for RNF, and 67 and 69 for RF males. By contrast, roughly two-thirds of the waking time of RF persons is spent at work. Since, with the exception of RF persons of low status, there are no significant differences in total waking hours (and this is not enough to account for the observed differences), it is clear that the non-agricultural worker has a longer potential time for leisure than does the agricultural worker, at least on the workday.

Some attention was given to status differences in types of contact in referring to a combined residential area–status group difference. The status differentials in interpersonal contact are now examined within each of the three residential areas, though it is recognized that each test is not independent of the others in a sampling sense.

First of all, there are few status differences by residence in the proportion reporting some daily contact or in mean time spent in the several types of personal contact or contact situations (Tables 1–4). None of these status differences is significant in more than one of the three residential contexts. Urban groups of high and low status, in fact, show no significant differences in exposure to types of contact, and there are no significant differences in average time spent in personal contacts or contact situations between RNF or RF males of high and low status. Among urban inhabitants, males of high status have a greater mean contact in a pure-client relationship, and consequently in all impersonal contacts, than do urban males of low status. The same status differential is observed for RNF males, but it is not statistically significant. As noted, this probably is largely a consequence of differences in exposure to clients when at work.

There are somewhat more significant differences between high- and low-status groups in variances of time spent in personal contact and contact situations, even though there are few significant differences between them in average time spent in types of contact. None of the differences is observed in all residential settings, however.

Urban males of high status have a greater variance in contact with close intimate friends than do those of low status, but the latter have a greater variance in contact with good friends than do those of high status. The status difference in variance for all friendship contacts therefore disappears. High-status RF males, in contrast to high-status urban males, have a greater variance for contact with good friends than do those of low status; but the reverse, although not significant, is found for close intimate friends among RF males, so that the status difference in variance for all friendships also disappears for RF males. The apparent pattern then seems to be one where high-status urban and low-status RF males show higher variance for contacts with good friends. This difference could well be a function of how high- and low-status males define "good" as compared with "close" friends— the distinction is difficult, in any case.

Urban males of high status have substantially greater variance in all impersonal contacts than do males of low status, but the difference is accounted for by the fact that high-status males have a greater variance in pure-client contacts, since low-status males have a substantially greater variance in contact in patterns of cordial recognition. Urban males of high status also show greater variance in the total time on their job than do those of low status. Both these patterns occur for

RNF males, although they are not statistically significant. Hence white-collar workers are probably less homogeneous in their personal relations than are manual workers (in the non-agricultural situs).

The failure to reject the major null hypothesis about status differentials in interpersonal contact or in exposure to types of situation, independent of residence, is a surprising one, given both a general expectation of class differentials and the existing literature on them.

Only a few of the many possible reasons for this failure are mentioned here. The first is that differences in measurement account for the difference in conclusions. Most previous studies use some attribute of persons, such as their membership in certain groups, or a characteristic of their behavior, such as number of personal visits or meetings attended, as measures of personal contact and participation, and they also focus more on organizational structure. The present study measures times spent by the individual in a type of contact or situation. These are different dimensions of behavior. The time spent in many activities can be a negligible proportion of one's day: for example, the time spent in voluntary associations or in formal community organizations usually occupies only a very small proportion of a man's weekly, much less daily, time.

A second explanation is that our data are for very small samples, so that real, but small, differences may go undetected. Moreover, we examined only employed married males aged twenty to sixty-five; other age-sex—marital-status groups may show these expected differences. If this is the case, generalizations must be appropriately qualified. Fourth, the selection of our population in a southern locale may account for some differences, since it might be argued that the "more rural South" places high emphasis on primary relationships. This, conceivably, could affect the absolute allocation of time to a particular type of contact; but just how such an argument would apply to a failure to secure relative differences in residence-status comparisons is far from clear. Fifth, the limitation of our data to a single workday may limit our conclusion—the day-off could show a quite different pattern, although preliminary analysis suggests that this is not the case. Furthermore, a record of activity over an extended period might conceivably confirm the differences found in other studies in our population. Many previous studies measure contact for weekly, monthly, and even longer intervals. Generally, the longer the time, however, the less time "other-than-daily contact" will occupy of a person's total interaction time. A once-a-week contact with a friend, on the average, should account for less of the total weekly time than a daily contact, unless the time spent in the weekly contact is considerably longer. Finally, our measure of status is a simple dichotomy of white-collar and manual-worker status groups. Such a gross distinction may mask true differences in status. On the other hand, the more status is refined in terms of specific operational indicators such as occupation, the more it may reflect non-status differences in the indicator.

The major findings with respect to status differences in types of interpersonal contact and exposure to contact situations are as follows:

1. There are no significant status differences in the proportion of respondents who had some contact or exposure, mean amount of contact or exposure, or variance in contact or exposure in types of interpersonal contact or time spent in contact, independent of residence.

2. When only the non-agricultural residential settings are considered (urban and RNF), there similarly are no clear-cut significant differences in the proportion with contact, mean amount, and variance in interpersonal contact or exposure to contact situations. High-status urban and RNF males both may have a greater mean contact and variance in a pure-client relationship and in total time in job situations than do low-status ones. These differences may be a function of only some white-collar jobs, however.

With respect to residence differences in exposure to different types of contact situations the major findings are as follows:

1. A higher proportion of urban employed married males than of RNF or RF males, regardless of social status, was exposed to mass media on their workday, and with greater mean exposure time.

2. Significantly more of the urban and RNF males (non-agricultural workers) than of RF males, regardless of social status, had some exposure to secondary situations, and they likewise had both higher mean exposure and variance in exposure to secondary situations.

3. There are no significant differences by residence in the proportion of persons who spent some time in isolation. But all RF males, regardless of status, spend significantly more time in isolation than do urban males, and they have a significantly greater variance in isolation as well.

4. The average time spent on the job was significantly greater for RF than for RNF or urban males, regardless of status.

Differences in types of interpersonal contacts for residential settings may be summarized as follows:

1. While almost all men had some exposure to primary contacts during the workday, the average urban employed male had a significantly greater average time in primary contact than did his RNF or RF counterpart, regardless of status. There was no such significant difference between RNF and RF males. Primary contact time *may* occupy a somewhat smaller proportion of the total interaction time for urban and RNF males than it does for RF males.

2. Urban males do not show a greater amount of primary contact in all specific types of primary contacts, however. There is almost no significant variation in average daily contact with intimate kin and association with close intimate friends by residence. The major differentiating type is contact with a work associate or client. A significantly larger proportion of the urban than of the RNF or RF males, regardless of status, had contact with a close work associate or client on their workday, and they spent a greater average amount of their daily time in such contacts.

3. Urban and RNF males are more likely to have a greater mean amount of impersonal contact on their workday than are RF males. This impersonal contact consists largely of contact in the client-role relationship.

Sociologists who speculate about the findings of this paper may be tempted to use the findings to show that the differences between residential groups in the United States have almost disappeared, but, of course, the study was not designed to demonstrate this, since no comparative historical data are available. Others may use them to show that the ideal typical description of the decline of the kinship relationship in urban areas has been exaggerated, much as Axelrod has done in a recent paper.[7] This interpretation is similarly suspect, inasmuch as no bench-mark data are available for temporal comparison.

For those inclined to speculate about the theoretical implications of the findings, two conclusions appear of special relevance. The first is that the agricultural–non-agricultural situs distinction appears to discriminate better with respect to differences in personal contact than does the type of residential settlement. This observation is in keeping with that made by Sorokin and Zimmerman about thirty years ago:

> . . . Rural sociology is in the first place a sociology of an occupation group, namely the sociology of the agricultural *occupation*. Such is the first and fundamental criterion of differences between the rural and other, particularly urban, communities. From it follow a series of other differences between the rural and the urban communities, most of which are causally connected with the above difference in occupation.[8]

The second observation is that the theoretical constructs conventionally employed to type urban and rural interpersonal relations and contexts do not lend themselves too readily to research. And, when they are translated into operational terms, the findings apparently vary for subclasses of a general construct. Thus, for example, only the "pure-client" relationship appears to have much discriminatory power in the "secondary" or "impersonal" relations construct. It is not maintained here that these operational constructs are the most satisfactory for theory—they probably are not—but rather that more attention must be given to the analytical discrimination of constructs in theoretically based research investigations on differences in interpersonal contacts or relationships.

NOTES

1. The statement by Georg Simmel generally serves as a prototype; cf. his "The Metropolis and Mental Life," trans. in Kurt H. Wolff, *The Sociology of Georg Simmel* (Glencoe, Ill.: Free Press, 1950).
2. For a fairly complete summary of the early literature see P. A. Sorokin and C. C. Zimmerman, *Principles of Rural-urban Sociology* (New York: Henry Holt & Co., 1929), and P. A. Sorokin and Clarence Q. Berger, *Time-Budgets of Human Behavior* (Cambridge: Harvard University Press, 1938).
3. Sorokin and Zimmerman, *op. cit.*, pp. 48–58, 49, 51–54.
4. Among the most recent representative urban studies in this area, pertinent are Morris Axelrod, "Urban Structure and Urban Participation," *American Sociological Review,* XXI (February, 1956), 13–18, and Wendell Bell and Maryanne T. Force, "Urban Neighborhood Types and Participation in Formal Associations," *American, Sociological Review,* XXI (February, 1956), 25–34. This relationship, commonly observed in urban areas, is not always verified in rural community studies; for example: "The white-collar groups had the highest scores for all three types of participation, although their superiority was less marked for informal than for formal and semiformal participation" (Otis Dudley Duncan and Jay W. Artis, *Social Stratification in a Pennsylvania Rural Community* [Pennsylvania State College School of Agriculture, AES Bull. 543 (1951)], p. 38).
5. Among urban and RNF males, professional, technical, and kindred workers; proprietors, managers, and officials; sales workers; and clerical and kindred workers are the white-

collar, non-agricultural occupations designated as "high status." All other occupations are "low status." Among RF males, all farm proprietors and managers are designated "high status"; all tenants, sharecroppers, and laborers "low status."

6. The conclusions of this study are limited by the selection of the particular population and by the criteria of allocating time among types of contact and types of situations. Alternative measures of contact or measures of interaction might easily result in different conclusions. Suppose, for example, that one knew the total number of persons seen (or met) during a day; urban persons probably have more such contacts in a day. Or suppose that the urban person works with a close friend more often than does a rural person; this does not preclude his also having a large number of indirect social contacts at work or contacts with persons he never even sees. While not all forms of social contact which are said to discriminate among persons in different environments are analyzed here, it should be clear that concepts like impersonal and personal contacts or indirect and direct contacts permit meaningful comparisons only if their operational referents are specified.

7. *Op. cit.*, pp. 17–18.
8. *Op. cit.*, p. 16.

MIGRATION TO AMERICAN CITIES

Charles Tilly

This book emphasizes the role of migration in the building of an urban world. Migration spells change for the people moving and change for the city as a whole; it marks every aspect of the city's operation. The next three articles consider migration to cities in the contemporary United States, in nine-teenth-century England, and in modern Africa. With the United States of today, we are dealing with a country where rural-to-urban migration is rapidly losing importance as compared with movements from one metropolitan area to another. My article sums up the main trends in recent American migration to cities and discusses their impact on the city itself.

When trying to put American migration patterns into perspective, we face the old half-full, half-empty problem. If a glass contains half the wine it could contain, it is both half full and half empty. But the two sound quite different and may lead us to different conclusions. Chain migration, urban villages, and people from rural areas are common in American cities, as they are in the rest of the world; this article's discussions of the Puerto Rican migration, the exodus from the Appalachians, and the moves of black migrants from the rural South describe patterns that might make American cities seem like cities everywhere else, although slowly moving away from the traditional type: the half-empty interpretation. In the article, I emphasize the half-full interpretation of the same facts: the new patterns of mobility which are emerging as intercity migration becomes dominant, the tendency of migrants to have relatively high education and occupational skill, the importance of job opportunities as stimulants to migration. I also point out that the immediate impact of migration on segregation, crowding, crime, and personal disorganization has been greatly overrated; these things are built into the structure of the city. Over the long run, the pattern of migration to the city strongly affects the whole urban condition—for example, through the creation of segregated urban villages grouping together people of the same national origin, as opposed to the sorting of the population by social class. But in the short run, these are simply facts of life to which the individual migrant must adapt.

Since they invented urban life eighty centuries ago, men have been moving incessantly to cities, and from city to city. Times of great urbanization are times of mass migration. The migration of our own time, which is urbanizing the entire world, far surpasses that of all previous ages in numbers of men and in geographic scope. The most spectacular surges to the city are now occurring in Asia, Africa, and South America. But even in North America, after a hundred years of irresistible urbanization, the bustle of migration continues. Americans move, and move, and move. For a century or so, about one American in five has moved every year. Much of the novelty of California reflects the fact that over two-thirds of its huge adult population has come from other states. Migration is creating new societies in North America as well as elsewhere.

North American migration differs from the Asian or African varieties because so many of the newcomers to any American city have spent so much of their lives in and around other cities, or at least in close touch with them. Practically no migrant to Cincinnati or San Francisco faces the kind of change experienced by a Nubian newcomer to Cairo or a Kohistani just arrived in Karachi. With increasing exchanges of inhabitants among cities and a dwindling share of the total population in rural areas, the great majority of migrants to most American cities now come from other urban areas.

Migration itself drained the rural areas and fed the cities. Up to 1910, the number of people in American agriculture actually grew steadily as the area of settled farms expanded. From 1910 to 1940 it remained fairly constant. Since 1940, the far-reaching mechanization of farms, the squeezing out of small producers, and mass departures of tenant farmers from the land have cut the farm population by two-thirds. By 1967, barely eleven million people—less than six out of every hundred Americans—still lived on farms. Even when the number of people on farms was growing or constant, those people had children at a rate fast enough to produce a substantial surplus for migration to the city. When the numbers of farms and farmers began shrinking around World War II, that only speeded up the exodus.

Combined with mass migration from overseas and natural increase in the cities, this unremitting movement off the farm helped American cities grow much faster than the countryside. The cities' share of the total population went from a fifth in 1860 to almost a half in 1910, to around three-quarters today. Most of the rest live in small towns rather than on farms. Will the vanishing of the rural population mean the disappearance of migration? Not at all. Movement of people

Reprinted by permission from Chapter 13 by Charles Tilly in *Toward a National Urban Policy* edited by Daniel P. Moynihan, © 1970 by Basic Books, Inc., Publishers, New York.

among cities will surely continue, and may well accelerate. Yet it does mean that the very triumph of the city will eliminate something which has been part of urban life since cities began: the attraction of the farm boy to the metropolis, and his transformation into an urbanite.

The geographic pattern of migration within the United States looks like a Persian rug: some well-defined main lines, some dominant colors, but within them intricate swirls, contrasts, and interweavings. Until a few decades ago, we could have described the chief flows of migrants within the United States as two or three well-defined streams going from south to north and two or three others going from east to west. Even then it would have been important to remember that every one of these streams was the net effect of a very large movement of migrants in one direction and a smaller but still substantial movement back in the opposite direction.

Nowadays, the map of migration flows is changing in two ways: first, more and more migrants are leaping hundreds or thousands of miles from city to city without regard for the old, established paths of migration; second, while the aggregate movement toward the north and (especially) toward the west is continuing, migration is actually scooping up the people in the interior of the United States and throwing them out toward its edges. As oddly as the fact fits the conventional picture of Americans as dwellers in great plains, two Americans out of every five live in metropolitan areas touching deep water: the two oceans, the Great Lakes, or the Gulf of Mexico. The great majority live within a hundred miles of deep water. And that deep-water band is gaining population far faster than the rest of the country. The rapid rise of California, now the most populous of all the states, sums up the movement toward the west and toward the sea.

Why do Americans move around the way they do? Migration depends on three factors: opportunity, information, and cost. The greater the opportunities elsewhere and the greater the flow of information about opportunities, the greater the migration; the higher the cost of mobility, the less the migration. At the broadest level, this comes to saying that improving communication, increasing ease of travel, and the growth of a diversified national labor market promote rising mobility. More narrowly, it amounts to the observation that the closer two places are together, the more extensive the existing contacts between them, and the greater the difference in opportunities between them, the heavier is the flow of migrants between them. When it comes to the individual, the probability that he will migrate to any particular place (or that he will migrate at all) depends on the fit between his needs or qualifications and the opportunities available in that place, the channels of communication he has with that place, and the ties or investments he has in his present location.

Most of these statements would be little more than truisms if it were not for the fact that occupational information, opportunity, and cost by themselves account for much of the American pattern of internal migration. Job opportunities produce the main flows of migrants in most parts of the world; they certainly do so in the United States. Whatever else may influence their decisions to move, the overwhelming majority of families migrate when the breadwinner is taking a new job or looking for work. When pollsters ask newcomers to a city why they came, the newcomers usually answer in terms of jobs. Long-distance migration normally speeds up in times of economic expansion and slows down in times of economic contraction. And we can estimate the flows of migrants among American cities with remarkable accuracy simply by using information about local levels of employment.

This does not mean everyone behaves the same way. Precisely because groups and individuals vary in terms of their access to information about distant jobs, the opportunities actually open to them, and the costs of leaving their present homes, their patterns of migration vary as well. Young Americans just leaving school, for example, ordinarily have up-to-date skills, a wider than usual knowledge of job opportunities, and few ties to hold them in place. Predictably, they have especially high rates of long-distance migration.

Compared with whites, American Negroes and Indians start out with less education on the average, face discrimination in hiring, suffer greater unemployment and less job stability, and get different, inferior information about available jobs. As a result, the pattern of migration varies considerably by race. Again, men with plenty of education and technical skill, like engineers or economists, are more likely than other people to be in demand for distant jobs, more likely to belong to national professional networks which distribute information about jobs and job candidates, more likely to be able to quickly reorganize their lives in a new city; and in fact long-distance migration is much more common among highly educated and skilled Americans than among the general population. Finally, a person's present location affects the cost and the attraction of moving somewhere else; depressed areas lose migrants heavily, and prospering areas gain them. So a man's age, race, skill, and present location all profoundly affect the chances that he will move—and if so, how and where.

Because of all this, migrants (especially long-distance migrants) are superior to the general population in education, skill, and occupational desirability. They come disproportionately from the age groups with the most vigor and the highest education—the late teens and early twenties. Migrants to cities coming from other cities or from small towns tend to be above the average in education and occupational skill in the communities they leave behind. They even tend to rank higher in education and occupation than the population already in the city to which they move. People moving off farms are a little different. They are not consistently better off than the people they leave behind; both the least and the most educated predominate in the younger ages, the least educated in the older ones. They tend to be even younger than other migrants, and they are on the whole below the standard levels of education and occupational skill for the city's population. But migrants from farms are only a small fraction of the people coming to any particular city; in recent years, their arrival has not deeply affected the urban population's level of qualifications.

Along with the definite statistical differences in migration by age, sex, race, skill, and present location come differences in the experience of migration itself. There is a great gap, for example, between the migrating business executive and the migrating day laborer. The executive has a job in the new city nailed down well in advance. Often he is transferring from one office to another within the same firm. He has plenty of experience with organizations and cities, which makes settling into the new place easy. We might call this a cosmopolitan style of migration.

The day laborer, on the other hand, rarely has a definite offer of a job before he comes. He does not usually move as far as the executive. It is much more likely that friends or relatives told him about general chances for employment in the new city, and that he came to that particular city especially because there were already friends or relatives there to help him out. They do help him—with housing, work, and getting around the city—and they form the nucleus of his social life long after his arrival. We might call this a local style of migration. The distinction between cosmopolitan and local styles of migration is quite a general one. In America, the local style is more common among people with less education, members of racial minorities, and people from rural areas. It promotes the formation inside the big city of little villages of persons linked by kinship or common origin.

Of course, these two ways of organizing migration exist throughout the world. In most countries outside Europe and North America, some variant of the local pattern predominates. In those countries, the expanding cities have often grown out from a compact, western-style nucleus organized around trade or colonial administration, heavily populated by foreigners, and segregated from the native population. Their growth through the local style of migration helps produce cities grouping numerous transplanted villages around a cosmopolitan core.

In the United States, the cities have commonly grown out from nuclei of trade or manufacturing without the same sort of distinction between natives and colonizers. They have had arrangements of transportation and communication making access to the center from the less crowded spaces at the periphery quick and easy. The growth of American cities through the cosmopolitan style of migration combines with these other factors to produce cities grouping cosmopolitan suburbs around a core containing what villagers there are.

This geographic arrangement of American cities shaped a phenomenon which fascinated urban sociologists for years: the fairly regular sequence by which an underprivileged group of migrants first settled together in the downtown areas of high congestion and rundown but cheap housing, then moved step by step away from the center as its members got better jobs and higher incomes, and mixed with the rest of the population in the process. It happened to many groups of immigrants from Europe: Greeks, Italians, Jews, Poles. It is still happening to North American migrants: Puerto Ricans, French Canadians, Kentucky hill people, West Virginia miners. Whether it is happening in the same way for Negroes, Indians, or Mexican-Americans, however, is a question full of doubt and anger.

Unfortunately, our reliable knowledge of American migration breaks down at this point. Some analysts feel that every group of migrants to American cities (whether from overseas or inside the United States) goes through the same general process of economic and social integration into the city's life, and that differences in the migrants' wealth, culture, and acceptability to the host population simply accelerate or retard the general process. Others think that this was true of the great waves of migration from Europe five to ten decades ago, but that decreasing demands for unskilled labor and solidification of racial discrimination in our cities have changed the situation entirely. Still others argue that every national or racial group has worked out a somewhat different arrangement with American society, depending on the state of the economy at their arrival, on the enemies they faced, and on their resources, culture, and leadership.

We can see some of the reasons for this disagreement by examining three prominent recent groups of migrants to American cities whose members have often arrived with little money and few of the skills which urban life rewards. Let us look at Puerto Ricans and Appalachians briefly, and at Negroes in greater detail.

Since Congress radically restricted overseas immigration in the 1920's, few people without high educational or occupational qualifications have been able to enter the United States permanently. Puerto Ricans are an exception, because their land's status—first as a colony, then as a more autonomous Territory, and now a Commonwealth—gave them American citizenship and the right to move freely to the mainland. Few came until the end of World War II. Then the opening of inexpensive air transportation between San Juan and New York combined with a strong demand for workers in New York to attract thousands of migrants per year. The new movements from Puerto Rico to the United States ran around thirty or forty thousand per year until the 1960's, when they dropped to less than half that rate. The actual number of people migrating was much larger, since families and individuals moved back and forth easily and constantly. The number of people going in one direction or the other depended heavily on the relative prosperity of Puerto Rico and the United States at the time; things were good enough in Puerto Rico in 1963, for example, to produce a net movement of over five thousand persons back to the island.

By that time, not only New York, but also Philadelphia, Boston, and other East Coast cities had significant Puerto Rican settlements, complete with shops, churches, and Spanish-language movie houses. Puerto Ricans unquestionably started at the bottom in most of those cities. They had the worst jobs, the highest unemployment rates, the lowest incomes. Their very high birth rates, furthermore, kept Puerto Rican families large, meant that a large proportion of their members were outside the labor market, and made them exceptionally dependent on public assistance to supplement their incomes. Despite slow shifts toward prosperity, these things are still true.

Yet the coming of the Puerto Ricans is too recent for us to assume that they are stuck at the bottom. Many of the traditional early signs of a group's success in America are already appearing among the Puerto Ricans of New York: Puerto Rican baseball stars, politicians, and teachers; prosperous small businessmen; people with good jobs leaving Spanish Harlem behind and moving into richer neighborhoods of no particular nationality. So far it is still possible (if by no means proved) that Puerto Ricans are following more or less the same path as their predecessors.

Appalachia is a large band of mountains, hills, and adjacent river plains which cuts diagonally across the eastern United States. It covers important and backward parts of the states between North and South—Kentucky, Tennessee, and others. Pioneers pushing west from the Atlantic coast settled the region a century and more ago. They and their descendants organized it in small family farms growing enough to keep their residents alive, and not much more. Early in this century coal mines opened up through much of the region; they provided jobs for many of the extra hands the prolific families produced. They could not absorb all the excess population, however. The region has been exporting migrants to northern cities like Cincinnati, Detroit, and Chicago for decades.

Since World War II, however, the automation of some mines, the closing of many others, the mechanization and commercialization of farming, and the growth of modern industry along rivers like the Ohio have driven and drawn families by the thousands from Appalachia. Like the Negroes who came from the plantation areas farther south, these white migrants had little education, few job skills of particular use in the big city, and not much experience with urban life.

Most of the people leaving Appalachia went where they already had close friends and relatives. The friends and relatives recruited them, just as the new-comers in turn would later recruit more migrants from back home. From the middle 1950's, they have formed their own villages within northern cities, notable for their overcrowded, rundown houses, their country music, their local mountain-eer bars, and the used cars kept in condition for the trip back home. For even more so than the Puerto Ricans, the people from Appalachia often dream of returning home, often make trips back, and often stay there for good. As a result, they are one of the most mobile groups in American cities. In Chicago, which may have 30,000 recent migrants from Appalachia, one school in an Appalachian neighbor-hood had 1,500 children who entered or left during the school year for every 1,000 who stayed the entire year.

Because they are transient, because the people from the same region who make good in the city aren't labelled as "hillbillies," and because the migration is so recent, it is hard to say what course the integration of people from Appalachia into American urban life is following. Careful follow-up studies of earlier migrants from rural Kentucky indicated that after some trial and error most of them settled down, remained in the city, acquired better jobs than they had at home, and began to disappear into the general population. Whether in a time of accelerating flight from Appalachia and continuing expansion of Appalachian communities within big cities this will keep on happening is still an open question.

The twenty-two million Negro Americans include a vastly larger number of urban migrants than the Puerto Ricans or the Appalachians. Their fate worries many Americans, white and black. Many of the worries are confused by the false notion that Negroes are like the recent Appalachian migrants in coming mainly from southern farms. From World War I on, a huge number of Negroes *did* move from the rural South to big cities of North and South. But the big move is almost over. Within the United States, Negroes are now more heavily concentrated in cities than whites are. They are especially concentrated in big cities like Chicago, New York, and Los Angeles. Like so many popular ideas about cities, the notion of the Negro as an urban neophyte comes from a confused memory of events already past.

While the great move out of the South was going on, it formed three great streams: the first up the East Coast through big cities like Washington, Baltimore, Philadelphia, and New York; the second from the Gulf of Mexico toward the Great Lakes and other big cities such as St. Louis, Cleveland, and Chicago; the third westerly from Texas and Oklahoma to California. Nowadays, however, more and more Negro migrants are moving from one northern metropolitan area to another; fewer and fewer are moving directly from the rural South to cities of the North and West. Malcolm X came to Harlem like many other Negro youngsters, but he came from near Detroit via Boston. During the late 1950's the majority of Negro migrants to big northern metropolitan areas like New York or Boston were coming from other metropolitan areas. Only a fifth of the 1960 nonwhite population of American metropolitan areas consisted of persons born on farms: even fewer of the people now on the move come from farms.

If the persistent vision of Negroes as displaced sharecroppers didn't get in the way, this wouldn't really be hard to understand. For one thing, not many Negroes are left on the farm. In 1960, there were little more than 200,000 Negro farmers in the states of the Deep South. Just over half of them were sharecroppers. Over a third of those farmers left the land during the following five years, and took their families with them. But as much as that massive exodus changed the character of the Southern rural population, it did not overwhelm the big cities to which the departing farmers were moving. Even if every single Negro living on an American farm in 1960 had moved to a metropolitan area within the following five years while other kinds of migration kept their pace, Negroes coming from farms would still have been a minority among the Negro migrants into the average metropolitan area.

Besides, job opportunities attract many more people from one metropolitan area to another each year than they induce to move into metropolitan life for the first time. Metropolitan residents have more of the skills and information which make long-distance migration feasible. They are more often involved in national, rather than local, labor markets. Since highly skilled occupations tend to produce geographically extensive labor markets, as the average occupational level of Negroes has risen in recent years, so has the frequency of their long-distance city-to-city movement in response to better job opportunities.

What about the differences between Negroes and whites in these respects? Even today, Negro migrants come from farms and from regions (like the Southeast) with generally low educational levels more often than white migrants do. These geographical differences are disappearing fast. Almost everywhere in the United States, Negroes, on the average, get less education and hold poorer jobs than whites. These differences are far from disappearing.

No one should be surprised, then, to learn that the average Negro migrant comes to the city with less education and occupational skill than either the white migrant or the bulk of the urban population. But compared to the Negro population already in the city, the average Negro migrant has a distinct advantage in age, occupation, and education. In short, once we make allowances for the national pattern of discrimination, we find that the same general rules hold for both white and Negro migration.

Now, this is a hard conclusion for many Americans to swallow, because they have the habit of blaming so many of the Negro American's troubles on migration. For example, many people have noticed and deplored the high rates of desertion, separation, divorce, and illegitimacy among Negro families. One widely-accepted explanation is that the strains of migration to big cities from the South commonly broke up families. But there is really no general evidence that long-distance migrants in America or anywhere else have more unstable family lives than other people. Such wisps of information as we have about recent Negro migrants to big cities suggest that their families may actually be more stable than the rest. The instability of Negro families is more likely created by the grinding unemployment and economic insecurity they face in the city than by the disruptive effects of migration.

Likewise, many people have explained the fact that American Negroes have higher rates of conviction for major crimes than whites do by pointing to the personal upsets and deprivations produced by migration. Here the evidence is a little stronger than for family stability, and again it points the other way: recent migrants are less likely to commit crimes than are long-time residents of the city.

Finally, the great riots in the Negro ghettos of Los Angeles, New York, Detroit, and other big cities since 1963 have stunned and puzzled many Americans.

Observers, both black and white, have often felt that one of the main factors behind the riots was the venting of frustration by disappointed newcomers from the South. The information from the Los Angeles riot of 1965, however, showed that the rioters arrested were mostly long-time residents of the city. Furthermore, very few of them had ever been in trouble with the law before.

The picture which is taking shape, then, does not show displaced individuals and families shattered by migration and therefore taking up crime and violent protest. It shows almost the opposite. It seems to take Negro migrants quite a while before they adopt the ways of the city; that means crime for a few, unstable family lives for more, participation in racial protest for others, wealth, power, and success for a handful, quiet misery for a great many. Migration does not produce these effects. Organized discrimination does.

The differences in opportunity between Negroes and whites appear from the moment of arrival in a new city. The white migrants to an American metropolitan area settle all over it, and especially in the suburbs. The Negroes go overwhelmingly to the central sections of the central city. Why? Well, the multiple forms of discrimination which make it so hard for Negro families to rent or buy housing in predominantly white areas produce much of the difference. For the Negro newcomer to a city, the main choices are the ghetto, the area next to the ghetto, or a fight. Other factors reinforce this segregation. By and large, housing in American metropolitan areas becomes more expensive with increasing distance from the center; people with little money to spend therefore cluster near the center. With average incomes barely half those of whites, Negro families rarely can afford to go very far out from the center. The problem of traveling to work in the central city enterprises which employ Negroes in any number sets another limit on the choice of dwellings. Finally, the tendency of those migrants who come to the city through contacts with friends or kinsmen to settle first with them or near them, as well as the tendency of other Negro families to seek protection and familiar surroundings near the ghetto, add a measure of self-segregation.

Few things are now working against this formidable phalanx of factors promoting segregation; some prosperous Negro families do move out of the ghetto, the legal supports of housing discrimination are falling away, and in the long run the fact that on the whole Negroes share the standard American preference for solid individual houses and gardens will no doubt win out. But up to now, American metropolitan areas have shown no real signs of desegregating. Migration and segregation have produced two fundamental changes in the character of American metropolitan areas, one unmistakable and the other easy to miss. The unmistakable change is the rapid rise in the proportion of the central city population which is Negro. If recent rates of increase continued until 1980, Chicago's population would be almost half Negro, Cleveland's 55 per cent Negro, and nineteen out of every twenty persons in Washington would be Negroes.

The subtle change in the character of American metropolitan areas is the increasing whiteness of the suburbs. Huge numbers of whites have moved into metropolitan suburbs, but almost no Negroes. Thus the share of Negroes in the suburban population has fallen. Increasingly white suburbs ring increasingly black central cities. The pattern of migration to American cities has obviously helped create the drastic and hurtful segregation of white from black. But without extensive discrimination in employment, education, and housing the process of migration would not operate as it does. The comparison among Puerto Ricans, Appalachians, and Negroes leaves unclear whether we ought to expect Negroes to follow the paths out of central city ghettos taken by Italians, Poles, and Irishmen. Still, the comparison makes two facts all the clearer:

1. The heavy presence of racial discrimination makes the exit from the ghetto slow and painful.
2. Many of the circumstances thought to be consequences of migration are really effects of the organization of life in the city itself.

It is possible, although by no means certain, that over the next few decades united Negro action and determined governmental intervention will wreck the structure of discrimination in jobs, schools, and housing. If that happens, much of the racial distinction, and racial tension, between cities and their suburbs will disappear. Even after that, however, the general distribution of jobs, housing, and land uses within American metropolitan areas will tend to concentrate the poorest and most alien newcomers downtown and the wealthier ones outside the center.

At the same time, we can expect the migrant from the farm—and even from the small town—to virtually disappear. For a great many reasons, it is unlikely that the rural migrant from overseas will replace him. A constantly mounting proportion of the new arrivals will be lifelong urbanites from other American metropolitan areas. An increasing number will come from metropolises outside the United States. The distances most of them travel from the old city to the new will increase; moves from coast to coast will become commonplace.

Somewhere in the future there is a possible alternative to the ceaseless flow of persons from city to city. Modern means of communication are making it increasingly practical to transmit only part of a man—his words, his voice, or his image—over long distances. So far the availability of substitutes for transmitting the whole man, like television and interlocking computers, has neither slowed down American internal migration nor stayed the rise of travel by automobile and aircraft. The substitutes could well become so workable that it would no longer make sense for men to travel three thousand miles for a meeting, transfer from one office to another, leave home to go to work, or even migrate in order to take a new job. An organization with its communication center in Chicago might have most of its workers on the Atlantic and Pacific coasts. By that time, we could reasonably expect the long-distance migration which is so much part of the present American scene to subside, and the sheer attractiveness of a particular city to become a much larger determinant of migration to it. Over a much longer run we could reasonably expect the same pattern to cover the entire world.

POPULATION CHANGE AND
THE VICTORIAN CITY
J. A. Banks

Although England was already one of the world's most urban countries in 1840 (when Banks' account begins), the next sixty years brought her as much urban growth as had occurred in all her previous history. The growth of large-scale industries and a number of other changes that went along with it created a great "implosion"—people and activities concentrated in a few locations as never before.

The development of the industrial city of Manchester gives some idea of what was going on. Manchester was a crucial center for the rapid growth of manufacturing (the "industrial revolution"), which began in England some time around 1750. Until 1800 or so, Manchester had practically no factories at all; it served as the focal point for thousands of merchants, manufacturers, weavers, spinners, and other industrial workers scattered through the country-side of Lancashire. Only after 1800 did industry and population concentrate in the city itself and the widespread manufacturing of the rural areas begin to decline.

Increasing reliance on steam power, the development of the factory as a work place, the growth of large firms, and, eventually, the building of railway networks channeling goods and people to a few locations all contributed to the "implosion." Manchester's population growth reflected this history: about 20,000 people in 1750; 95,000 in 1800; 400,000 in 1850; 765,000 in 1900. Although her rate of growth was roughly the same (about 3 percent per year) from 1750 to 1800 and from 1800 to 1850, in absolute terms the rise from 95,000 to 400,000 in the first half of the nineteenth century was the greatest the city ever experienced.

Manchester became the textbook case of the grimy, crowded industrial city: the Coketown of Charles Dickens' Hard Times, *a prime source of examples in Engels'* The Condition of the Working Classes in England. *But many other English cities went through the same evolution after Manchester. Banks' article on the Victorian city sums up their experience. He asks how the great move to the city occurred and what changes in the quality of life it produced.*

Banks is inclined to doubt the most pessimistic portrayals of the crowding, filth, and disorganization of the nineteenth-century cities—not so much on the grounds that they did not occur as on the grounds that they were only part of the picture, and that living conditions in cities often compared favorably with those in the villages from which many migrants came. He backs up his argument by pointing out how many young people migrated freely to the city and suggests that both job opportunities and the chance to escape from close parental supervision made cities attractive to the young. He goes on to say that once they were in the city, people (especially women) began to change. He sketches out the way both the adoption of birth control and the growth of political militancy among women may have developed from the new urban experience. All in all, he considers the growth of the Victorian city to have transformed English life.

Between 1841 and 1901 the population of England and Wales more than doubled, rising from 15,914,148 to 32,527,843 persons.[1] Inevitably this growth was not distributed evenly throughout the country. When the period began, the agricultural and industrial revolutions of the previous century had already made their impact on the social life of the people in the form of a great expansion of town dwelling, yet over half the population still lived in what for convenience may be loosely termed "rural" as compared with "urban" districts. When the period ended this proportion had fallen to about one-fifth, and it has remained more or less at this level ever since.[2] The last fifty years or so of the nineteenth century, that is to say, were years of the consolidation of a development of urbanisation in a society which fifty years before had been agrarian. Towns of over 100,000 inhabitants increased from 6 in 1841 to 30 in 1901—only London had been this large in 1801. Towns of 50,000 to 100,000 inhabitants, of which there had been 5 in 1801, increased from 22 in 1841 to 49 in 1901.[3] Many rural areas, whole counties even, became depopulated in the sense that by 1901 their populations were smaller than they had been in 1851.[4] A simple graph or histogram showing the expansion of urbanism[5] should, therefore, be interpreted as indicating rather more than a mere change in the proportions living in urban as opposed to rural districts. Behind the rising steps lies a history of definite movement into and out of the towns, but with the balance in favour of the former.

To the Victorians this pattern of rural-urban migration and the accompanying growth of town life was probably more obvious in England and Wales than might have been the case had the island been geographically much larger. A journey across the north of England from Liverpool to Leeds, for example, could pass through two other major cities, Manchester and Sheffield, and not one of these is more than forty miles from the next. Sheffield, moreover, is at the northern end of another such journey, less than forty miles from Nottingham, which is less than fifty miles from Birmingham. Of course, all these towns were large for their time in 1801, having more than 20,000 inhabitants, but by 1901 even the laggard amongst them was over six times as big. In such a relatively small total area the growth of population rapidly made the English a nation of townspeople. The Victorians, indeed, created a new civilisation "so thoroughly of the town" that it has been said to be the first of its kind in human history.[6] The task of this paper is to examine what this notion of such a civilisation entails as a sociologist sees it, especially by reference to the demographic aspects of the society.

Reprinted by permission from "Population Change and the Victorian City" by J. A. Banks, *Victorian Studies*, 11 (1968), pp. 277–289.

I

That the quality of life in the town is different from that in the country has often been attributed to population growth in terms of density. The movement into the towns in the nineteenth century inevitably meant that more people lived in the same space. Thus, London, always in the vanguard, already housed 20.9 persons to the acre in 1801, but even London doubled this number over the hundred years. 112 other towns with populations of 4,000 persons and over in 1801 had increased their densities from 12.5 to 22.9 to the acre by 1891. 170 towns of from 2,000 to 3,999 inhabitants in 1801 increased from 5.8 to 13.5 over the same period, while 224 towns of from 1,000 to 1,999 inhabitants increased from 3.0 to 10.6.[7] A growth in size was accompanied by an increase in density; and such figures have regularly been interpreted by social historians as the background cause to much of the misery, squalor, and vice which were found in the Victorian cities at this time. Thus G. Kitson Clark has written of them that they were "singularly ill prepared" to receive the millions who went into them.

> Suitable housing did not exist and the additional numbers were crammed into every nook and cranny from attic to cellar of old decaying property, or into cottages run up hastily in confined spaces with little or no access to light and air. Water and sanitation were often not provided at all, and where they were provided there was often a judicious mingling of cesspools and wells with an occasional overstocked graveyard or active slaughter house to add to the richness of the mixture. Since many industrial processes now needed coal furnaces, and by this time probably most domestic fires burned coal, from many towns, particularly in winter, a heavy sulphurous smoke cloud was emitted to combine with other atmospheric conditions to make the fogs which were such a feature of Victorian England, and which probably slew their thousands. Such conditions were not new, nor probably were they inherently worse than what had existed before. . . . But as numbers increased so these evils increased in the area they affected, and probably certain factors in them, as for instance the problems of the provision of water and the disposal of sewage, came to be less manageable and more pregnant with danger.[8]

Or again, William Ashworth has put the beginning of town planning in Britain into the context of growing public recognition, or at least middle-class recognition, that the towns of the 1840's constituted a social problem of considerable magnitude.

> Even if he were not his brother's keeper, every man of property was affected by the multiplication of thieves; everyone who valued his life felt it desirable not to have a mass of carriers of virulent diseases too close at hand. . . . It was morality (or, more exactly, criminality) and disease that were causing concern. Overcrowding and congestion, poverty, crime, ill health and heavy mortality were shown to be conditions commonly found together . . . there was nothing new in the existence of congested criminal quarters. In this as in other matters it was the changed scale of things that gave to an old problem the appearance of something new.[9]

The growing density of the population in the cities produced acute overcrowding, which in its turn was the cause of social evils, growing awareness of which led to the rudiments of a Welfare State.[10]

This paper challenges the argument implied in such descriptions, without necessarily becoming involved in the debate over the impact of the industrial revolution on the level of living of the working class at this time. Accepting the position that what Eric Hobsbawm has called the "pessimistic" and the "optimistic" schools have latterly been overshadowed by agnostics,[11] it is admitted that the evidence available shows that the economic circumstances of some sections of the population improved, while those of others declined without being sufficient in quantity and coverage to determine on what side the balance lay. What is challenged here is whether the people concerned *felt* the hardships of town life so acutely, in the sense of comparing them adversely with life in the countryside. The sociologist is bound to ask why it was that people continued to move into towns if conditions there were so manifestly worse than elsewhere. Undoubtedly it is the case that some of the worst urban areas were inhabited by the Irish and that migration from Ireland was in large measure a consequence of destitution in Irish rural areas. Irish vagrants, for example, seem to have constituted a large proportion of those figures of the migrant unemployed which Hobsbawm has used with such telling effect in his presentation of the anti-optimistic case (pp. 78–79); but at no Census date between 1841 and 1901 did the Irish-born population of England and Wales rise above three per cent of the total population.[12] To give overwhelming emphasis to the fate of such a small fraction, in the description of the social life of the time, would seem to paint an unduly biassed general picture, however much on moral grounds it is admissible to show compassion for the individuals concerned, whose circumstances were dreadful beyond belief.

The alternative, therefore, must be to explore the possibility that the movement into the towns was a direct response to some feature of town life which was attractive to the rural population of the nineteenth century. Economic opportunities, clearly, there must have been, since the industrial revolution was an urban rather than a rural phenomenon; but such opportunities should not be interpreted as implying that the economic state of the rural areas was necessarily worse than that of the urban and hence drove people into the towns in search of work. One assessment of migration patterns in Victorian England has concluded that "both in North and South the rise and fall in the movement of population from the rural areas had little to do with agricultural prosperity and depression,"[13] although there is other evidence that emigration abroad was related to long term economic decline in the rural areas of Cornwall and Gloucestershire.[14] A sociologist might thereupon suggest that some attempt should be made to examine the quality of town life to determine whether it was superior to that in the countryside, not so much perhaps in terms of material levels as in terms of those social relations, which in this context the eminent French sociologist, Emile Durkheim, called in 1893 a "dynamic or moral density" (*densité dynamique ou morale*).[15] Indeed, one implication of this position is, that it would tend to make the series of changes we call the industrial revolution a result of urbanisation, in the sense that the rate of growth of industry, as well as its initial establishment in the towns, would seem to be dependent upon the *social attractiveness* of town life. Stripped of its other nuances this was essentially Durkheim's claim. Eager to refute the assumption of his day that the division of labour was the driving force behind social change, he put forward a sociological plea for considering "moral" density to be intimately connected with physical density (*la densité materielle*), each influencing the other and both responsible for the growth of specialisation and the division of labour in society. In a series of deductions from the assumption that individuals possess a need for as intimate a social contact with one another as they can find (p. 239), he demonstrated that a denser population increases the possibility of greater intimacy and also makes possible a diversification of interests and functions in social life. The outcome is that such diversification, as a matter of fact, occurs in the form of economic, political, and social specialisation.

Empirical justification for this point of view is, to be sure, very difficult to obtain except in a very broad sense. Thus, although the Registrar General's "dictionary" of occupations is not altogether a reliable guide because of variations in linguistic usage in different parts of the country at different times, it is the best guide we have, and it identified about 15,000 distinct occupations in 1901 as compared with only 7,000 in 1851.[16] The population had doubled and the number of occupations had more than doubled in fifty years. The overwhelming number of new occupations, it can be safely assumed, were urban occupations, and urban densities had grown much faster than rural densities,[17] some of which had certainly declined. Such figures, taken together, suggest that there is at least a tenuous relationship between specialisation and density, although of themselves they do not indicate which is the cause and which is the effect. In any case there is no hint here of any measure of that elusive concept *densité morale*. Durkheim, indeed, spent the rest of his professional life wrestling unsuccessfully with the attempt to get a clearer understanding of what is implied in the idea and others like it;[18] and, it must be admitted, sociologists and social anthropologists studying urban-rural phenomena have added little to what he achieved. But for all that there appears to exist a general consensus amongst them that the urban and the rural differ in important respects in the nature of the social relationships which they display.[19]

II

For present purposes it will be assumed that some kind of "moral" density exists, even though it is beyond the resources of the author to demonstrate it quantitatively through the content analysis of a sample of documents. In its place an analysis of social relationships in the Victorian city is offered by reference to what is known of the kinds of people who moved into the towns during the period under review and to demographic data generally. Most migration, it should be emphasized, was over short distances.[20] E. G. Ravenstein, who was probably the first to emphasize this fact, asserted that even long-distance migration was undertaken in stages. Among the Irish, for example, he said, "some of them landed at Liverpool, and gradually worked their way through Cheshire, Stafford, Warwick, Northampton, and Birmingham, whilst another stream, and perhaps the more voluminous one, passed through Plymouth, Hampshire and Surrey."[21] The concept of short distance is, of course, meant to be comparative. Some migrants went a long way, even further when railway traffic became commonplace, although the general effect of the railways on the pattern of migration was negligible in this respect since their greatest effect was that many more people moved a short way.

Thus it is likely that the impact of migration on the towns, apart from augmenting the numbers of townsfolk and increasing their physical density, was not at all impressive, except perhaps in certain of the ports. Local dialects would not have presented the kind of problem that existed for long-distance migrants, and it seems reasonable to assume that the rural hinterland for most towns provided a population more easily assimilated into urban life than likely to influence it by remaining aloof and apart. Clearly, there were exceptions. Liverpool in 1881 contained only 81 per cent English-born inhabitants, as compared with West Bromwich, Norwich, Ipswich, Leicester, and Nottingham with over 98 per cent English-born; and 12.8 per cent of the Liverpuddlians were Irish (Ravenstein, pp. 173 and 176). The existence of a relatively large, Roman Catholic "enclave"[22] in a predominantly Protestant area gave Liverpool a characteristic ethos which has set it off as different even to the present day. At a time when working-class attendance at church was minimal, the fact that the Irish continued the habit of going to church regularly gave it an influence in the life of the city. Possibly "worship with their fellows, led perhaps by an Irish priest, was one of the few familiar and comforting things available to them in ugly industrial England";[23] but the effect was to maintain a sense of community, of having interests in common which were different from those of their neighbours, and which influenced not merely their religious, but also their political life. The only Irish Nationalist candidate ever elected to Parliament from an English constituency, T. P. O'Connor, was returned for the Scotland Division of Liverpool in 1885 and held the seat until 1929 (Jackson, p. 122). What the example of Liverpool emphasizes is that it was *exceptional* for migrants to carry their way of life into a town in the sense of it remaining an abiding source of strength and separateness. Rather was it that the town's way of life became theirs.

This is perhaps more strikingly emphasized by reference to the age structure of the population. As Weber put it (p. 280), it was a matter of "common observation" in the nineteenth century that migrants to the cities were "chiefly young people." The statistical evidence in support of this conclusion is not altogether as strong as Weber alleged, since there were cases of marked losses from rural areas of women aged over 35 in the period 1881–1901.[24] Nevertheless, it does seem to have been generally true that girls of from 15 to 20 and men of from 20 to 35 formed the great bulk of migrants from the countryside at this time, and probably earlier. Economic explanations were usually put forward to account for this movement, although the emphasis therein was not necessarily placed on destitution on the part of the migrants. Thus, H. L. Smith's discussion for Charles Booth of the influx into London asserted that "the countrymen drawn in are mainly the cream of the youth of the villages, travelling not so often vaguely in search of work as definitely to seek a known economic advantage."[25] Moreover, even here there was an emphasis on an attraction in London beyond what he called the "gigantic lottery of prizes." What brought them to live in the city was "the contagion of numbers, the sense of something going on, the theatres and the music halls, the brightly lighted streets and busy crowds—all, in short, that makes the difference between the Mile End Fair on a Saturday night, and a dark and muddy country lane, with no glimmer of gas and with nothing to do. Who could wonder that men are drawn into such a vortex, even were the penalty heavier than it is?" (Smith, p. 75).

For women one of the attractions may have been marriage, and indeed the fact that women were more likely than men to be short-distance migrants, was explained categorically in terms of "the marriages which take women into a neighbouring town" (Weber, p. 278). Presumably this is meant to imply that some country women married town dwellers, possibly following men who had moved earlier from their village; but there may have been a marriage attraction in the town from the possibility that in spite of the more unfavourable sex-ratio there (Weber, p. 286), a woman's chances of marriage may have been better, because both men and women married at younger ages in the town than in the country and a larger proportion of them altogether married. Again an economic explanation has been put forward for this, namely "the degree to which women find industrial occupations" which was claimed to be "one very powerful factor in determining the marriage-rate."[26] It is open to question, however, whether economic opportunity in the case of women, especially when linked with migration from home, might better be interpreted as a means of independence from the often severe restraints on behavior inherent in rural family life. In this respect the Victorian town might be said to have resurrected for its own purposes the medieval adage, *Stadt Luft macht frei.*

As early as the 1830's, it should be noted, observers had been commenting on the growing economic independence of children in urban, working-class families,[27] and Engels in 1844 referred to the practice on their part of paying their parents a fixed sum for board and lodging, keeping the rest of the wages for themselves. Occasionally they moved out from their parental home to set up house for themselves, either alone or with a friend.[28] Charles Booth, at the end of the century, wrote similarly of the "weakening of family ties between parents and children" which he thought had occurred during the twenty years previous to his survey. "Nowadays the home tie is broken early. . . . The growing independence on the part of the children is frequently spoken of."[29] In all, this economic opportunity may be seen as a determining factor but only in the sense that it made such independence possible. That some sections of the population migrated in search of it has been taken here to indicate that they found the freedom from traditional family ties attractive.

The demographic consequences of this development are also of some significance. With a relatively younger population marrying earlier, and with a larger proportion of the population marrying, the Victorian towns might have been expected to show a higher birth-rate and a larger completed family than prevailed in the countryside. On the whole, however, the opposite was the case,[30] and in certain comparisons the difference was marked.[31] This is particularly noticeable when the analysis is conducted in occupational, rather than in urban-rural terms. Amongst the working class the highest fertility, as demonstrated by the 1911 Family Census data, was held by mining families, with those engaged in agriculture second. Both groups were engaged in rural pursuits and both had a higher fertility than the average for unskilled workers taken as a whole. Textile families, on the other hand, were low in fertility, below the average for skilled workers, taken as a whole.[32] A movement of women from the countryside into the textile towns might hence be seen as involving a transition to a type of family life which was very different from that of their family of origin, and this was all the more emphasized once people began to restrict the size of their families; for in the 1860's the practice began first in the towns, or at least amongst urban occupations, and proceeded much further there (Innes, Table XIV, p. 43).

Of course, as is well known, this vital revolution was started initially and proceeded in the nineteenth century most rapidly amongst the upper and middle classes. It was only later that it was adopted by the working class. However, even amongst the middle classes it was an urban rather than a rural phenomenon, the 1911 census showing that farmers and graziers had larger families throughout the period 1861–86 than any other section of the middle class. Indeed their families were larger than those of the working-class textile workers (Innes, Table XVIII, p. 60). Thus the distinction between town and country in this respect was a distinction which existed independent of social class, and however much later developments in the countryside may have invalidated many more recent urban-rural comparisons,[33] it can hardly be denied that the formative years of British urban civilisation witnessed a change in the character of the evaluation of children in the family, which has been revolutionary in its impact on the position of married women in society and hence on society generally.

For present purposes it is not necessary to go into the factors responsible for the inception and spread of family limitation. What is rather more to the point is, that one facilitating means appears to have been the comparisons which members of the middle class were able to make of their own levels of living at different times with those of their immediate neighbours and acquaintances.[34] Hence what Norman E. Himes called "the democratization" of birth control might possibly be explained not so much by the publicity which was given to the Bradlaugh-Besant trial and which he thought to be important,[35] as by the comparisons which members of the urban working class were able to make of their situation with that of their wealthier neighbours. This may also have been related to the pattern of migration into the town, to the degree that many of the young girls from the country originally went into domestic service, and it is possible that the very great growth in the demand for such servants on the part of the middle class between 1851 and 1871[36] provided an economic opportunity for migration at that time. Later, it is true, the supply of domestic servants declined, especially amongst girls under twenty.[37] However, by that time the lesson had been learned, at least in the sense that some of the middle-class standards and aspirations had been adopted by the working class. It is not suggested here that they learned to use birth control from being employed in the middle-class families. So far as it is possible to tell, working-class birth control is a twentieth-century practice, on the whole, and there seems to have been a "conspiracy of silence" on the issue on their part long after the Victorian age had come to an end. Nevertheless, there can hardly be any doubt that by the end of the century working-class women were expressing a need for relief from the burden of too frequent childbearing, as their letters to the Women's Co-operative Guild showed;[38] and in this respect the demand for emancipation on the part of working-class women followed a generation later than that made by the wives and mothers in the middle class.

III

Thus, Hobsbawm's argument for the earlier period—"on a gloomy interpretation, the popular discontent of the early nineteenth century makes sense; and on an
optimistic interpretation it is almost inexplicable" (p. 124)—is a clear *non sequitur.*
The discontent of women with their traditional lot of childbearing and child-
rearing, in families of an average size of at least six children, arose not because they
had now become worse off than their mothers and grandmothers had been, but
because they saw themselves worse off than they might be. It is, of course, true that
such discontent did not manifest itself in the kind of collective organisation intent
on reform that Hobsbawm may be presumed to have had in mind; but it seems
equally true that the feminist movement as such was organised to claim equal rights
with men in the educational, occupational, and political fields, in response to social
changes which made manifest that there was a large section of the population for
whom such rights were essential. There is no question that they were claiming rights
which had once been theirs and latterly lost. The issue, indeed, centred around a
demographic fact, namely that throughout the nineteenth century there was a great
growth of "surplus" women. Already by 1841 there were 358,976 more women
than men in England and Wales. By 1901 this number had increased to 1,070,015,
and the sex-ratio had risen over sixty years from 1.046 to 1.068 women to each
man.[39]   Although about one-third of these were below the customary age for
marrying, the number who could never marry while monogamy lasted was large and
grew disproportionately throughout the century.

A traditional agricultural society could possibly cope with such a problem in
that there is always productive work in and around the homestead for an unmarried
woman to do and so augment the family's worldly goods; but the kind of pecuniary
calculations which are typical of urban industrialisation effectively separate home
and work for the middle and working class alike, making home activities overwhelmingly a form of consumption and work a form of family income earning. The
problem of the surplus woman, accordingly, was that of finding some place for her
in such a civilisation; and the feminist movement obtained its greatest impetus from
the need to find for spinsters and widows, especially of middle-class origins, outlets
for their energies which would also be remunerative.[40]   For working-class women
the factories already existed, and where there were no factories they could find
employment as dressmakers, admittedly at very low wages. The danger here was
that they might easily drift into prostitution, the great social evil of the Victorian
era, and there was always a section of the feminist movement which saw its task,
ideologically speaking, as that of a struggle of woman versus man. Hence although
organised feminism was led by middle-class women it was never a class movement,
and some of the issues it adopted, such as the abolition of the Contagious Diseases
Acts and the ending of the double standard of sexual morality, were clearly not of
direct advantage to middle-class women.[41]   It is, that is to say, an error to regard
social protest as indicative of deterioration in the situation of those who mount it.
Urban life, by bringing ever larger numbers of people in close proximity to one
another, increased the possibility of invidious comparisons, and it was this which
produced social movements aimed at an even better future for all.

Again, it is to be expected that towns might differ in such respects according
to the degree to which the sex-ratio, for example, and the numbers of surplus

women varied markedly from the national average. Thus, Middlesborough was selected out for special mention by Ravenstein in 1885 on the ground that "its rapid growth, the heterogeneous composition of its population, and the preponderance of the male sex, recall features generally credited only to the towns of the American West" (p. 215). Does this mean that in the face of aggressive masculinity feminism was a movement which found it difficult to take roots there? Historians have apparently found no reason to comment on this point,[42] and clearly a much more intensive study of such questions than has been presented here would be necessary to decide the issue. In so far as a town like Middlesborough could be shown to display characteristics of "moral density," distinct from what obtained generally, and more like what was typical of the American frontier, added emphasis would be given to the analysis of urban life in Durkheimian terms. Thus, although little in the way of "proof" of Durkheim's position has been presented in this paper, it is to be hoped that it has demonstrated the general usefulness of such a sociological framework of analysis in the examination of the Victorian city. It was, indeed, in the anticipation that sociological theorising could be shown to be illuminating to social historians that the topic was selected for consideration.

NOTES

1. United Kingdom Registrar General, *Census 1961, England and Wales Preliminary Report,* H.M.S.O. (London, 1961), Table 6, p. 75.
2. John Saville, *Rural Depopulation in England and Wales, 1851–1951* (London, 1957), Table VI, p. 61.
3. Details obtained from B. R. Mitchell, "Population and Vital Statistics 8, Population of the Principal Towns of the United Kingdom, 1801–1951," *Abstract of British Historical Statistics* (Cambridge, 1962), pp. 24–27.
4. Details obtained from Mitchell, "Population and Vital Statistics 7, Population of the Counties of the British Isles 1801–1951," pp. 20 and 22; cases of county decline in England were Cornwall, Huntingdonshire, Rutland, Somerset, and in Wales, Anglesey, Breconshire, Cardiganshire, Montgomeryshire, and Radnorshire. See also Saville, Table V, pp. 56–57. For details of rural decline in two counties of growing population, see Richard Lawton, "Population trends in Lancashire and Cheshire from 1801," *Transactions of the Historic Society of Lancashire and Cheshire,* CXIV (1962), 197–201, and Fig. 20.
5. See, for example, Mary P. Newton and J. J. Jeffery, *Internal Migration* (General Register Office, Studies in Medical and Population Subjects, No. 5), H.M.S.O. (London, 1951), histogram on p. 9.
6. Thomas W. Freeman, *The Conurbations of Great Britain* (Manchester, 1959), p. 1.
7. Thomas A. Welton, "On the Distribution of Population in England and Wales, and its Progress in the Period of Ninety Years from 1801 to 1891," *Journal of the Royal Statistical Society (JRSS),* LXIII (1900), 529 and 533.
8. *The Making of Victorian England* (London, 1965), p. 79. The implication is that this covers the period 1821–51. For a sample of contemporary documents of the 1840's see "A Gazateer of Disgusting Places" in E. Royston Pike, *Human Documents of the Industrial Revolution in Britain* (London, 1966), pp. 305–335.
9. *The Genesis of Modern British Town Planning* (London, 1954), pp. 47–48.
10. Maurice Bruce, *The Coming of the Welfare State* (London, 1961), chs. iii and iv; F. D. Roberts, *Victorian Origins of the British Welfare State* (New Haven, 1960), ch. i. Notice that Asa Briggs does not mention the population issue in his "The Welfare State in Historical Perspective," *European Journal of Sociology,* II (1961), 221–258.
11. *Labouring Men* (London, 1964), pp. 64 and 121. Although he concludes that the "negative case is now pretty generally accepted," and although he himself has contributed to it in

the tradition of the pessimistic school, chapters v, vi, and vii of this book comprise an excellent and fair survey of the debate.

12. John A. Jackson, *The Irish in Britain* (London, 1963), p. 11.
13. A. K. Cairncross, "Internal Migration in Victorian England," *The Manchester School of Economic and Social Studies,* XVII (1949), 75.
14. Ross Duncan, "Case Studies in Emigration: Cornwall, Gloucestershire, and New South Wales, 1877–1886," *Economic History Review* (Social Series), XVI (1963–64), 1.
15. *De La Division du Travail Social,* 3rd ed. (Paris, 1911), p. 238.
16. Interdepartmental Committee on Social and Economic Research Guide to Official Sources, No. 2, *Census Reports of Great Britain, 1801–1931,* H.M.S.O. (London, 1951), pp. 31 and 34.
17. Welton, Summaries 1 and 2, pp. 529 and 533.
18. Talcott Parsons, *The Structure of Social Action,* 2nd ed. (Glencoe, 1949), chs. viii–xi, *passim,* and ch. xviii, pp. 708–714. A very careful and accurate survey of Durkheim's position on moral density is given in L. F. Schnore, "Social Morphology and Human Ecology," *American Journal of Sociology,* LXIII (1957–58), 620–634. See also Harry Alpert, *Emile Durkheim and his Sociology* (New York, 1961), pp. 91–93.
19. See the useful summary in Ronald Frankenberg, *Communities in Britain* (Harmondsworth, 1966), pp. 286–292.
20. Arthur Redford, *Labour Migration in England, 1800–50* (Manchester, 1962), *passim;* Adna F. Weber, *The Growth of Cities in the Nineteenth Century* (London, 1899; reprinted Ithaca, 1963).
21. "The Laws of Migration," *JRSS,* XLVIII (1885), 183.
22. 23 per cent of Roman Catholic places of worship in England and Wales in 1851 and 1861 were found to be in Lancashire (William G. Lumley, "The Statistics of the Roman Catholics in England and Wales," *JRSS,* XXVII [1864], 183).
23. Kenneth S. Inglis, *Churches and the Working Classes in Victorian England* (London, 1963), p. 121.
24. See the summary conclusion in Welton, *England's Recent Progress* (London, 1911), p. 9.
25. "Influx of the Population," in Charles Booth, ed. *Life and Labour of the People in London* (London, 1892), III, 120.
26. William Ogle, "On Marriage-Rates and Marriage-Ages, with special reference to the growth of population," *JRSS,* LIII (1890), 268.
27. See the evidence cited in Ivy Pinchbeck, *Women Workers and the Industrial Revolution, 1750–1850* (London, 1930), p. 313.
28. *The Condition of the Working Class in England,* trans. and ed. by W. O. Henderson and W. H. Chaloner (Oxford, 1958), pp. 164–165. Notice that Harriet in Disraeli's *Sybil* left her parents to set up lodgings with a friend because she was tired of supporting her family.
29. Charles Booth, "Notes on Social Influences and Conclusion," final vol. of *Life and Labour of the People in London* (London, 1902), p. 43.
30. D. V. Glass, "Changes in Fertility in England and Wales, 1851 to 1931," in Lancelot Hogben, ed., *Political Arithmetic, a Symposium of Population Studies* (London, 1938), pp. 161–212.
31. Francis Galton, "The Relative Supplies from Town and Country Families to the Population of Future Generations," *JRSS,* XXXVI (1873), pp. 19–26.
32. John W. Innes, *Class Fertility Trends in England and Wales, 1876–1934* (Cambridge, 1938), Table XIII, p. 42.
33. See the useful discussion in Peter H. Mann, *An Approach to Urban Sociology* (London, 1965), pp. 96–105.
34. Joseph A. Banks, *Prosperity and Parenthood: A Study of Family Planning among the Victorian Middle Classes* (London, 1954), ch. ix.
35. *Medical History of Contraception* (London, 1936; reprinted New York, 1963), pp. 239–245. For an alternative assessment of the effect of the trial, see Joseph A. and Olive Banks, "The Bradlaugh-Besant Trial and the English Newspapers," *Population Studies,* VIII (1954), 22–34.
36. Banks, *Prosperity and Parenthood,* ch. ix and pp. 83–84.
37. United Kingdom Registrar General, *Census of England and Wales, 1901, General Report with Appendices,* H.M.S.O. (London, 1904), pp. 95–96.

38. *Maternity, Letters from Working-Women collected by the Women's Co-operative Guild* (London, 1915), pp. 18–190.
39. United Kingdom Registrar General, *Census 1961*, p. 75.
40. Joseph A. and Olive Banks, *Feminism and Family Planning in Victorian England* (Liverpool, 1964), ch. iii.
41. Joseph A. and Olive Banks, "Feminism and Social Change—A Case Study of a Social Movement," in George K. Zollschan and Walter Hirsch, eds., *Explorations in Social Change* (Boston, 1964), pp. 552–554.
42. Cf. Asa Briggs, *Victorian Cities* (London, 1963), ch. vi.

AFRICAN URBANISM, MOBILITY, AND THE SOCIAL NETWORK

Peter C. W. Gutkind

Gutkind's work gives us a fine example of the anthropologist's ability to see the forest in a single acorn. In one perspective, this paper is about a single peripheral neighborhood of Kampala, Uganda. In another perspective, it is about all rural people in cities. Gutkind uses the idea of "network" rather imprecisely to refer to the whole set of relationships surrounding a single individual; he uses it to escape the rigidity of categories like "tribe" or "lineage." Each person, in Gutkind's formulation, builds his own social relations with the people and the operating rules available to him.

The biggest distinction which results is between people whose networks are association-based and those whose networks are kinship-based. Gutkind points out that the majority Ganda are able to build networks based mainly on kinship, and to rely on them very extensively in their urban problem-solving. The non-Ganda have fewer relatives and compatriots around and rely more heavily on sets of other people built up from contact in local bars, within neighborhoods of the same tribal background, or at work. Both Ganda and non-Ganda, however, make out in the city by building such networks; they tend to maintain contact with their places of origin through remittances of part of their earnings, visits back home, and extension of aid to others from the same setting. Indeed, many of them return home permanently from Kampala after having spent a few years in the city. The net migration to the city is a by-product of a large circular flow of migrants, only a minority of whom stay permanently.

Behind the discussion of Ganda and non-Ganda in the parish of Mulago is a larger argument about the nature of African cities. Gutkind rejects two common notions which we have discussed several times earlier in this book: (1) the idea that African cities are in a "transitional" position halfway between a strictly personal, traditional social structure and an impersonal, differentiated, rationalistic one; (2) the idea that the villager coming to the city undergoes a radical severing of social ties, and then after isolation and

turmoil gradually builds up familiarity with the urban way of life. To both
ideas he opposes his portrayal of urban Africans as building new structures
out of old elements already quite available to them.

In recent years African urban studies have changed from the survey type,[1]
the documentation and description of basic demographic and social characteristics,
to a more analytical type of inquiry and presentation. Thus a number of conceptual
schemes are now being tested. Southall[2] and Banton[3] have tried to apply basic
sociological concepts, such as analysis of role relationships, to African urban
systems. Southall,[4] too, has raised questions regarding macro and micro analysis
both as to approach and method of investigation. Mayer,[5] and Wilson and Mafeje[6]
have used group and social network analysis as has Epstein[7] in a particularly lucid
presentation. Both Forde[8] and Mitchell[9] have summarized past approaches and
suggested new lines of inquiry. While most of these new studies have been penned
by social anthropologists and sociologists, geographers,[10] demographers and planners[11] have also shown an interest in comparative African urban studies.

African urban studies have achieved a place in comparative African sociology
in part because an ever larger number of Africans have decided to seek alternative
ways of making a living. This almost always means leaving the rural areas for a short
or prolonged residence in town. While Africa remains the least urbanized of the
continents, an urban environment has become the social and economic habitat for
possibly 9%–11% of the continent's population. In political terms, and as social
pace setters, the influence of the larger African urban centers is considerable.[12] The
growth of modern facilities in such towns is turning them into the showpieces of
the new African nations.

Thus Peter Marris writes:

With the approach of independence, the people of Nigeria began to look more
critically at their Federal capital, and saw in its congested lanes of ramshackle houses a poor reflection of their aspirations. As the Minister of
Lagos Affairs remarked, "It is the mirror through which foreigners make their
initial appraisal of Nigeria." The condition of central Lagos, he said, was
"humiliating to any person with a sense of national pride."[13]

While it is not always easy to obtain reliable statistics on urban growth and
rural-urban migration, particularly since independence, observers are generally
agreed that the annual post-independence increase is considerably above that of
previous years. What is also said to be a significant and new development is the
larger number of Africans, particularly those with some years of urban residence,
even if broken by frequent visits to kin and friends in the rural areas, who are
staying for a longer period and will, probably, make the urban areas their permanent home. Thus Plotnicov has shown for his Jos (Northern Nigeria) data that
Africans are increasingly reluctant to maintain close rural ties and even more
reluctant to retire to the rural areas.[14]

Reprinted by permission from "African Urbanism, Mobility, and the Social Network" by
Peter C. W. Gutkind, *International Journal of Comparative Sociology* 6 (1965), pp. 48–60.
Footnotes renumbered.

If this is so then there is clearly developing an African urban way of life—an urban system. It will then have to be approached and studied as such.[15] To do so we have to be mindful of Gluckman's solid guidance: "Urban life exhibits sufficient regularities for us to extract systematic inter-connexions which we can arrange to exhibit a structure and we can study how this structure changes."[16] He goes on to point out that: "The starting-point for analysis of urbanization must be an urban system of relations. . . . We have to start with a theory about urban social systems; but these systems are to be seen as made up of loose, semi-independent, to some extent isolated, sub systems."[17]

While we can expect a considerable increase in urban population,[18] largely of those individuals who are engaged in a futile search for wage employment, it remains to be seen what ties Africans will maintain with the rural areas. Mitchell has pointed out that the cycle of rural-urban-rural migration can perhaps be best understood in terms of centrifugal and centripetal forces.[19] However, what keeps a man in town and what draws him back (*pro tem*) to his rural home will be increasingly determined by economic rather than social ties. Even where cash crops are under cultivation, as in Buganda Province or in Ghana's cocoa belt, providing a steady if uncertain return, it is increasingly the fashion for the owners to employ migrants while they seek additional wage employment.[20] Should an agrarian revolution develop in Africa, i.e. a major shift from subsistence to surplus cropping, cash cropping on small or large units, an ever increasing number of Africans will seek employment in non-agricultural activities. Then for a large number of urban Africans the break with the land and rural traditions is likely to be complete and final.

Of course, it is probably far too early to indicate exactly the salient characteristics of African urban society in the years ahead. At present urban life in Africa is marked by certain well-known characteristics which were shaped in the immediate pre-independence period. In East Africa's urban areas, particularly since the second World War, the population is usually composed of many tribal groups living in either peri-urban areas or on designated housing estates within the towns. Demographically, the urban population is composed primarily of unmarried young men and few women. Africans come as "target workers" to acquire money and perhaps some new skills but return to their rural areas when it suits them or when their agricultural activities demand it. But more stay longer in town and fewer return to the rural areas.

If these characteristics are a correct assessment of the situation, then *urbanism as a way of life* will become an increasingly distinctive feature in the transformation of Africa. I think it is unsatisfactory to use the convenient label of "transitional societies" to describe the present total social system of African societies as passing through an intermediate phase from being less rural to being more urban. Many complex and yet unidentified processes are at work which may occur at different times and in different contexts from one society to another. The key issue is to find out how change and modernization take place. Central to this discussion is the fact that change and modernization often radically alter the patterns of social relations to bring about a different network of individual and group relations. This transformation is viewed by some observers as productive of negative and anomic characteristics. The individual and the group have been lifted out of the matrix of a complex system which was dominated by primary relations shaped by kinship, close interdependence and group reciprocity. The break with rural life is sharp and abrupt. However, this view ignores "how fluid the traditional (tribal) situation was" and that "individuals and groups were constantly on the move, communities dissolving and crystallizing again in new patterns."[21]   Thus quite obviously it is false to pose the rural tribal system as a system of clearly understood reciprocal relations marked by maximum integration and the urban system as one of maximum fluidity, amorphousness or unbridled individualism. A closer and more analytical presentation would reveal that an urban society is as integrated as any other type of community but that integration takes place around different variables.

Thus extended kinship is not necessarily incompatible with African urban society; nor does the mobility of Africans invariably weaken *all* traditional kin and group ties. The question really is what aspects of traditional social organization are both useful and adaptable to new conditions? In what follows I hope to indicate some of the characteristics of urban social networks[22]   and to suggest how such networks are shaped by the extent and type of rural-urban-rural mobility. My data is taken from the all-African parish of Mulago, one of a number of parishes which make up the peri-urban area of Kampala, Uganda, East Africa.[23]

The area from which my data is taken contains an extremely heterogeneous African community representative of some twenty-five tribes. The parish of Mulago, which borders on Kampala, is one of about twelve parishes (*muluka*) which are part of the *kibuga*, the headquarters or capital of the Kingdom of Buganda. The *kibuga* in turn is a sub-county (*gombolola*), a number of which make up a county (*saza*). On the south, Mulago borders on the predominantly non-African and modern commercial capital of Uganda. To the northwest and east, Mulago is part of a larger sub-county. In 1948 the population of the *kibuga* as a whole was 34,337 and the parish of Mulago 2,500 (estimated). That part of the population of Mulago which was surveyed between 1953 and 1958 amounted to 1339 people, i.e. about 53% of the estimated total. Almost 75% of the African residents of the *kibuga* are Ganda while the rest come from other parts of East Africa. Over the years the parish has steadily become more congested with all the characteristics and features of a slum area. Many of those who live in the parish work in Government and business offices in Kampala; others work at the large and nearby Mulago Hospital and others operate shops and services in Mulago itself.

There is considerable mobility in and out of the parish and also from one part of Mulago to another. Firstly, there is a steady stream of Africans settling in the parish from outside Buganda Province. Likewise many people leave Mulago to return to the rural areas. Secondly, due to the fact that the parish is part of Buganda Province, many Ganda constantly move in or out of the parish. Thus between November 1953 and March 1954 slightly over 10% had left Mulago while just short of 17% were newcomers and 8% had returned to the parish for the second or third time.

Thirdly, there was a good deal of mobility within the parish. Almost 11% of the residents, most of whom had been in Mulago from 9 to 30 months, had moved once since their first arrival; 6% had moved twice and 4% more than twice. Over 61% of those who moved within the parish were non-Ganda. When further interviews were carried out between November 1957 and March 1958, the intake into the parish amounted to 31% (17% newcomers and 14% returnees), whereas only 12% of those who had been interviewed between November 1953 and March 1954 had left Mulago. This intake into the parish was reflected in an overall increase of the population of the *kibuga* to 52,673 by 1959 and of Mulago (now enumerated separately in the 1959 Uganda Census) to 3767; an increase in eleven years, over the 1948 estimate, of 66%. The estimated population of the *kibuga* in 1964 is 65,000 (up by 23%) and of Mulago 4,200 (up by 13%).

These broad characteristics of mobility and population growth are closely linked, particularly the former, to the types of social networks in Mulago which are either kin-based networks or association-based networks. This distinction turned out to be useful when analysing certain characteristics of those more permanently resident (i.e. primarily Ganda) in Mulago (although frequently interrupted by *brief* visits to nearby rural areas) and those (primarily non-Ganda) who moved in and out of the parish, often staying away many months before returning to village or town. Thus Table 1 indicates that non-Ganda, who have been in and out of Mulago over a period of up to 8 years, up to March 1954, frequently return to their rural homes. While Ganda can see their kin and friends virtually whenever they wish, and rural kin and friends come to see them in Mulago, non-Ganda must make a special effort to return home. This they do often although Table 2 indicates that compared with the 1953−54 sample, the 1957/58 group had moved less frequently.

TABLE 1
Frequency of Visits to Rural Areas[a] (50 Miles and Further) of Non-Ganda Males 18 Years and over, 1953−1954 Sample

		Time Span			
After Every 3 Months of Residence	*After Every 6 Months of Residence*	*After Every 12 Months of Residence*	*After Every 24 Months of Residence*		*Sample Total*
41%	49%	8%	2%	100%	100

[a]Of at least 2 weeks but no more than 3 months.

TABLE 2
Frequency of Visits to Rural Areas (50 Miles and Further) of Non-Ganda Males 18 Years and over, 1957−1958 Sample

		Time Span			
After Every 3 Months of Residence	*After Every 6 Months of Residence*	*After Every 12 Months of Residence*	*After Every 24 Months of Residence*		*Sample Total*
30%	26%	38%	6%	100%	100

For a Ganda to visiting the rural areas does not mean that he must give up his employment or otherwise, significantly, pulling up his roots. Non-Ganda ties with urban life are thus frequently broken and on each return they must find new lodgings, new jobs and perhaps new friends. While they are not necessarily rural-oriented, the fact that they come without their families continues to tie them to a kin-based network which forces them back to their rural homes. However, while living and working in an urban area they are tied to a non-kin associational network which has resulted from their contact with members of the same tribe, or their work or neighbourhood associations. Each one of these contacts produces a set of network relations which are operative at different times and under different conditions. At times these networks overlap when tribe and composition of the residential neighbourhood are the same,[24] or when members of the same tribe are employed together. However, association-based networks need not be linked to common tribal background.

Perhaps the most outstanding example of a non-tribal network is the beer bar.[25] There are anywhere from six to ten bars in Mulago. At weekends and at the end of the month small rooms are crowded with customers. Various varieties of African beers are brewed by women, a number of whom have developed a reputation for their excellent beer—beer which has body and gives the drinker the feeling that he is consuming more than mere liquid. Each bar may be filled with 5–25 people and on a really crowded day many more sit outside the room on benches placed in the courtyard. On such occasions men and women of every tribe represented in the parish will sit together and jostle and joke with one another. It is a favourite place to pick up a woman and make whatever arrangements are desired. Friends made at work or in Mulago will frequent the bar as a group. At the start of an afternoon or an evening out, men can be seen playing a card game or any number of other African games. Some beer sellers set aside a little corner or open place for such regular customers. There is much coming and going, much joking and shouting and occasionally dancing. Europeans and Asians are often mocked in informal and spontaneous mime. Men and women discuss the affairs and personalities of the parish. They make cutting remarks about other tribes; they debate on a high moral plane thieves and prostitutes. Men give money to help out those who plead special needs in casual conversation. Newcomers use the occasion to make contacts, to seek lodgings and jobs.

As the afternoon and evening wears on, and as men and women drift in and out of the bars, the excitement and commotion heightens. Minor fights and bottle smashing occur. Those more sober will try to restrain those more excitable and persuade them to go home. Casual contacts and friendships made earlier will dissolve in anger, accusations and sudden violence. Property might be smashed and heads broken. Thieves and confidence tricksters will then ply their successful trades. Tribal feelings will be expressed more bitterly and factions will line up. But when it is all over the same people will return the next day and the next weekend seeking companionship and friends.

These informal associational networks extend into the community as a whole. Drinking clubs and credit societies are often born in beer bars. They may last for months until they break up to be re-formed at a later date. For the newcomers a beer bar is a central point of contact. For men it is a place to find a woman; for the down and out it is a way to pick up a drink and some money. For many more it is a way of recreation, of showing off and a debating union where personal and group problems are discussed—but never resolved.

Another common feature of Mulago's non-Ganda is to belong to small credit societies, of perhaps 4–8 members, which allows each participant in turn to receive a share of the wages of all other members at the end of each month. As the penalty for absconding with the money is likely to be a severe beating, should the culprit be found, members of such credit societies tend to be linked in mutual aid and close association. The composition of three such groups was based on friendships made at work rather than on tribalism. Yet another nontribally based form of association are groups of young men who join together to employ a young girl or older woman to cook for them. Towards this end they pool their resources. Such groupings are very loosely knitted types of association. Yet they should be seen as a particularly suitable structure as men can enter and join such groups without complex contractual and obligatory commitments. The existence of such groups is often attractive to newcomers who do not know their way about but through a friend can join a "supper club."

Other networks are based on residence in a tribal enclave whose members, usually non-kin, aid each other in many ways. Such enclaves often give a strong emphasis to a "we-group" feeling which is expressed in the manner in which they refer to other groups. Not infrequently they appoint one among them as a leader and spokesman. In doing so members of such tribal settlements have developed a more structured type of associational network which supports the individual in meeting virtually every contingency he might face. An example of this would be how members of a Luo settlement, comprising 8 men, two of whom had their wives and small children living with them, came to the aid of one of their number who had been arrested and fined in the sub-county court. His fine was paid by others of his settlement. In turn he was asked to find employment for a newly-arrived Luo because he was a minor foreman in the Public Works Department. As this request was made to him during a period of economic recession he was not able to locate employment. The other Luo of his settlement accused him of wanting to be paid for his services. A mock court was established and he was asked to move elsewhere—a step he finally took after having fallen ill and believing this to be due to witchcraft.

This event also illustrates that ethnicity is not always a sufficiently strong bond even under conditions of extreme heterogeneity in urban areas where ethnicity acts as a protective measure *vis-à-vis* the politically and socially dominant Ganda.[26]

Association-based networks are adaptable. They provide the non-Ganda from far away, and resident in a foreign setting, with friendship, mutual aid and support. To stand alone is impossible. The need for a supportive structure for a non-Ganda immigrant is on the mind of many. Out of several hundred interviews, virtually all of which make the same points, the following two are typical examples:

A

"When I first arrived in Mulago I looked for any person of my tribe I knew. I was lucky to find a friend and I stayed with him for three weeks before I found a place for myself. I had a little money when I arrived but after four days in Mulago almost half of it was stolen. My friend introduced me to his friends (not all of whom were of the same tribe) to ask for jobs. Eventually I found work as a sweeper in a big office.

"I now live with a group of young men only one of whom is a member of my tribe but two others work in the same office as messengers. We go to work together because one of them has a bicycle and I can ride with him. We cook for each other because we cannot pay for help. When a member of my tribe goes home I give him messages for my wife and if I have any money I will give some of that too.

"I am now trying to get better work where I can get more money. So I went to see a Ganda friend of mine. He likes me because I can speak his language. But I do not really like the Ganda people because they treat us all with contempt.

"On Sunday I play football. I have joined a club and pay one shilling every three months. There are people from many different tribes in my club but we get on well together. I sometimes get tired of living here and having to buy all my food. If I get tired of work I go home but I always come back."[27]

B

"I haved lived in Mulago for almost one year. It is the longest time that I have been away from my country. But I expect to go home for leave next month. The first time I came to Mulago I only stayed two months before I went home. But I came back again and stayed longer. I came back to Mulago because I had friends here and I knew that they would let me sleep with them.

"I sometimes go with women but there are not many here in Mulago. I have never been with a Ganda woman because I do not have money to pay them.

"Not long ago I was beaten up by another man and I took a complaint to the parish chief. I took a friend along with me to help to introduce me to the chief. The Ganda chiefs are not like our chiefs so I knew that he might not listen to me.

"Whenever a friend of mine goes home I give him money for my wife. I get this money from my friends but I always pay them back.

"I have some friends but they are not like the friends at home. They are just friends. You cannot trust your friends because they might spoil your name or beat you. In my home I am not beaten and if that should happen I will go to the chief and he will punish the culprit."[28]

What appears to be significant about these accounts is the fact that associationally-based networks provide a migrant non-Ganda with the instrumentalities to obtain a home and a job. Some networks are really class networks. As a migrant repeatedly returns to Mulago, or elsewhere in the *kibuga*, he gradually selects his friends according to similar skills, wealth and education. Such relations generally cut right across tribal background. Thus in Mulago there was a "Monday Night Club" composed of 4–10 members representing five different tribes. Most of the members were foremen, on public works, junior medical orderlies, junior clerks or small-scale artisans. When they met, usually on a rotating basis at a member's house, they just talked about anything that came into their minds. They aided each other both financially and with their labour, such as on the occasion when two members had help from the others to build extensions to their houses. When they met, which was irregular, they were always well dressed and in conversation they would debate the failures of other people, their bad habits and manners and the aspirations they had for themselves.

As his field of contacts extends, the migrant shifts from one kind of network to another. Friends become enemies and enemies friends. Much of the internal mobility within Mulago could be traced to acts of violence or accusations of theft or uncertain love affairs which badly disrupted the individual's relations with neighbours, fellow tribesmen or friends.

Participation in many different associations, such as credit clubs, recreational associations or beer drinking clubs, does not provide the individual with a set of clearly defined relationships which have predictability and regularity over time. Such relationships can be broken by all manner of means. Having visited his rural home means, in most cases, that on his return to Mulago he will have to start all over again the complex process of finding a home and a job. His past friends have gone; his job has been taken by another. Under such conditions men latch on to any type of organization and relationship which they consider suitable for their immediate and short-range needs. An associationally-based network in this sense is a particular kind of structure which lacks the formalness and cohesiveness of kin-based networks. Association networks must provide the individual member with concrete benefits of assistance and protection. Yet at the same time the unique feature of these networks is that they are constantly manipulated by their participants; this means that they are ever shifting and possess an amorphous quality which is reduced to a more structured situation only by the fact that such networks always exist. They can best be isolated by means of following the activities of specific individuals rather than by tracing collective activities.

If we now turn to kin-based networks we shall see that they are associated with quite different characteristics. In the first case kin-based networks are only established when either mobility is low or when circumstances favour their establishment, despite rural-urban-rural mobility. The latter is illustrated by the Ganda residents in Mulago, the vast majority of whom move frequently and easily in and out of Mulago. This is clearly indicated in Table 3. Thirty-one per cent visited their

TABLE 3
Frequency of Visits to Buganda Rural Areas (Within 70 Mile Radius[a]) of Ganda Men[b]

	1 Visit to Rural Area	2 Visits	3–5 Visits	6–8 Visits	8 or More Visits	Totals
Per month	6	11	14	—	—	31
Every 2 months	3	11	16	4	2	36
Every 3 months	1	10	14	4	4	33
	10	32	44	8	6	100

[a] Exclusive of those visiting within a 10 mile radius of Kampala.
[b] Both single and married men over 18 years.

kin and friends from once to five times per month; 36% up to 8 times every two months and 33% between 2 and 8 times every three months. This is in strong contrast with non-Ganda migrants.

Those Ganda who were married, but had left their wives at home, had frequent visits from them and other kin and friends when they found it difficult or inconvenient to leave Mulago. Weekend visiting in both directions was very common. Food was generally brought to Mulago by a rural visitor or a parish resident brought some back to his urban home. It was also very common for a parish resident to bring back a young child, perhaps his brother's child, to look after for a short or prolonged time. Not infrequently a steady stream of kin and friends would visit a Mulago resident and stay with him for a few days or weeks. Such visitors would expect hospitality which involved the host in considerable extra expenditure. This was, not infrequently, resented and formed the basis of bitterness and strained relations.

Most Ganda occupy higher economic and status levels than non-Ganda. This gives them better and more secure employment. In addition many Mulago Ganda own cotton and coffee gardens, looked after by kin or friends or non-Ganda migrants, which give them further incomes. In the parish virtually all shops are owned by Ganda, a fact which is resented by non-Ganda who claim that the former cheat them.

Thus economically and politically the Ganda dominate the parish. Few of them extend their contacts socially to non-Ganda. Most Ganda live on or near the "main street" running north-south through the parish. Non-Ganda live in close proximity but avoid close contact with Ganda. Between December 1953 and July 1954 one Ganda houseowner evicted three non-Ganda tenants to make room for Ganda renters. Ganda women who have too frequent contact with non-Ganda men are criticized and made to feel inferior. At the same time most beer brewers are Ganda women whose clientele are predominantly non-Ganda. In this way and through the authority of the Ganda chief, Ganda and non-Ganda residents are tied into overlapping association-based networks, politically and economically.

Ganda society in Mulago rests on kin-based networks. Although a Ganda lives away from his home he is never far away from its influence. Indeed, the village, via its individuals, extends into Mulago. The basic Ganda social unit in Mulago is, typically, a man and his wife and children or a man and his older children. Numerous other combinations also exist, such as two brothers whose sister cooks for them or a brother and sister, both employed in Kampala, sharing a household. It is less usual for a man to share his household with any of his wife's relatives although there are some cases of an older sister-in-law helping a Ganda shopkeeper. Few Ganda live alone.

When ceremonial and ritual occasions arise, birth, marriage or death, Mulago Ganda invariably return to their rural homes to participate. Shops are then closed and those employed in Kampala seek leave for a day or two. It is true that such easy urban-rural-urban movement is made possible because of the proximity of Mulago to the Ganda rural-interland. But it is also possible because of the substantially greater wealth of the Ganda who can afford to maintain a town house and a country estate. Non-Ganda who generally hold inferior jobs cannot move back and forth as easily although their tribal home may not be substantially further away than that of many Ganda.

In addition the Ganda have imported into the urban areas not only a network of kin-based relations but also those corporate institutions which make up the total structure of Ganda society. Thus in the peri-urban area of Kampala, Ganda own land in exactly the same manner as they do in the rural areas although they use their urban land for different purposes. Some land in the *kibuga* is held by virtue of the official offices held by the owners. The way the land is administered in the urban area has something in common with its administration in the rural area. Land disputes are handled by the judicial institutions of the Ganda.

Furthermore, the fact that most Ganda in Mulago and elsewhere in the *kibuga* are never far removed from others who are of the same clan (whatever the operational importance of this grouping is at present), reproduces the basic structural categories of Ganda society in town. For Ganda, therefore, urbanism as a new and distinct way of life becomes simply an extension of the structure, operation and the values of Ganda society as a whole. In this sense urban Ganda, while anchored in a kin-based network, are also part of an association-based urban network. Such a network is fashioned by new opportunities and demands, by new forms of differentiation, stratification and competition resulting from economic, political and social transformation.

For the Ganda, urbanization and urbanism as a way of life has not resulted in an abrupt break with the past. For urban Ganda, the model of the desirable society continues to be the traditions of the main features of Ganda life and culture. The urban non-Ganda, however, must construct for himself a pattern of social life and organization designed specifically for urban, and thus non-traditional, conditions. To achieve his ends he must participate in a network of contacts and associations which are radically different from those of his kin-based rural environment. As he progressively stays for longer periods in town, urban life presents itself as a more desirable social model and, presumably, a more clearly structured social order.

In this paper I have tried to point to a distinction between kin-based and association-based networks. These two models of social organization should not, however, be seen as mutually exclusive. They meet and overlap at numerous points. They are designed to meet different conditions. A kin-based network is designed to meet the demands of reciprocal roles; an association-based network is designed to meet, flexibly, new situations to which role responses are yet uncertain. Southall, I believe, is one of the first to attempt an analysis of comparative rural (kin-based) and urban (association-based) role functions. He writes:

> Our hypothesis is that the empirical, commonsense distribution between town and country life may be given sociological precision by determining certain features of role structure in each case. In general, town life is characterized by role-relationships that are more narrowly defined, more specific, more unequally distributed between persons, more extensively developed in latent role structure, more numerous as a whole in relations to persons who are themselves living at a high spatial density, and more fleeting in their duration over time. In short, the passage from rural to urban conditions is marked by a rise in the density of role texture.[29]

While this might be a fruitful way of analysing a complex system of behaviour, I believe that the social network concept allows for the documentation of how in practice the individual and the group manipulate various roles both simultaneously and separately. In this respect social network analysis points to the way in which role performance is a part of the operation of a system, or a series of systems. To achieve a better understanding of how participation in various types of networks determines and structures specific roles, i.e. ethnic, kin, political, economic or recreational roles, micro-analysis is likely to point the way.[30]

NOTES

1. For example: *The Social Implications of Urbanization and Industrialization in Africa South of the Sahara*, Paris, UNESCO, 1956. Acquah, I., *Accra Survey*, London, University of London Press, 1958. Leslie, J. A. K., *A Survey of Dar es Salaam*, Oxford University Press (for East African Institute of Social Research), 1963. Southall, A. W. and Gutkind, P. C. W., *Townsmen in the Making*, East African Studies No. 9, Kampala, East African Institute, 1957.

2. Southall, A. W., *The Theory of Urban Sociology*, typed Ms., n.d. (about 1956) and "An Operational Theory of Role," *Human Relations*, Vol. 12, No. 1, 1959, pp. 17–34.

3. Banton, M., *Role Congruence and Social Differentiation Under Urban Conditions*, Seminar on Social Structure, Stratification and Mobility With Special Reference to Latin America, Rio de Janeiro, June 1962, Pan American Union, Document 5 and "Role Theory and Urbanization," Paper presented at Symposium 26, Werner-Gren Foundation for Anthropological Research, Burg Wartenstein, Austria, August-September 1964, pp. 14.

4. Southall, A. W., Introductory Summary, in *Social Change in Modern Africa*, A. W. Southall (Ed.), London, Oxford University Press (for International African Institute), 1961, pp. 25–30.

5. Mayer, P., *Townsmen or Tribesmen*, Cape Town, Oxford University Press (for Institute of Social and Economic Research, Rhodes University), 1961.

6. Wilson, M. and Mafaje, A., *Langa: A Study of Social Groups in an African Township*, Cape Town, Oxford University Press, 1963.

7. Epstein, A. L., "The Network and Urban Social Organization," *The Rhodes-Livingstone Journal*, No. 29, June 1961, pp. 29–62.

8. Forde D., "Background and Approaches," in *Urbanization in African Social Change*, Edinburgh, Centre of African Studies, 1963, pp. 1–6.

9. Mitchell, J. C., *Theoretical Orientations in African Urban Studies*, Paper presented at the seminar on The Anthropology of Complex Societies, Association of Social Anthropologists, Cambridge, June 1963, 27 pp.

10. Steel, R. W., "The Towns of Tropical Africa," in *Essays on African Population*, Barbour, K. M. and Prothero, R. M. (Eds.), London, Routledge and Kegan Paul, 1961, pp. 249–78; Hamdan, G., "Capitals of the New Africa," *Economic Geography*, Vol. 40, No. 3, July 1964, pp. 239–53, "The Growth and Functional Structure of Khartoum," *The Geographical Review*, Vol. 50, No. 1, Jan. 1960, pp. 21–40; De Blij, H. J., "The Functional Structure and Central Business District of Lourenco Marques, Mozambique," *Economic Geography*, Vol. 38, No. 1, Jan. 1962, pp. 56–77; Mabogunje, A. L., "*Yoruba Towns,*" Ibadan, University Press, 1962, "The Growth of Residential Districts in Ibadan," *Geographical Review*, Vol. 52, No. 1 Jan. 1962, pp. 56–77; Morgan, W. B., "The 'Grassland Towns' of the Eastern Region of Nigeria," *Transactions and Papers* 1957, Publication 23, Institute of British Geographers, London, Philip, 1957, pp. 213–224.

11. Zaremba, P., "The Urban Development of West and Equatorial Africa," *Africana Bulletin*, No. 1, 1964, pp. 105–134; Georgulas, N., "An Approach To Urban Analysis for East African Towns With Particular Reference to the African Population," *Ekistics*, Vol. 18, No. 109, December 1964, pp. 236–440.

12. Gutkind, P. C. W., "The African Urban Milieu: A Force in Rapid Change," *Civilizations*, Vol. 12, No. 2, 1962, pp. 167–195; Sklar, R. L., "A Note on the Study of Community Power in Nigeria," Paper Presented at the Annual Conference of the African Studies Association, Washington, October 1962.

13. Marris, P., *Family and Social Change in an African City*, London, Routledge, 1961, p. vii.

14. Plotnicov, L., "Modern Urban Population Formation in Nigeria," Paper Presented at the Annual Meeting of the American Anthropological Association, Detroit, 1964, 8 pp.
15. Gutkind, P. C. W., "African Urban Family Life and the Urban System," *Journal of Asian and African Studies*, Vol. 1, No. 1, 1965. In press. (About 10 pp.)
16. Gluckman, M., "Anthropological Problems Arising from the African Industrial Revolution," in *Social Change in Modern Africa*, A. W. Southall (Ed.), London, Oxford University Press, 1961, p. 68.
17. Ibid., p. 80.
18. Hance, W. A., "The Economic Location and Functions of Tropical African Cities," *Human Organization*, Vol. 19, No. 3, Fall 1960, pp. 135–136; *The Geography of Modern Africa*, N. Y., Columbia University Press, 1964, pp. 52–57.
19. Mitchell, J. C., "The Causes of Labour Migration," *Inter-African Labour Institute Bulletin*, Vol. 6, No. 1, Jan. 1959, pp. 12–46.
20. Richards, A. I. (Ed.), *Economic Development and Tribal Change*, Cambridge, Heffer, 1954, pp. 119–140, 161–223.
21. Southall, A. W., *op. cit.*, 1961, p. 2.
22. The concept of network has received considerable attention in recent years by Barnes ("Class and Committees in a Norwegian Island Parish," *Human Relations*, Vol. 7, 1954, pp. 39–58), Bott ("Conjugal Roles and Social Networks," *Human Relations*, Vol. 8, 1955, pp. 345–84), Jay ("The Concepts of 'Field' and 'Network' in Anthropological Research," *Man*, Vol. 64, September-October 1964, pp. 137–39), Srinivas and Béteille ("Networks in Indian Social Structure," *Man*, Vol. 64, Nov.-Dec. 1964, pp. 165–168).

As a model the concept of social networks has been suggested as particularly suitable for the analysis of mixed and complex groupings. The concept of social structure postulates numerous but interdependent enduring groups and highly specific categories, groups and classes. Srinivas and Béteille suggest that the distinction between social structure (enduring groups—those with "a high degree of consistency and constancy") and networks "is primarily one of boundaries. A group is a bounded unit. A network, on the other hand, ramifies in every direction, and for all practical purposes, stretches out indefinitely. . . . The character of a network . . . varies from one individual to another." (p. 166)

Such a formulation allows more adequately for a description and analysis of many semi-independent social situations which result from disturbances and struggles, so much the mark of African urban life. In this sense a network "has a dynamic character. New relations are forged, and old ones discarded or modified. This is particularly true of rapidly changing societies in which individual choice plays an important role." (Srinivas and Béteille, p. 166). The objective, then, of network analysis is to "chart the type and the channels of interaction between persons and the extent of regularities which give a minimum of order and coherence to social life in communities which have no clear structure of discrete groups." (Southall, 1961, p. 25.)

The concept of social structure sprang from the work of social anthropologists working in relatively static and ethnically homogeneous communities. Few such communities are now being studied by anthropologists. As societies change they take on a new and different kind of complexity—a complexity which is increasingly the outcome of the way individuals, as individuals, manipulate a variety of situations and social relations. This in turn is the result of an ever widening field of choices which the individual can make in social, economic and political life. This is the essence of change and modernization which gives rise to new networks which cut across and involve change over the entire system. (See: Mair, L., *New Nations*, London, Weidenfeld and Nicolson, 1963, pp. 11–31).
23. Fieldwork was carried out between April 1953 and July 1955 and August 1956 to August 1958, while on the staff of the East African Institute of Social Research, Kampala, Uganda. For a description of the peri-urban area of Kampala see: Southall, A. W. and Gutkind, P. C. W., *Townsmen in the Making: Kampala and Its Suburbs*, East African Studies No. 9, East African Institute of Social Research, Kampala, 1957. Second Edition.
24. Gutkind, P. C. W., "Urban Conditions in Africa," *The Town Planning Review*, Vol. 32, No. 1, April 1961, pp. 20–31.

25. Southall, A. W. and Gutkind, P. C. W., 1957, op. cit., pp. 57–63.
26. Gutkind, P. C. W., "Accommodation and Conflict in an African Peri-Urban Area," *Anthropologica*, N. S. Vol. 4, No. 1, 1962, pp. 163–173.
27. From my unpublished field notes, October 1954.
28. *Ibid.*, February 1957.
29. Southall, A. W., 1959, op. cit., p. 24.
30. Southall, A. W., 1961, op. cit., pp. 25–30. In a forthcoming publication on Neighbourhood Units in Mulago, Kampala, I hope to apply some of the suggestions put forward by Southall.

THE CIVIC BOND

Richard L. Meier

"The Civic Bond" is the only selection from a longer work in this whole book, although some of the other articles first appeared as chapters in collections of essays. I have stayed away from snipping because it is important to let each author make a rounded and self-contained statement of his position. But Meier's chapter does come close to standing by itself. It sweeps across such a range of materials and ideas that it would be a shame to leave it out. The book it comes from, A Communications Theory of Urban Growth, *is a treasury of ideas about cities and urbanization. The ideas are all connected in one way or another with the central idea of the city as the locus and the result of complex systems of communication.*

The "civic bond" is whatever attaches individuals to cities. At one time or another, the whole range of human ties—love affairs, blackmail, neighborliness, business convenience, the hope for vengeance—have attached particular people to particular cities. In this essay, Meier tries to identify among them the recurrent, durable, and strong ties which have some special association with big cities. He goes at the question in three steps. First, he reviews some of the alternative theoretical schemes which might be useful in identifying the basic civic bonds: ecological schemes, communications schemes, and so on. Second, he makes a rapid survey of the whole movement of urban scales and forms from the historical beginning of cities to the present, attempting to single out what was happening as major changes in scale and form occurred. Third, he puts his conclusions together in a provisional synthesis. The closing paragraphs neatly summarize the synthesis.

Instead of resummarizing Meier's summary, let me mention a few ways in which his conclusions complement and extend the analysis of cities and urbanization that I have laid out earlier in this book. When Meier talks about the close connection between the growth of cities and the intensification of communications, knowledge, and controls, he is talking about standard consequences of carrying on large-scale activities which are widely dispersed in space; those are the city-builders. A number of his remarks, however, point to the other side of the relationship: to the ways that the presence of cities facilitates the carrying on of large-scale activities extending far beyond the cities themselves. He speaks of trade, conquest, routine government, religion, and the production of new cultural forms. He could speak of manufacturing as well. The causal connections run both ways:

    Then Meier introduces an important distinction between the incentives for geographic clustering in general and the incentives for the special sort of cluster we call the city. Clustering occurs in general, according to his analysis, because "face-to-face interaction, which is most efficient by far in creating and maintaining groups, requires proximity." But very large clusters occur because people carry on extensive, complex activities involving many individuals at once, and such activities both require and produce concentrations of communications, knowledge, and controls. The city is a device for carrying on face-to-face interaction and large-scale activity at the same time. It consists of numerous face-to-face groups, some brought into the city from outside and some created within the city, only weakly linked to each other but bound together by common involvement in the public sphere. Each of these groups has, of course, its own internal bonds. But the true civic bond, in Meier's analysis, results from transactions in the public sphere.

What justification is there for a metropolis to exist at all? Why doesn't humanity distribute itself over the earth's surface roughly in proportion to the concentration of natural resources which give it succor? Why should people congregate in a manmade desert and disperse to abodes on its fringes in daily cycles? What forces keep a metropolis from diffusing into the countryside where the population pressures are felt less severely? Why should people agglomerate into larger and larger urban complexes whose outlying strands are beginning to join up with their neighbors, thus presaging vast blobs and webs of urbanism covering the maps of the 1970's, 1980's and beyond?

Such questions have been asked before. They are almost always, however, raised in a metaphorical sense, more as paradoxes than as problems worthy of investigation. They are framed as "straw men" by the proponents of answers of one kind or another. Let us instead take the questions seriously. Just as the physicists have explored the nature of the forces that hold particles together in the atomic nuclei despite the tremendous repulsions built up by the proximity of like charges,

Reprinted by permission of the Joint Center for Urban Studies of M.I.T. and Harvard from "The Civic Bond" by Richard L. Meier in *A Communications Theory of Urban Growth* (Cambridge, Mass.: M.I.T. Press, 1962), pp. 20–44. Figures renumbered.

the chemists have asked the same questions about the bonds that tie atoms together into molecules and crystals, and the physiologists have investigated the properties of protoplasm that are responsible for maintaining the cell as a separate entity, the cohesive forces that hold people together in a city are subject to study and analysis. Analogous questions have led to discoveries in these other fields that have been highly illuminating, but for cities they have thus far led to rather feeble explanations. The reason, perhaps, lies in the way the social sciences have crystallized into academic disciplines. The economists, sociologists, political scientists and geographers all have a little bit to say on the matter, but their contributions don't jibe. The sum of four lines of argument is not a whole picture; it remains just four disparate lines of argument. If social anthropology and human ecology are added to the list, no improvement in integration is obtained—two more lines do not yield a finished blueprint.

In any search for a satisfying explanation of human clustering of the kind that has resulted in metropolitan aggregations, the properties of a satisfactory theory or representation must be taken into account.[1] Normally persons concerned with the understanding of urban problems accept causal and teleological explanations for collective human behavior. An acceptable causal theory must demonstrate a plausible linkage between events—such as the adoption of certain innovations by a community and its subsequent growth into a city—which also have a bearing upon situations expected to be encountered somewhere else in the world. A teleological explanation for the construction and organization of cities would imply that they were determined by some basic collective goal. Thus a new nation may have to create a proper capital, and a new city might thereby come into being. Normally, however, the creation of cities cannot be considered an *end* or goal of societies, but only a means to a variety of ends sought by some important sub-populations. Therefore causal theories and explanations will predominate over the teleological kind.

Whatever explanations are advanced should be compatible with the theories that are presently employed for comprehending physical, biological and social events. The first-order generalizations that can be identified, inferred, counted over time, or measured for intensity must, of course, also be included as the content of a theory. What would all these constraints permit as an outcome?

One aim in explanation will be that of expounding the properties of certain "conservation principles" which enable the tracing of outputs and inputs and the establishment of sets of accounts. Such principles, however, apply strictly to equilibrium or steady-state conditions, so that the conditions for a step-by-step accumulation of structures and traits within a growing community—an evolutionary or developmental theory—also need to be elaborated. Sometimes several successive inferences may be needed to jump from the observed phenomena to the theories. The first step in making inferences will be taken up in this chapter. . . .

MODELS OF MAN

One approach is to probe into pre-history and discover the origins of human *association in space*—the linking together of many households. A description of the growth process that is both parsimonious and internally consistent will be undertaken. It is not an easy task because most authoritative statements are carefully hedged nor is there any strong pressure to economize upon words.

Nevertheless, after viewing many cities in many places over a long period of time some common properties suggest themselves. They may be described in brutally simple fashion by using natural analogies with which any person would be familiar. For example, the *complementary* properties of individual human relationships (male and female, father and child, mother and child, speaker and listener, giver and receiver, etc.) tend to hold people together once an exchange has taken place. Proximity, therefore, leads more often than not to more proximity. Small units of population (primitive bands) may experiment with the division of labor, which implies the formulation of new roles and new kinds of interdependency, until some units survive long enough to add still newer ones. Once this process has reached the point where another push restores a modicum of balance, the new small community is like a novice bicyclist who has just managed to launch himself. He may veer from left to right, not being sure of where he is going, and may very likely founder at the first bump. But on some trial the task will be mastered, and very soon thereafter the novice will be learning how to add new tricks to his repertory which enable him to move with real speed. Once the number of interlocking roles reaches a critical value a community lasting many generations may be expected—one that understands its internal structure well enough to reproduce it in the form of a colony.

Colonies have a great competitive advantage over the random clusterings in their immediate neighborhood because they are endowed with a formula that has already succeeded in a similar environment. The improved security and permanence due to the internal order that had been achieved may induce some neighboring tribal units to imitate this organization. They would, of course, attempt to start with roles drawn from their own culture and combine them with those they borrowed. By this trial-and-error process, stretched over thousands of years, many independent routes to community were found. Some of these communities happened by accident (or intent, in the case of a few colonies) to be located at what became the crossroads for peaceful interaction among individuals from various communities. Whenever a great variety of persons had opportunity to meet, the chances of finding a complementary relationship were high. When the exchange of goods and skills was encouraged, the cities arose first in open valleys surrounded by a region of comparatively high population density. If the interaction was ritualistic and encouraged pilgrimages, or if it was the result of conquest at the perimeter of the community's territory that led to an accumulation of slaves and hostages, the location of the most urbanized central place was often less accessible.

This theory is fundamentally ecological and parallels descriptions of symbiosis and more complex forms of interdependence in nature. A diagrammatic representation is provided in [Figure 1] of (a) the formation of bonds between individual units, and (b) the susceptibility of bonds, once formed, to dissolution. The bonds between groups are shown to be both more fragile and more lasting than individual bonds (which, with a trivial number of exceptions, can last something less than the average human lifetime). A small fraction of the bonds formed between households, clans, guilds, clubs, and the like are long-lived. These groups

A. Bonds formed between individuals with complementary interests

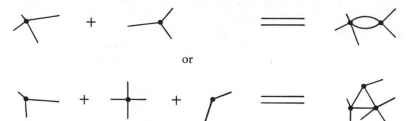

or

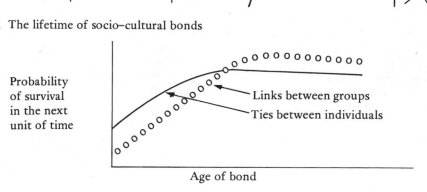

B. The lifetime of socio–cultural bonds

Probability
of survival
in the next
unit of time

Links between groups

Ties between individuals

Age of bond

C. Building in conflict together with cooperation

A. Persons with previously developed interests and skills form voluntary coopera-
tive combinations––dyads, triads, and larger. However most individuals retain
other public links, and this results in a society with a mass of relationships.
Bonds are continually dissociated and reformed within the network of individuals and relations.

B. Bonds between individuals (as represented in A) become stronger as they grow
older until a relatively constant attrition sets in. Bonds between groups (coalitions) are initially ad hoc and brief. They become quite stable when individual
bonds exist between leaders, and even more long-lived when the relationship becomes institutionalized.

C. Dissociation rate is increased when functional conflict is imbedded in the group.
Groups are then more sensitive to environmental change, and the over-all social
system appears to be more adaptive.

Figure 1. Cohesion through Complementary Functions

may accumulate and interlock to form complex institutions that sustain themselves over many human generations. It can also be argued that the formation, dissolution, and reestablishment of interdependencies of the short-lived variety are particularly suited to adaptive reorganization of the member population. It is probable that bound units would be situated much more closely to each other spatially than those not bound, but thére is no way of deducing this from elementary ecological theory. Ecology offers only one approach to the kind of theory that can be inferred from history. The difficulty with it is that the range of assumptions is not economical and that information which would permit detailed projection into the future cannot be collected. Ecology says nothing about what combinations of roles will not work and why they fail. A more complete formulation would incorporate some principles of economics in order to explain the successes and failures.

Economists start off with abstract concepts like utility or welfare that are intrinsic to individuals (or households). The welfare of one person may interact with that of others through exchanges in the market place or the political arena. Economists recognize transport as an important cost, and in regularized exchanges such costs are assumed to be minimized. Thus the tendency for households to cluster is asserted to depend heavily upon the cost of transportation. If all the households simultaneously maximize their utilities, and transport cost declines, then a strong tendency to agglomerate should result.

Similarly political scientists recognize that the exercise of power falls off with distance, because the further away a rule-breaker is from the focus of authority the more difficult it is to confront him with evidence of his crime and initiate a communal demonstration that this crime does not pay. Thus personal desires for collective security, personal power, and satisfactions of other wants (whose relative strengths can be deduced from previous behavior) have effects that diminish over distance in a fashion not dissimilar to that exhibited by gravity.

The competition in the market place and the struggle for power and influence together suggest that *conflict does not of necessity prevent an aggregation from being stable.* Combinations of conflict and cooperation in relations between individuals and groups can bind together a greater diversity of traits and skills than pure cooperation. This is shown in diagram form in Figure 1 c.[2]

The complications encountered with the *complementarity* concept when it is employed to explain a larger number of varieties of human clustering have encouraged some to investigate an alternative set of basic assumptions. They turn to classical physics for suggestions concerning basic assumptions and elementary processes, recognizing that atoms and larger pieces of matter also tend to cluster and that the reasons for aggregation are well understood. In physics the particles may have electric, magnetic, and gravitational fields which fall off in intensity as a function of distance. Positive and negative varieties of electric and magnetic fields exist, attraction is exhibited in the case of complementarity, repulsion occurs in case the particles have the same charge. Gravitation is a much weaker attractive force that operates so as to pull toward the center of mass when all charges have found their complements. Thus, by analogy, individuals wandering into the gravitational field of an existing agglomeration are either (a) deflected in their course to some extent, (b) pulled into a satellite arrangement, or most commonly, (c) attracted to the agglomeration itself. Any accidental aggregation in a widely diffused population would then be expected to accumulate population over time. These models of human interaction have been developed by J. Q. Stewart and co-workers.[3]

When the simplicity of the basic assumption is considered, the gravitation analogy "explains" a remarkable amount of human clustering. It has been applied successfully to problems of traffic analysis, marketing, inter-city communications, etc. Moreover, whenever additional information is considered, such as the existence of barriers to the movement of population, or the effort required to move, these allowances tend to yield even closer predictions than before. If the analogy is extended, so that the accumulation of wealth in population centers on a per capita basis is equated to the masses of the respective particles in physics, further improvement may be noted. The spatial properties of this field theory are depicted in Warntz's diagrams and maps (Figure 2).

It must be remembered, however, that classical physics became obsolete among the *avant-garde* in the physical sciences during the late 1920's. As the physicists began to probe inside the atom they encountered an increasing number of paradoxes that could not be explained with field theories. The system constructed by Newton, Faraday, Maxwell, Hertz and their successors was reconstructed as a quantum theory by Bohr, Einstein, Fermi and others. The field theory was not disproved, because it fitted quite well in the region to which it was originally applied and is used every day by the engineers in their designs, but it could not be extended successfully into the domain of the sub-microscopic. In the place of the field theory came a statistical mode of theorizing which could, with the expenditure of some effort, explain all that had been explained before but could also cope with the bonds that held atoms together in stable molecules, and the nucleons in the nucleus. The quantized concepts made possible a stronger, more powerful theory and they quickly came to monopolize the attention of investigators on the rapidly expanding frontier of science. Quantization was applied not only in physics and chemistry but also in biology where *genes* and *cells* (sometimes also *enzymes*) were discovered to be the appropriate quanta for the study of organisms. The social sciences have not yet reached a stage where such a quantum theoretical approach has been developed, although many of the essential insights have been developed.

According to quantum theories the bonds between two different elementary units are created by the sharing of some units which are still simpler and smaller. Thus protons and neutrons in the nucleus are bound to each other by the cloud of mesons which they share as satellites. The chemist's atoms share electrons for the most part, although complementary charges also contribute for some atoms. The sharing of genes by individuals in a population is what holds it together as a species and permits the population to survive in a relatively hostile environment.

What is implied by the acceptance of quantized theory for explaining the civic bond? In this case the transmission of separate *messages,* identifiable features of social transactions, corresponds most closely to the genes, electrons, and mesons in analogous theories. The more rapidly messages are exchanged the stronger the bond between two individuals or groups becomes. The more internal communication there is in a city, the more coherent it must be. Nevertheless the acceptance of

A. Population potential for Great Britain in 1951

B. Contours of potential near a small population center

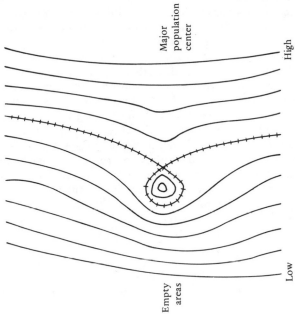

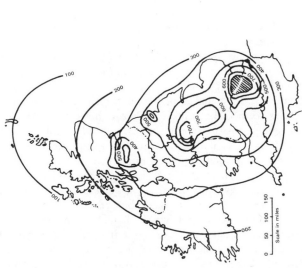

This diagram is from J. Q. Stewart and W. Warntz, "Physics of Population Distribution," *Journal of Regional Science* I, 1958, 110. It expresses the population potential for Great Britain in thousands of persons per square mile.

The population potential of any given place appears to be closely related to the intensity of social interaction once equilibrium with the social environment has been achieved. The peak potential in a city can reach well over a million person-miles.

A saddle point is created adjacent to the small population center in the general direction of the major one. The ridges are likely locations for transport and communications links.

Figure 2. The Mapping of Population Potential

a mode of thinking current in other parts of science leads only to a series of hypotheses each of which must be tested by the study of history and through contemporary investigations. If this kind of explanation survives such tests it will become possible to pursue a conjuncture of method in all the sciences. Students would then need to acquire many fewer principles; they would need only remember how the concepts are fitted to observable physical, biological, and social phenomena. Cities, too, can be fitted into the same general scheme.

What are the quantized properties of urban culture that seem to result in cohesion? It is necessary to deduce from the fact that urban aggregations have come into being that some features of the internal interaction must have been present. In Figure 3 the functional relationship to each other of the factors of *interaction frequency, distance,* and *cohesion* of specific social bond formed is represented graphically. For (a) one need only assume that individuals and groups locomote through the environment at a given average velocity and possess a relatively constant radius of observation for the individual units to spot each other in the course of explorations. The closer they are to each other the greater is the likelihood that messages would be transmitted between them. Ritual exchanges may be made in the form of gifts, offerings, or tribute, but barter is another important possibility. The bond that results is a residuum of interdependence that remains even when communication is broken off. In (b) the "stickiness" of interaction is represented. Familiarity breeds interdependence while too great frequency of contact results in stress (more will be said about this in later chapters). In (c) these principles are combined so as to show cohesion as a function of home-to-home distance. The distance at which attraction and repulsion are balanced will determine the population density of the urban aggregation.

The arguments have thus far presumed that the strength of socio-cultural bonds is measurable. The strengths can be established in much the same manner as in the physical world. Instead of using graded force to pull apart a test sample, those who work in the social sciences will observe how much money or other scarce resources is needed to attract one group away from another. Alternatively, they might ask what is the frequency with which one type of bond (e.g. friendship) is broken as compared to another (which might be a trading relationship)? Kinship bonds are the strongest, yet every society makes provision for the breaking and re-formation of such bonds. Cities seem to be stuck together with the more fragile bonds of acquaintanceship, neighbor relations, employment, guild membership, citizenship and the like. Nowadays we can infer a great deal about the relative strength of bonds from interviews with residents and new migrants.

The relatively unusual emphasis placed in the foregoing discussion upon a transactional, or quantized, model follows from the observation that a much larger volume of data is coming to hand than has been available before. In the past, the nearest approximation to such a model resulted from the biggest forays into the gathering of data—the origin-destination surveys carried out in conjunction with traffic and land use studies. Messages are much more numerous and varied than trips, but they can be treated in an enlarged origin-destination framework. On many occasions in the succeeding discussion, however, especially when relevant data are scarce, the more classical ecological and field theories for the organization and integration of cities will be employed.

A. Interaction frequency as a function of distance in the absence of barriers

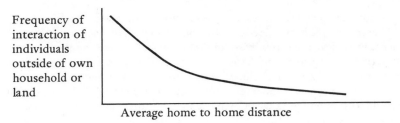

B. Attraction and repulsion as a function of frequency of human contact

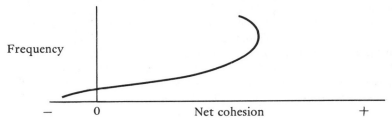

C. Attraction and repulsion as a function of distance of separation

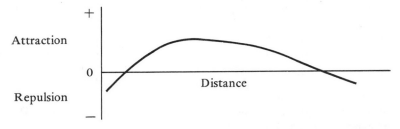

A. People must move through space so that their paths intersect more frequently than would be expected from random movements in the vicinity of the respective homes.

B. Enemies and strangers meet rarely. Increased frequency of contact leads to the discovery of complementarities and social bond formation, but a saturation must occur because otherwise population would become too densely packed to survive.

C. Repulsion at very short distances is needed to prevent suffocation and therefore the destruction of the community, while repulsion at great distance is quite natural since a major share of such persons are absolute strangers competing for some of the same scarce resources.

Figure 3. Some Elementary Human Interaction Relationships Required for Community Growth

CULTURAL SOURCES OF COHESION

Any comparison of cultures will reveal that some favor city life more than others. The records left by Greek civilization show that very strong emotional attachments were developed for cities, and civic service became the most prestigious form of activity. Despite the widespread expression of such values, the urbanized portion of the population is believed never to have exceeded 30 per cent, the remainder living in villages and even some isolated farmsteads.[4] In contradistinction, the Old Testament Jews when living in a very similar environment were taught to abhor the wickedness of cities. Cain, for example, was said to have built the first city (Genesis, 4:17), and Sodom and Gomorrah were destroyed by the wrath of the Lord. Abraham left Ur to live in a promised land, and his household owed no allegiance to cities.

For the Jews, Jerusalem constituted an exception. It contained the Temple, and provided a center for religious pilgrimages. During the short periods when it was also the capital of a small kingdom, it must have resembled other cities of the period in the East. These centers had a temple and a god that represented the independent entity of the city, just as the households had their own worship which reinforced the unity and continuity of the family. These old cities had a king's household, and a citadel to guard the main gate. There was also a bazaar, or market, which attracted traders from far territories. The city was also closely linked with tributary villages which provided the staples of life.

This is a relatively mature form for cities, however. Their origins can be discerned two or three millennia earlier when such institutions existed in a barely identifiable state.

Let us imagine the condition of human society before man began to make inscriptions and records. At that time we find population distributed over the earth's surface according to the density of natural resources, mainly food and water supplies. Since there was little storage of food, populations were forced to range in search of food in the off seasons. This is a state of organization known as an "unspecialized food gathering society." What factors caused such a population to cluster and condense in the early city?

Revolutionary changes in human organization began to be evident about 9000 years ago, after a period of rather rapid climatic change due to the receding glaciation. The appearance of the village-farming community on the "hilly flanks of the Fertile Crescent," and probably also in adjacent areas with a similar variety of animal and vegetable resources, marked a transition that was to proceed with astonishing speed—as compared to the development of technique among the earlier cave dwellers—to the development of cities. The wheat plant and several legumes were domesticated first, and the dog and the goat seem to have kept company with humans during this period, but arguments remain as to whether these animals were truly domesticated. The first permanent open settlements were established near year-round sources of water at points which allowed the hunters to range up to timber line or down into the dry plains while still maintaining garden plots in the loess soils left behind by the glaciers. They could be watered by the streams if rain was insufficient. Early Jarmo, as reported by Braidwood and coworkers,[5] contained as many as twenty tightly packed households, was continuously occupied over centuries at a time, and reoccupied in a sequence lasting six millennia.

Once such settlements had found ways to sustain themselves over the seasonal starvation periods normally experienced by the most primitive societies, an acceleration in the acquisition of new techniques was possible. Somewhere in this vicinity (e.g. southwest Asia) sheep, pigs, and cattle were tamed, barley was cultivated, and dates, olives, flax seeds and perhaps also pistachios and almonds were brought under village control. Thus within one or two thousand years a diversity of habitats could be occupied by communities which, because of the special resources that lay within a day's travel from the village, became semi-specialized. The appearance of herdsmen at the end of this period seems now to have been an offshoot of the mixed farming village. The herd-tending specialization was borrowed perhaps by migratory food gatherers and hunters of the gazelles that roamed the plains.

Within the villages forms of specialization other than agriculture and herding evolved. Clay figurines, bracelets, and carefully worked stone vessels have been found. So have evidences of mat weaving and basketry together with asphalt (probably used for waterproofing of baskets), glazed hemispheric depressions for heating water with hot stones, tool making for agriculture, mortars and pestles for grinding parched seeds, etc. These technics, for which evidence exists in the form of artifacts, are mentioned primarily to show the extent to which life was becoming more elaborate. The presence of obsidian and marine shell beads, available only from distant sites, strongly suggests continuous trading activity, although their absence in some sites of that same period indicates that the trading was not highly organized. In other words, trading was not an activity that was intensively pursued as a part of the division of labor until somewhat later. The invention of pottery seems to have taken place within a thousand to fifteen hundred years after the first permanent settlements. Adams[6] argues that a somewhat laggard specialization evolved in the alluvial plains. The latter were less troubled by the long-term effects of erosion (no doubt accelerated greatly by the domestication of the goat) and were influenced by many different developments from the piedmont area because the plain was more readily accessible than a neighboring portion of the piedmont which required traversing a ridge or a canyon. Fishing in streams and lower lakes seems to have become important. About 6500 years ago towns and clusters of villages employing primitive forms of irrigation appeared for the first time. They were located at the confluence of rivers in the plain of the Tigris and Euphrates, so that an extra form of transport, that of canoe, raft, or barge, was made available to these settlements. In the towns political and social stratification developed, and over time, temples became the dominant public works.[7]

The argument that bond-formation between humans is encouraged by the acquisition and retention of knowledge and that the product of this knowledge tends to accelerate the exchange of artifacts and messages which inform humans about each other, and thereby causes an elaboration of the variety of bonds as well as strengthening those that are most used, is not contradicted by what is presently known about prehistory. It is still rather premature to assert with confidence that a common path exists for man in his progress toward civilization but there are strong hints adduced from the record that, wherever the transition to cities is achieved, certain steps have followed in sequence. Hundreds of books trace in detail the structure of ancient cities in Mesopotamia and Egypt and from these patterns many reviewers have attempted to deduce typical stages in the urbanization of those ancient cultures. Recently much more evidence has been accumulating regarding cultures in northwest India, and thinking has been reorganized about the time sequence in Crete and China, all of which has strengthened the "common path" theme, but some of the most striking confirmations have been achieved by the archeologists and linguists concentrating during the 1950's upon the New World. Since they are not yet widely heralded, but have recently been carefully reviewed,[8] the detailed analysis of the evolution of the civic bond will follow American patterns. The physical environment within which cities evolved may be more familiar. Differences between the Old World and the New will be taken up after the sequence in the latter has been traced.

Parenthetically it might be mentioned that acquisition of knowledge of terrain and the movements of big game, occurring *simultaneously* with the development of improved weapons, coincided with the evolution of a society of big-game hunters who followed the migrations of their quarry. Most of the innovation seems to have been concentrated upon the techniques of bringing down animals much larger than man himself. Now, in the light of subsequent history, we see these three or four millennia of human experience, out of perhaps nine or ten altogether in North America, as an heroic diversion from the mainstream of development. The hunters encountered disaster when the climate changed and the game disappeared. The main long-term contributions came in the form of tuber and seed collecting by the more sedentary populations (perhaps only the women originally) which in turn led to domestication of plants and the development of the arts of pottery making and basket making. They led to an enhanced integration of agriculture and equipment for food preservation and finally to village farming.

Perhaps the crucial phase was enacted along the seacoasts of South and Central America. The densest populations could be supported at rocky shorelines that were rich with shellfish, crabs, etc. Pelagic species were available in season. These resources permitted a relatively sedentary society for food gatherers, but one which was challenged by "El Nino," the occasional shifting of ocean currents which causes a drastic reduction in marine resources and brings torrential rains to the Andean valleys.

Already by 3000 B. C. at least two varieties of beans, an even larger variety of gourds and squashes, and several fruits were incorporated within the diet of a desert-dwelling community so that it must be inferred that these plants were domesticated. This was well before the introduction of pottery or of maize. Organized irrigation would seem to follow as a logical next step after domestication. Since the soils of the West Coast of South America are easily worked with animal bones (the amateur archeologists in Great Britain have shown that ditch-digging with antlers and shoulder bones requires only 50–70% more man-hours than with modern pickaxe and shovel in a compact chalk soil) these irrigation techniques probably evolved quite early. By about 1000 B. C. it appears that all the water-courses from present-day Ecuador to north central Chile must have been settled and farmed.

The domestication of plants and animals made it possible to accumulate enough wealth to construct permanent dwellings and relegate the caves and temporary shelters to the men on hunting expeditions. Equipment for the grinding of maize or the leaching of manioc, too heavy to be carried on treks, could then be developed and installed. As the risks of starvation decrease, and the opportunities for human interaction are expanded, perhaps half the time available to adults could be devoted to social participation and trial-by-error approaches to manipulating the immediate environment. Such efforts could be easily extended to include the basic community relations. The first towns seem to have had ritual functions combined with the transfer of gifts. Taxation for public purposes and barter in the market place came later.

THE EMERGENCE OF CITIES

Proximity, it seems, led to an accumulation of shared experiences and interhousehold communications were therefore accelerated. Within a span of only a few generations some sites were enabled to grow into towns with temples, markets, and wide-ranging commercial contacts. Through commerce, war, and slavery, a distillate of the specialized experiences of each town—the plants and animals it domesticated and the handicrafts that it perfected—were distributed throughout a region. Then communications was elevated to a more abstract plane. Leaders, merchants, and heads of important households could not be several places at once so they were forced to delegate their power by using symbols such as seals and maces. Accounts also became so complex that they could not be trusted to memory, so a symbolic record was resorted to in shops, temples, and leading households. Written symbols, the new medium of communication, released unsuspected potentials for control and for the accumulation of experience.

A few of the favorably situated towns evolved into city-states with defense perimeters, temples, and vassal communities. This transition seems to have occurred with extraordinary rapidity, within the course of a few generations. In the cities the alternating periods of crisis and prosperity forced the standardization of relationships of role between rulers and the priesthood, as well as the merchants, artisans, freemen, and slaves. Improvisations led to precedents, precedents followed repeatedly became customs, customs became laws, and the responsibilities and duties became codified. Whereas the language of the hunter and the farmer was suited to the detailed description of the natural environment, the language of the city became equally explicit in its designation of social roles, public rituals, sites, artifacts, and events.

The profits flowing from aggregation filtered down to the common man, who was still predominantly a farmer and part-time fisher, hunter and herbalist. There was a structure of authority above him so that he understood his special duties and responsibilities in times of war and peace. He no longer needed to make his own weapons and armor. Although his attention was concentrated upon the growing of staples there were scores of domesticated plants available for rounding out his needs. The seasonal rituals and the exchange of spouses were coordinated at the village level, the calendar and market in the town, and the protection from invaders in the city. In the earliest civilization a person was tied to a site by law and custom, and he was conditioned to paying taxes.[9]

The New World turned much later than the Old to domestication of animals. Dogs everywhere seem to have tamed themselves with little effort on the part of humans. Goats were tamed very early in the Near East, perhaps with the first village-type settlements. Sheep, cattle, donkeys, and pigs appeared not long thereafter. A remarkable range of domestication was already evident in Egypt and the

Fertile Crescent by the time the Greek cities were being founded. Use of the horse, and then the camel, came later, and the idea of cart and chariot seemed to be contingent on the concept of a beast of burden transporting people and goods over a dry plain. The art of navigation developed early in the Near East, since most urban societies developed on river trade routes, whereas the Mayans seem to have undertaken trade about two thousand years ago, and it was not until a few centuries before the advent of Columbus that the Caribs began their Norse-like forays into the Antilles. Beasts of burden, such as llamas and alpacas, were impressed into service but were used in large numbers only when cities were being linked into large empires, as with the later Incas. In any case, they were not used as mounts. The other domesticated animals in America—turkeys, ducks, guinea pigs, and dogs bred for eating—could not function as mobile capital in the same way that goats, sheep, pigs, cattle, and horses did in Eurasia. In case of emergency the early American peasant was forced to fall back upon tubers that were purposely left in the ground, or reefs of shellfish that were held in reserve.

The first lifelong city dwellers in ancient times seem to have broken loose from many features of the rural pattern of life. Attempts were made to tie a man to a craft in the same manner that a serf was tied to the land, but many more opportunities were open for him to change his assigned role and his allegiances to superiors. The variety of demands put upon him was too complex to be regulated completely by custom. The citizen spent much more of his time in public, seeing many more people, including representatives of strange cultures that were apparently the equal of his own, and quite a few incomprehensible barbarians as well. The citizen engaged in a wide range of affairs, and was therefore better informed. In general, his attachment to his city was proportional to the extent of his participation in its affairs. Leading citizens, who may be thought of as an aristocracy, had conflicting obligations to household, clan, friends, social class, and figures of authority. Thus cities were particularly vulnerable to divisions within themselves, a condition that was ultimately resolved by transferring the contest for power to a higher forum, that of imperial politics. Some far-sighted individuals insisted upon a more comprehensive set of common experiences in the form of general education. Economies of scale became even more evident in education than in defense and commerce, so that almost all the higher schools, the academies and the training institutions, were conducted in the largest and best-established cities.

If this portrayal of the evolution of cities is to be balanced, and an explanation for the unevenness in progress is to be adduced, the diseconomies of the agglomeration of people and activities need mention. Periodic variations in the availability of resources, especially fresh water, discouraged and inhibited aggregation, so that larger populations were quite unstable until the metropolis was able to create and maintain its own waterworks system (as in Mayan settlements or in Rome and its colonies). When still larger numbers were assembled in one place sanitation usually became the limiting factor upon growth. Centuries of experience were needed before the incidence of epidemics could be associated with the provision for the disposal of wastes and maintenance of the purity of the water supply. Similarly, the problems of food allocation, fire, the safety of structures, policing, riot control and the like get out of hand as the number of residents exceeds 50,000–100,000 persons. The forging of institutions capable of coping with these emergencies economically requires generations of experience, and an improper start in any given direction of development virtually precluded any solution of the problem by that society.

In sum, the attraction of city life became stronger as time spent in *public* and *professional* activities, as distinguished from time spent reflectively on matters of *personal* concern, or in *familial* interactions, increased. Larger aggregations of people were permitted to evolve in competition with other sizes because knowledge accumulated and was reflected in increasingly selective and precise institutional controls that reduced the diseconomies of aggregation. Shared symbols, rituals, and practical experience generated civic bonds with strong emotional overtones. The increases in knowledge, communication, and the specification of coordinated behavior were outcomes of proximity of residence, but so were famines, epidemics, and street riots. When these latter were brought under control the government of a nation moved out of the palace and into the center of a city that was soon to expand to the proportions of a metropolis.

The foregoing sketch of the stages of evolution of human agglomeration is not intended to pass as history. Although it is based upon present archaeological and anthropological accounts and employs their chronology and some terms of their language, it is actually a foreshortened description of the inferences that follow from the set of assumptions introduced initially. The portrayal is a reasonable generalization rather than a strict representation of what is known. Archaeology and history are able to deny many lines of evolution, but the patterns implicit in what has been asserted are not disproved by the theses the pre-historians and the historians have deduced.

THROUGH COMMERCE TO THE METROPOLIS

Even after four or five thousand years of evolution in Asia, North Africa, and Europe, involving the creation of many uniquely urban arts, cities prospered and declined, and were rebuilt or replaced by other cities.[10]

What can be said to be the prime causes of decline? How often does factionalism become so irreconcilable that only the generals can rule? How soon does decline set in after the army is turned over to mercenaries whose demands for pay and plunder are continuously more difficult to meet? What happens when the currency is debased and the traders are no longer welcome in foreign ports, and farmers, impoverished by increasing taxes put upon land with declining fertility, are driven to revolt or to take up residence as a proletariat? The increasing dysfunction of the society with various strata and castes selfishly exerting their own small vetoes regardless of the consequences for the society as a whole certainly must reduce the capability to meet threats from aspiring neighbors and the barbarians at the border. Would not the exposure to many religions, revealing that no city's gods were omnipotent, lead to a diminution of patriotic fervor as well? Is not the general loss of facility in the communication arts—despite the occasional outstanding cultural contribution produced when decline is already advanced—due to polemics between dissident scholars and to the fragmentation of the academies and ateliers as well as to the impoverishment of the patrons and the loss of the economic security they provide? The momentum of growth in population and physical size may cause a few cities to overshoot the capabilities of the culture to fuse them into a coherent unit.

When the influence of Roman cities upon the countryside waned, large populations perished, and the remainder were again distributed over the map more or less in proportion to the availability of resources. The urban arts that had been drawn into Rome from the whole civilized world would have been lost at the time of its fall were it not for their partial transfer to cities in the East, to the Byzantine culture and the Arabs, and to the monasteries in the North. The Arabs, moreover, had begun to receive substantial infusions from India and China. Growing commerce, and later a wave of refugees from depredations of the Turks, brought about a rediffusion of the arts to cities of the Mediterranean and, with some lag, to the North also. Merchants in those centers demonstrated an avid devotion to communication—drawing, mapping, painting, sculpture, mathematics, astronomy (mainly astrology), and eventually printing—that went far beyond the needs for staying in business.

In feudalistic times a large city might contain 15,000–50,000 residents. Each (with the exception of a handful of trading cities providing interregional services) dominated a hinterland that could be covered within several days on horseback and was settled by 30 to 100 times the population of the city itself. About 90% of the total population lived in agricultural villages and manors which encouraged division of labor but supported very few skilled artisans, while the remainder lived in towns. The latter could be reached by practically all the population in one day of travelling, while villages were located so that a return trip could be made between manor and village in the same day. Communication in that period, with its extreme dependence upon ascribed status and face-to-face meeting, was limited to the transport of items that could be carried on one's person. Risks of interception by lawless persons were high and wolf packs roamed the forests, so that convoys were often felt to be necessary. The use of writing or records was minimal unless religious and governmental functions were superimposed upon commerce—conditions that normally gave a city primacy for its region. Net migration to the growing city was a gradual process that was interrupted by epidemics, famines, wars, and often held back by tolls and regulations.[11]

The ebb and flow in city life observed in the West has also characterized the histories of China, Japan, and India. Evidence of trends in the New World cultures is still very incomplete, since its archaeology has received less attention and the cultural development was cut off before even the parallels to Hellenistic urbanity had been achieved. From the evidence that is available to us, however, it is easy to see how the fortunes of primate cities varied with the effectiveness of tax collection from the provinces. Such cities rested upon a base of political power maintained by military operations. Most of the surplus funds were spent where it was convenient to those that held power. All the services that money could buy were therefore clustered around the palace. The common services, the kind found in any provincial city, were assigned to various precincts in the capital. Commerce had status well below that of the nobility, so that it was considered just another service which could be taxed and regulated.

The regeneration of trade between centers seemed to lead to remarkable urban growth (Figure 4). What is it about commerce that induces people to agglomerate? Commerce is founded upon a series of transactions between buyers and sellers, each of whom benefits to some degree. The standard transaction

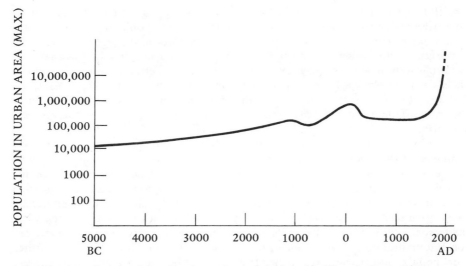

Figure 4. Maximum Size of Urban Clusters during the Historic Period. The early history of cities would probably show some irregularity in size, but population estimates are too crude to make it apparent. The explosion under way at present is obviously unprecedented in its acceleration and will lift humanity into a new dimension of mass interaction.

requires a short period of time for negotiation and is conveniently restricted to one locale. Once an interregional marketplace has come to be recognized, shiploads and caravans of products must be redistributed over short periods of time. At this scale of operations it is evident that both buyer and seller require services in the form of transport, warehousing, banking, accounting, security, etc., which they pay for out of the gross returns from the transaction. As in primate cities, artisans will set up their shops at sites calculated to capture a share of the gross profit. In commercial cities, however, many craftsmen will also be encouraged to produce for export. This may mean either a bonus for superlative proficiency in the art or a profit from quantity production. Increasing quality and volume enhance the flow of trade, and trade in turn makes greater demands for the standard services.

Reference has already been made repeatedly to economies of scale—the savings in the factors of production that are brought about by increasing the volume of output. We may expect the fruits of the improved unit efficiency to be shared by the producers, in this case in the mercantile city, and the consumers wherever they may be. A good part of these profits are obtained by mercantile enterprisers who endeavor to look for further opportunities for investment. If that investment is made in the city itself, the city will be creating jobs. It will attract three main types: *foreigners* from the other ends of the trade routes who live in enclaves of sojourners, *refugees* from the conflicts and ruthlessness of empire-building who will prefer these cities to other places that are open to them, and *townspeople* and *peasants* up to several days' journey away who have come in search of opportunity. If the investment is made in mines or colonies the growth of the mercantile city is delayed until resources above and beyond the investment have been transferred back to the city. It is important to note that wealth and the prospects of wealth serve as a magnet for population. The attractive force falls off with distance, but not by any simple geometric rule. A better measure yet is that it falls off inversely with the cost of movement. However, if any record could be made of the *frequency of contacts* with various locales, it would appear that this measure would yield an even better prediction of the attraction of the city for migrants.

The external economies that have also been mentioned refer to gains that are obtained from linking the production activities so that the byproduct, or even waste product, of one becomes the raw material of another. They may become sizable when basic production techniques are subject to few lapses and have good prospects. Then niches for new enterprises are created which are so much dependent upon one or more major producers that the best location is in the back yard, so to speak, of the latter. Geographical separation of the interdependent activities became more feasible after modern science and technology introduced substitutes for the byproducts that could be made available, if ever the primary supply should fail.

A good illustration of these effects was provided by printing when it was gaining a foothold in the cities of Western Europe. When only a dozen or two copies of a book were required, it paid to reproduce it by means using professional scribes. However, when hundreds could be sold, as was the case for recognized classics in university locales, printing was much the cheaper process. Here was a change in technology which brought economies of scale. The demand for books was highly elastic so that soon various kinds of contemporary treatises were sought by printers and booksellers. Papermakers, binders, engravers, artificers and dyers were all already in existence but their fortunes were advanced considerably by the boom in printing. The external economies here permitted the production of current material, eventually even philosophic journals, as a byproduct from Bibles, Aristotle, Galen, and the scholastics. The indirect effects, which also fall within the definition for external economies, such as the spread of literacy and learning, are not so localized. These indirect economies are due to the small adjustments in behavior, the opportunities to learn and to apply that learning, which flow through the channels of commerce and the technology of war.

It has been hinted along the way than an attractive "pull" upon the migrant is often reinforced by a "push" from the environment. The *push* postulates calamities and Malthusian pressures which force the people out of their homelands if they are to survive at all. Cities can sometimes be inundated with refugees, and in that case it is not so much the existence of an attraction but the lack of a suitable barrier that results in population growth. Some time after the influx has arrived opportunities for using the low-cost labor supply will be exploited and both income and wealth may begin to rise proportionately to population. Perhaps the best contemporary example is that of Hong Kong. The *pull* of a city is proportionate to the advance in wealth and income that it has achieved over and above the average levels in the countryside to a level below subsistence or whatever are the minimum limits set for "decency" or "tolerability." In actual observations the effects of "pull" and "push" can be distinguished only under extreme circumstances. Most of the time motives are mixed and the respective models consequently are woefully imprecise.

COHESION EXPEDITED BY EXCHANGES

The central problem, as it was understood at the beginning of this chapter, is that of discovering the sources and the fundamental units of the relations that are generated and maintained in an urban network. Some illumination was obtained from recent history, from economic argument, and from evolution, but all this was evidence of a qualitative kind. More compelling explanations for strengthening the relations are sought in the intensification of communications, the accumulation of knowledge about nature, and the formulation of specific social controls regulating public behavior. Language and commerce must be heavily involved. With that kind of suggestive material at hand it is possible to assemble a deductive system which promises not only to explain the civic bond in terms of more basic assumptions but to assist in the measurement of key parameters in urban socio-cultural systems.

The basic unit seems to be that of the *transaction*. The central concept is clear enough so that the precise delimitation of what constitutes a transaction can wait. It implies exchange between individuals or groups participating in a society. The exchange may involve goods (even spouses, as mentioned earlier) or services, but not necessarily. A transaction *always* involves some communication of information and, indeed, before the argument is completed, it will be seen that the transfer of information provides one of the most convenient criteria for determining what is and is not a transaction.

Consider the simplest case between two individuals in an urban context. Each remembers the time, place, content, and result of the meeting. Each recognizes the other actor according to name, social role, and function. It is a shared episode in two independent streams of experience. In a city many transactions are encouraged to take place between perfect strangers, in order to foreshorten the amount of time required for completion. The amount of communication needed is reduced by the specification of institutional contexts such as the market or the school, which create standard sets of expectations in each actor.

A series of transactions between two strangers has some interesting consequences. For one thing, they cease to be strangers. Each develops a more specific set of expectations regarding the behavior of the other. Formalities and assurances of good faith become redundant, and so are dropped. The later transactions are streamlined affairs as compared to mutual hesitancies involved in the first of the series. Each party comes to depend upon his set of expectations with regard to the other. (In high-density slums people are thrown together by chance. The result appears to a third party to be not too savory. However, the dissolution of these relationships by transferring the people to low-density housing on the urban fringe often leads to a strange emptiness of life which sociologists have called *anomie*. After living in the slums for a while almost everyone comes to depend upon his neighbors, either for the exchange of pleasantries and small helps or as objects upon which he can expend his aggressions. Bonds are formed in either case; the first is coordinative and relatively symmetrical, while the latter is polar and asymmetrical.) The rest of his behavior seems to take this stabilization of expectations into account so that relatively elaborate strategies dependent upon it can be developed successfully. These interdependent expectancies, as defined by time, place, name or designation of parties, context and content, are the relations that make up the network that lies behind civic organization. In order to isolate public affairs we must leave aside the bonds between persons within the household and other primary groups. In urban public life almost all the relationships start, as has been assumed here, from the interaction of strangers.[12]

The scientist, always in search of simple yet reaching explanations, would like to conclude that the strength of the bond takes the form of a *preference* for one situation among several, for one group among many, for a distinctive location, and a particular role at any given time, but this preference on the part of an individual or group is matched by a preference for them held by the institutions or individuals on the other side of the transaction. Thus reciprocal preferences form a bond. Non-reciprocated, or competitive, preferences can also exist; they can be bonded together in space by third parties who oscillate from one camp to the other. Preferences can be handled in contemporary economic theory as an aspect of *utility*. Utility may be thought of as a vector—a resultant of identifiable component vectors that act upon the choice mechanism by pulling in many different directions. Each component may be listed according to strength or direction very much like words in a lexicon. Such a utility, once it has been created, can be measured by creating a set of real choices in an environment of controlled risk, as described by Davidson, Suppes, and Siegel.[13]

As a *preference,* the relationship of A to B can be ranked with all the relationships in the class, which in this case might include all persons contacted publicly. However, quite different wants and gratifications can be compared with the preference for contact. Thus, seeing the teacher may be deflected by the introduction of the superior alternatives of playing a game or getting something to eat.

Starting from standard initial conditions, i.e., a context and stranger-to-stranger interaction, the scientist would like to be able to predict the strength of the bond that evolves. Certainly the strength will be a function of the *number* of transactions that have occurred, and the perceived *utility* at the time of the transaction for both A and B will be significant. There will very likely have to be introduced a parameter reflecting the amount of reinforcement (learning) obtained independent of the utility, and another parameter for the decay of the reinforcement over time (forgetting), which would be affected by the reward that was experienced. Even this would not be exhaustive because both A and B have primary relations in families or other private groups which can affect their secondary relations as virtual strangers and in addition they may acquire insights from observation and deduction that change the structure of their preference scales independent of social experience.

In theory all these events and parameters are countable and measurable, because they occur in public and are presumably not significantly influenced by the presence of a third party who might serve as an observer. Starting from individuals A and B, however, the measurements make predictions about behavior that are not very precise. Because of the limitations of scientific approaches for understanding the formation of bonds that affect spatial behavior of humans, "common sense" must be relied on to predict human behavior; however, the scientific techniques may be used for the microscopic analysis of specific mistakes made in these common sense judgments. Discovering the source of the mistake leads to correction of the error in most instances. Despite the time and space devoted to the discussion of the means for measurement, it is important to remember that prediction of bond strengths over a population like a city starting from such micro-theory is not feasible; the respective uncertainties accumulate and loom too large.

Almost everything that has been said about transactions between individuals applies as well to transactions between groups. The existence of a human group, whether it be a friendship group, a work group, a study group, or any other, presumes repetitive reinforcement of the bonds between individuals (which would otherwise decay due to "forgetting"). The relative strength of the bond connecting a member to other members and to the group as a whole (i.e., identification with its collective aims and activities) can be measured by the quantity of a given inducement (e.g., money, hierarchical status) required to get him to cut off his relationships voluntarily. Sometimes these relationships come to be valued as highly as life itself, but that is rare. A group can engage in transactions with non-members as individuals, with other groups, or with organizational entities on a still higher plane. Again interdependencies will result from a sequence of transactions that tend to bring people together in space so as to renew the contacts. *Face-to-face interaction, which is most efficient by far in creating and maintaining groups, requires proximity.*

As soon as inter-group relations are considered in the social fabric, however, a new kind of transaction may occur. Individuals may be transferred between groups. Even in the pre-dawn of civilization it was necessary for households to arrange for out-breeding. Hostages and harems served many of the same purposes. At a later date it became possible for persons to participate in groups outside the household. An outside observer would see them oscillating from one circle to another in the vicinity of their homes. Groups are linked into organizations through just such exchanges. The greater the number of working memberships an individual maintains the greater is his contribution to social cohesion. Thus one expects to find that the strength of the attachment to the city is a function of the number of "joiners" that have come onto the scene. This assumes, of course, that the person with multiple memberships is accepted by the respective groups and is an active participant.

THE ARGUMENT RECAPITULATED

The first problem that arises in achieving a systematic description of the metropolis is that of understanding and explaining the differentials in density, labor productivity and land value that distinguish a metropolis from rural communities in the same society. This description should be undertaken in terms of simple, isolable, and preferably manipulable, phenomena. What is the agglomerative force that seems to be at work maintaining these differentials in the face of diffusion and conflict? In common with other systems of thought, the source of cohesion was sought in the periodic, quantized exchanges between independent observable units.

The first resort was to explore recorded history, analyzing briefly the gradual transition from a relatively homogeneous distribution of population relative to resources—as was evident in primitive and medieval times—to the establishment of a metropolis. An intensification of *communications, knowledge* and *controls* seemed to be highly correlated with the growth of cities. The bonds that tie individuals to the city seem to result from the conservation and accumulation of some concomitant of these factors.

Similar explorations of underlying economic principles suggested that external economies (referred to more frequently also as "complementary of social function") resulting from changes in activities are most available to neighbors, because information concerning the opportunities arrives there first. Opportunities also appear at linkage points in communications systems and entrepreneurs located there obtain access to several independent sources of information first. Thus change encourages change in the vicinity of a communications focus, and activity is piled upon activity within a small amount of space, subject only to diseconomies associated with intense land use such as congestion, public disorders, and epidemics. The latter can be reduced by means of services, like police or public health, with extremely selective controls. If, as is usually the case, these services are subject to economies of scale, agglomeration is assisted further.

The evolution of the utility of agglomeration was traced back into pre-history. Certain givens about human beings, their genetics, primary relations necessary for nurture, the formation of coalitions for purposes of defense, and the exchange of goods, seem to lead necessarily to the accumulation of knowledge in the households surviving the longest and to the selection and recombination of the most useful elements of culture by successors and off-shoots. Once village life based upon agriculture had been established the accumulation of techniques visibly accelerated. Villages grew to towns, and towns to cities, in short order, and the need for records required the use of written symbols. The latter caused a new spurt in accumulation of knowledge, and an increased amount of *public* activity, as distinguished from private and familial activities.

A similar analysis of the evolution of a bond between two individuals, previously strangers to each other, suggested that the quantum involved is a *transaction,* an event involving at least the transfer of information, but possibly also the transfer of goods. For an individual the bond that develops from repeated transactions is an aspect of *utility,* a preference for that kind of control as against others that are possible, but the aggregate strength of the network of urban relations cannot be assembled from measurements of private utility and related parameters. Human groups may be linked together by means of shared individuals so that at higher levels of organization peculiar kinds of transactions must be considered. The counting of transactions, and an assessment of the traces of cohesion they leave behind, must take into account structural levels, i.e., civic cohesion is brought about by transactions occurring in the *public* sphere, rather than the family, clan, or friendship group.

NOTES

1. The argument touches at this point upon philosophies of science. It recognizes that a body of experienced investigators has evolved procedures for maximizing the reproducibility of observations and modes of interpretation which minimize the appearance of paradoxes. No single philosophical scheme has been settled upon, nor need it be at this stage because none is yet at the point of making fine distinctions. Cf. J. R. Kantor, *The Logic of Modern Science,* Bloomington, Indiana: Principia Press, 1953, Pts. I and IV; R. B.

Braithwaite, *Scientific Explanation*, London: Cambridge University Press, 1953, Chs. 1–3. For insights well ahead of his period see K. J. W. Craik, *The Nature of Explanation*. Cambridge University Press, London, 1943.

2. The theoretical arguments underlying this assertion, based upon game theory considerations, have been very persuasively assembled by Thomas C. Schelling, *The Strategy of Conflict*, Cambridge: Harvard University Press, 1960.

3. J. Q. Stewart and W. Warntz, "Physics of Population Distribution," *Journal of Regional Science 1*, 1958, 99–123.

4. R. E. Wycherley, *How the Greeks Built Cities* (London: Macmillan, 1949), p. 14.

5. Robert J. Braidwood, Bruce Howe, *et al.*, *Prehistoric Investigations in Iraqi Kurdistan*, Studies in Ancient Oriental Civilization No. 31, Chicago: Oriental Institute and University of Chicago Press, 1960.

6. Carl H. Kraeling and Robert M. Adams, eds., *City Invincible*, Chicago: University of Chicago Press, 1960, p. 26.

7. In a sociological evaluation of the evolution of cities, based in part upon analysis of the structure of such contemporary "feudal" cities as Khatmandu and Timbuktu, Gideon Sjoberg in his book *The Pre-Industrial City* (Glencoe, Ill.: Free Press, 1960) accepts V. Gordon Childe's basic criterion of civilization: cities come into being only after techniques for preparing permanent, coded records have been employed. This basis for deciding the transition from prehistoric town to primitive city is extremely sensitive to archaeological and cultural evidence, but it sometimes contradicts common sense because it places such developments as those leading up to the Incas into the "precivilized" category of cultures which are incapable of building true cities. Fustel de Coulanges in *The Ancient City* (New York, Doubleday Anchor, 1956) attributes the evolution of urban cohesion to community-wide religious practices but he has not made out a persuasive case when judged by the levels of explanation that we have set for ourselves here. Religious beliefs during this early period appear to have been extremely flexible—many of the omens were blatantly manipulated, even by moderately superstitious elites—so they simultaneously aided and hindered the establishment of cities. Lewis Mumford in *The City in History* (New York: Harcourt, Brace and World, 1961) has chosen to neglect some of the currently available information and can therefore conclude that a city is a cultural mutation (obviously deleterious in its effect!) which occurred only once and diffused somehow to the New World.

8. G. R. Willey, "The New World Prehistory," *Science 131*, 1960, 73–87.

9. A fascinating illustration of the historic process is now coming to light in the studies of the Yoruba, a West African tribe with a low level of literacy that has had a tradition of agglomerating in units of 10,000 to 100,000 persons. Arab accounts from 1066 A.D. onwards describe cities in West Africa, some on the Moslem frontier and some beyond. When the Portuguese arrived in 1486 they found Benin city which contained, according to accounts, anywhere from 15,000 to 100,000 persons, depending upon the season, the fortunes of war, and the biases of the estimator. From the fifteenth to the nineteenth century many cities disappeared, but quite a few lasted the whole period, so that continuity of existence was comparable to that observed in other parts of the world. The Yoruba were particularly vulnerable to the slave trade of the early nineteenth century because agglomeration made them easier to capture while at the same time their inland location cut them off from European weapons.

   The Yoruba have always been organized in kin groups, each of which operates as a land-holding corporation in which adult males hold shares. Positions of prestige exist primarily within this kin group. Workers on the land live in the city as much as they can, the actual time depending upon distance, which may be as much as thirty miles. Everyone is expected to be present for kin group meetings and festivals. Trade and craft specialization within the city are extensive, and the markets are well organized with impersonal dealings between middlemen predominant. The city was governed by chiefs subsidiary to a king.

   The old cities of the Yoruba, however, leave very little for the archaeologist to work with. The temples were of wood and are not large. There were no major public works such as roads or aqueducts, with the possible exception of walls and defense points. The streets were rectilinear (signifying that they were originally military camps or colonial settlements) but the compounds within the block were not standardized.

For over a thousand years most of the Yoruba have adhered to an agglomerative pattern. During that period they successfully resisted evangelical Mohammedanism and, though added to the British empire, only marginal elements accepted Christianity. Perhaps this is because their cities have been 95 per cent or more Yoruba, with most of the aliens being servants rather than merchants and craftsmen. They were thus prevented from experiencing the kind of cumulative progress that derives from agglomeration elsewhere in the world. In many ways the Yoruba resemble the Mayans, who lived at roughly the same latitude, but the Yoruba lacked materials with permanence.

Cf. "Urbanism in West Africa," Kenneth Little, ed., especially the contributions of R. J. H. Church, W. Bascom, and P. C. Lloyd, *The Sociological Review* 7, July 1959, 131 pp.

10. George R. Stewart in his novel *Years of the City*, Boston: Houghton Mifflin, 1955, portrays the founding, growth, temporary significance, decline and disappearance of a typical Greek city of middle rank that lasted perhaps seven or eight generations. He held assiduously to classical sources but in the arrangement of material illustrated some of the contemporary theories about the transformations of cities. This work represents a careful, yet colorful, illustration of the way larger social processes affect all the facets of public behavior.

11. R. E. Dickinson in his *City Region and Regionalism: A Geographical Contribution to Human Ecology* (London: Oxford University Press, 1947) provides a rather detailed picture of medieval German urbanization and urban influence. A well-organized general restatement with English and French examples in a more modern idiom is provided by J. C. Russell, "The Metropolitan City Region of the Middle Ages," *Journal of Regional Science 2*, 1960, 55–70.

12. The concepts that suggest the way to such theorizing have been around for some decades. It is likely therefore that these thoughts have been expressed elsewhere at an earlier date. When they were articulated here as a framework for urban organization I sought some prior statement. Thus far I have found only a rather early formulation by George Devereux, "A Conceptual Scheme for Society," *American Journal of Sociology, 44*, 1940, 687–706. He foresees some of the arguments appearing in Chapters Seven and Eight as well. Very likely other statements will be called to my attention.

13. D. Davidson, P. Suppes, and S. Siegel, *Decision Making: An Experimental Approach* (Stanford: Stanford University Press, 1957); J. S. Chipman, "The Foundations of Utility," *Econometrica, 28*, 1960, 193–224, provides a review of the underlying axioms and their implications for measurement. He points out, for example, that if membership in one commodity cannot be substituted for by others, then utility cannot be measured by a real number equivalent to a market price (i.e., a given number of *utiles*) but only by a vector that can be rank-ordered in a list of vectors.

Selected Readings on Cities

CITY AND SOCIETY

(This heading includes studies of the influence of cities, of relationships between city and hinterland, and of regional arrangements of cities.)

Armstrong, Lincoln, and Rashid Bashur. "Ecological Patterns and Value Orientation of Lebanon," *Public Opinion Quarterly*, 1958 22: 406–415.

Braudel, Fernand. *Civilisation matérielle et capitalisme.* Paris: Colin, 1967. A virtuoso history and analysis of European capitalism by one of the masters.

Braun, Rudolf. *Industrialisierung und Volksleben.* Zurich: Rentsch, 1960. The transformations of upland and rural life as Zurich's textile industry expanded.

Briggs, Asa. *Victorian Cities.* London: Odhams, 1963.

Centre de la Méditerranée Moderne et Contemporaine. *Villes de l'Europe méditerranéenne et de l'Europe occidentale du Moyen Age au XIXe siècle.* Saint-Brieuc: Les Belles Lettres; Annales de la Faculté des Lettres et Sciences Humaines de Nice, nos. 9–10. Conference proceedings of better quality than the usual, including valuable sketches of the internal organization of European cities in the past.

Charrier, Jean-Bernard. *Citadins et ruraux.* Paris: Presses Universitaires de France, 1970, Que sais-je? A compact essay on urbanization and rural-urban relations.

Chaunu, Pierre. *La civilisation de l'Europe classique.* Paris: Arthaud, 1970. A synthesis covering some of the same ground as Braudel's but with a greater emphasis on thought and the arts. Like Braudel's tome, lavishly illustrated.

Cipolla, Carlo M. *Literacy and Development in the West.* Baltimore: Penguin, 1969. A small, well-polished gem of a book, with many implications for (but few direct references to) urbanism.

Clark, Peter, and Paul Slack, eds. *Crisis and Order in English Towns, 1500–1700.* London: Routledge and Kegan Paul, 1972. A collection of first-rate studies of individual cities.

Clark, S. D. *The Developing Canadian Community.* Toronto: University of Toronto Press, 1962.

Davidovich, V. G. "On Patterns and Tendencies of Urban Settlement in the U.S.S.R." *Soviet Geography* VIII (1966): 3–31.

Delumeau, Jean. *Vie économique et sociale de Rome dans la seconde moitié du XVIe siècle.* Paris: Boccard, 1959. 2 vols. Bibliothèque des Ecoles Françaises d'Athènes et de Rome, 184. Excellent on grain supply, banditry, and their connections.

Deutsch, Karl. "Social Mobilization and Political Development." *American Political Science Review,* 1961, 15.

Duncan, Otis Dudley, et al. *Metropolis and Region.* Baltimore: Johns Hopkins University Press, 1960.

Everitt, Alan. "The Marketing of Agricultural Produce." In Joan Thirsk, ed., *The Agrarian History of England and Wales, 1540–1640.* Cambridge, England: Cambridge University Press, 1967, 466–592. As unlikely as it may seem, this and several other articles in the volume make excellent reading for anyone interested in the influence of the city on the countryside.

Fogelson, Robert M. *The Fragmented Metropolis: Los Angeles 1850–1930.* Cambridge, Mass.: Harvard University Press, 1967. Sociologically informed urban history.

Forman, Shepard, and Joyce Riegelhaupt. "Market Place and Marketing System: Toward a Theory of Peasant Economic Integration." *Comparative Studies in Society and History* 12 (1970): 188–212. Covers a wide range of sources, in addition to offering an important argument.

Fourquin, Guy. *Les campagnes de la région parisienne à la fin du Moyen Age.* Paris: Publ. de la Faculté des lettres et des sciences Humaines de l'Univ. de Paris, 1964. A splendid study of the influence of a great and growing capital on the medieval countryside.

Friedmann, Georges, ed. *Villes et campagnes.* Paris: Colin, 1953.

Garigue, Philippe. *La Vie familiale des canadiens français.* Montréal: Presses de l'Université, 1962.

Goldberg, David. "The Fertility of Two-Generation Urbanities." *Population Studies* 12 (1959): 214–222.

Harris, Marvin. *Town and Country in Brazil.* New York: Columbia University Press, 1956.

Hsiao, Kung-Chuan. *Rural China: Imperial Control in the Nineteenth Century.* Seattle: University of Washington Press, 1960. How a vast empire maintained local power.

Innes, Harold A. *The Bias of Communication.* Toronto: University of Toronto Press, 1951.

Jones, A. H. M. *Athenian Democracy.* New York: Praeger, 1958.

Kantor, Mildred B., ed. *Mobility and Mental Health.* Springfield, Ill.: Charles C. Thomas, 1965. Combination of reviews of literature and reports on research.

Köllmann, W. *Sozialgeschichte der Stadt Barmen im 19. Jahrhundert.* Tübingen: Mohr, 1960.

Kunkel, John. "Economic Autonomy and Social Change in Mexican Villages." *Economic Development and Cultural Change* 10 (1961): 51–63.

Lapidus, Ira. *Muslim Cities in the Later Middle Ages.* Cambridge, Mass.: Harvard University Press, 1967.

Lopreato, Joseph. "Economic Development and Cultural Change: The Role of Emigration." *Human Organization* 21 (1962): 182–200.

408   *Cities*

Lowenstein, S. F. "Urban Images of Roman Authors." *Comparative Studies in Society and History* 8 (October 1965): 110–123.
Mehta, Surinder. "Some Demographic and Economic Correlates of Primate Cities: A Case of Revaluation." *Demography* 1 (1964): 136–147.
Miles, S. W. "An Urban Type: Extended Boundary Towns." *Southwestern Journal of Anthropology* 14 (1958): 339–351.
Morrill, Richard L. *Migration and the Spread and Growth of Urban Settlement.* Lund Series in Geography, Human Geography No. 26, 1965.
Morse, Richard M. "Some Characteristics of Latin American Urban History." *American Historical Review* 67 (1962): 317–338.
Murphey, Rhoads. *The Treaty Ports.* New York: Macmillan, 1972. A brief, readable introduction to the Western wedge into China.
Nash, Manning. *Machine Age Maya.* Menasha, Wisc.: American Anthropological Association, 1968.
Pach, S. P. "Die Getreideversorgung der ungarischen Städt vom XV bis XVII. Jahrhundert," *Third International Conference of Economic History, Munich 1965* I, 97–108. Paris: Mouton, 1968. One of a set of dense papers on urban food supply.
Pourcher, Guy. *Le Peuplement de Paris.* Paris: Presses Universitaires de France, 1964. INED Travaux et Documents No. 43.
Pred, Alan. *The External Relations of Cities During 'Industrial Revolution.'* Chicago: Department of Geography, University of Chicago, 1962. A general essay plus a study of Goteborg, Sweden.
Rudé, George. *Hanoverian London, 1714–1808.* London: Secker & Warburg, 1971. An outstanding student of protest and rebellion tries his hand, very surely, at continuous urban history.
Russell, J. C. "The Metropolitan City Region of the Middle Ages," *Journal of Regional Science,* 2 (1960): 55–70.
Shryock, H. S., Jr. *Population Mobility within the United States.* Chicago: Community and Family Study Center, University of Chicago, 1964.
Szabo, Denis. *Crimes et villes.* Paris: Cujas, 1960.
de Valdeavellano y Arcimis, Luis Garcia. *Sobre los burgos y los burgueses de la España medieval.* Madrid: Real Academia de la Historia, 1960.
Vidich, Arthur J., and Joseph Bensman. *Small Town in Mass Society.* Princeton, N.J.: Princeton University Press, 1958.
Vogel, Ezra, *Canton under Communism: Programs and Politics in a Provincial Capital, 1949–1968.* Cambridge, Mass.: Harvard University Press, 1969. A sociological reconstruction from outside of China—something like putting together a ship inside a bottle, and something like doing history.
Weber, Adna F. *The Growth of Cities in the Nineteenth Century.* Ithaca, N.Y.: Cornell University Press, 1965. Reprint of an old standard first published in 1899.
Wheatley, Paul, "The Significance of Traditional Yoruba Urbanism", *Comparative Studies in Society and History,* 12 (1970): 393–423.
Wilensky, Harold L. and Charles N. Lebeaux. *Industrial Society and Social Welfare.* New York: Free Press, 1965. Paperback edition with new introduction. Implications of the urban society for the dispossessed.
Wilkinson, Thomas O. "Urban Structure and Industrialization." *American Sociological Review* 25 (1960): 356–363.
Wood, Arthur. "Political Radicalism in Changing Sinhalese Villages." *Human Organization* 23 (1964): 99–107.
Würzbacher, Gerhard. *Das Dorf im Spannungsfeld industrialler Entwicklung.* Stuttgart: Enke, 1954.

THE ORGANIZATION OF CITIES

(The following items emphasize participation in the life of the city, differentiations of space, time, and social position. There are a few discussions of urban order or disorder.)

Agulhon, Maurice. *Une ville ouvrière au temps du socialisme utopique: Toulon de 1815 à 1851.* Paris: Mouton, 1970. Working-class organization in a French port city during political turmoil and early industrialization.

Allen, William Sheridan. *The Nazi Seizure of Power: The Experience of a Single German Town, 1930–1935.* Chicago: Quadrangle, 1965. Although this book is often read for the history of the Nazis, it can well be read for urban power structure.

Back, Kurt. *Slums, Projects, and People.* Durham, N.C.: Duke University Press, 1962.

Balandier, Georges. *Sociologie des Brazzavilles noires.* Paris: Colin, 1955.

Banfield, Edward C. and James C. Wilson. *City Politics.* Cambridge, Mass.: Harvard University Press and M.I.T. Press, 1963.

Banton, Michael. *West African City: A Study of the Tribal Life in Freetown.* London: Oxford University Press, 1957.

Barnes, J. A. "Network and Political Process." In *Local Level Politics,* edited by Mark Swartz. Chicago: Aldine, 1969.

Bartholomew, Harland. *Land Uses in American Cities.* Cambridge, Mass.: Harvard University Press, 1955.

Beijer, G. *Rural Migrants in Urban Setting.* The Hague: Nijhoff, 1963. Mainly bibliographical, Western Europe only.

Bennassar, Bartolomé. *Valladolid au siècle d'or: Une ville de Castile et sa campagne au XVIe siècle.* Paris: Mouton, 1967. The French style of urban social history applied to golden-age Spain.

Berger, Bennett. *Working Class Suburb.* Berkeley: University of California Press, 1960.

Berry, Brian J. L. "Internal Structure of the City." *Law and Contemporary Problems* 30 (Winter, 1965): 111–119. A quantitative geographer's view.

Bettelheim, Charles, and Suzanne Frère. *Auxerre en 1950.* Paris: Colin, 1950.

Bordua, David, ed. *The Police.* New York: Wiley, 1967.

Caplow, Theodore, Sheldon Stryker, and Samuel E. Wallace. *The Urban Ambience.* Totowa, N.Y.: Bedminster, 1964. Study of local social relations in San Juan, Puerto Rico.

Chapin, Stuart F., Jr., and Henry C. Hightower. *Household Activity Systems—A Pilot Investigation.* Chapel Hill: Center for Urban and Regional Studies, Univ. of North Carolina, 1966.

Chevalier, Louis. *Classes laborieuses et classes dangereuses.* Paris: Plon, 1958.

Chevalier, Louis. *Les Parisiens.* Paris: Hachette, 1967. A brilliant, opinionated combination of literary and social history by a man who has turned away from demographic analysis after doing it well.

Chombart de Lauwe, Paul-Henry. *Des hommes et des villes.* Paris: Payot, 1963. A close discussion of the small scale in big cities.

Chrisman, Miriam Usher. *Strasbourg and the Reform: A Study in the Processes of Change.* New Haven, Conn.: Yale University Press, 1967.

Clark, S. D. *The Suburban Society.* Toronto: University of Toronto Press, 1966. All suburbia (all "urbia" as well) seen in, through, and from Metro Toronto.

Cobb, Richard. *The Police and the People.* Oxford: Oxford University Press, 1970. Essays on the ordinary people of Paris and elsewhere in urban France, as they dealt with the police from 1780 to 1820, and as the police dealt with them.

Coleman, James S. *Community Conflict.* Glencoe, Ill.: Free Press, 1957. A synthetic review of the literature.

Conot, Robert. *Rivers of Blood, Years of Darkness.* New York: Bantam Books, 1967. A stirring, thorough journalistic account of the Watts riot and its background.

Coult, Allan, and Robert Habenstein. "The Study of Extended Kinship in Urban Society." *Sociological Quarterly,* 1962: 141–145. Brief review of the literature.

Couturier, Marcel. *Recherches sur les structures sociales de Châteaudun, 1525–1789.* Paris: SEVPEN, 1969. Demonstrates the blending of demographic and class analysis which is now emerging in European social history.

Crissman, Lawrence. "The Segmentary Structure of Overseas Chinese Communities." *Man* 2 (June, 1967): 185–204.

Deyon, Pierre. *Amiens, capitale provinciale.* Paris: Mouton, 1967. Already a standard work on early modern urban history.

Dobriner, William M., ed. *The Suburban Community.* New York: Putnam, 1958.

Dore, R. P. *City Life in Japan.* Berkeley and Los Angeles: University of California Press, 1958.

Dorsett, Lyle W. *The Pendergast Machine.* New York: Oxford University Press. A short study of Kansas City politics in the great days of Boss Pendergast.

Dynes, Russell. "Rurality, Migration and Sectarianism." *Rural Sociology* 21 (1956): 25–28.

El Kordi, Mohamed. *Bayeux aux XVIIe et XVIIIe siècles: Contribution à l'histoire urbaine de la France.* Paris: Mouton, 1970. Another well-executed French urban history.

Epstein, A. L. *Politics in an Urban African Community.* Manchester (England): Manchester University Press, 1958.

Ferdinand, Theodore N. "The Criminal Patterns of Boston Since 1849." *The American Journal of Sociology* 73 (July 1967): 84–99.

Foote, Nelson, et al. *Housing Choices and Housing Constraints.* New York: McGraw-Hill, 1960.

Fried, Marc, and Peggy Gleicher. "Some Sources of Residential Satisfaction in an Urban Slum." *Journal of the American Institute of Planners* 27 (1961): 305–315.

Gillion, K. L. *Ahmedabad: A Study in Indian Urban History.* Berkeley and Los Angeles: University of California Press, 1969.

Glazer, Nathan, and Daniel P. Moynihan. *Beyond the Melting Pot.* Cambridge, Mass.: Harvard University Press and M.I.T. Press, 1963.

Godechot, Jacques. *The Taking of the Bastille.* New York: Scribner's, 1970. Valuable not only for the great revolution but also for the social life in Paris in 1789.

Goheen, Peter G. *Victorian Toronto, 1850 to 1900: Pattern and Process of Growth.* Chicago: University of Chicago Department of Geography, Research Paper no. 127. A detailed analysis in the style of today's quantitative geography.

Gulick, John. *Tripoli: A Modern Arab City.* Cambridge, Mass.: Harvard University Press, 1967. Traces the history and the physical and economic changes that have occurred since the fourth century B.C.

Gutkind, P. C. W. "African Urban Family Life." *Cahiers d'études africaines* 3 (1962): 149–217.

Handlin, Oscar, ed. *Children of the Uprooted.* New York: G. Braziller 1966.

Hapgood, Hutchins. *The Spirit of the Ghetto.* Edited by Moses Rischin. Cambridge, Mass.: Belknap Press of Harvard University Press, 1967.

Hayden, Tom. *Prelude to Riot: Official Violence and Ghetto Response.* New York: Vintage, 1967. An account of conflict in Newark, by a man much involved.

Howe, Christopher. *Employment and Economic Growth in Urban China, 1949–57.* Cambridge, Mass.: Cambridge University Press, 1971.

Hoyt, H. "Growth and Structure of Twenty-one Great World Cities." *Land Economics* XLII (July 1965): 53–64.

Janowitz, Morris, ed. *Community Political Systems.* Glencoe, Ill.: Free Press, 1961.

Jones, Emrys. *Towns and Cities.* London: Oxford University Press, 1966. Geographic analysis over a wide range of space and time.

Kaplan, Harold. *Urban Political Systems: A Functional Analysis of Metro Toronto.* New York: Columbia University Press, 1967. Extensive theoretical analysis à la Talcott Parsons, plus important information on metro politics.

Keller, Suzanne. *The Urban Neighborhood: A Sociological Perspective.* New York: Random House, 1968.

Kerr, Madeline. *The People of Ship Street.* London: Routledge and Kegan Paul, 1958.

Kuper, Leo, et al. *Durban, A Study of Racial Ecology.* New York: Columbia University Press, 1958.

Lachiver, Marcel. *La population de Meulan du XVIIe au XIXe siècle (vers 1600–1870):* Etude de demographie historique. Paris: SEVPEN, 1969. Rich, precise demographic history of a small city.

Lane, Roger. *Policing the City: Boston, 1822–1855.* Cambridge, Mass.: Harvard University Press, 1967.

Leggett, John. "Uprootedness and Working-Class Consciousness." *American Journal of Sociology* 68 (1963): 682–692. Differences in expressed attitudes among Detroit workers.

Lewis, John Wilson, ed. *The City in Communist China.* Stanford: Stanford University Press, 1971. Expert observations by Western experts and Easterners as well.

Lieberson, Stanley. *Ethnic Patterns in American Cities.* New York: Free Press, 1963.

Liebow, Elliot. *Tally's Corner.* Boston: Little, Brown, 1967. Almost participant observation of a Washington street corner.

Litwak, Eugene. "Geographic Mobility and Extended Family Cohesion." *American Sociological Review* 25 (June 1960): 385–394.

Lyford, Joseph. *The Airtight Cage: A Study of New York's West Side.* New York: Harper and Row, 1966. Life on and just off the streets.

McEntire, Davis. *Residence and Race.* Berkeley: University of California Press, 1960.

Manteuffel, Tadeusz. *Barcelone: Centre économique à l'époque des difficultés, 1380–1462*

Paris: Mouton, 2 vols. The great Mediterranean trading city in a time of splendid near-independence.

Marris, Peter. *Family and Social Change in an African City*. London: Routledge and Kegan Paul, 1962.

Masotti, Louis H., and Don R. Bowen, eds. *Riots and Rebellion: Civil Violence in the Urban Community*. Beverly Hills, Calif.: Sage Publications, 1968. Emphasizes the sorts of studies which grew out of American ghetto protests in the 1960's.

Mayer, Philip. "Migrancy and the Study of Africans in Towns." *American Anthropologist* 64 (1962): 576–592.

Mitchell, J. Clyde, ed. *Social Networks in Urban Situations*. Manchester, England: Manchester University Press, 1969. How the urban anthropologists are now using network notions, especially in non-Western settings.

Momsen, Ingwer Ernst. *Die Bevölkerung der Stadt Husum von 1769 bis 1860*. Kiel: Geographische Institut, 1969. Careful demographic history.

Moore, William, Jr. *The Vertical Ghetto: Everyday Life in an Urban Project*. New York: Random House, 1969. A participant observer's report worth comparing with Rainwater's study of the same place, listed below.

Morill, W. T. "Immigrants and Association: The Ibo in Twentieth Century Calabar." *Comparative Studies in Society and History*, 5 (1963): 424–448.

Nelson, Joan. "The Urban Poor: Disruption or Political Integration in Third World Cities?" *World Politics* 22 (1970): 393–414.

Orleans, Peter, and William Russell Ellis, Jr., eds. *Race, Change, and Urban Society*. Beverly Hills, Calif.: Sage, 1971. Urban Affairs Annual Review, No. 5. A compendium of current work.

Osofsky, Gilbert. *Harlem: The Making of a Ghetto*. New York: Harper and Row, 1966. Splendid social history.

Polsby, Nelson W. *Community Power and Political Theory*. New Haven, Conn.: Yale University Press, 1963.

Rainwater, Lee. *Behind Ghetto Walls*. Chicago: Aldine, 1970. Description and analysis of a giant wasteland: a St. Louis housing project.

Reimer, Svend, and John McNamara. "Contact Patterns in the City." *Social Forces* 36 (1957): 37–141.

Sainsbury, Peter. *Suicide in London*. London: Chapman and Hall, 1955.

Shostak, Arthur B., and William Gomberg, eds. *Blue-Collar World*, Englewood Cliffs, N.J.: Prentice-Hall, 1964. Varied essays on working-class life in American cities.

Spear, Allan H. *Black Chicago: The Making of a Negro Ghetto, 1890–1920*. Chicago: University of Chicago Press, 1967.

Suttles, Gerald D. *The Social Order of the Slum*. Chicago: University of Chicago Press, 1968.

Taueber, Karl, and Alma Taueber. *Negroes in Cities*. Chicago: Aldine, 1965. Concentrates on extensive and ingenious manipulation of census tract statistics for American central cities, 1940–1960.

Tilly, Charles. "Occupational Rank and Grade of Residence in a Metropolis." *American Journal of Sociology* 67 (November 1961): 232–330.

Chapter

5

Changing the City

INTRODUCTION

Urbanists are utopians, and utopians are usually urbanists. When Tomaso di Campanella, a Dominican monk, set down his sketch of the ideal social order in 1623, the title came out *City of the Sun, an idea of the Platonic Republic*. It takes the form of a dialogue between a Grandmaster of the Knights Hospitallers and a Genoese sea captain. The sea captain has come back from a long voyage in the course of which he blundered into an unknown land dominated by the City of the Sun. A priest-king rules the city, assisted by three princes representing Power, Wisdom, and Love. The citizens' daily routines and division of labor, the sea captain reports, spring from well-defined principles of virtue. And the layout of the city itself—the seven concentric circles separated by stout walls, the educational tableaux on the walls, the prescribed locations of gardens, temples, dormitories, and public places—represents a clear vision of theocratic socialism.

When Frank Lloyd Wright sketched his Broadacre City and Le Corbusier sketched his Radiant City, each of them was just as definitely combining a physical arrangement with a moral order, and just as surely casting his vision as an urban community. Those who strive to define the good life can hardly avoid doing it in terms of designs for cities. Those who design cities cannot avoid adopting and imposing, however unconsciously, a vision of the good life. In that sense, the choice among destruction, rebuilding, and observation which Claudel offered us at the beginning of this book is a false one: the poet-observer is the person most likely to articulate the vision on which the others will act.

Where, then, shall we find any room for systematic analysis? Everything depends on whether human social arrangements display detectable regularities and whether we regard them as displaying regularities. If not, the systematic analyst has no distinct contribution to make. The scholar-poet will only serve as chorus. If so,

413

the systematic analyst will, in the long run, be specially fitted to saying whether a given action will, indeed, have the consequences its proponents intend or claim. He will be almost as fitted to saying what actions will favor or forbid a desired consequence.

In this chapter, we cover the distance from short-run practicality to long-run speculation. The majority of the articles are not utopian in scope or style, yet they illustrate the special value of analysis as a way of determining whether the means and ends at hand really do join as they are supposed to. They do so, on the whole, with limited objectives and short-run outcomes in view. There are also a few essays on large questions—questions so open as to be hopeless as guides to immediate action. Yet they, too, are fundamental to the future of cities. We can only know the consequences of the choices they pose in the very long run.

They are choices of orientation, of conception, of research strategy. They amount to bets on the nature of the urban reality and on the features of the urban environment which will prove manipulable. Following a normative approach to urban structure, for example, means betting (to some degree, though there are still ways to hedge the bet) that creation and absorption of a certain way of life will turn out to be the crucial urban phenomenon, the one which triggers the development of certain spatial arrangements, certain kinds of social relationship, and so on. In advance, we cannot be sure. We leap in the twilight, if not in the dark.

Better concepts will supply some of the needed light. This book's approach to the conceptual problem has been to sort out five different ways of dealing with communities, cities, and urbanization. Each has a measure of coherence. They are the ecological, normative, locational, interactional, and holistic conceptions of these phenomena. Each has some merits and, in the present state of expertise, some serious drawbacks.

I have tried to give roughly equal representation to the first four lines of argument in the reprinted articles. Holistic statements are, I will admit, few and far between. If I have taken special delight in expounding the interactional view of community-city urbanization in my own sections of the book, it is not in order to propose that interaction is their eternal essence, but to show that we already have available some moderately consistent and interesting notions about one crucial aspect of the tangled phenomena the word "urbanization" calls to mind.

Were I legislating usage for urbanists, I would rule out holistic and normative conceptions of urban phenomena as too unwieldy and too susceptible to circular argument. I would force a choice among locational, ecological, and interactional vocabularies. If the choice finally fell on the locational ideas, then urbanists could treat changes in norms, population distributions, and interaction patterns—each coherently identified—as causes, effects, and functions of changes in the spatial distribution of activities rather than lumping them all together. In fact, the ecological conception of community-city urbanization has some priority in terms of simplicity, established usage, and convenience in the collection of data. The current generation of demographer-ecologists, however, has so far fumbled the problem of bounding communities consistently and has wavered in its fidelity to net migration and natural increase as the fundamental processes of urbanization.

With an acceptable procedure for bounding communities and a reasonable model of the interaction of net migration, natural increase, and urban growth, we could turn without sighs to the big job: the construction of a theory of urbanization. Given an ecological starting point, the theory would amount to a series of interdependent statements about the causes and conditions of the varieties of migration and natural increase which amass more and more people in larger and larger communities. In the long run, urbanists would again want to specify how changes in norms, shifts in the spatial distribution of activities, transformations of interaction (not to mention technological innovations, increases in wealth, or new forms of coercion) relate to the ecological process. They will do well to keep clear distinctions among them.

THE POSSIBILITIES OF CHANGE

Nowadays, no one can really escape the city. The hunters and trappers of Canada's Arctic ship their pelts to cities, draw their supplies via aircraft cased in cities, and wonder what the people in Ottawa, Toronto, or Yellowknife are going to do to them next. Likewise, the city can escape no one. Every farmer who shifts his main crop from wheat to rye influences the cost to the urban consumer of wheat bread and rye bread. Every suburbanite who moves into the woods five miles further out from the factory in which he works stretches the metropolitan area just a bit in that direction: in a small way he generates a new demand for highways, telephones, and fire protection. Every city council which allocates tax money among schools, roads, and public welfare shapes and reshapes the lives of all the city's residents. *Whether* to change the city is an idle question; every one of us changes it with each breath he takes. (Given the nature of atmospheric pollution, we can take that figure of speech literally.) The question is how deliberately—and in what way—to intervene in order to create a better kind of city.

Such a question knots together technical, philosophical, and political problems. Ideally, what do we want from our cities? That is largely a philosophical problem. What would it take to approach the ideal? Broadly speaking, that is a technical problem. How should we resolve conflicts over ideals and means of attaining them? That problem is mainly political. The philosophical, technical, and political problems are knotted together for two reasons: first, because the way we handle one of them sets stringent limits on the way we can deal with the other two; second, because a certain way of getting things done and of distributing power is normally part of the ideal vision. If our ideal city does its work through wide consultation and participation of its citizens, it will no doubt take widespread participation and redistribution of power to bring it into being.

The sort of systematic urban analysis represented in this book concentrates on the technical problems: how to get from here to there. It does not deal comprehensively with the philosophical and political problems. Yet social scientific treatments of the city have a special contribution to make toward changing the city. They help trace out the further implications of changes which appear quite desirable or undesirable in themselves, but which may have the opposite effects on the city as a whole. Furthermore, they help to assess the likelihood that a given means will actually bring a desirable outcome into being—and, conversely, they help to identify the alternative means for producing that outcome. They are less likely to be helpful when it comes to developing a new moral sense of the good life, persuading others of its worth, bringing together the essential resources, people, and leadership, or keeping the whole transformation running smoothly from day to day. The special role of social scientific analyses, where they are valid, is to help relate means and ends.

Let us be clear about the urbanist's responsibilities. Anyone who advocates a given course of action starts from philosophical assumptions and political preferences. When it comes to recommending a particular method of community organization or urging the building of a new kind of transport system, an urbanist bears more than the average responsibility for the philosophy and politics built into his proposal; the weight on his shoulders is greater because other people often give greater credit to the ideas of a specialist, even when he is outside his true area of specialization. In fact, the urbanist's systematic knowledge gives him little advantage in dealing with questions of philosophy and politics. The limits to his knowledge, however, do not absolve him from blame for promoting bad means or bad ends.

The papers in this chapter raise the philosophical and political questions, but they focus on the technical questions. As they appear in the papers, the questions take this form:

1. *Philosophical*: What kind of city do we need?
2. *Technical*: What are the likely outcomes for urban life of alternative ways of changing the city now being proposed? What are the points of intervention which will make the greatest difference?
3. *Political*: Who should control the decisions, and how?

On the whole, our authors respond to the philosophical question with pluralism and skepticism. They want a city in which people will have the freedom to pursue a number of different ends, not necessarily all compatible with each other. They are skeptical of any unitary, fixed master plan for the production of happiness. And they are willing to assume that people know what they want out of life, even if they do not know how to get it. All this leads to a view of the city as an assembly of devices for the accomplishment of human objectives—not as a work of art, an expression of natural law, or a machine tuned to some single task. The approach is characteristically American. At its worst, the approach produces the conclusion of "hands off"; since this is the mess people made, it must be the one they wanted. At best, it leads to the reasoned consideration of the appropriate forms of city for different patterns of human activity that we find in Kevin Lynch's essay.

TECHNICAL PROBLEMS

The technical discussions in this book will disappoint anyone looking for grand schemes or for strictly practical advice, as they fall in between. Even within their special territory of means-end analysis, the claims and the accomplishments of the papers are modest. There are few principles concerning the operation of cities which the analysts have established so unmistakably that they are willing to bet other people's lives on them. William Michelson's discussion of the implications of urban research findings for the construction of low-income housing, for example, cautiously points out the ways in which housing needs and preferences vary with life cycle, family pattern, and several other factors; he draws out some of the implications of these variations for urban planning. Yet the state of existing knowledge of these matters does not permit any more than gentle nudges to the planner's elbow.

I should say it more strongly. We know scandalously little (either in general or in particular) about what differences various programs of housing, public assistance, health care, or education actually make to the lives of people supposed to benefit from them. For perfectly understandable reasons, the agencies which sponsor and administer such programs do poor jobs of measuring their actual effects. The pitifully sparse information available on the fates of families displaced by urban renewal illustrates this weakness. So does our inability to say anything very convincing about the common but dubious assertion that "high" welfare payments in New York or Chicago are attracting migrants from poorer sections of the country. (Earlier I gave my reasons for thinking that assertion wrong, but the fact is that clinching evidence one way or the other does not exist.)

We cannot expect the operating agencies to conduct dispassionate evaluations of these matters. For one thing, they have too much invested in success, or the illusion of success. An urban renewal agency, for example, has little practical alternative to issuing early statements which are so optimistic as to guarantee that any serious later evaluation would make its leaders out to be knaves or fools. Without the early appearance of optimism, they could do nothing at all. Nor do they have the expertise. Yet governments, high and low, constantly base policies of intervention on assumptions about their effects on the lives of the people involved.

There lies the urbanist's dilemma. A national government will spend billions, a city council millions, a planner thousands, and make a substantial but hardly predictable difference to the lives of city-dwellers regardless of what the researcher says. When that much is at stake, surely a little systematic knowledge is better than none at all. Yet in many regards the researcher's ability to guide change or anticipate its results is at least as bad as everyone else's. Might it not be better to press on with the investigation in order to be able to act intelligently ten or twenty years from now? After all, that way the urbanist will be able to avoid exaggerating how much he knows, becoming a huckster and a fixer, losing the detachment and skepticism necessary in distinguishing between real results and wishful thinking.

ACTION RESEARCH

Like all true dilemmas, this problem permits no pat solution. One of the more creative responses to the dilemma, however, emerges from the articles in this chapter. It is to study actual interventions in areas about which the social scientists already claim to know something, to trace out the effects of those interventions systematically, and to compare those effects with the ones the initiators of the intervention were trying to produce as well as with the ones existing theories might have led one to expect. Alonso's brief comparison of "historical" and "structural" theories of urban form, for example, is quite theoretical. Yet it leads easily to a program of systematic observation of urban renewal which will at the same time provide precious information about the difference renewal actually makes and indicate which line of theorizing about land use makes more sense. Presumably both results should make it easier to act a bit more effectively the next time.

Action research focused on the consequences of actual interventions promises several payoffs for further efforts to change the city. It is a means of getting information about what conditions are really like among ordinary people: what hardships they face, what grievances they feel, how they experience the efforts of others to help or to manipulate them. It is a means of finding out which possible levers for concerted action produce detectable effects, which ones will not budge, and which ones are not attached to anything significant. It offers some promise of anticipating the consequences of the next change before it begins. It points to improved means of determining whether the current action is having the effects its supporters, critics, or perpetrators claim—and thus perhaps of modifying or stopping it on the way. And it even leads to conclusions concerning the effectiveness of different ways of organizing to promote, block, capture, or alter a planned change.

The article in this chapter by Tilly and Feagin gives a modest illustration of the potentialities of action research. It follows a small housing experiment in Boston for several years and simply compares what happened to people in that program with what happened to similar people having different experiences with housing. Nothing fancy; just a conscientious effort to match families with each other, keep in contact with them through an important move, record and tabulate the changes they faced. The comparisons yielded substantial evidence of important differences between the consequences of relying on the private market, living in public housing, and moving into new housing at subsidized rents. I wish I could say that important innovations in housing policy resulted from our investigation; they did not. Yet the existence of this modest study makes it harder to argue that the private market will meet the needs of the poor, or that mixing income levels in the same new housing will generate conflict among residents and degradation of the property.

PRESSURE POINTS FOR CHANGE

This study and others like it raise the question of pressure points: where to touch the city in order to get the largest amount of change for the effort invested. The largest choice we face is between (1) intervening in individual lives one by one, and (2) acting directly on big structures such as the system of transportation or the labor market. A service which helps families find housing suitable for their needs in the existing market follows the first choice; a general program of rent control follows the second.

Each of the choices has significant costs. Although the person-by-person approach permits the adjustment of services to individual needs, it often rests on the implicit assumption that there is something wrong with the individual or family which needs correction, it lends itself to inhumane treatment of the helped by the official helpers, it often involves large invasions of privacy, and it tends to be so costly that only a few people get the assistance they need. Although the big-structure approach tends to have wide impact on the whole city, it ordinarily requires a big, complicated, slow-moving (not to mention self-serving) organization; it creates local injustices and inefficiencies by neglecting the problems of the particular person or moment; and it tends to be vulnerable to swings in the political and economic climate.

Why not try to combine the advantages of both? The problem is how to do it without combining the disadvantages as well. Large welfare bureaucracies meting out assistance case by case combine the two approaches; much of the time they turn out to be sprawling, ramshackle, inhumane devices for keeping the poor in their place. Two other ways of combining the approaches look more promising in the light of this book's studies: (1) organizing relatively small subcommunities of people with common interests within the city, making sure the subcommunities have political, economic, sociological, architectural, and engineering expertise at their disposal, and assuring them a strong say in the big decisions which affect them; (2) developing programs which put flexible resources in the hands of the people who need them without dictating the details of their use. The development of advocacy planning, the use of community organizing as a political strategy, and the adoption of universal family allowances fit the prescription.

POLITICAL PROBLEMS

Who will decide, and how? The strategies I have just mentioned put the local and short-run decisions under the control of the people most directly affected by them. But what about the general, long-run decisions: at which level to set family allowances, how to finance them, which rules of eligibility will apply, and similar decisions. Where they address this fundamental political question, the papers in this book do not agree. In general, their pluralism, populism, and skepticism point away from the planning decision made by the powerful expert who is somehow insulated from politics and toward the dispersion of powers of consultation, veto, and review in the hands of ordinary citizens. This implies a willingness to live with the decisions ordinary people make (even when "we" know better) and a determination to tip the advantage away from groups who buy or inherit political power. None of this is new; all of it belongs to a great North American political tradition.

Any urban researcher seeking to follow these leads, however, will soon face weighty political realities. One of them is finding a base from which to work. Most large-scale, deliberate interventions in the city are carried out by those who hold power, or on their behalf. The investigator attached to the organization which carries out a program of rehousing, job training, or road construction will tend to have substantial resources and access to inside information. He will also tend to have trouble freeing himself from the organization's definition of what it is doing, in getting objective information on how much difference the program actually made, and in publicizing negative results.

The investigator attached to the organized opposition to a program (or to the groups it is supposed to affect most directly, whether they are organized and opposed or not) can maintain his distance and help redress the political balance; but he faces the problems of getting access to the essential information, of finding the resources to do his work, and of carrying on any investigation at all in the presence of strong reasons to commit his efforts, his resources, and his reports of findings to the cause at hand.

Yet the "neutral" solution of a research organization attached to a government, a university, or a charitable institution characteristically has the difficulties of guaranteeing no access to the essential data, of having to attract the attention of its investigators away from enterprises they find more absorbing, and of compromising their autonomy and neutrality in the search for resources. No matter which of the three solutions he adopts, an urbanist who begins to study an open question takes the chance that his findings will, if publicized, damage the group which has supported him. Any base at all, in short, places restrictions on the researcher.

The second political reality is that other people play the major part in deciding which "urban problems" deserve serious attention at the moment. I am not thinking merely of the ability of governments, corporations, and big organizations to keep "snoopers" away from their unsavory practices. That is only one part of a general process. At a given time, only a very small number of the conditions which might be defined as a "serious problem" by one standard or another actually receives public recognition. The set changes from year to year: the "preservation of open space" appeared to be a large urban problem in the America of the 1950's, but somehow dissolved as an issue in the 1960's. At the risk of irreverence, I suggest that even the "problem of pollution" may well fade away—not as a reality, but as a major target of collective action—by the 1980's.

The rise and fall of urban problems is a political process in which interested agencies, entrepreneurs, and slogan-wielding public figures play a large part. So do unplanned events like a series of riots or an international crisis. It is an important process, because it strongly influences the programs of service agencies, the availability of research support, the interests of students and researchers, the curricula of educational institutions, and the volume of information available concerning the phenomenon under discussion. As I write, the urbanist who suspects that cement sidewalks or buildings more than twenty feet tall are damaging people's lives will have trouble finding support for his inquiries. He will most likely have to convince a number of other people that what he is concerned about is really an "urban problem," somehow attach it to one of the currently accepted urban problems, or carry out the work on his own. (If these examples seem cynical, silly, or tendentious, remember that in the 1950's, when the so-called flight of middle-class families to the suburbs was commonly thought to be a major urban problem, smog was no more than a bad joke about Los Angeles. The accepted definitions of the two conditions have changed far more than the conditions themselves.)

All this means that organized intervention in the city is a political process. The study of organized intervention in the city is also a political process. The evaluation of organized intervention in the city is likewise a political process. That is as it should be. The quality of people's lives is at stake.

ARTICLES IN THIS CHAPTER

The articles fall into two unequal sets: four articles (Michelson, Tilly and Feagin, Alonso, Fried) deal with different forms of deliberate intervention in North American cities; two articles (Tilly, Caro Baroja) present ways of thinking about cities which are full of promise but which have not been used extensively so far. Two reasons led me to exclude interesting essays concerning the building of new cities in poor countries, planning in Holland, neighborhood programs in China, and other relevant activities outside of North America. First, the political context of planning and intervention is so important that a few selected articles could do little more than establish that the Japanese, Germans, Brazilians, and others do indeed handle their problems differently from each other. Second, the overlap of themes among the papers I have selected should make it easier for the reader to begin distinguishing among well-attested findings, common assumptions which are open to question, and conclusions which take the analysts beyond the boundaries of reliable knowledge.

SOCIAL INSIGHTS TO GUIDE
THE DESIGN OF HOUSING
FOR LOW INCOME FAMILIES
William Michelson

In this report to a national group of housing and planning specialists, William Michelson makes a straightforward review of established variations in housing needs. He does it as a way of suggesting how the planning of housing should vary with the populations involved. Architects and planners have, of course, always designed different sorts of housing for different sorts of people, depending on their notions of what those people wanted, needed, or could be sold. Michelson's innovation is to check those notions against what the people involved actually say and do. Michelson gently uncovers a vicious contradiction: while the big differences in the housing people now occupy in American cities depend on income, the fact is that housing needs and desires themselves vary insignificantly by income: life cycle, life style, family structure, value orientations, and local customs make the big differences. As a result, only high-income families have the chance to adapt their housing to their particular needs and desires. Nor have American planners and architects done much to redress the balance. Michelson pushes for redress.

What's in a title? Every word in the above title has a special meaning to me. For example, when I use the words "Social Insights," I envisage ideas, observations, knowledge of relationships involving human beings. I do not necessarily envisage *direct* answers to bothersome questions. The housing and redevelopment official is well aware of the range and nature of such questions, and the precedents for their solutions. I don't pretend to stand in the place of such officials, but rather desire to present the import of what could loosely be called basic research—an endeavor divorced from administrative exigencies and one that may possibly come up with answers not readily apparent during crisis situations.

"Design" is another crucial word in this title. I won't concern myself primarily with either the condition of housing or its management. My concern is the way in which space is molded to house people and to separate them from other people and from the various activities in which they participate within the greater urban area.

Also important in this title is the word "Guide"—"guide the design. . . ." I present the following insights with great seriousness and with constructive intent. At the same time, I am only too aware of the variety of factors that enter into a policy decision. Social insights ought to *guide* decisions on design, but not to *determine* these decisions any more than any other factor taken in isolation.

However, perhaps the most crucial term in the title is "Low Income", since it represents both a peculiar set of problems and, at the same time, a diversion. Families with extremely low incomes have troubles. Everyone who has worked with public housing is familiar with them. There's no need for me to repeat them here. Yet low income families are a lot of other things as well. Their values differ. They are at different stages in the life cycle. And even if all the above factors *were* the same, local customs differ. Characterizing people apart from their economic level has great importance for the design of housing. While one can't ignore the real problems of low income, a preoccupation with this one factor diverts attention from understanding serious problems in housing which stem from other causes.

Indeed, in two analyses I have made of people's housing desires—one in the

Reprinted by permission of the publisher and the author from *Critical Urban Housing Issues: 1967* (Washington: National Association of Housing and Redevelopment Officials, 1967), pp. 60–68.

Boston area[1] and the other a nationwide survey originally conducted by the University of Michigan's Survey Research Center[2]—what people professed to want in housing bore no relation at all to their social or economic level, but rather related closely to certain aspects of their values, family patterns, life styles, and the like. Therefore, I think it might be useful to outline below what I mean by these factors and to summarize some of the insights currently available in what is still an underdeveloped field of research.

STAGE IN THE LIFE CYCLE

Perhaps the most obvious of these factors that are independent of income is one's stage in the life cycle. By this, I mean a person's or family's position with respect to age, marriage and child-rearing. It makes a big difference in housing whether a man is newly married, has a family of school-age children, or is a retired widower.

It is generally agreed that the upper floors of high rise apartments are no place for families with children.[3] When children leave this type of family nest to play outside, they leave parental observation and control completely behind. You can't follow a child's progress in city streets and playgrounds from the twentieth floor the way you can from the second story into a yard or smaller public open space. While (lower) Park Avenue mothers seem able to stay with their children (or at least send the maid), such supervision is difficult to expect from a working mother, a mother with one or more even younger children in the family, or a mother who just isn't around—all distinct possibilities in low income housing. Therefore designs which attempt to avoid high rise living for families with children are well advised. While the physical plan of housing can't be expected to cure socially derived problems, certain problems are no doubt aggravated by inappropriate housing for famlies.

At the other end of the scale, some people have argued that older people whose children have grown up and left home and who may also be widowed, desire to give up whatever housing they may own and move into a centrally located multiple dwelling. My own feeling, however, is that to these people, centrality of location is much more important than type of accommodation—just as it may be to a young single person. Even if they no longer need their space, many senior citizens do *not* wish to leave behind their homes, but since they can't have both house and location today, some choose the latter; and their numbers are large enough to constitute a small market. Indeed, an excellent study of movers to newly built, downtown, high rise apartments, often on redevelopment sites, shows that the overwhelming majority of older movers, came from apartments that just weren't as centrally located, not from single or duplex homes.[4] Therefore, the *location* of housing units for older people should be thoughtfully considered.

A second issue concerning older people is whether housing units for the aged should be designed in homogeneous blocks or integrated with units intended for other age groups. The design problems here are the size, mixture, and location of dwelling units inside appropriate buildings. There is no clearcut answer. When older people live primarily among themselves, their interests rapidly turn morbid—to each other's illnesses and funerals. Yet, when integrated with younger people, the aged cannot insulate each other from the feeling of dread with which young adults often regard old age. Indeed, one recent study shows that morale may be higher when older people are isolated from others.[5] However, perhaps the best solution may be what's found in the privately developed old-age communities where the age required for residence is relatively low. Here there are some people present who are still in the prime of life to set the tone for a group which otherwise has the protective qualities of a homogeneous old-age group.

FAMILY PATTERNS

A second way of characterizing people is by their family pattern. Even within specific income brackets, families follow a number of different patterns. There are the standard, so-called "nuclear" families of father, mother, and children. There are families where the mother is the only adult consistently on the scene. There are families of many generations and there are others where much activity takes place among a wide variety of relatives in the same generation; both the latter are often called by the name "extended family".

A variety of evidence from several cultures indicates that extended family patterns are most easily sustained in high density residential areas, often with mixed land uses. For example, Herbert Gans paints a picture[6] of the now well-known West End of Boston, where Italian-Americans were aided in meeting kin in the same age group frequently and spontaneously by the high density of the housing and by the mixture of commercial facilities among the residential units. To these people, frequent and intense contact with kin was more important than any more impersonal activity such as occupational achievement. Problems were encountered by some families who, when their income allowed it, left the neighborhood for typical suburbs not realizing the change it required in their daily family pattern.[7] Also, children sent to Cape Cod by a well-meaning philanthropy were struck with what they felt was the loneliness of life there.[8]

A study of the move from an old, low income, high density section of London to a low density housing estate in the outskirts[9] demonstrated a great change in family patterns. Whereas formerly, relations between different generations in families had been extremely strong, with members of the extended family providing strong assistance in times of economic and medical stress, after the move these people had to rely on less personal, more official sources of aid. Indeed, in a low density area, with few or no other relatives within easy reach, the lives of these people changed drastically. Unable to maintain intense extended family relations, they started to accumulate and value possessions, to "keep up with the Joneses". This, in turn, required a new and rational accounting both for money and time. Many people may regard such a social change as desirable; others, not. But it is important to note that the relation between family patterns and housing design, while not by any means fixed, is not wholly random. What must be kept in mind is that if you consciously change the spatial form of people's physical environment, you are more than likely to cause a change in their social environment.

From some of my own research, I have found that the closer to a person's home his friends now live, these friends often being relatives and neighbors, the higher the density of the residential area he considers ideal. Similarly, the more frequently a person sees his intimate friends, particularly if they are neighbors and relatives (implying the pattern of life just sketched), the more likely he is to desire small-scale enterprises and institutions around him.

What does all this mean for the design of low income housing? The lives of some potential candidates for it now are strongly influenced by frequent, spontaneous, and meaningful personal relations in high density, but deteriorated neighborhoods.[10] Indeed for many of these people and others as well, even if they don't have large or stable families, kinship has been the primary source of aid and information in migrating to and living in a particular city.[11] If their way of life is felt worth protecting (a value judgment), then replacement housing can be designed which will provide for a mixture of housing units in close proximity to each other which can accommodate people in various stages of life, with occupancy determined by people's interaction patterns, rather than by more formal criteria. One could conceive of designing buildings and filling them with occupants on the basis of the family ties and friendship patterns of the particular people involved.

Another English study demonstrates just how hard it is to reassemble extended families when housing isn't oriented to mixing generations, where the density is low, and where units are allotted impersonally.[12] Making available opportunities for small, specialized business enterprises to mix in with new housing in an appropriate manner would not only reinforce the family patterns, but would also counter many of the economic losses often sustained by small business in relocation.[13]

It thus behooves the housing official to consider the role of the family and close associates in people's daily social activities when planning the design of housing. There is room for much experimentation in this area.

LIFE STYLES

Certainly the family patterns just discussed have much to do with people's life styles. But there is more to life style than family pattern. An additional important element is a person's use of time. What does he do with the hours that he is free to spend as he wishes? What does he value doing which can be encouraged or hampered by his spatial surroundings?

Some people prefer to spend their time away from home taking advantage of public and private facilities, cultural and otherwise. In Greece, for example, the home is literally only a place to hang one's hat; the Greeks prefer to spend their time in cafes, theatres, and other places where people congregate. In the United States, one prominent writer has argued that people intensely devoted to their careers prefer the close-in apartment for just such a reason, while others with an opposing life style prefer the family-oriented and distant suburb.[14] Other people prefer to spend their time in and around their homes in active pastimes. Still others prefer to watch television and drink beer. It is easy to picture life styles in extreme patterns—the suave, hard-working career man who uses all the cultural facilities of the downtown to his advantage versus the dedicated, reliable family man who spends his time in workshop, yard and countryside to better his brood. Depending on which life style the particular people involved desire to pursue, it may make a big difference whether housing is planned within easy access to a variety of commercial and recreational facilities, whether housing units are arranged so that a family can pursue active and possibly noisy pastimes without radically impinging on neighbors, or whether housing consists of the bare essentials. As a previous commentator pointed out, we are unlikely to inspire very many pioneer-style, handyman fathers in high rise apartments.[15]

In the nationwide survey I referred to before, people who recently moved from an apartment to a single family home but who now regard such a move as a poor idea, differ from their more satisfied counterparts in that they are significantly less likely to do things so many homeowners cherish—have cookouts at home and participate in workshop activities. Similarly, those people interviewed who lived in uncrowded areas and who desired to live closer to the center of their city were significantly more likely than the general population to enjoy theatre and concerts, but less likely to enjoy hunting—two quite different uses of time.[16] Thus, the degree of accommodation of people to their housing is very much related to the ease with which their life styles can find full expression in the surrounding physical environment, since housing design by definition creates varying separations of people from other people and from activities.

VALUES

Another relevant characteristic of people, apart from their economic status is their values (more precisely value orientation, so as to avoid confusion with such issues as "net worth"). People's daily behavior and strivings are guided in large part by general, abstract goals or rules which they've accumulated through past experiences and associations. One can value convenience, privacy, beauty, safety, achievement and many other things. The relation of such values to the design of housing can be illustrated in a recently popular book on cities, *The Death and Life of Great American Cities* by Jane Jacobs.[17] Mrs. Jacobs makes a number of intriguing suggestions about design, but a consistent reason behind most of them is that these arrangements would curtail crime. Mrs. Jacobs values safety very highly, so much as to make this value a basis for design, ahead of such other values as beauty or convenience. And some designs such as high density walkup apartments over stores, typical of Greenwich Village, may satisfy this value better than others.

In my Boston area study,[18] the more people valued efficiency and speed, the more likely they were to prefer living in higher densities (albeit mostly in single houses) and having low travelling times to nonresidential land uses. The less this value meant to them, the lower the densities and the higher the travel times desirable. These two aspects of housing design were not indifferently related to people's values, although the usual high level of preference expressed in surveys for the single home did turn out to be independent of people's values and other personal characteristics. Furthermore, people who value privacy not surprisingly prefer lower residential densities. In addition, people to whom social class differences are very important, whatever their own class level, prefer smaller scale stores and institutions (boutiques and chapels where they can be accorded some attention, not supermarkets or cathedrals).

Values are hard to measure, and even social scientists rarely agree on their precise nature. Yet values are irrepressible characteristics of people which have a bearing on the design of housing.

LOCAL CUSTOMS

A final factor needs no special elaboration. There are some characteristics of people which are idiosyncratic to a local area, but must still be reckoned with in housing design. In Lagos, Nigeria, for example, a rehousing scheme ran into problems because the planners hadn't realized how important it was for the women of the area to act as traders; not to do so would have destroyed their images of themselves as worthwhile adult females.[19] Urban anthropologists can often be of assistance in providing this type of information.

To this point, I have outlined five characteristics of people—stage in the life cycle, family pattern, life style, values and local customs, which offer insights into the design of low income housing and which at times are neglected in the single-minded pursuit of the concept, "low income". But satisfactory expression of these characteristics in appropriate designs may create problems at present, because it may well be that these designs are either too expensive (in land or dollars or both) or even impossible to build, given current technology. But I would not, on these grounds, forget about them. Essentially, people's housing and activity needs are spatial needs, and while our imaginations and our policies may permit shaping space in only restricted ways today, some of which may be impossible to provide in low income housing, there is every reason to expect that we are capable of shaping the space that groups of families with particular characteristics need or desire in new, more practical ways in the future. Instead, the erection of Habitat 1967 in Montreal this year heralds such a trend. There is a strong feeling that the architect, Moshe Safdie has created an environment which offers all the spatial characteristics of a single family home in a high density, easily constructed, urban setting.

But before we can revolutionize housing design, we need considerably more insights, thoroughly documented, than those currently available on the relation of people's many characteristics to their spatial surroundings. Low income housing can be a strong producer as well as a consumer of such insights. In the great variety of housing which exists, certainly many variations of the separation of people from others and from activities abound, and the nature of accommodation of many kinds of people to these various surroundings can be studied and made the basis for future technological innovation and benefit.

I would, therefore, put great stress on research as a concomitant of every new housing project. But it would be more subtle than to investigate the traditional concerns of crime and health or whether people's housing "condition" had bettered or worsened. What we really need to know is the extent to which changes in the *design* of the spatial environment affect the way people lead their lives—what they do, where they do it, and with whom they do it. On these, the real effects of housing hinge. On knowledge of these, we can build appropriate housing.

Since however, most plans made in the past and contemplated in the future involve some amount of change in environment for people, some mention must be made of change as a phenomenon, even though it is not a "social" characteristic of anyone. A fruitful study in Boston brought out that forced relocation—the loss of a home and often of a close-knit network of associates has an emotional effect on people comparable to the loss of a member of the family, only without the benefit of a funeral to cope with internal feelings. A great percentage of the people studied, even with minimal prior attachment to their former area, evidenced emotional and even physical reactions for an extended period after they were forced to move.[20]

Furthermore, one characteristic of working class people compounds the problems of accommodation. Their social and physical world, even though it may be intense and rich in a deteriorated area as suggested, is usually limited. They are often suspicious and distrustful of other people with whom planners might justifiably lump them. Their new neighbors could be Martians for all they know, even though they might have previously lived in an adjacent area. People are wary of public housing if only on the grounds that they think their new neighbors will be incompatible, and then this often guides their subsequent actions, making true the prediction.[21]

Any kind of public policy presupposes that the benefits outweigh the costs. This is no less true for housing policies, although often value judgments are involved in weighing cost and benefit. If, however, the true social costs of housing change are reckoned and felt worth bearing, it is still possible to minimize these costs through recognition of the source of problems and the adoption of ameliorative measures. Perhaps we could benefit from "redevelopment funerals" of some kind! Certainly, both the design and the administration of replacement housing can reflect a sympathetic understanding of the formerly narrow world of its new resident.

In summary, adequate design for low income housing involves considering far more about people than their income. Insights based on stage in the life cycle, family pattern, life style, values and local customs may help differentiate between the advisability of alternate physical designs. Indeed, since spacial separations from people and activities are ultimately the commodity involved in design, the optimal design of future housing can be aided by systematic study of people's accommodation to the spatial characteristics of today's housing. But all this presupposes change, which if considered necessary, needs be made as painless as possible through knowledge of the people involved.

NOTES

1. A full description of this study may be found in "Value Orientations and Urban Form", unpublished doctoral dissertation in Sociology, Harvard University, 1965. Some aspects are summarized in "An Empirical Analysis of Urban Environmental Preferences", *Journal of The American Institute of Planners*, Vol. 32 (1966): 355–360.
2. The study was conducted at the University of Michigan by Professor John B. Lansing and his staff. His basic report is *Residential Location and Urban Mobility: The Second Wave of Interviews*, Ann Arbor: The University of Michigan, Survey Research Center, Institute for Social Research, 1966. My secondary analysis of this data, just completed, is as yet, unpublished. I am grateful to Professor Lansing for making available his data.
3. A suggestive discussion of this is found in Anthony F.C. Wallace, "Housing and Social Structure: A Preliminary Survey with Particular Reference to Multi-Storey, Low Rent Public Housing Projects", Philadelphia: Philadelphia Housing Authority, 1952 mimeographed. Many of Wallace's ideas were recently upheld in a pilot study by Leon Kumove, *A Preliminary Study of the Social Conditions of High Density Living Conditions*, Toronto, 1966, although Kumove found a surprising high degree of "neighboring" in apartment houses with children. Garden style apartments appeared to breathe more activity into men than did high rise.

4. Janet Abu-Lughod, "A Survey of Center-City Residents", in Nelson Foote, Janet Abu-Lughod, Mary Mix Foley and Louis Winnick, *Housing Choices and Constraints,* New York: McGraw-Hill Book Company, Inc., 1960, pp. 387–447.
5. Mark Messer, "Engagement with Disengagement: The Effects of Age Concentration", paper read at the annual meeting of The American Sociological Association, Miami Beach, Florida, August 28–September 1, 1966.
6. Herbert Gans, *The Urban Villagers,* New York: The Free Press of Glencoe, Inc., 1962.
7. Communicated by Dr. Florence R. Kluckhohn, who is conducting studies of families of Irish and Italian ethnicity in the Boston area.
8. Gans, *op. cit.,* pp. 22–23.
9. Michael Young and Peter Willmott, *Family and Kinship in East London,* London: Routledge and Kegan Paul, Ltd., 1957. The same general factors are noted as at work in Lagos, Nigeria by Peter Marris in *Family and Social Change in an African City,* Evanston, Ill.: Northwestern University Press, 1962.
10. An excellent discussion of the general phenomonon is by Marc Fried, "Transitional Functions of Working Class Communities: Implications for Forced Relocation", in Mildred B. Kantor (ed.), *Mobility and Mental Health,* Springfield, Illinois: Charles C. Thomas, 1965, pp. 123–165.
11. See for example Charles Tilly and C. Harold Brown, "On Uprooting, Kinship, and the Auspices of Migration", to appear in *International Journal of Comparative Sociology,* Guy Pourcher, *Le Pouplement de Paris,* Paris: Presses Universitaires de France, 1964, see esp. p. 182 and John S. MacDonald and Leatrice MacDonald, "Chain Migration, Ethnic Neighborhood Formation, and Social Networks". *Milbank Memorial Fund Quarterly,* Vol. 42 (1964) pp. 82–97.
12. Peter Willmott, *The Evolution of a Community,* London: Routledge and Kegan Paul, 1963.
13. Basil Zimmer, "The Small Businessman and Relocation", in James Q. Wilson (ed.), *Urban Renewal: The Record and the Controversy,* Cambridge, Mass.: M.I.T. Press, 1966, pp. 380–403.
14. Wendell Bell, "Social Class, Life Styles, and Suburban Residence", in William M. Dobriner (ed.), *The Suburban Community,* N.Y.: G.P. Putnam's Sons, 1958, pp. 225–47.
15. Wallace, *op. cit.*
16. From the unpublished material cited in footnote 2.
17. Jane Jacobs, *The Death and Life of Great American Cities,* N.Y.: Random House, 1961.
18. See footnote 1.
19. Marris, *op. cit.*
20. Marc Fried, "Grieving for a Lost Home", in Leonard Duhl (ed.), *The Urban Condition,* N.Y.: Basic Books, Inc., 1963, pp. 151–71, as well as Fried, "Transitional Functions . . ."
21. See, for example, Chester Hartman, "The Limitations of Public Housing: Relocation Choices in a Working Class Community", *Journal of the American Institute of Planners,* Vol. 24 (1963): 283–96 as well as the previously cited works by Gans and Young and Willmott. A very general statement of the social phenomenon involved is brilliantly stated by Edward C. Banfield in *The Moral Basis of a Backward Society,* N.Y.: The Free Press of Glencoe, Inc., 1958.

An excellent discussion of many of these phenomena, among others, may be found in Alvin L. Schorr's *Slums and Social Insecurity,* Washington, D.C.: U.S. Department of Health, Education and Welfare, Social Security Administration, Division of Research and Statistics Research Report No. 1.

BOSTON'S EXPERIMENT WITH
RENT SUBSIDIES

Charles Tilly and Joe Feagin

The brief report by Tilly and Feagin on a small housing experiment in Boston illustrates the strengths and weaknesses of evaluation research. The results are modest both because of the program's limited scope and because of the number of questions we left open. Nevertheless, the study provides comparisons between the experimental program and the immediately available alternatives to it. It also yields criteria for choosing among rent subsidies, the construction of new dwellings, and several other ways of delivering housing to poor families under various operating conditions. The comparative design of the evaluation gives it strengths which an examination of the experimental program alone would not have provided.

But this little evaluation took a surprising amount of energy and money. Feagin, several other people, and I spent a substantial part of our time on it for three years and spent over 20,000 dollars in the process, most of it in the form of salaries to interviewers, coders, and other researchers. Perhaps we were inefficient. Still, considering that the study of the experiences of only forty families in one well-defined experimental program took that kind of effort, imagine what it would take to pin down the effects of building a major highway, or guaranteeing the annual incomes of a thousand Chicago families!

In fact, this little study points up a dilemma that every urban researcher faces sooner or later. In the short run, there is almost always some better use for the resources the research uses up. The payoff, if there is one, ordinarily takes place elsewhere and over a longer term. The money and effort we put into our investigation might have provided sound housing for another half-dozen families during the two years the intensive investigation lasted. As it is, the families involved got almost no tangible benefit from our work: a bit of information about what was going on, some pressure on the authorities to continue their subsidies once the experimental period was finished, nothing much else. The practical benefits of the research, if they occur, go to people who get better housing in the future through rent subsidies and similar programs. There also may be some future benefits of a more indirect sort, due to the small contribution the research makes to our general understanding of housing and residential change. But there it is: evaluation research almost always consumes resources which at the moment could be better used to help someone whose need is urgent then. And if no one ever puts the results of the research into action, the resources are doubly wasted. This is a strong argument for evaluation research which specifies the costs and benefits of the practical alternatives available at the time (which our Boston study did, to some extent) and which feeds back rapidly into action (which, I fear, ours did not—at least not rapidly).

Within the last few years several new housing programs for low-income families have been authorized by Congress. Before these low-income housing programs came into existence, an experimental rent subsidy program in Boston anticipated many of their features and characteristics. From 1964 to 1967, forty large, low-income families, who had been displaced by public action, paid the rents they normally would have paid in public housing for lodging in three newly constructed nonprofit developments built mainly for middle income families. Evaluation showed that the experimental rent subsidy program met its objective—providing sound, attractive housing to low-income families without major difficulties and at moderate cost. Such rent subsidy programs have important implications for certain persistent problems of housing policy—relocation, desegregation, economic integration, and code enforcement.

Until recently low-income families displaced by urban renewal or other public actions have generally faced a choice between unsubsidized housing in the private market and subsidized housing under public ownership. Those who opted for the private market either moved into substandard dwellings elsewhere in the city or paid significantly more for their new housing than for the old, or both. Those who went to public housing normally found themselves in large, segregated, institutional developments populated entirely by families who had also gone through a lengthy process of administrative screening. The experience of the movers in the private market has intensified the feeling that urban renewal essentially displaces slums instead of eliminating them and victimizes the helpless in the process. The experience of those who have moved to public housing has fostered the accusation that urban renewal segregates the poor and stores them out of sight.

Within the last four years, several new housing programs designed for low-income families have been authorized by Congress, each involving income redistribution in the form of federal housing subsidies. However, some "low-income" programs, such as the 221 (d) (3) Below Market Interest Rate program and the new Rental Housing Program, are not real alternatives to public housing, because the limited federal subsidies involved mean that housing generally cannot be rented for sums that many families in the public housing income range can be expected to pay.[1]

Currently, the two major low-income programs that seem to provide workable alternatives to public housing and the substandard private market are the Rent Supplement program and the LHA Leasing program.[2] The Rent Supplement program, created by the 1965 Housing Act, is administered directly through federal agencies, bypassing local housing authorities; the program relies on private groups to build and manage low-rent housing developments. Contracts for rent subsidy payments are made directly between the FHA and private owners. Hedged in by a growing number of restrictions on eligibility requirements, construction costs, and

Reprinted by permission of the *Journal of the American Institute of Planners* from "Boston's Experiment with Rent Subsidies" by Charles Tilly and Joe Feagin, *Journal of the American Institute of Planners,* 36: 5 (September 1970). This discussion is based on a lengthy report submitted to the Boston Housing Authority in 1969: Charles Tilly, Joe R. Feagin, and Constance Williams, "Rent Supplements in Boston" (Joint Center for Urban Studies of Harvard and M.I.T., 1969). The research was made possible by the Boston Housing Authority and the Department of Housing and Urban Development.

maximum rentals, this program has so far provided only a small percentage of the number of housing units originally authorized.

Unlike the Rent Supplement program, the Section 23 Leasing program is administered through local housing authorities. This approach provides for leasing by the LHA of existing housing units from private owners, followed by the subleasing of these units to tenants who would otherwise qualify for public housing. Also in its early stages, this leasing program has great potential for meeting the housing needs of low-income families.

Before these low-income housing programs came into existence, an experimental rent subsidy program in Boston anticipated many of their features and characteristics.[3] What is more, it worked. This article reports on the costs, effectiveness, and policy implications of the Boston program.

THE BOSTON PROGRAM

Until 1964, the Boston Housing Authority had put most of its energy into large public housing developments. Then it began an experiment with rent subsidies, financed by the federal Department of Housing and Urban Development with funds allocated by Congress in the early 1960's for experimental housing programs. For the three-year period from 1964–1967, forty large, low-income families displaced by public action (thirty-five of them black, five mixed or white) paid the rents they would normally have paid in public housing, but lived in apartments or row houses in one of three newly constructed 221 (d) (3), middle income developments. The three projects were sponsored by non-profit organizations with a definite interest in Boston's black community and were located in the ghetto or on its fringe. Two of them were, in fact, side by side in the midst of a cleared site within a major ghetto urban renewal project.

Thus, the Boston rent subsidy program dealt with a common situation in what may become a typical way. Although its designers did not realize how typical it would become when they were planning in 1963, certain critical features of their resulting program were prophetic: (1) provision of housing for families displaced by public action; (2) restriction to families with incomes low enough for admission to public housing; (3) payment of rent subsidies to development owners on behalf of selected tenants; and (4) substantial local housing authority control over tenant selection, rent, and administrative procedures. Subsequently, both the Rent Supplement program and the LHA Leasing program incorporated some of these features. Both were designed for poor families with incomes in the public housing range; both have facilitated housing poor families displaced by public action. (The Rent Supplement program formally focuses on such families.) Both programs involve federal rent subsidies. Under the Rent Supplement program, subsidies are (typically) paid directly to the development owners; while under the LHA Leasing program, they are indirectly paid through the local housing authority. In regard to the fourth characteristic, local housing authority control, the Boston experimental program was similar to later LHA Leasing programs though it differed substantially from current Rent Supplement programs. This is an important point to emphasize, since such LHA control generally means local public control over tenant qualifications, administrative procedures, and housing standards.

The experimental rent subsidy program differed from currently existing Rent

Supplement and LHA Leasing Programs in several other respects. The Boston program, unlike the Rent Supplement program, was not as severely hemmed in by federal restrictions on construction costs, maximum market rentals, and housing amenities—limitations that have not only virtually eliminated the possibility of building qualifying housing that will attract the income mix of the Boston experimental program but also made the "Rent Supplement program generally unworkable for new construction in major central cities outside the South and Southwest."[4] The Boston program reflected greater flexibility in this regard, a flexibility to which the Rent Supplement program will probably have to return, if it is to serve a large number of low-income families.

The Boston experiment differed from many current LHA Leasing programs in (a) its involvement with new construction (the Kaiser Report recommends an expansion of the leasing program to include new construction) and (b) its contractual arrangements (the private owners, or their managers, played an important role in selecting tenants and in the administration of the Boston project).[5]

The BHA program was also prophetic in that two circumstances associated with its implementation seem characteristic of many local projects built under subsequent low-income housing programs including: (1) a very high proportion of Negro families as participants; and (2) housing built on a renewal site, frequently in or near a ghetto area.

The three ghetto developments involved in the BHA program, newly constructed 221 (d) (3) "middle-income" housing, varied in design (Charlame Park Homes and Marksdale Gardens were mainly row houses while Academy Homes consisted of two- and three-story apartments), but all three were attractive and convenient. Largely because of their locations, they attracted mostly black tenants—close to 90 percent.

The forty families were scattered throughout the three developments, occupying about one unit in eleven. Aside from a few administrative accidents, the only segregation was due to the families' need for larger apartments, which were clustered to some extent; but there were no areas that could reasonably be labeled "rent subsidy areas." So far as we could determine, no areas ever were labeled that way by local residents. Nor were the recipients of rent subsidies ever singled out by their neighbors as a separate class of people.

The normal rents in Charlame, Marksdale, and Academy ran from $85 to $150 per month. For the forty families, the Housing Authority paid the difference between those rents and the amounts they would normally pay in public housing. The rent subsidy averaged about $51 per month per family.

The experimental rent subsidy program lasted three years. Because of the construction schedule, the last families moved in when it had little more than a year to run. At the end of the three-year period, thirty-five families of the original forty still remained in the program. Three had, in effect, been evicted for bad housekeeping; two more had, so far as we can tell, dropped out voluntarily. When the program officially ended, the BHA simply shifted the remaining families to a new leasing arrangement so that none of them had to move from the dwellings they were currently occupying. By September 1968, three of the thirty-five families had sufficient income to pay the full rent themselves; altogether, then, 88 percent of the families who started the program in 1964 and 1965 were still in their dwellings three or four years later.

THE EVALUATION

Our systematic observation of the Boston subsidy experiment ran from June 1964 (two months before the first families moved into their new dwellings) to June 1966 (eight months after the last families moved in). During that time we stayed in close contact with the people running the program, examined records of the Boston Housing Authority and several other agencies dealing with housing low-income families, collected general information about the Boston housing market, and interviewed a number of officials and local leaders concerned with housing and other problems of Boston's ghetto. Our largest effort, however, went into a series of interviews with the forty families in the rent subsidy program and with other families chosen for comparison.

The comparison samples included three important housing groups: families who moved into public housing; families who found dwellings in the private market; and a group of higher income families who moved into the same three developments as the rent subsidy families. Interviews were conducted both before and after the housing moves. Because of the ghetto location of the projects in which rent subsidy families were to live, most of the families we interviewed were black.[6]

In general, our investigation showed that the experimental rent subsidy program met its objective of providing sound, attractive housing to low-income families without major difficulties and at moderate cost. The selection process, it is true, was excessively cumbersome, partly as a result of being grafted onto the Boston Housing Authority's regular procedures for placing families in public housing. But once families had joined the program there was little that could go wrong. The chief mishap was the eviction of three families, allegedly for "bad housekeeping," by the local management. Such cases seem to point to the desirability of putting even more control over the conditions of tenure and renting in the hands of the public housing authority. In general, the subsidy families kept their dwellings in good condition; they paid their rents regularly and from every point of view fulfilled their obligations as tenants. In short, the administration of the program did not present any exceptional problems, and it required much less apparatus than the running of public housing developments does.

What about the administrative and subsidy costs of the experimental subsidy program particularly as compared with other housing alternatives? We have no usable information on the cost of providing standard housing for low-income families through income redistribution or direct intervention in Boston's private housing market. However, we do have some comparative data on the apparent costs of three programs being operated by the BHA: (1) large project public housing; (2) leased housing; and (3) experimental rent subsidy housing. We stress *apparent* here, because the data have two important flaws: (1) they deal with current costs for units already on hand, rather than the cost of adding new units; (2) they do not genuinely reflect the differences in administrative costs among the programs. Figures indicating costs per unit per month are shown in Table 1.

The low subsidy of the non-elderly public housing units comes largely from the fact that many were built some years ago, when construction costs were substantially lower than today. As Table 1 shows, the public housing subsidy rises regularly with the recency of construction; the apparent costs of recently con-

TABLE 1
Apparent Costs of BHA-Low-Income Housing Programs[a]

| | Costs ($) per Unit per Month | | |
Program	Current administrative costs	Current federal subsidy	Total
Public housing			
Non-elderly units built 1940–54	7.40	24.87	32.27
Elderly units built 1960–63	7.40	62.12	69.52
Elderly units built 1966	7.40	75.52	82.92
Other BHA programs			
First nine private units leased (first three months)	7.37	50.56	57.93
Estimated cost of first thousand 221 (d) (3) units leased	7.37	54.00	61.37
Experimental rent subsidies in 221 (d) (3) units	7.37	51.01	58.38

[a]Calculated from figures provided us by Frank Donahue, Director of Finance and Accounts, Boston Housing Authority.

structed public housing for the elderly *greatly* surpass those of leased housing and the experimental rent subsidy housing. Based on these data on elderly units, one would also expect subsidy costs for newly constructed non-elderly public housing to be much higher than they were fifteen or more years ago.[7]

The average rent subsidy of $51 per month, plus estimated administrative expenses, brought the cost of the experimental program to about $58 per unit per month. Rent subsidies of the type involved in the BHA experimental and leasing programs appear to be a somewhat less expensive method of adding dwellings to stock available to a local housing authority than construction of new publicly owned developments. Yet these figures on the Boston experimental program do not include an additional hidden rent subsidy, a result of construction of the housing projects being financed under the 221 (d) (3) BMIR mortgage program; inclusion of this additional subsidy, difficult to calculate, might increase the total subsidy per unit to the $70-$80 range, closer to that for recent public housing.[8] Moreover, whatever cost advantages rent subsidies have over public housing programs are only for the short run of five to ten years. In the long run, obviously, capital costs per unit of publicly owned housing decline, even if maintenance costs rise, while rent subsidies tend to rise with average rents; the financial advantage of one over the other will depend on borrowing costs, durability of publicly owned housing, and rate of increase in rents in the local area.

In addition, public construction of housing does guarantee the addition of new housing, accessible to low-income families, to the housing stock. Rent subsidies like those in the BHA experimental program do not. The Boston experiment essentially opened up to low-income families forty units that would have been built anyway, would have had the same locations, and would have been occupied by middle income families. Yet a rent subsidy program on a much larger scale than this experiment and directed toward new dwellings, could certainly encourage construction that would otherwise not occur.[9]

But what of the effect of the moves on the low-income families themselves? All rent subsidy and comparison families participating in the Boston experiment came from the ghetto or its fringe. Most remained within the ghetto or on its fringe after the move. This was particularly true of the rent subsidy families; all remained in or near the center of the Roxbury area ghetto. Respondents in the comparison housing samples, those moving into private, public, and 221 (d) (3) housing (without subsidy), tended to report somewhat greater contact with whites after the move yet so did the rent subsidy families. Actually, none of the housing alternatives we examined produced a significant amount of residential integration.

The moves did, however, produce important changes in the quality of the housing people occupied and in their feelings about the housing. Almost everyone in every housing category, private or public, moved into somewhat better housing than he had before—better in terms of structural soundness, space, comfort, and the family's satisfaction with it. The general enthusiasm of the rent subsidy families is illustrated by the data in Table 2, which presents the post-move comparisons of present and previous residences made by the rent subsidy wives and the public housing wives in our sample. Both groups are composed of black respondents; a few white and mixed-race families have been omitted from the two samples to increase comparability. It should be noted that at the time of their selection (in 1964–1965), public housing was the only major alternative, outside the private housing market, available to these low-income families.

Examining the two columns for the rent subsidy wives, it is clear that on every item the proportion liking their 221 (d) (3) apartments better than the last places they had lived far exceeds the proportion not liking them as much. This is particularly true of the items bearing on space, design, safety, quietness, and childrearing features of the new 221 (d) (3) environment. In each of these cases the "like it better-don't like as much" differential and the absolute percentage exceed the comparable figures for the public housing sample, although the public housing figures also indicate overall satisfaction with the new environment. In only one case is the "like it better" percentage for the public housing sample greater than that for the subsidy group. This is in regard to the issue of rent paid. Some of the subsidy families also had minor complaints about the design of their new dwellings, but their general attitude toward rent subsidies was quite enthusiastic. One articulate respondent commented: "It helps a lot to know that you can live happy and decent like one who can really afford it."

Moreover, we found that most people in each of our housing samples cut some informal social ties when they moved and slowly made new friends afterward. Those who moved into the private market (and thus had the greatest control over their new locations and relied most often on friends and relatives in the search for housing) appear to have cut the fewest ties; those who moved into public housing appear to have cut the most. In the new neighborhood, our data suggest that the subsidy families joined in local affairs faster and more actively than those moving

TABLE 2
Comparison of Present and Previous Residence, after the Move[a]

Compared to the last place you lived, do you like "x" better, worse, or the same (selected dimensions)	Rent Subsidy Wives (N=35)		Public Housing Wives (N=24)	
	Percent replying "like it better"	Percent replying "don't like it as much"	Percent replying "like it better"	Percent replying "don't like it as much"
The size of this place	91	3	75	4
The outside of the building	94	3	75	13
The amount of rent you pay	66	26	96	4
Amount of space you have to invite friends over	91	6	67	8
As a place to bring up children	83	3	58	17
Nearness to public transportation	60	20	42	25
Schools	40	26	33	17
Class of people who live near	46	3	21	25
The quietness of the street	86	9	29	46

[a]"About the same" and "can't say" responses have been omitted from the tabulations in this table, but can be calculated by subtraction. The data are for the Negro families in the two samples.

into other types of housing. The net effect of the move appears to have included a heavier involvement in neighborhood activities.

Contrary to some published criticisms of the rent subsidy approach, we could detect no signs that higher income neighbors of the subsidy families singled them out as a special group, or that any special frictions developed from grouping together households with different income levels. Of course, the income differences were not as great as might be expected; moreover, middle income families, the overwhelming majority of families in the developments, had seen enough of the housing problems of poor Negroes to react favorably to the general principle of government rent subsidies.

IMPLICATIONS FOR PUBLIC POLICY

Rent subsidies of the type involved in the Boston experiment, along with those in the closely comparable LHA Leasing programs, have many advantages as an instrument of housing policy. Some of these advantages are shared with federally financed programs that bypass local housing authorities, particularly the Rent Supplement program, but many are not. So far we have concentrated on whether rent subsidies under the auspices of a local housing authority work, without too much bother and expense, as a means of providing sound housing for poor families. In our view, they certainly do. We should also consider their implications for other persistent problems of housing policy: relocation, desegregation, economic integration, code enforcement, and special-need households.

The subsidy families in the Boston experiment, and many of those in other housing markets with whom we compared them, were being relocated as a consequence of urban renewal in and around the ghetto. Our findings indicate that the families who relocated through the private market had the smallest personal adjustment to make, because they continued a routine they already knew well from previous moves. Low-income families moving into public housing and 221 (d) (3) developments had greater adjustments to make; in almost every respect the families moving into 221 (d) (3) dwellings were far happier with those adjustments.

Several features of rent subsidies (from this point on, we will take this phrase to include both the experimental Boston program and LHA Leasing arrangements) make them handy tools for relocation of poor families. They are flexible: in all but a very tight market they can be used to rapidly increase the number of units available for relocated families. They give redevelopment and housing authorities the means to assure that relocated families receive dwellings in good condition. Furthermore, location of dwellings is not a great problem. In principle, it makes little difference whether they are scattered or clustered, central or suburban. The main limit in all these respects is the state of the city housing market.

Whether or not rent subsidy programs produce racial desegregation in housing depends entirely on location of the subsidized units. The Boston program did not produce any substantial amount of desegregation. Programs working with the existing stock of housing, even if run by people committed to equal opportunity, are likely to feel the subtle pressures that produce current forms of residential segregation—if only because the equal opportunity policy itself will affect which units are offered to the public authority for leasing or subsidy. A greatly expanded program of rent subsidies, especially if it concentrated on new 221 (d) (3) middle income dwellings or their equivalent, would have a strong impact on the pattern of racial segregation *only if* the developments were distributed around the city. The more scattered the units, the greater the desegregation, as long as a substantial proportion of the families involved belonged to racial minorities. A policy of clustering, on the other hand, would tend to perpetuate, or possibly even consolidate, the ghetto.

The Boston experiment did produce a small measure of *economic* integration, since families of somewhat different income levels lived together without notable difficulty. We have no reason to believe that it could not happen on a larger scale. This feature of rent subsidies deserves further scrutiny, because the Boston arrangements were especially favorable: a relatively narrow income gap; a very low proportion of poor families; no notable racial difference between the two groups. We suspect that significantly changing any one of these conditions would reduce contact between families receiving rent supplements and their neighbors. We also suspect that it would take a *huge* change in these conditions to produce systematic hostility between the two groups. The best way to find out is to carefully examine cases in other cities in which the proportions have been different, the income differentials larger, the racial cleavage more definite.

It is also hard to judge the effect of an expanded program of rent subsidies on the *quality* of a city's housing. For the particular dwellings involved, local housing authority control over rent payments and tenure would help maintain landlord concurrence with building and health codes. Such a program ought to reduce the demand of very poor families for substandard dwellings, but whether landlords would respond to rising vacancy rates by improving, converting, abandoning, razing, or reducing rents on their properties is hard to say. No doubt a combination of all of these would occur, and the net effect would be a modest improvement in housing quality.

This brings up a danger many people have seen in rent subsidies. What if they gave unscrupulous landlords an opportunity to collude with inspectors in setting high rents and low standards? The association of rent subsidies with housing built by nonprofit or limited-dividend corporations, as in the Boston experiment, does not pose much of a threat. But what about slum properties operated for maximum profit? There is a risk here, and it will take some policing. Nevertheless, the local housing authority operating a rent subsidy program under its own control has several advantages over the city's code enforcement officer. It is offering something precious to a slum landlord: a guarantee of continuous rent payments. It can negotiate the rent directly, with plenty of experience behind it, for many units at a time, rather than relying on piecemeal landlord-tenant agreements. The LHA can supervise maintenance, or it can contract with a third party for maintenance.

Households with special needs may not be so well served by rent subsidies. Old people are perhaps the best example. Housing built specifically for the elderly often has such features as ramps, few and easy stairways, low cabinets, and specially equipped bathrooms. Although there are excellent reasons for avoiding construction of large enclaves of buildings for old people, there are also many advantages— social, practical, financial—to producing such dwellings in small clusters. Rent subsidies do not easily lend themselves to this purpose. They work best providing for households who need the sorts of dwellings that *normally* come onto the market but that, without subsidy, would be beyond the households' means.

CONCLUSION

In fitting rent subsidies, under the auspices of local housing authorities, into the spectrum of available means to assure that every poor family has sound housing and maximum freedom of choice, the framers of public policy face two major decisions. The first decision is between public ownership and management, on the one hand, and rent subsidies (including leasing), on the other. The second is between the use of housing already available and the creation of new dwellings. Public ownership gains in attractiveness when the demand for publicly subsidized housing is relatively constant; rent subsidies seem more viable when that demand varies.[10] Available housing is most likely to meet public needs when vacancy rates and turnover are high, discriminatory barriers few, and average quality of housing good; new construction makes greater sense in cases of tight markets, extensive discrimination, and low housing quality. Therefore, rent subsidies in existing housing are likely to work best where demand for publicly subsidized housing is quite variable, the housing stock good, discrimination weak, and the market relatively loose. A program like the one tried in Boston—combining rent subsidies with earmarking newly constructed units—is likely to reach its maximum effectiveness where the housing market is tight and discriminatory, the housing stock inferior, and the demand either somewhat less variable or far greater than can be met with current public resources.

NOTES

1. This is not to say that some low-income families will not benefit from these programs, especially those in the upper range of the public housing level. The as yet untested Section 235 Homeownership Program (1968 Housing Act) will probably serve families in this same income range. See, President's Committee on Urban Housing, *A Decent Home* (Washington, D.C.: U.S. Government Printing Office, 1968), pp. 60–79.
2. Even these programs do not reach the poorest of American families.
3. Actually, the technical name of the Boston program was "rent supplements"; to avoid confusion with the somewhat different government program now bearing that name we have referred throughout to the Boston experiment with the term "rent subsidies."
4. For a critical review of the current Rent Supplement program, see, *A Decent Home*, p. 65.
5. *Ibid.*, p. 79. Technically, private owners can play an important role in the tenant selection process under the Section 23 program, although so far that function has usually been in the hands of the LHA.
6. Most of the statistical analysis in the larger report, on which this summary is based, deals with the 129 families in the several housing groups that were best matched with regard to income, size, and composition, and with whom we had comparable interviews both before and after the move. One hundred and twenty of these families were Negro.
7. We have no reason to expect any substantial difference in subsidy between the rent subsidy and leasing programs for 221 (d) (3), although Table 1 shows an apparent difference of almost $3 per month. We have good reason, on the other hand, to expect the administration of leasing scattered private units to cost more than the administration of leasing units in 221 (d) (3); however, the data in Table 1 seem to indicate the opposite conclusion.
8. There are, of course, hidden subsidies involved in public housing, such as local tax concessions.
9. The new Section 236 Rental Housing program makes an attempt to do this, but it provides for only limited subsidies and probably cannot reach the same income levels as public housing.
10. Although public ownership gains in attractiveness in situations of more or less constant demand, this does not mean that rent subsidy programs in private housing are necessarily unattractive in many such situations.

THE HISTORIC AND THE STRUCTURAL THEORIES OF URBAN FORM: THEIR IMPLICATIONS FOR URBAN RENEWAL

William Alonso

William Alonso's comparison of the implications of historical and structural theories of land use for the consequences of urban renewal takes on a problem of much larger scope than our Boston evaluation. It consequently steps back much farther from the individual people involved. Alonso points at the theoretical premises of urban renewal as it was being conducted in the early 1960's. He finds a deep assumption of the validity of the venerable "historical" theory of urban form—which has high-income metropolitan families moving outward because new housing can only go up on the open land at the edges, and new housing is what they want. He gives strong reasons for doubting the strictly historical theory. They amount to reasons for doubting that renewal will bring higher-income families back to the central city. As an alternative, he offers a structural theory, which yields different predictions for the future and for the consequences of urban renewal.

The argument has two edges. It is a critique of the unconscious assumptions of policy, which shows that the assumptions have important practical consequences. It is also a proposal to test alternative theories through the natural experiment of urban renewal. A decade later, we can see that Alonso was right: the higher-income families did not come back, mainly for the reasons that he outlined back then. At that time, his argument was an unpopular one. Now there are new assumptions and rationalizations which call urgently for the same sort of analysis: the idea that neighborhoods are likely units for organization and collective action, the argument that decentralization will produce services more responsive to the needs of ordinary people, the notion that street crimes are making big cities less habitable than they used to be. Big, expensive programs for changing cities rest on these assumptions. Perhaps they are right, but they certainly have not received enough rigorous analysis for us to be sure.

William Alonso has developed these arguments more extensively in his book Location and Land Use *(Cambridge, Massachusetts: Harvard University Press, 1964). There is an important effort to reconcile the two kinds of argument to be found in a book by Edgar Hoover and Raymond Vernon,* Anatomy of a Metropolis *(Cambridge, Massachusetts: Harvard University Press, 1958), which is a well-known study of the New York metropolitan region.*

An explanatory theory of urban form has been developing in recent years that provides an alternative to the classic theory developed by R. Haig (1926)[1] and by Park and Burgess (1925).[2] The new theory has emerged so gradually and it differs from the older theory in apparently so slight a degree that it has gone unrecognized as being in conflict with the older theory. Yet the difference is a most important one not only from a scientific point of view but also for the vast urban renewal program that is so vigorously being pursued by our cities. This program is implicitly based on the older theory, and depends on its validity for its success. Should the new theory prove more nearly correct, there is grave danger that much of the current renewal effort will fail.

Both theories are interested in a broad range of urban phenomena but it will be useful to focus on a paradox that has intrigued students of American cities since the turn of the century. This is that land values tend to drop with distance from the center of the city, while family income tends to rise with distance. The paradox is, then, that the well-to-do live on cheap land while the poor live on expensive land.

The older theory explains this phenomenon in terms of the passage of time, and may be called an *historical theory*. In brief, it holds that as a city grows the houses near the center of the city become old and therefore unsatisfactory to high-income families. The rich then build new houses where open land is available which, of course, is on the periphery of the city. Those of lower income then move into the vacated houses. The moving parts of this theory are the aging of structures, sequential occupance by income levels, and population growth, for the number of low-income families must increase to provide a demand for the houses vacated by the well-to-do. The urban area grows much like a tree in cross-section, by means of a growth ring which leaves behind old, rigid tissue. Land values do not play an essential part in the argument and seem to receive slight mention in recent statements of the theory although earlier writers placed emphasis on speculation to explain high central land values. Homer Hoyt, whose sector theory is an important variant of this type of theory, explains: "The wealthy seldom reverse their steps and move backwards into the obsolete houses which they are giving up . . . As they represent the highest income group, there are no new houses above them abandoned by another group. Hence the natural trend of the high rent [high rent for dwellings: it should not be confused with high land values] area is outward, toward the periphery of the city."[3]

In spatial terms the clearest statement of the historical theory remains the "concentric zones hypothesis" of Burgess. The Burgess theory is the spatial equivalent of the filtering process or trickle-down theory of the housing market according to which new houses are built only for the well-to-do but in time pass on to those of lower income. Thus, society provides housing for the poor not by building directly for them but by letting the wealthier absorb most of the depreciation costs before the house is handed on.

By the historic theory, then, the location of the rich depends on the availability of land. Residential urban renewal, whatever its original statement of intentions, has taken on a typical form. It clears decayed housing in the center of urban areas and replaces it with more expensive housing, confident that the

From William Alonso, "The Historic and the Structural Theories of Urban Form: Their Implications for Urban Renewal," *Journal of Land Economics*, 40 (© 1964 by the Regents of the University of Wisconsin), pp. 227–231.

newness of the buildings will attract those of high income. The previous low-income residents are thus displaced and move elsewhere, typically away from the center. In effect, it makes land available in the center for high-income housing, while still endorsing the trickle-down view of the housing market. If correct, this means that Americans will no longer follow each other like lemmings from the center to the suburbs and then to the exurbs as population grows and buildings age. Rather, this centrifugal expansion will now be turned inward and the growth ring will be near the center. The suburbs, as time goes by and buildings age, will become available to those of lower income. But of course the new central housing built by urban renewal will in time age also and the wealthy will once again be on the move. If they are not to go to the suburbs again urban renewal will have to provide them with buildable land near the center. Logically this should be the land ringing the areas now being renewed, which will by then be occupied by the oldest structures. Following this reasoning, urban renewal in the long run will be a ring expanding outward *through* the urban mass, leaving behind a gradient of housing that ages toward the center and pushing against the oldest housing of the urban area until the center is once again the oldest and the process starts again. Thus, the simple movement outward of high income to the suburbs will be replaced by a convection flow like that of boiling water in a pot.

This is a very simplified view of the distant future of urban renewal. It is clear that the moving ring of renewal cannot always be of the type used today. Institutional devices may be modified to permit renewal by the free market and less direct governmental intervention. Depending on a host of factors, such as the quantity and condition of the housing stock and the structure of the demand forces, rehabilitation may become more important. For the process to work there must be a balance of the rates of population growth, new construction, aging of buildings, and the structure of demand, according to income, age, and type of families. If there is, for instance, a very rapid increase of low-income demand, the filtering process may not deliver enough dwellings to the lower sector of the market and overcrowding, invasion, and accelerated social obsolescence will result. In the extreme case, as in the developing countries, there would result a complicated alternation of high- and low-income rings. If, on the other hand, population growth slows down or the structure of income rises rapidly at the bottom, there would be a softening of the demand for old, central accommodations so that the centrifugal growth may leave a hole in the center, manifested in high vacancies, lower densities, reconversions, and the other phenomena of "gray areas." This appears to be the case in metropolitan areas and of course is the ideal situation for urban renewal according to the historical theory.

But the practice of urban renewal is based on the assumption that if high-cost housing is offered in the center, it will attract high-income people. Recent investigators have suggested that the peripheral position of the rich may be the result of the structure of market forces rather than the consequence of historical development. That is to say, that the rich may be in the suburbs because they prefer to be there rather than because they have nowhere else to go. In the words of Vernon and Hoover, "higher-income people use their superior purchasing power to buy lower density housing, but at the cost of a longer journey-to-work."[4] Note that in this explanation it is lower density rather than newness that makes the suburbs attractive to the wealthy.

The reason for the preference for ample space over shorter journey-to-work becomes clear by the simultaneous consideration of the value of land, the cost of commuting, and travel and space preferences. Most Americans prefer to have ample land, as shown by the popularity of the single-family home and as anyone can learn merely by talking to people. As with all desirable things that can be bought, the wealthy tend to buy more land than the poor, all other things being equal. Coupling this greater purchasing power with lower land prices away from the center, it is clear that the savings in land costs are far greater for the rich than for the poor. For instance, if one would buy 10,000 square feet and the other 2,500, a drop in price of 50 cents per square foot would mean a savings of $5,000 for one and only $1,250 for the other.[5] Consider now that such a move would cost $500 per year in added commuting costs: this would represent 20 cents per square foot for the poor man but only 5 cents per square foot for the wealthy one.[6]

If typical American tastes are a liking for ample land and a relative willingness to commute, it is clear that more distant but cheaper per-square-foot sites are more attractive to the wealthy than to the poor. Accessibility, which diminishes with increasing distance, behaves as an "inferior good;" that is to say that, although accessibility is desirable, people as they become wealthier will buy less of it because they prefer to substitute for it something else (land). Such inferior goods are not rare: for instance, the per capita consumption of wheat and its products has declined steadily in this country as people in their affluence prefer to substitute meat and other foods for bread.

This explanation of the more-land-but-less-accessibility phenomenon may be called *structural* to distinguish it from the Burgess-Hoyt historical explanation in that it represents the working out of tastes, costs, and income in the structure of the market. It does not rely on the historical process although this process is undeniable and has been a strong influence reinforcing the structural forces. To put it another way, the structural theory says that a city which developed so quickly that the structures had no time to age would still show the same basic urban form: low income near the center and high income further out. The structural theory is not an alternative to the historical theory; rather, they are complementary. Thus far, both have acted in the same direction. But now urban renewal, relying entirely on the logic of the historical theory, has set them at odds for, while it provides central land, it cannot afford sufficiently low prices to permit low densities[7] so that the structural forces will continue to pull high-income people (and therefore new construction) to the suburbs.

Under these conflicting circumstances the net result of urban renewal will be unclear, particularly because the structural forces depend on tastes and these are very difficult to evaluate. For instance, the fragmentary evidence I have seen of societies where apparently no great value is placed on ample land for the home (*i.e.,* societies in which the rich do not occupy very much more land than the poor) suggests that there the rich tend to live near the center. This is in agreement with the structural theory because, as there is no attraction in the substitution of space for accessibility, greater purchasing power is used to buy accessibility. Indeed, there is in the United States a substantial minority of the well-to-do that does prefer accessibility to space and this minority lives in luxury apartments or town houses in the central areas. Much of the demand for the new construction of urban renewal is undoubtedly attributable to previous neglect of this sector. It is also instructive to follow the location of middle-class families through their life cycle: the young couple lives in a central apartment, moves to the suburbs as the family grows, and returns to the center after the children leave home, thus reflecting their changing space-preferences with changing family size.

Taste or preference for space are possibly words too weak to denote what is really meant by this key variable of the structural theory. Rather, the nature of the demand for space in this country seems to be a deeply ingrained cultural value, associated not only with such functional needs as play space for children, but also with basic attitudes toward nature, privacy, and the meaning of the family. A preference so deeply rooted in a culture is not likely to change suddenly. But in the last three years there has been a startling increase in the proportion of new dwellings in multiple structures and it has been suggested that this reflects such a change of taste. Whereas from 1954 to 1956, 89 per cent of new dwellings were single-family homes and only some 11 per cent of new dwellings were in multiple structures, the current rate is well over 30 per cent. Have the well-to-do, who are the consumers of most new housing, begun to prefer accessibility to space? In a sense this may be the case: as metropolitan areas have grown bigger and roads more congested it may be that some have come to feel that the commuting trip is too long and have returned to central locations. However, the prospective vast road building and mass transit improvement programs may again reduce time-distances (much as the popularization of the automobile did in the 1920's) and re-establish the almost complete preponderance of the single family house.

But there is another explanation, more powerful than that of distances, for the increase in apartment construction. We have mentioned the convection-flow life cycle of the American middle-class family. The young and the old need apartments while it is those in their thirties that power the demand for single-family homes. Those reaching the age of thirty these days are those who were born in the Great Depression when the birth rate fell dramatically. Thus, in the 1960 to 1970 decade there is less demand for single-family homes because there are 9 per cent fewer people coming into their thirties than in the 1950 to 1960 decade. But this situation will change sharply in 1970: there will be an increase of almost 40 per cent among those reaching their thirties in the 1970–1980 decade over the 1960–1970 decade. Thus, we may attribute much of the shift from single to multiple dwellings to temporary changes in the age composition of the population rather than to fundamental changes in taste and we may expect that these changes will be short-lived.

Urban renewal is a magnificent opportunity to reshape our cities. Today there is money, public support, legal power, and human energy of a scale that could not have been imagined a few years ago. The urgency of urban problems and the many years of frustration of those concerned with them have naturally led to a rush of activity now that the means are available. In spite of the conviction of the planning profession as a whole that comprehensive planning is necessary, too often urban renewal has consisted of one project and then another, with no overall plan. It is precisely this lack of a comprehensive urban (*i.e.*, metropolitan) plan that has obscured the implicit theoretical structure of renewal, for a comprehensive plan is the marriage of the goals of a community with an understanding of the structure of the community. The implicit exclusive reliance on the historical theory (which is incomplete without the structural theory) raises the danger of large-scale failure through a lack of understanding of the workings of the urban system and a misinterpretation of the structure of demand. It is a false empiricism to scoff at theory as too abstract. Empiricism requires an evaluation of results and it will be many years before the long-range effects of current experiments in urban renewal become clear. At a time when we are so vigorously rebuilding our cities it is important that we be as intelligent as possible about it. We must make explicit the theories of urban structure under which we are proceeding. If the historical theory by itself is correct, current renewal procedures stand a good chance of success. But if it needs the complement of the structural theory, current renewal projects are skimming a narrow and specialized sector of demand which will soon dry up. In many cities stand acres of cleared land awaiting development and investors face time lags of years from the inception to the completion of development. The reaction-time of the urban renewal process is too slow to permit a purely pragmatic approach. Vacant land and vacant buildings are frightening possibilities.

NOTES

1. Robert M. Haig, "Toward an Understanding of the Metropolis," *Quarterly Journal of Economics,* May 1926.
2. Ernest W. Burgess, "The Growth of the City" in *The City,* editors, R. E. Park and E. Burgess (Chicago, Illinois: University of Chicago Press, 1925).
3. Homer Hoyt, *The Structure and Growth of Residential Neighborhoods in American Cities* (Washington, D.C.: Federal Housing Administration, 1937), p. 116.
4. Edgar M. Hoover and Raymond Vernon, *The Anatomy of a Metropolis* (Cambridge, Massachusetts: Harvard University Press, 1959), p. 169.
5. Of course, greater quantities will be bought at the more distant location because of price elasticity, but the essence of the argument is unchanged and it is simpler to view the quantity of land bought by each individual as unchanging with location.
6. The analysis of the effect of income on location is developed more fully in my *Location and Land Use* (Cambridge, Massachusetts: Harvard University Press, 1964).
7. Even in cases in which extraordinary subsidies (in excess of 90 percent) afford the redeveloper central land at a price comparable to that of suburban land in order to permit low densities, the resulting pattern has been more urban (ten or more families per gross acre) than suburban (four or less families per gross acre). The subsidy per family of providing 100-by-100-foot lots at suburban land prices in a renewal area would be in the order of twenty to forty thousand dollars.

FUNCTIONS OF THE WORKING-CLASS COMMUNITY IN MODERN URBAN SOCIETY: IMPLICATIONS FOR FORCED RELOCATION

Marc Fried

The study of Boston's West End by Marc Fried singles out one of the major costs of urban renewal: the forced relocation of families which are rooted in their old neighborhoods. The West End, whose working-class families Fried describes, has long since disappeared in favor of high-rise apartments. His objective is not simply to show that many people suffered from their forced relocation and that their suffering had something to do with the patterns of working-class life. Those findings in themselves constitute important arguments against the wholesale razing of residential areas, but Fried's analysis also reveals significant variations in preparation and response within the West End population. In fact, some families were quite prepared to move and even profited by the move. By specifying which sorts of persons suffered, prospered, or fared indifferently under relocation, Fried helps fashion a new policy.

As contrasted with earlier policies which assumed that moving to newer housing was always a good thing, Fried's policy would probably minimize relocation; it would vary the extent and pattern of both razing and relocation with the populations involved; and it would give the local people a strong say in what happened to their area.

That sort of conservative policy has many attractions at face value, but it also leaves important questions unanswered. What about housing which has simply outlived its usefulness? In European and American cities many people still live in decayed nineteenth-century structures which were built without central heating, electricity, or indoor plumbing. Should the buildings remain standing if someone wants to live in them? What about the many working-class neighborhoods where the average family moves every year or two? What about the fact that most poor people, when asked, say they would rather live somewhere else, in a better neighborhood? What about the substantial minority of the West End population who had most of their friends outside the West End, who were indifferent or hostile to their neighbors there, and who were at least thinking of moving out (see Fried's tables 4, 5, and 7)? If Fried's analysis persuaded us that all relocation was bad, we would begin trying to conserve things the people involved did not want to conserve. Forced relocation is the enemy. But then the problem becomes the one William Michelson poses earlier in this chapter: how to build a city in which people differing greatly in needs and preferences all have a choice and a chance.

Adaptation to residential displacement depends upon a variety of psychological and social factors. More specifically, it appears to be a function of preparedness for change. Certainly, the characteristics of the prerelocation environment—their attractive or disturbing qualities—are bound to influence the motivation to adapt to a new environment. Similarly, the situational characteristics of the new environment are likely to influence the ease or difficulty of coping with the transition. Nor is there any doubt that variations in personality are related to the manner and

Reprinted by permission of the *Journal of the American Institute of Planners* from "Functions of the Working-Class Community in Modern Urban Society: Implications for Forced Relocation" by Marc Fried, *Journal of the American Institute of Planners*, 33: 2 (March 1967). This report is part of a study conducted by the Center for Community Studies (Department of Psychiatry of the Massachusetts General Hospital and the Harvard Medical School); the research is supported by the National Institute of Mental Health, Grant No. 3M, 9137–C3.

effectiveness of adaptation to new situations. History and current experience, however, suggest that the critical mediating factor is the readiness to accept the challenge implicit in displacement experiences. Such preparedness is a function of the meaning of predisplacement and postdisplacement situations rather than of any single and objectively definable attribute of personality or environment. Thus, in attempting to understand the impact of forced relocation on the population of a working-class community, it becomes necessary to understand some of the central functions and widespread meanings of working class community life.

The transition from rural peasantry to urban working class within recent generations appears to be one of these widespread past experiences for many working-class populations.[1] Community relationships in working-class life provide the stability required by rural peasants who have only recently experienced a major transition to an industrial society which offers few meaningful life situations to lower-status groups other than a narrow range of job opportunities. In this context, forced dislocation and relocation must be viewed as a major disruption for many working-class people. More specifically, residential displacement creates a situation requiring adaptive capacities which are differentially distributed among the populations of working-class communities. These varying adaptive capacities, in turn, may be seen as representing a series of stages in the process of learning to cope with the unique demands and opportunities of the urban, industrial environment.

MIGRATION AND SOCIAL MOBILITY

In the history of Western economic development and social change, there has been a frequent recurrence of that phenomenon which assumed such unusually massive proportions during the nineteenth and twentieth centuries: the movement from rural to urban areas. Immigration from Europe to the United States may be seen as one phase in this more general pattern. Although there was significant migration to urban centers within European countries, the United States provided both the industrial and agricultural frontiers which attracted the greatest proportions of the disaffected peasantry of Europe. During the half century after 1870, the proportion of immigrants in the United States remained fairly constant. As land became less easily available and the composition of the immigration changed, the great majority of migrants from Ireland, Italy, Poland, Greece, and Russia settled in the cities where they became industrial workers. In fact, throughout this period, the majority of the working class appears to have been of first or second generation immigrant origin.[2]

Lipset and Bendix[3] have pointed out, on the basis of a number of recent studies, the widely similar rates of upward social mobility in many highly industrialized countries and the continuous process of replacement of the lowest-status workers by migrants from rural areas. If the large proportion of relatively recent migrants within the working class is considered, it suggests that a relatively large proportion of the working class is "comprised of a group of people who have only recently experienced a dramatic transition from peasants to industrial workers and, who within a short generational span, are likely to go through an equally marked, if less sudden, transition within the class levels of urban, industrial society."

THE WORKING CLASS COMMUNITY

Through what resources are these transitions effectively accomplished, enabling a series of adjustments to take place in a relatively orderly and meaningful way? The locus of both stability and change in these patterns of adaptation must be sought in the working-class community. By the working-class community, we mean those ports of entry for the foreign and domestic migrant which have appeared in every major urban area in all industrial countries. Many of these areas are designated as "slums" on the basis of physical deterioration. But, since the work of William Foote Whyte,[4] interest has been rekindled in the relationship of physical location to potential social cohesion (neighborhood, community) in the working class.[5] It is the social system of the working-class community, and not the society as a whole, which accepts and absorbs the immigrant from the rural regions of the United States, Europe, and elsewhere. It is the working-class community which provides a basis for social interaction and for a common identity despite diversities of ethnic origin. It is the working-class community which also allows for gradual adaptation to the altered environment and to the radically different sets of expectations which eventuate in preparedness for social mobility within the larger industrial society. In this light, we can see the working-class community as a vast processing mechanism. It is a port of exit as well as a port of entry. The different elements of working-class experience, however, differ in their effects upon assimilation into the urban environment of industrial society.

The fact that adjustment to an industrial work role is essential for earning a livelihood initiates the process of adaptation. The opportunities for actual and potential mobility provided by work situations are effective assimilating forces due to the greater rewards (extrinsic or intrinsic) of higher status occupations. Thus the forces which most drastically and directly facilitate cultural preparedness for leaving the working-class community and assimilation into the larger society are also the forces which most immediately affect occupational mobility and readiness for transitions in social roles.

On the other hand, the greatest impediments to assimilation and mobility for the transplanted rural migrant arise from working-class patterns of social relationship. These relationships are distinctive *one,* by virtue of being predominantly oriented to the collectivity, *two,* through the importance of an accepted position in the community based on territoriality and kinship, and *three,* because of a local orientation which sharpens the distinction between comfort within familiar networks and discomfort in the world of strangers outside the community.

These orientations and the patterns of social organization which embody them are the bulwark of working-class communities. The similarity of these orientations, if not the patterns of social organization themselves, to the dominant orientations of the peasant community is a primary factor in allowing for effective adaptation to that striking transition experience from peasant to worker. But for the working class in general, the transition to a higher occupational and social status is far less attractive than it might be, because it implies less involvement with the solidary and rather comprehensive social networks which are typical of working-class community life and social organization. Coming to terms with the opposing influences from assimilation and mobility aspirations, on the one hand, and from the commitments to and collective meaning of community life, on the other, is the major adaptational problem associated with social mobility for the working class.

Not infrequently, the working-class community exercises so powerful an influence on its members that residential mobility is delayed until long after upward social mobility is a realistic potential or an accomplished fact. It is hardly surprising that those communities which are most effective in enabling the first transition from peasant to worker to take place meaningfully for immigrants and for their children, readily become so stable and socially significant to their members that they provide a basis for resistance to further change or displacement.

WORKING-CLASS SOCIAL RELATIONSHIPS

The single finding which emerges most consistently from studies of the working class is the central importance of locally-based social relationships. The term which most comprehensively characterizes the social relationship pattern typical in the working-class community is the "close-knit network."[6] The close-knit network pattern involves a high rate of interaction among a cluster of people rather than discrete, diadic interpersonal relationships, a sense of closeness and fairly binding commitment, and local residence of network members. Close-knit networks may include family; extended kin; neighbors; local shopkeepers; and members of the same church, club, or settlement house. What is common to the various close-knit networks is not their basis in kinship or in common enterprises but rather the ready availability (made possible by residential contiguity) of members, the binding set of expectations for mutual assistance, and dependability in emergencies and in daily encounters, in sorrow and in joy, in routine contact or in the presence of conflict.[7]

The structure of social affiliations of the working-class community can be described as an overlapping series of close-knit networks situated in a single geographical or residential area. The social effectiveness of the close-knit network pattern and the psychological effectiveness of group identity depend upon *one,* a conception of the group as the legitimate source for defining goals and evaluating decisions, and *two,* the immediate, concrete availability of other group members. The importance of these patterns is further reinforced by their similarity to the pattern of social relationships in peasant communities. The stability of the close-knit network is, in large part, responsible for facilitating the adaptation of inmi-grants to the working-class community. This stability, moreover, is due not only to the security and satisfaction provided, but also to the exclusion of alternative forms of security and satisfaction, affiliation, and participation. The working-class focus on group identity as a primary source of personal meaning[8] implies that, although the individual may participate in other groups and derive an expanded sense of meaning from other involvements, the core of his identity must be located within a single group or network. Other commitments and involvements inevitably lead to a greater sense of option, of alternative resources, and thus to increased individuality. Variations in commitment to and exclusive affiliation with a close-knit network are, therefore, evidence of the level of psychological and social preparedness for change, and appear to be among the important indicators of readiness to move outside the working-class community.

In this light, any sudden and extensive change in the population of the working-class community, such as is brought about by forced relocation, can be seen as a most important crisis. Even given the familiar delays in the accomplishment of relocation, there is insufficient time to manage the major adjustments to a new way of life. Thus, it is a crisis of considerable proportion for a great many people in any working-class community, and the total response to it is bound to be strongly influenced by prior experiences and achievements in coping with the urban, industrial environment.

Like any crisis of transition, forced relocation provides opportunities which may facilitate adaptation at a new level of functioning, or fixation within and regression into comforting patterns of the past, or even complex combinations of regression and adaptive achievement.[9] While a majority of the working-class community may experience the sudden and drastic disruption of forced relocation as a crisis, it is likely to have quite different consequences for different individuals depending on their psychological, social, and cultural readiness for meeting this challenge. The extent of such differences and their sources are the issues to which the remainder of this paper is addressed.

THE STUDY

The West End of Boston was an ethnically-differentiated community of approximately 12,000 persons (about 2,700 families) in the heart of Boston, similar in its essential characteristics to working-class communities in other urbanized countries.[10] In April, 1958 the City of Boston took title to fifty acres of this area, mostly residential property, which represented the largest part of the physical base of the community. This was the beginning of the last stages of a long battle to remove these residential units as part of the city's urban renewal program.

In studying the impact of relocation in this area, we selected a random sample of 585 respondents for interview before and after the relocation. From this sample, we were able to interview 473 women (81 percent) before relocation and 502 (87 percent) after relocation.[11] In all, there were 435 women from whom we obtained both pre- and post-relocation interviews. The interviews covered a wide range of behavioral and attitudinal information: demographic data, residential experience, community activities, social affiliations, family relationships, child orientations, and personality data.

Previous analyses of the comparative data from pre- and post-relocation interviews have shown that a marked cognitive and affective reaction took place which can properly be referred to as grief.[12] Its manifestations were quite similar to the characteristic patterns of grief and mourning for a lost person. Not only were they intense and deeply felt but they were also of long duration and, for some people, quite overwhelming. Severity of grief was consistently and strongly related to many variables of spatial and social commitment to the community but less clearly associated with variations in the realities of the postrelocation situation. In effect, these data pointed up all of the binding involvements of working-class community life: the localism, the sense of familiarity and home, relationships to other people of the close-knit network type, and a host of other characteristics discussed or implied in the literature on the working class. As in other situations of loss, however, most people manifested remarkable powers of recuperation despite their experience of grief. Clinically, we know that losses can be handled in a great variety of ways. Some of these methods of coping with loss are quite successful and some quite tragic. While important losses always seem to leave their scars, for many people these are submerged in the process of adapting to new situations and experiences, and for some people the loss proves to be an opportunity for defining a new set of goals and a more satisfying level of adjustment. Thus, despite the overt and widespread evidence of grieving for a lost home as a consequence of forced relocation, there remain a number of questions concerning the sources of effective coping behavior.

The analysis of adaptation and coping behavior is a complex issue. For this purpose we shall use the subjective experience of the individual regarding the changes which relocation has wrought in her life. The index of postrelocation success or failure is based on two separate questions. One of these is a global multiple-choice self-estimate: "Taking everything into account, are you satisfied with the change from the West End? Would you say you are satisfied, dissatisfied, or that it made no difference?" The second question, separated from the first by numerous other items about current residential experience, is open-ended: "Has your life changed since moving from the West End? Would you say: In almost every way, In many ways, In a few ways, or Hardly at all?" and linked to this: "What are the main things that have changed?" In analyzing the open-ended question for the present purpose, we used only a rating of these responses into the categories: Happier, Ambivalent, Mixed, Unhappier.[13] The index itself is a simple combination of the responses to these two items concerning satisfaction and happiness. Thus there are three final categories which serve as the dependent variables for analysis: Adjusted-adapted, Mixed reactions, and Unadjusted-unadapted. The Adjusted-adapted category includes those people who have adjusted to the new situation, in the narrow sense of accepting the realities of life, and have also adapted to it in the broader sense of actively fitting personal wishes and environmental situations to one another.

EFFECTS OF PRERELOCATION ASSIMILATION STATUS

The conception of the working-class community as a processing mechanism implies that there will be an array of individuals in different stages of transition to dominant American social, cultural, and psychological patterns. Solely on objective criteria of nativity and nativity of parents, the West End contained a wide range of individuals at different stages of assimilation. The foreign-born were numerous (33 percent), but those who were born in the United States of foreign parents formed the largest category (42 percent). A small group (9 percent) were of native birth with one foreign parent. The native groups of native parentage comprised 17 percent of the residents.

As we would expect on the basis of the discussion of transition experiences and readiness for change, there is a consistent and powerful difference in adjustment-adaptation when we consider objective status attributes (occupation, education, income, assimilation status) as indicators of preparedness for this transition. The higher the status, the larger the proportion who have been able to cope successfully with the social changes implicit in relocation. When we take account of two such factors as education and occupation or education and assimilation status, we find quite extreme differences in adjustment-adaptation; 72 percent are ad-

TABLE 1
Adjustment-Adaptation Index by Education and Occupation
(percent adjusted-adapted)

| | Education | | |
Occupation	High school or beyond	9–11 years	0–8 years
Highly Skilled	72% (46)	50% (12)	-- (5)
Skilled	32% (37)	36% (36)	19% (26)
Semi-skilled	28% (35)	42% (48)	19% (57)
Unskilled	30% (10)	31% (29)	20% (51)

TABLE 2
Adjustment-Adaptation Index by Education and Assimilation Status
(percent adjusted-adapted)

| | Education | | |
Assimilation Status	High school or beyond	9–11 years	0–8 years
Native U.S. Both parents U.S.	56% (36)	42% (31)	25% (8)
Native U.S. One parent U.S.	38% (16)	29% (14)	14% (7)
Native U.S. Parents foreign	38% (60)	36% (67)	17% (46)
Foreign born	53% (17)	44% (16)	22% (86)

justed-adapted among the high education-high occupation group while only 20 percent of the low education-low occupation group fall into the adjusted-adapted category.[14] Similarly, 56 percent of the group with relatively high education and native birth with native parents are adjusted-adapted compared to 22 percent of the low education-foreign-born group. When education is controlled, however, assimilation status does not yield a completely linear relationship to adjustment-adaptation,[15] revealing the need to consider subjective factors which modify the implications of such objective attributes as nativity.

EFFECTS OF PRERELOCATION ORIENTATION
ON ADAPTATION TO CHANGE

There is little doubt that prerelocation orientations to the communal area as a whole and to specific roles and relationships within the area were critical for relocation readiness.[16] There are negative associations between many indicators of high prerelocation commitment, involvement, and participation, and satisfactory and effective post-relocation adjustment-adaptation. Thus, only 26 percent of those with very positive feelings about the West End were able to adjust effectively to the postrelocation situation; but 51 percent of those with ambivalent or negative feelings were satisfactorily adjusted. Similarly, 26 percent of those who designated another area as "home," and 54 percent of those who said they had no particular home were satisfied and happy in the postrelocation situation. Feelings about West End neighbors shows an even more striking effect: 21 percent of those who were strongly positive about their West End neighbors and 60 percent of those who were negative were adjusted. Evidently, prerelocation orientations to the area and to specific relationships within the community are critical determinants of postrelocation adjustment and, by implication, central indicators of readiness for change.

TABLE 3
Adjustment-Adaptation Index by Prerelocation Feelings about Neighbors

	Adjustment-Adaptation Index			
Feelings about Neighbors	*Adjusted-adapted*	*Mixed-conflicted*	*Unadjusted-unadapted*	*Total*
Superlative	21%	21%	57%	75
Positive	33%	22%	46%	224
Ambivalent-indifferent	41%	27%	33%	79
Negative	60%	20%	20%	20

Adjustment is not so strongly related to kinship contacts as it is to prior orientations to the West End and to neighbors. Forty-three percent of those with rare contact with siblings prior to relocation were adjusted-adapted, as compared with 25 percent of those with frequent contact, a smaller difference than that produced by prior attitudes toward the neighborhood. Either family relationships per se were of less importance than other foci of commitment or, for many people, the mandatory and obligatory character of these relationships may have been a source of considerable ambivalence. By contrast, the more flexible and optional affiliation with close-knit networks, a structure which we have suggested as the focal unit of social organization in the working-class community, is more clearly associated with postrelocation adjustment-adaptation. The data show that 22 percent of those with extensive close-knit network ties, and 52 percent of those with minimal close-knit network ties were successfully adjusted to the postrelocation situation.

EXTRA-COMMUNITY ORIENTATIONS

Commitment, involvement, and participation in a local area represent important dimensions of social and spatial orientations. But these are only selected aspects of the fabric of conceptions and feelings about the social and physical world.[16] The world view of most people in the urban, working-class community is highly parochial and turned inward and the salience of the community is a function of the relationships which are excluded as well as of those included. The framework for this inward-orientation and delimited area of familiarity and comfort is provided by conceptions of the world outside the community. By the same token, these conceptions are likely to be part of the perspective which defines preparedness for change and are bound to have considerable bearing on the process of coping with relocation. These data reveal that the effect of extracommunity orientations during the prerelocation period on subsequent adaptation is clear and consistent. The greater the familiarity with the world outside the immediate community, the more clear the perception of social and spatial dimensions of the universe beyond the physical and psychological boundaries of the West End, the larger were the proportion who experienced relocation with both satisfaction and happiness.

This proposition may be viewed from several vantage points. One central variable is the extent to which interpersonal relationships were locally based in the community. Among those people whose interpersonal relationships were primarily local before relocation, 22 percent were satisfactorily adjusted after relocation but among those whose interpersonal contacts were predominantly nonlocal, 54 percent were in the adjusted-adapted group. The extent to which alternative residential areas are within the scope of consideration is another aspect of the degree to which one's life-space is rigidly bounded by the community. This is usefully revealed by prerelocation plans to move out of the West End: 62 percent of those who had planned to move, 52 percent of those who had been thinking about it, and only 24 percent of those who had definitely planned to stay were well adjusted.

Finally, one of the most direct expressions of ideational preparation for the social change implied by moving out of the working-class community lies in attitudinal differences from typical working-class views. When we combine several social attitude questions into an index based on these differences, we obtain an implicit index of social mobility orientation.[17] A similar pattern of relationship emerges between this index of prerelocation social mobility orientation and postrelocation adjustment-adaptation: 26 percent of those who showed minimal social mobility orientation and 53 percent of those who received a maximal rating on social mobility orientation fell into the adjusted-adapted category. Thus, whether

TABLE 4
Adjustment-Adaptation Index by West End Dwelling of Five Closest People

West End Dwelling of 5 Closest People	*Adjustment-Adaptation Index*			
	Adjusted-adapted	*Mixed-conflicted*	*Unadjusted-unadapted*	*Total*
All West End	22%	23%	55%	177
Mostly West End	33%	25%	42%	76
Equal—mostly outside West End	45%	16%	39%	71
All outside West End	54%	18%	28%	39

we consider the world outside the community on the basis of the distribution of interpersonal relationships, anticipations of alternative dwellings beyond the community, or attitudes which are more congruent with the views of people outside than inside the community, the effects on postrelocation adjustment are consistent.

In brief, readiness for transition from the working-class community is manifested in a variety of interrelated, but independently significant ways.

Coping with the transition to a new social and residential experience, leaving a familiar and beloved place, undertaking a struggle with challenges which were not sought and which so often go beyond available psychological or social resources necessarily pose extremely difficult problems. *The fact that less than one third of the entire sample was both satisfied and happy with the change indicates how small a proportion of the population of a working-class community is ready for this transition.*

EFFECTS OF SOCIAL RELATIONSHIPS
IN THE POSTRELOCATION SITUATION

Two related but distinct elements among those characteristic of social relationships in the West End were positive attitudes toward neighbors and a high degree of localism. By localism we mean the extent to which a person's close friends live in his immediate neighborhood. Less than 25 percent of the sample revealed any signs of negative reactions, ambivalence, or even indifference toward his West End neighbors, while 73 percent had all, or most, of their closest relationships (excluding spouse, parents, or children) with people living in the West End. In view of the importance of these characteristics in the prerelocation situation, it is important to determine the effect of changes in them after relocation.

Two years, roughly the mean interval between prerelocation and postrelocation interviews, may not be long enough to reestablish neighbor relationships as widespread or as positive as those which were obtained in the prerelocation situation. Nevertheless, a large proportion were well-disposed toward their new neighbors and expressed quite positive feelings about them (although they often commented forlornly, that it was really not the same as in the West End).

In view of the fact that sociability is a personality attribute which is likely to persist in a variety of circumstances, it is hardly surprising to find some tendency for those who were more positive toward their West End neighbors to be more frequently positive about their current neighbors. Nor is it surprising to find that there is a rather steep decrease in adjustment-adaptation with increasingly negative feelings about current neighbors (47 percent adjusted-adapted among the positive group, 17 percent adjusted-adapted among the negative group). Of greater importance, however, is the persistent effect of prerelocation feelings about neighbors on the effectiveness of postrelocation adjustment in spite of variations in current feelings about neighbors.[18] The more positive the prerelocation feelings about neighbors, the weaker is the influence of current feelings about postrelocation neighbors on adjustment-adaptation. Among the people who were extremely positive about their neighbors in the West End, 35 percent of those who are also positive about their new neighbors, and 10 percent of those who are negative about their new neighbors are well adjusted. But at the other extreme, among those

TABLE 5
Adjustment-Adaptation Index by Prerelocation and Postrelocation Feelings
about Neighbors (percent adjusted-adapted)

Prerelocation Feelings about Neighbors	Postrelocation Feelings about Neighbors		
	Positive	*Ambivalent*	*Negative*
Extremely positive	35% (40)	4% (26)	10% (9)
Positive	45% (111)	24% (87)	11% (26)
Ambivalent-negative	62% (40)	33% (41)	28% (18)
Total	47% (191)	23% (154)	17% (53)

people whose feelings about West End neighbors were negative, ambivalent, or
indifferent, there is a larger difference in the proportion which is adjusted-adapted,
depending on current feelings about postrelocation neighbors; 62 percent of those
who are now positive and 28 percent of those who are now negative are well
adjusted.

The existence of close-knit networks in the working class is, as we have
indicated, dependent on the contiguity of close persons. Upon relocation, there
were many efforts to maintain or to establish continuity with the past.[19] Some
people moved to sections in which relatives or former neighbors had already found
apartments; others tried to reestablish close relationships patterned after their West
End experience with their neighbors in the new residential area. Nevertheless, only
rarely was it possible to reestablish all or any significant part of the West End
close-knit network with the same individuals.

The effects of changes from prerelocation to postrelocation in the degree of
close interpersonal relationships which were locally based are small but clear and
consistent with other associations. Those people whose closest relationships had
previously been confined to the West End show a uniformly low level of satisfaction and happiness in the new situation whether they now have close people locally
available (26 percent) or not (21 percent). This is the group who were so thoroughly embedded in the West End and in traditional patterns and concrete associations

TABLE 6
Adjustment-Adaptation Index by Localism of Prerelocation and Postrelocation
Closest Persons (percent adjusted-adapted)

Localism of Prerelocation Close Persons	Localism of Postrelocation Close Persons	
	Mostly local	*Mixed or dispersed*
All West End	26% (39)	21% (132)
Mostly West End	46% (15)	30% (60)
Equal or mostly outside West End	35% (17)	51% (88)

that any adaptation was difficult. Among those people who had most, but not all of their closest relationships within the local area, the differences are greater: those who have again established a predominantly local pattern of close relationships are more frequently adjusted-adapted (46 percent) than those whose closest persons are now more widely dispersed (30 percent). The fact that their predominantly local relationships did not wholly preclude close interpersonal relationships with people outside the area suggests greater flexibility and a somewhat greater readiness for transition. For some of this group, at least, there seems to have been the possibility of successfully transposing a familiar pattern despite the fact that different individuals were involved. However, among those who had, in effect, rejected an exclusively or predominantly local pattern of social relationships in the prerelocation situation, increased localism after relocation is associated with *decreased* adjustment-adaptation. Those individuals who did not conform to the modal prerelocation pattern of localism were not only unlikely to establish it anew after relocation but they appear to have experienced localism as a "regression" to a familiar but unwelcome past. In short, whatever pattern of social relationships was established after relocation, the frequency of adjustment-adaptation was strongly conditioned by transition readiness, as reflected in neighborhood orientations in the prerelocation period.

In stressing the impact of changes in social relationships on the effectiveness of adjustment to the experience of relocation, we have focused on that factor which has been of central importance in the lives of the great majority of working-class West End residents. It is evident that relocation necessarily entailed the disruption of dominant patterns of interpersonal contact for most of the former inhabitants. As indicated earlier these patterns of social relationship were functionally effective in stabilizing the transition from peasantry to working class and in allowing a subsequent transition from working class to middle class to take place coherently and meaningfully. However, as we have seen, a great many people from this working-class community had not yet reached the stage of readiness for the latter change.

Hypothetically, relocation can be conceived as an opportunity for change, for greater assimilation, for social mobility. *However, the freedom to use these opportunities must first be achieved internally and become an aspect of the individual's adaptational potential.* Some people disregard the features of opportunity and obtain a modicum of stability from reestablishing familiar patterns in new residential areas. But only a small proportion of the working-class community seems to have reached that stage of readiness for these transitions which allows them to move into higher status areas, to accept or seek out a higher level of social status, and to develop a different pattern of interpersonal and community orientation which, together, imply a high degree of assimilation and integration into the dominant urban, industrial way of life. For the most part, at least for several years after relocation, they neither wanted to nor appeared able to utilize the experience of forced residential change as an opportunity to achieve a pattern of life in closer accord with American middle-class ideals.

EFFECTS OF RESIDENTIAL CHANGES

While relocation is an important instance of forced *social* change in the working class, other significant types of changes are also brought about through relocation. The most obvious of these is the change in residence. The clearest opportunity provided by forced relocation, of course, is to improve the status of one's residential area.[20] While the majority moved into areas which were working-class or lower class, 42 percent moved into lower middle or upper middle-class areas. Naturally, there is a strong association between the status of the postreloca-tion residential area and social class status. Thus, 62 percent of the high occupation group moved into middle-class residential areas and only 35 percent of the low occupation group moved into these areas. There is also a clear relationship between the residential status of the postrelocation area and adjustment-adaptation: at the extremes, among those who moved into clearly middle-class areas, 43 percent are adjusted-adapted while only 20 percent of those who moved into lower-class areas are adjusted-adapted.

We have now to consider the various factors which influence both residential status and adjustment-adaptation as well as the relationship between them. Simul-taneous examination of social status variables, postrelocation residential status, and adjustment-adaptation, discloses different relationships among the subgroups. Thus, the association is strongest for the higher status people: they show considerably larger proportions of adjustment-adaptation with higher postrelocation residential status. On the other hand, for the lowest educational and the lowest occupational groups, the proportions who are adjusted-adapted are slightly higher in working-class areas than in the middle-class residential areas.

PLANS FOR MOVING

We have previously shown that educational and occupational position are important variables as indicators of preparedness for social change. A more direct and similarly patterned indicator of such preparedness is found in pre-relocation plans to move out of the West End. Among those who evidenced their preparedness by clearly anticipating the move (Planned to move) there is greater frequency of adjustment-adaptation in middle-class areas (64 percent) than in working-class areas (47 percent). However, among those who definitely planned to stay (and who would, thus, be viewed as unprepared for the change) and among those who had been thinking about it but had made no plans or efforts to leave (indicating their reluctance to depart despite ideational assimilation), there are no differences in adjustment-adaptation associated with postrelocation residential status.

The interaction among the several central factors in effective adjustment to

TABLE 7
Adjustment-Adaptation Index by Prerelocation Plans to Move and Postrelocation Residential Status (proportions adjusted-adapted)

| | Prerelocation Plans to Move | | |
Postrelocation Residential Status	Planned to move	Thinking about moving	Planned to stay
Middle-class	64% (25)	50% (34)	26% (103)
Working-class	47% (19)	52% (21)	23% (199)

the relocation experience is also revealed by the relationship between prerelocation aspirations, postrelocation residential status, and adjustment-adaptation. Social mobility orientation, as we would expect, is associated both with postrelocation residential status and with adjustment-adaptation: the higher the social mobility orientation, the more likely was the individual to move to an area of higher residential status; and the higher the social mobility orientation, the larger the proportions of adjustment-adaptation. But whether or not there is evidence of social mobility strivings, the experience of higher residential status shows a small association with higher levels of adjustment-adaptation. Thus, it is not the fulfillment of prerelocation status aspirations but the achievement of objective improvements which leads to higher rates of adjustment-adaptation. Moreover, it suggests that although social mobility orientation is undoubtedly associated with preparedness for social change, it is not a primary manifestation of readiness for transition to the world of the middle class.[21]

TABLE 8

Adjustment-Adaptation Index by Postrelocation Residential Status and Prerelocation Social Mobility Orientation (proportions adjusted-adapted)

| | *Social Mobility Orientation* | |
Postrelocation Residential Status	*Minimal mobility orientation*	*Maximal mobility orientation*
Middle-class	32% (120)	50% (42)
Working-class	25% (194)	43% (37)

A similar result which is due to a similar constellation of factors is the association between prerelocation residential aspirations (conceptions of an ideal dwelling), postrelocation residential status, and adjustment-adaptation. In general, the higher the residential aspiration, the larger the proportions who are adjusted-adapted (although, among the group with unrealistic fantasies of great luxury, there is a slight decrease in proportions adjusted-adapted). But the effect of middle-class residential status on adjustment-adaptation is greatest among the group with minimal residential aspirations. *Thus, as in the case of social mobility orientations, objective improvement in the postrelocation situation does serve to counteract some of the general tendency toward low levels of adjustment-adaptation,* but this result is most apparent for those who could least anticipate the possibility of these residential improvements.[22]

That objective improvement in residential status counteracts or compensates for a small part of the social dislocation implicit in forced relocation from a working-class community seems clear. Where there is a shift from positive feelings about the prerelocation residence to negative feelings about the postrelocation residence, the change to middle-class residential status is still associated with higher levels of adjustment-adaptation. Even when relocation is associated with increased household density, the rate of effective adjustment is higher in the middle-class

TABLE 9
Adjustment-Adaptation Index by Postrelocation Residential Status and Change
in Close-knit Network Contacts (proportions adjusted-adapted)

| Postrelocation Residential Status | *Change in Close-knit Network Contacts* | | |
	Minimal pre- and post-	*Minimal-moderate pre- and increased*	*Moderate-high pre- and decreased*
Middle-class	80% (10)	44% (71)	26% (80)
Working-class	42% (45)	36% (80)	16% (105)

residential status shift (40 percent) than for those who moved to working-class areas (19 percent). *However, improved residential status seems least effective in reversing the impact of changes in social relationships which were due to relocation.* This is evident with respect to changes in close-knit network relationships. Among those whose commitments were minimal and who continued to have minimal close-knit network contact after relocation, the differences in adjustment-adaptation with residential status are very great (80 percent in middle-class areas, 42 percent in working-class areas). But for those whose prerelocation experience involved a moderately high or very high degree of close-knit networks, there is little difference in adjustment-adaptation according to postrelocation residential status. In fact, the association between change in close-knit network contact and adjustment-adaptation remains extremely powerful and drastically reduces the significance of residential status changes except for the group who had little involvement with close-knit networks before and after relocation.

CONCLUSIONS

Throughout these data, the critical significance of preparedness for social change in coping with forced relocation is revealed again and again. Such preparedness may be manifest in objective indices of status, in social orientations to working-class patterns, in conceptions of the world outside the working-class community, or in personality resources which facilitate adaptation to change. *It is particularly striking that such prerelocation evidences of preparedness for change are the most important factors determining postrelocation adjustment-adaptation and tend to dwarf the importance of postrelocation situations and experiences. However, objective experiences of improvement with relocation can partly counteract the effects of lack of preparedness for the change.* Preparedness for change most particularly signifies an ability to utilize the wider range of options offered by "the open society" and to maximize the achievement of goals and aspirations. Objective improvements, whether in residential status or in household density or in other living conditions, are clearly more frequently associated with satisfaction for those who were ready to use the relocation situation as an opportunity for an increased range of choices. But those random or subtly selective factors which led to objective improvements despite the apparent lack of preparedness for this transition also provided some sense of unanticipated achievement which facilitated effective adjustment.

The one drastic and widespread change, the adverse effects of which showed little modification due to objective improvements of any type, was the almost inevitable shift in patterns of social relationship. The organization of social relationships through close-knit networks is a primary component of social integration in the working class. By the same token, it is a primary focus of disruption when the community is rapidly destroyed because of extremely rapid social change. And forced relocation is the most extreme and precipitate of these social changes. The willingness to relinquish this characteristic pattern of working-class social interaction and commitment is a primary, virtually an ultimate, manifestation of preparedness for transition to the world of the urban, industrial, middle-class society. But most people in working-class communities, here and elsewhere, seem quite unwilling to relinquish these patterns. In fact, many people who were otherwise ready for assimilation and social mobility were restrained from realizing these changes because of the binding power of their close-knit network ties. Given a long span of time, we assume that most of these people or, at the very least, their children would have developed the inner resources which would allow them to make the transition with meaning and satisfaction. But the social and residential dislocations associated with urban renewal occur almost at a single point in time. As the effects of these dislocations appear in post-relocation adjustment and adaptation, we can see rather direct evidence of the various stages and diverse factors involved in preparation for leaving the communal life of the working-class community. In effect, dislocation and relocation serve as prisms which array the population along the axis of adjustment-adaptation according to their preparedness for change prior to relocation. Only a very small proportion, indeed, is clearly ready to utilize the opportunities implicit in this form of social change. Thus, the unwelcome demands forced upon the population obtrude themselves with particular force and clarity. This is the setting for a major crisis of transition, a crisis which few working-class people are ready to meet.

NOTES

1. This statement, of course, is not directly applicable to the Negro working class. However, the importance of relatively recent experience in rural community life for a large proportion of the Negro working class does provide a comparable, if not identical, base.
2. While it is impossible to obtain precise figures for different status levels among employed males, a comparison of the different occupational groupings given by the census for native white of native parentage contrasted with native white of foreign parentage and foreign-born white makes it clear that the majority of low-status occupations must have been held by the foreign-born and their children. See for example N. Carpenter, *Immigrants and Their Children* (Washington, D.C.: Government Printing Office, 1927); E. P. Hutchinson, *Immigrants and Their Children, 1850–1950* (New York: John Wiley and Sons, 1956); and S. Lieberson, *Ethnic Patterns in American Cities* (New York: Free Press of Glencoe, 1963). Studies of discrete organizations—see J. S. Ellsworth, Jr., *Factory Folkways: A Study of Institutional Structure and Change* (New Haven: Yale University Press, 1952)—and of industries—see D. Brody, *Steelworkers in America: The Non-Union Era* (Cambridge: Harvard University Press, 1960)—support this conclusion on a more local level and further indicate the gradual infiltration of immigrants and their

children into the semi-skilled and skilled manual occupations. For a similar view see S. Lipset and R. Bendix, *Social Mobility in Industrial Society* (Berkeley: University of California Press, 1959) and S. M. Miller and F. Riessman, "The Working Class Subculture: A New View," *Social Problems,* IX (1961), 86–97.

3. Lipset and Bendix, *loc. cit.*

4. W. F. Whyte, *Street Corner Society* (Chicago: University of Chicago Press, 1943, revised 1955) and "Social Organization in the Slums," *American Sociological Review,* VIII (1943), 34–39.

5. The work of Park and his students was responsible for the earlier interest in community and neighborhood influences. R. E. Park and H. A. Miller in the book, *Old World Traits Transplanted,* (New York: Harper and Brothers, 1922) were quite conscious of the significance of immigrant ideas for allowing a slow process of adjustment by the erection of barriers to a more immediate impact of the demands of "Americanization." However, Whyte's study introduced important considerations of unique patterns of social organization to a greater extent than did any of the earlier studies. And subsequent work has continued to bear out and to implement his observations. See for example M. Fried, "Grieving for a Lost Home," in L. J. Duhl (ed.), *The Urban Condition* (New York: Basic Books, 1963); M. Fried and P. Gleicher, "Some Sources of Residential Satisfaction in an Urban Slum," *Journal of the American Institute of Planners,* XXVII (November, 1961), 305–315; H. Gans, *The Urban Villagers* (Glencoe: The Free Press, 1962); C. Hartman, "Social Values and Housing Conditions," *Journal of Social Issues* (Summer, 1963); R. Hoggart, *The Uses of Literacy* (London: Chatto and Windus, 1957); J. M. Mogey, *Family and Neighborhood* (New York, Oxford University Press, 1956); and M. Young and P. Willmott, *Family and Kinship in East London* (Glencoe: The Free Press, 1949).

6. E. Bott, *Family and Social Network Roles, Norms and External Relationships in Ordinary Urban Families* (London: Tavistock Institute, 1957).

7. A primary focus in describing the social relationships of the working class has been on familial ties. See for example, A. Cohen and H. M. Hodges, "Characteristics of the Lower-Blue-Collar-Class," *Social Problems,* X (1963), 303–334; Gans, *loc. cit.;* Miller and Riessman, *loc. cit.;* L. Rainwater, R. P. Coleman, and G. Handel, *Workingman's Wife: Her Personality, Work and Life Style* (New York: Oceana Publications, 1959); and M. Young and P. Willmott, *loc. cit.* Some recent results have begun to suggest that family relationships involve no greater interaction in the working class than in the middle class—see for example, Eugene Litwak, "Occupational Mobility and Extended Family Cohesion," *American Sociological Review,* XXV (1960), 9–21—and that family relationships are important to the extent that they facilitate the development of secure local affiliations (Fried and Gleicher, *loc. cit.*). In any case, the critical issues devolve on (1) the salience of a limited set of social relationships, and (2) the orientation of these relationships to an ascriptive pattern (regardless of its derivation from kinship ascription) within the framework of rigidly defined (although informal) reciprocal sets of obligations. For a critical review of the limitations of such concepts as "close-knit networks" see S. N. Eisenstadt, *The Absorption of Immigrants,* (London: Routledge and Kegan Paul, 1954).

8. Fried, "Grieving for a Lost Home," *loc. cit.*

9. The literature on crisis and adaptation to crisis is still quite small and deals with only a narrow range of crises. Several of these studies, however, open new areas for study and conceptualization and provide some of the foundations for further work. I am particularly indebted to Erich Lindemann, both in his formal presentations and in the course of many discussions, for my understanding of the issues involved in adaptation to crisis and its relation to health and illness. See E. Lindemann, "Mental Health in the Environment," in Duhl (ed.), *loc. cit.;* "Psycho-Social Factors as Stressor Agents," in J. M. Tanner (ed.), *Stress and Psychiatric Disorder,* (Oxford, Blackwell Scientific Publications, 1960); "Symptomatology and Management of Acute Grief," *American Journal of Psychiatry,* (1944) pp. 141–148; and E. Lindemann and L. Dawes, "The Use of Psychoanalytic Constructs in Preventive Psychiatry," *Psychoanalytic Study of Child,* VII (1952), 429–448.

10. For a list of studies of working-class communities in other urbanized areas see Marc Fried, "Transitional Functions of Working-Class Communities; Implications for Forced Reloca-

tion," in Mildred Kantor (ed.), *Mobility and Mental Health* (Princeton, N.J.: D. Van Nostrand, 1964), footnote 10 and References.

11. Unfortunately, not all of these 473 women were interviewed while still living in the West End. The sample was selected on the basis of every fifth card in the files of the relocation office. These files were based on a house-to-house survey done several months previously with 99 percent of their interviews completed. By the time interviewing began and, in the course of interviewing, people started to leave the area at an increasing rate. Thus, 32 percent of the prerelocation interviews were actually done right after the family had moved out of the West End. In these cases where "voluntary" relocation antedated the interview, prerelocation issues were handled retrospectively. But in these instances, "retrospective" generally refers to between several weeks and several months after moving.

12. Fried, "Grieving for a Lost Home," *loc. cit.*

13. We shall not take up the theoretical issues involved in the ideas of satisfaction and happiness. However, the data reveal an interesting contrast related to the theoretical issue. A much greater proportion (57 percent) report that they are satisfied than give evidence that they are happier (21 percent). A comparison of the items which are related to each of these questions suggests that Satisfaction-dissatisfaction indicates adjustment in the narrower sense. It implies that the postrelocation reality situation has not been too bad and that, in any case, the person has accepted the change as an integral feature of current life. Happiness-unhappiness, on the other hand, appears to stir up a longer range conception of oneself, of one's situation, and of the satisfactions and meanings of the past. Generally speaking, prerelocation variables are more strongly related to the Happiness-unhappiness dimension; and postrelocation variables are more strongly related to the Satisfaction-dissatisfaction dimension.

14. Throughout the treatment of data, results are reported in the form of percentage differences. Tests of significance have not been performed for each table. However, a hypothetical 2×2 table with marginals equally distributed would reach the .05 level of significance with a X^2 test when the percentage difference is 11 percent. Occasionally, the term "significance" is used when the results are so overwhelmingly powerful that, by inspection alone, it is clear that a statistical test would indicate significance well beyond the .01 level of probability. It should be clear, however, that the rationale for interpreting percentage differences lies primarily in the consistency of relationships with similar or meaningfully interrelated variables. Thus, regardless of the strength of any given relationship, it is used interpretively only if similar relationships militate against the likelihood of a chance correspondence among two or three variables. The other criterion employed throughout is that of linearity in the relationship. True linearity is difficult to obtain when there are many cells in a table and, thus, the number of cases in some cells is severely reduced. Nonetheless, any marked deviation from a linear pattern is treated as a negative instance. Similar relationships among several tables, therefore, refer to (1) similar direction of relationship when two related variables are run against a third, (2) an arbitrary minimal difference between the extremes of 15 percent, (3) linearity in the relationship when there are more than two subcategories in the variable. As will be evident, these are the minimal criteria employed and no instance of relationships reported is limited to these minimal demands.

15. There is a tendency for those who are American-born with one foreign parent and, to a smaller extent, for those who are American-born with two foreign parents to show smaller proportions of adjustment-adaptation than do the extremes of assimilation status. These discrepancies can, however, be explained by introducing some of the complexities of transition-readiness which are not wholly, at least in any simple sense, a function of objective status attributes. The group with one foreign parent has consistent problems in adjustment; there is considerable evidence to show that their decision to remain in the West End, in spite of their objective "readiness" to make the transition, was due to intragroup and interpersonal conflict and intrapersonal insecurity. On the other hand, the very large group who are native-born with two foreign parents is the model community group and shows the most intense commitment, the most extensive participation, the greatest consistency in sharing the urban-working-class form of group identity. For a larger proportion of this group than for any other, therefore, the loss of the West End was a most severe disruption and an irremediable experience of separation.

16. In referring to "the communal area" we imply that the geographical area defined as the West End was also a physical basis for social organization. As we shall show in subsequent reports, this is the case although the relevant area was not uniformly circumscribed by the entire population. Gans in *The Urban Villagers, loc cit.*, suggests that this sense of a larger "West End" area was a product of the reaction to relocation. Not only do the internal relationships in our data indicate that this was not the case, but other and earlier reports about the area describe or imply a generalized sense of a common spatial-social region. See J. F. Dineen, *Ward Eight* (Boston: Waverley House, 1963) and R. A. Woods, *Americans in Process* (Boston: Houghton Mifflin Company, 1902).

17. This index is based on six items which define characteristic goals and ideals associated with either "typical" middle-class orientations or mobility strivings *per se*. Three of these items are drawn from R. Centers' *The Psychology of Social Classes: A Study of Class Consciousness* (Princeton: Princeton Univ. Press, 1949) and show strong social class associations. In our data all six items are strongly associated with social class differences.

18. In all of these analyses which involve simultaneous consideration of three different variables, the figures in many cells are quite small. Thus, the conclusions must be viewed more tentatively. As with the previous results, however, the consistency of the findings provides a fairly substantial basis for interpretation.

19. Fried, "Grieving for a Lost Home," *loc. cit.*

20. A very large proportion of the residents of this area were not primarily oriented to the low rents nor, on the basis of their incomes, need they have been. Rents were, however, extremely low in the West End and any residential change almost necessarily meant increased rental costs. In fact, the difference in rental cost for a dwelling unit in a higher or lower status area would have been relatively small compared to the difference between West End rents and any other feasible apartment rents. Moreover, as Chester Hartman has shown, in his article, "Social Values and Housing Orientations" in the *Journal of Social Issues* (Summer, 1963), there were various indications of residential and housing desires which went beyond the opportunities offered by the West End. These remained unfulfilled, to a large extent, however, because they meant leaving the area which was of greater importance than the qualities of housing per se.

21. To clarify this in detail and to present the evidence for this view would carry us far afield. In brief, social mobility orientation is not a primary manifestation of preparedness for social change for several reasons: (1) some of the people who show strong mobility desires are quite unrealistic and the desires represent vague fantasies rather than progressive assimilation and adaptive achievement, and (2) social mobility from the working class frequently moves by slow, step-wise increases in educational and occupational status which antedate any self-conscious desire for or even ideational assimilation to middle-class status. This does not, of course, mean that some working-class people may not self-consciously desire social mobility and prepare themselves for meaningful and integrated transition. In the normal course of events, these are the people who regularly do move out of working-class areas at the point in time when this can most consistently correspond with other status changes. In the situation of forced relocation, however, we observe the entire array of those individuals who have not yet reached this point although their plans to move do provide evidence that some of this population were on the verge of making this transition.

22. Further analysis reveals yet another condition of variation. Among the group with higher education the fulfillment of pre-relocation residential aspirations leads to larger proportions of adjustment-adaptation. For the group with low education (0–11 years schooling), those with low aspirations are more likely to be adjusted-adapted if they move into a middle-class area.

METROPOLIS AS ECOSYSTEM
Laurence Tilly

"Metropolis as Ecosystem" is the only selection in this book by a full-fledged biologist. Tilly specializes in the intensive study of fresh-water ecosystems. (A representative report of his work appears in "The Structure and Dynamics of Cone Spring," Ecological Monographs, 38, Spring, 1968.) Here, however, he sketches what would be involved in not only insisting that big cities are ecosystems (which hundreds of authors have done recently) but actually performing a bio-ecological analysis of their structure and dynamics (which no one has done with any thoroughness). It turns out to be an enormous job, both because of the system's complexity and because of the present unavailability of data. It also turns out to be an important job, because it is more likely than the other means available to pinpoint the probable effects of changes in transport, waste disposal, construction, and other technical procedures on the chances for survival of the city's inhabitants and of what remains of their natural surroundings.

Two fundamental facts about cities come out more clearly in Tilly's article than they have elsewhere in this book. The first is the extraordinary dependence of life within the city on processes and materials far outside it. One example is the importance of oceanic algae—crucial suppliers of oxygen—to the very breath of urbanites. Another is the predominance of fuels, especially fossil fuels, drawn from elsewhere in the total flow of energy within the city. Anything which upsets the flow of these precious resources will disrupt urban life. Of course, all ecosystems depend on all others to some degree. The city is simply an extreme case of that dependence. The second fundamental fact is the unusual prominence of one-way (rather than circular) flows of matter and energy within the cities; the results are large dumps of abandoned material and energy, high ratios of imports to consumption, and extensive waste. Tilly's presentations of these special features of cities are not alarmist, but matter-of-fact. Nevertheless, he reminds us firmly that the cities we are building already threaten to commit ecocide, if not suicide.

When thinking about man's largely self-made urban problems, it is easy enough to overlook a most basic consideration—that man lives in an environment, part natural, part manufactured, and that his relationship to the parts of that environment, and of the parts to each other, can be ignored only at the risk of mutual destruction.

It is common-sense ecology that organisms have characteristic places to live. Fish are found in water, moles in the ground, since different organisms have

Reprinted by permission in revised form from "Metropolis as Ecosystem" by Laurence Tilly, *GW, The George Washington University Magazine,* 6:2 (Winter 1969–1970), pp. 21–25.

different requirements for life that must be supplied by the environment. In the process of drawing upon their environments for such requirements, living things leave characteristic marks upon their surroundings. Ecologists use such marks as clues to the active presence of particular organisms or association of organisms. Some of these escape notice in ordinary observation, but even the novice naturalist can recognize the hill of an ant, the burrow of a rodent, or the nest of a bird. Such structures represent adaptive modifications of environment by organisms. They represent matter moved and energy expended in the struggle for survival.

Man as an organism characteristically inhabits the specialized combination of unusual burrows, hills, and nests called a city ("metropolitan area" or "metropolis" gives a better sense of scale, and perhaps most accurate would be "ecopolis"). The human organism has spent enormous energy moving materials to construct shelters in a social setting. Early man was evidently a relatively large, erect, warm-blooded, semi-tropical animal adapted to living in social groups along the edges of forests. Like other animals he was subject to environmental vagaries such as drought, food shortage, and predation by other animals, so early populations probably lived in equilibrium with their environments. Natural selection favored the development of intelligence directed toward learning behavior. Culture, developed in association with intelligence and social behavior, evidently conferred adaptive advantages on the groups possessing it, since culturally integrated groups gradually increased their populations. Such social organization seems to have been possible especially where the environment supplied food in greater than usual abundance so that specialization other than food gathering and cultivation could be pursued by parts of the population. About five to six thousand years ago social aggregations achieved a point of sufficient specialization and independence that sociologists now recognize them to have been cities. Even the early city was a complex array of interacting units integrated into a functional whole. From the perspective of an ecologist, such a system of organisms and surroundings in interaction is an *ecosystem,* parallel in many ways to the more or less natural units in which other organisms live.

Ecosystems are units which include organisms and environment in inter- action. A classic example is the lake ecosystem. Viewed as an ecosystem, a lake is more than a hole full of water. It is more than the place and the organisms in it. It is a superiorganistic unit that has an organization, structure, and function. Like an organism it may be dissected (in imagination and in fact) for an understanding of its parts and functions. The nonliving parts of most importance in the lake ecosystem include the medium itself, the water, all the materials suspended and dissolved in it, the mud and other mineral deposits forming the bottom, and the sunlight which penetrates the water. The important living components include the members of the food chain: tiny suspended green plants, small suspended plant eaters, predators, larger predators, and finally, the decomposers. The energy flow is generated using the matter of the system which is in continual movement through the cycles of the food chain.

Interconnections and interdependencies exist between the living and the nonliving in all ecosystems. In a lake the oxygen of the water is related to the penetration of sunlight and to its interception by green plankton. Oxygen is released by green plants exposed to sunlight as one product of the food making process. In general, the more plants intercepting sunlight, the more oxygen there will be. However, the more plants there are, the less light penetration there will be, so limits are reached. Further, the minerals found in the lake water influence the kinds of green plants that can grow. Some kinds produce more shade than others, hence their presence precludes the appearance of other species and influences the pattern of oxygen (and other mineral) distribution. The connectedness of components could be discussed at length. The important point is that the real world is extremely webby, and the ecosystem is a convenient perspective for examining its webbiness.

The metropolis, like all ecosystems, involves organisms and environment in interaction and, like other ecosystems, can be analyzed in terms of its structure and function. It has its own array of living and nonliving parts moving the matter and expending the energy which constitute the major part of the metropolitan activities, and which also operate to regulate those activities.

While the metropolis is obviously a man-centered ecosystem, it has minor species of importance, such as pets, parasites, and commensals, as well as man's intentionally or accidentally cultivated or tolerated plants. While it is difficult to estimate the historical role of organisms such as the rat, the fly, and the microbes they may transmit to man, the evolutionary successes of these and many other creatures are tightly bound to the activities of man and to his success as a species.

Natural systems from which man is excluded tend to be more diversified in species. Theoretical reasons as well as empirical observations support the idea that ecosystem stability is positively correlated with species diversity. In general, where man has moved in, he has upset system stability and destroyed diversity through his activities in cultivating the soil, harvesting natural food organisms, and occupying the land. Like other ecological dominants, *Homo sapiens* increases at the expense of other species.

The metropolis is a dependent ecosystem. Like an anthill community, a city is dominated by one species but dependent upon and connected to many more. Aside from the obvious connections the city has with food organisms and organisms of industrial and pharmaceutical importance, it is subtly but restrictively tied to the whole biosphere. For example, the city is absolutely dependent upon oceanic algae. Cities act as giant consumers, ingesting organic matter and oxygen and disgorging volumes of carbon dioxide. Something approaching 70 per cent of the world's oxygen supply comes from the oceanic algae. Without diffusion of oxygen from the oceans, the cities would asphyxiate.

The metropolitan environment includes not only the physical and chemical features of the ordinary ecosystem: components of air, water, soil, food, and building materials, but also those elements that make the ecosystem extraordinary. Besides materials man-the-animal needs for survival, he surrounds himself with uncountable numbers he has imported, dug up, or manufactured. His is a world of two-by-four trees, concrete rocks, conditioned air, and artificial light. Most of his physical world is in some way culturally modified. Man is not alone among the organisms in his behavior in modifying his physical surroundings and importing and manufacturing exotic materials. Bees, for example, build complex hives of remarkable order and strength and proceed to air condition them by pumping their wings. Prairie dogs excavate extensive burrow systems including "root cellars" where they cache provisions for seasons of food scarcity. Man's activities differ from those of other such organisms not in kind but in degree.

The profound difference in kind lies in man's potential realization of the influence of his actions on the environment and in his ability to vary his actions in response to it. Man's awareness of his position in time and space reveals new dimensions of environment—the purely cultural dimensions of mind and imagination. For the first time in any significant degree, the organisms become creator of and subject to forces interposed between the cause and the effect, between the stimulus and the response. The *idea* of the cause itself evokes an effect; the *idea* of the stimulus can itself elicit a response. An idea has an impact far out of proportion to the material and energetic investment it represents. It often appears that in man an idea or an "image" can become a complete substitute for the physical entity it may be supposed to represent. The myriad ideas and images about the metropolis that exist in the minds of the inhabitants are prime movers of the activities which characterize city life. As yet depressingly little is known of how the physical entities, the ideas related to them, and the human organisms' responses are interconnected in anything approaching a predictable manner. Studies of these interconnections are absolutely essential to the understanding of the ecology of the metropolis.

Despite this fundamental gap in knowledge, it is still possible to begin at least to draw some outlines for an ecological picture of the metropolis. And it is an important undertaking, for unless increasingly more is known about how the components of the metropolis interact, attempts to deal with each component separately will be decreasingly productive. All ecosystems require a continuous supply of energy to power their activities. Since no energy-requiring process is 100 per cent efficient, the amount of energy available to do useful work diminishes with time and must be replenished. Cities exploit two main energy flow pathways. The first is the human food chain mainly involving transfer of energy from sun to green plants which directly or indirectly become available as food for man. The second line of energy flow is the fossil fuel path. Fossil fuels such as coal and oil were formed eons ago when solar energy was stored in the bodies of organisms that died and were buried before decay could be completed. Supplementary energy may come from electricity generated from water or atomic power.

To speak about energy flow is necessarily to speak of matter movement. The two are inextricably linked. For energy to be expended, matter must be moved and vice versa. The energy in foods or fuels is locked in the chemical bonds of matter and is transformed into the movement of human bodies, blocks of concrete or automobiles, and eventually into heat. An important distinction is that while energy is degraded and becomes unavailable, the ashes of matter are at least potentially available to be enriched with energy and moved again and again. Since the amount of matter in the biosphere is limited, it is obvious that some of the movements have to be circular if energy is to continue to flow. In cities, however, the flows of matter as well as those of energy tend to be undirectional and, therefore, wasteful.

Matter is brought into the city by a root system of roads, rails, and air corridors. It is channeled into maintenance, new growth, exportable manufactures, and, after some delay, into worn out discards that tend to accumulate in ever increasing quantities in the dung-heap trash piles which ring our metropolitan areas. Substances which make up living tissue do tend to be recycled, but in peculiar concentrations and with notable losses. For example, phosphorus appears to be everywhere the most critically scarce element related to the process of energy fixation, yet it is extremely abundant in sewage effluent. It tends to be deposited in the ocean depths at rates greater than natural recovery processes presently balance. The net result of the phosphorous waste is two problems compounding each other: both the loss of an essential element in short supply and that loss as a contributor to water pollution. Other substances used primarily in activities that are cultural in the broad sense of the term flow to the waste pile. Dumps for such substances are likely to be places of high deposit and little return.

Ecologists who are students of "natural," which is to say "non-human," ecosystems have found it useful to analyze them in terms of energy flow. The relatively few analyses attempted suggest that a few components are responsible for the major portion of energy flow, so that one may safely ignore minor components in generalizing about the function of ecosystems. So far, only very fragmentary attempts have been made to analyze human ecosystems in comparable terms. For obvious reasons the most complete treatments deal with primitive cultures and not with cities.

If the metropolis is really homologous (alike in all essential respects and not merely similar in some respects) to other ecosystems it should yield to the same sorts of analyses designed for understanding "natural" ecosystems, and the most useful of those have been examinations of energy flow and matter movement.

To construct an energy flow analysis for a metropolitan ecosystem it is necessary to determine a full set of input-output relations for each set of components which use energy and matter. A budget may be established for each component subject to energy income and expenditure according to the equation $I = H + Y + G$, where: I = Income; H = Heat; Y = Yield, and G = Growth. This applies to any component, living or nonliving, that uses energy. A logical place to begin in such an analysis would be with a component whose losses were products escaping the system, for example, manufacturing industries whose products are exported. In such a case the "income" would be in the form of raw materials and power. The principal expenditures would be in products manufactured, heat generated as a result of the inherent inefficiency of all energy transfer processes, and the energy value of minerals used in maintenance and repair, as well as the so-called "by-products" and "waste products" of manufacturing.

Abel Wolman has developed a partial input-output budget for a hypothetical American city of one million. I have used his data, handbook data on calorific equivalents, and some considered guesswork, in converting his figures to an energy flow estimate for the city. Table 1 contains the converted and estimated flow rates. The justification for making such a conversion is that the weights of materials are not so representative of their ecological significance as are the energy requirements.

By far the major budget item is the fuel which powers the cultural activities of the metropolis. Flow directed toward strictly biological activity constitutes only about 4 per cent of the total shown. The budget should also include estimates of commercial exchanges of raw materials and manufactured goods. A more complete accounting of energy flow would include a detailed schedule of disbursements, such as the fraction of total energy directed toward each of the major ecosystem components that could be recognized as elements of the structure of a metropolitan ecosystem. For examples of some of the flow paths that might be of ecological interest, see Figure 1.

TABLE 1
Energy Budget for Hypothetical Metropolis of One Million Inhabitants
(billions of kilocalories per day)

In		*Out*	
Item		*Item*	
Food	More than 3	Sewage	1
Fuel	72	Carbon monoxide	0.8
		Hydrocarbons	1.2
Raw Materials and imports	More than 5	Refuse	5
Totals	80	Totals	8

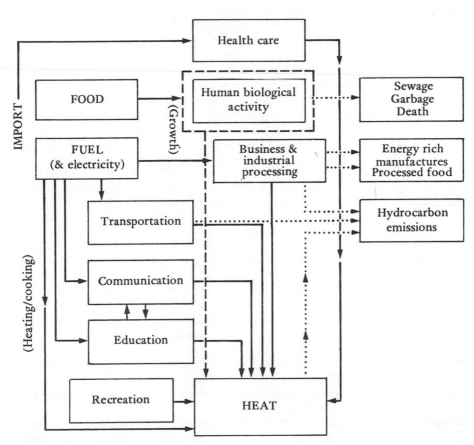

Figure 1. City Energy Flow

The structure of an ecosystem depends on the spatial and functional placement of parts relative to the whole. Obviously, then, the structure of any ecosystem is related to the number of components which can be defined—and to the number of interactions in which each component may participate. The practical consequences of such a definition is that no complete description of structure is possible, and one focuses upon "effective" components and factors.

Figure 1 presents an oversimplified diagram of energy flow pathways which would be an important aspect of the structure of a city ecosystem. No attempt has been made to depict components or flow paths in proportion to each other, although that would be highly desirable. In a conventional ecosystem analysis one would be interested in the relationship between the magnitude of the "standing crop," or inventory, and the energy flow through each component. Data may be available for documenting such relationships but have not been put in usable form as yet.

The components pictured might be organized into four major categories as attempted in Table 2. These categories are: the biological, the biocultural, the cultural, and the regulatory. The categories are not mutually exclusive; the same components may appear in more than one category. When this happens, different features of the same component are being emphasized.

This table is not an attempt to be exhaustive, only suggestive. The criterion for inclusion of a component is its probable involvement in energy flow. Different ecosystem functions would require the consideration of different components.

If one is interested in the spatial relations of parts of the metropolitan ecosystem, one might attempt to correlate the distribution of individuals, families, social groups, or institutions with other components or factors. For example, a great number of sociological studies have attempted to analyze the distribution of such groups as racial minorities in terms of dwelling type, proximity to center city, income, and so on. The computer has made possible the examination of relationships among matrices of factors and components, thereby extending the possibilities for correlation analyses of ecosystem structure.

TABLE 2
Components and Categories of Metropolis Ecosystem Structure

Biological	Biocultural	Cultural	Regulatory
Food	Building materials	Education	Government
Water	Transportation materials	Government	Money
Sewage	Communication materials	Recreational	Home and family
Carbon dioxide	Heating, cooling, cooking	Religious	Communications
Oxygen	Manufacturing	Personal services	Church and religion
Other biological elements	Health care		Folkways and mores
			Pollutants

It is obvious that the metropolis is among the most complex of ecosystems. It is also painfully obvious that the metropolis is among the ecosystems most in need of comprehensive study. There is no need to dwell on the problems of metropolitan life discussed in great detail elsewhere. Air and water pollution, strangulation by car and road, intermittent power failures, disintegration of neighborhoods, and over concentration of population are but a few. Seen from the perspective of ecological analysis, many such problems are related to each other and to the larger question of human ecosystems now in a perilous state of disequilibrium. We are just becoming aware that we may have modified our environment beyond the limits of tolerance.

A bioecological analysis of the metropolitan system appears to be justifiable in terms of both theory and need. Need is sorely and immediately evident in those cases where metropolitan ecosystems are interfering with natural ecosystems. The example of the lake given earlier is hardly typical of such polluted lakes as Lake Erie, whose natural balance has been knocked askew by the wastes of the man-made ecosystems that border it. Development of theory will not guarantee any immediate remedies but should provide organized, comprehensive ways of thinking about the metropolis as an interrelated whole, not merely a series of discrete problems to be approached individually.

Only in recent years have urban sociologists recognized the analytical utility of the ecosystem model derived from biological ecology. In 1964 Otis Dudley Duncan made a strong case for the application of such a perspective to the examination of cities and other human social structures, yet biological ecologists have not widely explored human ecology in its broader ecosystem complexity despite general appeals that have been made by practicing members of the profession. Perhaps the reluctance to expand such investigation stems from the general difficulty of starting interdisciplinary programs in educational institutions or from the immensity of underwriting so mammoth an undertaking. The often discussed and desired National Institute of Ecology would be an appropriate agency to initiate and support such an important enterprise. Whatever the mechanism, it seems fair to say that only in the light of the more comprehensive view of ecosystem ecology will the negatives of anti-pollution and anti-population find appropriate, positive antidotes.

THE CITY AND THE COUNTRY: REFLEXIONS ON SOME ANCIENT COMMONPLACES
Julio Caro Baroja

Caro Baroja's reflections recall the historical sweep of the essay by Lewis Mumford (Chapter 2). The leading questions are normative—they deal with alternative ways of life. Caro Baroja speaks of many topics in the course of a rich and evocative survey of Mediterranean history. Perhaps the central issue is the character of the division between city and country in that part of the world. Caro Baroja makes us aware of the length and continuity of urban experience in the Mediterranean, the extent to which the structures of the city have created those of the countryside, the persistence of hostile stereotypes of city and country which reveal little of the actual difference between them but which disguise varying moral views of the world which have importance in their own right. Most significant for our purposes, he shows how anthropological observation of the present and historical observation of the past combine to give us the power to deal with the largest, most persistent traits of urban life.

It is impossible to conceive a general plan of studies of the social structure of the peoples of the Mediterranean which does not investigate the role of the city. Such investigations would, I believe, modify to a large extent some of the commonly accepted ideas regarding the significance of urban and rural society in the development of communities; this, in spite of the fact that this ancient contrast between the city and the country is a source of almost all the speculations of historians and anthropologists in their endeavours to sketch the general character of Mediterranean society.

The classic authors were much impressed by this contrast. Varro in his famous treatise on agriculture said that in this world there are only two forms of life for man: the urban and the rural. He added that the rural life is not only prior to urban life but is also more noble and better, since it is given to us by divine nature, whereas urban life is the work of man.[1] The scheme which he proposed presents the ancient form of life as also more moral and more in keeping with religious principles, while modern life is more wicked and ruled by artifice. This scheme is indeed older than Varro. When Aristophanes tried to show in 'The Clouds' the difference between the good life of old and the modern life of the city, he took as a prototype of the one, Strepsiades, a pious man, industrious and economical, who loved country life, and of the other his wife and his son, city people, addicted to all sorts of diversions, extravagance and superfluities.[2]

Now Aristophanes was only repeating a commonplace of the Athens of the time in homage to his traditionally-minded public. Yet this commonplace has lasted to our day: in the city are found vice, corruption and artifice; in the country the ancient virtues, and still more than in the countryside of one's own land, in the countryside of distant regions which have a smaller number of cities. Caesar said at the beginning of his 'Commentaries' that the more isolated people are more courageous while those who are accustomed to commerce and an easier life are less manly.[3] Tacitus was of the same opinion and there are critics who consider his 'Germania' no more than an illustration of this thesis of the corruption of Rome, the city *par excellence,* contrasted with the natural morality of the countryside, represented by the Germans.[4]

Similar ideas are found in sixteenth century Spain in Granada, in the time of

Reprinted by permission from "The City and the Country: Reflexions on Some Ancient Commonplaces" by Julio Caro Baroja, translated by Carol Horning, in *Mediterranean Countrymen* edited by Julian Pitt-Rivers (Paris: Mouton, 1963), pp. 27–40. Footnotes renumbered.

the uprising of the Moriscos against their oppressors, the *Cristianos Viejos*. The authors who have left accounts of the rebellion report that those Moriscos who lived in the city were rich men given to trade and immersed in a life of luxury; they would have liked liberation more than anyone, but they lacked mettle, while the neighbouring mountains, the rough Alpujarras, sheltered men less refined, but more unyielding and capable of warlike activities.[5] The observations of these historians corroborate the ideas of the Renaissance moralists, the heirs of the Greeks and the Romans. Fray Antonio de Guevara was a Spanish moralist of the 16th century who enjoyed a remarkable vogue during his lifetime and who is considered one of the founders of 'Euphuism'. He is famous moreover because he embellished his work with citations from authors and classical books invented by himself, thereby demonstrating an aristocratic contempt for pedantry. The life of this ingenious divine, who came to be a bishop, was spent at court. But in 1539 he published a treatise *Menosprecio de corte y alabanza de aldea* in which he eulogized village and small town life and criticized the city, not only from a moral point of view but also on account of the ills and inconveniences which he experienced at court, the highest expression of urban life.[6]

The tradition reaches down to the nineteenth century where we find the first sociologists to study the characters of urban and country life. Though they believed themselves to be 'scientific', they were not free from the influence of the past.

I wish to return once again, however, to the Classical world to draw into the discussion new elements from authors whose reflexions upon the dichotomy, freer perhaps than ours from the weight of erudition, yet possess great insight.

II

The Greeks, in spite of their pride of race, admitted that the Mediterranean was a little sea and that the people who lived around it were but a small part of humanity. In the 'Phaedo' Plato ironically compares the Mediterranean with a puddle of water and its peoples with noisy, croaking frogs. There could not be a less flattering analogy: from the Hellespont to the Columns of Hercules nothing is to be seen but frogs and ants floundering around their narrow puddle, and these humble animals are the Greeks, the Phoenicians, the Carthaginians, the Egyptians, the Jews, the Romans and the Iberians.[7]

In order to understand the structure of this world as seen through the eyes of an ancient Greek, consider another text of Plato. Plato thought that after the deluge only three political orders were established in all the known world: the simplest and most rustic in the mountain heights, and a second, somewhat later in time, on the slopes of the same mountains. Little by little men living on the lower slopes acquired self-confidence and courage, and then, the third and most modern political order was formed, on the plains.[8] Several centuries later Strabo considered it necessary to add two more orders: that constituted by those who live in the coastlands and that of island dwellers, and he developed the idea that as man finds the courage to approach the sea, he creates a larger variety of forms of government and a diversity of mores and customs.[9] The Platonic thesis, synthesized by Strabo, is founded on the classical image of the world of Mediterranean man. But this image lends itself to an historical and moral interpretation. For, according to this idea, among the societies of the time there remained representatives of earlier, different modes of life. The most 'primitive' would be those who still lived in the manner of the Cyclops, that is, in a state of pristine innocence, while the most modern—the inhabitants of coastal cities—affected artifice and corruption. In order to show the extension of the classical thesis it might be recalled that among several peoples of southern Europe (some of whom are not Mediterraneans) the idea persists in that certain territories which constitute the boundaries of their universe there formerly lived creatures very similar to the Cyclops, even in their physical characteristics. Thus, for example, in the heart of the Basque Country, among the inhabitants of the south of Guipuzcoa, a mythical being, the 'gentil' is found who, according to popular belief, lived in the neighbouring heights and compared to whom the peasant considered himself a man of knowledge.[10]   Actually, the myth served to place the peasant midway between an hypothetical state of primitive anarchy, supposedly prechristian, and the state of corruption associated always with the life of ports and towns. He thus remained in the centre of his moral world.

(B)	(C)
primitive anomia	modern corruption
('gentil' in the mountains)	(seaports and cities)

x

ego

(A)

The ancients established, then, several theses concerning the nature of the origin of rustic and urban life, theses which are echoed in more modern epochs and which present a geographical or spacial side, an historical or temporal side and a moral side. I present them in the adjoining diagram.

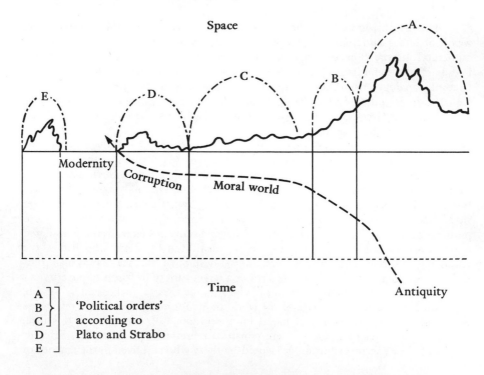

A ⎫
B ⎬ 'Political orders'
C ⎭ according to
D   Plato and Strabo
E

In spite of the classical authors' insistence on the particular quality of rural as opposed to urban life, they had very distinct ideas on the close relations of the city with the country and on their necessary connections. And it is worth noting that when they do the work of sociologists (rather than historians, geographers, or moralists), they begin to see clearly something that can be defined as a linking of functions between the city and the country.

III

Consider a third text of Plato, found in the *Republic*.[11] Socrates makes, in this, his typical analysis of the composition of the polis. He creates a chain of connected elements from the most elementary and everyday need to the most superfluous luxury. Nourishment, lodging, and clothing are the human needs producing the labourer, the mason and the weaver, and in addition, the clothier. The principle of the division of labour gives rise to the existence of specialists in each craft. There are, therefore, several kinds of labourers, herdsmen, and townsmen. There are also different kinds of traders: some trade by sea, others by land. The volume of trade also produces varieties of traders and merchants.

'But', says Socrates, 'we are not considering the basic essentials, merely, of a city, but a city in all its luxurious splendour'. The luxuries increase their dimensions since they require activities still more considerable than do necessities. Thus in the polis we find actors, dancers, men of affairs, those who labour to enhance feminine beauty, and wet-nurses, schoolmasters, hairdressers, barbers, cooks . . . On the other hand, luxury arouses a covetousness which induces war, in a way that causes a whole military system to be created, to grow and to fortify itself. In company with soldiers and their chiefs come the armament dealers, the entrepreneurs and manufacturers of arms. The polis, then, is a bizarre assemblage of men, united by interlocking interests. In the text of *The Republic* there is not the smallest concession to utilitarianism, because the author (or Socrates himself) clearly recognizes that simple necessity cannot be everything in urban life, and that the city is governed by pleasure and power—in a word, vices.

On the other hand there are continual relations between the market place, the port where the businessmen gather, the surrounding plains and even the mountains which close the horizon. The man from the country is influenced constantly by the life of the townsman. The complaints of Aristophanes' Strepsiades show the individual side of these relations. But the collective side now merits our attention.

IV

I wish to pose the following two questions: (1) to what extent is this classical dichotomy valuable as a basis for the study of contemporary Mediterranean societies? (2) to what extent is one able to speak of continuity in the same societies? Using archaeological criteria it is easy to demonstrate the greater antiquity of country life, the antiquity to which Varro assigned the highest degree of nobility. But between the date when the first farmers appeared along the borders of the sea and that of the so-called urban revolution, the lapse is significant for the archaeologist and prehistorian, but less so for those who are dedicated to the study of historical societies. Thus I am surprised to see social anthropologists make use of archaeological criteria.[12]

A short time ago Cadiz celebrated its third millennium.[13] Some other Mediterranean cities were already in existence when Cadiz was founded. Others are more modern, but the more famous are at least as old. Athens or Rome, Naples or Syracuse, Marseille or Malaga, Jerusalem or Seville have undergone many crises and changes, have had moments of ascendancy and decadence.

In chronicles and local histories the idea is always reflected that cities express a continuity which cannot be found in nations. I believe that the local chroniclers had a clearer view than certain historians of the nineteenth and twentieth centuries who have tended to deny the importance of continuity. When at the end of the 17th century a Spanish magistrate wrote a first-hand account of the riots of the city of Messina against the Spanish, he did not hesitate to take as the base and principle of his report the personality of Messina from the time of its founding right up to the era in which he wrote.[14] Consciousness of the historical continuity of the polis has perhaps always remained alive in southern Italy.

There remain several historical and anthropological problems with regard to the spirit of continuity. This spirit is inconceivable without a large number of traditional institutions, which the moralists did not consider when they characterized city life. Among these institutions are several established in accordance with what some sociologists call 'small groups,' which others have named 'intimate face-to-face associations,'[15] that is to say, the institutions which follow are most characteristic of 'small groups.'

In a number of cases the rural communities of the Mediterranean have an eponymous ancestor, a known founder, and so do the cities. Sometimes he is an obscure tribal chief who is more or less mythical; sometimes he is a royal chief, like Alexander or Constantine or one of those warlike Muslim founders of ephemeral states that Ibn Khaldun studied with insight.[16] For several centuries lineal descent was a notable influence in the Mediterranean city. In the Middle Ages and even later in Italy, Spain and elsewhere, there are examples of cities thrown into civil strife, of bands organised around lineages and directed by aristocratic chiefs supported by their kindred and numerous clients.[17]

The same sense of solidarity based upon traditional principles is found in the religious life of the city. Festivals in honour of gods of purely local character occupied a place of importance in the lives of the Greeks and the Romans. In the life of cities of the Middle Ages and even of our own day festivals in honour of saints play an important part. Philologists, historians and folklorists have studied the calendar and have described in great detail the public and private celebrations of the great cities. Up to recent times the different quarters of Spanish cities were distinguished as to their religious character. They formed *parroquias* (parishes) or *colaciones* and the fact of belonging as neighbour to a determined quarter required a man to participate in the parish life organised by a series of brotherhoods and religious associations. One can even point to a parish law which has been little studied though it is full of interest. The most characteristic urban trades, those producing necessities as well as those furnishing luxuries, were regulated, until the end of the *ancien régime*, by sodalities of a pious nature, whether in pagan or Christian territories.[18]

From the end of the Middle Ages the peoples of all Catholic Europe celebrated an occasion which sums up the spirit of city life, the festival of Corpus Christi. During this festival men, organised in sodalities, venerated the body of

Christ. The whole range of offices and occupations which characterise the city are represented in the celebration of 'Corpus Cristi.'[19] All the guilds take part in the procession from the goldsmiths and lapidaries who make the most luxurious products to the gardeners and labourers of the neighbourhood. Even the physical form of the city is a manifestation of this will to submit to a traditional order; not only in the medieval Christian city laid out geometrically but also in the Muslim city with its more irregular contours, each activity has its prescribed locality, each man has his place in accordance with an hierarchical order. The aristocrats occupy one street, the jewellers another, a third the cutlers, the tanners live beyond the walls and the despised Moors, Jews, and prostitutes live in a state of segregation.[20]

Nevertheless, it is in this urban society that the moralists and the historians have found examples to defend the classical thesis of the city dwellers' failure to respect ancient traditions. Let there be no mistake. It is not in the secularized city of the nineteenth century that sociologists found the first grounds for establishing distinctions such as that drawn up in Tönnies' memorable thesis on the *Gemeinschaft* and the *Gesellschaft* or that of Durkheim on the difference between mechanical and organic solidarity.[21] The principles of secularisation, of breaking with tradition and of a purely contractual organization are found in the antique city. But they are not the only principles there. Yet the commonplace has had enough influence to give that impression.

During the epoch when Fray Antonio de Guevara was writing, and even a few years earlier, several Portuguese writers were comparing an ideal type of country *fidalgo* (nobleman), who preserved the virtues of ancient times, to the man of the city or port, engaged in colonial enterprises. These authors condemn the thallassocratic *élan* with which Portugal, in spirit comparable to ancient Greece, launched herself during the fifteenth and sixteenth centuries.[22]

VI

It is true that the moralists' position vis-à-vis the city is due to the presence of some elements which threaten to destroy the traditional order in a way not possible in the country. But even seen from this limited viewpoint, I think, the classical thesis is less than profound for several reasons. I have examined so far those values of city life which like the traditionalists we may call 'positive.' Now it is necessary before considering the characteristics of rural society to point to come of the 'negative values' of the same city life, those which justify, from the classical point of view, the city's lack of moral prestige.

All cities are characterized by the presence of a social class which has been well defined by the Latin word 'plebs.' At times the 'plebs,' or plebeians, have been the object of prejudices similar to those which have been aimed against racial and religious minorities; the plebeian has been stereotyped according to some of his public activities. In the lands of the Mediterranean it was common for the 'plebs' to indulge in periodic agitations of a revolutionary character against the established social order, especially during periods of famine. Then, furious mobs would rally to the call of some man unknown until that day, a leader born to a tragic destiny. The urban revolutions of the Mediterranean peoples have been the subject of classical accounts in various languages, and it would be worth while to make a comparative study of these accounts to determine the common traits of these struggles.[23] The existence of urban revolutionary plebs has given moralists and traditionally-minded historians a leading argument against the city. The same common people must be considered, then, in other spheres of activity.

In examining an English literary review recently I was interested in an article, by an author unknown to me, defending the thesis that several analogies may be established between that which has been observed in the popular quarters of the cities of southern Italy and that recorded in the lewd and elegant novel of Petronius.[24] I do not know which passages of Petronius are most appropriate to establish the comparison, but from what I know of the life of some of the ports of southern Spain it is possible to find the same characteristics in the slums from one century to another. At times this homogeneity of the slums has inspired historical theories. For example, societies of criminals, like the *germanía* of Seville in the sixteenth century and the Neapolitan *camorra* of the nineteenth, bear a strong resemblance. The first fashioned itself upon the statutes of the artisans' guilds. According to Don Luis Zapata, in order to gain admission it was necessary to submit proof as to the purity of one's blood.[25] Perhaps the statement disguises a criticism of his contemporaries' obsession with pedigree. But there is no doubt that Cervantes, in *Rinconete y Cortadillo,* presented a picture of the *germanía* which is comparable, almost in its smallest details, to the descriptions of the *camorra* of the Italian authors of the nineteenth century, one at least of whom throws the responsibility for the *camorra's* very existence on to the malevolent power of the Spanish.[26] However, this kind of historical imputation which would credit the introduction of homosexuality and such other evil customs into 15th century Italy to the Spaniards has been denounced by Benedetto Croce.[27]

The slums of Mediterranean society have had unity since the earliest ages, and this is due to that same basic structure which is associated by Socrates and Plato in the passage which opened our characterisation of the polis, with, as its essential element, the pursuit of pleasures.

The rapid growth of certain activities in the polis always produces analogous results, as for example in Portugal at the time of the greatest thalassocratic expansion, the first half of the sixteenth century. The humanist Clénard in a detailed letter listed the following traits, contrasting them with other European societies:

1. Abandonment of agriculture,
2. Abandonment of industry to foreign hands,
3. Development of slavery,
4. Famine,
5. Hypertrophy of pretensions to nobility,
6. Relaxation of morals.[28]

A whole country remains submerged in a state of 'corruption' synonymous with the 'modernity' which the classical writers considered the final consequence of urban life. But modernism of this sort can appear in any age. The vices of the city are as modern as the complaints and curses of the prophet against the worldliness of Babylon.

But what remains to be said about the antique 'virtues' of the countryside?

VII

Perhaps the most famous to sing the praises of country life was Horace. Everyone remembers his poetry. But the poet, always enigmatic, put the eulogies into the mouth of a usurer, a point which is surely worth a second thought.[29] Consider again Varro's statement regarding the nature, divine in origin, of country life. The labours of the peasant are loved by the Gods, and when public men suffer from disappointments, they seek solace in the calm of the countryside. This is the classic commonplace once more.

But is the primitive simplicity of country life, clear to the poets and moralists, a reality around the Mediterranean? I am very sceptical about this, even if the question is phrased in the modern terms of *Gemeinschaft.* I believe in other words, that just as the ancient Mediterranean city displays contradictory characteristics from the moral point of view, there may be social structures in the country which are not primitive, traditional, closed, etc. When Aristotle described the best site for a city ruled by a monarch, as contrasted with that best suited to an aristocratic or a democratic city, he gave us a model for parallel analysis with regard to forms of rural society, which can, in fact, be distinguished as functions of different social and economic regimes.[30]

The economic system in force during the greater part of the Middle Ages in most of the countries of western Europe, and even during other periods, best corresponds to the aristocratic regime. The principle of local self-sufficiency was the key to this system, whose attributes were most marked in certain mountainous regions. Towers and castles were raised overlooking the field: the chiefs of rural cantons were nobles who are described in the literature as the most typical embodiments of ancient tradition. But let us come down from the crags, the valleys and the passes of the mountains. On the fertile and abundant plain is something very different. We have come from the *saltus* to the *campus,* called in the Latin *campania,* by the Arabs the similar word *canbaniyah* and by the southern Spaniards 'la campiña.'[31]   Here, ever since early times, there have been large agricultural exploitations. Already in the age before the Roman conquest on the borders of Guadalquivir there were rural estates of considerable size. The Andalusian *latifundia* of Roman and Visigothic times and those of the period of the caliphs of Cordova are well known. After the reconquest, the Christians redivided the land upon an equally lavish scale. Today the great estates subsist as if men, like the land, were guided by the hand of a blind destiny or τύχη.[32]   The same may be said of other Mediterranean countries. Now, the great estate is a result of divisions made by conquest and capitalist speculation, which lead to an organization of agricultural work in keeping with rational principles and with economic planning upon a certain scale. The *latifundia* of the South exist as a function of the city and its commerce. The production of cereals, wines and oils must be industrial. This has nothing to do with a primitive state of man, imposed by the teachings of the gods together with a simplistic ethos, nor with an aristocratic principle of autarky. Equally, the great estate or exploitation of the plains contributes to the development of city 'pleasures'—even forcibly.

Max Weber attributed the decadence of Rome to the fact that its economic life was based on slavery, and that this system was not able to support the requirements of the great cities.[33] This thesis may be discussed and even challenged, but at least it must be granted that the ancient great estate imposed on those who worked it a condition of diminished social personality, until they came to be considered as simple 'vocal' instruments according to Varro's definition.[34] In a countryside possessing such economic characteristics a labourer could have the same traits as those attributed to the urban plebs, which can even supply labour for agriculture. It must not be forgotten that many of the Mediterranean cities numbering several thousand inhabitants are composed in large measure of journeymen who are contracted or engaged by the day in a sort of human market: this happens today as it did in the times of the New Testament.[35]

In a countryside characterised by the great estate, the subversive conditions are, then, similar to those which are found in the city. The history of rural unrest in the Mediterranean is a long and complex one. In my country there is a series of examples well suited to a comparative study: from the agitations of the starving who revolted in Andalusia in the time of Philip IV with the cry of 'Long live the King and down with bad government,' up to the revolts at the beginning of the century.[36]

I am not very familiar with the studies of modern sociologists and anthropologists on southern Italy, nor have I any experience of the life of that nation. But I can assert that there are astonishing resemblances between what is described in the letters of P. Villari,[37] in several books by A. Niceforo and by others and on the other hand the Spanish accounts of this same period in Southern Spain which were dictated by the concern to resolve the problems which were so alive at the end of the 19th century[38] and which, perhaps, exist today. In the countryside of the south one can detect a state of anomia manifested on the one hand in a lack of adjustment to urban codified culture (a lack expressed in the rates of illiteracy and illegitimacy) and on the other hand in an indifference to the values of a traditional life in religious matters, etc.

VIII

Though not myself a social anthropologist, I have treated a subject which is of theoretical importance to social anthropology. I have attempted, in the observations I have made above, to stimulate discussion and research rather than to reach, myself, any scientific conclusions. I am obliged to recognise that in spite of the objections I have outlined there is a real dichotomy between the social forms of the city and the country, and I accept the reality of many of their traditional attributes. I must also stress the wide acceptance of the judgements of the classical moralists by the people themselves.

If, for example, I were to ask a bourgeois of the city of Malaga what are the qualities and faults of the country people, the response would be moulded in accordance with the ancient commonplace—equally if I were to ask a peasant from the sierra about the people of Malaga. But the men of the plain who live close by the city, even the farmers, have urbanised tastes and an eye for luxury. The spirit of thrift, the aptitude for hard work and the capacity to renounce all diversions are found among the mountain people, those who live farther from the city, such as the peasants of Alhaurín who lack the urban refinements of vivacity, finesse and the art of pleasing. They are called *catetos,* a term equivalent to many employed in Spain, such as *paleto, grullo, payo, payés* (from *pagense* (*m*)), *isidro, jebo* etc. The *catetos* are near relatives of the men whom the late Professor Redfield found in some Mexican communities and who styled themselves, less euphemistically, *tontos*, that is to say *fools*.[39]

In summary, I believe it would be worth while to study the peoples of the Mediterranean in terms of the structural and functional relations between the two elements of the dichotomy, paying more attention to the historical reality than to the abstractions of the moralists and their disciples, the sociologists. The general problems of the culture and society of the countryside and of the city are not easily discussed without taking into account the dimensions and constituents of the Polis or its equivalent. Following Socrates I believe that one must examine the essential ties which relate those who may be considered the characteristic representatives of *rusticitas* with those who typify *urbanitas*. Their cultural universe is conditioned at each point in time by the strength of the traditions which link them to their past.

NOTES

1. Varro, *R.r.* I, 1–4.
2. It is in the first verse of 'The Clouds' that Strepsiades eulogizes the life he used to lead in the country before he married 'the niece of Megacles, son of Megacles.'
3. Caesar, *B.g.* I, I, 1.
4. The German philologists have emphasized most strongly the edifying character of 'Germania,' while the French seem more circumspect in this regard.
5. Caro Baroja, Julio, *Los moriscos del Reino de Granada*, Madrid, 1957.
6. Guevara, Fray Antonio de, ed., Madrid, 1915.
7. Plato, *Phaedo* 109a–b.
8. Plato, *Leges* III, 677a–687a.
9. Strabo, *Geogr.* XI, 4, 3 (501).
10. The author who has made the most conscientious investigation of the 'gentiles' is the prehistorian and folklorist J. M. de Barandiarán. Julio Caro Baroja, *Los vascos*, Madrid, 1958, pp. 355–357, 392–393.
11. Plato, *Republic* II, 11–13 (369b–373d). On war and the army, II, 14, 373d–374d.
12. Redfield, Robert, *The primitive world and its transformations*, Ithaca, 1957, pp. 23–25 *et passim*.
13. The date for the founding of Cadiz is given by Vellerius Paterculus (1, 2, 4) as the year 1110 B. C.
14. Lancina, Juan Alfonso, *Historia de los reboluciones (sic) del senado de Messina*, Madrid, 1692, pp. 4–9.
15. 'Intimgruppen' (K. Durkmann), 'Primärgruppen' (Ch. H. Cooley) etc. 'Soziologie.' Herausgegeben von Professor Dr. René König *Das Fischer Lexikon*, Frankfort, 1958.
16. On the founding of Alexandria, Strabo XVII, 1, 6 (792). Julio Caro Baroja, 'Aben Jaldun y la ciudad musulmana' in *Etudios mogrebies* Madrid, 1957.
17. The struggles which took place in Toledo in the 16th century between the lineages of Silvas and Ayalas and those of Quiñones and Ponces in Seville are well known. Manuel Danvila, *Historia critica y documentada de las communidades de Castilla*, I, Madrid, 1897, pp. 90–91, 129–135 etc.
18. The Greek festivals studied by A. Mommsen, the Roman treated by W. Warde Fowler, and others of antiquity may be taken in conjunction with those of Christian cities even without following any formal scheme of comparison in order to yield some strictly sociological regularities.
19. We do not possess a good study of the festival of 'Corpus Cristi' and its relation to the idea of *corporatio*.
20. On the characters of Spanish cities I have assembled several essays in my book, *Razas, pueblos y linajes*, Madrid, 1957.

21. I cannot discuss the extent to which the ideas of Durkheim, Tönnies, etc. are based on the ideas of the ancient moralists. But I firmly believe they have submitted to their influence and even to that of the prophets of Israel, thundering against Babylon in the biblical text. The Sacred literature of the Jews has, to this day, exercised an enormous influence on the ideas of European peoples and the Old Testament is still a source (little recognized) for many an historical, sociological and anthropological theory.

22. The critique of the 'modernity' of the times, from this point of view, is very well expressed in several of the poems of Francisco de Sá de Miranda (1481–1558). For example in letter V to Antonio Pereira, where the author makes the surprising assertion that the French life of this time was more *à l'ancienne*:

> Inda hoje vemos que em França
> Vivem nisto mais á antiga;
> Na vila o vilão se abriga
> Onde tem nome e herança
> Vive i da sua fadiga.

(*Poesias* ed. by José Pereira Carmes (Oporto, n.d.) p. 99 (Strophe 27). In letter VI (to Don Fernando de Menezes) he abhors Seville as an example of the modern city (ed. cit. pp. 103–110). Hatred of modernism was joined to a hatred of the sea, full of dangers, as a road to corruption. André de Resende is another who, in his poems, expresses a similar point of view:

> Os galeões, navios e naos cheias
> D'ouro, de prata, seda e gente avara
> Ao fondo vão do reino das sereias.

Obras, Coimbra, 1849?, p. 295 (vv. 97–99 of the satire II against those who look for temporal profit). Epistle IV on Lisbon (pp. 378–383) is a manifestation of the same moral attitude:

> O brocado, a téla, a seda
> O crédito e a moeda
> O tracto e a mercancia.
> toda a droga e especiaria,
> Alli se acha a santimonia,
> Virtude e são sacrificio
> Alli confusão e vicio
> E quasi outra Babylonia.

These are typical views (p. 380 strophe 7).

23. One might point, as an example of a typical revolution, to that which Masaniello led in Naples. Besides the classical accounts there is a veritable reportage of the same event in the 'Cartas de algunos PP. de la Compañía de Jesús sobre los sucesos de la Monarquía entre los años de 1634 y 1648' VII (*Memorial histórico español* XIX, Madrid, 1865, pp. 23–26, 28–55, 60–62, 76–78, 85–117, 135–140).

24. Wall, Bernard, 'Some contemporary Italian writers' in *Horizon* XIV, 1946, p. 321.

25. Zapata, Luis de, 'Miscelanea' in *Memorial histórico español* XI (Madrid, 1859), pp. 49–50.

26. Caro Baroja, Julio, 'La germanía y la camorra' in *Razas, pueblos y linajes*, pp. 325–335.

27. Croce B., *La Spagna nella vita italiana durante la Rinascenza*, (Bari, 1917), p. 248.

28. Cerejeira M. Gonçalves, *O Renascimento em Portugal-Clenardo* I, Coimbra, 1917, pp. 113–125, 125–156; II, Coimbra, 1918, pp. 12–16.

29. Horace, *Ep* I, 2, 67–70.

30. Aristotle, *Politics* VII, 11, 5 133, b.

31. Caro Baroja, Julio, 'En la campiña de Cordoba' in *Razas, pueblos, linajes . . .*, p. 233.

32. See the study referred to in the previous note, pp. 233–259.

33. Weber, Max, 'La decadencia de la Cultura antigua' in *Revista de Occidente* XXXVII, July, 1926, pp. 25–59.

34. Varro, *R.r* I, 17, I.

35. Saint Matthew XX, 1–16.

36. For instance, the revolts of Seville, Córdova and Granada etc. About the former there is a letter of May 26, 1648 in the 'Cartas de algunos PP. de la Compania de Jesus . . . ' VII (*op. cit.* note 23.), pp. 184–188.

37. Villari, Pasquale, *Le lettere meridionali ed altri scritti sulla questione sociale in Italia,* Rome-Turin-Florence, 1885.
38. Niceforo, A., *L'Italia Barbara contemporanea* (Studi ed appunti), Milan, 1898.
39. Lewis, Oscar, *Life in a Mexican village. Tepoztlan restudied,* Urbana, 1951, pp. 430–431. Redfield, R., *The little community. Viewpoints for the study of a human whole,* Chicago, 1955.

Selected Readings on Intervention and Urbanism

This list includes discussions of the texture of urban life, planning, the forms of cities, metropolitan population redistribution, and the future of urban organization.

Alonso, William. *Location and Land Use.* Cambridge, Mass.: Harvard University Press, 1964. Phrased in terms of economic theory, with strong operational implications.

Altshuler, Alan A. *Community Control: The Black Demand for Participation in Large American Cities.* New York: Pegasus, 1970.

Argan, Giulio C. *The Renaissance City.* New York: Braziller, 1969. A brief, well-illustrated analysis of the princely planned city.

Banfield, Edward C. *The Unheavenly City: The Nature and Future of Our Urban Crisis.* Boston: Little, Brown, 1968. As the preface says, "This book will probably strike many readers as the work of an ill-tempered and mean-spirited fellow."

Bascom, William. "Some Aspects of Yoruba Urbanism." *American Anthropologist* 64 (1962): 699–709.

Bellush, Jewel and Murray Hausknecht, eds. *Urban Renewal: People, Politics and Planning.* New York: Doubleday Anchor, 1967.

Beyer, Glenn H. *Housing and Society.* New York: Macmillan, 1965.

Bloomberg, Warner, Jr., and Henry J. Schmandt, eds. *Power, Poverty, and Urban Policy.* Beverly Hills, Calif.: Sage Publications, 1968. General essays and authoritative reviews of current work.

Bracy, H. E. *Neighbors: Subdivision Life in England and the United States.* Baton Rouge: Louisiana State University Press, 1965. Comparative study of two suburbs.

Buchanan, Colin D. *Traffic in Towns.* Penguin Books, 1963. A shortened version of the controversial report on the automobile in England, and what to do about it.

Chapin, F. Stuart. *Urban Land Use Planning.* 2d ed. Urbana: University of Illinois Press, 1965.

Choay, Francoise. *L'Urbanisme: Utopies et realities.* Paris: Editions du seuil, 1965. An anthology of major ideas about the planning and reshaping of cities.

Clinard, Marshall B. *Slums and Community Development.* New York: Free Press, 1966. Much on intervention and self-help, especially in the United States and India.

Crecine, John P., ed. *Financing the Metropolis.* Beverly Hills, Calif.: Sage, 1970. One of the Urban Affairs Annual Reviews (no. 4, to be exact), with their usual bibliography-laden summaries of subproblems.

Davies, J. Clarence. *Neighborhood Groups and Urban Renewal.* New York: Columbia University Press, 1966.

Dickinson, Robert E. *The West European City: A Geographical Interpretation.* London: Routledge and Kegan Paul, 1951. Mainly detailed discussions of changes in the physical form of selected cities since the Middle Ages.

Fogelson, Robert. "White on Black: A Critique of the McCone Commission Report on the Los Angeles Riots." *Political Science Quarterly* 82 (September 1967). An exemplary critical use of systematic knowledge about cities.

Freeman, T. W. *The Conurbations of Great Britain.* Manchester, England: Manchester University Press, 1959.

Gans, Herbert J. *The Levittowners.* New York: Pantheon, 1967.

Gans, Herbert J. *People and Plans.* New York: Basic Books, 1968. Reflective essays by one of the most thoughtful and well-informed commentators on American urbanism.

Gibbs, Jack, and Leo F. Schnore. "Metropolitan Growth: An International Study." *American Journal of Sociology* 66, (1960): 60–66.

Goldstein, Bernard. *Low Income Youth in Urban Areas: A Critical Review of the Literature.* New York: Holt Rinehart and Winston, 1967.

Gottman, Jean. *Megalopolis.* New York: Twentieth Century Fund, 1961.

Gutkind, Edwin A. *The International History of Urban Development.* New York: Free Press, 1964–1973. Monumental, profusely illustrated, concentrated on the form of cities. The volumes to date treat (1) Central Europe; (2) Alpine and Scandinavian countries; (3) Spain and Portugal; (4) Italy and Greece; (5) France and Belgium; (6) The Netherlands and Great Britain; (7) Poland, Czechoslovakia, and Hungary; (8) Bulgaria, Romania, and the U.S.S.R.

Hall, Peter. *The World Cities.* New York: McGraw-Hill, 1966. Beautifully illustrated quick survey of a half-dozen major metropolises.

Hirsch, Werner, ed. *Urban Life and Form.* New York: Holt, Rinehart and Winston, 1963. Another review of the big issues in urban studies.

Howard, E. *Garden Cities of Tomorrow.* London: Faber and Faber, 1965. A new edition of a nineteenth-century classic which incited green-belt planning, Lewis Mumford, and other twentieth century wonders.

Jacobs, Jane. *The Death and Life of Great American Cities.* New York: Random House, 1961.

Kozol, Jonathan. *Death at an Early Age: The Destruction of the Hearts and Minds of Negro Children in the Boston Public Schools.* Boston: Houghton Mifflin Company, 1967.

Lapidus, Ira M., ed. *Middle Eastern Cities: A symposium on Ancient, Islamic and Contemporary Middle Eastern Urbanism.* Berkeley and Los Angeles: University of California Press, 1969. First rate brief introductions to the urban Middle East, past and present.

Laslett, Peter *The World We Have Lost: England Before the Industrial Age.* New York: Scribners, 1965. A searching, debunking review of the evidence on "Traditional agrarian" society.

Le Corbusier. *When the Cathedrals Were White.* New York: McGraw-Hill paperbacks, 1965; the first English edition 1947. A poetic testament from a great architect-planner.

Lynch, Kevin. *The Image of the City.* Cambridge, Mass.: M.I.T. Press and Harvard University Press, 1960.

Mackensen, R., and J. Chr. Papaleskas. *Daseinformen der Grosstadt* Tubingen: J. C. B. Mohr, 1959.

Meyerson, Martin, ed. *The Conscience of the City.* New York: Braziller, 1970. Topical essays of superior literary and intellectual quality.

Michelson, William. *Man and His Urban Environment.* Reading, Mass.: Addison-Wesley, 1970. A systematic exploration of urban physical arrangements on social life.

Moynihan, David P. *Maximum Feasible Misunderstanding.* New York: Free Press, 1969. Acid analysis of citizen participation in urban renewal.

Murphey, Rhoads. "City and Countryside as Ideological Issues: India and China." *Comparative Studies in Society and History* 14 (Spring, 1972).

National Association of Home Builders. *Urban Renewal; a Selected Annotated Bibliography.* Washington, D.C.: National Housing Center Library, 1965.

Pinkney, David H. *Napoleon III and the Rebuilding of Paris.* Princeton, N.J.: Princeton University Press, 1958.

Reps, John W. *The Making of Urban America: A History of City Planning in the United States.* Princeton, N.J.: Princeton University Press, 1965. Rich with pictures and maps.

Robson, William A., ed. *Great Cities of the World: Their Government, Politics and Planning.* New York: Macmillan, 1957.

Rodwin, Lloyd, ed. *The Future Metropolis.* New York: Braziller, 1961.

Smith, Page. *As a City Upon a Hill: The Town in American History.* New York: Alfred A. Knopf, 1966.

Sternlieb, George. *The Tenement Landlord.* New Brunswick, N.J.: Urban Studies Center, Rutgers University, 1966.

Strauss Anselm. *Images of the American City.* Glencoe, Ill.: Free Press, 1961.

Thernstrom, Stephan. *Poverty, Planning and Politics in the New Boston: The Origins of ABCD.* New York: Basic Books, 1969.

Thompson, E. P. *The Making of the English Working Class.* London: Gollancz, 1963. Rich analysis of the quality of local life and the nature of working-class aspirations in early industrialization-urbanization.

Tilly, Charles. "Reflections on the Revolution of Paris." *Social Problems* 12 (Summer, 1964): 99–121. A provisional synthesis of studies of the form and personnel of rebellion in Paris from 1789 to 1848.

Toynbee, Arnold. *Cities on the Move.* London: Oxford University Press, 1970. Sweeping observations of urban history, analyses of our own time, and glimpses at the future, by the world historian.

Tunnard, Christopher. *The Modern American City.* Princeton, N.J.: Van Nostrand, 1968. The social and technical context of contemporary planning, with documents.

Turner, Roy, ed. *India's Urban Future.* Berkeley: University of California Press, 1962.

Vernon, Raymond. *Metropolis 1985.* Cambridge, Mass.: Harvard University Press, 1960. A review of the New York metropolitan study.

Warner, Sam Bass, ed. *Planning for a Nation of Cities.* Cambridge, Mass.: M.I.T. Press, 1966.

Webber, Melvin, et al. *Explorations into Urban Structure.* Philadelphia: University of Pennsylvania Press, 1964.

Wheatley, Paul. "The Significance of Traditional Yoruba Urbanism." *Comparative Studies in Society and History* 12 (1970): 393–423.

Williams, William Carlos. *Paterson.* New York: New Directions paperback, 1963. A poet's powerful reconstruction of a city's metamorphoses.

Wilson, James Q., ed. *The Metropolitan Enigma.* Cambridge, Mass.: Harvard University Press, 1968. Essays often opinionated, by professional students of American cities.

Wilson, James Q., ed. *Urban Renewal: The Record and the Controversy.* Cambridge, Mass: M.I.T. Press, 1966. A comprehensive reader.

Zucker, Paul. *Town and Square from the Agora to the Village Green.* New York: Columbia University Press, 1959.